Snohomish County: An Illustrated History

David A. Cameron, Charles P. LeWarne, M. Allan May,
Jack C. O'Donnell, and Lawrence E. O'Donnell

Artwork by Bernie Webber

 Kelcema Books LLC, P.O. Box 107, Index, Washington 98256

PUBLISHED BY
Kelcema Books LLC
P.O. Box 107
Index, WA 98256

ISBN 0-9766700-0-3

Library of Congress Control Number: 2005923327

Printed and bound in the United States of America

Editor: David A. Cameron
Manuscript Editors: David A. Cameron, Lynne Grimes
Proofreaders: Jane Wyatt, David A. Cameron
Indexer: Lynne Grimes
Design: James D. Kramer design services, Everett, WA 98208

Table of Contents

Acknowledgments

We gratefully acknowledge the contributions of the following organizations and individuals:

Louise Lindgren, Snohomish County Department of Planning and Development Services; Tony Stigall, Roger Kelley, and Dennis Frimml, Snohomish County Department of Public Works; Fred Bird, Snohomish County Department of Information Services; Snohomish County Executive's Office; Snohomish County Council; League of Snohomish County Heritage Organizations; Margaret Riddle and David Dilgard, Everett Public Library; Jan Hollenbeck, Mt. Baker-Snoqualmie National Forest; Alderwood Manor Heritage Association, Darrington Historical Society, Edmonds-South Snohomish County Historical Museum, Gold Bar Historical Society, Granite Falls Historical Society, Index Historical Society, Lake Stevens Historical Society, Marysville Historical Society, Monroe Historical Society, Monte Cristo Preservation Association, Mountlake Terrace Historical Society, Mukilteo Historical Society, Museum of Snohomish County History (formerly the Snohomish County Museum & Historical Association), Sky Valley Historical Society, Snohomish Historical Society, Sno-Isle Genealogical Society, Stanwood Area Historical Society, Stillaguamish Valley Genealogical Society, Stillaguamish Valley Pioneers Museum, Darrington Ranger District, Tulalip Tribes of Washington, the Sauk-Suiattle Tribe, the Stillaguamish Tribe, the Snoqualmie Tribe, Helene Cameron, Monte Holm, Marie Little, Joyce Wans, Norma Joseph, Lawrence Joseph, Katherine Joseph, Karen Prasse, Dennis Conroy, Victoria Harrington, Laura Cameron Behee, Middy Ruthruff, Ann Tuohy, Henry Gobin, Maxine Gressett, Priscilla Shipley, Nellie Robertson, Tom Gaskin, Bob Laz, Carl Gipson, Diane Janes, Bruce Brown, William Morris, Dave Larson, Cathie Currie, Darlene Huntington, Nancy DeCoteau, Edna May Savory, Walt Taubeneck, Doris Cannon, John Mattson, Toby Langen, Mary Ann Moeller, Ann Collier, Joni Sein, Grace Fisk, Pauline LeWarne, and Loren Kraetz.

Introduction

Each individual sees and interprets this world from a unique point of view. For native peoples and old-timers, the pace of change in Snohomish County in a single lifetime has been drastic. A newcomer's frame of reference is the way the land looks now, and the years of old growth logging and primitive travel by water and dirt road exist only in museum photographs. For each person the basic forms of the mountains, river valleys, lakes, and shoreline seem never to change. As for the climate, by the dark, wet days of November, most wish it *would* change.

Because of its complex environment Snohomish County is not an easy place to characterize. It is a land with several personalities. From the densely populated southwestern lowlands close to Puget Sound, life focuses on the east side of Lake Washington, cultural and sporting events in Seattle, and the southbound commutes forth and back along the always jammed and under-construction lanes of Interstates 5 and 405. People in Everett to the north along the lowlands have trouble realizing that.

Everett became the largest city in the county, won the county seat from nearby Snohomish in a heavily contested election, and hoped to draw the commerce of the region toward its downtown and deep water harbor. Limited in its growth options by its location on the peninsula (formed by the estuary of the Snohomish River), Everett found its outlet also to the south. Especially after the Boeing Company began development next to Paine Field in the 1960s, Everett found its wealth and opportunities shifting, and the lowlands became a continuous strip of development from Smokey Point north of Marysville, filling in southward down the freeways to join with the bedroom communities adjoining Seattle.

Toward the northern border, the agricultural lands at the mouth of the Stillaguamish River and the surrounding hinterlands felt cut off and isolated from all of their neighbors south of the Tulalip Indian Reservation. Clinging with Scandinavian tenacity to their rural and small town preferences, they prospered on dairy cattle and deep alluvial soils. When travel to the county seat in Snohomish took five days by steamboat via Seattle, they tried to secede, but were outmaneuvered by the political connections of Snohomish founder Emory C. Ferguson. Those thoughts still simmer at times in the breasts of shoppers headed across the Skagit County line for the malls covering the fertile fields of Mount Vernon.

Upstream from Stanwood, Arlington, Granite Falls, and Monroe live the most isolated of the county's residents, those who have moved easterly away from the urbanization of the lowlands to create communities in the three very separate Cascade Mountain river valleys formed by the Skykomish and the forks of the Stillaguamish rivers. To many of them, government in Everett is far away and dominated by the cities and suburbs -- more a nuisance taking their money and forcing regulations with little in return, that is, until roads need repair or economic help is required to deal with heavy unemployment caused by a decline in their resource based industries. Travel is time consuming, with chain store malls far away. People here are more self sufficient and more deeply influenced by the extremes of weather and scenery. They see the pressures of population growth now moving in on them from the west along the highway corridors. Some fear it, while others welcome the chances to open their holdings to development. "Property rights" and dreams of a new rural county hampered with few restrictions have surfaced and resurfaced as Monroe, Lake Stevens, Granite Falls, and Arlington now are becoming a part of "Pugetopolis". Attempting to govern, characterize, or create a sense of unity in a region of such differences always has been difficult -- and probably frustrating -- for those who have tried.

The Natural Setting

I t may come as a shock then when we begin to realize how recent are these physical forms which we take as permanent. Geologically (as well as historically), this is one of the newest parts of North America. Beneath the ground of what many magazines have called "America's most livable" regions it is also one of the most violent and unstable.

This came about because around 250 million years ago the North American continent began to move toward the southwest. Between Europe and North America, the Atlantic Ocean had started to grow, spreading apart with massive eruptions of lava from the earth's crust. As it grew, it pushed the North American continental plate toward Asia. Meanwhile, the Pacific plate slipped toward the northwest and headed for what now is Alaska. Between them currently is the surviving remnant of the Juan de Fuca plate, which extends from northern California to the northern tip of Vancouver Island. Since the surface crust of the earth is of a constant size (rather like the cover on a Mariners baseball), when one plate expands, another has to contract. Thus the continental plate eventually began a process of absorbing the Juan de Fuca plate, driving it downward in a subduction zone. This process continues.

As the plate moves, it creates a trench down which the lighter ocean floor slides toward the hot center of the earth at a rate of two inches per year. After a million years, some 31 miles have been absorbed. After 30 million years, that becomes 930 miles, which is farther than a drive from here to Billings, Montana or Salt Lake City, Utah. Over these long expanses of geologic time, islands and subcontinents which had been in the Pacific were drawn in to the advancing coast, sucked down, and melted. When lighter surface rock of the doomed plate eventually plugged-up that trench and filled it, a new trench

1

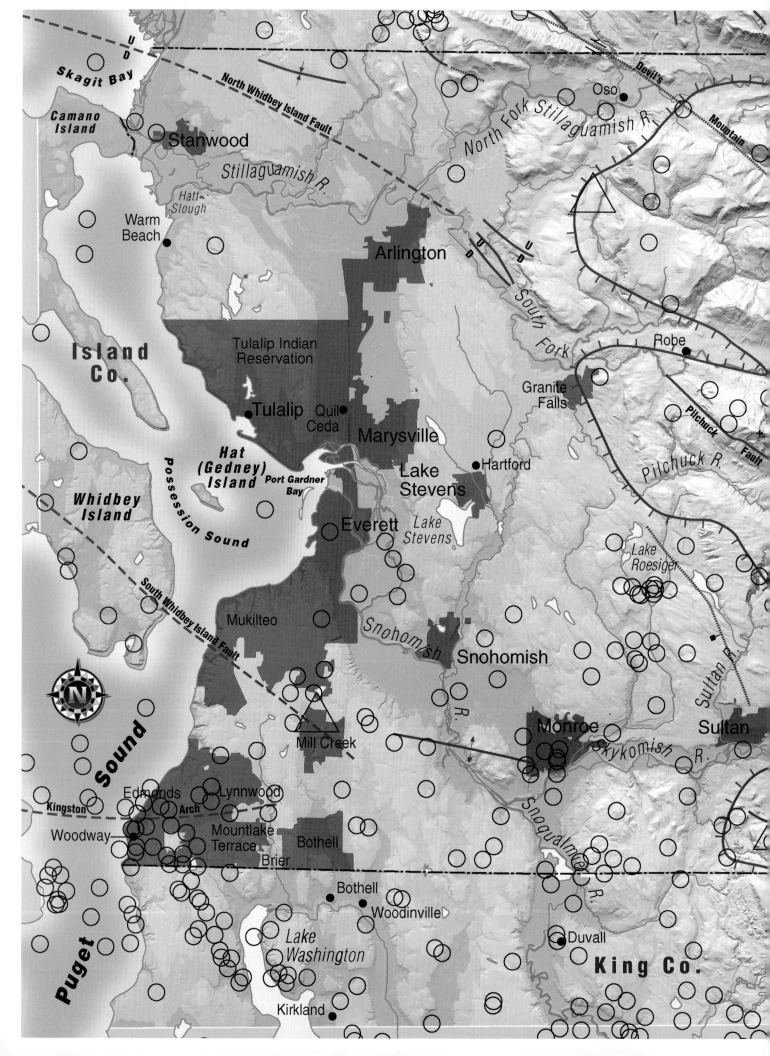

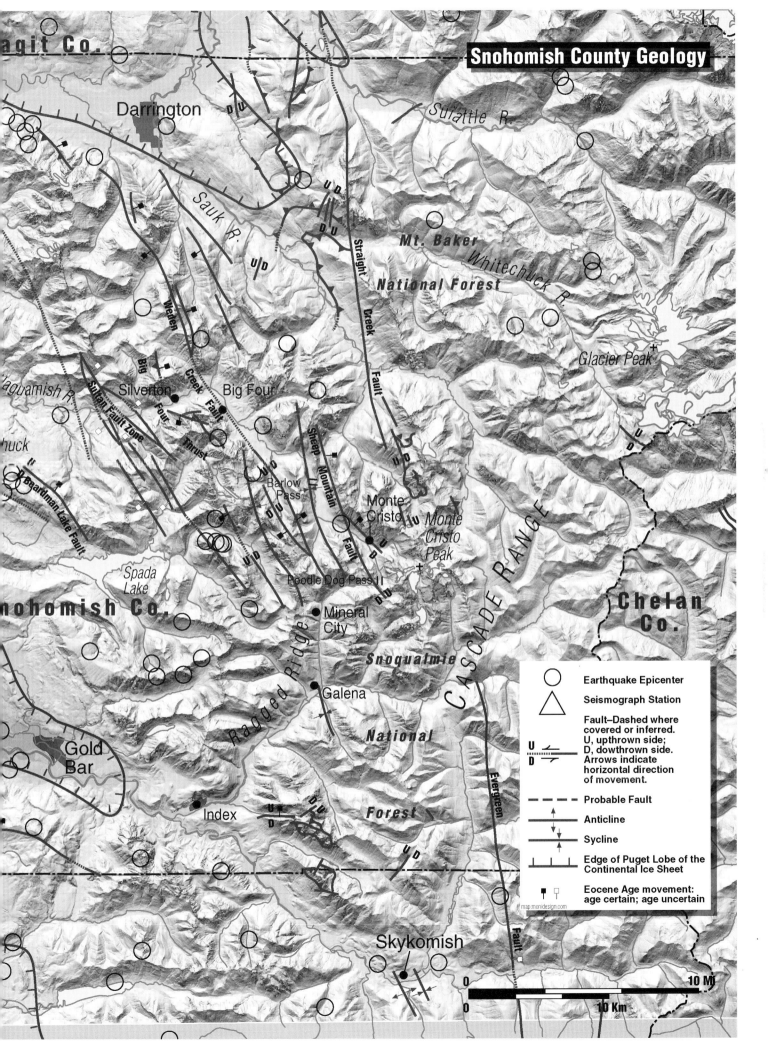

Snohomish County Geology

Skagit Co.

Darrington

Suiattle R.

Sauk R.

Mt. Baker
Whitechuck R.
National Forest

Glacier Peak

Weden

Big Creek Fault

Big Four

Straight Creek Fault

Silverton

Big Four Thrust

Sultan Fault Zone

'aguamish R.

huck

Boardman Lake Fault

Sheep Mountain

Barlow Pass

Monte Cristo

Monte Cristo Peak

Fault

Poodle Dog Pass

CASCADE RANGE

Chelan Co.

Spada Lake

Snohomish Co.

Ragged Ridge

Mineral City

Snoqualmie

Galena

National

Gold Bar

Forest

Index

Evergreen

Skykomish

Fault

Legend

○ Earthquake Epicenter

△ Seismograph Station

U ⟍⟋ Fault—Dashed where
D ⟍⟋ covered or inferred.
U, upthrown side;
D, downthrown side.
Arrows indicate
horizontal direction
of movement.

– – – Probable Fault

——↕—— Anticline

——↕—— Sycline

—⊥⊥⊥— Edge of Puget Lobe of the
Continental Ice Sheet

■ □ Eocene Age movement:
age certain; age uncertain

map:monidesign.com

0   10 Mi

0   10 Km

then formed farther to the west, or another already existing one took over. In this way new pieces of land became attached to the continent, beginning around 205 million years ago.

Before the continent began to move, its edge was roughly the boundary of present day Idaho and Montana. Then Washington began to arrive. First a piece named the Intermountain terrane linked up to form what are now the Okanogan High-lands (the rolling, scenic foothills of the Rocky Mountains, comprising the north-eastern quarter of the state east of the Okanogan River and north of the Columbia Basin). Next (around 100 to 90 million years ago) came the North Cascades ter-rane. This probably was a group of islands

Stratovolcano Glacier Peak is twice as high as Mt. Pilchuck but seldom seen due to its eastern position along the Cascade crest. Pumice from its eruptive past has been found as far east as Saskatchewan and Montana. (Courtesy David Cameron)

rather than a single land mass, and it joined the Intermountain terrane to create a new section roughly from Snoqualmie Pass northward, running up Puget Sound to Victoria and including all of the present-day county. However, the Insular terrane arrived at nearly the same time and drove deeply into the North Cascades, followed later by the Pacific Rim terrane. That was fourth and last, compressing and folding the earlier ones, becoming a new source of rock for the western edge of the county before it stopped.

Broken and twisted by the pressures of the two newer arrivals, the mountains of the North Cascades were deeply fractured and sliced, as shown by the Straight Creek fault. It runs north and south, on a line east of Monte Cristo and Darrington into Skagit County.

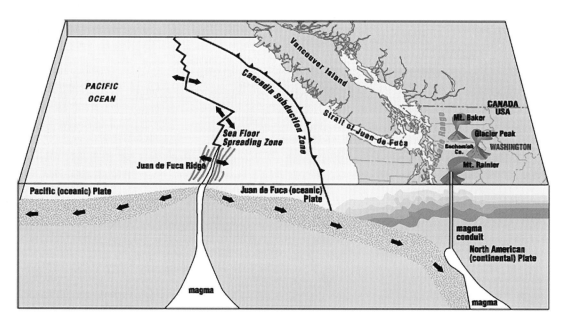

Map compiled from United States Geological Survey (USGS) data.

Rocks west of the fault appear to have been shifted 68 miles to the north of their counterparts east of the line. The smaller Evergreen Mountain fault parallels it east of the Beckler River in the southeastern corner of the county, while the Sultan, Weden Creek, and Sheep Mountain faults follow the same course in the central portion.

During the period from 55 to 37 million years ago, most of the county from Arlington south was under water, influenced by sediments running down from the mountains. Fossils of this Eocene period portray a climate favorable to tropical broadleaf evergreens, mixed with layers of sandstone, shale, volcanic ash, and coal. Evidence of this is found in the seams of Coal Creek, in the slopes of Stillaguamish Peak some 1,500 feet above the town site of Silverton. Unlike Bellingham, Black Diamond, Cle Elum, and Centralia, however, there were no commercially valuable deposits of soft, bituminous coal found in the county when this was in demand as a fuel for steam engines late in the nineteenth century.

A thoroughly violent period followed. From 35 to 17 million years ago subduction into the trench along the Insular terrane began to produce a chain of huge volcanoes down the length of the present mountain system. As the ocean floor is pushed under the North American plate and heats up, it turns to liquid and expands. This in turn causes the crust above to buckle and rise, letting out the magma as lava. If it carries steam from water trapped in the sinking rocks, it can be explosive, producing gray andesite or lighter-colored rhyolite. The violent stage ended perhaps when the descending crust broke off and ended the supply of water for steam.

There followed a warm, wet period, when great flows of hot, liquid basalt covered the Columbia Basin east of the Cascades a mile deep. In western Washington the Olympic Mountains rose on our western skyline. Between the Olympics and Cascades, the Puget Sound Lowlands gradually began to form, perhaps due to the ongoing movement of the Pacific plate heading toward the north and the North American plate grinding inexorably toward the southwest. Great blocks of rock sheared off and were broken by this twisting, causing them to fracture and drop. Judging by the frequency of shallow earthquakes in the area, this process continues. Hundreds of small quakes happen each year, most of them far too small to feel. To date in historic times there have been only a handful of significant earthquakes centered in Snohomish County. These include a 4.3 magnitude near Sultan on January 5, 1932, followed by a 5.7 southeast of Granite Falls

Volcanic Activity on Glacier Peak Since the Last Ice Age

Years Ago	Events
13,500	Possible collapses and large lahars, large eruption
13,000	Growth and collapse of the dome, large eruption
12,500	Large eruptions of ash
7,000	Possible collapses and lahars
6,500	Large eruption with small eruptions of ash
6,000	Large lahars and large eruption
5,500	Growth and collapse of the dome with a large eruption
3,000	Dome growth and possible collapse, along with lahars and small eruption
2,000	Dome growth and collapse, two small eruptions, lahars
1,000	Dome growth and collapse, five small eruptions, lahars
Recent	Steam eruptions, small lahars, small volume ash eruptions

Based on information from the United States Geological Survey

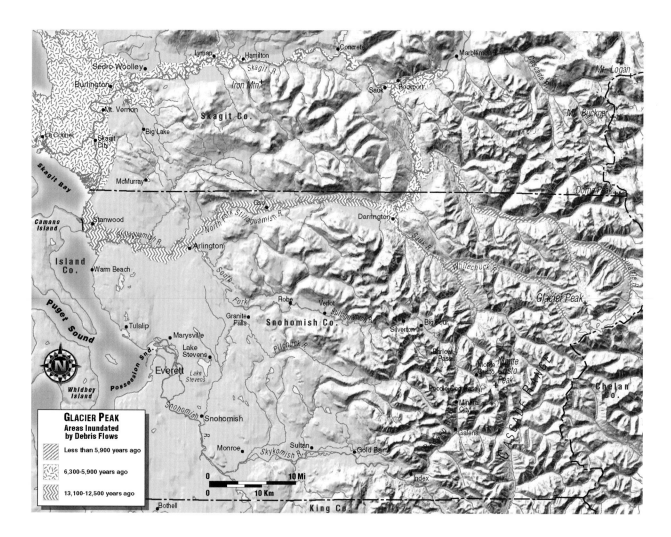

GLACIER PEAK
Areas Inundated
by Debris Flows

Less than 5,900 years ago

6,300-5,900 years ago

13,100-12,500 years ago

later that year on July 18; a 5.0 near Hartford on March 25, 1955; a 4.0 east northeast of Monroe on November 1, 1969; and a 4.1 southeast of Darrington on November 23, 1971. The deep intraslab 7.1, 6.5, and 6.8 quakes of April 13, 1949, April 29, 1965, and February 28, 2001 caused moderate damage to county structures, as they were centered in southern Puget Sound. Due to a very small population and a lack of records, there is no evidence of damage from the events of June 1869, December 7 and 12, 1880, or the powerful 7.4 north Cascades earthquake of December 14, 1872. Geologists pinpoint the last great subduction zone earthquake off the Pacific coast as having occurred on January 27, 1700. These monster events with magnitudes of 8.0 and above are estimated to occur every 300 to 500 years.

Fertile eastern Washington hills of windblown loess soil deposits which became the rolling wheat fields of the Palouse Hills show that the climate then turned dry 15 million years ago. These deep, easily eroded lands are the home of modern dry land farming operations, providing major export crops from the Pacific Northwest.

Violent new life began in the Cascade volcanoes three million years later, resuming a process which continues to the present and led to the eruption of Mt. St. Helens on May 18, 1980. Once again water laden sediments were sinking into the western trough, this time though at less of an angle. As a result the new peaks generally were well to the east of the old western Cascade volcanoes. These earlier mountains had subsided when they lost their base of hot, steam filled magma and now were replaced by our more familiar ones.

Some eruptive sites fizzled out after a single emission, such as the Whitechuck cinder cone, but around 750,000 years ago the great stratovolcanic mass of Glacier Peak came into being. Of the five major volcanic peaks in the state, Glacier Peak is the oldest, with Oregon's Mt. Hood next in age at less than 700,00 years. It also is the least known. Because it lies so far to the east and is in an area of other peaks in the 8,000 foot category, Glacier's 10,451 foot summit is screened from view by the front range of the Cascades behind the foothills bordering the Puget Sound Lowlands. In addition, no roads approach its base. Long hikes up Forest Service trails into stunning alpine views of the Glacier Peak Wilderness Area provide the only access.

At first this volcano's hot lava flowed to the east, bordering Lime Ridge. Then, as its dimensions grew, the glowing material crested over the top of the ridge and spread down into the Whitechuck River southeast of Darrington before coming to a halt. Its powdered pumice and water-borne glacial debris gave the stream its Chinook jargon name of "white water." To the east and north the Suiattle River was pushed against the bulk of Miners Ridge.

The last major eruption of Glacier Peak was a landmark event. Approximately 11,200 years ago a series of nine or more separate outpourings spewed pumice to depths of at least 12 feet a dozen miles from the peak and created an atmospheric cloud which carried ash through central Idaho and into Montana. In addition, one third of a cubic mile of pumice moved down into the valley of the Whitechuck River. Geologists use this ash layer as a dating device, as with the later eruption of Oregon's Mt. Mazama. Unlike that volcano, whose collapsing dome filled with water and created Crater Lake, the summit of Glacier Peak remained largely intact. Winds blowing over the pumice deposits on dry summer afternoons still can create clouds of dust, causing passing airline pilots to radio in reports of what appears to be forest fire smoke. Although there have been no more recent eruptions of the mountain on that scale, there still are springs of water heated by underground magma at Sulphur, and Gamma creeks around the edges of the peak. Popular Kennedy hot spring was covered by a landslide during a major storm in October 2003. Debris flows (called lahars) may constitute more of a danger to nearby residents than lava and ash. In the fifteen thousand years since the last ice age glaciers retreated from the vicinity of the peak, geologists have evidence of major flows around 13,000 and 6,000 years ago. Some of that material with its consistency of wet concrete reached Puget Sound. One such event came down the Whitechuck and Sauk rivers and filled the site of Darrington. It blocked the main channel of the Sauk River from flowing down what is now the north fork of the Stillaguamish River valley and created a huge lake. Eventually, the debris eroded away on the north edge, causing the Sauk River to flow northward instead along its present channel into the Skagit River. The danger of lahars continues, primarily along the upper reaches of the Suiattle and Whitechuck rivers, as the acidic waters of the Cascade volcanoes weaken the cone rock to where it may crumble and slide down the mountain either of its own accord or due to earthquakes. An eruption also can trigger such a flow, as with Mt. St. Helens in 1980. Scientists have concluded that the largest credible lahar would require perhaps a third of the upper cone to collapse and slide. Such an event could send debris down the Sauk and Skagit valleys to the Skagit flats in several hours. For the Sauk River again to flow down the North Fork Stillaguamish valley its channel would have to be blocked to a depth of perhaps 30 feet, most likely to occur only after a series of eruptions and debris flows coming down the Suiattle River to its confluence with the Sauk just north of the Snohomish-Skagit county line.

Two million years ago the ice ages began, the Pleistocene era. As the climate grew cooler and wetter, glaciers began to grow. Each winter they advanced a little farther, and each summer melted back a little less. In time the Cordilleran ice sheet moved down from the British Columbia mountains, filled the Fraser River valley and the Straits of Georgia, and worked its way south through the Puget Sound Lowlands. As the ice moved, additional glaciers advanced down the valleys of the Cascade Mountains, scouring out their distinctive U-shaped valley sidewalls and floors. How many times this occurred, no one knows, as later episodes destroyed the evidence left by previous ones. Perhaps the second to the last ended 100,000 years ago, followed by the usual interglacial warming and drying time. Limited evidence suggests that much of the present western portion of the county then was covered by a large body of fresh water known to geologists as Lake Snohomish.

It is known that the most recent invasion of the ice climaxed about 15,000 years ago, and that its Puget Lobe extended as far as Toledo, south of Olympia. This Fraser Glaciation brought a sea of ice to a depth of almost a mile across the western third of the county, roughly the same height as Mt. Pilchuck! As this enormously heavy mass of ice moved it carried with it debris ranging from house sized boulders to finely ground sediments. When the ice quickly melted back it left these deposits to annoy gardeners, lawn makers, and well drillers, but to delight those in the sand and gravel industry— making this the county's most valuable mineral resource.

For those who live along the scenic bluffs bordering Puget Sound and for many others along steep hillsides or attempting to maintain railroad and highway rights-of-way, the glacial inheritance is a decidedly mixed blessing. A large lake had filled the low lying Sound lands as the advancing ice blocked normal flow patterns, its sediments creating a thick layer of clay. Over this impermeable layer came one of loose sand washed off the glacial ice in its seasonal melting. Then when the ice lobe began its retreat back to the north, it left that layer of glacial till spread over the top as mixed size hardpan. In the years since, a thin soil layer has been

Lake Stevens is the county's largest, with Mt. Pilchuck to the east. Glacial ice, which dug out the lake, once was as deep as the 5,000-foot mountain. (Courtesy David Cameron)

created to blanket these strata.

Glacial strata may be exposed along the bluffs of the coast line, especially in the southwestern portion of the county where the edges of steep drop offs and gullies provide sweeping views out over the sound and privacy from any close neighbors. However, when severe winter storms with their rain, snow melt, and strong wind saturate the ground and loosen vegetative cover, these soil layers can create an environment of landslides and resulting property damage. Water may percolate through breaks in the till, load up the unstable sands, and be blocked from further sinking by the impermeable clay silts. When this happens the sand may liquefy and slide, covering railroad tracks below and eroding people's yards. In some years this has resulted in millions of dollars of damage, blockage of roads, and engine crews finding parts of their trains swept over the breakwater and into Puget Sound.

Along the edges of the glacial lobe the ice dumped its load in lateral moraines, long ridges of gravelly deposits. These moraines, the lower mountains rounded off by the grinding action, and the U-shaped valleys show that the last glaciation curved around the mountains from roughly the Whitechuck River where it enters the Sauk River, westerly down the north fork of the Stillaguamish River to turn southward around Twin Lakes east of Arlington, and then up the south fork of the Stillaguamish River to Verlot. Rounding Iron Mountain east of Granite Falls, the ice followed the line of the Menzel Lake Road toward Lake Roesiger, but then angled southeasterly along Blue Mountain to create Wallace Falls and extend up the Skykomish River to "Zeke's Hill" where U.S. 2 wraps behind Mt. Persis on its way east toward Index.

Blocked by the ice, Cascade rivers turned into deep lakes extending far back into the mountains and up the sides of the valleys, leaving deposits of blue clay to trouble future road builders. As the ice retreated, rivers returned to wander across the flattened lowlands toward Puget Sound instead of having to work along the edges of the blockage. The Skykomish, for example, had been forced to flow south into the Proctor Creek drainage. Glacial moraines are seen here and also at Sand Hill east of Granite Falls on the south fork of the Stillaguamish River. That one is so high that the first automobile road headed east up its steep slope was filled with zigzags, sometimes requiring Model T Fords to work their way up backwards. It still is a challenge when snow covered and frosty in winter.

Melting of the ice was not uniform. Some deposits lasted longer than others and were surrounded by deposits of glacial debris (or tills). Finally, they too disappeared, leaving holes into which water naturally drained, creating lakes as large as Stevens and Goodwin and smaller ones such as Martha and Silver.

During interglacial periods moisture decreases and temperatures rise. By 10,000 years ago, the water (earlier tied up as ice) had melted, and the sea level rose to 300 feet above where it had been at the height of the ice age, when the Pacific coast line had extended 30 miles to the west from where it is now. As the Strait of Juan de Fuca re-opened and the sea levels rose, salt water also returned to Puget Sound.

These waters gradually created a rich blend of microenvironments of shallow tidal flats between the mainland and Camano Island, estuaries and deltas at the mouths of the Stillaguamish and Snohomish river systems (which were influenced by tidal flows up their

Salmon in Snohomish County

By Roger Kelley

Eighteen thousand years ago Puget Sound and Snohomish County lay 4,000 feet beneath the glaciers of the Cordilleran ice sheet. The frozen landscape of glaciation was followed by a period of rapid temperature increase. As the temperature increased, the ice melted, creating rivers that were milky with the sediments of "rock flour", heavy silt created by the constant grinding action of a moving glacier on the landscape. These rivers moved with tremendous force and little resistance through valleys of glacial outwash carrying huge boulders, creating and abandoning channels as they constantly migrated across a wide floodplain.

During the ice age and the warming period that led to the retreat of the glaciers, the salmon lived in Beringia, an ice-free region stretching from Northwest Alaska to Siberia, or in ice-free streams of the Columbia River basin. Gradually, over a period of about 10,000 years, the climate cooled and the salmon began to migrate to the rivers of Puget Sound and Snohomish County.

The environment the first salmon entered bore little resemblance to Snohomish County today. The hot, dry climate of the post-glaciation era left riverbanks with little vegetation to cool the water or stabilize the riverbanks. This lack of cover increased stream water temperature to a point that was too warm to sustain salmon and deprived them of the insects that fall from the plants into the water, a large part of the fish's diet.

Even with these conditions, a few salmon managed to spawn. Their offspring survived the pounding of the gravel-filled and silt-laden rivers by migrating to calmer off-channel branches. These areas, adjacent to the mainstream rivers, provided calmer waters for young fish, but often dried up when channels changed, leaving them prey for predators. Yet, the salmon persisted.

Manu Esteve 2001

As the climate continued to cool and the environment stabilize, the native plants we see today began to dominate the landscape. Hemlock and western red cedar grew along rivers and streams, their roots stabilizing the banks and shade from their branches cooling the water. As trees died and fell, pools were created where salmon rested and hid. Huge logjams eventually created sloughs and off-channel areas. These also slowed the water, allowing sediments to settle to the stream bottom and increasing the supply of nutrients.

As the rivers and the landscape changed, so did the salmon. As each species evolved, they developed lifecycle traits that led to the utilization of all areas of the watershed. Chum and pink salmon spawn in the lower reaches, migrating to sea immediately after leaving their gravel nests. Coho prefer smaller tributaries and branches farther inland. Because of their jumping ability, coho use streams that are inaccessible to other salmon. Chinook are the largest species, spawning in the larger tributaries and mainstream rivers. Sockeye migrate to a lake immediately after spawning, where they stay for about one year before migrating down to the saltwater.

Our county's streams and rivers have changed dramatically since the end of the last ice age and continue to evolve. Natural pressures include flooding, scouring of the stream bottom, landslides, new channels forming as a stream meanders across a flood plain, plus trees and other vegetation falling into the water. These processes are being magnified, hastened, and altered by our increasing population.

Through logging and agriculture, the industries which helped create Snohomish County, humans unknowingly contributed to the decline of the salmon runs. In the late nineteenth century rivers were cleaned of individual logs and jams which prevented navigation of the rivers but had provided salmon with protection from predators, created rearing ponds, and helped lower the water temperatures. Logging next to streams led to bank erosion. Larger amounts of silt smothered salmon eggs and clogged fish gills. As shade trees were removed from stream banks, temperature increased to a point that salmon could not tolerate. As farms and dairies began to be established in the fertile river valleys of the Snohomish, Stillaguamish, and Skykomish rivers, land was drained, streams relocated and straightened, and dikes built as protection against floodwaters. Today there are approximately 50 miles of dikes protecting nearly 20,000 acres along the Snohomish River and its sloughs. In the Stillaguamish watershed the course of the river was diverted from its original course into Hatt Slough. These changes provide security for homes and properties but prevent fish from reaching spawning or rearing grounds.

As the human population increased, the fish that once were plentiful in county streams decreased. This steep decline came to public attention in May 1999 when chinook salmon throughout Puget Sound were listed as a threatened species under the federal Endangered Species Act. Bull trout were added five months later.

The factors which led to the decline of these and other fish species are tied directly to Snohomish County's popularity as a place to live, work, and raise a family. To accommodate the county's increasing population more bridges, roads, schools, businesses, and homes must be built. This construction has altered the habitat which sustained the salmon for centuries.

Today, rain that once took days or weeks to reach a creek or stream now travels the same distance in hours, creating water volumes and velocities that destroy salmon nests ("redds") and flush young fish out of rearing areas. Culverts needed to build roads over creeks can become barriers to fish migration. Wetlands that filtered and slowed water and kept streams flowing year round have been filled. Snohomish County's creeks carry pollution from homes, businesses, streets, pets, and parking lots. Removing native plants from banks continues to cause erosion and increase water temperatures. All of these actions and others have reduced or eliminated the habitat required to maintain healthy fish populations and left us with difficult choices if the salmon are to survive.

Information from Lichatowich, Jim. *Salmon Without Rivers: A History of the Pacific Salmon Crisis.* Island Press, Washington, D.C., 1999.

channels and over their marshes), bays at Tulalip and Port Gardner, and open areas of beach sand and cobble to the south.

Into these waters came the five varieties of Pacific salmon: chinook, coho, chum, pink, and sockeye. Neither the Stillaguamish nor the Snohomish rivers is home to the sockeye, but they may be found in the waters draining into the Skagit system to the north and in those streams feeding Lake Washington to the south, including those from southern Snohomish County. Lake Washington also holds runs of chinook and coho. All these anadromous fish are born in fresh water and migrate to the ocean to mature, returning late in life in huge runs up the rivers and streams to spawn once and die. Unlike the single cycle of the salmon, anadromous trout of the steelhead, cutthroat, and Dolly Varden varieties may return several times to lay their eggs. Fresh waters of the county also hold native resident populations of these trout, along with Arctic grayling, white fish, sturgeon, and sculpins.

Puget Sound is home to the small smelt and herring, along with flounder, cod, rock cod, perch, skates, small sharks and the awesome orcas, or killer whales. Crab, clams, oysters, mussels, and barnacles may be found, along with porpoises, seals, and sea lions. Ducks, geese, and grebes are abundant, especially along the tidal flats in north county. Inland are loons, eagles, hawks, ospreys, blue herons, ravens, owls, grouse, pigeons, doves, herons, waterfowl, and varieties of shore and songbirds.

Among the land animals, black bear and occasional grizzlies are native, as are white-tailed deer and elk. Mountain goats inhabit the high, rocky country to the east, while beaver and muskrats find homes near water, Marten and fisher roam forested areas, and big cats of the lynx, bobcat, and cougar varieties are resident. Coyotes have adapted quickly to the human presence, sharply increasing their populations. Grey wolves periodically are seen in the Cascades.

As the land slowly warmed and a layer of humus developed over the glacial till, trees began to cover the once barren and devastated area. Lodgepole and then white pines came first, followed by immense stands of Douglas fir. Western red cedar and western hemlock are better adapted to growth in the shade of the towering firs, however, and the old growth forest up to approximately 3,000 feet in elevation came to be dominated by them. When fires burn or storms blow down stands of trees, Douglas fir can re-establish itself, especially on drier lands, as it is prolific in producing cones with viable seed. Pacific silver fir is abundant at the higher levels of this temperate western hemlock zone, with deciduous trees also found in wetter areas and those which have been disturbed. Here are red alder, cottonwood, and big leaf maple, with understories of salal, ferns, and often damp tangles of vine maple.

Above the hemlock lies the Pacific silver fir zone, ranging in elevation from 2,000 to 4,200 feet, depending upon local conditions. Here there is a mix of Douglas fir, noble fir, and

Misty trees near Blanca Lake are typical of the old growth forest which covered virtually all of the county before 1860. (Courtesy Louise Lindgren)

western hemlock, with western red cedar and western white pine also among the silver fir. At higher elevations the pungent Alaska cedar and mountain hemlock also appear, with some open sub-alpine meadows.

From 4,200 to 5,500 feet is the mountain hemlock zone, with subalpine fir, Pacific silver fir, Alaska cedar, and (in drier sites) lodgepole pine. Upper elevations often are spotted with mixes of species, with understories of heaths, brightly blooming asters, and members of the rose family. For much of the western Cascade range, the continuous forest ends around 4,600 feet, with outcrops and rock faces, talus slopes, and snowfields predominating. Alpine meadows and lakes, glaciers, and exposed rock (covered much of the year by snow) dominate the high country.

Primarily in the lower elevations and along the open margins of the forests in pre-European contact times, a substantial number of root and berry plants were found which were utilized for human nourishment. A few open prairie areas existed, caused by natural and aboriginal human burning. In historical times these included Woods and Cochran's prairies along Woods Creek north of Monroe, Kent on Portage Creek south of Arlington, Sauk at the base of Prairie Mountain northeast of Darrington, and Allen at the site of today's Evergreen State Fair grounds and Valley General Hospital in Monroe. Deep in the mountains the higher ridges contained large open areas of meadow, the home of later ripening berry fields favored by bear and Native Americans alike in their preparations for winter. In the late nineteenth and early twentieth centuries herds of sheep were grazed here as well, temporarily expanding the range of the natural grasses. This practice came to an end when wool prices dropped in the face of human-made synthetic fibers, starting with rayon in the early 1930s.

Tiger lily, blue common camas, and wild carrot have edible roots, as do bracken, wood, and sword fern. [*Note: The creamy white meadow death camas, Zygadenus venenosus, is a lethally poisonous plant sometimes found near the blue. Some tribal people vigorously weeded it out so that there was no confusion between the two.*] The varieties of huckleberry and blueberry, salmon berry, salal berry, raspberry, tiny native strawberry and blackberry, thimbleberry, blackcaps, and elderberry abounded, ripening first close to Puget Sound and then progressively toward the higher elevations as the season advanced. Hazel nuts, rose hips, kinnikinnick, wild plums and crabapples, and a variety of plants with leaves and new shoots also were utilized for food. Many of the berries were gathered by the early American settlers, but most now have been supplanted by exotic introduced varieties raised commercially or let run wild, such as the Himalaya blackberries, which create dense and thorny thickets on both roadsides and vacant city lots.

In the Puget Sound Lowlands, which comprise roughly a third of the county's 2,098 square miles (larger than the states of Rhode Island and Delaware and half the size of Connecticut), the dominant features are the three river valleys, with their deep soils of till and silty lake deposits. These are underlain by sands and clays, often requiring complex

Clear waters of the North Fork Skykomish River at Index, framed by Mts. Index and Persis, continue to provide important habitat for salmon and steelhead trout. (Courtesy Louise Lindgren)

systems of drainage to run off the effects of constant seasonal rains and frequent November flooding.

The Stillaguamish in the north created a long, glacier carved valley from near present day Darrington westerly to its mouth near Stanwood, until the main channel gradually changed its course southward to empty into Port Susan through Hatt Slough. Its south fork begins in steep mountains north of Monte Cristo, cutting sharply through treacherous Robe Canyon and past Granite Falls before more gently meeting the north fork at Arlington. Because its narrow, rugged valley east of Mt. Pilchuck is drenched with heavy rains, water levels quickly rise, and clay deposits are washed into the stream bed, making fish survival more difficult than on the river's far more productive north fork, which is known for its winter steelhead fishing.

Dominating the southern section of the county is the Snohomish River complex, created from the Snoqualmie River and its immense drainage basin in King County joining with the Skykomish River, which runs close to the south Snohomish county line to the rivers' juncture in the Tualco region near Monroe. Steep breaks through bedrock on the south fork of the Skykomish River produce spectacular Canyon, Eagle, and Sunset Falls, readily seen from U.S. 2 and passing passenger trains. The river's north fork cuts its way through bedrock more gradually and provides a traveler's route almost to the crest of the Cascades. The Sultan and Pilchuck rivers drain the Sultan Basin and south side of Mt. Pilchuck, emptying into the main stem at Sultan and Snohomish respectively. Where the Pilchuck River enters the lowlands and curves south it comes within a mile of the South Fork Stillaguamish River as it brushes Granite Falls and heads north. This created a short

Looking east over Everett in the 1960s. Cascade Mountain peaks on the skyline include Whitehorse, Three Fingers, Big Bear, Liberty, Pilchuck, and the corner of Glacier Peak. Urban areas lie in the Puget Sound Lowlands and the lower mountain valleys. (Courtesy Everett Public Library)

portage between the two systems which was used by Native American peoples in their dugout canoes almost into the twentieth century.

Deep in the Cascades, the Sauk River differs from the others in that its dominant flow is to the north, joining the Skagit River near Rockport in Skagit County. Its south fork forms at Monte Cristo, then drops steeply to join the north fork at Bedal. The north fork of the Sauk, as of the Skykomish, forms a natural travel route from its thundering falls above Bedal to Indian and White passes, where easterly flowing streams head down toward the Columbia River. Above and below Darrington the Whitechuck and Suiattle rivers bring their glacial and pumice laden waters into the Sauk, again with a short portage possible westerly to the headwaters of the north fork of the Stillaguamish River.

Although stories abound that the way summer in the county may be told from winter is that the rain is warmer in July, the area really does have a typical period of dry weather and warm temperatures. The problem is that those weeks start late and end too early! Its mid-latitude West Coast marine climate is heavily influenced by the presence of the Pacific Ocean, whose moisture comes ashore from the southwest and west during the rainy season due to the rotation of the earth. In the drier months the Pacific atmospheric low pressure area moves northward, allowing the late spring high to form. Temperatures average nearly 76 degrees Fahrenheit during July in the extreme northern and southern coastal areas from Stanwood and Mukilteo down to Edmonds and Woodway, cooling toward the Cascades. January readings average about freezing near the salt water and drop sharply to around 16 degrees in the mountains northeast of Darrington.

Rainfall is influenced very much by the topography. To the west the Olympic Mountains create a rainshadow effect extending along the western lowlands, where Everett averages some 35½ inches per year—almost entirely as rain. As the winds carry the clouds easterly, they are forced to rise first over the foothills and then the full heights of the Cascade range. Monroe (at the edge of the hills) averages 46¾ inches; Darrington (behind the first range of mountains) averages over 80 inches, and the notoriously wet shoulders of Mt. Pilchuck have averaged 144 inches at Verlot. Perhaps 200 inches could fall near the Cascade crest, mostly as winter snow. Three-quarters of the precipitation falls from October to March, as the often dry autumn ends with high winds and constant rains. November usually is the worst month for flooding, especially around Thanksgiving. Early snowfalls quickly melt off with torrential tropical rains from the Hawaiian Islands, creating serious damage along the courses of the rivers. To date the "100 year flood" levels are measured from a memorable week in 1897, which wrecked much of the county's transportation system and washed away the town of Sauk City at the mouth of the Sauk River in eastern Skagit County. Recent major floods also have occurred in November 1975, December 1980, twice in November 1990 and in October 2003.

Winter snow levels vary generally from 1,500 to 2,500 feet, with the higher peaks in the 6,500 to 7,000 foot range remaining blanketed in scenic white year round. Much of the winter lower level snow pack is wet and heavy, again causing damage to structures and bridges and routinely closing access to the high country until late spring and early summer melt.

Frequently, a "Puget Sound convergence zone" is created by the action of the southwesterly winds sweeping around both sides of the Olympic Mountains, bringing rain and high winds into the county while leaving areas on either side dry and calmer. However,

Snohomish County is too far south to be affected by the effects of cold winter winds and ice storms blowing down the Fraser River into Whatcom and Skagit counties, and the county also misses some of the extreme winds along Hood Canal and the Strait of Juan de Fuca. Easterly winds during the summer may bring low humidity and high fire danger from across the mountains, while in the fall heavy fogs drift across the lowlands from Puget Sound, often burning off in late morning to reveal a sparkling landscape, building a reservoir of pleasant memories to carry its residents through yet another round of autumn rains.

The Native Americans

As the glacial ice retreated northward and higher up the mountain valleys, the climate was cooler, wetter, and more humid than the present. Then, into this area of thin soils and pine forests, hunting bands of people began to appear. They may have come into the Puget Sound area from the north, perhaps down the Fraser River, or from the unglaciated areas along the lower Columbia River and the Cowlitz River in southwestern Washington. Humans also may have occupied the region prior to the last glaciation, but any evidence of that would have been destroyed.

The archaeological record is far from complete, especially in what now is Snohomish County. The rising sea levels and land rebounding from the weight of the ice, then a climate of warm, acidic rain destroyed most artifacts of organic origin. The tremendous alterations in the last 225 years (resulting from catastrophic death rates among the native peoples from foreign diseases), followed by rapid urbanization and cutting over of the ancient forest cover for houses, farms, businesses, and highways make scientific interpretation of the past most difficult.

Drawing upon archaeological work throughout the Puget Sound and upland river regions, it appears that people were here 12,000 years ago. Little evidence (primarily stone tools) remains even for the past 5,000 to 10,000 years. Four differing tool traditions have been identified along the northwest coast of the United States. These are the fluted point (or Clovis, as it is known elsewhere in North America); the stemmed point; the pebble tool (or Olcott); and the microblade. The fluted point is very widespread around the continent, and possibly the type used by hunters at the Sequim Manis mastodon site on the Olympic Peninsula. These projectile points also have been found on the surface near Olympia and Chehalis, as well as on Whidbey Island. The Manis site has 10 layers dating from 12,000 to 6,000 years ago, with the fluted point probably in the 10,000 to 9,000 period. Most likely it spread down the Columbia River and then up to Puget Sound.

Even less is known of the stemmed point, but its dates are about the same. It may have developed among the ancestors of the Sahaptin-speaking peoples of the interior and spread from the Great Basin culture area down the Snake River and the Columbia Rivers to the ancestors of the Chinook-speaking people. It was used primarily for hunting.

The third tradition, the pebble tool (or Olcott), is widespread throughout the Puget Sound region, northward into the Queen Charlotte Islands of British Columbia, and southward to the Oregon coast. It holds a local distinction, as the Olcott site lies on the south fork of the Stillaguamish River drainage upstream from Arlington, where remains

In 1905 William We-allup was drying salmon for winter, a regular part of the yearly food cycle, done over open fires and later in smokehouses. Predictable fish runs, along with a very wide range of tools and technologies to catch them, made salmon the dietary staple. (Courtesy Everett Public Library)

were found on several terraces above the river. Artifacts of this style date from approximately 9,000 to 10,000 years ago (at the maximum) to approximately 5,000 years ago, a period of warming and drying, with Douglas firs dominating the forests. Flakes used for scrapers, leaf-shaped points, antlers for woodworking, polished soapstone, and bits of obsidian have been found. Most of the tools were made from basalt and siltstone. It appears that the people fished as much as hunted, perhaps spreading their culture from the salt water up the rivers and streams and into the mountains as the salmon spawning grounds advanced and the climate improved. The pebble tool culture may have originated in western Siberia in the Kamchatka Peninsula and around the Sea of Okhotsk, spreading around and southward down the Pacific coast where the salmon were plentiful. By 3,500 years ago there is some evidence of people ceremonially potlatching and using masks, practices which continue to the present. These were the ancestors of the present Coast Salish people.

Lastly, the Microblade tradition arrived from the north. It featured small, sharp blades (which might then be inset into handles for easier cutting) struck off from a central stone core. Evidence of these tools and their users' orientation toward the sea for subsistence has been found in southwestern Washington by 7,000 years ago. Within another 2,000 years, the people who carried these several tool kits and ways of living had adapted, mixed, and created the bases for a flourishing culture focused on the exploitation of both sea and land resources.

For a better understanding of the development of Native American culture, archaeologists classify the time from at least 12,000 and down to 5,000 years ago as one of generalized hunting and gathering. People then lived and traveled in small groups, based in the river valleys during the winter and obtained food from rivers and higher elevation lands during the summer. Late in the season, they moved into the foothills and Cascade Mountains for big game and berries. Tool making and food preservation activities would be in temporary base camps and probably followed traditional annual routines, varying with the availability of food. Now extinct species (such as bison, mastodon, and caribou) were hunted, along with present ones, but there is no evidence of deep piles of shellfish middens or substantial dependence on salmon. Those would come later.

From approximately 5,000 to 2,500 years ago, the period is defined as one of the development of specialized resource use. During this period there are more differences apparent between the people who lived along the salt water and those whose homes were in the upstream river valleys. Higher sea levels may have covered earlier remains along island beaches and the river mouths. Trade with people living east of the Cascade Mountains was undertaken, based on remains of tool styles and materials which were used on the Columbia Basin and found here. Contact with people on the coast also may have been important. The seasonal patterns of obtaining food continued, as tools became more refined and large permanent winter village sites developed along the bays and river systems. Anadromous fish were a major source of food, and populations grew with better winter storage techniques.

Shaping a western red cedar log into a well balanced and maneuverable dugout canoe took a great amount of skill and labor. Models varied from large sea-going designs with high prows to break the waves to long, slim versions suitable for ascending and descending white water rivers. (Courtesy David Cameron)

These patterns continued. From 2,500 to 250 years ago the population reached its maximum density, with stable communities from the salt water islands to the heads of Cascade river navigation. Trade, resource utilization, and technology reached their peaks.

In 1774 Spaniard Juan Perez reached Nootka Sound on the west coast of Vancouver Island, followed by the British explorer James Cook in 1778. In late spring 1792 George Vancouver's expedition members were the first Europeans to sight what was to become Snohomish County. With these observers' written reports begins the ethnohistoric cultures period, roughly the last 225 years on the Northwest Coast.

Vancouver did not find a culture untainted by European contact, even though no other foreigners yet had stepped ashore. In the few ensuing years since the first Nootka encounters, the waves of almost unimaginable numbers of deaths already had begun. Europeans had experienced the deadly cycles of bubonic plague beginning in the fourteenth century, met new diseases with their explorations of the coasts of Africa and then Asia, and in the millennium before then had been on the receiving end of outbreaks which had begun in central Asia and traveled the Silk Road and caravan routes into the Roman and Byzantine empires. Surviving populations had developed limited immunities to many of these pestilences, but the North American population had none.

The Northwest Coast culture area, stretching from southeastern Alaska to northern California along a narrow strip 1,500 miles long between the Pacific Ocean and the mountains, was the home of perhaps 200,000 people. Within a century that figure had dropped by 80 percent, a devastating reduction double that of Europe's Black Death. From one of the densest populations of non-farming people in the world, it became a shattered

19

remnant of survivors unable to stop or even deeply influence the incoming tide of European settlers.

Major disease outbreaks have been charted, beginning probably with smallpox carried aboard the Spanish Heceta/Quadra expedition of 1775. This pandemic killed perhaps a third of the native people. It was followed by another wave in 1801, carried from the interior Plains people to the Columbia Basin and then to the Pacific. A little over two decades later either smallpox or measles took another ten percent in the "Mortality" of 1824 and 1825. Five years later malaria appeared at Fort Vancouver near the mouth of the Columbia River, spreading southward along the Willamette River and into California. While it did not move north into the cooler Puget Sound region, it did take away perhaps 85 percent of the Lower Columbia people. Americans brought this scourge, either by fur trappers arriving from the Mississippi Valley or sea-borne traders aboard the vessels "Owyhee" and "Convoy." With the area largely depopulated, Americans seeking new land would flock into the Willamette in the decades following, and only slowly moved northward toward Puget Sound when the best selection was taken.

Smallpox ravaged the northern people in 1836 through 1838, perhaps also visiting the central Washington coast, but not documented in Puget Sound. During the 1840s Americans by the thousands followed the Oregon Trail to Fort Vancouver, while the Hudson's Bay Company developed Fort Nisqually at the mouth of that southern Puget Sound river. With the immigrants came more varieties of disease: dysentery, measles, typhus, influenza, and the common cold. In spring 1848 they worked their way through the Sound peoples from the Nisqually up to Fort Victoria, killing many more.

Fortunately the Hudson's Bay Company also brought vaccination for smallpox, stopping outbreaks in 1853 and again in 1862–1863. These epidemics took many victims on either side of Puget Sound, but no longer in this area, although the Lower Skagit people were especially hard hit. Measles reappeared in 1868 and 1874.

In the case of smallpox, those who survived carried an immunity. This could not be passed on to their children. Thus the disease would spread into the newer population and strike the young, a pattern similar to that of Europe. Living in communal houses helped transfer the contagions, while traditional patterns of sweating and then bathing in cold water might induce pneumonia.

In the mid- and late-nineteenth century, chronic illnesses, introduced venereal disease, alcoholism, and depressing cultural changes brought on by the restrictive life on reservations brought on a continuing drop in population. For those people continuing to live in their traditional valley areas, medical services and white community support were virtually non-existent.

For the Lushootseed-speaking population, which included those living from the Skagit River south to Olympia and east to the Cascade Mountains, estimates are that 11,835 people lived here prior to European contact. That number had dropped to 3,549 in the 1870 census. In 1984 it had risen to 15,963, and even higher if members of the then federally unrecognized tribes were included. The people here fared far better than many others, as the overall Northwest Coast population fell from its pre-1774 estimate of 200,000 to a low of 33,000, with virtual extinction of native culture in the sections to the south where malaria had taken its toll.

Although Europeans contacted the Northwest Coast people in the 1770s, the first face-to-face meeting here between the two did not occur until June of 1792, when the

British scientific and diplomatic expedition led by Captain George Vancouver entered the western waters and made landfalls. He noted the considerable effects of disease on the population and that they already possessed metals. In 1827 the Hudson's Bay Company established Fort Langley at the mouth of the Fraser River, followed by Fort Nisqually northeast of present-day Olympia. There was no permanent fur trading or agricultural post between those locations. Roman Catholic missionary fathers Francis Norbert Blanchet, Modeste Demers, and then J.B.Z. Bolduc passed through to work with the Sound peoples between 1839 and 1843 but did not establish permanent missions and thus had little lasting influence. It was not until after the United States had taken over ownership of the Oregon Country south of the 49th parallel in 1846 and the Washington Territory was created in 1853 that there was any substantial attempt to contact the native peoples or to gather information about their numbers, settlements, or ways of life. Almost 25 more years passed before Northern Pacific Railroad survey crews even entered the eastern approaches and crossed the Cascade passes. Much could change in the lives of the native peoples before any written records were kept.

Given the relative ease of water access and the great difficulty of overland travel, the large amounts of food available from the sound and rivers, and the amount of mountainous terrain in what became Snohomish County, it was natural that people lived along the waterways. Thus, the greatest population density was along Puget Sound and its two river estuaries. As upriver distances increased, population tended to decrease—a pattern duplicated by later American settlement.

The political boundaries of Snohomish County, however, later were drawn in the north and south along township survey lines rather than natural river drainages. Following the Cascade crest to divide Snohomish from Chelan County was logical to the east, as was utilizing the middle of the channel between Whidbey Island and Camano Island to separate Island County to the west, but to the native peoples the lines made less sense. Their lives centered about the water. The islands and mainland shore made a more logical unit, as did each river drainage. Thus in historic times four main tribal groups occupied most of the county, with two others utilizing smaller portions. Land use was more complex than American deeds and title, however, and after the Treaty of Point Elliot in 1855, that traditional pattern soon was destroyed.

Along the shores of Puget Sound from Warm Beach in the north to Richmond Beach in the south and up the Snohomish River to the vicinity of Monroe lived the Snohomish people. They also had villages and camps on Hat Island, the southern half of Whidbey Island from Bush Point down, and most of Camano Island. The Stillaguamish ("Stoluck-wha-mish") lived along the Stillaguamish River drainage and both of its forks, while the Skykomish ("Skai-wha-mish") inhabited the Skykomish River from Sultan to above Index on the river's north fork. To the northeast the Sauk-Suiattle ("Sah-ku-mehu") people occupied the drainages of the Sauk and Suiattle rivers. Snoqualmie ("Snoqualmoo") people had a village on the east side of the Snoqualmie River near present day Duvall in King County and bordered the Snohomish villages near Monroe. In the northwest the Kikiallus ("Kik-i-allus") had the primary rights to the northern portion of Camano Island and the mainland near Stanwood, with the majority of their territory in Skagit County to the north. The Lower Skagit had villages and rights on northern Whidbey Island. All of these groups spoke the Lushootseed language, one of the Coast Salish family. It was subdivided into northern and southern dialects, with the dividing line along the

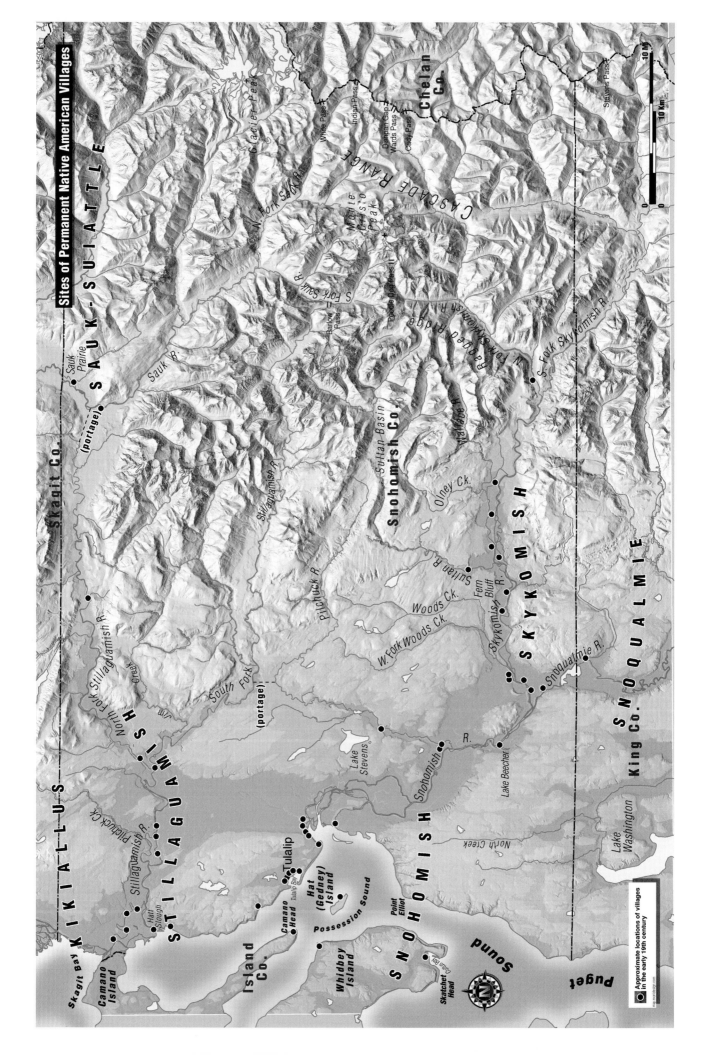

Sites of Permanent Native American Villages

SAUK-SUIATTLE

Skagit Co.

Chelan Co.

CASCADE RANGE

Stevens Pass

White Pass

Indian Pass

Dishpan Gap
Wards Pass
Cady Pass

N. Fork Sauk R.

Glacier Peak

Monte Cristo Peak

Sauk Prairie

Sauk

(portage)

Sauk R.

S. Fork Sauk R.

Barlow Pass

Poodle Dog Pass II

Ragged Ridge

N. Fork Skykomish R.

Stillaguamish R.

Snohomish Co.

Sultan Basin

S. Fork Skykomish R.

Mallace R.

Olney Ck.

SKYKOMISH

Pilchuck R.

Sultan R.

Fern

Woods Ck.

Skykomish R.

Skykomish Bluff

W. Fork Woods Ck.

Snoqualmie R.

South Fork

North Fork Stillaguamish R.

Creek

(portage)

Lake Stevens

Snohomish R.

Lake Beecher

King Co.

SNOQUALMIE

Lake Washington

Lake

North Creek

KIKIALLUS

Skagit Bay

Camano Island

Stillaguamish R.

Pilchuck Ck.

Hatt Slough

STILLAGUAMISH

Camano Head

Tulalip

Tulalip Bay

Hat (Gedney) Island

Possession Sound

Point Elliot

Island Co.

Whidbey Island

Oaks Bay

Skatchet Head

SNOHOMISH

Puget Sound

N

Approximate locations of villages in the early 19th century

10 Km

10 Mi

Snohomish River basin. The Snoqualmie people were speakers of the southern form, everyone else in the county and those along the Skagit River basin speaking the northern. People on the western side of Puget Sound spoke Twana, a related language.

Snohomish people say that wherever there is a present city, the native people earlier had a village. That statement largely is true, especially for the towns built along rivers. However, there were far more villages in the county during early pre-contact and contact times than there are present communities. Hebolb, located at Preston Point at the mouth of the Snohomish River in north Everett, was the major village in Snohomish territory, a site reported to have been fortified with a palisade against the slaving raids of the Lekwiltok Kwakiutl and others of present day British Columbia.

On Whidbey Island villages were found at Bush Point, Cultus Bay, and Sandy Point. Others were at Camano Head (destroyed by a huge landslide around 1820) and Hat Island. Mainland villages included Warm Beach (probably at Spee-bi-dah); perhaps four at Tulalip; Priest Point; an area between Priest Point and Quilceda; Quilceda; and upriver at the present city of Snohomish.

The S'dodohobc band of the Snohomish, who lived in the Monroe region, had village sites near the present S.R. 203 bridge to Duvall and two more along the south side of the Skykomish River. Along the Pilchuck River the Kwetlibubc band's villages were near Snohomish and Machias, while the Stk'talidubc band had its villages across from Sultan on the south side of the Skykomish River and probably also at Fern Bluff east of Monroe and Beecher Lake near Cathcart. A village at one exit of the Stillaguamish River on Hatt Slough may have been occupied by people associated with the Snohomish.

The Stillaguamish people also claim this site (named Sp-la-tum), and note that it had a chief named Zis-a-ba. It served as a meeting place for the Stillaguamish and various other peoples. Other villages were near Stanwood, Florence, south of Florence, three more in the lower valley, Kent Prairie south of Arlington, plus Trafton and Hazel on the north fork of the river.

Skykomish people had their villages at Sultan, probably Startup, then Gold Bar and Index. Perhaps others lived above Index on the north fork of the Skykomish, but there is insufficient evidence to tell. The Sauk-Suiattle villages were at the mouth of the Suiattle River where it enters the Sauk River in Skagit County and at Sauk Prairie, northeasterly across the river from Darrington. A busy summer site was at Bedal, where the Sauk River divides into its north and south forks.

Each village was composed of long, multi-family houses built of cedar planks attached to permanent large cedar posts. They averaged 40 to 50 feet in width and 80 to 100 feet in length, although the potlatch house (used for ceremonies rather than for daily living) could be much longer. In recent times one at Tulalip was 115 feet long, another at Guemes Island some 250 feet, and Old Man House of the Suquamish tribe was 500 feet in length. Normally they had single pitched roofs with openings which could be covered over with boards to regulate the smoke rising from inside fireplaces and rain coming downward. Mat partitions divided the house into separate areas for families. Doorways opening to the outside were covered with cedar planks or the ever handy mats, which also were used for wall hangings and floor covering. These were made from woven tules and cat tails. Bed platforms were located along the sides, with storage platforms above them accessible by ladders. Here were kept the all important dried winter foods, along

Lushootseed Language
Provided by Tulalip Tribes Cultural Resources Department

Lushootseed (Puget Sound Salish) is spoken by tribal people whose ancestral territory extends from the Skagit and Nooksack Rivers in the north to the Nisqually in the south, and west along the Sound to Squaxin Island and the adjacent mainland. It is part of the Coast Salish group of related languages, which includes Lummi, Twana (spoken in the Hood Canal area) and Halkomelem (spoken in the southeast regions of Vancouver Island and on the southwest part of mainland British Columbia).

Though they share a common ancestor, the Coast Salish languages are not mutually intelligible. For example, about 40% of Twana words have easily recognizable cognates in Lushootseed, but other characteristics of the languages are so different that each must be learned as a "foreign" language by speakers of the other. The Coast Salish languages in turn are part of the larger Salish family of languages, which are spoken in interior British Columbia, Montana, Idaho, and Eastern Washington.

United States government records from the middle years of the nineteenth century document 41 Lushootseed-speaking tribes, each with its own dialect distinctive enough to identify its speakers as being from a particular group but all mutually intelligible throughout Lushootseed territory.

The most striking differences between dialects distinguish the Southern group from the Northern group on the basis of pronunciation and vocabulary.

Of the dialects attested in the mid-nineteenth century, at least ten are still heard today: old stories are still told to enrich people's understanding of their experiences; ceremonial occasions are opened and closed with ancient words whose very sound is considered a blessing in itself; and certain teachings are most effectively shared through the medium of a language whose grammar encodes the cultural values by which human life in this region has governed itself for thousands of years. Lushootseed nowadays may also be heard in classrooms, for several tribal groups, among them the Tulalip Tribes, whose reservation is just west of Marysville, offer language instruction in local schools.

Intricately woven baskets designed for a variety of uses, vertical mat house dividers, and warm fur clothing were found throughout the Lushootseed-speaking area. (Courtesy David Cameron)

In pre-treaty Snohomish County, four main groups of people lived along the river courses between the Cascades and the Sound: the Snohomish (sduhub_, a name possibly related to the Lushootseed word for *man*, stub_), whose subgroups include the Skykomish (s¬ix°ab_, Upriver People), the Monroe People (sdutuhub_, a name probably related to sduhub_), and the Pilchuck People (k°i©abab_, Red River People [*Pilchuck* means *red water* in Chinook Jargon]); the Snoqualmie (sduk°albix°, the Moon People, whose name comes from the mythic account of their beginnings); the Sauk and Suiattle River People (sa´k°bix° and suya©bix°); and the Stillaguamish (stulɑk°ab_, the River People).

The -amish (=ab_) and -omish (=ub_) suffixes mean *people*, and the -mie (=bix°) suffix means *a homogenous group or cluster*. Around 1900, a sound-change occurred in Lushootseed, and the nasal consonants, *m* and *n*, were replaced by *b* and *d*. However, many tribal, personal and place names had been recorded for United States government purposes before the sound- change occurred. Thus we have *Snohomish* surviving in English, while it has become sduhub_ in modern Lushootseed.

The main features of the landscape, the Cascades and the Sound, were known in Lushootseed as simply "the mountains"and "the salt water." The word for *mountain* is sbadil, and the plural is sbadbadil. Lushootseed has separate words for salt water and fresh water. *Salt water* is ±°alį, and this was used for both the Sound and the Ocean. The word for *fresh water*, q°u´, is forms the name for a confluence of rivers, q°u´alq°u´.

Like all of the Salish languages, Lushootseed makes use of a group of suffixes that add the meanings of whole words to the roots they are affixed to. For example, the suffix =qs means *nose* and by extension *point*, (both something sharp and a point of land jutting out into the water). Mission Point on Tulalip Reservation is known in Lushootseed as skayu´qs, Ghost (or Corpse) Point, because it was in that location that the dead were laid to rest. In the same way, Priest Point is called in Lushootseed ¢©a´qs, Rock Point; and Marysville is s¨ɑ´qs, "something hung over a point."

Another suffix frequently found in place names is =ali, meaning *a place where something is found*. White Horse Mountain is įubaliali, perhaps related to the verb įubɒ, to go across the mountains. Hat Island is known as ¢ɑ¢ɒsɒli, interpreted by elders as a *place where children are found*. One explanation for this name is that the island may have been where the wool dogs were bred and raised, to keep the line pure from interbreeding (¢a¢as is the word for *child*).

In pre-reservation times the largest Snohomish village was hibulɒb, located on Preston Point at the mouth of the Snohomish River in what is now Everett. A fortified village surrounded by a palisade, it contained the largest ceremonial longhouse in this area, as well as four other longhouses, each 100 feet long by 40 feet wide, and many smaller dwellings. It was only after the Reservation had been established that Tulalip became headquarters for the Snohomish people. The name, dx°lilap, is formed from a prefix, dx°-, meaning *direction* or *motion*, a root, lil, meaning *far*, and a suffix, =ap, meaning *end* or *bottom* . It is sometimes difficult for people today to find a way to combine all the concepts in all the parts of a word and come up with a single meaning; but one that has been proposed for dx°lilap is *far to the end*, referring to the fact that in order to reach the end of the bay (to the south), one must make one's way east around a long sand bar before turning south.

Everett is known as d£ɒ¨ig°ɒd. d£ɒ¨ means *it must be* or *it would seem*, and =ig°ɒd is a suffix referring to the inside of a body and by extension to the inside of any small place; by another sort of extension it can refer to mental or emotional processes: but how to put these together and come up with a meaning for d£ɒ¨ig°ɒd ? The meanings of some names are simply not recoverable even in part. q°ɒ§sidɒ´, (Quilceda), a creek that runs through north Marysville and has given its name to several businesses, a street and a school, is a mystery to modern Lushootseed speakers.

Some names are just single words applied to a place. Carnation, an important village of the Snoqualmie people, is tulq, *mussel* ("Tolt"), because freshwater mussels were found there. (If we were to redraw county lines according to ancestral concepts of habitation, the King-Snohomish county line would not exist.) But sometimes these single-word names can give us a surprise: Mt. Pilchuck, for example, is bɒlalg°ɒ´, *belly button*. Both the names we understand and those that we do not make us realize that people have been thinking about this Snohomish County landscape for thousands of years and that there is a heritage of human experience draped over every lake, mountain, shore and landmark, not just at s¨ɑ´qs, where this draping was commemorated in a name.

with extra blankets and other items of personal wealth. In front of the sleeping platforms were lower ones for seats and also for slaves to sleep if the regular areas were full. Fires often were shared between families and located near the sides, as the middle was kept open for an indoor passageway.

Ownership of the house might be by a single man or perhaps several, and symbols of their guardian spirits were carved on the house posts. Frequently everyone in the house was related, with leadership in the hands of a single wealthy man. Where several houses made up a village, one of those household heads was regarded as its overall leader. Primary loyalties lay with the family and village, as there was no political system unifying all the people into a tribal or geographical unit. Individuals inherited from their parents rights and privileges associated with the family and birthplace. Each village had recognized areas where its members had exclusive and shared rights through kinship ties to gather food and fish, and each individual had rights acquired through birth and marriage to utilize other areas as well.

Thus the winter fishing area bordering the village would be its exclusive territory to use, but others from nearby communities might also be able to fish there in the remaining seasons if permission were given, and those who were related to members of the village also had the right to be there. This moving about to obtain food according to the progress of the seasons and the runs of the fish led to friendships, social ties, and a feeling of unity among peoples, increased by the custom of marrying someone from outside the village.

When the Americans arrived and required the people to sign treaties in 1855 (in order for title to their lands to be taken by the United States government and the people moved to the Tulalip Reservation), the federal officials sought to appoint chiefs and sub-chiefs and to assign villages to tribal groups. This system of organization and control was not the traditional practice, nor was thinking of land and water resources in terms of exclusive private boundaries. The right to use what was there and the fact that those rights could be shared and changed through marriage and succession were the conflicting native view.

The natural environment produced enough food to allow development of a very high culture, but without the surpluses which agriculture would have provided. As a result, native people developed a yearly cycle of activities based upon the availability of fresh foods and the necessity to preserve enough for survival during the late autumn and winter

Temporary shelters made of overlapping mats to shed rain were made in a variety of sizes, depending upon the needs of people in fishing, gathering, and hunting sites. Notice the salt water canoe with its high prow and the small, one-person model. (Courtesy Everett Public Library)

Travel by canoe was done on the Sauk River until roads and logging railroads began to penetrate the upper valley in the 1930s. This is Martha Tommy poling her way upstream. (Courtesy Darrington Historical Society)

months before the coming of new plants and the annual anadromous fish runs.

For the Snohomish bands this began in April and May, with the availability first of sand rushes and then sprouts of the salmonberry. Clams, cockles, fishing on the sound, and hunting added to the menu. As summer approached, first salmonberries ripened, followed by the small wild strawberries appearing on river banks and then the islands and uplands. Clamming, fishing, and hunting continued. Blackberries and blackcaps ripened in July and August, followed by salal, blueberries, and mountain huckleberries. By late August, hunters had begun their trek into the Sultan Basin for elk. Early autumn brought salmon season, especially upstream from the present town of Snohomish, as upriver fish had lost some of their fat and could better be preserved for winter. Fall hunting for deer, elk, and bear went on in the Sultan Basin, the Pilchuck drainage, and along the upper reaches of the Skykomish River. During hunting time, many people gathered upstream near Woods Creek and Allen's Prairie to preserve fish and game and gather from the acres of hazelnuts, cooking with piles of heated flat stones covered with cedar boughs and earth.

Mountain goat hunting in the country above Index began in September, along with gathering of the tasty blueberries ripening in the higher elevations. Berries were dried in cakes for reconstituting as stewed fruit after a main dish of fish or just eating as is, while the goats provided a major source of wool for the making of clothing by the Sauk and blankets throughout the area. With the onset of October storms the people left their temporary camps of mats and wooden shelters and returned to the winter villages. During the months of cold rain and snow they hunted and fished nearby, worked on the repair and creation of necessary articles, and joined in the important season of winter ceremonials. Steelhead trout returned during January to the Pilchuck, Skykomish, Snoqualmie, and Stillaguamish drainages, and preparations were made for another year of life.

This cycle was followed in its essentials by all of the groups. Among the Sauk-Suiattle, for example, the tribal council met in early spring to assign tasks to families for the coming year. Among the upstream peoples the emphasis was more on hunting and mid-season berry gathering. They were in a less favorable environment for obtaining large amounts of food and were more dependent upon good fish runs, although the fish there were easier to preserve. When horses were introduced, it then was possible to cross the mountains to the upper Wenatchee River to catch and sun dry early winter steelhead. Later, the horses were returned over the passes to eastern Washington and allowed to roam freely during the winter until rounded up by young men and boys the following early summer. This could make for some memorable trips, as Leo Brown recalled being told by the Wenatchi people that the animals had wandered off toward Spokane. It was his job to take off after them and bring them home to the Sauk River.

Root foods also were important, especially tiger lily and wild carrot, along with bracken fern. These were gathered and the plants cared for in areas such as Kent Prairie near the forks of the Stillaguamish River and at Sauk Prairie to the point of an incipient agriculture. When potatoes were introduced in the early 1840s from trade with the Yakama people and the Hudson's Bay Company, they quickly supplanted the wild species.

A wide variety of techniques were used to take fish, including weirs, traps, gaffs, spears, gill nets set from canoes, rakes for smelt and herring, and communal baskets for flounders. Weirs and traps were especially ingenious in their construction, with varia-tions for depth, width, and power of the stream flows. Preservation was by drying on racks in the open air or under cover, along with smoking in the open or in smokehouses. Shellfish also were dried, with strings of clams especially valuable trade items for goods from upstream and eastern Washington people.

Deer, elk, and bear were valuable for their hides as well as their meat and were obtained through the use of bows and arrows, deadfalls and traps, as well as driving them off cliffs, as the Sauk-Suiattle people did with elk above Monte Cristo Lake. Mountain goats were similarly

William Shelton actively kept alive tribal culture and traditions, served as chief of police, and was known throughout the region for his carving. Story poles he created became popular sites for visitors in downtown Everett and at the state capitol building in Olympia. (Courtesy Everett Public Library)

driven. Seal were hunted by the Snohomish. Their oil was important for fat in the diet, as was that of elk and deer for the upriver people. Spears were used for beaver, while slings were effective against many birds. Waterfowl were hunted with bow and arrow, trapped with nets, and driven into fixed nets, where they could be dispatched in large numbers.

Food was cooked in watertight, coiled baskets. Water was poured in, then hot stones dropped inside to raise the temperature. Steaming in pits also was common, done out-doors in a hole heated by a fire. Ashes were scooped out, the food placed carefully inside, and then the items covered with boughs and earth, with a fire started on top to add heat. Roasting by an open fire was popular for fish, large clams, and many meats, while deer meat sometimes was roasted by wrapping pieces in cedar bark (along with some grease) and placing it on hot stones.

Inner bark from the western red cedar was a major source of material for clothing. During the chilly winter weather, coastal women wore a breechcloth of soft shredded bark under a bark knee length overskirt. When warmer weather arrived, the breechcloth was set aside. Upper-class women wore a buckskin shirt, which came down to below the knees and usually had long sleeves. Shells and otter fur were used for decoration, with strings of shells sewn under the arm and both used around the neck opening. Knee-length leggings and skin moccasins could be worn for inland or mountain travel. Lower ranking women wore a cedar bark skirt to below the knee, but without the skin shirt. Woven basketry caps were obtained in trade from the Klickitat: brimless, twined, and conical in the Plateau style; or the Cowichan of Vancouver Island, which were large and brimmed. Married women among the Snohomish wore snugly fitting soft basketry hats without brims, held on with skin straps. For rain, a long cape of cedar bark was worn, covering the body down to the hips. Bear and seal skin capes also were worn by both sexes.

Skins and wool, sometimes along with cedar bark skirts, were utilized in the interior, where the weather often was cooler and walking through undergrowth required more protection. Deerskin breechcloths were worn, as were moccasins for rugged land travel. The Sauks, living in a drier, more extreme climate, preferred Plateau-style garments similar to those of eastern Washington and did not wear shredded cedar bark.

Men used similar materials, again with class differences. A skin breechcloth, long leggings, and shirts with elbow length or no sleeves decorated often with otter fur, along with an otter fur belt lined with buckskin were common for inland winters. Lower ranking men might just wear a blanket during cold times. Men often went nude for summer.

Additional protection from the elements came from capes of bear and seal skin, as well as blankets woven from a variety of fibers. These included highly prized mountain goat wool, hair clipped from a species of dogs kept for that purpose by the Snohomish, or down from fireweed plants mixed with that from wild ducks. Men also had winter hats of animal skins: raccoon for the Snohomish and young mountain goat for the Skykomish. These latter ones had the horns and ears still intact. Children also had fur caps or strips of beaver wrapped around their heads.

Hair was worn long and braided for women, knotted and tied in the back for men. Women also practiced tattooing, while both sexes painted themselves for decorative and religious purposes as well as for protection from the elements. Unlike most neighboring people, ear rings and labrets were not worn, except for the Snoqualmie women, who pierced both ears and septum.

Differences in rank were apparent by a person's manner of speech, actions, and general behavior as well as more obvious clothing and the amount of respect accorded by others. There were high and middle classes of free people, as well as a low class of slaves who had been taken as captives in war. The practice of slave-holding ended with the Treaty of Point Elliot in 1855, well before it was forbidden throughout the rest of the United States following the Civil War. Slaves often did the same work as free individuals, but they were trained to do only specific tasks or parts of them and banned from knowledge of the whole. They also were excluded from many social and religious customs and could be given away as wealth. Edith Bedal and Jean Bedal Fish recalled how their grandfather (Wa-wet-kin, chief of the Sauk-Suiattle people) would tell them of being given half a dozen slaves from his saltwater hosts as a matter of respect when he traveled down to visit them.

Upper class people had more wealth and privileges, but also more rules to follow. Marriage, for example, was expected to take place with a suitably high-ranking person from outside the tribal group, conducted with formal negotiations initiated by the groom's family, and confirmed with the exchange of presents. Feasting, perhaps a large gathering from both peoples if the individuals were of enough importance, and then setting up their household in the groom's village followed. This made for an alliance between families, one which gave privileges and also worked to reinforce the couple's commitment to the relationship. After the first baby was born the parents often went to visit the bride's family, and she might then begin to address her husband's parents as her own. If a spouse died, the survivor was expected to remarry someone in the family of the deceased person. All women and almost all men married. The relative age was not important; instead, social class, diligence in work, strength, and intelligence counted for more.

This system of seeking a spouse from beyond the indiviudal's village, band, or tribe resulted in a very complex system of personal rights to obtain food or other resources, claim hospitality, and travel, as well as acquiring more tangible objects of personal use and others such as family names and ceremonial roles. People traveled regularly during the seasons when berries ripened, big game was hunted, and when specific fishery locations were in use. This increased contact between groups.

Marriage might also occur between a member of a village west of the Cascades and one from across the mountains, as with a Sauk finding a spouse among the Wenatchi, Entiat, Klickitat, or Inchelium tribes. Travel over the passes was common during the later summer and early autumn months, usually for trade but sometimes also for raiding by eastern Washington tribes or the far-ranging Thompsons from British Columbia. Major routes included by canoe and foot up the north fork of the Skykomish River and over Cady Pass, as well as ascending the North Fork Sauk River and crossing at Indian Pass. Both of these routes led to the Wenatchi people.

Other passes utilized were the Klawhat, Suiattle, Buck Creek, and High on the Suiattle River system; White on the north fork of the Sauk; and Dishpan Gap, Wards, Saddle Gap, and Wenatchee on the north fork of the Skykomish River. Local people also used Cascade Pass to the north and Union Gap, Stevens Pass, and Deception Pass in the south.

When horses were introduced to the peoples of eastern Washington, their use spread also to suitable territories in the west, primarily the Snoqualmie through their trade with the Klickitat people. Prior to that time (and continuing where horses were a rarity) people maintained trails for foot travel or if easier, walked along or in the waters of the rivers. Trading strips of dried clams, lengths of shell money, and other transportable western items for obsidian and chert projectile points, plus obtaining minerals for paints and mountain goat hair for weaving, led to ties between individuals and villages. These were more important to the Skagit and southern Puget Sound tribes than to those in Snohomish County, but trade and intermarriage were significant

Rushes were gathered and sewn together with thread made from nettles, using a long, curved needle. These resulting mats were utilized for a wide variety of purposes, including covering canoes to protect them from the sun and for wearing to keep off the rain. (Courtesy David Cameron)

here, as shown by excavations of Plateau materials at local archaeological sites and high quality obsidian from as far away as central Oregon and northern California used by the Mis-skai-whwa of the neighboring upper Skagit River.

Canoe travel within the area was made easier due to the development of portages from the Sauk to the North Fork Stillaguamish River at Darrington, from the South Fork Stillaguamish River to the Pilchuck below Granite Falls, and on Whidbey Island at Greenbank—handy there not only in normal times but also to evade northern raiders when they came south into Puget Sound. Overland trails included a route from Tulalip to Marysville, one from Marysville to Lake Stevens via Cavalero's Corner for berry gathering, another from Woods Prairie north of Monroe to Fern Bluff on the Skykomish River, and from Gold Bar into the Sultan Basin, probably along Olney Creek.

Without metal tools for trail maintenance, the Sauks carried well wrapped coals in baskets, using them to set fire to tree trunks and tangles which had fallen across the path. As a result, many people were very well traveled. Jim Brown, last chief of the Sauks, had visited Spokane and traded furs at Spokane House, joined in the busy traditional trading activities of Celilo Falls on the Columbia River, had seen the lower Columbia region, and exchanged goods at Port Townsend. Alki Beach in West Seattle also was a popular site for trade, while on the east side Sauks visited the post at Lake Chelan and summered at Lake Kachess near Snoqualmie Pass.

When people returned in late fall from their travels and securing food for their winter supplies it became time for the winter ceremonials. Life was surrounded and strongly influenced by spiritual powers to an extent not often understood by later observers. Differences between the tribes also added to the complexity. For example, the Snohomish and other coastal people followed *syowen*, while the Snoqualmie and Sauk practiced *sqalaletut*. Spirits were associated with many animals, specific locations and unique natural features in the environment, along with the elements found in nature. These spirit powers might be obtained by individuals who sought them and could be both beneficial and dangerous, depending upon how they were treated and who had them. A shaman would obtain powerful ones for healing and killing, while others sought non-shamanistic (or "lay") spirits to aid them in their daily lives.

This seeking often began in early childhood and might continue onward into puberty. It was done by young people of both sexes, and required a strong discipline of fasting, seeking, and being alone in the outdoors. The spirits would appear in human form initially, but later could assume whatever shape they wished. A song, a dance, and other personal information would be imparted, along with the power which the spirit had to bestow. Information thus obtained was kept to one's self, save that a child might talk over the experience with close elders for advice on how to treat what he or she had learned.

Spirits lived in their own land, but would come to aid the person who had obtained them when called. The exception were the shamanistic spirits, who always accompanied the shaman and made him a person to be treated with respect and caution due to their presence. In the winter, however, the spirits returned to the earth. A person who had obtained one as a youth would, in later life, be alerted that it had come back to him for the first time when he became ill or when things far out of the ordinary began to happen to him. When a shaman confirmed that the cause was supernatural, then the person affected was obliged to host a dance and distribute gifts.

Invitations were sent out to people of surrounding villages, who brought food and presents for the occasion. The host and his relatives accumulated wealth and food also, and after the rituals of receiving, demonstrating, and interpreting his newly returned power, there was a sharing of spiritual gifts followed by a distribution of material ones.

Personal skills, the accumulation of wealth, and the widely praised traits of hard work and perseverance were all associated with the acquisition of guardian spirits. They also had to be heeded and might be lost. If that occurred, a person might become seriously ill or die, problems that only powerful shamanistic spirits might reverse. At death, a very dangerous time due to the power of ghosts to steal the souls of living persons, the bodies of high-ranking people were placed in canoes mounted in trees or for lower ranking ones, buried in the ground. Personal effects of the deceased would be given to others, with some offered through fire to be of use in the spirit world. If all were done properly, the spirits would be satisfied. After a period of time it was customary to exhume the bones of the deceased, clean and wrap them, and then rebury them in their final resting place. A potlatch then would be given in their memory.

Potlatching (from Chinook jargon, "to give") was a key social event among the people, a way of recognizing the differences in rank and status of individuals and families, a system whereby goods and food were widely distributed outside the immediate family group and village, and as an occasion which brought people together from distant places to gather basically on a friendly basis. The practice flourished throughout the Northwest Coast cultural area and has been analyzed for a number of differing groups.

In the nineteenth century when British and American goods entered the economy, those living near trading posts or with substantial products to trade with them brought even more desirable items into the potlatching cycle. This calling together of guests, enjoyment of games, contests, and gambling, followed by the feasting and distribution of gifts

Narrow Trails
By Edith Bedal

The narrow trails I have seen
Along the hills of the Cascades
In all those far away places where I have been
The colorful flowers bloom in all the glades.

There is the trail up to blue Round Lake
The place of the Indian myths.
Those rocks and caverns in the wake
Of dawn show pale blue and grey.

On in the cool October night
Plays the northern aurora borealis
From horizon to the zenith
Blue light gleams, cracks, and hisses.

There are the narrow trails
From the beginning to the many ends
They follow up the hills and vales
Through fir, cedar, and hemlock bends.

Through the many mountain heights
Like White Pass shining against the azure blues
Only to see secluded and unknown sights
The narrow trails lead me on to places ever new.

helped spread news of status changes among the entire community of peoples. Winter spirit dances and memorials to the dead were frequent, but also potlatches were held to commemorate a marriage, when new names were acquired through inheritance or accomplishment, after a girl attained puberty, sometimes after a bride's return to visit her family, after a successful hunting expedition, and when the salmon returned in the summer.

Presents were distributed according to the rank of the recipient: the richer and more powerful receiving theirs first and on down the social scale. In this way, people had their positions ratified among the group. The greater the amount given away, the greater the prestige of the hosts, who had worked to make new wealth items such as blankets and canoes for two years or more. In turn, those receiving gifts were expected to invite their hosts to a future potlatch and return the amount with interest. This distribution had several other effects, such as the realization that wealth objects owned by a person sometime would be passed on to another and by the same token new ones would be received, that foods and objects such as beautifully made baskets which a family might not be able to obtain for itself could be given to them by others, and also that the obtaining of powerful helping spirits and hard work were publicly rewarded.

All of these traditions changed drastically after 1855, with the implementation of a federal reservation system designed to remove native peoples from their lands and place them on small, out of the way parcels. Title to their lands then would be transferred to the government, surveys completed, and the region opened to American settlement. What then would be the fate of the natives was less clear.

In the early nineteenth century there was an active trade between the tribes and the British-owned Hudson's Bay Company, based at Fort Vancouver on the north bank of the Columbia River and then extended with the opening of Fort Langley and Fort Nisqually. The company stayed out of internal native affairs and concentrated on obtaining furs. Snohomish and other people traveled by canoe to the forts, returned with European goods which entered trade channels, and had some contact with both French Roman Catholic and American Methodist missionaries, along with passing traders and company employees.

The boundary settlement with Great Britain in 1846, followed by the massacre at the Whitman mission near Walla Walla, led to the creation of Oregon Territory by Congress in 1848. As a part of the organic act it was stipulated that native rights of person and property would not be impaired until a treaty was signed. However this quickly was violated by the Donation Land Claim Act of 1850, which provided that white male citizens of the United States could obtain title to 320 acres, with an additional 320 for a wife in her own right. Native people, African-Americans, and Hawaiians (of whom a number worked in the fur trade) were excluded. The best lands in the fertile Willamette Valley of Oregon quickly were taken up in these square mile chunks, and newly arriving American settlers began to move north up the Cowlitz River to Puget Sound in order to locate suitable claims.

In 1853 Washington Territory was created and Governor Isaac Ingalls Stevens appointed to organize its legal system. As governor in Olympia, Stevens also acted as *ex officio* Superintendent of Indian Affairs. The federal Bureau of Indian Affairs had been organized as a part of the War Department in 1824, then transferred to the newly created

Department of the Interior in 1849. Its primary purposes were to extinguish native land titles and try to resolve the problem of what then to do with the affected people. During the 1850s the solution was to isolate them on small tracts of land where they would be free from the contaminants of American society such as alcohol and prostitution, teach them how to create new lives as self-sufficient farmers, and replace their belief systems with Christianity. Traditional beliefs, economic systems, and means of governance were considered of no value.

Stevens felt great pressure to negotiate treaties and remove the danger caused by friction between incoming American settlers and natives desirous of maintaining their rights. In March 1854 he was advised that Snohomish men had murdered

Many people, especially in the eastern parts of the county, did not move to Tulalip but instead remained on ancestral lands. Susan Bedal, daughter of Sauk-Suiattle chief Wa-wet-kin, raised her family at their homestead near the forks of the Sauk River, in earlier times an important tribal fishing site. (Harry Bedal photo, 1908, Bedal collection, courtesy Astrida Blukis Onat)

William Young on his way between Skatchet Head at the southern tip of Whidbey Island and his destination at Port Ludlow across Puget Sound. A posse sent to apprehend the killers was fired upon, resulting in the death of Dr. Wesley F. Cherry, one of the owners of the Tulalip Mill Company on Tulalip Bay.

Personally organizing and leading an expedition northward to Whidbey Island and the Snohomish River, Stevens ultimately was unsuccessful. His forces burned stockades at Skatchet Head where Chief S'Hoot-soot and some 300 people lived and one on the mainland along the river, also destroying Snohomish canoes. Most of the native people fled for safety, some to Olympia and Fort Steilacoom, and told a sharply differing story. According to them a drunken Young drew his sword, killed Sh-its-hoot, and broke another man's leg, whereupon the son of Sh-its-hoot avenged his father. Another Snohomish man, Sle-hua-huat, then stole Young's money.

Out of this experience came a process Stevens would follow the next winter when he began a vigorous program of treaty conferences. On his way to Whidbey Island he had stopped at Seattle for men and further information. There he had met with Pat-ka-nim and part of the Snoqualmie tribe, along with members of the Suquamish, all of whom happened to be in town. In a firm speech he designated Pat-ka-nim as head of the Snoqualmie tribe and Chief Seattle head of the Suquamish, requesting them to maintain the peace. He had appointed Col. Michael Simmons as Indian Agent to act for him, as he himself would be going to Washington, D.C. to learn the "Great Father's will toward them." If their people behaved, he would take care of them. If not, arms would be used. Simmons and Pat-ka-nim then selected a dozen men as sub-chiefs, followed in like manner by Seattle, who spoke of his good feelings toward the Whites. Pat-ka-nim followed "very unwillingly," according to observer George Gibbs, who was on this expedition and wrote the account for Stevens.

A similar process occurred a week later on Whidbey Island, when the governor summoned the Skagit tribal members to meet with him and help in apprehending the fugitive Snohomish. When George Sna-ke-lum and many of the Skagits refused, Stevens instead appointed Goliah as chief and chose six sub-chiefs, demoting Sna-ke-lum to that rank.

On December 7, 1854 Governor Stevens followed his instructions from the Bureau of Indian Affairs and organized a five man commission to reach agreements with the tribes of Washington Territory and the neighboring Blackfeet of Montana. In a series of treaties, negotiated between December 26, 1854 and January 31, 1855, that mission was accomplished for the northwestern region. Locally, delegates from the native groups were summoned to Point Elliot at present-day Mukilteo to hear the terms of the proposed agreement and then sign it. In keeping with his instructions to simplify the wide number of tribes, bands, and villages, Stevens divided the people into four units based on the main river drainages. Seattle was to represent the Duwamish and Suquamish populations, Chow-its-hoot the Nooksack and Lummi, Goliah the Skagit, and Pat-ka-nim of the Snoqualmie the Snohomish, Skykomish, and Snoqualmie systems. These "chiefs" were to maintain order and carry out the terms of the Treaty of Point Elliot, assisted by appointed sub-chiefs. If they failed in their task, they would be replaced.

The scene at that January 22 meeting was very confused, given the short notice to people, the fact that the treaty was written in legal English (although negotiations all were handled in the Chinook trade jargon of English, French, and some native words), and that the government officials had very little knowledge of the actual populations or territories involved. Some, such as the Stillaguamish, just seemed to have been overlooked. Wa-wet-

Many Sauk-Suiattle and Stillaguamish men took part in the timber industry, especially driving cedar shingle "bolts" downriver from logging camps to the mills. These are Sauk men poling back upstream in 1914. (Bedal collection, courtesy Astrida Blukis Onat)

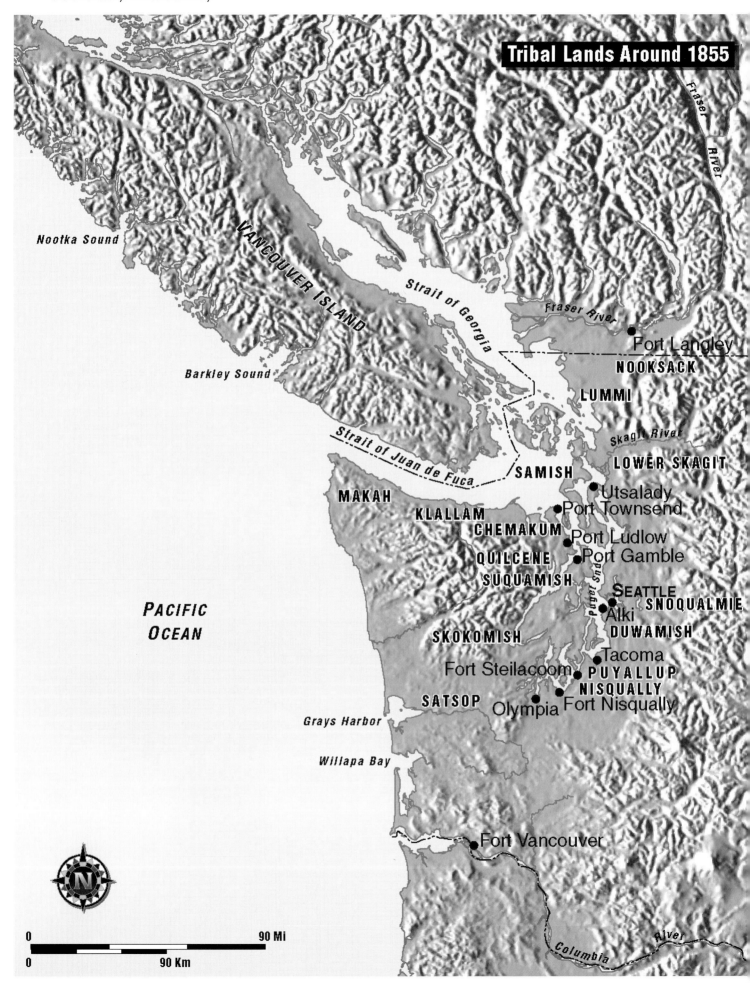

Tribal Lands Around 1855

Fraser River

Nootka Sound

VANCOUVER ISLAND

Strait of Georgia

Fraser River

Port Langley

NOOKSACK

Barkley Sound

LUMMI

Skagit River

Strait of Juan de Fuca

SAMISH

LOWER SKAGIT

MAKAH

Utsalady

Port Townsend

KLALLAM

CHEMAKUM

Port Ludlow

QUILCENE

Port Gamble

SUQUAMISH

Puget Sound

SEATTLE

SNOQUALMIE

Alki

DUWAMISH

PACIFIC
OCEAN

SKOKOMISH

Tacoma

Fort Steilacoom

PUYALLUP

SATSOP

NISQUALLY

Olympia

Fort Nisqually

Grays Harbor

Willapa Bay

Fort Vancouver

Columbia River

N

0		90 Mi

0		90 Km

Point Elliot Treaty Remembered

Courtesy of Priscilla Shipley

Suzie Dorsey, a member of the Stillaguamish and Skagit Tribes living at Trafton, who at the age of 83, on March 4, 1927, gave the following description of the signing of the Point Elliot Treaty:

I was just a girl of 13 years of age and was there at Mukilteo 1855 when the treaty was signed. I saw Governor Stevens and John Taylor was interpreter. There were lots of people there from all tribes, and lots of chiefs and sub chiefs. Governor Stevens told the Indians he would give them lots of money for their land. He told them to take off their hats. They never understood him so he came around to them and took off each of their hats and told them to call the same as he did "Hip Hip Hurrah," while he waved their arms with their hats.

I saw large poles, several of them around in the ground. Hung on them were ropes and loops as if to hang people. So Indians were scared, they thought that if they didn't do what Governor Stevens wanted he would hang them all.

I know that around Skagit Tribe where I lived the Indians were not driven from their homes right away after treaty, but what treatment were given to other tribes I never heard.

I know that at time of treaty each woman was to receive 20 threads, one thimble, one needle, ½ yard of each for shirt and leggings of calico, piece of blanket for shoulder and package of pins.

I know that Stillaguamish Tribe never joined Snohomish Tribe at time of said treaty for a reservation as each tribe by each river were to be given land separate for them and their families.

---

kin, leader of the Sauk, refused to sign after hearing of the terms. However, Dahtl-de-min, described as a sub-chief, did. This led to subsequent controversies over the latter's authority and also to his relationship with the tribe. As a whole, the Sauk group maintained that they were not signatories.

A 36 square mile township of land at Tulalip was reserved by the tribes for their use, along with several smaller reservations at Port Madison, Swinomish, and Lummi Island outside of what was to become Snohomish County. At Tulalip an agricultural school, doctor, and agency headquarters were to be provided by the federal government, with the native peoples moving to their new home within a year of treaty ratification. That ratification by Congress, however, did not happen until March 9, 1859, delaying the start of promised annuities and benefits.

Within months of Stevens' circuit of treaty conferences war broke out in Washington Territory, ignited first in September 1855 by the Yakamas, when American miners trespassed on reservation lands. Federal troops initially were defeated. By October the Nisqually had opened hostilities in the southern Puget Sound valleys, causing panic among the few white settlers. Although Pat-ka-nim initially had opposed the first American settlement on Whidbey Island earlier in the decade, he now sided with Stevens and fought against the hostile tribes.

Fear of northwestern Washington tribes' joining in the combat led to the creation of two new temporary reservations on Whidbey Island, well away from the fighting. County people were assigned to the one at Holmes Harbor, while the Skagit River tribes were to stay at Penn's Cove. Many reported as ordered, but they found the organization poorly run, little available food, and no reason to stay. In the spring most returned home to fish, hunt, and plant, the agents confessing that this was the best solution to the food shortage. Most of the upriver peoples never returned, but instead went back to their usual homes. In later years some moved down to Tulalip.

Warfare in the south Sound came to its bitter end in 1856, with serious casualties among the peoples of both sides. At Tulalip Chief Bonaparte reported there was great frustration with the government delay in treaty ratification and meeting its

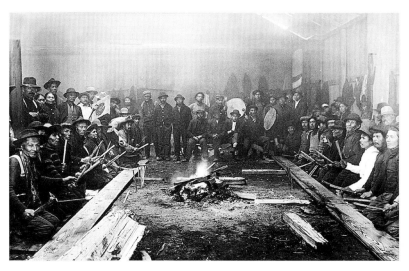

Gambling games, racing, and athletic contests have deep cultural roots among the native people. These men are enjoying the setting of their new longhouse, built at Tulalip in 1914. (Juleen photo, courtesy Everett Public Library)

commitments, a situation exacerbated by deep political divisions among the Americans over Stevens' Indian policy and how the war was handled. As the reservation was located on traditional Snohomish tribal lands, most of them did move to the site, along with a large number of Skykomish and many Snoqualmie.

Government payment of goods, however, did not begin until autumn of 1861, as the residents of the reservation found themselves caught up in the spoils system and corruption of the nineteenth century Bureau of Indian Affairs. Congressional patronage and growing territorial contempt for native peoples produced a climate where monies and supplies intended for reservation use routinely were skimmed off or removed from shipments. A case in point was that of steamship Captain Libby, who appropriated cloth bound for Tulalip women to enable them to do fancy work for resale. He was caught and had to repay the loss, but never stood trial for grand larceny. In the words of Congregational minister and Indian Agent Charles A. Huntington, "the law of public opinion in Washington Territory ignored the humanity of Indians and denied them any rights that white men were bound to respect."

Between 1869 and 1870 President Ulysses Grant attempted to save money by replacing civilian agents with some of the surplus Army officers left over from the recent Civil War; however, there was no change in overall poor management. Captain George D. Hill was assigned to Tulalip, and later as King County treasurer he was disgraced for corruption in that office. Of more significance was Grant's implementation of his "Peace Policy," a desire to end federal mismanagement by the creation of a Board of Indian Commissioners chosen from eminent men to advise on native affairs. As a part of this change in direction, religious denominations were assigned reservations to oversee and nominate their supervising agents. It was not a success, although the basics continued into the first third of the twentieth century.

In the case of Tulalip, the federal government contracted with the Roman Catholic Church to create the school promised in the Treaty of Point Elliot, a relationship which lasted from 1869 until 1901. Father Eugene Casimir Chirouse of the French order of the Oblates of Mary the Immaculate had left missionary work in the Yakima valley with the outbreak of hostilities in 1855 and was reassigned to the Tulalip area. He located first on Ebey Slough between Quilceda Creek and Priest Point in 1856, and then the following year moved onto the point itself, where a small community developed around the mission and school. In 1863 he moved both westward to Tulalip Bay and established his final location, dedicated to St. Anne. In 1868 the Sisters of Charity opened a program for girls. Education for the children at the boarding school was focused on Christian themes and basic occupational skills designed for assimilation into white culture. Traditional languages, religious practices, and values were to be eliminated by raising a new generation, isolating the children from their families. In his 1870 report, Chriouse noted attendance of 26 boys and 23 girls, but requested enough resources to enlarge his student body to 200 with a new school building. The government did not agree.

School children spent part of each day in manual labor and gardening, clearing land and raising much of their own food. Fund raising trips around the Sound where the boys put on musical performances brought in money for clothing and necessities. Agriculture, however, did not appeal to their elders, who preferred to fish for their livings or do subsistence work in lumber camps. They requested that Tulalip people rather than whites be hired for reservation jobs and that the trading post be tribally owned, but these were not granted. Traditional religious practices were banned, however, as were potlatching, the right to come and go freely, and the right to gather in groups—save for Sundays at church.

Chirouse left St. Anne's in 1878, transferred to Canada to give him a rest from his labors. He was succeeded by Father J. B. Boulet. Chirouse returned to Tulalip for a visit in 1891, with over 400 people camping there to welcome him back. The following year he died from the effects of a stroke.

In 1901 the federal government reversed its policy of reservation administration by religious groups and terminated the educational agreement. Dr. Charles M. Buchanan was appointed as superintendent and a new school erected in 1905. Eventually, Tulalip administered all native activities in western Washington until headquarters were moved to Everett by the Bureau of Indian Affairs and the boarding school closed in 1932. Children now are educated through tribal programs and the Marysville School District.

Government policy toward its native population varied over time, reflecting conflicting theories and public opinion. Potlatching, for example, originally was made illegal on the grounds that the

Roman Catholic Father Eugene Casimir Chirouse had charge of the Tulalip mision of St. Anne's and was contracted by the Bureau of Indian Affairs to operate its school for Indian children at Tulalip. Funds were scant, and the students did large amounts of physical labor as well as classroom work. Native traditions were actively discouraged. (Courtesy Everett Public Library)

people were impoverishing themselves by giving away goods to others and because officials did not recognize the reciprocity involved. Yet, federal actions always were bound by the constitutional power of signed treaties. These recognized tribal sovereignty with all rights not specifically transferred to the government retained by the native people. In addition, the government assumed a trust relationship, binding itself to consider the best interests of those who were considered members of recognized tribes. Here, that meant the signatories of the Treaty of Point Elliot.

In 1887 the Dawes Act established a system of giving individual private allotments of reservation land in an attempt to have the recipients take on the same roles and attitudes toward property as the Americans, thus reducing communal ownership. This policy already had begun at Tulalip and led to the sale and loss of many parcels.

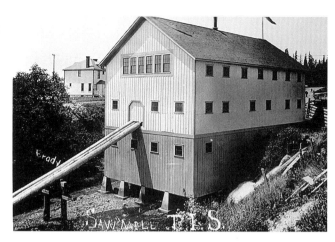

This water powered sawmill at Tulalip Bay was the first industry in Snohomish County. Built in 1853, it became federal property after the Treaty of Point Elliot in 1855 and served reservation needs until it was junked in 1906. (Brady photo, courtesy Everett Public Library)

The interior of the Tulalip mill shows its simple circular saw cutting a log into planks. No steam power to lift logs, move carriages, or shift sawn boards made the design simple but labor intensive and dependent upon stream flow. (Courtesy Everett Public Library)

For the Sauk people (who were unable to obtain a reservation and whose homes were burned in 1892 by whites who claimed their Sauk Prairie land) allotments along the unsettled Suiattle River seemed a viable option. There, under Chief Jim Brown, they were joined by the Mis-skai-whwa tribe from the neighboring upper Skagit and Cascade rivers, led by Captain Moses Tiatmus. However, these allotments later were deemed to be forest land rather than suitable for crops and turning native people into yeoman farmers, and most were cancelled in 1917. This action led to winter starvation and the marginal existence of many tribal members who had not patented their claims, a situation worsened by the affects of the great "Spanish influenza" pandemic at the end of World War I.

American citizenship was added to that of the tribe by act of Congress in June 1924 to all native people born in the United States, spurred by their roles in fighting for the country in the armed forces during World War I. Ten years later the Wheeler-Howard Act ended the policy of individual allotments, with surplus lands previously eligible for sale now reverting to tribal ownership. New Deal policies favored hiring of native people in the Bureau of Indian Affairs and the recovery of tribal lands. Shimakum, or Charles Jules, the last of the hereditary Snohomish chiefs, had died in the 1920s, and now the old system of naming chiefs was ended, replaced by governance through elected tribal councils. At Tulalip members of the various tribes were united into the new Tulalip Tribes of Washington.

In the early 1950s Congress determined to reduce the number of people in its trust relationship by pursuing termination of federally recognized tribes and relocating native people into cities to assimilate in the larger American culture. These attempts were not successful.

The late 1960s witnessed the extension of the civil rights movement to include those of Native Americans, as during the following decades a resurgence of native pride accompanied legal reforms and limits on efforts by the State of Washington to regulate tribal affairs. Religious freedom, educational and health programs, and tribal legal jurisdiction all were affirmed, but the most explosive issue was that of fishing rights.

United States District Court judge George H. Boldt ruled in 1974 after extensive testimony and research in *U.S. v. Washington* that the tribes retained their right to fish and to manage fisheries under the 1855 treaties, determined that they had the right to share equally in the opportunity to harvest fish in their traditional grounds, and found that the State of Washington could not interfere as long as the tribes were protecting the resource. The decision was upheld by the United States Supreme Court in 1979.

Although the tribes had worked actively to release salmon into Puget Sound to increase the runs and created their own hatchery programs, the non-treaty sports and commercial fishing interests were stunned by the requirement that their share of the fishery drop from roughly 90 percent to 50 percent. Great bitterness and scattered violence resulted as the new reality slowly was accepted. Also of importance was the court's ruling that the tribes had a legal role in the management of the watersheds where the salmon spawned. The future of the salmon and steelhead runs and the costs in land use restrictions as well as money necessary to preserve them were very active issues at the beginning of the new century.

Intensely debated are the ways of seeking financial support for much needed tribal programs, jobs, and economic development on trust lands. At Tulalip income has been received from some 200 residential leases on beach lands which were signed from the 1930s through the 1950s, along with leased tidelands for log booms. During World War II the federal government's condemnation of 2200 acres for an ammunition depot led to the later creation of the Boeing test site. This property came from private allotments of trust land, purchased by the tribe when surplused after the war and without the chance for previous owners to seek its return.

Federal grants for water, sewer, and hatchery programs also have brought money to the reservation, as has the practice of leasing privately owned allot-

In 1905 the B.I.A. opened a new boarding school at Tulalip. It too provided work and home making skills along with educational essentials designed to allow young people to fit into American society. (Courtesy Everett Public Library)

Working in the school laundry and kitchen taught self-discipline, responsibility, and family care, as well as reducing staff costs. It was expected that graduates would return to their families and serve as positive influences, but not that they would go on to higher education. (Courtesy Everett Public Library)

Spring Forest Flowers

By Edith Bedal

Going up Suiattle
Seeing early forest flowers,
All gorgeous trilliums.

    Splashing within groves
    Are dogwood, sweet twin flowers
    Underneath evergreens.

Through moss carpeted trails
Bloom delicate miner's lettuce
And queen's cup lily.

    By the rocks and streams
    In shady glens are blue violets.
    Miniature Johnny jump-ups.

In sunny open spaces
Blossom rose salmon berries
Starry white thimble berry.

    Wild strawberries, plums,
    Racemes of spicy Solomon's seal
    Hedged in by rare rocks.

Within cool shady nooks
Hidden beneath dark green leaves
Bloom purple ginger flowers.

    Around the curved trail
    In depths of pine and fir trees
    Grow the lovely cinquefoil.

Far across the canyon
Spring swollen cataracts tumble
Foaming down wide chasms.

    Stopping for a view
    Twisted stalk, pink lady slippers
    By our feet we see.

Small trees, golden moss
We pass as wearily we walked,
Arriving, there it is!

    With joy and relief
    To rest hunchbacked, sore shoulders,
    Canyon Creek, trail's end.

Note: Best time to see the flowers in bloom is in April and May.

ments for residences and salt water resorts, as formerly at Hermosa Beach. Many people continue to seek wealth from logging and the resources of the sea, while others work at the tribal businesses. Significant income is generated by individuals from the extensive business leasing at the Marysville entrance to Tulalip, where a hotel, recreational vehicle lot, gas station, and fast food restaurants are located. These are less controversial enterprises than those which are based on bringing onto the reservation non-tribal members to partake in highly profitable businesses such as gaming, fireworks, liquor and cigarette sales. The original casino was on privately-owned land and leased to the tribe, while "Boom City" (with its bustling Fourth of July trade) also is organized and run by entrepreneurial individuals. To the north, creation of the new Quil Ceda community with its destination shopping center and new casino has raised issues over land use regulations and the extent of tribal control over the taxing power. All these have aided employment and income, especially with their proximity to I-5, as their impact extends well beyond Marysville and nearby areas, making the Tulalip Tribes of Washington one of the county's largest employers.

In 1972 the Sauk-Suiattle tribe was accorded federal recognition, followed by the Stillaguamish in 1976. As an incidental part of their negotiations the Sauk people had their name officially changed to Sauk-Suiattle, reflecting the earlier disputed allotments along the Suiattle River.

Esther Ross carried out a superb publicity stunt to dramatize the Stillaguamish case when the Bicentennial Wagon Train (celebrating 200 years of American independence by crossing the United States) lumbered its way along I-5, past the tiny tribal office at Island Crossing. In a scene familiar to Western movie fans (but never true in Snohomish County) the Indians attacked the wagon train, symbolically of course, and the media carried their story nationwide. A key role was played by Llwellyn Goodridge, as the tribe finally obtained their legal status, a small trust land base, and the beginnings of their fisheries

Reviving traditional religous beliefs, restoring ceremonies such as those honoring the return of the first salmon of the year, and giving presents at gatherings for those who have passed away have helped to restore feelings of pride and confidence in native culture. Gloria St. James here blesses Tulalip First Salmon fishermen. (Courtesy Diane Janes)

program. Most recently the tribe razed its housing and attempted to arrange for its own casino, issues which have caused deep controversy.

It was not until 1999 that the Snoqualmies were successful in obtaining their federal recognition as a distinct tribe. This ruling was strongly opposed by the Tulalip tribal council, which had appealed the decision and also actively opposes attempts to form a separate Snohomish tribal organization. Some already recognized people at Tulalip see further recognition as a lessening of their share of federal trust benefits and treaty rights, while others question whether it should be extended to those who never endured the reservation experience. A dominating opinion is that the Tulalips legally represent the descendants of the tribes which signed the 1855 treaty, so why should any other groups of individuals be accorded that status?

With their legal rights reaffirmed, but still facing needs for economic opportunity, education, housing, health care, and nurturing of the young and elders, the native peoples continue to maintain their special cultural contributions in an increasingly urbanizing and changing county.

Although no longer the dominant source of food and employment, fishing remains a vital religious and cultural tie to tribal identity. The tribes have an important legal role in preservation and restoration of salmon habitat, as well as operating the Tulalip and Stillaguamish hatchery programs. (Courtesy David Cameron)

European and American Exploration

I t has been called the "Second Great Age of Discovery"—those decades in the late eighteenth century when Europeans and Americans charted coastlines and filled in maps. Three hundred years earlier, during the "First Age of Discovery," such mariners as Columbus, Magellan, and Cabot had located new continents, islands, and oceans. European settlement followed, but with vast areas remaining unknown. During the "Second Great Age of Discovery" Europeans and Americans ventured out for commercial gain and to fill in the gaps.

One challenging region ripe for exploration during this time was the enigmatic northwest coast of North America. There Russian fur traders from Siberia moved east and south along islands and coast, and Spaniards hoped to extend empire and religion north from established colonies in Mexico. After 1776 vessels flying the flag of the young United States entered northwest waters. Other nations came too, mostly to seek profits by gathering sea otter and other pelts valued in China. However, the dominant actor was Great Britain. The British sought wealth through trade and by extending geographic and scientific knowledge, factors that intertwined with their quest for a water route through the continent. Sir Francis Drake briefly had touched a region he called New Albion in the 1570s; although historians have long thought this was northern California, recent speculation suggests Drake ventured along the Vancouver Island coast. Two centuries later James Cook, John Ledyard, John Meares, and others of their countrymen clearly plied the northern coast. In 1792 their mantle passed to Captain George Vancouver, then in his mid-forties and seasoned by three decades at sea. That spring Vancouver, commanding HMS *Discovery*—a three-masted sloop-of-war—and the brig *Chatham*, entered the inland sea he would name Puget Sound. For a month his men charted its waters and named prominent features.

Vancouver's mission grew from a dispute with Spain that arose when the Spanish commander at Nootka Sound, located on present-day western Vancouver Island, seized a British ship. Tensions then eased, and Vancouver's task was moderated to accept the contested properties from Spanish officials. Along the way he was to explore the coast and possible inland waters in search of the Northwest Passage, the waterway rumored to connect the Atlantic and Pacific coasts. He was to claim any unknown lands for the United Kingdom.

Born to well-to-do parents in Norfolk, England, probably in 1757, Vancouver entered the British Navy at age 14 as an apprentice in James Cook's second expedition to the South Pacific Ocean. A few years later he was a midshipman on Cook's third voyage, which sailed north along the Oregon coast to the Bering Strait and Siberia. After Cook was killed in the Sandwich (Hawaiian) Islands, Vancouver, who was attacked while protecting his ship in the incident, returned to Britain. Commissioned a first lieutenant, he served in the Caribbean during the latter months of the American Revolution and its aftermath.

Late in 1790 Vancouver was selected to command the *Discovery* on its expedition along the northwest coast of North America. Instructed to receive the properties seized at Nootka, he was also ordered to acquire "more complete knowledge, than has yet been obtained, of the northwest coast of America." Specifically, the government wanted accurate information about any waterway which might "facilitate an intercourse, for the purpose of commerce, between the northwest coast" and "the opposite side of the continent, which are inhabited or occupied by His Majesty's subjects." He was to investigate "the direction and extent of all such considerable inlets, whether made by arms of the sea, or by the mouths of large rivers . . .." There were specific references to the rumored Strait of Juan de Fuca, named for a Greek sailor who had told of an opening he had entered two centuries earlier, and whatever sea or strait might lie beyond.

This generally accepted portrait of British Captain George Vancouver shows the diplomat and explorer who was the first European to enter Puget Sound waters. In June 1792 he landed here and claimed the surrounding land of New Georgia for his monarch, King George III. (Courtesy of the National Portrait Gallery, London)

With 101 crewmen aboard the *Discovery* and 45 more on the *Chatham* under Lt. William Broughton, Vancouver set out down the Thames early in 1791. During the voyage east around the Cape of Good Hope to Australia, the South Pacific, and the Sandwich Islands, the men encountered storms, illness, unfriendly natives, and occasional morale and disciplinary problems, along with ordinary routine chores. Vancouver proved to be a harsh, sometimes erratic, taskmaster.

In mid-April the expedition passed California and headed north. A chance meeting with the American Captain Robert Gray increased curiosity about waters beyond the Strait of Juan de Fuca and also alerted Vancouver to the possibility of the Columbia River, which he had passed on a cloudy day without noticing. Although Broughton later sailed up that river, Gray returned in the interim, and his discovery enhanced eventual United

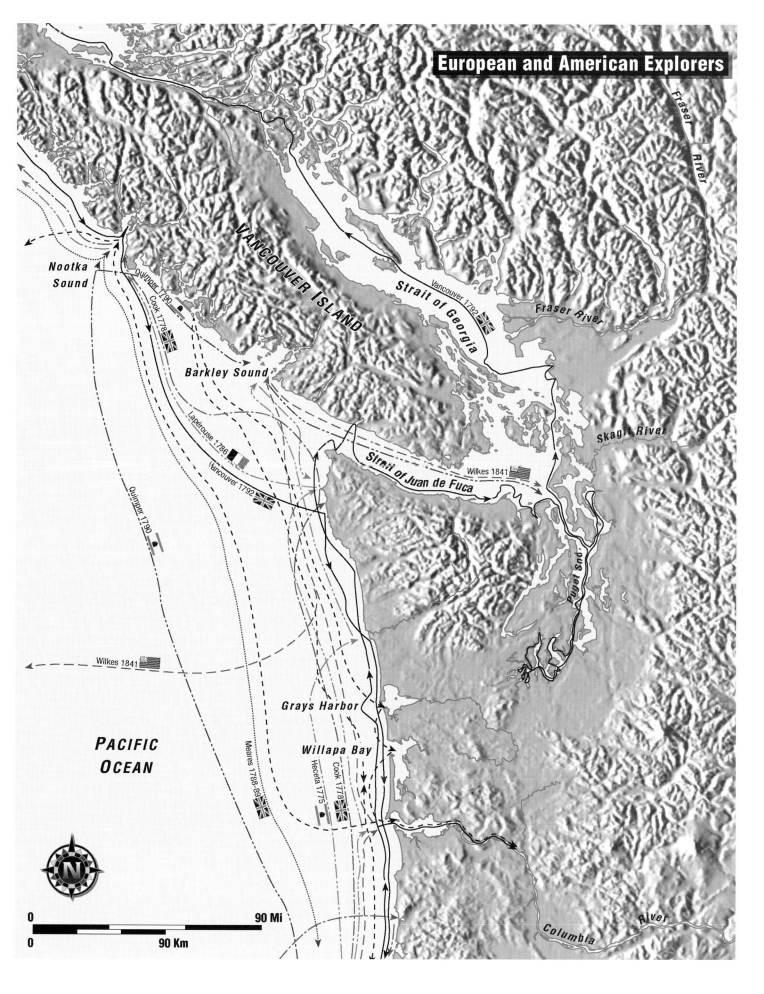

Fraser River

VANCOUVER ISLAND

Strait of Georgia

Vancouver 1792

Fraser River

Skagit River

Nootka
Sound

Quimper 1790

Cook 1778

Barkley Sound

Lapérouse 1786

Vancouver 1792

Strait of Juan de Fuca

Wilkes 1841

Puget Snd.

Quimper 1790

Wilkes 1841

PACIFIC
OCEAN

Grays Harbor

Meares 1788-89

Willapa Bay

Heceta 1775

Cook 1778

Columbia   River

N

0   90 Mi

0   90 Km

States claims to the region. Spanish ships also were in the area. They sailed through the Strait of Juan de Fuca, but then turned north instead of south, apparently underestimating the extent of that passage. They did leave the name Camano on certain features, however, one honoring Seigr. Don Jacinto Caamano, commander of the frigate *Aransasu*, which was surveying these waters out of their Mexican base at San Blas.

On April 29, 1792 Vancouver's ships anchored a few miles inside the Strait of Juan de Fuca. Several days later they moored near the entry to Puget Sound in a sheltered bay that he named Port Discovery after his ship; here the men erected tents ashore, made repairs, encountered native people, and explored the environs. They sighted and named Mount Baker before exploring farther south in the inland sea. The party divided into three groups at Restoration Point, a southern tip of present-day Bainbridge Island, which the explorers named on the anniversary of the British monarchy's restoration in 1660 after Oliver Cromwell's reign. Vancouver himself explored the middle section of the sound; a small sloop commanded by Peter Puget explored the southern reaches. Lt. Joseph Whidbey proceeded north to investigate the island that would soon bear his name and the nearby mainland. Whidbey found the Indians friendly, and presents were exchanged. Despite evidence of previous trade, these natives were clearly unaccustomed to meeting whites. He described an "eastern shore a shallow flat of sand, on which are some rocky islets and rocks, runs out, until within half a mile of the western shore forming a narrow channel . . . in nearly a NNW direction, for about three leagues."

Late in May the groups reunited. The passage from Port Townsend to Tacoma was named Admiralty Inlet, in honor of the supervisory board of the Royal Navy. Early June was spent in a region which would become a part of Snohomish County. There a negligent apprentice caused the *Chatham* to run aground. Helped by the *Discovery* crew and a flood tide, the brig later set sail once more. Weather and "great fatigue" slowed exploration. The crewmen fished, enjoyed onshore recreation, and on June 4 celebrated the birthday of King George III. That Monday they were given "as good a dinner as we were able to provide for them, with double allowance of grog to drink the King's health." Early that

Vancouver's sloop "Discovery" and brig "Chatham" are shown on the coast in this drawing from the expedition. (Courtesy British Columbia Archives)

afternoon the commander took the action he had been anticipating when he led several officers ashore to a spot possibly on Tulalip Bay on today's Tulalip Indian Reservation. Amidst formalities that included "a royal salute from the vessels", a 21-gun salute, according to one member of the *Chatham* crew, Vancouver took possession of "New Albion" from 39 degrees 20 minutes north to the entrance of the Strait of Juan de Fuca, including islands in the straits and the interior sea. He named the land New Georgia and the sea the

Archibald Menzies' Journal

An important member of Vancouver's party was 38-year-old Archibald Menzies, a naval surgeon who had previously sailed in the Pacific and would become a noted botanist. Menzies described the present Snohomish County shoreline, a minor disaster, and Vancouver's formal claiming of the region in his journal as edited by C. F. Newcombe:

In the morning of the first of June we weighed anchor & finding the Arm a little to the Northward of us divide into two branches, we stood up the Eastermost which soon in the afternoon we found to terminate in a large Bay with very shallow water & muddy bottom, on which the Chatham who was about two miles ahead of us got aground owing to the inattention or unskillfulness of the leadsman, for on sounding afterwards they found they had run over a flat of near half a mile or so very level that there was not more than a foot depth of water difference, yet the leadsman passed over this space without perceiving it, till they struck, which was upon an ebb tide, & it afterwards fell about five feet—they carried out a small Anchor three hawsers length from the Vessel & after heaving tight waited the return of the flood tide which about 11 floated them without having received any injury, when they hauled out and brought to in deeper water.

Next morning we had rain & foggy weather, which continued till about noon. In the forenoon we both weighed & with a light northerly air returned down the arm till we came a little below the point of division & then anchored near the eastern shore abreast of a small Bay formed between two steep sandy bluffs into which we found some small streams of fresh water empty themselves, which was rather a scarce article hitherto in our different explorings. We also saw some of the long Poles already mentioned erected upon the Beach.

In the evening the two Boats returned after having carried their examination to the termination of the western branch which was named Port Gardner & which like the rest they found to end with Shoal water surrounded by low land. In this arm they saw two Villages pretty-numerously inhabited with Natives, they supposed there might be upwards of 200 in each, & they behaved very peaceably. They found Oak Timber more abundant in this arm than any we had yet explored & the country to the westward of it they describe as a fine rich Country abounding with luxuriant lawns, cropped with the finest verdure & extensive prospects teeming with the softer beauties of nature as we have already mentioned in our view of it from Port Townsend.

We remained here the two following days with fine pleasant weather. The latter being the King's Birth Day, Capt Vancouver landed about noon with some of the officers on the South point of the small Bay where he took possession of the Country with the usual forms in his Majesty's name & named it *New Georgia* & on hoisting the English Coulours on the spot each Vessel proclaimed it aloud with a Royal Salute in honor of the Day.

We both weighed anchor early on the morning of the 5th & with a moderate breeze from the northward made Sail back again out of the Arm after having explored its different branches.

C. F. Newcombe, ed., *Menzies' Journal of Vancouver's Voyage, April to October, 1792*; (Archives of British Columbia, Memoir No. V). Victoria, B. C.: William H. Cullin, Printer to the King's Most Excellent Majesty, 1923, pp. 44-45.

Gulf of Georgia for his king. Possession Sound was named to honor the event. The large broad bay became Port Gardner for Sir Alan Gardner, a vice admiral who had been Vancouver's mentor, and that to the north was Port Susan, quite likely for Gardner's wife.

Vancouver's description might also apply more broadly to today's Snohomish County: "The inlet here terminated in an expansive though shallow bay, across which a flat of sand extended upwards of a mile from its shores; on which was lying an immense quantity of drift wood, consisting chiefly of very large trees. The country behind for some distance, was low, then rose gradually to a moderate height; and, like the eastern shores of the inlet, was covered with wood, and diversified with pleasant inequalities of hill and dale . . . the whole presenting one uninterrupted wilderness."

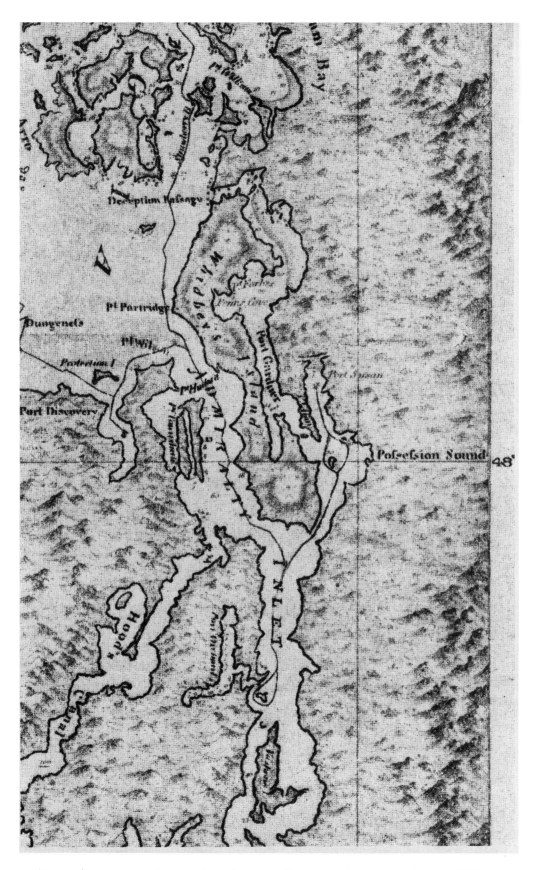

This map from Vancouver's report shows Possession Sound and the site of the June 1, 1792 grounding of the "Chatham" in Port Susan.

Vancouver had eyes to the future: "The serenity of the climate, the innumerable pleasing landscapes, and the abundant fertility that unassisted nature puts forth, require only to be enriched by the industry of man with villages, mansions, cottages, and other buildings, to render it the most lively country that can be imagined; whilst the labour of the inhabitants would be amply rewarded, in the bounties which nature seems ready to bestow on cultivation."

Archibald Menzies, the expedition's botanist who was destined to become renowned in his field, rhapsodized over the flat lands near Everett: "A Traveller wandering over these unfrequented Plains is regailed [sic] with a salubrious and revivifying air impregnated with the balsamic fragrance of the surrounding Pinery, while his mind is eagerly occupied every moment on new objects & his senses rivetted on the enchanting variety of the surrounding scenery where the softer beauties of landscape are harmoniously blended in majestic grandeur with the wild & romantic to form an interesting & picturesque prospect on every side." Thus the first Europeans to view Snohomish County described the land.

The morning after the ceremony a light breeze allowed the ships to sail out of Possession Sound. A friendly Indian chief cautiously brought fruit and dried fish aboard to exchange for trinkets. Despite unfavorable winds, the ships worked north, eventually beaching at just south of the present international boundary at Birch Bay. Then Vancouver continued on to the rendezvous at Nootka Sound where the issues revolving about the conflict with Spain were discussed, though not thoroughly resolved. Vancouver continued explorations in Alaska before returning around Cape Horn to Britain in October 1795. Thereafter he prepared his journals, defended himself from accusations by a disgruntled former crewman, and battled increasing illness. In 1798 he died and was buried in Petersham, England.

Vancouver's voyage into the sound he named for Peter Puget occupied little more than a month out of a 4½-year voyage. Yet, it defined major outlines of the coast and waters, and outstanding physical features were named. For all his observations, Vancouver did not note the rivers that flowed into Sound and ocean, including the Columbia, the Snohomish, and the Stillaguamish. The climactic event of those weeks took place in Snohomish County when he landed to claim all such lands for his country.

Over the next half-century, Great Britain and the United States survived as the major players in what would be called the Oregon Country, that vast land between Spanish California and Russian Alaska, the Pacific Ocean and the crest of the Rocky Mountains. In a peculiar but pragmatic arrangement, the two nations jointly occupied the region for the nearly three decades between 1818 and 1846. Most of that time Britain's Hudson's Bay Company dominated the economy and politics from its regional headquarters at Fort Vancouver on the north bank of the Columbia River. Fort Langley at the mouth of the Fraser River to the north was opened in 1827, followed in 1833 by Fort Nisqually on southern Puget Sound, and then Fort Victoria on Vancouver Island 10 years later. Company boats plied Puget Sound, including the *Beaver*, the first steamer in Pacific Northwest waters. These passed by but gave little formal notice to the eventual Snohomish County shoreline. As fur trading waned and increasing numbers of white settlers entered the region, it became clear that Americans would supplant British dominance. This reality was confirmed by the 1846 treaty, which established the 49th parallel and the Strait of Juan de Fuca as the border between British and American lands and resulted in H.B.C. offices transferring to Fort Victoria.

That agreement resulted in part from a second great exploration of Puget Sound. By the 1830s, forward thinking Americans in the federal government were anticipating a maritime survey that would be worldwide in scope and include the Oregon Country. Scientific expeditions sponsored by national governments were not unique, with those led by England's James Cook and the Americans Lewis and Clark among notable predecessors. But, "like many government projects," historian David Buerge commented, this proposal "was sired by hope and born in controversy." Congressional doubts, politics, and apathy brought delays until the United States Exploring Expedition was authorized in 1838. It would become better known as the Wilkes Expedition, after the name of its leader.

Lt. Charles Wilkes was given command primarily because he had some scientific interests and expertise; he was neither of high rank nor regarded as an able leader of men. Possibly he would have preferred an expedition composed entirely of naval officers, but a distinguished and varied array of scientists was among the 490 men who set out. An essential goal was to obtain scientific knowledge worldwide, but developing American interests overseas made commercial possibilities a major factor. Sailing out of Norfolk, Virginia and then New York harbor with six ships late in the summer of 1838, the expedition ventured to South America, the Antarctic, South Pacific Islands, and Hawaii before touching the west coast of North America.

Charles Wilkes, Commander, USN. (Courtesy of Washington State Historical Society)

Aboard the sloop-of-war *Vincennes*, Wilkes led his men into the Strait of Juan de Fuca on May 1, 1841; just as Vancouver had a half century earlier, they anchored in Discovery Bay before proceeding to survey Puget Sound and surrounding landforms. Impressed by both, Wilkes headed overland to the Hudson's Bay Company headquarters at Fort Vancouver. He returned to Fort Nisqually in time to celebrate with ceremony and frivolity the first Fourth of July in what would become Washington State.

Wilkes then divided his men into separate parties to explore specific areas. Two groups went overland, one across the Cascade Mountains and the other towards Grays Harbor, while a small maritime party headed to survey Hood Canal. The task of exploring the waters and shoreline of Admiralty Inlet was assigned to Lieutenant Commander C. Ringgold, who commanded the *Porpoise*. The ship was a 230-ton gun brig, previously used and modified by Wilkes.

At Nisqually on May 13, 1841 Wilkes prepared Ringgold's specific orders. Starting his explorations near Vashon Island, he was to move "north, examining and surveying all islets, and the shores of both sides of the straits, particularly all those bays etc., that afford shelter for vessels, not only as harbors, but for temporary anchorage." Upon reaching Whidbey Island, Ringgold was instructed to "pass into and survey Possession

Vancouver had served under Rear Admiral Sir Alan Gardner in the West Indies, and it was Gardner who recommended him for command of the British expedition to Nootka Sound. Port Gardner Bay is named for him (Courtesy Everett Public Library)

Sound to its extreme end, and all its inlets, etc." The crew was instructed to keep meticulous records, to make correct triangulations, to measure latitude, longitude, and altitude, barking or whitewashing large trees for markers. Full soundings were to be taken daily and tides measured. The men were to sketch the land. Commercial potential was to be noted: "You will endeavor to obtain all the information that may lay [*sic*] in your power, relative to the geological formation, and capabilities of the soil for agriculture . . . also all minerals . . . All water-courses and brooks that may afford water for shipping will be particularly noticed." Nor were the indigenous people ignored; records were to indicate "the names of the Indian tribes, numbers, and extent of districts belonging to them, it is desirable to get; all curiosities, etc., you will of course preserve."

The small party sailed north—investigating Whidbey Island—and then turned east, noting "much good land." They gave the name Saratoga Passage to the strait separating Whidbey Island from the island he called McDonough, both terms honoring a War of 1812 naval hero and his flagship at the battle of Lake Champlain. The former name remained, but the latter was forgotten when, a few years later, a British officer designated the island Camano, apparently to recognize the Spanish presence.

Vancouver already had dubbed the waters between that island and the eastern shore "Port Susan." Wilkes's men praised its deep waters, except for the shallower northern portion which was "an extensive marsh and mud-flat" with a creek passing through. They measured a nine-mile, land-locked shoreline, reaching 3½ miles across.

Wilkes accepted Vancouver's name of Possession Sound to describe the passage between Whidbey Island and the mainland; it was four miles long and 2½ miles wide. A "fine stream" (most likely the Snohomish River) emptied into the sound, but it had four mouths, none deep enough "to admit boats at low water" possibly because a bar or flat extended across the entrance. Ringgold's crew encountered "many canoes" carrying Indians, some possibly from the southwest. Their dress resembled that of others the men had seen. They wore leather hunting shirts, beads, and shells, and the women also wore brass bells and trinkets. Some had brass rings on wrists and fingers and a few were tattooed. Several were draped in blankets fastened by wooden pins around neck and shoulders. The Americans thought the people "filthy" and coated with dirt, conjecturing that they suffered from bronchitis or "tubercular consumption."

The men measured Port Gardner Bay as being six miles square, with anchorage only on the south side. At its center lay Gedney's Island, a mile and a quarter long and a third of a mile wide with a shoal off the southwest point. The point marking the southern boundary of Port Gardner where "the bank drops off suddenly" was named Point Elliot. Elsewhere he found little suitable anchorage. Further south, the man labeled two small points Point Edmund and Point Wells, the latter for a crewmember.

After spending more than nine weeks at their task, on July 20 Ringgold and his crew rejoined Wilkes at New Dungeness on the Strait of Juan de Fuca. Their report became the basis for that portion of Wilkes's narrative which described this area of the Sound. Other regions received greater consideration from Wilkes and his writers, but the shoreline destined to become Snohomish County received their general praise. Within a few years white lumbermen, settlers, and prospectors would fill in the details of the county's river valleys and inland areas.

The Territorial Period 1849–1889

P romises of gold, land, and timber brought Americans to the Pacific Northwest during the territorial years. Many left the east coast and headed for the placer gold mines of California, working there until the easy money played out and they heard of better opportunities to the north. Others arrived in San Francisco to set up businesses supplying the miners, then branched out. Some crossed the country to Oregon's Willamette Valley, finding the best land taken early and so crossing the Columbia and working their way up to the sheltered inlets and deep harbors of Puget Sound. Many retained family and community links with their original homes, and their experiences and advice frequently brought others to join them. Natives of Maine, New York, and Kansas, joined by those who had tested life in Iowa, the Dakotas, and Michigan were joined by immigrants from Canada, Norway, and most of the European countries. Overwhelmingly the early newcomers were young, male, Caucasian, and single. Early relationships were established with the daughters and families of the Native American population, and new families formed. In later years more Caucasian women, Chinese men, and African Americans arrived, and the former majority of biracial and native residents found themselves marginalized in what by statehood was becoming a society more urbanized and industrialized than any other portion of the American west.

Snohomish County was typical of how settlers in western Washington developed their resources, commerce, and settlement patterns, but it also displayed significant differences. It had no major timber milling center of its own, what was to become its major city did not even exist until after 1890, and for a time in the 1870s and 1880s it was a center of literary and scientific culture focused a dozen miles up the Snohomish River.

Chelan Co.

Cascade Range

Glacier Peak

Sulattle R.

Whitechuck R.

N. Fork Sauk R.

Sauk Prairie

Sauk R.

Monte Cristo Peak

Monte Cristo

S. Fork Sauk R.

Mineral City

Cadi Pass

Hubart Peak

Snohomish Co.

Skagit Co.

Barlow Ridge

N. Fork Skykomish R.

S. Fork Skykomish R.

Silver Cr.

Index

Hazel

Starup

Wallace

Gold Bar

Stillaguamish R.

Mt. Pilchuck

Sultan

Sultan R.

South Fork

Pilchuck R.

Lake Roesiger

Woods Ck.

Skykomish R.

King Co.

Cicero

North Fork Stillaguamish R.

Trafton

Granite Falls

Three Lakes

Forest Glade

Woods Prairie

Tualco

Snoqualmie R.

Duvall

Haller City

Arlington

Snohomish City

Park Place

Snoqualmie R.

Bryant

Pilchuck Ck.

Kent Prairie

The Big Burn

Kellogg Marsh

Getchell

Marysville

Smith Island

Steamboat Slough

Lake Stevens

Fort Ebey

Snohomish R.

Marshland

Shorts

Cedarhome

Stanwood

East Stanwood

Stillaguamish R.

Silvana

Norman

Florence

Ebey Slough

Preston Point

Port Gardner

Lowell

Centerville

Hat Slough

Warm Beach

Kayak Point

Tulalip Indian Res.

Tulalip

Tulalip Bay

Hat (Gedney) Island

Priest Point

Port Gardner Bay

Mukilteo

Lake Washington

Skagit Bay

Camano Island

Island Co.

Whidbey Island

Possession Sound

Point Elliot

Brown's Bay

Edmonds

Puget Sound

56

From late summer 1852 through late spring 1853 a wave of relatives and other land-seekers followed Isaac N. Ebey to the fertile, open prairies of northern Whidbey Island. In the rain shadow of the Olympic Mountains a community of several hundred people developed. When Washington became a territory in 1853, Island County was formed to include all the land on Whidbey and Camano islands, plus the eastern mainland of what would become three counties (Snohomish, Skagit, and Whatcom), as well as the San Juan Islands. Samuel Hancock had explored first the Snohomish River and its tributary Snoqualmie in 1849, leaving an analysis of natural resources and his first sight of Snoqualmie Falls. He joined the Whidbey settlers, claiming land near Crockett Lake, and then in 1854 also checked out the lower Stillaguamish River and its south fork.

When gold fever brought the Forty-niners to California it also brought Andrew Pope and W.C. Talbot from East Machias, Maine. They imported shiploads of lumber around Cape Horn from their family timber businesses but soon realized that closer and more dependable sources of trees were needed. Rejecting the Portland area because of the treacherous bar at the mouth of the Columbia River, they decided on the sheltered harbor of Port Gamble near the mouth of Hood Canal and directly across the Sound from what would become southwestern Snohomish County. In 1852 they created the Puget Mill Company and opened their first mill the following September, shipping four million board feet of lumber in 1854. Four years later a second mill was added, and then the first one totally replaced with another able to saw 160,000 board feet a day. This output was aggressively marketed in California, Hawaii, South America, China, Australia, and any other spot around the Pacific Rim which would pay for a cargo. Joined by other equally voracious operations in such booming sites as Port Blakely, Port Ludlow, Seabeck, Utsalady, and Seattle (although these could not match the power and connections of Pope and Talbot), the millmen needed millions of board feet of trees felled and floated to their saws.

With miles of saltwater frontage and two river valleys (which extended deeply into the interior to the Cascade Mountains), Snohomish County could provide much of that future timber. The price also was right. Two legal difficulties stood in the way, however. The first was that ownership of the land still was in native hands until the Treaty of Point Elliot was signed in January 1855, on the beach where Frost and Fowler soon would build their store, saloon, and hotel and call the place Mukilteo. Ratification by Congress would not occur until 1859. The second was that the system of land acquisition by logger and farmer alike was complex, slow, and totally underfunded. Little of the government lands obtained by the treaty could be purchased outright, as no surveys had been completed. The original Donation Land Claim Act of Oregon Territory in 1850 had been extended into Washington Territory upon its organization in 1853, whereby surveyed land could be purchased at a cost of $1.25 per acre. Congress, however, only allotted survey money at a rate of $8 per acre, when the actual cost of the job in rugged, tree covered western Washington ranged from $12 to $20. The Preemption Act of 1841 was amended in July, 1854 to allow a person to file on 160 acres of unsurveyed land and eventually prove up on it by building a home and cultivating, the price also $1.25 per acre. This was the procedure widely adopted here and was similar in requirements to the 1863 Homestead Act. In 1878, the Timber and Stone Act attempted to reduce the red tape by allowing individuals to purchase 160 acres outright at a cost of $2.50 per acre, the whole procedure to be completed within 60 days.

While these laws were intended to encourage settlement, in actuality they often delayed it and played directly into the hands of mill company and logger theft. Unable quickly to obtain title to a stand of trees, the timbermen simply stole them off public lands and corrupted the officials charged with enforcing the law. This was especially true of the Timber and Stone Act and of the Puget Mill, which paid men to file on and purchase lands with the sole purpose of turning over title to the company. A system of fines was tried whereby the companies reported the amount stolen and then paid a penalty ranging from fifteen cents to $2.50 per thousand board feet, but it did not really come to an end until the Northern Pacific Railroad became concerned that its granted lands also were being raided. The railroad had received a strip of land 20 miles wide, in alternate sections, through each state and one forty miles wide through the territories. As the line had surveyed a route across the Cascades down the Skagit River, a sizeable amount of this county's land also was unavailable for claiming. By 1873 the Northern Pacific had stopped the major land corruption, and 10 years later finally built across Stampede Pass to Tacoma, thus freeing up more land for settlement.

Pope and Talbot also took advantage of the disputed sale of lands set aside for support of the University of Washington. In an apparent deal to benefit both the mills and the university, the Reverend Daniel Bagley was authorized as land commissioner to sell parcels at $1.50 per acre. In 1862 the Puget Mill Company picked up acreage near the future site of Edmonds as part of its total of over 17,000 around the Sound and eventually acquired a substantial amount of southwestern Snohomish County.

In 1877 it also purchased at half price the bankrupt Utsalady sawmill, which Lawrence Grennan and Thomas Cranney had operated since 1856, and where virtually all of the Stillaguamish valley timber was sawn. On the previous November 4 their mill manager had boarded the steamer *Pacific* at Utsalady, carrying with him the funds and credits needed to pay mill and shipyard bills in San Francisco. He was among more than 250 passengers aboard the sidewheeler, which was lost off Cape Flattery in one of the Northwest's worst marine disasters. In a night-time collision with the sailing ship *Orpheus* the hull of the old, rotten *Pacific* split open and quickly sank, leaving only two survivors, one of whom later died of hypothermia. Captain of the doomed ship was J.D. Howell, formerly a Confederate naval lieutenant and brother-in-law of President Jefferson Davis. Lost also were funds from local logging camps, businesses, and individuals, along with the first grain shipment from the area and a quarter of a million dollars in gold from miners boarding in Victoria. Grennan had died in 1869, and Cranney now failed financially in the months following the wreck.

It took almost to the end of the territorial period before county millmen were able to compete with the giant exporting cargo mills—

Dr. Wesley Cherry joined with Charles C. Phillips and John Gould to build the first industry in the county, a small water powered saw mill at Tulalip Bay. Cherry was killed shortly after while serving in a posse (see Chapter 2), and the mill became the property of the United States government following the Treaty of Point Elliot in 1855.

Territorial volunteers under Col. Isaac Ebey fortified a small island at the the head of Ebey Island to block hostile Indians from reaching Puget Sound. This strategic location is shown in the middle of the channel to the right of the numeral 4 in a later map. Over the years the island virtually has disappeared. (Courtesy Everett Public Library)

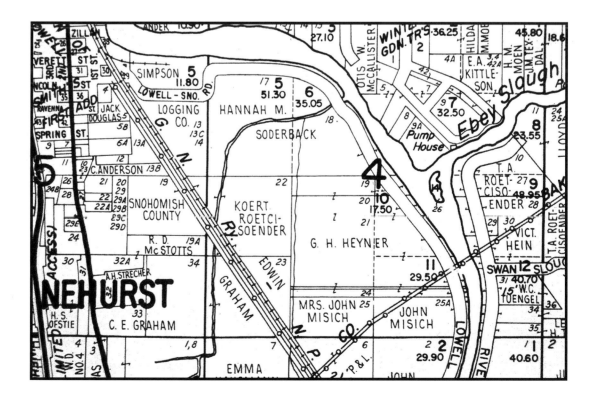

although, in the case of the pioneering Tulalip mill company on Tulalip Bay, the problem was the Treaty of Point Elliot rather than business rivalry. Charles C. Phillips, John Gould, and Dr. Wesley F. Cherry, all of Whidbey Island, decided in 1853 to erect a small water powered mill at the mouth of the creek where George Vancouver probably had refilled his water casks 60 years earlier. At this time the land was claimed by Jehiel H. Hall, who donated his water rights, timber, and five acres to the group. In turn he received a quarter interest in the venture. Unfortunately for the little mill, it was put into production just as San Francisco lumber prices fell in the aftermath of the gold rush, and then the treaty negotiations were held. Tulalip was reserved for the native peoples, too late to save their cemetery at Skayu Point from desecration. Eventually the mill owners would receive long-delayed compensation for turning their plant over to the government. Under federal control its circular saw would continue to produce lumber for the needs of the reservation until finally being junked in 1906.

The second attempt to develop a sawmill, this time one more dependably powered by steam, was built by David and Jacob Livingston halfway between Mukilteo and the future site of Everett in 1863. It failed two years later. In 1872, Jacob Livingston platted the town site of "Western New York" on his portion of their land near present day Harborview Park, but this also was unsuccessful and later vacated.

Unresolved issues and white trespass, resulting from Governor Isaac I. Stevens' hurried treaty making, led to the outbreak of war east of the Cascade Mountains in 1855, which spilled over into the west that autumn. To block hostile forces from descending the Snoqualmie and Snohomish river route to Puget Sound the territorial government raised volunteer troops under Colonel Isaac Ebey and recruited heavily at Port Townsend and Whidbey Island. Supported and guided by Pat-ka-nim's Snoqualmie and Snohomish tribal forces, in November Ebey's contingent moved up the Snohomish River to the spot where Ebey Slough forks off to begin the Snohomish delta region. There the troops constructed a blockhouse surrounded by a timber stockade on a small island, effectively sealing off all river traffic through the spring of 1856, when their term of enlistment expired. As there were no roads, the soldiers had boarded the schooner *A.Y. Trask*, which was towed upstream by the 85-foot iron propeller steamer *Traveler*. These were the first known commercial vessels to enter the Snohomish River.

Quickly reorganized in spring 1856 as the Northern Battalion of three companies, and now under the command of J.J. Van Bokkelin of Port Townsend, the combined force moved south up the Snoqualmie River into King County, erecting a series of forts along the way. Pat-ka-nim's men, well armed and supplied by the territorial government, surrounded and entered an encampment of Snoqualmie who were being urged on to fight by several visiting Klickitat men from eastern Washington. Two of the three Klickitats were executed before the third agreed to cooperate and talk. With the heads of the dead men sent down to the whites as a sign of his good faith, Pat-ka-nim's party headed south down to the White River, where they attempted to capture Nisqually leader Leschi and end the fighting. Warned by a barking dog as the men approached, Leschi escaped, and battle ensued. The outnumbered Snoqualmie and Snohomish fighters inflicted more casualties than they suf-

Pat-ka-nim, appointed chief of the Snoqualmie tribe by Governor Isaac I. Stevens, sided with the territorial government in the 1855-1856 Indian War. His force from the Snoqualmie and Snohomish tribes took an active role in the fighting. (Courtesy Everett Public Library)

Emory C. Ferguson settled along the Snohomish River in 1860 and became not only the father of the town, but also the leading figure in the county of Snohomish for the next three decades. His original prefabricated home still stands above the river bank. (Courtesy Everett Public Library)

fered before they pulled back, short of ammunition. Pat-ka-nim had opposed the first attempts by A.B. Rabbeson and Thomas Glasgow to claim land on Whidbey Island, but he had since visited San Francisco and seen the power of incoming settlement and chosen to support the eventual victors. That role brought acclaim from the white Americans, but decidedly mixed feelings among Native Americans.

There was great concern for personal protection from Native Americans even after the end of fighting in September 1856. War broke out again in eastern Washington a year and a half later, lasting until the Spokane, Coeur d'Alene, and Palouse tribes were badly defeated in the battles of Four Lakes and Spokane Plains in September 1858. With the additional delay by Congress in ratifying the Treaty of Point Elliot until the spring of 1859, few settlers were eager to take up new claims in the county. Individual cases of violence on both sides continued to occur for many years. Notable were the murder of settler T.P. Carter in 1860 by three Snohomish tribal members trying to rekindle the fighting and the shootout between the families of Sultan John and the Taylors at Sultan in 1884 which left one wounded on each side. That incident was sparked by the Taylors' objection to the band's dogs running loose on land claimed by the white family. In 1876 federal troops patrolled the upper Skagit country, successfully intimidating members of the Sauk-Suiattle tribe who bitterly objected to loss of their lands to white settlers, insisting unsuccessfully that their representatives never had signed the Treaty of Point Elliot.

Northwestern gold entered the picture in March 1858. Word filtered south from the Fraser River country just across the 49th parallel that placer gold discoveries were rich and easily worked, the native peoples were friendly, and the country looked richer the farther north one went, as in California a decade earlier. Immediately a rush began from not only the Puget Sound region, but also from the south, where over 20,000 Californians took passage to Victoria for the new diggings. However, the boom quickly collapsed, with high water inundating the river bars when the summer snow melt began, difficulty of travel up the unbelievably hazardous Fraser Canyon, and few more worthwhile sites to mine. It did lead to the creation of a new government, the colony of British Columbia, but for Americans it proved a sharp disappointment. As the tide of gold seekers quickly ebbed back down the river, a substantial number either decided to look around the Sound for new opportunities or lacked the money to travel any farther. Among them was a young carpenter from New York via California named Emory C. Ferguson.

Finding employment at the small community of Steilacoom, Ferguson became part of a group of investors interested in obtaining from the legislature the franchise for a ferry across the Snohomish River. Congress had allotted money to construct a military road along the east side of Puget Sound to connect Fort Steilacoom in the south with Fort Bellingham in the north, a route to run inland from the coast to allow communication in case the powerful British navy should send ships down from its base at Esquimalt on Vancouver Island. The "Pig War" dispute between the United States and Great Britain over rival claims to the San Juan Islands had not erupted into fighting, but that situation was far from resolved.

The proposed road was constructed into King County, but by the time it reached the Snohomish River it had degenerated into a rough, muddy trail. It crossed Kent Prairie near the future site of Arlington and then disappeared in the swamp southwest of the site of Bryant near what would become the Skagit County line. Contractors convinced inspectors that the road indeed was passable for wagons as specified by shipping one up the "road" in parts on the backs of pack mules, paddling it across the river, and then assembling it on the north bank as proof of their work. The Army official traveled up from Steilacoom by canoe, observed the vehicle, and approved payment. At Fort Bellingham, commander Pickett (later of Gettysburg fame) spent his allocation building a road and bridge in the opposite direction.

Nevertheless, a ferry made sense to Ferguson, even though his partners backed out of the proposal. In 1859 they had sent Edson Cady, Hiel Barnes, and Egbert Tucker up to the site to stake claims for them. In February 1860 he visited the site, and in April shipped up a pre-fabricated house to make "Cadyville" his permanent home. He took Barnes' claim to the west on the north bank, adjoining Cady's to the east toward the Pilchuck River. Tucker's across the river to the south soon was taken over by John Harvey. Still thinking of gold, Ferguson raised money and supplies from Port Townsend and Whidbey Island supporters to construct a road and trail up the Snohomish River, then follow the Skykomish and finally the North Fork Skykomish River to Cady Pass over the Cascade Mountains, intending to drop down to Lake Wenatchee, the Columbia River, and then turn northward to the Similkameen and Kettle river strikes. Cady followed the old Native American trading route part way in the fall of 1859, and then a crew of white and native men improved the trail to the crest the following summer. Ferguson and Cady made the entire round trip later that year but returned empty handed, disappointed at the small amount of gold being found. That was the end of the road building. Ferguson now turned toward developing his property, while Cady began carrying freight aboard his river scow, the *Minnehaha*.

Meanwhile, the federal customs collector at Port Townsend, Morris H. Frost, had become familiar with possible business sites around the Puget Sound and concluded that the Point Elliot treaty signing location would make an excellent spot for a store and saloon. It lay on the water route between the settlements at Seattle and Bellingham Bay, would be close to large Native American populations, and would be near the mouth of the Snohomish River. He convinced Jacob D. Fowler to leave his similar business at Ebey's Landing and move over to the mainland to become his operating partner. In July 1860 Frost made his claim, followed in September by Fowler, who erected the buildings along the beach and named the spot Mukilteo, or "good camping ground."

Loggers such as Alexander Spithill and John Elwell had looked over the timber along the salt water, while a few of the men who had served as volunteers during the upriver expedition had decided to come back over to seek claims or cut trees along the delta, and so the Frost and Fowler operation had some willing customers. As winter rains settled in and logging ceased, they also had a market for a hotel, which became a popular seasonal address for many men in the timber business. It also was the logical place for mail to be

Morris H. Frost sensed the business possibilities of the Point Elliot location where the 1855 treaty had been signed. In 1860 he claimed land there and became a rival to Ferguson. (Courtesy Everett Public Library)

Jacob O. Fowler was convinced by Frost to join him at Point Elliot and take the leading role in managing their new store, hotel, and saloon. Fowler named their site Mukilteo, which became briefly the first county seat in 1861. (Courtesy Everett Public Library)

dropped off. In 1862 Mukilteo became the county's first post office, with Fowler appointed the first postmaster.

During 1860 the area still was part of Island County, with government at Coupeville and court held at Port Townsend as part of Judicial District 3 (until 1868). With the nation in grave crisis leading toward civil war, a number of the settlers along the Snohomish River wished to participate in that year's divisive elections. Seventeen votes were cast unofficially and sent to Coupeville, where they were too late to be counted. Frustrated by the situation, a petition meeting was organized and hosted by Emory C. Ferguson where the men requested the territorial legislature create a separate mainland county. Frost and Fowler also may have sent their own. The timing was excellent!

Once again gold and silver had been discovered, and new thousands of eager miners poured into eastern Washington territory, headed for the Boise Basin, Idaho City, and Missoula. Walla Walla surged to the lead in population, most of which supported the Democratic party and had no interest in the issues affecting Puget Sounders, who over-whelmingly supported the victorious Republicans of Abraham Lincoln. Fearing domination of the territorial legislature by those eastern mining interests, a proposal by Territorial Councilman Paul K. Hubbs of Port Townsend to create a new county in his district already had passed by the time the Snohomish men had paddled their canoe down to the capital with their petition. (Two years later, Congress finally would shuck off the entire mining area to create an oddly shaped and culturally divided new Idaho Territory, leaving the Republicans firmly in control in Olympia for the next three quarters of a century.)

Effective January 14, 1861, Snohomish County came into existence. The county's temporary seat would be in Mukilteo, until elections could be held in July. The county's first officers were Jacob Summers (sheriff); Emory C. Ferguson, Henry McClurg, and John Harvey (commissioners); Jacob D. Fowler (auditor); Charles Short (judge of probate); and John Harvey (treasurer). A rough census of the non-native population listed 49 men and no women, the majority located near Mukilteo, Snohomish, and Tulalip.

On March 12, 1861 the county commissioners met at Frost and Fowler's store to conduct their first business: receiving and accepting a petition for the county to build a road from Snohomish City up the Snohomish and Skykomish rivers to Woods Prairie (near the future site of Monroe) and rejecting Fowler's request to grant him a license to sell a small amount of liquor, holding that they only had authority to issue full licenses for the fee of $300. Salem Woods (of Woods Prairie) was appointed assessor, with Fowler taking over as treasurer. C.M. Stilwell received appointment as justice of the peace for the Mukilteo precinct, Ferguson for the Snohomish one. At their second meeting on May 6, the county was divided into two voting precincts, ballots to be cast at the store for the Mukilteo precinct and at Ferguson's house for Snohomish. Salem Woods now became sheriff. Frost and Fowler agreed to the full liquor license, while Ferguson and Cady were licensed to operate their ferry across the river at Snohomish.

The first election on July 8, 1861 would set the tone of county politics for many years to come. Ferguson showed his skill by organizing 17 votes for his site, while only 10 were cast for Mukilteo. In addition to that victory for Snohomish, Republican Colonel W.H. Wallace had been appointed governor of Washington Territory by President Lincoln. Wallace had been one of the five members of the original group formed to acquire that ferry in 1859! Ferguson was an active Republican, but Morris Frost and Jacob Fowler

Beachfront Mukilteo provided the only civilized amenities for the county's all-male
white population during the early 1860s. Its early dominance faded as Snohomish rose, even though it
boasted of a number of county "firsts". (Courtesy Everett Public Library)

Democrats; and it was obvious which way political patronage would flow into the new
county. Frost, an older man of culture and education originally from New York (as was
Ferguson), consistently would be outmaneuvered, and his settlement would decline in
importance.

In 1862 Sheriff Woods conducted an official census of the county's non-native
population and listed 44 residents aged 23 to 58, averaging slightly over 33. There were
no women or children. Morris Frost was 55, Jacob Fowler was 24, Father Eugene Casimir
Chirouse was 40, Emory C. Ferguson and Henry McClurg were both 29, Edson Cady was
34, and Salem Woods was 31. Twelve were born in New York state, another 12 were
foreign born, and only three were born west of the Mississippi River.

That shortage of white women soon led to the creation of families where the father
was white and the mother Native American. Later in 1862 Louisa Fowler was the first
child born to such a couple in the county, her mother Mary having the first of her four
daughters. Neil Spithill followed, his father Alexander of Scottish descent and his mother
Jessey of white and Native American heritage. Over the next decade there were far more
families of mixed heritage than of white only, and the alliance with a native family not
only brought the obvious benefits of a woman with a large support system of relatives
who knew how to live in the country (and usually had her own canoe at a time when that
was the prime means of travel), but also of a man who had the skills to fit into the new
and increasingly dominant American culture.

White women did not begin to appear permanently until spring 1864, when Mary E.

Sinclair accompanied her husband Woodbury to Ferguson's settlement, which (since 1861) officially was named Snohomish City. The couple purchased the Cady claim. Sinclair formed an unsuccessful partnership with Clendenning to open a store there. In November on the lower Stillaguamish River Maria L. Marvin accompanied her husband Captain Daniel Marvin to file on land along the river, joining John Silva, Willard Sly, and George Nevils, with James Cuthbert arriving the next year. All of these men had native wives.

Logging was active along the lower waterways, with Eugene Smith and Otis Wilson obtaining a contract from the Puget Mill Company to cut their timber at Brown's Bay near the future site of Meadowdale in 1862. That done, in 1863 they moved their operations up the Snohomish River to Lowell. There Smith would create a base, and after a brief sortie to the Coeur d'Alene mines in 1865, develop both a future townsite and an important logging and milling operation. By 1864 timber was being cut at the mouth of the river by Spithill, Preston, and others, while Martin and Joseph Getchell arrived to join Smith at Lowell. In 1863 James Hatt with his Native American wife moved to Hatt's Slough on the lower Stillaguamish and began logging for the Utsalady mill, selling their business to William Douglass in 1866 and filing a land claim. Thomas Runnels opened a logging camp in either 1864 or 1865 to cut timber on Irvine's Slough at what later became the site of East Stanwood. In 1868 he sold out to S.G. Record. James Duvall also opened a camp along the Stillaguamish River before transferring southward to the Snoqualmie, later to

Timber harvest dominated the early economy. Trees were felled by hand, moved by ox teams along skid roads to the water, then floated to large saw mills at Port Gamble and Utsalady. (Courtesy Stanwood Area Historical Society)

have the town of Duvall named for him.

In October 1864 Henry Marshall had located the first land claim in the Stillaguamish Valley at what would become Florence. In 1866 he left, selling out to James Perkins, the man who would later turn Florence into a thriving community. Perkins was a veteran of the Fraser River gold rush, along with his partner Gardner Goodridge. Broke and unemployed, they had found work with Grennan and Cranney's Utsalady mill. From 1862 to 1864 they cut timber on Camano Island, then moved operations north of the site of Stanwood and were the first to float logs down the river and over to the saws. Perkins then returned to Utsalady, while Goodridge decided to file a land claim on Florence Island on the south bank of the Stillaguamish River and keep logging with William Moore. Goodridge developed a successful farm but was aggressive in clearing his land, which included a tribal cemetery. His wife Polly, granddaughter to a Stillaguamish chief, convinced her angry fellow tribal members that the desecration of their graves was not worth a major battle, thus saving Goodridge's life. Another cemetery later was destroyed on the Matterand claim a short distance downstream. The settlers had little regard for traditional Native American burial or other religious rites.

Dennis Brigham located at what would become the Bayside section of Everett in 1862, followed by Erskine D. Kromer next to him two years later. He was an operator on a telegraph line being constructed northward along the Pacific coast to link up with Alaska and Russia, but when the engineering feat of laying a telegraph cable across the Atlantic ocean was completed in 1867 the business collapsed, with its wires reaching only into British Columbia. With Taylor and Bagleys' store and saloon and a cluster of men logging at the mouth of the Snohomish River at a site briefly named Habolum at Preston Point,

Grennan and Cranney's steam sawmill at Utsalady began operations in 1858 and stimulated logging activity on the lower Stillaguamish River starting in the early 1860s. Sailing ships carried lumber and spars to markets as distant as China and Europe. (Courtesy Stanwood Area Historical Society)

66

Snohomish city in the 1860s was just a riverside clearing. On the left is Emory C. Ferguson's Blue Eagle Saloon, with the Sinclair home to the right. (Courtesy Everett Public Library)

the county created another voting precinct of "Ebey Slough" in 1864. It was joined by Qualco (later called "Tualco"), the fertile region between the Skykomish and Snoqualmie rivers above Snohomish City. Here from "the forks" upstream were located Salem Woods, Henry McClurg, Charles Harriman, and others attracted to the rich bottomlands. All of these men had native wives.

Among the more interesting arrivals in 1864 was Dr. Henry A. Smith, the county's first physician. He had served as a surgeon in the 1856 war, and his farm and orchard at Smith Cove on Elliott Bay in King County had been damaged during the fighting. His goal was to establish a flourishing farm on Smith Island, a part of the Snohomish River delta. In the spring of 1865 he diked some 65 acres, planted fruit trees, constructed a flood and water control system, and attempted to prove the viability of marshland reclamation on the Netherlands model. Root crops, potatoes, rhubarb, and fruit trees flourished, as did the number of visitors seeking medical treatment or a chance to visit with his attractive daughters. He also provided the nearby Tulalip Indian Reservation with medical services. However, in 1870 he decided to return to the Seattle area to provide better schooling for his children, and with neglect the farm system soon deteriorated. When a dike failed in

Steamers of the Puget Sound "Mosquito Fleet" provided freight and passenger transportation to salt water and river communities, vital in the days before railroads and paved highways. Shallow draft sternwheelers such as the "Gleaner" could run in close to the shore and readily back off sandbars when the tide rose. (Courtesty Stanwood Area Historical Society)

1877, the farm was destroyed.

In 1865 the Civil War came to an end. The times improved noticeably, and people once again began to move to Puget Sound. On Florence Island near the mouth of the Stillaguamish River Robert Fulton opened a trading post. He expanded it in 1866 with a saloon and place to stay. He named this site south of the future location of Stanwood "Centerville." Fulton soon sold to John Gould, who in turn sold to George Kyle. Kyle obtained the first post office there, with himself as post master. The Stillaguamish precinct was established in 1867.

In Mukilteo regular steamer service now was provided by the sidewheeler *J.B. Libby*, built in Utsalady in 1863, while Frost and Fowler acquired and built a small fleet of vessels for trading on the Sound, including the *Gazelle* and in 1868 the sloop *Bee*. Alexander Spithill also planted the first orchard there. Runnels' logging camp was busy at the mouth of the Snohomish, then transferred operations north to the Stillaguamish, while upstream at Lowell Rueben Lowe opened a house of prostitution with Native American women. Ferguson had obtained the second post office in the county in 1863, constructed his Blue Eagle, with its combined saloon/hotel/store/post office/courthouse/ residence building, married Miss Lucretia Morgan, and allied himself with Benjamin Stretch. With Stretch as sheriff of the county and Ferguson in a variety of roles including territorial representative in Olympia, together (for the next 20 years) they would dominate politics to the advantage of the Snohomish valley.

On the problem side, virtually everyone was rich in land, timber, stumps, and high hopes but poor in terms of actual money. Unlike many other counties, virtually no steady cash came in from the outside, as there was no federal customs house or troop garrison, no territorial capital, prison, or university, and not even a seaport—much less a bank. Snohomish County for its first two decades was quite similar to the Willamette Valley of Oregon in the 1840s, where those traveling the Oregon Trail arrived with little gold or silver and paid their expenses in bushels of wheat they grew on their new farms. Here it was a matter of settling accounts with the mill companies after the log rafts reached Port Gamble, Utsalady, or Seabeck and totally depending upon mill men measuring the logs and setting their price. This resulted in a colonial economy run largely on barter and good faith. Much of the economic activity was circulated in scrip, kept on books as unpaid debt or credit, and traded not on the basis of bushels of wheat from the Oregon prairies but rather on local hand-split red cedar shingles from the surrounding forest. Bundles of these were produced with a home made wooden mallet in one hand and a sharp splitting froe in the other. In the small cabins and riverside shacks this was the prime evening and wintertime activity. Loaded up onto the occasional steamboat, they provided a labor intensive source of income when sold at Port Gamble, Utsalady, or Seattle. This poverty also extended to the ability to pay taxes, from which there was virtually nothing to build a public road, pay officials (no one wanted to be judge of probate, which took a lot of time and paid virtually nothing), or finance a school. Most of the income for county government came from liquor licenses, of which there were eight

Eugene Smith logged at Brown's Bay and then made his home at Lowell. Near Beverly Park this camp shows his crew's use of peeled logs as primitive rails for easier ox skidding of the heavy timber on primitive trams. Smith utilized a long log chute down to the river, where he later built his own mill. (Courtesy Everett Public Library)

by the end of the decade. Saloons were a fixture at every settlement and with every store, considered a frontier necessity.

In 1869 the county's first school did open at Snohomish, with Miss Robie Willard teaching a three month session at her friend Mary Sinclair's house. Only a few of the 22 children in the valley attended, all in the primary grades. The salary cost $188.59, paid in paper money "greenbacks," which were worth around 60-cents on the dollar. A small tax had been levied on property since 1861, had been collected since 1866, and took that long to accumulate enough to pay for the instructor.

The 1870s began with a census of most of the county. It indicated a total non-reservation population of almost

Until World War I county roads were unpaved, muddy ruts in the wet months and dusty tracks when dry. Travel was so bad that northern settlers tried unsuccessfully to secede rather than have to take days to visit the county seat in Snohomish. (Courtesy Granite Falls Historical Society)

585, with three-quarters of the residents Caucasian. There were also 54 Native Americans, 89 a blend of both Caucasian and Native American, one African American, and three Chinese men (all of whom were employed as cooks). The African American was identified as Isaac Sharpe (born in New Jersey and age 42); the Chinese cooks were identified as Wah Ah (age 31), John Hop (age 21), and Lewis Wah (age 25). Native people living in the upper valleys also appear not to have been counted. Two census precincts were listed, Stillaguamish with its post office at Utsalady, and Cadyville, which included the rest of the county.

An interesting aspect of the census is that the enumerator found 14 men employed as gold miners. Near Sultan the Skykomish River bars were being worked for placer gold, which led to creation of a new voting precinct and a small store run briefly by Alonzo Low. Fourteen logging camps provided most of the jobs in the county, which found itself bankrupt and unable to pay its bills. Eugene Smith erected a popular store at Lowell, along with a flume down the steep ridge behind the settlement to carry logs off the hill and into the Snohomish River. As population grew there, the Ebey precinct was dissolved and reorganized as Lowell, named for Rueben Lowe's home town in Massachusetts.

In 1871 for the first time most settlers began obtaining title to their claims. Ferguson took the opportunity to lay out a plat for Snohomish City, although there were few buyers, and Eugene Smith obtained a post office for Lowell. Smith was postmaster. Timber prices were down, though, and he fell on hard times, with the Getchells and the Puget Mill Company after him for their money. When prices improved he was able to settle those debts.

Roads throughout most of the territorial period were only hacked-out routes dodging trees and swamps. These roads were seldom wide enough for a team of animals and often impassable due to mud. Heavy goods were sent by steamboat on the lower rivers, while people normally traveled by canoe. Nevertheless, a road was put through in 1871 to connect Snohomish City with the Skykomish valley, and a bridge was authorized across the Pilchuck River—although not completed until 1877, and then only with donated local labor and money.

While traveling along Puget Sound, a fateful wind caused George Brackett to put his canoe ashore for safety in the southwest corner of the county, where Pleasant Ewell had built a cabin on the first bench back of the beach in 1866 and then sold to Frost, Fowler, and Fowler's brother Nat. Brackett liked what he saw and returned in 1872 to buy the claim in turn and become the eventual founder of Edmonds.

In 1871 the county's first divorce was finalized, *Mary Ann Harvey v. John Harvey*. First marriages in the county had been a triple wedding by Father Chirouse on September 4, 1864 between George Olette of Kitsap County and Nancy Navard, Peter St. Louis and Mary Sally Navard, and John Peter Fryberg and Helen Dayton. On June 20, 1865 probate judge R.C. Fay married Henry Valentine and Sarah E. Lewis, while the first Snohomish City nuptials were on November 17, 1866 between Marcel L. King and Adelaide C. Boyington. Woodbury B. Sinclair officiated as probate judge. The year 1871 also witnessed the death of Mrs. Emmerentze Taftezon on October 22. She was born in Norway in 1792, the year of Vancouver's arrival in Puget Sound. Her son, Zachariah Martin Taftezon, was one of the first settlers on Whidbey Island, arriving in December 1849 or January 1850, having become the first settler of Norwegian ancestry in the territory. Mrs. Taftezon and her daughter Bernhardine arrived in 1865 to join Martin. In 1868 she, Bernhardine, and her son-in-law Eilert Graham homesteaded at Hatt's Slough. Emmerentze was the first white person to die and be buried in the Stillaguamish valley. She also was the second white woman in the county to lose her life. The first was Mrs. Edna Peden in July 1870. She drowned when the canoe in which she was riding to visit a friend struck a snag and overturned in the Snohomish River.

Millions of dollars were lost far down the Pacific coast in 1872 when San Francisco mining stock prices collapsed. This financial panic kept lumber prices dull for much of the decade. In Snohomish, however, Ferguson's continuing efforts to build his place into a legitimate community were paying dividends, as business had improved to the point where the sternwheeler steamer *Zephyr* was making weekly trips up the river from Seattle. On their adjoining claim the Sinclairs platted a second section of townsite lots at an angle to Ferguson's, causing an odd bend at Union Street, while at the foot of Maple Street to the east William Romines bought the River Side Hotel in an attempt to dominate the hospitality business. He was opposed by Isaac Cathcart, who had arrived in 1869 to make money logging and then invest it in the Exchange Hotel, eventually branching out and working with Ferguson to become the wealthiest man in the county by statehood. Romines' fate was the exact opposite, ending up in poverty and killed accidentally by a railroad velocipede while walking the tracks. There was money to be made in the hotel, saloon, dance hall, prostitution, and gambling business, especially when the loggers were paid and hit town for the weekend.

A far more beneficial asset to the community was the arrival of Dr. Albert C. Folsom: scientific, literate, and a brilliant former army surgeon. His life had collapsed, generally attributed to a failed romance, and he became perhaps the best-loved man in the county until his death in 1883. Working without care for profit, he gave his life for the people around him and teamed up with Eldridge Morse in 1876 to create the county's first newspaper, *The Northern Star.*

The number of school districts doubled in 1872, as the original Snohomish District No. 1 was divided first into a second district in 1869 for the Park Place area on the lower Skykomish River (although no classes yet were held), and then the next two districts were created in the Stillaguamish valley. Florence became District No. 3, with classes held in Willard Sly's workshop before the first building was erected. Centerville became No. 4, although the district was unable to pay its teacher Ann R. Hancock that year for the 30 week term she taught the eleven students. Lowell began classes for its six students with Mrs. Hyrcanus Blackman teaching, then organized District No. 5 in 1873, utilizing a small building at the foot of Main Street donated by Eugene Smith. Mukilteo became District No. 6 in 1874, opening an excellent building with maps, charts, and patented desks for the students. Tualco No. 7 at "the forks" also was organized that year, along with Mt. Forest No. 8 up the Snoqualmie River at Cherry Valley.

Important arrivals to the county in 1872 included James P. and Maria Comeford to operate the Tulalip trading post; the three Blackman brothers from Penobscot County Maine: Alanson, Elhannan, and Hyrcanus; and the return from Maine of John Elwell and his sons, most notably Tamlin. The Comefords would create Marysville (named for Maria) around their trading post and liquor business next to the reservation, while the others would come to dominate the timber industry in the county. For now, the Blackmans went to work for Eugene Smith in Lowell, which he and his wife Margaret along with Martin and Olive Getchell platted in 1873.

Thomas Ovenell left England for the California gold rush at age 13, arriving in the lower Stillaguamish valley in 1874. The family still farms the original 122 acres purchased from James and Louisa Caldon for $2,500. (Courtesy the Ovenell family)

Snohomish was distancing itself from the other settlements as the largest community in the county in the early to mid-1870s, but it also was evolving into a complex society led by educated men who were extremely interested in cultural and scientific developments of the day. In 1873 they formed the Athenaeum Society and elected Ferguson president. Other officers included John Davis, Hugh Ross, Thomas F. Marks, Eldridge Morse (the county's first lawyer), M.W. Packard, and Dr. A.C. Folsom. The Roman emperor Hadrian had created the first Athenaeum, a center of literary and scientific learning dedicated to the goddess Minerva. Similar institutions spread throughout the empire, and in nineteenth century America the idea was revived. The members pooled their books to create a library of some 600 volumes as well as to develop what became the largest and finest museum collection in Washington Territory. Morse's excursion into the newspaper business three years later reflected these interests and concerns in its columns, many of which were written by Folsom.

At this point, there still was no organized church in the county save for Father Chirouse's mission at Tulalip, so the Athenaeum provided a forum for discussion. In 1874 Morse, Ferguson, and Folsom joined with Sheriff Benjamin Stretch and blacksmith W.H. Ward to create the Free Religious Association, an influential group of free thinkers. Perhaps growing cultural influences, along with the fact that now both Lowell and Mukilteo had schools, helped convince County Commissioners Eugene Smith, Morris Frost, and James Long to dedicate one third of the county's revenue from liquor licenses to support of the schools in 1873. Financial panic resulting from the collapse of Jay Cook's plan to complete the Northern Pacific Railroad was leading to hard times, though, and timber prices were not good, so the following year the commissioners reverted to tradition and ended that brief assistance. Then too there was the murder of Charles Seybert.

Serious crime was quite rare, and this crime was particularly unsettling in that the killer was Seybert's son, who had used an axe recently purchased at Smith's store across the river from their Ebey Island home. Defense lawyer Eldridge Morse tried to show an abusive father and husband who had struck his pregnant wife Mary Sis-que-qua, this atmosphere contributing to young Edward's mental slowness and later violent outbursts. Seybert was a six-foot one inch college graduate from Pennsylvania whose first wife (and mother of sons Bernard and Edward) Caroline lived in San Francisco. He had served in Colonel Ebey's volunteers and was a man of some means; now married to Mary Sis-que-qua, he held a large 152 acre farm on both sides of the river at Lowell, arriving there before Eugene Smith, and had served three years as county sheriff. Morse proved his point to the jury—innocent by reason of imbecility—and the boy was released on $1,000 bond to his mother, who may have taken him to live with her and her elder son Bernard in California. Charles and Mary's daughter Johanna later was orphaned by the death of her mother but grew up to be a strong and influential woman at Tulalip.

The county had no jail and no budget for apprehending and holding suspects, much less for lengthy trials. Delinquent property taxes had to be assessed a 25 percent interest penalty and collections energetically pursued to cover the legal costs for young Edward's proceedings.

On the brighter side, a small rush of miners staked claims and organized themselves on Silver Creek near the headwaters of the north fork of the Skykomish River. They had followed the old Cady route eastward, prospecting the side creeks and finding significant deposits in the silver, gold, and copper bearing rock of the western Cascade Mountain mineralized zone. Ineffective processing equipment and total lack of transportation facilities doomed their efforts to develop any paying mines.

At the northern section of the county rumblings of discontent were heard about the slow pace of road building, as one was needed to improve travel up to the Skagit valley across the flats. Severt Brekhus arrived on the Stillaguamish, following the Taftezons in what soon would become a solid stream of Norwegian immigrants into the valley, and logging was bustling at a pace equal to that of the Snohomish valley to the south. Meanwhile, Snohomish could boast of a new school building, the organization of the Ladies Union Sewing Society, and an impromptu county fair.

The winter of 1874-1875 was a hard one, the Snohomish River freezing solid and stopping all steamboat and canoe travel. Cold weather began at Christmas and lasted some six weeks. With logging shut down this provided an opportunity for Eugene Smith to host a Lowell holiday dance which a large number of Snohomish residents attended, traveling on ice skates!

Later that year the Blackman brothers opened their first logging camp, Lot Wilbur moved to Snohomish to become the county's first druggist, and a well organized county fair was held on grounds near the northwestern corner of Snohomish. At Centerville James Caldon bought up the Robert Freeman claim on the north side of the river. Here he erected his new Pioneer Hotel and saloon and also became postmaster, leaving the original site of Centerville on the South Pass of Florence Island to be abandoned and largely forgotten. Meanwhile James Comeford began buying up large land holdings immediately adjacent to the eastern boundary of the Tulalip Indian Reservation along the mouth of the Snohomish River.

Mukilteo dominated 1875, however. After a brief boom and bust, Mukilteo was vying to become the Puget Sound terminus of the Northern Pacific Railroad. The terminus, unfortunately, went to Tacoma instead, and only a branch line as yet linked that town with Kalama on the Columbia River. Nevertheless, Mukilteo showed a major spurt of development. Frost and Fowler had salted down salmon caught off Point Elliot, but now a partnership of Rheinbruner and H.C. Vining established an operation which shipped barrels of the fish to the east coast, the first county products sold there. Rheinbruner dropped out the following year, but Vining persevered until 1877. Joseph Butterfield had put the county into the beer business with his creation of the Eagle Brewery in 1875, and the following year it was purchased by Frost and Fowler. Their product was sold all over the Puget Sound country, as were the patent medicines produced by Lot Wilbur up at Snohomish.

Summer 1876 was a time of celebration, for this was the centennial year of the United States. A grand exposition was held in Philadelphia (home of the Declaration of Independence), where, among other marvels, Alexander Graham Bell showed off his miraculous new telephone. In Snohomish County it also was a time of accomplishment, a year when people felt good about the future and about what they already had achieved. To do justice to the occasion, Eldridge Morse was appointed by the commissioners to create a history of the county, which was presented at the festivities in Snohomish. In January he had begun printing *The Northern Star*, only the third paper to be published north of Seattle. (The first had been the *Northern Light*, which flickered briefly during the 1858 gold rush through Whatcom, while the second was the *Bellingham Bay Mail*, which soon moved to La Conner and became the long-lived *Puget Sound Mail*.) With the able assistance of Dr. Folsom and a policy of welcoming anyone who wished to join in open discussion through the press, the quality of the publication was outstanding. In its pages the affairs of the county were recorded, as well as descriptions of Morse's extensive travels throughout the Sound country. It almost was too good to last. With a population base of perhaps 400 around the town and barely a thousand in the county to support the costs, when depression came Morse's limited business ability was unable to keep it afloat past May 1879.

Snohomish had become far more than a one-man town centered about Emory C.

Salmon had been the staple fish for the tribal people and early settlers alike. In the mid-1870s Mukilteo was home for the first commercial fish packing plant in the county to ship barrels of salmon to the East Coast, followed by the territory's first cannery in 1876. Economic depression soon shut down its operation. (Courtesy Lindgren/Cameron collection)

Ferguson, although he still was the dominant individual. Lot Wilbur now took over as postmaster, for example, and when the county auditor disappeared overnight it was Morse who replaced him. A second attorney also had arrived, William M. Tirtlot, a disabled Civil War veteran of strong religious beliefs. A new Snohomish County Telegraph Company was organized to tie the town in to Western Union via wire to Lowell and then Port Gardner, where Erskine Kromer was the operator again. Ferguson was president of the company, with Kromer, Henry F. Jackson (the Lowell operator), and Isaac Cathcart vice presidents. None could understand Morse code, so tape printers were used.

More business meant better communication on the river as well. The *Nellie*, a new sternwheeler 85 feet in length, became a favorite of the town and also made some upriver trips, as did the *Fannie Lake*, while the older *Zephyr* declined. A road toward Sultan was authorized, as was a bridge across Hatt's Slough, the first on the Stillaguamish

Another sign of culture in the town in 1876 was the formation of the first church in the county beyond St. Anne's Mission. Snohomish was a business-oriented town: Presbyterian with its emphasis on hard work and moral living was its religion of choice. The Reverend J.R. Thompson was in charge of the new church from his base in Olympia, while the mission board provided $500 to go along with the locally donated $1,000 in money and labor. Thompson would preach once a month, two lots were contributed for a

75

building, and ground was broken in December. Hugh Ross, Royal Haskell, Lot Wilbur, and Ferguson were among the church society officers.

The Masons became the county's first fraternal organization that year, organizing Centennial Lodge in honor of America and soon erecting a hall which could be rented out for court-house offices. While men began construction of a building to house the Athenaeum, woman officers of that society began raising money for a piano for the group. Teacher and Athenaeum vice president Mrs. Bell also created a music program for the Snohomish school, in the process raising enough money through their public performances to purchase an organ—the district's first musical instrument.

Tied up on the north bank of the river at Snohomish in 1877, the 80-foot long steamer "Nellie" awaits her next load of passengers. She began service the year before, carrying people and supplies from Seattle as far as the lower Snoqualmie. In 1876 she came within a mile of Falls City, but her relatively deep draft of almost five feet kept her normally on the downstream runs, where she was a popular favorite. (Courtesy Snohomish Historical Society)

Snohomish County now also had its own district court and twice yearly sessions. These were held in the hall of the River Side Hotel, subject to interruption by guests trying to use the bar and facilities. In one case the judge fined a lodger for contempt of court for snoring so loudly that he could be heard outside the thin walls of his room.

Financially, 1876 also was a memorable year for the timber business, as log prices were high, at least eight camps were running near Snohomish, and the Stillaguamish was bustling. On the Pilchuck River Bennett & Witter erected a small water powered sawmill, only the third in county history.

A highlight of the year was the third, large county fair held at the fairgrounds, with the prize winners lauded in *The Northern Star*. Isaac Cathcart found a wife, and the town celebration of their nuptials was the biggest yet seen. At Christmas a tree was erected at the River Side Hotel, and the townspeople gathered to give presents to the children and hear addresses by the Reverend McFee and

Before the advent of gasoline engines and electricity farm work was heavily labor intensive, especially dairying and during harvest time. Itinerant single men formed the backbone of the labor force, making possible the manpower required by the timber, agricultural, and later railroad industries. (Courtesy Stanwood Area Historical Society)

William Tirtlot, who often filled in at the Presbyterian church.

Things were going equally as well along the Stillaguamish, where two major developments occurred. The first was the arrival of O.B. Iverson, Civil War veteran of Norwegian ancestry, who joined a survey party in the valley and decided the place had promise. He returned to the Dakotas (where he had been active in politics and in bringing immigrants to that territory) and convinced a number of Norwegian families to return with him to the more moderate climate of northern Snohomish County. This began an ongoing stream of Scandinavians, who quickly began to develop farms and enter the logging business, creating a strong ethnic heritage in the lower valley. Nels Eide, Nels P. and Peter Leque, Anders J. Brue, Peter Gunderson, Jacob Brekhus joining his brother Severt; Ole Matterand, Ingebregt Stenson, Olanus Olson, Styrker Erickson, and Lars Larson were some of those early arrivals, along with Thomas Jensen from Germany, who settled at Island Crossing.

Thomas Jensen filed on his homestead in 1878, working winters in San Francisco to earn money for it. His original house is in the foreground, with the second to its left, the first farm in the Island Crossing area. Today his descendants produce field corn, peas, and vegetable seed. (Courtesy the Jensen/Grimm family)

The second key development was the decision of Coupeville merchant Daniel O. Pearson to leave Whidbey Island and search out the length of the Stillaguamish and its south fork for a suitable site to relocate his retail establishment and his family. He decided on the north bank of the river across from Centerville, ordered lumber for a store and wharf from the Puget Mill Company, and the next spring brought in stock for his business to the tune of $4,000 from San Francisco and Portland. When James Caldon died, his wife Louisa could not qualify for his Pioneer Hotel liquor license and run the saloon because she was a Native American, and the law tried to protect them by preventing the sale of alcohol to or by natives. Therefore, McLoughlin and McNamara took over the Pioneer Hotel and liquor business, while D.O. Pearson became postmaster. He satisfied the postal officials' objections to having too many "Centervilles" by renaming his site "Stanwood," for his wife Clara's maiden name.

Rounding up loose cattle on Florence Island for sale as butchered beef to logging companies led J.H. Irvine to open a rival store in 1879, increasing trade in the small settlement, but at the expense of Pearson. A comment of the times was that if people had cash they went to Irvine's. If they did not, they would go to the more understanding Pearson for credit. Irvine became rich, while the Pearsons almost lost their livelihood in the great depression of the 1890s.

As there were only a few narrow, muddy tracks passing for roads in the county, and railroads were as yet a dream, the rivers and their larger tributaries continued to be the

Norwegians Discover Centerville

By Karen Prasse

O. B. Iverson emigrated from Norway at age 12 with his family and grew up in Iowa. He served in the army in the Civil War and then in Dakota Territory. After returning to Iowa in 1866, his crops were destroyed in a hailstorm. He tried again in South Dakota. Iverson was a man of many occupations in addition to farming. After returning from Norway as an Immigration Officer in 1874, the grasshoppers devastated his South Dakota farm, and he decided to visit the west coast in search of a place to re-settle.

He arrived in San Francisco by train. There he was warned that the Puget Sound had neither soil nor climate fit for farming, but he didn't like California either, so he boarded an English revenue cutter as a clerk and arrived in Olympia on March 15, 1875. The next day he visited the Governor, Etisha P. Ferry. The Governor referred him to the officials who kept the field notes and records about Washington Territory, and he spent the next few weeks studying them to prepare for excursions into undiscovered areas to find a suitable place to farm with his family and Norwegian friends.

His writings include humorous anecdotes about his search for good farmland. In August 1876, he was invited to accompany Deputy Surveyor Shoecraft on his trip to survey two townships on the Stillaguamish River. Capt. Budlong and his sloop, the "Albatross," were chartered for this voyage of discovery. On August 3rd, 1876, the surveying party set out from Olympia. Following is the 1920 version of his first arrival in the Stillaguamish Valley.

O. B. Iverson and his family. (Courtesy Stanwood Area Historical Society)

We had a fair wind until past Tulalip when the wind died down and thunder clouds came up in the south, and a few very large drops of rain fell. The center of the electric disturbance was quite distant, judging by the time between the dull flash and the distant rumbling....but no storm or wind came and it was quite dark before we reached the flats but the tide being high, and in our favor, we decided to risk the snags, and take the chance of finding the channel in the dark. We started by compass, and Captain Budlong knew about the snags at the mouth of the river, and said we could keep it by sounding. There was five or six feet of water over the flats, but he said the channel was deeper.

At last we found the channel. We took down the sails which were useless anyway, having no wind, and with two men on the sweep (long oars) we made headway. But it was dark. The Professor [Washington P. Frazier of South Bay, Washington, second in command] said it was "opaque." Sam said, "Yes that was the right word for it. It was like a democrats understanding. Joe, who thought he was a democrat, said it was a d-d lie, and Tom said that he believed Joe, as he had never known one that had any.

But now something happened to drive attention away from and end this intelligent discussion. We were in the channel all right, we knew that by the depth of the water. During the flashes of lightning we had observed a very large white snag, and this snag seemed to stay by us. Either we were standing still or the snag was following. The professor on the lookout said that it was a floating snag, but the boys at the oars said they could outrow any d-d snag, and they did put on some extra steam but whenever we had a flash there was the snag. Joe, who was from Louisiana said it was a ghost snag, that there were lots of them in the Mississippi, but whenever they showed themselves it meant disaster. This was pleasant. About that time we began to notice a peculiar noise above. It sounded like scraping metal against metal. The sloop standing rig was wire and the professor began to explain that when it would discharge a spark of lightning into the ground or into the water, or anything else that might be in the way. This was more pleasant than the ghost. I think on the whole we were a badly scared lot, but fortunately it was dark. Jim had found what he thought was the professor's alcohol, but had made a mistake and got the coal oil can and took a hurry drink, and after he got his breath he made some unprintable remarks. I found a blanket and went to sleep.

When I woke up in the morning the sloop lay high and dry in the middle of Davis Slough. With the mast against the telegraph wire that crosses it, and the ghost snag close by.

This discovery made something of a nick in the professor's electric theory, but he repaired it by explaining that friction produces electricity and the friction of the jib stay against the telegraph wire produced electricity, and he was correct in his diagnosis.

But we were hungry for grub rather than science and after cooking and eating breakfast on a sand bar among some snags, most of us decided to go to Centerville by land. We could see the town. There was no mistake about that. We saw three buildings and there was only a nice grass prairie between us that we could see. We did not all take the same path, there being no path. Nearly half-way across the prairie the professor being behind, called lustily for help. He had fallen into a blind slough. Only his intellectual head appeared in the grass. We had to turn back and extract him. He might or he might not have got out unaided. The slough or ditch was not much more than a foot wide on the surface and completely covered by thick grass but it was near three feet wide at the bottom and about five feet deep, with the nicest, stickiest kind of gray mud at the bottom. We traveled with more circumspection after that.

Before we reached the town we found the river where it splits, part flowing south into Port Susan and part north into Skagit ot Utsalady Bay. We made a lot of noise and attracted the attention of Bob Freeman, who was Jim Calden's deputy and he came with a boat and took us across the river to town, which was then Centerville and is now Stanwood.

The city at that time consisted of Jim Calden's hotel and saloon or more properly saloon and hotel, because the saloon was much larger part. It stood on the bank of the river with the dyke for the front porch. It was quite a long and wide building, one story. Rather more than half was saloon the other half divided into kitchen and dining room, with several shed built bedrooms back of the main building. The other buildings in town were Henry Oliver's house (now part of the hospital) and Jack Irvine's cabin in the brush about where Thompson's wagon shed now stands. That was about all. I almost forgot, Oliver had a barn about where the post office stands and a pig house on the site of which the first church was built and later Ketchum's store. The town did not interest me much but the river did. When we crossed it there was a strong current down stream like any sane river would run. The next time I looked at it the insane thing ran just as furiously upstream. I began to think that either I or the country was crazy.

In the afternoon we met the hotel proprietor. He had been up all night skinning some loggers at poker. For his ability at this kind of work he was named "Skinny Jimmy." He was a straw colored slim, good looking Englishman and a pretty good fellow too, if you refrained from playing poker. Centerville was the head of navigation for sailing vessels. We stored most of our baggage. Budlong and the "Albatross" returned to Olympia. Before he left, we having lost our lantern, gave him the coal oil as it was not good to drink, Jim having tried it.

We loaded as much of our goods as we thought we needed into two shovel nose canoes that we chartered from a chief with the poetic name "Splitlip Jim" who owned several canoes and squaws, and had a sort of monopoly of transportation on the river, and with two squaw propellers on each canoe we scooted up the crazy river at a great rate to the foot of the big jam and camped.

The story continued with a valuable original account of the lower Stillaguamish River valley. He describes the log jams, the trip in the Indian canoe, and what it was like to camp without modern backpacking equipment.

Later he, Leque, and Nels Eide purchased what is now known as Leque Island. In September, after first arriving in Centerville, Nels Eide and O.B. Iverson went to Olympia to arrange the purchase of Berry's logging camp and possibly the rest of the island it was located on.

They began the arrangements and then proceeded to McNeil Island, where they met the Leque and Christensen families who recently arrived from South Dakota. They knew from previous correspondence that they were there looking for land to farm, but to make ends meet, were currently occupied with the provision of ship's knees. Iverson brought Leque to the island:

We put in the afternoon inspecting the island and Leque agreed that it was worth more for farming purposes than the whole Henderson Bay country. We now made a memorandum of agreement to secure title to the whole island, and to divide it equally as near as possible, Eide taking the north end, Leque next, then Danielson, leaving the south end to me on which the house was located. Also to share all expenses equally. It remained to secure title and subdue the land but the conquest of the Stillaguamish by the Norsemen had begun.

only feasible means of transportation. Yet, they also had serious problems. Eugene Smith had sawn and pulled leaning and fallen trees out of the way enough to drive logs from Lowell down Steamboat Slough to Priest Point at the mouth of the Snohomish River as early as 1864, but that was an easy task compared to the mass of tangled logs and debris which faced travelers and log drivers on both the Stillaguamish and Skagit rivers. These long masses of blocking wood required arduous portaging for canoe travelers and effectively stalled upriver settlement until they were removed. The quarter-mile long one on the Stillaguamish began at river mile six. It was not until April 1877 that the clearing project began, financed by local residents and businessmen, and the job took until November when high water finally floated the snarled jungle down to the Sound. That accomplished, the line of settlement swiftly began to move upriver past Florence toward Norman and Silvana, where two more jams existed. From here water levels normally were too shallow for steamboats, so shipping of supplies largely was an expensive monopoly of skilled Stillaguamish tribal members with their canoes.

Down at Mukilteo, 1876 was the year of the first salmon cannery in Washington Territory, the forerunner of a huge industry which eventually would help destroy the once great native salmon runs on Puget Sound and the Columbia River. In June George T. Myers came up from the Columbia to organize Jackson, Myers & Company. It was reported that other products also would be processed, but that seems not to have occurred. That year, too, the pioneering business of Morris Frost and Jacob Fowler failed, perhaps due to too many debtors not paying their bills. It was placed in the receivership of V.B. Stacey. Under his leadership, the town had a brief boom, with new owners for the Eagle Brewery and lessees for the cannery, along with construction of new houses, the arrival of several new families, and the reopening of the old hotel. It was over as quickly as it began however, as 1879 and 1880 were gloomy with depression and business failures.

Upriver at Snohomish, 1877 started out as a good year, with the Athenaeum and the Presbyterian church finished, school for the first time held on the Pilchuck River, and Ferguson deciding with his father-in-law H.D. Morgan to take over the Bennett & Witter sawmill. This they improved with a new dam and machinery, and the following year they constructed the first plank road in the county out to the mill from town. Along the river over a million shingles were produced, logging was bustling, and the first mention appears of farmers above the forks growing hops.

However, the good times were ending. California lumber prices collapsed to the point where Puget and the other mill companies no longer were buying logs, and the economic viability of the county depended upon the income from selling its timber. It still was very much a colonial economy shipping out raw materials and receiving back finished products with no control over pricing. Seasonal high water broke log booms on the Skykomish, and the loosened logs were swept down to the Sound, boom drivers and steamboat men desperately trying to round them up before they were lost. (Each log was branded with a hammer so it could be identified by its owner, similar to a cattle brand.) This year the county fairgrounds remained silent: the event a smaller one held in October at the Athenaeum building.

A severe epidemic of diphtheria also began, causing Dr. Folsom to delay his retirement, which had been planned due to a severe injury to his eye. Children died, sometimes whole families of them, as desperate parents without any effective medicines sought helplessly to ease their suffering. Samuel Howe and his wife lost their five youngsters in five weeks, and even the Fergusons lost a daughter, while Mrs. Ferguson barely survived. Snohomish school closed due to a lack of money, log prices fell to their lowest rate in history ($3.50 per thousand board feet in 1879), population growth stagnated or fell, Eugene Smith's logging operation at Lowell was burned out by arson, *The Northern Star* closed its doors, and the hard times lasted until 1882.

On the positive side, 1878 was the year the Reverend Christian Joergenson arrived in Stanwood as a mission clergyman to the burgeoning Lutheran settlers. He expected to remain briefly, but instead remained for the rest of his life. The energetic congregation prospered spiritually if not financially during the depression, laying the foundation for the first church in the valley in 1878—although, it was not completed until 1885. This was the first church built by Lutherans in the far west, a white painted structure with a golden brown steeple which lasted until the devastating Stanwood fire of 1892.

Several interesting cultural developments occurred that year. Snohomish organized a cornet band, the sign of some civic pride, and for the first time there is the rise of organized sport. The Snohomish "Pacifics" baseball team donned uniforms to play teams from Lowell and Port Gamble, thus beginning a town tradition which would last for a number of years and

Most early homes were one or two rooms, often of board and batten construction with shingle roofs. Crops were planted among the tree stumps after logging, as clearing land was laborious and expensive. Group photographs usually were taken outside with people neither moving nor smiling, as glass plate negatives required long exposure times. (Courtesy Granite Falls Historical Society)

produce twentieth century major league players. In the nineteenth century, however, the Pacifics challenged teams throughout the Sound country and as far away as Portland during the 1880s.

Elsewhere around the county, at their Marysville site the Comefords began a new trading post in 1877 and opened it still uncompleted in 1878. A post office was established with J.P. as postmaster, and the following year School District Number 10 was created on Woods' farm two miles to the east. Across the reservation line the agent had enough of the log drivers' rowdiness and tore down their seasonal shacks at Priest Point where they had assembled the log rafts for towing over to Port Gamble or up to Utsalady. That ended a long tradition.

Racial and cultural relations between native and non-native women and men were an issue which troubled Judge Lewis at the 1877 District Court session, as territorial law forbade interracial marriage. Lewis, described as a "terror of evildoers", demanded not that this law be enforced, but rather that Caucasian men living with Native American women but not married to them either formalize that relationship with a county marriage ceremony or be prosecuted for immoral behavior. The percentage of interracial families was declining rapidly with the influx of settlers, but still there was a significant number of such relationships—perhaps a third of the couples in the county. As a result, the number of marriage licenses shot up from 12 in 1876 to 38 in 1877–1878, then dropped to 9 in 1879, and 1 in 1880.

A small number of Chinese men were employed as construction workers for Ferguson and Morgan's mill in 1878, while a number of Chinese placer miners also were recorded as working with Caucasians in the Sultan area. Significant numbers of workers now were leaving southern China to work on North American railroad projects, but as yet that development had not reached the county.

In 1880 the depressed conditions continued. Stanwood now produced grain from diked fields north of town and erected a new school, which helped focus attention on its community prospects, while Florence also began to grow. New voting precincts were created to separate Centerville/Stanwood from the upstream Stillaguamish, and another briefly existed at Silver City for the miners 'on Silver Creek off the North Fork Skykomish. On the main Skykomish River John Nailor and his wife claimed land at the mouth of the Sultan River and found their place a way station for passing miners.

In 1878 J.P. and Maria Comeford opened their trading post near the Tulalip Indian Reservation on the north bank of the Snohomish River delta and named it "Marysville." A post office and nearby school quickly followed. (Courtesy Everett Public Library)

These are members of the Snohomish "Pacifics," the county's first professional baseball team, as they appeared in 1884. The "Pacifics" played the top teams in the Pacific Northwest and began a century-long tradition of great players to come from Snohomish. Standing are John Delfel, W.R. Booth, Clayton Packard (umpire), Oliver Dunstan, C.A. Missimer (scorer), and Homer Moore. Seated are H.F. Jackson (manager), Archie Anderson, R.O. Welts, J. Van Bowen, and J.W. Fobes. (Courtesy Museum of History and Industry)

In 1881 B.C.W. Schloman and his mother went on upstream to the forks of the Stillaguamish River in the ongoing search for unclaimed valley bottomland to farm, establishing a post office at their home. She was the first white woman to live in the Arlington area. Later they went down to Silvana, returning in 1890. In order to transport their cows upstream, two canoes were lashed together and a level platform built between them. The native men were creative, if expensive.

Mrs. H.W. Illman became the first white woman in the Sultan vicinity that year, while down at Edmonds George Brackett obtained a post office. He had requested the name be "Edmunds" for the Vermont senator, but the paperwork came back with an "o" instead, and so it remained.

Railroad rumors and economic conditions both began to pick up in 1882, beginning a boom which lasted for the next decade and brought major development to the county. The Northern Pacific Railroad would be crossing the Cascade Mountains to create a direct link between Puget Sound and the East rather than depending on the branch line northward from Portland and Kalama to Tacoma, so developers' hearts began to beat faster as opportunities beckoned throughout central and northern Puget Sound counties.

Prices for both crops and timber now were on the rise, with two camps running for Eugene Smith, three for the Blackman brothers, and two for Tamlin Elwell (one with partner Henry F. Jackson on the Pilchuck). More men and animals logging meant more markets for hay, vegetables, butter, and eggs. The Blackmans had invented a new wheeled logging car which could be pulled out along wooden rails, first by oxen and later by a steam engine. This replaced dragging the entire dead weight of logs along the ground on a skid road and quickly became popular. The Blackmans also started construction of a large steam sawmill at Snohomish and began to experiment with steam powered donkey engines for bringing the logs to the rails. Their next step would be steam powered locomotives. With these developments, the county was entering the age of industrialized timber production and Snohomish establishing its base as a manufacturing center.

At the county seat in 1882 a new paper appeared to replace the defunct *Northern Star*. Clayton H. Packard was the driving force behind the *Eye,* going through several partners. On July 4 Pattison's ferry across the Skykomish began operation, making land travel possible above the forks into the Snoqualmie valley. On the same day, Snohomish beat Seattle in baseball 20-10 and collected a $30 purse, while others engaged in foot races and watched evening fireworks. The next month a group of athletes and horse racers came over from Tulalip and cleaned out the home town bettors. Snohomish even had enough tax money available to reopen school for 42 students in March.

On the Snohomish River the *Nellie* and the *Mabel* also competed for passengers and freight, while the new shallow draft *Alki* made runs to the settlers and camps far up the Skykomish and Snoqualmie. Beyond steamer range and at seasonal low water, however, travel still was by canoe for both freight and passengers.

Upstream from Centerville, Florence became an early center of Stillaguamish activity. Organizing the county's third school district in 1872, it flourished until the late 1880s. Part of the store to the left of the photograph still remains, but the main channel of the river now is long gone, flowing to the south through Hatt Slough. (Courtesy Stanwood Area Historical Society)

Along the Stillaguamish River the flow of settlers increased, with mail service to Silvana, then backpacked on up to people's homes as far as half a mile below the forks. There were no horses in the valley, and the only ox not in a logging camp belonged to Iver Furness. Still, there were some 350 residents now, and they were not happy with the domination of the county by Ferguson, Stretch, and the Republicans of Snohomish. That was especially true regarding the lack of suitable roads connecting the valley with the Snohomish and Skagit population centers. To conduct county business it took a valley resident five days, requiring a steamer trip to Seattle, catching the *Nellie* or *Mabel* there for Snohomish, completing the paperwork, then returning by the same route.

In 1883 Skagit County was formed from Whatcom. Only a few miles across the flats separated Stanwood from the Skagit River, and the northern tier residents decided to secede. Unfortunately for them, Ferguson was in the territorial legislature and not about to see his home territory sliced up. The attempt was cut off.

A bonanza befell Tulalip in January 1883, when the steamer *Josephine* suffered a boiler explosion off Kayak Point on her way northward to Mt. Vernon. Nine died and many were injured, including James Perkins of Florence. Survivors were pulled from the waters by native people in their canoes who had witnessed the disaster. The drifting overturned wreck was towed from off Hat Island to the reservation, where it was scavenged by the residents.

Just outside the reservation, James and Maria Comeford organized a major Fourth of July celebration to promote their new hotel building and draw attention to the settlement they were creating. Over in Snohomish, the day was a success in baseball, with the Pacifics taking the Seattle White Stockings, but in horse racing a rider accidentally was

84

killed. Later in the summer the Tulalip athletes and racers came back for a second round of events and betting, but this time they were the ones cleaned out.

Snohomish also had plays, two skating rinks, Isaac Cathcart's new opera house, and far too much open vice to suit the grand jury. During the hard times the Athenaeum had failed, so Cathcart picked up the property and turned the building into another saloon. Horse racing on the streets endangered pedestrians, and the flourishing brothels were becoming too obvious. However, little was done, as the economy of the town was largely dependent upon attracting the logger clientele. A new shooting club was formed, and local men volunteered to form a militia in case Chief Joseph's Nez Perce war caused a local uprising, but the governor turned down their services.

The Morgan & Son mill became the Morgan Brothers when H.D. sold his interest to his younger son, and then the two brothers opened the first sash and door factory in the county to augment their lumber production. Across the river from Snohomish there was a marked increase in draining the thousands of acres of marshland, digging and connecting a system of ditches along the southern and western portions of the valley. Reflecting this growth was the creation of school district No. 11 south at Marshland and No. 12 two miles upstream at Shorts', these in 1880 and 1881. Downstream on the east bank from Snohomish the Swans Trail and Fobes districts number 14 and 17 completed the school organization in the area by 1889.

Traveling up the Skykomish River one could go by land along a narrow, muddy wagon road across the mouth of the Pilchuck, pass the forks, note Pattison's ferry to cross over to the Snoqualmie valley, then proceed up to Park Place, finding both the hotel and saloon closed, but the small school and post office available. The road now ran as far as Fern Bluff, nearly half way to Sultan. As that area still was accessible only by canoe, when winter came and unusually severe weather set in, the few settlers and native families were cut off until the thaw, which caused damaging spring floods. During the harvest season near the forks the visitor could observe a bounty of hops being cut and shipped, especially at Harriman's, where not only his Native American in-laws found work, but hundreds of others as well. Until poor prices and infestations of hop lice ended active production at the end of the decade, hops were a major crop in the area. In 1886, for example, 1,200 native people harvested 17,000 boxes for downriver shipment.

Along the Sound at Edmonds George Brackett erected a separate building for his post office and began stocking a small amount of goods for sale. At the northern end of the county labor unrest led to the refusal of loggers to work the usual dawn to dusk hours at Jennings' camp on Port Susan,

The Stillaguamish Norwegian Lutheran Church congregation was organized in August 1876 by immigrants to the Centerville area. Their original church was laboriously built as scarce funds and time permitted. Painted white with a 60-foot golden brown steeple, it was completed in 1890. On the evening of May 31, 1892 it was burned in the Stanwood fire, with only the pews, organ, and a badly cracked bell saved. (Courtesy Stanwood Area Historical Society)

but they quickly were replaced with more docile hands.

From Stanwood Mrs. Ella C. Granger was asked to give up her teaching position and take over as the county's superintendent of schools, a position up to this time always held by a man, although Mrs. Bell had been offered the job the year before but left the county before she could fill it. Mrs. Granger had definite ideas about improving instruction throughout the county and the determination to carry them out. When she asked the county commissioners for $60 for a county-wide teachers' institute the next summer and was turned down, she carried it out for three days anyway, the gathering a great success for teachers in cooperation with the territorial university in Seattle. It only cost $40, with Mrs. Granger covering $10 of the expenses. That impressed the commissioners, who agreed in the fall to pay the bills. Also that year she opened a select high school in Snohomish to teach in effect the first year of what then was called "normal school," the training to become a teacher. This was not successful and only lasted one year. When she returned to her Stanwood school in 1885, however, she noted the number of county districts had grown to 18. Even if there were as yet no high school-level education in the county, most of the local teachers offered a wide variety of night courses for adults, and schools were utilized for both civic and religious gatherings.

This early logging locomotive was one of five built by the Blackman Brothers of Snohomish and the only one of which we have a photograph. Each was different, but all were designed to run on a wooden track with rails set eight feet wide, a carryover from the days when horse and ox teams required that much width. These were the only locomotives manufactured in Washington. (Courtesy Walt Taubeneck and Marysville Historical Society)

86

Steamboats in Snohomish County

By David Cameron

During the territorial period and early twentieth century rivers were the prime means of travel in the county. Native canoes always were vital, but steamboats provided cheap and efficient transportation of freight and passengers for settlers and townsfolk. Sidewheelers, sternwheelers, and propellers, they were well known and recognized for their idiosyncrasies and the personalities of their captains. When steam locomotives arrived, much of the passenger trade declined, followed later by the loss of freight revenue to the railroads. Automobiles, trucks, and diesel locomotives ended the age of steam by mid-century.

These are some of the steamboats which were associated with our county, part of the famed Puget Sound "Mosquito Fleet."

Name	Type	Dates	Notes
Alki	Sternwheeler, freight	1889-1920	Built at Utsalady. Used on highest reaches of the Skykomish River, reached Fall City on the Snoqualmie river in July 1883
Nellie Pearson	Propeller, tug	1900-1945	Built at Everett, renamed the Bee
Black Prince	Sternwheeler, freight	1901-?	Built at Everett, became part of the Everett Yacht Club
Calista	Propeller, passenger	1911-1924	Involved in the November 5, 1916 Everett Massacre. Built at Dockton, wrecked 1924
Cascade	Sternwheeler, mixed	1904-1922	Built at Snohomish, fastest boat on the Snohomish River after racing the City of Quincy in 1892
Chehalis	Sternwheeler, passenger	1867-1882	Built at Tumwater, active on the Snohomish River, foundered 1882
City of Everett	Propeller, passenger	1900-?	Built at Everett, ended up as the West Seattle Athletic Club clubhouse
City of Mukilteo	Propeller, ferry	1927-1945	Built at Seattle
City of Quincy	Sternwheeler, passenger	1878-1900	Built at Portland, active on the Snohomish River
City of Stanwood	Sternwheeler, freight	1892-1894	Built at Stanwood, burned
Delta	Propeller, passenger	1888-1910	Built at Stanwood
Edith R.	Sternwheeler, misc.	1883-1905	Built at Seattle, only 75 feet long, it reached the base of Snoqualmie Falls in the 1880s
Fanny Lake	Sternwheeler, freight	1875-1893	Built at Seattle, active on the Snohomish River, to Tulalip, Centerville. Burned 1893
Florence Henry	Sternwheeler, passenger	1891-1918	Built at Ballard, destroyed in Alaska. Active on the Snohomish and Skykomish rivers up to Sultan
Flyer	Propeller, passenger	1890-?	Built at Portland, Famous for her speed, on the Everett-Tacoma run after 1910
Fearless	Propeller, tug	1901-?	Built at Everett, converted to diesel
Gleaner	Sternwheeler, freight	1907-1940	Built at Stanwood for the Stillaguamish River trade. Sank 1940.
Grace Thurston	Propeller, tug	1899-1938	Built at Everett
Harvester	Sternwheeler, freight	1912-1938	Built at Stanwood for the Stillaguamish River trade. Wrecked 1938.
Independent	Propeller, tug	1899-1930	Built at Everett

Loma	Sternwheeler, tug	1909-1924	Built at Everett
Josephine	Sternwheeler, freight	1878-1883	Built at Seattle, blew up in Port Susan January 16, 1883
Majestic	Propeller, passenger	1901-1945	Built at Everett, later became car ferry
Mame	Sternwheeler, freight	1887-?	Built at Snohomish, first boat to ascend Skykomish to Sultan January 1888, converted into a barge
Manette	Propeller, passenger	1901-1923	Built at Everett
Monte Cristo	Sternwheeler, mixed	1891-1922	Built at Everett, ran on Snohomish and Skykomish as far as Sultan, beat the *Florence Henry* to Sultan in a famous race on May 22, 1892. To Skeena River, B.C.
Mary D. Hume	Propeller, whaler	1881-?	Built in Oregon, converted to tug boat, still running at mid-twentieth century
May Queen	Sternwheeler, passenger	1886-1920	Built at Seattle, active on the Snohomish and Skykomish rivers. Both she and the *Mame* were built by Captain McMillan, seventy five feet long and of very shallow draft for upstream travel
Nellie	Sternwheeler, passenger	1876-1910	Built at Seattle, beloved on the Snohomish River, rival to the *Zephyr*
Verona	Propeller, passenger	1910-1940	Built at Dockton. Scene of the I. W. W. massacre in Everett, November 5, 1916
Zephyr	Sternwheeler, passenger	1871-1907	Built at Seattle, active on the Snohomish River, converted to a tug boat

Information on these boats is based on Newell, Gordon R. *Ships of the Inland Sea*, Binford & Mort, Portland, 1951 and Whitfield, William. *History of Snohomish County, Washington*, Pioneer Historical Publishing Company, Chicago and Seattle, 1926.

Built in 1890 the speedy "Greyhound" dominated the run between Everett and Seattle at the turn of the twentieth century. (Ferguson album, courtesy Snohomish Historical Society)

Snohomish dominated the political, economic, and cultural affairs of the area. Emory C. Ferguson's Blue Eagle Saloon to the left (shown in 1884) served a variety of functions, including the site of county government. The white house to the right of center is that of Woodbury and Mary Sinclair. Mrs. Sinclair was the first permanent white woman settler in the county. (Courtesy Everett Public Library)

In 1883 the territorial legislature passed a controversial law allowing women the right to vote. Married women already had gained the right to own, sell, and bequeath property and to keep wages which they earned. Voting was taken away in 1887 by a court ruling on a technicality, whereupon the legislature re-passed it. The following year the supreme court again overturned the law. During those years of suffrage, however, county women took an active role on juries, in elections, and in political party affairs. Mrs. D'Arcy of Centerville was a delegate to the Republican territorial convention, while in 1884 the first jurors to serve were Parlisca Getchell, Susan N. Hilton, and Harriet Stevens. In the 1884 fall elections 87 votes by women were cast in the Snohomish precinct.

Low timber prices still plagued the market, closing many logging camps and causing economic problems. In Snohomish William Romines' saloon went broke, as did Stevenson's store, and most dramatically the Snohomish Trading Company store of Emory C. Ferguson—embarrassing, but not lethal to his dominant political power (although his old ally Sheriff Benjamin Stretch had to make deals with discontented Stillaguamish residents to obtain their votes).

With the county population now estimated at roughly 2,150 and that of Snohomish at 700, settlement increased up the interior valleys. A road from Snohomish was opened northward up the Pilchuck River, then through the Big Burn and down the South Fork

Stillaguamish River to Kent Prairie. Near the portage between the two rivers Joseph Enas had taken up a claim in 1883, to be followed in 1884 by George W. Anderson, William M. Turner, and F.P. Kistner. This was the beginning of the Portage settlement, soon to be renamed Granite Falls.

Lake Stevens also had settlers along the northeast shore, and they constructed a road through the timber to join the one up the Pilchuck. Farther east at Marysville William Westover cut a trail northeasterly and claimed land at Kellogg Marsh. Along the Stillaguamish Florence was becoming a rival to Stanwood, as F.E. Norton erected a store, the Corinth Hotel went up, and a townsite was platted. Farther upstream the first woman to settle permanently on the North Fork Stillaguamish River was Mrs. Collingwood, who with her husband took up a preemption claim three miles above the forks. On the Fourth of July 1884 they joined with Mr. and Mrs. Kent, her parents, and six others to celebrate the holiday with a picnic gathering at Kent Prairie. No longer would the river's north fork be called "Starve-out Valley" for the number of single men who tried to establish claims but found the isolation too difficult and had to return down below.

George Brackett joined the platters on August 24 that year, hoping to make money by developing his Edmonds townsite. On the Sultan River, placer miners at Horseshoe Bend hoped to divert the river and make theirs by washing gold directly out of the sand.

In the following year (1885) the Comefords platted Marysville, and its businesses began to grow. J.C. Lambert obtained his liquor license for the saloon, while Mark Swinnerton and H.B. Myers purchased Comefords store. Edmonds established its School District No. 15 with Miss Box instructing six students, John Nailor became post master of a new post office located in his Sultan home, and J.P. Anderson brought some 60 settlers up the Pilchuck River toward Marysville and Kent Prairie.

Two other events would have more lasting effects. In the first case, the Blackman brothers created the county's first shingle sawing machines. These developed into semi-automatic devices powered by steam, which allowed a sawyer to cut off uniform shingles at a speed as fast as he could reach to his left to pick the shingle off the saw and then trim it with another saw in front of him. The finished piece then was dropped to the floor below where a packer bundled them into bales. Speed was limited by the quickness of the sawyer, who required only seconds to produce a shingle—or, cut off his fingers. This device revolutionized shingle production. With a huge supply of western red cedar shingles on the market, cheap roofing materials now were exported throughout the Pacific rim and to the east coast, as a major step was taken toward industrialization in the county. The brothers also opened a store in downtown Snohomish, but then saw Isaac Cathcart's land clearing fire near his property south of the town spread into the timber and completely burn out the Blackmans' logging camp. In the next few years more fires would follow.

The second event of 1885 was far uglier. A growing anti-Chinese movement had developed in the West, fueled by a tight job market and tens of thousands of Chinese contract laborers who were brought to the Pacific coast to work on railroad construction. Without families and accustomed to working for very low wages, most planned to take their earnings back to help their relatives in a politically and economically deteriorating south China. On September 19 a mass meeting was called in Snohomish to discuss the expulsion of Chinese from the city. Ferguson chaired the meeting and opposed any such

On Ebey Island next to the slough Iver Johnson cleared, diked, and ditched to create his 166 acre farm. The Norwegian immigrant paid $1,000 in gold coin for the land, supplementing his income with fishing and trapping. Buildings erected in 1909 still are standing, and his descendants still farming. (Courtesy the Johnson family)

action, although most other speakers favored it, including popular young lawyer Samuel H. Piles, who later became a United States senator. A second meeting was held the following day and a committee selected to advise the unwanted men to leave, but the committee did not act, and the issue seemed to die down. Snohomish was not represented at the Anti-Chinese Congress which met in Seattle on September 28. The issue was kept alive, however, by the actions of the Knights of Labor, a rising union organization favoring expulsion of the Chinese as a way to raise falling wages, and by the deadline of November 1 adopted by the Congress for all Chinese to leave Washington Territory. In Snohomish Ferguson's defense of the Chinese was publicly ridiculed by *Eye* publisher C.H. Packard, who kept his columns full of scurrilous anti-Chinese material.

On November 3 well organized citizens rounded up all the Chinese in Tacoma, loaded them onto boxcars, and hauled them to Portland. Federal troops prevented similar action in Seattle. On February 7, 1886, however, the anti-Chinese organization moved quickly to load the Seattle population onto a waterfront steamer. Some were deported, the rest guarded to await a further boat. The next day an incident occurred between the Home Guard and the anti-Chinese demonstrators which left one man mortally wounded and four others injured, all anti-Chinese. This broke up the movement.

The following day in Snohomish the few Chinese still around were told to leave, and 18 did. Three remained, owners of a small laundry who had hoped to sell their business and promised to leave shortly. This caused persons unknown to set off a charge of powder under a corner of their building. No one was injured. Two days later, the last Chinese left, and Packard exulted, "Snohomish is at last a white man's town."

The night after the explosion a group of men led by J.H. Hilton, W.H. Ward, H.C. Petit and "other leading citizens" tore down the laundry building and were not disturbed in their work. Four men were indicted for conspiracy in the bombing: P.J. Cull, Jack Brooks, John Defel, and George Vivian, but they were not convicted for the crime, and neither was anyone else. Popular feeling was against the Chinese, but not in favor of violent expulsion. This was reflected by a territorial law in January banning Chinese from owning real estate in Washington. More punitive legislation was stopped in Olympia by the efforts of Ferguson and former judge Orange Jacobs of Seattle.

Snohomish was entering its best years in 1886, a period of growth and development which would last until 1890 and the rise of Everett. It claimed a population of some 800, which would have made it the fourth largest community on Puget Sound, behind Seattle, Tacoma, and Olympia. It also continued to flourish by catering to the logger trade, as an attempt at prohibition by local community vote was openly flouted and finally ignored. More genteel pursuits developed as well: the first advertisement for ice cream also appeared.

Memorial Day was celebrated for the first time, led by the new Grand Army of the Republic post of Civil War veterans and the Good Templars lodge, while the Odd Fellows built a large new hall. Charles Bakeman became the first undertaker and also built the first buggy in the county, a buckboard.

The Fourth of July was the main holiday celebrated in the late nineteenth century, and this year it was the turn of Florence to shine. The small Stillaguamish River town was making a run at Stanwood for commercial leadership of the valley and for several years was ahead, but then faded at the end of the decade. Settlement continued in the lower section, as Norman organized its School District No. 13 in 1882, East Stanwood/Cedarhome was founded in 1885 as No. 19, and Stanwood renumbered No. 18. Upstream growth continued steadily, Arlington schools tracing their origin to district No. 16 in 1884, and then Stillaguamish (Island School) No. 22 in 1887, Trafton No. 26 in 1888, and Oso No. 27, also in 1888. Lumber for the floor of the first school in the Arlington area was cut at the Utsalady mill, taken by river to the forks, then loaded onto mule back to be packed the last half-mile to the site.

Farther up the north fork, Oso began with the claim of J.H. Armstrong, while Fabian Sorrial demonstrated the transportation difficulties of the valley by backpacking fruit trees some 35 miles up river from Stanwood to his claim. Logging now began above the forks in 1886, as it did at the mouth of the Sultan River, where John Nailor established a ferry across it. On the Snoqualmie River 12 camps were running, and drivers even shot logs over the falls.

As 1887 began, people in the county became well aware that a new day of transportation and town building was dawning. Railroad rumors were in the air. The maneuvering was complex and occurred outside the county borders, but essentially Seattle businessmen and promoters wanted to tap the hinterlands with rail lines to bring in forest, mining, and agricultural products to be processed and exported from their city. They also hoped to become the terminus of the new transcontinental railroad being built with masterful planning and on a solid financial basis by James J. Hill of Minneapolis. To this end they began construction of the Seattle, Lake Shore and Eastern Railway north out of Seattle around Lake Washington, one branch headed easterly toward Issaquah and the other northerly into Snohomish County—specifically, Snohomish and then up the Pilchuck River toward the forks of the Stillaguamish, eventually to link up with the transcontinental Canadian Pacific Railway across the border.

Population reached around 3,200 in the county, J. Furth & Company of Seattle opened the first bank in county history in Snohomish, and a feeling of expectation was in the air. Farm production rose to out-produce local logging camp demand for the first time (diked flats along the lower Stillaguamish providing most of the crops), and the area ranked number one around the Sound in timber output.

On the Stillaguamish, Dr. Phelps arrived at Florence, the first permanent doctor in north county, and then moved up to Arlington. Nels K. Tvete opened a store and became postmaster at Norman, Stephen Cicero and a group of other Michigan immigrants poled their canoes up past the forks to claim land, William Aldridge and his wife were at Oso, Higgins at Hazel, and Mrs. Thomas Jefferson taught school at their Trafton site, later recalling the end of the road was 10 miles away and the store/post office 15 (at Silvana). In 1889 Gustav Nicklason arrived down at Cedarhome, opening a store and post office.

Stanwood made the big news, as Henry Oliver sold his land to W.R. Stockbridge of Puyallup, who formally platted the town and sold lots. A new blacksmith shop and a two story hall went up the following year, along with a riverside wharf and a sawmill. In 1889 Dr. Daniel McEacheran arrived, and Andrew B. Klaboe opened the second drug store in the county after Lot Wilbur's down in Snohomish. A new hotel, a hardware store, a waterworks from Lake Young four miles away, and a Methodist church also came in 1889, along with a brief visit by *The Stillaguamish Times* newspaper, which the next year moved on upstream to the forks and Haller City. These were the best years for Stanwood, which once again threatened secession before being placated by Snohomish.

To the south, Marysville also began to grow, as several small mills were constructed, the first by E.J. Anderson, followed by the Ford shingle mill in 1888 (which burned the following year), and the Cox brothers in 1889. With the probability of a railroad coming along the western edge of the county, Comeford's town site blossomed with a new store, a hotel, a number of new houses (including Comeford's, described as "magnificent"), and a school house for district No. 25. As with Stanwood, Marysville too would boom until 1890.

Across the bay at Mukilteo, life also was springing anew in 1887 with Coleman's new wharf and fish cannery, which refused to fire its Chinese workers. A new idea was developed by Walter Keyes, who decided to turn Mukilteo into a popular resort for visitors. In May he created an eventful opening with excursions from Seattle and Snohomish, two bands, and a picnic by the territorial Home Guard regiment. The following year Mrs. L. Thomas leased and remodeled his Bay View Hotel and sparked major interest in the community, which finally was platted the next fall. Investors were attracted, hopes were high for creating a playground for the new rich who would be developing nearby Everett, and those dreams carried over into the new decade and its grinding depression.

In the southwestern corner of the county George Brackett donated land for a second school in Edmonds in 1887. This building was 18 feet by 24 feet in size. A shingle mill went up in 1888, the first of what would become a series along the waterfront, and in 1889 the town exploded with

Granite Falls erected its first school of logs, one room with all grades taught by Eva Andrus. As travel was difficult and little money was available for any public services, the county developed a large number of mostly rural separate school districts. Land was donated for school buildings and the structures erected by the residents. (Courtesy Granite Falls Historical Society)

This view of Lowell shows Smith's log chute to the left. The square Great Northern Hotel dominates the center of the town, with the ridge above all cut-over land where Interstate 5 now runs next to the Evergreen Cemetery. (Courtesy Everett Public Library)

growth. A sawmill, hall, drug store, brick works, and a Congregational church also were erected.

Snohomish still dominated the action, though. New residents, job and profit seekers, and a large floating population associated with making money from the railroad crews flowed into the community. County population reached 6,000, with 1,200 inside the town limits of Snohomish, 2,500 in its precinct. Vice and crime were becoming more of a nuisance. One such instance occurred when "French Louie" chased saloon-owner Isaac Cathcart and his bartender through the streets of town, and Mollie "the lady stud poker dealer" Campbell and her husband headed the list of shady gamblers. Robberies and even occasional shootings occurred, causing the town fathers to license the gambling tables in 1888.

The town finally decided to incorporate in 1888, a process which had to be repeated only two years later, when the state law providing procedures for incorporation was declared unconstitutional. Money now could be found to operate the public school, after a fight over its new location and a shortage of funds for the last four years. The school opened in August with 100 students; and a year later, in December 1889, the school finally had a quality three-room building for its home. A rival to the *Eye* appeared on the streets when the *Sun* began publishing a weekly edition under George W. Head in 1888, and it went to a daily the following year. Meanwhile the *Eye* had absorbed the short-lived *Opinion*, and publisher Clayton Packard himself had made news first when Isaac Cathcart was acquitted of assault against him in 1883 and later when J.W. Gunn of the *Sun* failed to make stick a charge of criminal libel against him.

In other business developments, Jacob Furth reorganized his private bank into the First National Bank of Snohomish, locating it downtown in the first brick building in the county. The building still stands a century later. The same is true of Lot Wilbur's drugstore building; it was the second of brick which followed shortly after. Wooden buildings and factories were far more flammable than brick, as shown when the Blackman brothers' large saw and shingle mill along the river was burned by arson. A major tragedy was narrowly averted, as a crowd was gathered there to hear a political speech. Only courageous work by a bucket brigade stopped the fire from spreading to the town, but still 130 men were left unemployed. Undaunted by their loss, the brothers built an even larger mill to replace it, which opened in 1890 and continued as the industrial backbone of Snohomish.

On July 3, 1888 the Seattle, Lake Shore and Eastern reached the south side of the river, opposite town. Passengers crossed the river and boarded the cars for Seattle, turning what had been an all-day trip by steamboat into one of only 2½ hours. Due to more railroad politics, the bridge across the river was delayed at first, then quickly pushed to completion in September, only to be washed away by October flooding. It was rebuilt, however, and survey crews staked their way north up the Pilchuck valley. When Seattle burned in June 1889, Snohomish dispatched its new fire engine and crew by rail to help in the disaster. The Seattle fire also destroyed most of the railroad's survey field notes and delayed progress into the central part of the county. Train travel did not quickly end the steamboat business, though, as freight rates were far cheaper by water.

Along the proposed rail route the population grew steadily in 1888 and 1889. Maltby organized a school district in 1889, as did Getchell, the Burn, Forest Glade, Maple Grove (Carpenter), and Three Lakes. Granite Falls was organized in 1886 as district No. 21. Fernwood in the south organized in 1887, with Thomas Lake in 1888. Shoultes, north of Marysville, also was created in 1888.

Elsewhere around the county, Lowell shared in the general prosperity, as a new grocery store, wharf and the impressive Great Northern Hotel went up with its view overlooking the river and valley to the east, and a Congregational church was organized, meeting in Eugene Smith's new hall. Smith also invested in a large sawmill at the bend of the river, one with a capacity of 65,000 board feet a day. At the upper end of the valley, Park Place could boast of a new post office; although, when "the father of Monroe" (J.A. Vanasdlen) arrived that year, he recalled the site consisting only of an old saloon and two small buildings.

Upstream at Sultan, placer mining in both the Skykomish and Sultan rivers had been going on intermittently. In 1888 the steamboat *Gleaner* utilized high water to reach Sultan with freight, proving it could be done. The next year (1889) W.B. Stevens purchased the Pioneer Hotel, built a store, and platted a townsite.

Farther upstream early in the decade Frank N. Sparling had settled at what was to become Wallace (later renamed Startup). Gradually, his small home grew into a popular stopping place for passing miners; so, he developed a lodging house and decided to find a wife, not an easy task in territorial Snohomish County. He met Miss Eva Helwick of Ohio through the pages of *Heart and Hand Magazine,* and in 1889 they were wed at the fine new Penobscot Hotel in downtown Snohomish. Back in Wallace, he sold part of his land to

William Wait. Soon thereafter John F. Stretch opened a small store nearby, as the community began to develop.

A mile above the forks of the Skykomish River on the north branch, Amos Gunn took over a preemption claim and packed in supplies from Wallace. Later, his family would arrive. His wife, Persis, would name the site Index. Ten miles farther up the river, interest was perking up in the Silver Creek mines, and in June, a prospector named Joe Pearsall scrambled up Hubbart's Peak to see in the distance an ore outcrop which would become the site of Monte Cristo.

When the autumn vote for statehood took place on October 3, 1889, county opinion favored Olympia over Ellensburg and North Yakima for the state capital. In that same vote, county residents turned down prohibition (821 to 464) and women's suffrage (929 to 399), but approved the state constitution (1,202 to 130).

Not only were the territorial days ending, but so also the era of one-man domination of towns. Eugene Smith, George Brackett, James Comeford and, above all, Emory C. Ferguson were about to meet and be engulfed by men of capital resources, railroad power, and timber connections on a level the county had not yet seen.

1889–1900

When Washington achieved statehood on November 11, 1889, approximately three quarters of Snohomish County's 6,000 white settlers and its several hundred Native Americans lived along the Snohomish River and its tributaries. Snohomish City, the county seat, was easily the largest and most influential settlement, with busy newspapers, the county's only bank, and its easy access to King County via the Seattle, Lake Shore and Eastern Railway.

Lumbering continued to dominate all aspects of the local economy, evolving from the Civil War era small camps into an organized and systematic enterprise by the late 1880s. Steam locomotives and donkey engines were replacing oxen and horses, allowing tree cutting in more remote inland areas. At least 25 logging camps were scattered throughout the lowlands and the Cascade foothills. An estimated 150 million board feet were cut in the county in 1889. Mills tended to be rather small individually, except for Blackman Brothers in Snohomish. Collectively, the mills were emerging as big business, providing local processing rather than requiring export to Port Gamble or Utsalady as had previously been the practice. Saw mills produced 23 million board feet of lumber in 1889, while eight county shingle mills shipped millions of shingles each month.

The supply of trees still seemed limitless—even though estimates in those days suggested exhaustion of the resource within 60 years—and, the majestic lowland forests were being reduced with abandon. Loggers prided themselves in bringing down the huge Douglas firs and western red cedars. For several more decades pioneering photographers such as Darius Kinsey and his wife Tabitha documented trees of gargantuan size. Cedars up to 12 feet in diameter at three feet above the ground were not uncommon, and firs over eight feet thick at the butt were being cut on a regular basis. One cedar brought down near Arlington measured 68 feet in circumference and 23 feet in diameter.

Agriculture, originally a subsistence operation, found a willing market in the logging camps, providing a second source of county income. By the time of statehood in 1889, approximately 20,000 acres were under cultivation, with 90 percent of the farmlands located in the lowlands of the Snohomish and Stillaguamish river valleys. The diked tideland areas and bottom lands near Stanwood proved to be especially productive. Hay, oats, wheat, barley, and potatoes were major crops, having replaced the failed hops in the Tualco region. Fruits (such as peaches, plums, and blackberries) were also grown, but primarily for home consumption. There were several thousand head of horses, cattle, sheep, and hogs. Dairying, which would become the most extensive agricultural pursuit in the next century, was just getting started.

Sawing felled trees into the right lengths was the job of the "bucker." This was often difficult, due to tangled underbrush, steep slopes, and binding stresses on the downed tree. Cuts also might have to be made from the bottom up. For this hazardous work the bucker was paid less than a faller, loader, teamster, or blacksmith, who received top wages. (Courtesy Granite Falls Historical Society)

As with the timber industry, agriculture also was benefiting from increased mechanization. Improved horse-drawn hay rakes and mowers allowed the harvesting of larger plots. The threshing machine also was a major breakthrough, as hay and grains could be cut and processed in volume. By 1889 thanks to the boost in production made possible by machinery and the growing number of farms, the county was producing more agricultural products than it could consume.

Dependent on water transportation, most communities in the county still lacked much of a sense of overall cohesion. People identified more with their local valley rather than with the county as a whole, and the rivalry continued between Stillaguamish inhabitant's and the far more populous Snohomish region. Mukilteo, Edmonds, and the hinterlands had little political or economic clout. Towns were centers of social life and commerce, largely self-contained, and concerned with boosting their own growth through attracting new businesses and settlers. With only 180 miles of muddy, narrow, and often impassable roads tying together the valleys overland or paralleling the main rivers, travel still was slow and arduous—especially upstream and along tributary rivers or north-south overland.

Despite the lack of "connectiveness," a general sense of anticipation pervaded the county in 1889. This was a time of great western expansion, and Snohomish County shared in the entrepreneurial fever that was sweeping Puget Sound. James J. Hill, the great "Empire Builder" of the Great Northern Railway, was pushing

With most of the county covered by huge old growth timber, stump removal for farming and townsites was a daunting and hazardous task. Burning, horse-powered pullers, and explosive black powder were utilized, along with back breaking hand labor. Cut over land and "stump farms" were inexpensive compared to improved acreage. This is on the Hans Thompson farm east of Island Crossing. (Courtesy Loren Kraetz)

rails steadily westward across the plains and mountains of the Dakotas and Montana. Puget Sound appeared to be the target, and speculation abounded as to where the rails would meet salt water. Leaders of Puget Sound communities—and would-be communities—attempted to convince themselves and others that they had the perfect location for the Great Northern terminus. Stories spread of east coast investors prowling western Washington in search of locations for cities and industries. Rumors swirled about fantastic new mineral discoveries in the mountainous regions of eastern Snohomish County. There was considerable expectation everywhere that big things were about to happen.

Meanwhile, across the United States, a series of what, at first seemed to be unrelated events were really the pieces of a giant jigsaw puzzle that, when fully assembled, would change Snohomish County beyond the wildest dreams of its 1889 residents. A Tacoma

A Home in Washington

By Mabel Monsey

We came to Washington when it was yet a territory. Had we invested our money then in Seattle property, we would now have been wealthy. We took up our present home as a pre-emption 11years ago this fall, just two months before the pre-emption law went out. We took a 40-acre claim because we could by so doing get a very fine location, and in Washington location means much.

Our 40 acres was, when we located on it, within one-half or three-quarters of a mile from a good railroad and one mile and three-quarters from depot and post office. Shortly after we came here a school was established at Hartford. Until it was built I taught our children at home. There is still no church, though there are two Sunday schools, one at Hartford, and another three miles form us.

I shall never forget the feeling of perfect content that filled us as we came first to the place to be known in the future as home. We never once thought of the 40 acres of solid woods we must cut down and clear out. We were young and brave, my husband and I. We were ready to work hard in our struggle for a home. We had brought with us into the wilderness four girls ranging in ages from nine years to 18 months. With them to care for I would have little time to get lonesome.

When we first came to our Washington home a large fir log lay right in front of the door, fully eight feet through. We had to make a ladder to climb to the top of this log, and then walk down the log to a smaller one, and so on to the road. We could see nothing of the road, which passed two sides of our place, and was a good plank road leading to a new mill then being built at the lake [Stevens]. We knew that a beautiful lake lay on one side of us, the railroad and the mountains on the other side, yet all we could see was a forest all about us, and abounding in deer, bear and other game.

My husband had slept in the house the night before [we arrived] and numerous skunks had played in the room all night, much the same as young kittens would play. The same day I arrived with the children the kitchen floor was laid. It was then the first of November, cloudy, sometimes raining days; not cold. That first day after the kitchen floor was laid and a carpet put down in the sitting room, the loft overhead was filled with superfluous furniture, the bare walls were covered with pretty pictures brought from our far eastern home. The organ, sewing machine and two beds found place in that room, together with two large rockers and other chairs and a large box stove. The kitchen was also crowded full, and a woodshed was hastily built afterwards and more furniture stowed away in it, but all the furniture left in the woodshed came unglued, owing to the dampness of the weather. A bed room was next built on large enough for two beds, and we then took one out of the sitting room, giving us room for a table. We lived thus for one year.

We had a bank account to call upon for the necessities of life. One of the first things I did was to subscribe for a number of the best farm journals, a floral magazine, several ladies' magazines and journals and the leading county paper. Also, a good eastern paper and a first-class religious paper, some 11 or 12 altogether, and they have been welcome inmates to our home ever since.

All winter long my husband cleared land. The next spring I planted the best flower garden we have had since we have been here, and we had a very good garden. How we appreciated the first sunshine that came in and the increase of sunshine as more and more trees were cut down. That same year the mill near us bought our trees, and tree after tree was laid low, much of that timber coming back to us as lumber for a fine new house which we were building. Thanksgiving saw us in our new house with a crowd of merry makers about us.

Mabel Monsey (Courtesy Lake Stevens Historical Society)

The years went by. A boy had been born to us and had been buried. Another boy came and then twins, and then another girl and another boy, and still another girl, and now our family numbered 10 living children, eight girls and two boys, and two boys who had died, one in far away Ohio, one here.

We saw some hard times during the panic [1893-1897], but we were never more happy. My husband had to go away to work, but always at home to his meals and at night except two years and a half he was night watchman and ran the engine at one of the mills near us. But now we have a home that can be considered a home, yet we have but seven acres cleared and some 20 in pasture, which is full of stumps and logs laying about. We have 100 chickens, two fine cows and a horse. A school house was built on our land. The depot was moved to within half a mile from our home. There is also a store, two saloons and a hotel at this little burg, known as Hartford Junction.

We are a healthy, industrious, happy family, a reading and musical family. The organ has been replaced with a fine piano, and we welcome the rainy winter days with our ruddy fires and plenty of entertainment in our own home. We have never allowed ourselves to be too busy to read, write, play and sing, or be sociable. None of us worry, fret, or grumble. Yet, when we look over the past we cannot say to easterners, "Do as we have done," for it requires much perseverance, courage, pluck, grit, and patience. If husband and wife do not happen to share alike in this respect one or the other is apt to become discouraged. Then, as the years have gone by, all valuable land near town or railroad has been taken up, so the better way is to buy partly improved farms. People here sell our and go east of the mountains, while people east of the mountains, by which I mean eastern Washington, come here. The same case holds good as to California.

Hartford, Wash. Mabel H. Monsey, 1901

Mabel and her husband Captain John Monsey moved west from Ohio in 1888, then came to Hartford along the Seattle, Lake Shore and Eastern Railway. She was a writer of short stories, articles, and poems, as well as having a column called "Fordhart Corners" in the Seattle *Post-Intelligencer*, which brought in much needed income. In 1903 they moved back to Seattle in order to find adequate schooling for their growing family. The above remembrances come from a collection of her writings between 1891 and 1903 assembled by Edna May Savory of the Lake Stevens Historical Society.

mill owner and industrialist cruised past the shores of Port Gardner Bay in search of lumber lands for his burgeoning empire. As his wife sighed, "There goes our last dollar," a nearly bankrupt ship designer in Duluth, Minnesota watched his strange invention (a craft called a whaleback) slide down the launching ways to the waters of Lake Superior. Elsewhere, a fabulously wealthy and somewhat depressed New York oil baron was trying to figure out how to spend money as fast as he was earning it. Also, a lone prospector in the mountains of western Washington peered across a valley at a ledge, which seemed to ooze with silver laden ore. And, a young engineer was determining that a pass (known as Marias) provided a marvelous route through the lofty Rocky Mountains.

The Tacoma industrialist was Henry Hewitt. Although he had been in the Pacific Northwest for little more than a year, he had already established himself as one of the richest individuals in the new state. Having compiled a sizeable fortune as a contractor and businessman in Wisconsin, Hewitt headed to the southwest in the late 1880s. He landed briefly in the area of the current day Nogales, Arizona, where he was involved in an unsuccessful smelter venture. From there he migrated to Tacoma, where he became an organizer, partner and officer of the huge St. Paul and Tacoma Lumber Company. By the time of statehood Hewitt was one of Washington's leading industrialists. While searching for new timberlands to feed his mill, Hewitt had come across the Port Gardner peninsula. Bordered by Puget Sound on the west and the Snohomish River on the north and east, the peninsula struck the astute Hewitt as desirable property. There was ample water depth for deep harbor possibilities and substantial stands of timber on and near the peninsula. Interestingly, this area, which seemed to have such promising attributes, had no real town site in 1889. Perhaps three-dozen settlers were located there. After his explorations Hewitt kept the Port Gardner site high on his agenda.

The ship designer was Alexander McDougall, a Scottish-born ship captain who designed the whaleback to slice through the water with the decks awash. Shaped somewhat like a giant cigar, the revolutionary vessel could be built as a barge or self-propelled unit and did, in fact, resemble a whale's back when it was underway. Struggling against doubters, who scoffed at the design and described the bow as looking like a pig's snout, McDougall had nearly exhausted his resources when he finally launched his first whaleback barge in 1888. The vessel proved to be a successful hauler of goods on the Great Lakes, but McDougall did not have the finances to build another one. To keep his dream alive McDougall turned to east coast investors. Dealing with a New York financier, Colgate Hoyt, McDougall entered into an arrangement where he became a director and minority owner of a newly organized company to produce whalebacks. Located in Superior, Wisconsin and headed by Hoyt, the enterprise was named The American Steel Barge Company. By the end of 1889 more barges had been launched, and designs were underway for self-propelled vessels. Excited by their success, barge work officials began to

Generally regarded as the "Father of Everett," Henry Hewitt was the Northwest link with eastern capitalists who financed the city. A successful Wisconsin lumberman who moved to Tacoma in 1888 as a partner and executive in the powerful St. Paul and Tacoma Lumber Company, he became familiar with the potential of the Port Gardner peninsula and dominated its early development. (Courtesy Everett Public Library)

Though John D. Rockefeller was the major financier of early Everett, it is unlikely that he ever knew much about the project to build a new city on Puget Sound. He was drawn into the scheme by Charles Colby and Colgate Hoyt, who had the dream but not the money to start the city. Operating with Rockefeller's resource, the two, Colby in particular, were the conduit to Henry Hewitt. When the project began to collapse and Rockefeller became aware of the financial drain, he took action to remove Colby, Hoyt and Hewitt from positions of authority and initiated actions which eventually led to the discard of all his Everett holdings. One of the few reminders of Rockefeller's involvement is the Everett street which bears his name. (Courtesy Everett Public Library)

consider the possibility of locating a barge and ship building plant on a salt-water location. They hoped the whaleback would prove just as seaworthy—and profitable—on the high seas as it was on the Great Lakes.

Charles Colby, one of the company directors, headed a delegation to find the new barge works plant site. Following the "Go West" spirit of the day, Colby sought out the relatively untapped area of the Pacific Northwest. Colby, whose many business roles included chairmanship of the Northern Pacific Railroad executive committee, remembered Hewitt from the days when both were operatives in Wisconsin. Colby's journey led him to Tacoma, where he and his entourage called on Hewitt. Hearing of the shipyard idea, Hewitt began to extol the virtues of the Port Gardner site. Intrigued by Hewitt's zeal and apparent knowledge, the eastern financiers invited Hewitt to join them on the steamship *Queen of the Pacific* cruise to Alaska in July 1890. The trip, with captive audience, must have provided the perfect arena for Hewitt's abundant salesmanship skills. When the group returned to Tacoma, the idea for a shipyard on the Port Gardner peninsula had blossomed into a vision of a new Puget Sound metropolis. There would be the shipyard, a nail factory, a pulp mill, sawmills, railroad, dry dock, hotels, and warehouses. This city of diversified industries might rival New York City. At the very least, it would be the "Pittsburgh of the West." All that was needed was money—someone with even greater wealth than a Colby or a Hewitt to underwrite the project.

And, someone with that great wealth, the oil baron, did enter the picture. Having amassed the greatest fortune of any American in history through his monopoly over the nation's oil industry, John D. Rockefeller had the resources to make the dream come true. It was his money behind the American Steel Barge Company, and this was but one arm of his vast empire. He would be called upon by trusted underlings Charles Colby and Colgate Hoyt, who already were involved in a number of his enterprises, and he would be asked to finance a new city. Once Hewitt had completed a more thorough study of the Port Gardner area with the same enthusiastic conclusion, Colby and Hoyt conveyed the plan for the new city to Rockefeller. Soon Hewitt had the authority to spend up to $800,000 to acquire property.

The prospector who glimpsed the sparkling glitter through his field glasses was Joseph Pearsall of Mineral City, a small mining town on Silver Creek in the Cascade Mountains of eastern Snohomish County. Standing on Hubbart Peak between Silver and Troublesome creeks more than a mile above sea level in the late spring of 1889, Pearsall had spotted the red-gold glitter across the valley on a ledge that went from the valley floor to a mountaintop. He realized the stained sulphide rock might be galena, which not only contained lead but sometimes also silver and possibly gold. Trekking to the ledge far above the headwaters of the south fork of the Sauk River to take ore samples, he confirmed his conjecture. This evidence of mineral wealth and the need for a place to process it would, within a couple of years, be linked with the establishment of the new city on Port Gardner Bay.

The young engineer was John F. Stevens, a representative of the Great Northern. His company was eager to find the most feasible passage through the Rocky Mountains when Stevens identified Marias Pass in December 1889. The 5,213 foot high divide in northwestern Montana provided an excellent and unexpectedly low elevation route for the railway's plan to build a line to the west coast. It was an important milestone in the eventual construction of the railroad, which would cross both the Rockies and Cascades on its way to Puget Sound.

In September of 1890 Hewitt began to acquire property on and around the Port Gardner peninsula. Within a few months he had possession of about 5,000 acres. In negotiating with the local settlers, Hewitt promised industries as an incentive for these existing landowners to sell and/or give property to him. To Eugene D. Smith, the "Father of Lowell," he pledged a pulp mill. One set of landowners who had preceded Hewitt to the area were brothers Wyatt and Bethel Rucker and their mother, Jane. The Ruckers, just as Hewitt, were from Tacoma and had their own plans for a city. In August 1890 they had filed a 50-acre bay side plat for a town site to be known as Port Gardner. In deference to Hewitt's plan the Ruckers later withdrew their plat and transferred some of their holdings to him with conditions that bound Hewitt and his company to specific industrial developments. The contract, which outlined these conditions, is sometimes referred to as "The Remarkable Document." In subsequent years, it would continually haunt the backers of the new city.

By November 1890 the planned new city had a name. At a dinner party in the Colby home Hewitt suggested the name "Everett," which was the name of Charles Colby's 15-year-old son. The always-crafty Hewitt must have understood the benefit of endearing himself to the person who was chief connection between the Rockefeller money and his own pocket. Also, "Everett" did not give away the geographical loca-

Brothers Bethel (left) and Wyatt Rucker were already on the Port Gardner peninsula with their mother Jane when the plan to build Everett was developed. The Ruckers had planned to start "Port Gardner" on Bayside but agreed to join in with the more grandiose Rockefeller/Colby/Hewitt scheme. The Ruckers remained through the city's ups and downs, and descendants still live in the community. Banking, lumbering, a large mill on Lake Stevens, and Big Four Inn above Silverton were all Rucker ventures. (Courtesy Everett Public Library)

tion of the new town, a ploy that might discourage speculators from flocking to the area and driving up prices. In a further display of patronizing wizardry Hewitt rolled out a plan that showed the major north/south streets with names such as Colby, Hoyt, Rucker, and Rockefeller. And, not surprisingly, the main east/west thoroughfare, which intersected with those north and south avenues on its route from Bayside to Riverside, would be called Hewitt.

On November 19, 1890 articles of incorporation for the Everett Land Company were filed in Pierce County. Hewitt was the president. Although John D. Rockefeller's name was not included on the Board of Directors, the entire board was affiliated one way or the other with the Rockefeller interests. The new city was getting closer to reality, but a national recession extending into the first half of 1891 slowed progress.

Another important incorporation occurred on March 10, 1891 when the Seattle and Montana Railway was established. This company came into being when Nelson Bennett, a railroader who was cooperating with Canadians to develop a rail link from Puget Sound to the Canadian Pacific at New Westminster, British Colum-

The Everett Land Company headquarters originally were located on the southwest corner of Pacific and Oakes avenues, in 2004 the site of Bethany on Pacific. The Summit Hotel (later the Chapman Apartments) can be seen in the background. Later the company's structure was moved to Hewitt Avenue. When the Everett Improvement Company took over in 1900, they simply changed the sign to indicate the new owners. (Courtesy Everett Public Library)

This October 1891 view looking north on the Everett bay front shows the newly completed Seattle and Montana Railway. The photograph shows the small white house of the Rucker family, along with Miley and Henderson's false fronted store, home of the city's first post office. Owned by Great Northern's James J. Hill, the rail line was a significant link from Puget Sound to Canada. When the Great Northern Railway was completed over Stevens Pass in 1893, it connected with the Seattle and Montana, giving coveted regional access to Hill. (Frank LaRoche photo, courtesy Everett Public Library)

Social outings, trips to town, and courting were all made easier as county roads dried out in the late spring and more were built to link communities, although land transportation always was slow and limited to light traffic. (Courtesy Granite Falls Historical Society)

bia, sold his interest to Hill's Great Northern. The line had been completed from Fairhaven (Bellingham) to New Westminster when Bennett sold. Hill created the Seattle and Montana, and the rush was on to finish an approximately 70-mile rail connection between Seattle and Fairhaven. Much of the line, including the section from Seattle to Everett, would run along the bay front. The Seattle and Montana would connect the entire Puget Sound area with the Canadian Pacific, regardless of where Great Northern reached the Sound.

As the Everett plan neared the hatching stage, Snohomish County was experiencing substantial growth. The 1890 federal census listed 8,514 county residents, an increase of more than 2,000 from the previous year. In terms of population, the county was now ninth among the counties of western Washington. King County was the most populous with 65,443 inhabitants. Snohomish City, the county seat, completed incorporation in 1890 with an official population of 2,012. Edmonds incorporated that year, too, and welcomed Allen M. Yost and his family to the city. He would play a major role in its future. Upstream from Sultan, the plat of Wallace was filed in 1890, and the name Granite Falls given to the post office near the falls of the South Fork Stillaguamish River. A town site called "Outing" was platted along the shore of Lake Stevens the same year, but soon vacated.

In an effort to facilitate transportation between the growing areas, county citizens approved an $80,000 bond issue on November 4, 1890 to improve the narrow and frequently impassable county roads. Voters, however, failed to approve a bond issue for a new courthouse. Pressured by the needs of a burgeoning population, increased rent for meeting space in lodge halls, and new requirements brought by statehood, county commissioners issued bonds on their own authority. The courthouse would be two stories high, of brick, and located along Avenue D on lots donated by brothers Emory C. and Clark Ferguson. The $24,000 building was completed in early 1891. There was great pride in the use of local and state construction materials. Stone came from the Snoqualmie and Chuckanut (in Whatcom County) quarries, while the brick was made at the Bast brickyards in Snohomish. This impressive structure later served as a home first for the private Puget Sound Academy and then Snohomish High School before it was razed in 1938.

In those early days of statehood, county railroads were to urban development what the waterways had been during the territorial period. Since rail lines often paralleled water routes, this meant further development of established towns as well as the birth of new ones. It also could spell disaster for established towns not on the rail line. The arrival of the Seattle, Lake Shore and Eastern in 1888 had benefited Snohomish and prompted the beginning of Yew, later named Maltby, nine miles to the south. The line's extension north from Snohomish in 1890 gave rise to Machias and Hartford. Farther north, plats for Arlington and Haller City were filed on March 15, 1890 and April 24, 1890, respectively. These two communities were located near each other at the confluence of the north and south forks of the Stillaguamish River where the rail line would cross on its northward route. Both were financed by outside interests, but it was J.W. McLeod, Arlington's backer, who seemed to have the better

information. A contractor for the Seattle, Lake Shore and Eastern, he may have known in advance that the depot would be built at the Arlington site. Located south of Haller City and farther from the river, Arlington's advantage was its slightly higher elevation. It simply was too difficult for the steam locomotives to climb the grade in either direction if they started from a dead stop at Haller City. The depot placement was but one factor in the immediate and fierce rivalry between the two towns. By summer 1890, trains had reached the feuding settlements.

In 1890 Snohomish erected this fine brick building as the county's first real court house. With the loss of that function, the structure served first as home for the Puget Sound Academy and then Snohomish High School. It was razed in 1938. (Courtesy Everett Public Library)

In spring 1891 the Port Gardner peninsula showed the first evidence of becoming a town site. B.E. Aldrich opened the Workingmen's Grocery on Riverside, and soon a small commercial area of wooden structures, some with canvas roofs, developed at a location which would become the intersection of Pacific Avenue and Chestnut Street. In June 1891 P.K. Lewis opened a store on the bay front. Within a month another store and Everett's first post office were operating near Lewis. Meanwhile, half-way across the continent, the whaleback steamer *C.W. Wetmore*, named for another of the eastern financiers involved in the Everett project, was launched at Superior. A few months later, the vessel would arrive in Everett with much of the machinery for the city's early industries.

Closer to home, track laying for the Seattle and Montana Railway line was beginning from Seattle on the south and Bellingham on the north. In the southern part of the county the track-laying engine rounded Hamlin's Point near Edmonds in June 1891. In anticipation of the railroad, the Minneapolis Realty and Investment Company bought the Edmonds town site from town founder George Brackett in 1890 and began promising development activities: a new wharf constructed, a new office building erected, and an elegant hotel built, the Bishop, in honor of the company's president. Unfortunately, the anticipated land boom never materialized, and the company's holdings were eventually repossessed by Brackett. Edmonds would survive and eventually prosper, but without the involvement of Mr. Bishop and his company. Just north of Edmonds, the railway would pass near the vast holdings of the Mosher and McDonald Logging Company, which built its own small railroad to bring logs from inland to the salt water. Completion of the Seattle and Montana gave the logging company the option of shipping their logs out by water or by rail. A stop named Mosher, between present-day Picnic Point and Chenault Beach, was established. From Mosher the line was constructed north along the water to Mukilteo and then past the embryonic settlement on Everett's bay side. Marysville, the next town north, experienced the same growth fever as its railroad brethren. The town incorporated in early 1891 and elected merchant Mark Swinnerton as the first mayor. In subsequent years Swinnerton and his family would play influential roles in the town's development.

A few miles north of Marysville, near the point where the railroad crossed the Stillaguamish River, Silvana, which previously had been known as Stillaguamish, was selected as the area depot. The town site was laid out in 1891, and the next year the town's first business opened, L.P. Elverum's general merchandising store. A few miles north, the location of the Seattle and Montana line created great distress for Stanwood. Avoiding the lowest part of the flatlands, the rails were laid close to the hillside approximately one mile east of the town, and the depot was erected there. Although it was the largest settlement in the Stillaguamish Valley, Stanwood had been bypassed. Outraged by this shun, the community's farmers and merchants boycotted the line and turned to the steamship to transport their goods. They even bought their own vessel, the *City of Stanwood*. This venture, which showed early success, was short lived, however. The craft with a valuable load of hay and oats was lost in a January 1894 fire. While Stanwood fumed, the area around the depot would develop into the rival town of East Stanwood. The fierce competition between these two segments of the "Twin Cities" would rage for decades. Regardless of the emotions of the residents along the route, the Seattle and Montana was rushed to completion, with the final spike driven near East Stanwood on October 12, 1891.

This happy snow couple from Marysville shows a sense of play never far from the surface of settlers' lives. All-night dances, Fourth of July celebrations, skating parties, and excursions all helped lighten the busy routines of large families and work. (Courtesy Marysville Historical Society)

Meanwhile, after his discovery, miner Joseph Pearsall had taken into his confidence Frank Peabody, a fellow prospector who had contact with "men of means". Together they found not only that the ledges extended further into neighboring mountains, but also the results of their assays proved there was twice as much gold as the silver value in the ore. Initially they were funded by John MacDonald "Mac" Wilmans, a 31-year-old investor who already had made and lost considerable money in various business and mining ventures.

By 1890 several Seattle area investors, including Seattle *Post-Intelligencer* newspaper publisher Leigh Hunt, were involved. They named the district Monte Cristo, for the widely read nineteenth century French novel *The Count of Monte Cristo* by Alexandre Dumas. Unlike the adventure and romance which led the fictional hero to victory and great wealth, the problem here was more mundane and just as challenging: how to freight tons of ore from deep in the mountains to a center where it could be processed and the gold and silver bullion shipped. Realizing their original route over the rugged mountains southwest of Monte Cristo was not viable, the investors concentrated on a route up the Skagit River valley and then ascending the Sauk River, a major Skagit tributary whose south fork headwaters are at Monte Cristo. Plans were proceeding well in 1891, when it was noted that a low pass (later named Barlow for the engineer working on the railroad right-of-way) separated Monte Cristo from the south fork of the Stillaguamish river system, which led more directly to the Sound. The mining investors were familiar with the plans for a new city on the Port Gardner peninsula and concluded that a railroad down the south fork of the Stillaguamish very easily could veer off near Granite Falls and connect with Everett. They thought that perhaps the Everett backers would be interested in financing the railroad and a smelter in the new city. The Wilmans group contacted Hewitt, who sent mining engineers to check out the claims of the Monte Cristo men. Their report was favorable, and Hewitt soon was in touch with Colby and Hoyt. Further investigations by experts seemed to verify the mining potential, and in short order the Rockefeller syndicate added a Monte Cristo railroad and an Everett smelter to their plans. In addition they invested in the mining district itself, taking over most of the properties before the end of 1891.

At the Everett town site the pace was accelerating that fall. Although there was no formal announcement, it seemed certain that James J. Hill's Great Northern would reach salt water at Port Gardner Bay and Everett would be its terminus. This, coupled with stories of Rockefeller's millions pouring into the area, set the stage for boomtown Everett. The industries which Hewitt had promised, all owned by the Everett Land Company syndicate, were going up. Along the Snohomish River, construction of the Pacific Steel Barge Works, a division of the American Steel Barge Company, was underway. Work was proceeding on construction of the pulp mill along the Snohomish River in Lowell and the nail works on the Everett bay front. At least one local brickyard had begun production. The Everett Land Company was not yet ready to sell residential and business property, but others were. On one December day the Swalwell Land, Loan and Trust Company on Riverside sold $150,000 worth of lots. Hart's—Everett's first sawmill—fired up on December 10. The next week the first school opened with 26 students, and on December 21 the whaleback *C.W. Wetmore* arrived with machinery for the nail works, shipyard and pulp mill.

The year 1892 was a banner one for Everett. Houses and businesses were going up quickly to accommodate the thousands of new arrivals. Riverside developed more rapidly than Bayside, and the business section in the eastern neighborhood moved from the Pacific and Chestnut location to Hewitt Avenue, where more substantial structures were being erected. Bayside began to develop when the Everett Land Company finally started selling lots in March. Although Hewitt Avenue was rife with saloons, brothels, and gambling houses, the social institutions of more stable society also began to develop. Concerned about the need for law and order in this unruly town, the citizenry organized a provisional government known as "The Committee of Twenty-One" on March 21. When the city bragged of running out all its gamblers, other parts of the county observed that nobody was left in Everett. Another school was added, although it was still necessary to rent space for the rapidly increasing enrollment, and several churches were started. The

Although Everett's first Riverside commercial structures were located at California and Chestnut streets, Hewitt Avenue soon become the main business thoroughfare. A view west from Swalwell's Landing on the Snohomish River shows how Hewitt had developed by 1892. The brick Bank of Everett and Swalwell buildings across from each other at Pine Street were still standing in 2004, but the many wooden frame structures are long gone. The railroad crossing was for the Everett and Monte Cristo, which in the summer of 1892 was connected with the Seattle and Montana at the tip of the Everett peninsula. (Courtesy Everett Public Library)

pulp mill and nail works began production, the first telephone system went into service, several banks were started, and the shipyard was busily servicing the *C.W. Wetmore*, which had arrived in need of many repairs. Construction of the smelter, which would be known as the Puget Sound Reduction Company, was commencing near the tip of the peninsula north of the barge works.

With the gearing up of business and industry, workers also began to organize. Six labor unions had sprung up in Everett by fall 1892, including the painters and the carpenters. On Monday, September 5, 1892 some two years before it became a national holiday, Everett was the site of a Labor Day celebration. Many businesses closed for at least part of the day in observance of the festivities. A parade across town was followed by songs and recitations. The evening activities concluded with about 200 guests at the fireman's ball. By 1893 an American Railway Union had been formed in Snohomish with thirty charter members. The following year, 25 journeymen printers organized the Everett-Snohomish Typographical Union. The coming tough economic times of the mid and late 1890s would take their toll, but seeds had been sown for the strong labor movement which would emerge in the early years of the next decade.

Located on the Snohomish River near the northern tip of the Port Gardner peninsula, the Pacific Steel and Barge Works was the Puget Sound branch of the American Steel Barge Company on Lake Superior. It was designed to produce steel hulled vessels nicknamed "whalebacks", which were designed to offer minimal resistance to wind and waves. The barge works closed in 1894 after the production of just one ship—the "City of Everett". (Courtesy Everett Public Library)

When the Everett syndicate purchased most of the mines at Monte Cristo it erected a smelter for those and British Columbia ores on the hill above the barge works. The Puget Sound Reduction Company was purchased by the ASARCO trust and closed in 1912. Highly contaminated soil left from the smelter's operating days later led to an expensive, ongoing cleanup effort and demolition of homes built on the site. (Courtesy Everett Public Library)

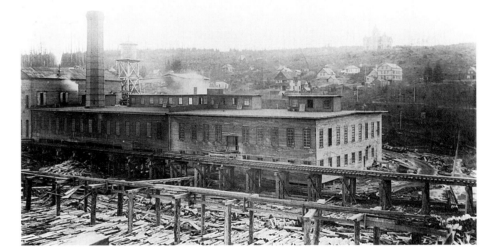

The Puget Sound Pulp and Paper Company mill, shown here in 1895, operated for over three quarters of a century and was the backbone of the Lowell economy. Originally a Rockefeller enterprise, it was owned for much of its existence by brothers William and Leonard Howarth and A.H.B. Jordan and known as the Everett Pulp and Paper Company. It was not uncommon for several generations of the same family to have worked there. The turreted structure on the hill is the Lowell School, designed by Everett architect Frederick Sexton, which served the community from 1894 until it was replaced in 1951. (Courtesy Everett Public Library)

The Puget Sound Wire Steel and Nail Company was located on the Everett bay front just south of Pier One and the later alumina dome. Although a successful enterprise, it was closed when financier J. P. Morgan organized the United States Steel Company and bought up competitors. Later the buildings housed a fish packing plant. By 2004 there was no trace of the structures. (Courtesy Everett Public Library)

Interest in the Great Northern took a leap forward when Hill arrived in Everett on February 16, 1892, and Hewitt tried to entice the "Empire Builder" into confirming that Everett would be its terminus. At a sumptuous banquet in the Bay View Hotel, next to the Seattle and Montana tracks, Hill stressed the importance of Everett, but he carefully avoided the commitment, which Hewitt and the Everett backers so dearly wanted to hear. In the meantime, on the bluff above the Bay View, the opulent Hotel Monte Cristo was being constructed. With its elegant turrets and expansive wrap around porch, it seemed to symbolize Everett's vision and hope perhaps more than any other structure. Hill may not have committed himself, but Everett still was the "Magic City", or on a more realistic level, the emerging "City of Smokestacks," a title it wore with pride.

While Everett longed for railhead designation, the Great Northern line was being pushed relentlessly toward Puget Sound. Once John F. Stevens had identified the best rail route through the Rocky Mountains, he was assigned the same task for the Cascades. After exploring the mountains above Lake Chelan and various other areas, he assigned his assistant, C.F.B. Haskell, to explore up Nason Creek from Lake Wenatchee, in September 1890. Haskell found the desired location and marked it by carving the words "Stevens Pass" on a large cedar tree, honoring his boss. He then followed the western descent to the south fork of the Skykomish River. In a later trip Stevens and E.H. Beckler confirmed the route as the best over the Cascades. While the pass itself was in King County, most of the rail line from there to the Sound was in Snohomish County. The race was on to complete the final leg of Hill's masterpiece.

Great Northern construction created almost frenzied activity. Several small towns, some of them temporary communities for rail construction and maintenance workers, sprang up along the western route. Wellington (renamed Tye after the 1910 snow slide disaster), Corea, Scenic, Martin City, Nippon (later renamed Alpine), Berlin, Grotto, Baring, and Halford were among the mountain stations that have all but disappeared today. Yet, not all the settlements were temporary. Index, near the confluence of the north and south forks of the Skykomish River, profited from both the railroad construction and nearby mining districts. Farther west, the town at Wallace, where a river by the same name entered the Skykomish, was disappointed in not getting a depot. Sultan, located at the confluence of the Sultan and Skykomish rivers, experienced a major boom. Even before the railroad, Sultan had attracted settlers because of the adjacent mining districts. The town was designated a rail construction supply station, and at times up to 1,000 men were employed. By the end of

Overlooking Port Gardner Bay at the corner of Pacific and Kromer Avenues, the Hotel Monte Cristo symbolized the grandiose dreams for Everett. This opulent wooden structure opened in 1892 to provide appropriate accommodations for visiting eastern capitalists. Originally it was to be called the Hotel Colby, but the name was changed during construction at Mr. Colby's request. The structure became Everett's first Providence Hospital in 1905 and was torn down in the mid-1920s when a new facility was constructed just to the east of it by the Sisters of Providence. (Courtesy Everett Public Library)

111

1891 its population was estimated to be between 800 and 1,000. The boom continued in 1892 with the addition of many businesses, including the Bank of Sultan.

Farther downstream, where the Skykomish and Snoqualmie rivers join to form the Snohomish River, more development occurred. The plat of Monroe was filed on February 5, 1891 and that of Tye City, March 22, 1892. The latter was on property crossed by the Great Northern right-of-way. A train depot was established in the vicinity, and the community of Monroe was underway. In the meantime the established town of Park Place was suffering because it was too far southwest from the new rail line. The problem was solved when John Vanasdlen, a co-filer of the Tye City plat and postmaster at the Monroe post office, had the post office and store physically moved by oxen to trackside. Later, other buildings would be relocated in the same fashion. Thus Vanasdlen would become known as the "Father of Monroe." Residents also participated in railroad construction activities. Barges 60 feet long and six to eight feet wide were filled with supplies and towed upriver by mules. Two brothers, Simon and Charles Elwell, built a 44-foot canoe to carry materials for railroad construction. Reportedly, the huge craft could hold up to 4,700 pounds.

For Snohomish the railroad was a bittersweet pill. As with other communities, it would profit from being on the route. However, at one point it had been the only county settlement connected by rail with the outside world. Completion of the Seattle, Lake Shore and Eastern, the Seattle and Montana, and now the Great Northern, meant that virtually every major settlement in the county now enjoyed that status. Some analysts reluctantly admitted that the Great Northern connection with Everett would solidify the new Port Gardner peninsula city's position for county pre-eminence, as geography, location and money were on Everett's side. From 1889 to 1893 Snohomish experienced much prosperity, with an estimated one million dollars invested in the community during that time. Yet telltale signs of trouble were apparent as early as 1892, when plans for a giant smelter allegedly financed by millionaire miners failed to materialize. As financial concerns grew, city revenues fell sharply. In truth, Snohomish was on its way to losing the county dominance it had exercised for the previous three decades. By 1893 Everett would have a population more than twice the size of Snohomish. Emory C. Ferguson, who had reigned over county politics from the time of its birth in 1861, would lose his clout to the likes of fellow Republican Francis Brownell (the young attorney sent by the Rockefeller interests to keep tabs on the Everett project). Just as Snohomish had wrested power from Mukilteo in the 1860s, Everett would wrest the power from Snohomish in the 1890s.

After years of struggle, the Great Northern finally was completed in early 1893. On January 6 the last spike was driven near Scenic, about 13 miles west of Stevens Pass in the Cascade Mountains. The long awaited rail link with the east was now completed, and it did not take James J. Hill long to reveal his terminus plans. His line did indeed reach salt water at Everett, but the western terminus would be Seattle, some 30 miles south via the Seattle and Montana, where he had been given great real estate concessions. Regardless of this disappointment, Everett and Snohomish County were now connected via rail with the markets of the east and midwest. The first through train reached Lowell on February 28. Less than a month later 40 railcars loaded with shingles from Everett's bay front Neff and Mish shingle mill rolled on to the Great Northern tracks. It was Everett's first full freight load to be sent eastward via rail.

112

An Editor in Snohomish

By George E. Macdonald

Known throughout the English-speaking world of radicals and liberals as the Grand Old Man of Free Thought, George E. Macdonald died June 21, 1944, aged eighty-seven. For half a century he had edited The Truth Seeker, Rationalist periodical in New York. Friend of Robert G. Ingersoll, of Clarence Darrow, of Ernst Haeckel, and of Sir Hiram Maxim. Mr. Macdonald war a careful and forceful writer, and when he turned to his autobiography, he revealed a fine sense of narrative and no less of good humor. Born In New Hampshire, he came to the Pacific Northwest in 1891 to serve as coeditor of The Eye, a newspaper at Snohomish, Washington, and a lively time he had of it. This firsthand account of life in a new Northwest town is taken from Mr. Macdonald's *Fifty Years of Freethought.*

When my wife and I arrived in summer 1891, the town of Snohomish, Washington, was not to be called a quiet hamlet. It was full of people, all moving. A desperado with a hotel hack seized us at the station, outside the business belt, and set us down in the center of population. While we gave admiring attention to a rider who managed his loping horse with a single line around the animal's jaw, C. H. Packard, editor and publisher of *The Eye*, who had induced the to come to Snohomish from New York, rushed up and named us.

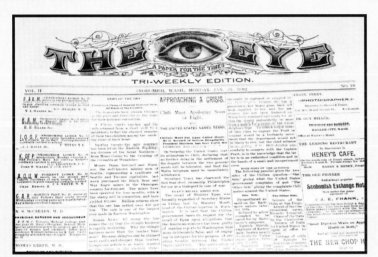

Packard had selected a room for us at the Maple House, a hotel hanging over the river, and to the Maple House we went. We saw that Main Street was closely companied for a little distance by the Snohomish river. Houseboats lined the shores.

After being introduced to the printers on the following morning, I inquired which type was dead and "threw in a case." It lay before me to learn what was news in this town and where to look for it, and then to divide my time between fathering it and putting it in press. Mr. Packard wrote a paragraph for *The Eye* introducing me as the new city editor. He did not forget to name certain well-known publications, *Puck*, *Judge* and so forth, to which I had contributed. The city editor, when city editing, went to the justice's court, or to the superior court, or to a meeting of the city council, or to the opening of a new store or café, or he might absorb an item from observation or interview, and returned with the proceeds to the office. He then turned his notes into copy, and helped to put them into type; he proved the galley with a towel wrapped around a planer, read and corrected proof, transferred the matter from the forms and locked them up, put the forms on the press, and perhaps took a turn at feeding. Before I became accustomed to press work, I spoiled a set of rollers try starting the press when they were lifted at one end. The sentiments that Packard managed to contain regarding a man, drunk or sober, who would start a press without looking at tho rollers, did him honor.

There was in our city another paper, the *Daily Sun*, upon which Packard looked with disfavor. The picture of its editor formed in the mind from the way Packard spoke his name fitted the man himself pretty well when one came to see him. He must have met with disappointments in life that had disillusioned him, for he had a saturnine countenance, a harsh laugh, and the morose outlook of a cynic. He was thought, in *The Eye* office, to be fit for treason, stratagems and spoils, and suspected of being on the outlook for opportunities for practicing them. Before I had ever laid eyes on the man, Packard one day said to me: "Here, Mac, is something on Frank Mussetter that I want you to write up." I asked: "What infamy has Mussetter been up to now" and Packard replied: "Why, God damn it—" and then outlined in expletives the character of Mussetter. Our contemporary, it appears, had suppressed or misstated facts of public interest in order, as it was our place to allege, to curry favor with a certain low element and put *The Eye* in wrong. Hence I wrote the editorial, unconsciously using fighty language, and our afternoon edition gave it circulation. The consequences were set forth in the next number of our publication, in an editorial which read:

A fierce-looking individual, loaded with several inches of adulterated, hydrant water and a big revolver, which he said he had borrowed especially for the present crisis, awaited the senior *Eye* man's return from breakfast last Saturday morning. The distinguishing features of the combination were those of Frank Mussetter, editor and reputed. owner of our at times luminous contemporary. Mussetter was evidently riled. He reads *The Eye* and thus keeps thoroughly posted on local and domestic affairs, although the scarcity of news and original editorial in his own paper might lead subscribers to doubt it. As we said before, Mussetter was riled. It might have been *The Eye's* scoop in exposing a priestly scandal and the Sun's supposed connection with the affair, but he didn't say so directly. Placing his good right hand in his pistol pocket, he inquired in a fierce, double-leaded voice fortified with beer if *The Eye* had a gun. Being informed that the chief engineer of this great moulder of public opinion was not in the habit of having such dangerous things in his possession when inside the city limits (vide Ordinance No. 4), Mussetter cautioned us to procure a weapon. He said he had come to shoot us; that he had borrowed a gun from Charlie Cyphers with that object in view, and he proposed to use it. He was informed that he would probably never flail a better opportunity than now presented; also that be was making a damn fool of himself. *The Eye* man explained that he was not a shootist, but would try to accommodate him with all the satisfaction he wanted in any other way. Mussetter averted that both he and his paper had been greatly hurt (and we don't doubt it) by *The Eye's* articles, the truthfulness of which he did not deny; and that be would be satisfied with nothing short of shooting us. However, he graciously concluded to postpone the killing, and gracefully withdrew, remarking in a four-to-pica tone of voice, that he would surely open fire the next time he met us, and that we had better be prepared to meet our God, or words to that effect.

Siwash Indians lived in wickiups along the banks of the Snohomish river, and paddled up and down the stream in dugout canoes. "Canoe" brings to mind a kind of small and light craft, generally employed for idle uses, such as taking a girt out on the Charles river in Massachusetts. I have seen a Siwash canoe probably 18 feet long and of four-foot beam, that carried the load of a moving-van, including the family. The Siwashes were savage as to their mode of life, but peaceable and friendly toward their fellow men. So far as I could make out, they had solved the problem of living without labor. With so many salmon in the stream they did not have to work; they went fishing.

Nevertheless civilization was in the process of absorbing them. Younger men went out as farmhands; the old men and women were most numerous in the wickiups. A government reservation at nearby Tulalip drew many away from the streams. Early settlers who, according to ancient history were deserters from British men-of-war had found their way up the rivers around Puget Sound and lived with the Siwashes, squatting on the land or buying it from the natives. The white men bought their Indian wives of fathers, brothers, or perhaps of husbands. The sale of a girl by her father to a man who said he wanted her for a wife was upheld by the courts as legal in this country, which in 1891 had been a state for only two years.

A young man settling there on a farm 70 years ago could make no better investment of his money or spare stock than to toy a wife with it, for the Indian women were good helpers about a place, and the children could be worked as they grew up. How many wives some of them bought I am not interested to know. The federal law that was passed for the abolition of polygamy in Utah in the 1880s did away with the plural wife system among these old settlers to Washington, who were expected to acknowledge the wife they had taken last and discontinue the others. They obeyed the law by establishing the senior spouse as wife. As regards the rest, it was said that to avoid inflicting hardships on them they were retained in the family as maids. None of the so-called squawmen lived inside the Snohomish city limits; they were ranchers. One of them, when his elder wife died, moved into town and married white. But he kept his ranch, and how large a population of secondary wives and their children the ranch maintained you could only judge from appearances. The man kept a general store in town. I saw one day a troop of mounted Indians galloping through the streets, and inquired of an older resident whether this was a massacre. He said no, it was only So-and-so's family going to his store for provisions…some of the best-looking girls in town were half or quarter Indian. The first year was the hardest, for *The Eye* was a Republican paper, and took sides in politics. Although I had been voting the Republican ticket since 1880, when it came to writing editorials I simply didn't know how. A book in *The Eye's* library, entitled *A History of the Republican Party,* was the source of all I wrote in defense of the GOP. By good luck the need for these editorials ceased; Packard espoused the cause of Populism and wrote with such zeal that *The Eye* thereafter was never short of timely political matter.

The Eye was a good paper too. We brought it out as a tri-weekly, filled with local and county news, and every issue had a real editorial; and all that had been in the tri-weekly went into the weekly edition, where the accumulated editorials made a full page, as in the best city papers. No man in the county had a better reputation for honesty and squareness than Packard. His probity was unimpeachable.

The Press is said to be for sale. I never heard of any schemer trying to buy the opinion of our paper, and I was myself corrupted but once. That was when a man just starting a game down the street and mistakenly supposing I was going to make an outcry over it, took me aside and said that as *The Eye* had always used him well, he would like to show his appreciation. He was opening a little place, he said, to give the boys a chance to get action on their money; and while it was not the kind of proposition that competed for advertising space, still the Press ought to be supported by all good citizens. Then to my surprise he passed me a 20-dollar gold piece.

As the first proffer of a bribe in my newspaper experience it produced in me a hitherto unknown reaction. On the spur of the moment one was not sure what one ought to do with the money or the base wretch offering it. While I mulled over the situation he invited me to step inside and see his little roulette layout. And now my course became clear. I changed the 20 into silver dollars and, picking number 27, told the

man who turned the wheel to let it spin. He complied and announced "little 2-0." The other plays which I then tried were like the first one, and in half an hour I walked virtuously forth, carrying with me none of the wages of corruption.

During my city editorship of *The Eye,* I made an excursion to a "future metropolis" which the prospectus called Ocosta-by-the-Sea. The attractive name was the gift of Tacoma realtors interested is adjacent lands. The promoters organized a committee to entertain the gentlemen of the Press. By error, invitations were sent to the newspapers in Seattle and Snohomish, promising transportation, hotel accommodations, and entertainment to editors and their wives "as free as air." The city editor of *The Eye* and Mr. Stinger of the Snohomish *Sun* answered the invitation by letter. The committee in rejoiner gave them to understand that railroad trains were waiting for them to hop aboard. But the conductors declined to pass the editors and their wives on the strength of the committee's promises; so each of the editors paid $20.20 for carfare. The further "hospitality" of the committee was enjoyed at an average cost of $15 per editor and wife. Ocosta, when reached, we observed to be a marsh, with raised wooden walks, to which the appearance of being lined with trees had been given by spiking evergreens, or small saplings, to the string pieces of the walks every 10 or 15 feet The editors stopped, looked, and gave judgment. Said Mr. Sanger: "We have walked into the jaws of a big fake."

The committee had made provisions for 50 guests, and 600 strangers were present. The committee compromised by selecting for its hospitality the newspapermen from Tacoma and points south, which did not include the Seattle and Snohomish editors…I never went back to see how Ocosta-by-the-Sea came out. After what I said about the place in *The Eye*, I couldn't look for an invitation to return, except to explain myself.

Nearer home, however, I witnessed the transformation of a wilderness into a city. Downstream a few miles from Snohomish there used to be a landing place called The Portage. Between the Snohomish river and the waters of Puget Sound lies a peninsula. Mud and sand flats at the mouth of the Snohomish river interfere with navigation. For that reason, at this place a few miles downstream from Snohomish city, freight and passengers formerly were taken overland to deep water on the Sound side, which was Port Gardiner. The Portage and Port Gardiner are now no more. When I reached those regions in 1891 a land company had bought the peninsula to start a city on. The ground had to be cleared by uprooting and burning stumps, and the first time I saw the place it was smoking, A few weeks later a wide planked thoroughfare a mile and a half long bearing the name of an avenue ran lengthwise the neck of land, and there being no buildings as yet, merchants carried on business in tents. They christened the place Everett, after a future New Jersey politician named Colby, whose father was chief promoter.

Word soon went out that the Great Northern Railroad, then under construction by James J. Hill, would have its western terminal at Everett. They built a wharf and advertised that whale-back ships from Duluth or Superior, in Wisconsin, would soon make port there. It was going to be the first city of the Sound, with Seattle second. Everett never fulfilled 10 percent of its ballyhoo. Nevertheless, in a remarkably short time it had a resident, maybe, for every stump that had been pulled, or a population of 7,000, twice that of Snohomish, while the Everett Land Company controlled county politics and patronage.

Until the city of Everett was built up, just a few miles away, Snohomish had been the county seat and the center of traffic for the region. Now business departed. The hotels emptied, houses became vacant, the merchants lost their trade, labor was idle. The election went against *The Eye,* which without the city printing must take in its sign as official city paper. Advertisements disappeared from its pages or were run free to economize on composition and boiler plate. Lawyers and lodges, moving away, withdrew their cards. The character of the population changed and fewer knew or cared for *The Eye* as the historic county paper. Two other journals survived in Snohomish: *The Democrat,* which fed on public pap, and *The Tribune,* which had been bought by a couple of enterprising young men who knew what sort of a paper such a town as Snohomish was destined to become, a village of families, would read.

In past times, if I said to Justice Griffith, our best source of local news: "Have any items of news come under your judicial cognizance today?" he was likely to reply. "You may say that out-of-town relations bummed a Sunday dinner off our local society leader, Mrs. Barnum, yesterday." That was just the kind of news Packard and I overlooked, and it was the sort, less cynically worded, that the young fellows of *The Tribune* featured. A woman could not go for a horseback ride on the Pilchuck road without getting her name into *The Tribune.*

Conducting *The Eye* was a two-man business no longer and likely to become less so. I communicated with my brother in New York, who said that *The Truth Seeker,* which he then edited and on which I had worked, stood in need of my services. I then let Packard know that I was leaving. He fain would have condoled with me over the outcome of my venture into country journalism, but I wouldn't dole. I felt like repeating to Snohomish and its remaining people the formula of the departing guest: "I have enjoyed my visit very much, and it was kind of you to have me."

In other railroad developments, the Northern Pacific had taken control of the Seattle, Lake Shore and Eastern in early 1892 as a means of securing a rail line to Canada. Meanwhile, another railroad called the Snohomish, Skykomish and Spokane, or more commonly the "3S," was building a line from Snohomish to Everett on the north bank of the river, crossing at Lowell. When Hewitt saw this as a potential link for the run from Monte Cristo, he quietly purchased a controlling interest and absorbed it. On July 19 the rails of the "3S" were tied into those of the Seattle and Montana at the tip of the Everett peninsula near the smelter. Shortly before that connection, Hewitt's new Everett and Monte Cristo Railway Company was incorporated with a capitalization of $1,800,000. The basic route for the Everett & Monte Cristo would be from the mines down the south fork of the Stillaguamish River to Granite Falls and then over to a connection with the Northern Pacific (former Seattle, Lake Shore and Eastern) at Hartford, a mile north of Lake Stevens. This would lead down to north Snohomish and then utilize the former "3S" right-of-way for the final leg to Lowell, Everett, and the smelter.

The railroad was completed in September 1893, when the engineers and construction crew finally overcame the challenges of building through the South Fork Stillaguamish River's deep and narrow Robe Canyon east of Granite Falls and up the grade to Monte Cristo. The town site of Monte Cristo was filed by the Everett syndicate and lots sold. A five-story plant was built to reduce ore from the various mines to concentrate for processing at the Everett smelter.

Entering 1893, the Everett boom still was in full swing. The Polk Company produced the community's first city directory in January and estimated the town site's population as 5,452. Snohomish was the county's second largest community with an estimated population of 2,500. Other population estimates in that first Polk directory included: Stanwood (1,000), Edmonds (700), Arlington (500), Sultan City (350), and Mukilteo (300). The next year's directory added Marysville (700), Monte Cristo (400), Hartford (300), and Haller City (400). Arlington, Haller City, and Edmonds were noted as centers of lumber and shingle manufacturing. Arlington also was described as an area where much land was being brought under cultivation, while Stanwood was noted as a rich agricultural district. Mukilteo was mentioned as a port of call for steamers, and Sultan City was considered a distribution center for mining camps.

Other 1893 county developments included the filing of the plat of Index on April 25. Three months later a huge fire destroyed virtually everything in town except the Great Northern depot and station house. A wagon road was built to connect Hartford with Everett. The expansion of agriculture throughout the county led to the development of the Farmers' Alliance, which by spring 1893 had lodges in most every rural locality. The Alliance was a precursor to the Populist movement, which would sweep through the county a few years later. The mining town of Silverton, located on the Everett and Monte Cristo Railway a few miles northwest of the town of Monte Cristo, was platted.

The year 1893 also saw the birth of the county poor farm. This home for the indigent was built near Monroe on a site later occupied by Valley General Hospital. Costing $4,500, the two story wooden structure had 20 beds. The charge was to "Keep, clothe, properly care for and furnish medicine for each of the county paupers at 85 cents a day, except such as may be suffering from contagious disease." Overseer John Conway was paid $100 a month to administer the operation and provide services. The poor farm was serving 26 individuals, including four females, by the end of the decade and continued in operation well into the twentieth century. While the number of residents—or "inmates" as they were called—was not large, the dire admonition that, "You're going to end up in the poor farm," carried a special meaning in county lore.

On the economic front, mining captured the romantic spirit, but lumbering was still the county's dominant activity. Logging camps abounded to feed the many shingle and lumber mills. In 1893 the county shingle output was reported to be 313,830,000 with a value of $417,932. Everett alone was reported to have produced 92,000,000 shingles

Public social services were rudimentary at best. In 1893 the county constructed its Poor Farm on Allen Prairie west of Monroe, providing shelter for 20 people. Shown here in 1909, it later became the site of Valley General Hospital. (Courtesy Monroe Historical Society)

and 23,300,000 board feet of lumber. The county demonstrated the pride in its forest products industry with its contributions to the 1893 World Exposition in Chicago. The Mosher and McDonald Logging Company provided 16 timbers, all 42 inches in diameter and up to 44 feet long, to be used in the construction of three Washington State buildings at the fair. These logs were placed in a manner to create a magnificent log cabin effect in the lower 15 feet of the massive structures. Snohomish's E.C. Ferguson contributed a section of 18-inch fir bark for display. It was reported to be the thickest bark ever known. Loggers from Arlington furnished a 200-foot tall flagstaff, which was said to be the largest on the fair grounds.

In April 1893 the city of Everett incorporated, and a city government came into being. The roadblock to incorporation had been removed when the Everett Land Company finally acquired valuable tidelands whose ownership had been in dispute. Thomas "Ed" Dwyer was elected mayor, and the first meeting of the new government took place on May 9. Just as the Everett government was getting started, the county government was in a state of turmoil. Bitter rivalries between the Republicans, Democrats, and Populists had left the county with representatives from each party in various offices. There was little compromise, and the three-cornered fight over issues such as taxes nearly tore the county apart. A dispute over who should pay how much contributed to lower tax receipts. Wages of certain county workers were reduced, but the pay of others was increased. This situation heightened the anger and suspicion already prevalent at the courthouse.

The year had begun well locally, but by spring disturbing economic developments were beginning to send a pall across the nation. The New York Stock Exchange trembled in May and then crashed on June 27, 1893. It was the beginning of the "Panic of 1893," the worst depression to that point in the nation's history. By the end of the year an estimated 4,000 banks across the country had closed, 74 railroads were in receivership, and nearly 15,000 businesses had failed. Snohomish County was a microcosm of the national picture. The Minneapolis Realty and Investment Company, which had its grand

118

plans for Edmonds, was among the many businesses that collapsed. Log and lumber prices fell, with the ensuing closure of camps and mills throughout the county. The effect rippled into nearly every aspect of community life. The shortage of funds for county government resulted in employees receiving warrants that were worth 90 cents on the dollar. Stanwood's Methodist minister, R.K. White, resigned because he could not live on a salary that had slid to 26 cents a day. Ida Stephens of the Monroe area remarked that you could buy a yard of calico for a nickel—if you had a nickel.

The panic was particularly hard on new enterprises such as the Everett project. Three of Everett's five banks were closed by December 31. Most industries were operating intermittently, if at all. To complicate matters further, the entire mining/smelting scenario was showing ominous signs. The difficulty in transporting ore from mine to smelter, concerns about the quantity and quality of the ore, and the national collapse of precious metal prices were raising questions about whether the operation ever could be profitable. The Everett Land Company failed to meet the Rucker Brothers "Remarkable Document" requirement of erecting a sawmill within 18 months, and thus began a series of revised

deadlines, each of which the Land Company failed to meet. Dutifully the Ruckers would report each failure and then enter into another amendment. Eventually Everett Land Company Manager Schuyler Duryee would acknowledge that the multiple amendments were no fault of the Ruckers and a credit to their patience.

As the fiscal picture worsened, the Everett Land Company slid into critical financial woes. Officials of the company disagreed about the measures that should be taken. Henry Hewitt wanted to wait out the tough times, but this was not acceptable to his colleagues. Pressured by the Rockefeller forces, he resigned as president and in 1894 was not even re-elected to the Board of Trustees. Colby and Hoyt attempted to take charge, but their leadership floundered when the Land Company could not pay the interest on its bonds,

The Sunset Telephone Company began Everett's first telephone system in Novermber, 1892 with 50 to 60 subscribers. Within a few years there were half a dozen separate companies, each with its own lines and operators. Where rival companies served the same area, businesses had to have two separate numbers. City Livery and Feed Stable in Snohomish, for example, could be reached at both Independent 452 and Sunset 117. (Courtesy Everett Public Library)

most of which were now held by Rockefeller. The oil billionaire, who, by some reports, had been drawn into the project during a time of personal distress, was now aroused to action. He summoned Frederick Gates, a trusted financial advisor, to extract him from the mess. With Colby and Hoyt relegated to secondary roles, Gates, a former Baptist minister, came to Everett to carry out his superior's order. Gates was not a cut and run operative. Over the next few years he methodically and skillfully maneuvered the various Rockefeller-owned enterprises into positions of consolidations and sales. It would take him nearly a decade, but eventually Gates would untangle Rockefeller from the Everett/Monte Cristo web and from some accounts turn a profit in the process.

If the "Panic of 1893" were a concern at the local level, it certainly wasn't indicated in the year-end issues of the Everett newspapers. Under the headline "IN STRONG SHAPE", the December 28, 1893 *Everett Herald* related the "voluntary retirement" of Henry Hewitt as Everett Land Company president and the appointment of Charles Colby to the position. Praising both men and others involved in the company, the *Herald* concluded that "Everett's prestige is unequalled by any new city in the United States." *The Everett News*, with reference to attributes of the nail works, pulp mill and smelter, was equally upbeat. *The News* pointed to the impressive production by Everett's 12 lumber and wood products manufacturing plants and the four shingle mills, which it said were cutting half a million shingles per day. While the news media's search for optimism may have been admirable, the "Panic of 1893" was very real—and, it was not confined to 1893. Its effects continued well into mid-decade.

Ironically, many new county mills and lumbering projects were being established in 1894, when the market trend was downward. Most were fairly small operations. Hope for the forest products industries took a leap forward in 1895 with a report that midwestern lumbering magnate Frederick Weyerhaeuser would be visiting the Puget Sound area. Meanwhile, shingle manufacturers were surpassing the sawmills as the major forest products producers. August 1895 figures from the assessor's office indicated that eight of the county's 11 sawmills were operating, and the total output was about 60 percent of capacity. Forty of the county's 41 shingle mills were in production with a daily output of 1,640,000 shingles.

Two of the county's major industries reached milestones in 1894. The first carload of ore—one that came from the Deer Creek area near Silverton—was shipped on the Everett and Monte Cristo Railway. The ore arrived at the Everett smelter on January 2. Thus, the railroad and the smelter finally were in operation. On October 24, 1894 the whaleback steamer *City of Everett* was launched at the Pacific Steel and Barge Works. A crowd estimated at 10,000 gathered to watch the steel-hulled vessel slide into the waters of the Snohomish River. Nearly 350 feet in length, the *City of Everett* was, up to that time, the largest ship ever built in the Pacific Northwest.

The county's agricultural picture experienced changes during the mid-1890s. In parallel with the forest products expansion, farming was increasing despite the county's depressed economy. An 1895 County Assessor's statement reported 2,450 farms. Oats were the most common grain, with 5,000 acres under cultivation.

The county's ideal environment for dairying had brought that activity into prominence. The county's first creamery was established in Snohomish in 1894, but it did not succeed. Several other successful

Only one ship ever was produced at the Pacific Steel Barge Works. The steel hulled "City of Everett" was launched on October 24, 1894 as a crowd of thousands watched. At 346 feet in length and 2504 tons, it was up to that time the largest ship yet constructed in the Puget Sound region. Reportedly, it was the first American steam powered ship to pass through the Suez Canal and circumnavigate the globe. The "City of Everett" was lost in the Gulf of Mexico in 1923. (Courtesy Everett Public Library)

creameries, however, opened within a year. The two which emerged as the most widely known were in Monroe and Stanwood. The latter city's operation, the Stanwood Co-Operative Creamery, was particularly renowned. Started in 1895, it was out of debt within a year and using up to 7,000 pounds of milk per day. The creamery took first place at the 1896 Pierce County Fair and first place at the State Dairy Association conclave two years later in Ellensburg. Poultry raising also came into being during this time with the opening of a "chicken ranch" in 1894, but it would be well into the twentieth century before poultry became an important agricultural pursuit. The same was true for fruit growing. Strawberries, for example, were first shipped to Seattle in 1895, and a horticultural society organized in Sultan the previous year. However, fruit growing was not a major commercial venture until after the turn of the century.

While individuals and businesses struggled to survive the difficult fiscal times of mid-decade, a political struggle of a different ilk was raging. Everett's sudden emergence as the county's largest city resulted in a fight over the location of the county seat. In early 1893 there were indications that Everett had its eye on that symbol of leadership. In February of that year the Everett Land Company offered to pay half of the expense of a road to Granite Falls and to help other towns with better roads. Critics labeled this part of a scheme to court goodwill and make it appear the desire to move the county seat from Snohomish to Everett was a grounds well throughout the county. Several Everett organizations, including the Young Men's Democratic Club and the Business Men's Association, began to agitate for the switch. The movement gathered momentum in May of 1893 when the businessmen of Everett appointed a committee "to secure the county seat." Spurred by the committee, the Everett City Council proposed a special city election to approve the purchase of a courthouse site for $30,000. The measure passed by an overwhelming 615 to 22 vote, and Everett was clearly on the path to battle Snohomish.

On September 2, 1894 an Everett county seat petition with 1,884 signatures was submitted to the County Commissioners. This mandated the Commissioners to submit the matter to the electorate: November 6, 1894 would be the day of decision. The pre-election campaign included spirited and sometimes coarse debate. The *Everett News* editor labeled his counterparts at the Snohomish *Tribune* as "gibbering idiots," and the Snohomish newsmen responded in kind.

When the election finally took place, a delay of ballots and claims of fraud by both sides led to a canvass of the vote. The complicated and controversial review, undertaken in an atmosphere of mistrust and threats of violence, finally resulted in the Commissioners declaring Everett the victor. Records were to be moved to Everett by January 21, 1895. The Snohomish supporters, however, were not ready to concede. They carried the battle all the way to the Washington State Supreme Court, which decreed the returns had not been properly examined, and Snohomish still was the county seat. Now the Everett supporters retaliated and eventually were able to force the Commissioners to re-canvass the vote. This recount gave Everett more than the 60 percent majority needed for approval, and they declared Everett to be the "county seat on and after November 5, 1895." Snohomish once again was aroused, but neither side seemed eager actively to pursue a prolonged court battle that would unearth both sides' unsavory—and, frequently fraudulent—election activities. There was ample evidence, for example, that Everett had paid some Seattle residents $2.00 a person to vote. On the other hand, at least 200 of the

In 1895 the Stanwood Cooperative Creamery opened for business, processing milk from Stillaguamish Valley farmers and winning prizes for its top quality butter. Located on the hill above East Stanwood, its first president was the Reverend Christian Joergenson. (Courtesy Stanwood Area Historical Society)

Snohomish voters were known to be permanent residents of the Snohomish G.A.R. Cemetery. The State Supreme Court was back in the fray, however, and in December 1896 ruled that the October 1895 re-canvass by the Commissioners was valid. Everett had won. In January 1897 a long line of empty wagons arrived in Snohomish to cart the county records to the "City of Smokestacks." A new Romanesque-style brick courthouse was erected in Everett, and the Snohomish building began its second career as a school. Feelings between the communities ran high for decades, but eventually the fight would be forgotten to a point that reading about it years later was an exercise in comedy relief.

The county seat fight was not the only political activity making headlines in mid-decade. The nation's fiscal condition had led to the development of the People's Party, better known as the Populists. Roots for Populism could be found in the Farmers' Alliance, which had first been established in Texas in 1877 to lead the farmers against the practices of the huge and powerful railroad companies. By the 1890s Populists were an amalgamation of rural and urban citizens who called for reform that would give more power and protection to the "common man." Snohomish County, as much of the nation, was ripe for the Populist revolt. The dismal financial situation had convinced substantial numbers of county dwellers of their victimization by ruthless capitalists. Many felt their destinies were controlled by outside interests with no conscience and no concern for anything but profit. Actions such as the nail company's move to increase the price of nails from 85-cents to $2.80 with no increase in the workers' wages reinforced the Populist sentiment.

The Populists first appeared as a county political force in 1892. Two years later their candidates outpolled the Democrats for nearly every county office and seriously challenged the victorious Republicans. Washington State Republicans held their 1896 convention in Everett, but the bigger local story was the merging of the Populists and Democrats into a Fusionist party that captured every county office in the November election. The county sent Fusionists to the state legislature and helped elect Populist John Rogers the state governor. William Jennings Bryan, the Populist whom the Democrats had nominated as their presidential candidate, failed in his national quest, but he carried the county with a nearly two-thirds majority. The Populists' control in the county would prove to be short lived, however. Improved business conditions in the last few years of the decade, failure to hold together the rural and urban sectors, grand jury charges of county government graft, and the defeat of Bryan all contributed to the rapid decline of the movement. In 1898 the Republicans regained control of most important county offices. Bryan would carry the presidential candidate banner again for the Democrats in 1900, and he would even appear at Everett's nail works on April 6 to promote his cause. Then he would lose to President William McKinley again, and this time he would not even carry Snohomish County.

As the county slugged out its political battles, the local press continued to search for signs of improved economic conditions. In February 1895 *The Everett Herald* reported that Bureau Veritas, a French marine insurance rating company, gave the *City of Everett* its highest rating. Captain F. D. Herriman of the firm stated, "The whaleback is destined to control the commerce on the Pacific Coast and ocean at an early day. You people of Everett are fortunate in having the American Steel Barge Company's yards here. They will be taxed to their utmost capacity for the next few years." The January 4, 1896 edition of the *Everett News* described a large mill to be built on the Everett bay front and an *Everett Herald* of the same week cited activity at several Everett industries as proof that "Everett is in better condition today than at the beginning of 1895." This rosy assessment did not assuage the economic realities. The barge works never produced another vessel. The Everett smelter was more often closed than opened. Even its newspapers folded. Massive unemployment had followed completion of the Great Northern and Everett & Monte Cristo. The city of Snohomish collapsed economically. A broken Snohomish is poignantly described in the diaries of Philip Clayton Van Buskirk, a United States Navy career man who periodically visited the Puget Sound area in the 1880s and 1890s. Arriving in Snohomish in 1896 with the intent of retiring in the vicinity, Van Buskirk saw a place that had dramatically deteriorated since his visit in the early 1890s. His walk through downtown led him to observe, " . . . save here and there a group of vicious looking youngsters, very few people are in the streets . . . Wilbur's Drug Store, a fine brick building, appears alone to have held its own in the general dilapidation and decay which marks the Business quarter of Snohomish, altogether a woebegone, run down town."

Residents were encouraged by lumberman Fredrick Weyerhaeuser's visit to the county in 1895. Yet, no amount of optimistic speculation could conceal the real picture. Perhaps no single event made reality clearer than the 1895 financial collapse of Snohomish pioneer Isaac Cathcart. He had first settled in the town during 1869 as a tree faller in the logging industry. Over the years he branched into a variety of enterprises, building an empire that included farms, construction companies, telegraph business, a hotel, a store, mills, logging operations and land investment. In 1880, he completed an opera house, which became a center for Snohomish community social gatherings. There was even a town named for him on the Seattle, Lake Shore and Eastern Railway south of Snohomish. By the early 1890s he had amassed a fortune estimated at $500,000, and he was considered the wealthiest man in the county. In May 1895, however, listing liabilities of $50,000, he executed a trust mortgage in favor of his creditors, covering all his property. His assets were listed at $100,000—but that was on paper. In reality, little beyond the $50,000 was realized. Thereafter he was finished as a figure in county financial affairs. It was chilling proof that no one was exempt from fiscal disaster.

During this time of economic and political unrest several women's organizations came into existence. Excluded from the power structure of business and politics, the women focused on human needs and social reform. Churches and lodges, which proliferated during the 1890s, operated in a similar arena, but with different emphasis than the women's groups. One example was the Woman's Columbian Book Club of Everett, which was formed in 1894. Formal organization followed the group's successful effort in supporting Everett's first hospital. Once organized, they pushed for a public library, which through their efforts came to fruition in 1898. The determination of the group is evident in the statement of first president Alice Baird, "We do not mean to let a single year go by without doing at least one good thing for our city." Another group was the Everett branch of the Women's Relief Corps, organized in 1895. The purpose was to aid the aging Union Army veterans from the Civil War. Snohomish's Cosmopolitan Club began in 1898 as a child study group and sponsored a kindergarten. Under the leadership of individuals such as Margaret McCready, the club accomplished much. The Cosmopolitan and Everett Book clubs belonged to the State and National Federations of Women's Clubs, which became powerful forces during the first half of the twentieth century.

By 1897 there were signs of improvement. Frederick Weyerhaeuser visited the Puget Sound area again, and this time he brought as his guests about 70 leading lumbermen. There was no immediate impact in Snohomish County, but the prospects for investment by these industry leaders did buoy spirits. Public confidence leaped in 1897 when Klondike gold rush fever hit the local area. Although Seattle would become the Pacific Northwest outfitting and supply center for those headed north to Alaska, the excitement would uplift the entire Puget Sound area. Snohomish County residents were among those, too, who ventured north in search of gold. Most returned with nothing except stories of anguish. There were notable exceptions, such as East Stanwood's Henry "Klondike" Anderson, who returned to help found a bank and build a magnificent mansion overlooking the town, and Francis Giard, another East Stanwood resident who became a major landowner, farmer and businessman.

In spite of the ups and downs, Snohomish County was growing. The increase of Sultan's population, as reported in the January 7, 1897 edition of *The Everett Herald*, illustrated what was happening throughout the county. The town had grown from 1894 to 1896, and the population was now calculated at 780 for the precinct. More children continued to be enrolled in the public schools. There were 76 school districts in the county by 1897. By 1899, the number would increase two more with a total enrollment of

In 1894 members of the newly organized Woman's Columbian Book Club of Everett gave major support to the recently opened Everett Hospital, the city's first. Although the facility was forced to close and reorganize in the ensuing depression, the building at 3322 Broadway next was used as a home for Bethania College and then the location for Bethany Home for the Aged before it was demolished and replaced by a brick structure. Both the women's book club and Bethany continue to flourish. (Courtesy Everett Public Library)

more than 5,500 students. Everett's enrollment pattern, which showed a constant increase except for a small dip in 1894, was probably typical of county school growth. The city had 845 students in 1895 and 1,534 by 1899.

Interest in recreation and leisure activities increased also. Baseball, which had been played in Snohomish City as early as 1877, was the major sport. Shortly after Everett was established, there was a town baseball team, which lost to Snohomish by a score of 39 to 5. The premier local baseball player of the era was Snohomish's Walter Thornton, who made it to the major leagues as a pitcher for the Chicago Cubs, then called the Colts. Rugby football is reported to have been played in 1893, and Snohomish defeated Everett 10 to 0 in a celebrated 1894 football game. Horse racing had a foothold by the 1880s. In the mid-1890s both Stanwood and Snohomish boasted of busy horse racing tracks. Even in the tight money times, some of the purses were said to total $1,500. A bicycling craze swept the county in the late 1890s. By now, several communities had sufficient roads to accommodate the cycles, which included everything from the unicycle to the ten-tandem models. Marysville bragged of having two wheels (bicycles) for every 10 people in town. Golden Eagle wheels cost about $30.00, and the very popular Phoenix model went for $40.00. A whole culture of cycling etiquette developed and appeared in printed form. One of the favored biking routes passed through the famous bicycle tree near Snohomish, where a 12-foot high five-foot wide arch had been cut through a giant cedar. Countless bikers had their photographs taken at that spot.

On the business front, the county was launched into a new era of mining and related enterprises when its first load of ore arrived at the Everett smelter in January of 1894. By the beginning of 1895, Monte Cristo was thriving with nearly 200 town residents and several hundred workers living in the boarding houses at the mines. The mines, along with those in Silverton, were producing much of the 80 tons of ore the Everett smelter was processing daily. By December 1894 the smelter had produced 3,000 ounces of gold, 60,000 ounces of silver and 500,000 pounds of lead. Labor troubles, the rugged terrain and the harsh winter weather frequently hampered the mining operations, however. The section of the Everett and Monte Cristo Railway through Robe canyon east of Granite Falls was proving to be especially vulnerable to the winter storms and floods. A major storm and flooding in November 1896 knocked out much of the route. It quickly was rebuilt, and by April 1897, the Monte Cristo mines were producing 1,000 tons of concentrate per week. In June of that year the Monte Cristo mining district was hailed as being the most productive in the state, with record loads being shipped. Total output up to June 1 was computed to be 3,500 carloads of gold and silver

Walter Thornton of Snohomish pitched four seasons in major league baseball. He threw a no-hitter, and batted .312 before quitting in a contract dispute. He returned to create powerful Everett teams. Then, under the influence of evangelist Billy Sunday, he left for a 45-year career as a street preacher in Los Angeles. (Courtesy Dave Larson and Everett Public Library)

ore. Unfortunately, this celebration of productivity would be short lived. Torrential rains in November again caused a massive flood that destroyed the canyon portion of the railroad and tore out track and bridges all along the line.

Then, on December 11, 1897, Frederick Gates, Rockefeller's representative who was overseeing the Everett and Monte Cristo enterprises, announced repairs would not be made. Stating that the railroad and the mines "never paid dividends . . . and had not panned out," Gates put the non-Rockefeller mining operatives in an untenable position. No railroad meant no way to ship their ore. At Gates' mercy, they were forced to sell to him or be driven into bankruptcy. By 1899 Rockefeller had the mines as well as the railroad and smelter. Though he ultimately would prove to be interested in none of them, it would give him an enviable bargaining chip with potential purchasers of any one of them. The rail line would be rebuilt but not until Rockefeller, through Gates, had further solidified his position. There would, in fact, be a rebirth of mining from 1901 to 1903 as Rockefeller neared the end of his Everett/Monte Cristo involvement.

While mining faded, logging and lumber increased during the mid- and final years of the decade. Shingle mills, in particular, proliferated throughout the county. One of the most impressive collection of mills was along the Edmonds waterfront. This included the Hatch and Basner Company, which produced nearly 20 million shingles in 1895, and also featured an electric generator to provide lights for the mill and its owners' homes. Logs and bolts (sections to be cut into shingles) were floated down the county's rivers in enormous quantities. The 1895 drive on the Stillaguamish River was estimated at 20 million board feet. Logging companies were pushing small railroads farther into the timberlands as another means of getting the timber out of the woods. One of the men who took a leading role in these ventures was Joe Irving of Everett. Huge, physically powerful, and fearless, his exploits in the lumber business became the stuff of legend. By the end of the decade, an estimated 1,500 loggers were busily reducing the approximately eight billion board feet of standing timber in Snohomish County. Everett alone had 14 mills in operation, and more would soon be on the way.

It came as a distinct shock then when

Cycling became very popular in the 1890s and early years of the twentieth century, a sport enjoyed by both men and women alike. With safer models of bicycles and the extension of roads, people rode out for picnics and popular destinations such as Snohomish's famous "Bicycle Tree" south of town, which remained a local landmark until 1928. Its successor cedar across the road lasted until 2002. (Ferguson album, courtesy Snohomish Historical Society)

on February 22, 1897 outgoing Democratic President Grover Cleveland issued a procla-
mation creating thirteen forest reserves in the West, including over 21 million acres in
Washington State. Included was the Washington Forest Reserve of three and a half million
acres in the northern Cascades, including Snohomish County. Cleveland had tried in
1891 and again in 1893 to set aside portions of the nation's remaining uncut forestlands,
but had been blocked by Congress and westerners who regarded public lands as theirs to
exploit.

Local reaction was furious. Cleveland's action, " is a fitting finale to the public career
of the most contemptible and most generally despised man in the United States," roared
the Snohomish *Eye* on March 4, 1897. "Concerted efforts will be made to have the present
congress undo the damnable work of Cleveland," the *Eye* concluded. So they were, but
the resulting modifications still created the basis for beginning a program of federal
forestry, while excluding agricultural and mining lands and allowing for flexibility in
timber use, land exchanges, and utilization by local settlers. An immediate effect was the
end of homesteading within the boundaries of the reserve along the upper reaches of the
county rivers, causing many settlers to leave and isolating town sites such as Silverton,
Monte Cristo, Mineral City, and Galena City.

In celebrating the 10th anniversary of statehood on November 11, 1899, Snohomish
County could look back on a decade of phenomenal change. The population had tripled. A
city which had not existed in 1889 was now the county's largest. The same new city was
also the county seat, with approximately one third of the county's 24,000 people residing
there. The 1900 census also showed a population that was predominantly Caucasian.
Racial minorities comprised only four percent of the population, with the largest numbers
being "Indian, Japanese, Negroes and Chinese" in that order. Transportation had changed
dramatically. Riverboats, which reached their peak around 1892, had been replaced
largely by railroads as the major means of moving both people and freight. Telephone
systems had developed as a means of communicating.

Significantly too, the county had lost its frontier persona. Saloons, brothels and
gambling houses still existed, but social institutions of a more orderly society were now
prevalent. Where there had been few churches, there were now many. Methodists,
Lutherans, Baptists, Catholics, Congregationalists, and Presbyterians were among the
congregations that flourished. The numbers of schools had increased markedly. By 1900
there were 93 districts, 83 buildings, and county school enrollment had passed the 5,000
mark. High school education had been made available in several communities. Labor
unions had been organized and would become increasingly important in the coming
decade. There was a plethora of social organizations—from Masonic orders to an Eastern
Star's women's group. There were but three banks in the county in 1889. All three were in
Snohomish and all had been organized within the previous two years. In 1899 there were
banks throughout the county, with the largest number in Everett. Significantly, most
people were living in cities and towns. It was becoming an urban society with a large
working class, primarily in the forest products industry. In this regard, an urban geography pattern that would prevail for the next half century had been established. Except for
Lake Stevens, which developed a few years later, the largest communities in 1900 would
still be the largest in 1950.

Stanwood, with its developing neighbor East Stanwood, was the pre-eminent com-

THE MINES OF MONTE CRISTO

Aerial tramway buckets carried ore from the mines high above the town down to the concentrator and railway, the weight of loaded ones enough to bring back up the empties. Speed was controlled by brakes on an eight foot diameter iron wheel which still rests atop Mystery Ridge. (Courtesy U.S. Forest Service)

Far above Weden Lake, the Del Campo mine operators reported values in gold, silver, and copper. James and Dan Kyes with Sheridan McElroy constructed the precarious building. Nearby Kyes Peak is named for James' son Jim, who climbed it in 1920 as a Boy Scout and was lost in World War II commanding the U.S.S. Leary. (Courtesy Enid Nordlund)

Working conditions were extremely difficult and dangerous due to steep terrain and mountain weather. This log cookhouse near the entrance to Glacier Basin served both the Mystery and Pride of the Mountains miners. "X" marks show where men were found after a lethal avalanche. (Meyer photo, courtesy U.S. Forest Service)

128

Dumas Street was the retail and lodging heart of Monte Cristo. Paved with forty foot wide planking, it was partially supported by cribwork above the steep gorge of Seventy six Creek. (Gifford Pinchot, 1897, courtesy The National Archives)

The United Companies concentrator contained two sets of machinery, one for the Rockefeller-owned mines near Glacier Basin and the other for the Wilmans' operations on Wilmans Peak. From here the concentrates were sent down to the Everett smelter. (Ferguson album, courtesy Snohomish Historical Society)

Lifeline for Monte Cristo mining was the Everett & Monte Cristo Railway. Rainy season floods and rock falls caused continual disruptions in Robe Canyon, shown here at Tunnel 5. (Courtesy David Cameron)

129

munity of the lower Stillaguamish River valley. Noted for its large concentration of Scandinavian settlers, the community had an active social life centered around churches and lodges. It also had a new industry in 1898, The Friday Fish Company. Logging, lumbering and agriculture were still the major sources of revenue, but the new enterprise, though short-lived, was a precursor to the canning industry in the vicinity. Florence, once a thriving challenger to Stanwood, was on a downhill spiral, which eventually led to the loss of its own post office. A century later there was but one surviving store building and a handful of houses along the river bank as reminders of Florence's rich past. Even the river had shrunk at that location. The major flow was now through Hatt Slough to the south.

Arlington and Haller City had merged into the major community for that upriver vicinity. Essentially, Haller City succumbed over a period of years to its better-located neighbor. Businesses were moved south from Haller City to Arlington. In some cases buildings such as George Murphy's store were placed on huge rollers and completely relocated. The Haller City post office finally closed in mid-decade. The newspaper changed its name from *Haller City Times* to *The Arlington Times* after its move. By the end of 1899 virtually all the commercial establishments were in the Arlington section. There were efforts to combine the two school districts and to incorporate as one community. The former failed in 1900, but the latter would succeed three years later. Haller Street, near the river, and Division Street, which marked the demarcation between the two towns, would survive as reminders of the past. In 1899 Arlington had dairies and shingle mills as the chief industries. It served as the hub and banking center for smaller surrounding settlements such as Bryant (north on the Northern Pacific line), Pilchuck (a logging center on the creek of the same name), and locales up the north fork of the Stillaguamish (Trafton, Oso, and all the way to Darrington). On the south fork of the Stillaguamish, Granite Falls, never one of the county's larger communities, emerged as a gateway to the upper river mill towns of Robe and Gold Basin as well as the mining towns

Nicholas and Tekla Thomle brought their family from Norway in 1890 after their business was burned by arson. They are shown here with their Stanwood area home in the background, as travel by water was more convenient until after World War I. The Williams descendants of the Thomle family farm the original 56 acres in 2003, and part of the house also is in use. (Courtesy the Williams family)

Snohomish County in 1899

Marysville served as a center of logging, milling, farming, and commercial activity, expanding along the north bank of the Snohomish River estuary next to the Tulalip Indian Reservation. Stimulated by the railroad boom, the town incorporated in 1891. (Courtesy Everett Public Library)

of Silverton and Monte Cristo.

Everett was easily the county's most dominant city. Just north of it, Marysville was growing into one of the county's half dozen largest communities. Separated from Everett by the four channels of the Snohomish River delta, Marysville was free to develop without threat of absorption by its larger neighbor. At the end of the decade, Marysville had been incorporated for nine years. There were stores, hotels, churches, and its own bank, which also served Silvana and Norman.

Upriver from Everett and Marysville, Snohomish was firmly entrenched as the county's second largest community, a position it would hold for the next 50 years. With its varied commercial, lumbering, and agricultural enterprises, Snohomish was the hub and banking center for Machias, Hartford, Maltby, and Cathcart. Virtually all the Skykomish River towns (Monroe, Sultan, Startup, Gold Bar and Index) depended on Snohomish for banking services. Sultan, which had lost its bank during the panic days, also declined in population and influence after the Great Northern construction had been completed, although it would remain the major upriver community.

Monroe, despite its dependence on Snohomish for banking, had developed into the largest population center on the Skykomish River. With roots in the historic settlements of Park Place and Tualco, and the later plats of Tye City and Monroe, it benefited from the Great Northern, its proximity to fine timberlands, and the rich surrounding farmland. By the turn of the century Monroe boasted of a church, a hotel, four shingle mills, three saw mills, four general stores, a creamery, and a weekly newspaper, *The Monroe Monitor*. Lumber, livestock, butter, cream, and produce were the major exports.

South of Everett, Mukilteo and Edmonds remained the chief towns along the county bay front. However, Mukilteo, the place of so many firsts, could not be counted as a major county town by decade's end; nor would it be in the coming years. Land developments of the early 1890s, based on speculation that "Mukilteo was about to become the great playground for those who expected to grow suddenly rich at Everett," collapsed with other Panic of 1893 failures. A fish cannery operated briefly in the early 1890s, but it also

An evening in the parlor with piano music was a common middle and professional class enjoyment. Before recorded music, families made their own, gathering for singing, listening, and playing together with mixes of instruments. (Courtesy Everett Public Library)

The Broadway School, Everett's first, opened on December 14, 1891 with Emma Serepta Yule as its teacher. Later she became the district's first principal and from 1897 to 1900 served as superintendent. After leaving Everett, she worked in Alaskan schools, headed a college English department at the University of the Philippines in Las Banos, authored numerous articles, and wrote three books. (Courtesy Everett School District No. 2)

fell victim to the times. Edmonds, on the other hand, experienced greater success. It was a shingle-making center and even had a substantial iron foundry that manufactured large quantities of metal bands for bundles of cedar shingles. Edmonds was the largest community in the southern Snohomish County, a distinction it would hold for decades.

More elements of permanence had appeared in the major communities. Towns had well defined and generally passable main streets. Substantial brick business blocks had been erected on many of those. Roads and bridges, while still subject to the whims of nature, were more dependable. Water systems were becoming more common. Shacks and shanties were giving way to well-constructed frame houses. Newspapers were established that were still in existence a century later. *The Arlington Times*, *The Monroe Monitor*, *Marysville Globe*, and *The Stanwood/Camano NEWS* are local papers that can trace their origins to the 1890s. In short, towns looked like places here to stay.

One thing that had not changed was the male domination of society. Women were relegated to a secondary role in most aspects of public life. All positions of power in government and business still were held by men. After brief territorial rights the state constitution in 1889 had restricted women's voting to school elections. Full suffrage would not come until 1910; even at that, it would precede national suffrage by 10 years. Little credit was given to women for their role in holding the family together, raising the children, and working alongside their husbands on the farms. Education was one of the few lines of work in which women had the chance to excel: 70 percent of the county's teachers were female in 1900. Many, like Emma Yule, who rose to be the superintendent of the Everett Public Schools, were outstanding educators. There were the women, too, who organized associations to be of service in the communities. Yet, by and large, women were confined to a narrow, relatively unappreciated niche. It would be decades before they would begin to approach equality.

As the century drew to a close, two individuals who had so significantly influenced the county's past executed an agreement that would significantly influence the future. By prior arrangement, Rockefeller and Hill arrived in Everett on their private railroad cars in June 1899. Rockefeller was eager to unload the remnants of the Everett Land Company—the wharves, waterworks, street railway, and other properties—and, Hill, interested in Everett's future as it related to his rail line, was willing to buy. The two worked out a deal. Wyatt Rucker, whose "Remarkable Document" had continually held the Everett Land Company's feet to the fire, was the one who finally picked up the bonds of the failed company on behalf of the Minnesota railroad magnate. In short order Hill would reorganize the company into an agent for his Everett agenda.

1900–1918

James J. Hill's acquisition of the Everett Land Company would have an enormous impact on Snohomish County, as would another business deal he was working on at the same time. In a position of influence in the Northern Pacific Railroad (as well as owning the Great Northern Railway), Hill negotiated the sale of 900,000 acres of the Northern Pacific's prime Pacific Northwest federal land grant timberlands to Frederick Weyerhaeuser, his St. Paul, Minnesota neighbor. Weyerhaeuser, highly esteemed in the lumber industry, had long shown an interest in the wood products potential of the Puget Sound area. Bringing in fellow midwestern lumbermen (including W.H. Laird and Matthew Norton) to raise the $5.4 million required for the purchase, he formed the Weyerhaeuser Timber Company. This purchase would accomplish at least two things for the Snohomish County. Trusting in Weyerhaeuser's judgment, other midwestern timber magnates would be drawn to the area. Secondly, Weyerhaeuser himself now needed a mill site near his holdings, a search which would lead him to Everett. The purchase also meshed perfectly with Hill's plans. Convinced from the beginning that Everett's real future was in its nearby forests rather than in heavy manufacturing and metal processing, Hill proposed to make Everett a timber mill town. The logs from those forests would be processed into lumber and shingles to be shipped to midwestern and eastern markets via his railroads.

The Weyerhaeuser purchase and Hill's acquisition of the Everett Land Company both were announced in early January 1900. Soon, Hill reorganized the failed John D. Rockefeller enterprise into the Everett Improvement Company and placed a trusted confidant, John McChesney, in charge of the operation. The Hill/McChesney impact was immediate and impressive. The Hall-Hill shingle company was recruited to Everett before the end of January and soon was cutting 200,000 shingles daily. Lumberman David Clough (former governor of Minnesota) arrived via Hill's private rail car and was soon joined by his son-in-law, Roland Hartley. The two became owners and major investors in several lumber and logging operations.

By the end of 1901, Everett boasted of nine lumber mills cutting 1.25 million board feet per day and 13 shingle mills with a daily output of 1.5 million shingles. In 1902 Weyerhaeuser Timber Company made its appearance on the Everett bay front. The company began operations in the old Bell-Nelson mill, which it had purchased and upgraded. The lumbermen and the mills continued to arrive for the next decade. W.I. Carpenter, H.W. Stuchell, Thomas Robinson, C.A. Dean, Neil C. Jamison, Clyde and E. Q. Walton, William Hulbert, and Fred Baker were among the names that became synonymous with the Everett lumber and shingle industries. Clough and Hartley set a new standard in 1907 with a shingle mill hailed as the largest in the world. By 1908 the city's shingle mills, many clustered on the 14th Street dock which jutted into the bay, could produce more than six million red cedar shingles per day. Proudly re-proclaiming its "City of Smokestacks" nickname, Everett had a waterfront from the bay around the peninsula and up the river that was filled with mills, each with its own stack. By 1910 Everett was the kind of place Hill had envisioned. There were 11 lumber mills, 16 shingle mills, and 17 combination lumber-shingle operations, more than any other city in Washington.

While McChesney's main thrust was the development of Everett's mill town economy, he was busily involved in other enterprises also. In 1901 he organized the American National Bank and built the Everett Theater, a magnificent show place that far overshadowed any previous theater in the county. He facilitated the organization of the Everett Flour Company, which soon was producing hundreds of barrels of the "Best Ever-ett" flour each day. He brought shipyards and a brewery to the city, and in 1901 bought controlling interest in the Everett Railway and Light Company. Within four years he had reorganized the firm and merged it with other utilities to form the Everett Railway, Light and Water Company, an Everett Improvement Company operation.

Meanwhile, the four great industries from the Rockefeller era experienced various fates. The nail works became a victim of its own success. When the national steel trust, under J. P. Morgan's direction, evolved into the United States Steel Company at the turn of the century, it simply acquired and dissolved its smaller competitors. The nail works, which had thrived during much of its ten-year history, was thus eliminated. Despite McDougall's dream, the whalebacks did not conquer the world's oceans. The shipyard closed, having manufactured but one vessel, the *City of Everett.* The smelter, supplementing its Snohomish County supply with ore from other parts of the Pacific Northwest and British Columbia remained in operation, but its days were numbered. However, the Lowell pulp and paper mill survived and flourished. Because of its international market,

Speculation that James J. Hill's transcontinental Great Northern Railway first would reach salt water at the Port Gardner peninsula was instrumental in the founding of Everett. However, Hill then made Seattle his western terminus and did not take an interest in the city until after the collapse of the Everett Land Company. Then he played the leading role in transforming Everett into a town based on processing the county's forests of old growth timber. (Courtesy Everett Public Library)

the mill was less susceptible to the ups and downs of the local, regional and national economies. In 1900 it was turning out 18½ tons of finished paper per day. With more than 250 employees and an annual payroll of $165,000, it was the Everett area's largest manufacturing plant. Known as Everett Pulp and Paper Co. by this time, it was purchased two years later by brothers William and Leonard Howarth and A.H.B. Jordan. Ownership would not change again for decades, and the plant would operate for the next 70 years.

While McChesney toiled in this Everett realm, and the original Rockefeller industries took their courses, Hill continued local investment in his railroad. In a bold venture to eliminate several miles of switchbacks near the Stevens Pass summit, his crews punched a 2.6-mile tunnel through the mountain crest by the turn of the century. In 1900 he also completed a tunnel beneath Everett, which would bring the rail line more directly to the waterfront. He then set about to create the Delta Terminal and repair yards in northeast Everett along the Snohomish River. They were described as the largest Great Northern operation of this type west of Spokane. Hoping to export wheat and import silk, both of which could be hauled across the west on his railroads, he built an 800-foot by 144-foot dock on the Everett bay front in 1908. The dock was to be serviced by two new Great Northern ships, the *Minnesota* and the *Dakota*. At 28,000 tons each, they were the largest ships in the world at the time of their launchings. About the same time he also erected on Bond Street a stately new Everett train station. It featured huge paintings of Glacier National Park, which was along the railway route and being strongly promoted by the

After having purchased nearly 5.5 million dollars worth of prime timber lands in the Pacific Northwest from James J. Hill, the Weyerhaeuser Timber Company needed a mill in the region. In 1902 the company bought the Bell-Nelson Mill on Everett's Bayside for less the $250,000 and upgraded the dilapidated plant into an efficient sawmill capable of producing 50 million board feet of lumber a year. The mill was Weyerhaeuser's first in the Pacific Northwest and the first of several Everett Weyerhaeuser operations built over the next half century. (Courtesy Everett Public Library)

Snohomish County Now Was a State Leader in Lumber and Shingle Mills

Opened in 1915, the giant Weyerhaeuser Mill B complex on the Snohomish River in north Everett was the state of the art in its ability to process old growth logs. For half a century its annual capacity of over a quarter billion board feet of lumber was a key in making the company the dominant producer as well as the largest timber land owner in the Pacific Northwest. (Juleen photo, courtesy Everett Public Library)

Fourteenth Street Dock in Everett was the county's greatest concentration of shingle mills. Built on pilings out over the water, the mills cut millions of board feet of western red cedar and shipped rail car loads throughout the United States. (Courtesy Everett Public Library)

Below: Wagner and Wilson began operations in 1906 with the purchase of 3,000 acres of timber land and became the largest saw and shingle mill operation in the Monroe area. Finished products were shipped out on the Great Northern and Milwaukee railways. (Axtell photograph # 209, photograph #378L, courtesy Monroe Historical Society)

President Thomas Robinson and his wife Matilda lived at 2131 Grand Avenue in Everett in 1915. Directly beneath them lay their Robinson Manufacturing Company, with access to the tide flats and Norton Avenue via a planked trestle. It became the site of Naval Station Everett, with a cement bridge down to West Marine View Drive. (Courtesy Everett Public Library)

Mukilteo revived when the Crown Lumber Company located its huge plant along the waterfront, where ocean-going vessels could tie up directly to the dock. California owned, the mill was known for its hiring of Japanese workers who lived in a close community just east of the town. (Courtesy Pete Hurd)

The Theurer and Hambridge small shingle mill on the Oscar Sandman farm near Granite Falls was typical of scores of those which operated throughout the county in the first half of the twentieth century. Note the milk cans and cabbage proudly shown on the far left by Sandman. Lumber camps and mill crews were the chief markets for most local farmers, many of whom worked in the woods seasonally to augment their incomes. Jack Theurer is standing third from the right. (Courtesy Granite Falls Historical Society)

railroad to increase tourism revenue. From 1907 to 1911 Hill undertook a massive project of building a permanent seawall from Seattle to Everett to prevent his double track rail lines from washing out. Approximately 200,000 cubic yards of granite, quarried near Index and cut into chunks measuring six feet long, four feet wide and three feet thick, were used. Hoisted into place by a steam derrick, they formed a protective wall that was up to 14 feet high in places. The seawall served its purpose well; nearly a century later it was still there.

The boom created by Hill was not confined to Everett. Virtually the entire county was caught in a momentum that would bring phenomenal growth from 1900 to 1910. By 1908 there were an estimated 42 sawmills, 96 shingle mills, four sash and door factories, and a half-dozen box factories in the county. Much of the product was headed to San Francisco, which was rebuilding after the devastating 1906 earthquake and fire. The Everett Chamber of Commerce published a survey, noting the 1909 Snohomish County timber and lumber output had a total value of $15,708,546, making it the largest lumber and shingle-producing county in the state.

Many of the county operations were small, but there were sizeable concerns outside of Everett. The Rucker brothers, from Everett's early days, established a huge mill on the northeast shore of Lake Stevens in 1906. Capable of cutting 100,000 feet of lumber and 250,000 shingles daily, the enterprise employed more than 250, including the loggers and the logging railroad workers. The Crown Lumber Company, established in 1909 when the Nelson Lumber Company of San Francisco acquired the old Mukilteo Lumber Company, became the biggest employer in Mukilteo. Located on the bay front east of the present ferry landing, the facility used around 200 workers to produce more than 200,000 feet of lumber per day. The firm also owned a fleet of wooden steam schooners that carried much of the plant's output to foreign ports. Other large mills included the Wagner and

A Golden Age of Steam
Logging Locomotives

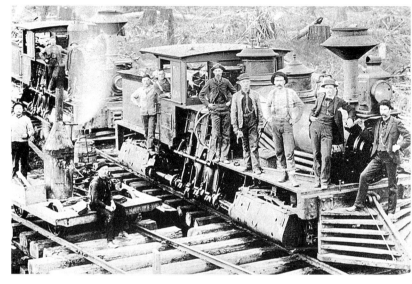

Top: The Stimson Lumber Company logged north of Marysville into the Stillaguamish valley during the 1890s, then was incorporated as the Marysville & Northern in 1904. Notice the home-made vertical boiler machine on the left, along with early model Shays. (Courtesy Bob Miller)

Middle: Johnson-Dean also used this Heisler design with saddle tanks, produced in Erie, Pennsylvania. The Heisler featured two huge cylinders set at 45 degree angles and meeting in a V shape beneath the boiler to power its gears. One is visible to the left of the crew. (Courtesy Bob Miller)

Bottom: This saddle tank model carried its own water for the boiler and was operating for the Danneher company at Darrington in the late teens. Danneher agreed to IWW demands for an eight-hour day, overtime pay, and better bunkhouse conditions, concessions which were bitterly opposed by other operators and perhaps led to his death under suspicious circumstances. (Courtesy Darrington Historical Society)

Previous page: Logging locomotives were light and powerful to pull heavy loads on steep grades. Over 2700 of these geared Shays were built between the 1870s and 1945. Johnson-Dean of Granite Falls in 1910 had a 17-year-old engineer (left) who learned steam mechanics with tractors on his father's Kansas farm. (Courtesy David Cameron)

Snohomish County in 1918

Wilson operation near Monroe, the Morgan Brothers mill in Snohomish, and the Robe-Menzel mill near Granite Falls.

To acquire the raw materials the mills were increasingly dependent on logging railroads, which spread like giant vines across the county. In his *Encyclopedia of Western Railroad History* rail historian Donald Robertson has identified 15 local railroads (excluding predecessor firms) which operated in the county after 1900. Those listed show a total track mileage of 608. While many of the railroads merely meandered from the mill or community into the woods, others reached from inland areas to the bay front. The Marysville and Northern, for example, was a Stimson Logging Company line that ran from north of Arlington to Ebey Slough at Marysville. The Admiralty Logging Company and Merrill and Ring Logging Company railroads were connected via a network with two bay front terminals, one near Meadowdale and the other between Everett and Mukilteo. Nearly all the small roads were standard gauge so they could hook up with each other and the major railway systems. The Three Lakes system east of Snohomish connected, in fact, directly with both the Northern Pacific and the Great Northern lines. In several instances the railroad names were still evident a century later. Admiralty Way is a street in the Paine Field area southwest of Everett, and Stimson Crossing marks the intersection of the rail line with Smokey Point Boulevard (old U.S. 99) north of Marysville. A large sign next to the rail line still identifies English as the north county community which developed near the English logging camp. The firm punched some 70 miles of railroad into both Snohomish County and Skagit County. The English name was largely lost, however, when Lakewood was selected as the name for the community post office.

The small logging lines were not the only railroads expanded during this period. The Seattle and International Railway Co. (S & I) started constructing a line from Arlington to Darrington in 1900. Before the work was completed in 1901, the Northern Pacific announced that it had taken over the S & I. Located on the flats between the Sauk River and north fork of the Stillaguamish River, Darrington was believed at the turn of the century to be located on the extension of a silver and copper mineral belt running from Money Creek in eastern King County northward through Index, the Sultan Basin, and Silverton. Using a new efficient rail-laying machine, Northern Pacific crews wasted no time in completing the 28-mile long line. Miners and prospectors, spurred by local promoter and eternal optimist Charles Burns, prowled the nearby mountains, but there was little to justify Burns' rosy outlook. Jim Price, an importer from the East Coast, was on the verge of opening a mine and smelter when he was shot to death by an enemy of his attorney father. The operation never opened. The Bornite Gold and Copper Company of Bangor, Maine spent $300,000 attempting to develop a copper mine but eventually gave up. Although the mining failed to meet expectations, the railroad was not in vain. It became the lifeline for the Stillaguamish River's north fork communities and the means for hauling millions of feet of logs and timber. By 1902 Darrington's U.S. Mill employed 100 men and was cutting 23,000 board feet of timber per day. Other mills and logging operations developed around the town and down the river valley between Darrington and Arlington. Fortson, founded in 1903, became one of the many lumbering centers along the Stillaguamish north fork. Darrington itself grew into the major town of the upper valley. John Montague built what was described as the leading store in the community. The town also included a hotel, two saloons, a lodging house, three mills, train depot, post office, a

143

church, a school and numerous residences by 1906. In these early years, Darrington was a true frontier outpost. In her history of the community, *Darrington: Mining Town / Timber Town*, Elizabeth Poehlman relates the story of two young teachers, both vying for the same position, who came to town in 1901 for an interview and stayed overnight at a boarding house. It seems that one of the overimbibing townsmen staggered into the boarding house after having fallen into a primitive privy. Resident Toby Freese later recalled that the inebriate "perfumed the place up a bit and by God, the next morning both those teachers left town on the morning train." But, drunks, teachers, and all, Darrington survived on its timber-based economy.

The new railroad also stimulated growth in Arlington. In 1903 the town incorporated. Capitalizing on its role as a rail center and its location near timberland and rich agricultural land, the community and its environs grew to a total population estimated at more than 2,000 in 1908. The mills in and around Arlington were producing 375,000 board feet of lumber and 18 million shingles monthly. Once again, Arlington provided a giant flagpole for a World's Fair. This time it was a 200-foot cedar spire for the 1904 exposition in St. Louis. On the home front the community was producing 7,500 pounds of butter per month from its highly regarded creamery. By 1908 there were five churches, a school system serving around 400 students, and numerous orders and lodges. The Arlington News Stand, Hotel Royal, and Arlington Steam Laundry were among the many establishments in the town's business section.

Saddened by the untimely death of his wife Josephine Larson of Florence, John Hals of Stanwood created in her memory the Josephine Old People's Home, later renamed the Josephine Sunset Home. Standing on ten acres of land donated by Hals to the Lutheran Church, it opened in 1908 at a cost of $10,000 and still provides its services to the region. (Courtesy Stanwood Area Historical Society)

Farther down the Stillaguamish, the twin cities of Stanwood and East Stanwood entered the new century with confidence. Maintaining its independence, Stanwood incorporated in 1903. The community also found an answer to its distance from the East Stanwood rail depot by building its own small rail line from the heart of town to the depot. Owned and operated by John Hall, the Hall &Hall Railroad began operation in 1904. Known locally as the "Dinky," the diminutive train hauled both freight and passengers between the two towns and was acclaimed by the national McClure Newspaper Syndicate as the shortest steam railroad in the world. Also in 1904 the Bank of Stanwood was established in the town's first brick building. The bank president was Henry C. "Klondike" Anderson, one of the few Snohomish County residents to return from the Yukon gold rush with a handsome profit. In 1905 the town got its first hospital and its first park. The next year electric lights came to town. In 1907 there was a library. The impetus for the library came from funds left by John Irvine in his will. The community prided itself in starting a school bus in 1908 and in hosting a visit by noted Norwegian explorer

When the Seattle and Montana Railroad built through the Stillaguamish Valley in 1891 Silvana was platted and businesses came. Because of its lowland location, the town and its surrounding farmlands are susceptible to seasonal flooding. (Courtesy Stanwood Area Historical Society)

Roald Amundsen that same year. Before the year was out the community had dedicated the Josephine Old People's Home. This facility for the aged was donated by local shingle mill owner Jon Hals in memory of his recently deceased wife. Stanwood also prospered from its location in a highly productive agricultural district. The "Gilt-Edge" butter from the Stanwood Co-Operative Creamery was known throughout the county. The Washington Canning Company, which incorporated in 1908 and opened the next year, canned 5,300 cases of fruit and vegetables in its first season. In 1910 the Pacific Coast Condensed Milk Company started a Stanwood plant which received 20,000 gallons of milk every morning. Initially the milk was boiled in the Stanwood facility and shipped to Mt. Vernon for canning. Later a full-fledged local condensery would be constructed.

The prosperity of the area was not confined to Stanwood. East Stanwood developed into a substantial community also, under the leadership of people such as C.J. Gunderson, who served variously as postmaster, merchant, banker, undertaker and chief town promoter. A town site plat was filed January 9, 1906 as the first plat of East Stanwood. Two new churches were built in the vicinity, and a cooperative store called the People's Union was opened. Undaunted by their rival's 30-plus year head start, East Stanwood forged ahead, even challenging Stanwood's status as the center for Norwegian pride by hosting a public lutefisk dinner billed as "all you can eat for 35 cents, children 20 cents."

Granite Falls, with its desirable location on the rail line connecting Monte Cristo with Everett, was another town experiencing growth. Population shot from around 50 in 1900 to almost 700 by 1905. Town incorporation occurred in 1903, and by 1906 there were a bank and several other businesses, including A.H. Moll's hardware and furniture shop and H.E. Jewell's photography studio. Numerous lumber and shingle mills operated in the vicinity. Also, the Wayside copper mine located near Granite Falls was a major producer from 1905 to 1910, sometimes employing as many as 100 men.

The communities of the Snohomish/Skykomish/Snoqualmie valleys also profited during the boom days of the early 1900s. Despite a major downtown fire in 1901, Monroe surged ahead. As with Arlington and Stanwood, Monroe benefited from its proximity to both good farmland and good timberland. The Monroe creamery opened the same year as the big fire and soon was producing both butter and cheese from milk it bought at 90 cents a hundredweight. The town incorporated in 1902 and opened its first hospital a year later, joining more than 50 downtown businesses. Nearly a thousand men worked in the logging camps and mills in the nearby area. Monroe even conducted its own fair, the first occurring on September 4 and 5, 1903. Shortly thereafter, C.J. Stuart, a foremost fruit grower and banker from Puyallup, was persuaded by the Great Northern to locate a large berry ranch near Monroe. By 1906 the Great Northern Fruit Company had 50 acres in berries at the Monroe farm. The 28-acre raspberry field was said to be the largest in the state. In addition there were seven acres of blackberries, five acres of strawberries and three acres of evergreens. The berries were shipped out in great volume. Some of the product, packed into specially designed refrigerator units, went by rail to markets in the Midwest. Another major agricultural industry was the huge Pacific Condensed Milk Company plant, which opened in 1908 with the capability of processing 250,000 pounds of milk daily.

When this plant opened in 1908, it was the first of the large milk condenseries in Snohomish County. Operated by the Pacific Coast Condensed Milk Company, the facility manufactured Carnation Milk. The factory was the company's seventh in Washington and Oregon and came into being after the Monroe Commercial Club actively solicited the company to locate in the community. With the capacity to process much greater quantities than creameries, condenseries were key to the growth of Snohomish County dairying. (Courtesy Monroe Historical Society)

Farther up the valley, Sultan continued to be the gateway for miners seeking riches in the basin to the north and east. The town incorporated in 1905 and was soon boasting of its graded streets and sidewalks, as well as other civic improvements. In the early 1900s Index experienced a mining boom that swelled the population to around 1,000. Even a 1902 fire, which consumed half the town, could not squelch the enthusiasm of the town being called the "Butte of Washington" because of the area's copper mines. The most productive mine was the Sunset, about 10 miles above Index. Its ore was being shipped via the Great Northern to the smelter in Everett. Another kind of mining would also bring employment and fame to Index. Large granite quarries begun by John Soderberg and T.S. Ellis would be used for major construction projects throughout western Washington. Index also became the home of Lee Pickett, famed photographer for the Great Northern.

Closer to Everett, the community of Marysville also shared in the boom of the early 1900s. Firmly entrenched as one of the half dozen largest communities in the county, Marysville would see its 1900 population of 728 nearly double in the next 10 years. Numerous mills, including the Ebey, Harrington, Smith, and Dexter companies were operating in the area by 1906. Farming increased in economic importance as the land around the community was cleared of timber. The town erected a city hall in 1901 and founded a new library in 1907. Sadly, the community lost two of its most prominent citizens in 1906 when H.B. Myers and Mark Swinnerton died. Both had been successful businessmen and civic leaders. Swinnerton had been the town's first mayor, and Myers had been on the first town council. Town flags were flown at half-mast in honor of the two.

Snohomish, still smarting from the county seat loss and its relegation to the number two position among county communities, would grow in the early 1900s, but not at the

Index was a busy site with over 600 residents in 1916, compared with 150 in the 2000 census. A granite quarry, saw and shingle mill, and nearby copper mines were the chief industries. This is Avenue A looking east through the business district from the Great Northern Railway tracks, which divide the town in half. (Lee Pickett photograph, courtesy Index Historical Society)

rate of many other locales. Nonetheless, the community remained an important shipping, industrial and commercial center. In 1902 the lumber and shingle business of Snohomish and vicinity was reported to have employed 700 men with annual wages of more than $550,000. The Maughlin Brothers Mill, Snohomish Logging Company, and Robert and Mack Loggers were among the largest of the many logging and lumbering enterprises. Snohomish's downtown bustled with hotels, stores, theaters, saloons, pharmacies and other businesses. The Wilbur Drug Company (oldest in the county), Herron-Sitton Dry Goods Company, Russell's Transfer, and New Brunswick Hotel (which in 1908 advertised

John Soderberg began quarrying granite rock at Index in 1904, and it found widespread popularity including use in the Everett post office and the state capitol building in Olympia. Granite and the skilled workers required to cut and finish it were replaced by the use of reinforced concrete, and the operation closed with the depression in 1932. (Lee Pickett photograph, courtesy Index Historical Society)

American plan rooms for $2.00 per day) were but a few of the downtown establishments. The town was proud of its schools, both public and private. The Puget Sound Academy, which occupied the old courthouse, was rated a foremost private institution. Snohomish built its own library in 1901 and then in 1909 became the recipient of a $10,000 grant for a Carnegie Library, one of three in the county. The others were in Everett and Edmonds, and all three buildings were in various public uses almost a century later. In 1903 the community was connected with Everett via an interurban service. The line utilized the old Everett and Monte Cristo tracks, which were by now a part of the Northern Pacific system. The cars ran 11 trips a day between the two communities.

Mukilteo experienced resurgence with the Mukilteo Lumber Company and its successor, Crown Lumber. By 1905, the town's population was estimated at 350, with 150 of those being Japanese who lived in a section unceremoniously known as "Jap Gulch." The breadwinners of the Japanese families were largely employees of the nearby mill. In 1906 the Mukilteo federal government lighthouse opened. In addition to serving as a beacon for mariners, the picturesque structure became a county landmark and the frequent object of photographs and paintings. The Puget Sound and Alaska Powder Company built a dynamite producing facility near Mukilteo in 1909. Located in a ravine northeast of town, the plant was described as the largest concern of its kind on Puget Sound. It was said the plant's production was a good index of county activity because the dynamite was used for local land clearing, rail work, and logging.

Clambakes have been an ongoing Mukilteo tradition, given the miles of nearby salt water beach and the enjoyment of sharing the results of one's digging. Community celebrations and fundraising activities alike benefitted from the occasions, this one taking place in 1914. (Courtesy Everett Public Library)

Edmonds maintained its position as the only south county community of substantial size. The string of shingle mills along the waterfront was the community's economic backbone, but there were additional industries also. The Washington Excelsior and Manufacturing Company and the Knowles Superior Wrench Company were among the other firms. The State Bank of Edmonds was created in 1907. The *Edmonds Review* newspaper attracted fame because its manager, Mrs. M.T.B. Hanna, was one of the first women to hold such a position in the United States. By 1908 the downtown included more than 50 business and professional establishments. There were four churches and a myriad of lodges and orders from Masons to Eagles. There were connections with Seattle by road, rail line and passenger boat. Also in 1908 Edmonds was officially elevated from a fourth class town to a third class city. The census accompanying this action showed a population of 1546. In 1910 Edmonds was the recipient of a $5,000 grant for the construction of its Carnegie library, largely

Many Japanese families came to work in the Crown Lumber Company sawmill on the Mukilteo waterfront, creating a community which lasted until the mill closed during the depression of the 1930s. (Courtesy Everett Public Library)

Grants from Scottish American steel magnate and philanthopist Andrew Carnegie led to the building of modern library facilities in Snohomish, Everett, and Edmonds. To the left of the Edmonds library are the fire bell tower and the town hall, shown here on August 5, 1918. When the library opened in 1911 town offices were relocated to its basement. New facilities for both were opened in 1962, and in 1973 the building became home to the Edmonds Historical Museum. (Courtesy Edmonds-South Snohomish County Historical Society)

Former Minnesota governor David Clough (right) and his son-in-law Roland Hartley led a major influx of lumber and mill men into the county. Hartley (below, left) was cruising timber north of Sultan: "On Sunday, August 16, 1908, we were close to a county road and wrote Nina [Clough] that if they would come up on the Saturday train, we would have a team meet them and bring them out to our tent and we would cook them a Sunday dinner. You can see the satisfied look on all but the cook, which look answers for itself". – Roland Hartley (Both photos courtesy Monroe Historical Society)

through the efforts of city librarian Rev. John Lockwood.

Fueled primarily by its timber assets, the county was moving ahead. However, the multimillion-dollar output of the timber industry did not mean that workers were basking in prosperity. The work, whether it was logging or milling, was strenuous and hazardous. Hours were long and the pay adequate at best. The real money was flowing into the pockets of the men who owned and operated the logging companies and the mills. This group, labeled the "sawdust baronage" by Norman Clark, author of *Mill Town*, a book on Everett's social history to 1916, included people such as David Clough and Roland Hartley. Meanwhile, the amounts pocketed by the local owners would pale in comparison to the profits rolling into the coffers of the absentee entrepreneurs, James J. Hill and Fredrick Weyerhaeuser. While the mill laborer toiled with the hope of someday buying a cottage on a 25-foot lot, he watched Clough and Hartley move into beautiful mansions on Everett's north Rucker Avenue. Had he visited St. Paul, Minnesota's Summit Avenue, the worker would have seen Hill's magnificent fortress, the largest home ever built in Minnesota, and the smaller but still impressive residence of next-door neighbor Weyerhaeuser.

In addition to meager pay, the workers, along with their bosses, suffered the ups and downs of a fickle market. About

By the time this photograph was taken from high atop Rucker Hill *circa*1915, Everett was the mill town which James J. Hill had envisioned. Lumber and shingle plants lined both the bay front shown here and the Snohomish River. In its earliest days as a planned industrial city, Everett was known as the "City of Smokestacks". The nickname was even more appropriate during the city's "mill town" era. (Courtesy Everett Public Library)

the time the mill was running steadily, a downturn would come. The collapse caused by the Wall Street panic of 1907 was especially severe. It would be two years of shutdowns, slowdowns and closures before the local timber economy found some degree of stability, while the county's mining industry never did. Boom and bust market uncertainties caused by the existence of far too many mills and their constant overproduction also contributed to the owners' reluctance to spend money for safety improvements or equipment up-grades. Working conditions, even in the best of times, were dangerous. Injuries and deaths were not uncommon. It was said you could always identify a shingle mill worker by his missing fingers. Feeding an open saw, the operator could easily lose a finger, hand, arm, or life with one slip. Additionally, many workers suffered from cedar asthma and other life threaten-ing dust allergies caused by the lack of blowers and ventilation, and there was no social safety net of insurance, medical benefits, or job retraining for victims or their families. Thirty-six of Everett's 224 deaths in 1909 were reported to have occurred in mills.

In this kind of atmosphere it was not surprising that Snohomish County became strongly unionized. They were numerous by the early 1900s, and they were not confined to the lumber industry. The Everett Central Trades Council was organized in December of 1900 and within four months included 27 trades and six local unions. Members actively sought better wages, improved working conditions and boycotts of firms using non-union labor. Everett became a staunch American Federation of Labor town, and unions were

Lumbering Dominated the County Economy

Left: As rails had replaced animals, so too their successors began to appear. This early solid-wheeled logging truck belonged to the Rucker brothers, who platted the town of Lake Stevens next to their mill. (Courtesy Granite Falls Historical Society)

Above: County homes were roofed with western red cedar shingles, produced by the millions each month for export around the Pacific rim. Although banned from some markets due to their fire hazard, their water and rot resisting qualities made them the local favorite for over a century until the old growth trees were gone. (Courtesy Marysville Historical Society)

Above: Spar trees and portable steam-powered donkey engines lifted logs into the air and onto railroad cars as technology ended the era of oxen and river rafting. (Courtesy Snohomish Historical Society)

Left: Most mills were located on the water, where steam tugs such as the *Tillicum* moved rafts of logs and finished lumber could be shipped either by ocean going vessels or rail cars. This 75 ton vessel had a 500 horse power engine and was owned by the American Tugboat Company of Everett. (Courtesy Marysville Historical Society)

active in other parts of the county too. Mills throughout the county were struck for higher wages by the "knotsawyers" and shingle packers in 1901. An Edmonds unit of the Shingle Weavers Union organized in 1903. When Labor Day came around there were parades and other festivities, the 1901 event in Everett starting with a parade of 900 men representing 14 local unions. A mass meeting then took place, at which the mayor addressed the workers, and this was followed with contests in field sports. Enduring periodic setbacks, organized labor would grow through the decade with the constant demand for better wages and working conditions—and, the intermittent strikes to accomplish the same. By 1910 there were at least 29 different unions in Everett alone.

There were notable exceptions to unionization, however. The Everett Pulp and Paper Company, one of the largest mills in the county, would remain non-union for decades. The plant, around which virtually everything in Lowell revolved, practiced a *modus operandi* that Don Berry, author of *The Lowell Story: A Community History* called "heroic industrialism." The work force included both men and women and was viewed by management as part of an extended family. Nearly all the workers lived in Lowell, and it was common for two, three and four generations of a Lowell family to become part of the mill's family. Mill manager William Howarth and superintendent A.H.B. Jordan were known for their benevolence and their involvement in community endeavors such as schools, youth organizations and hospitals. The generally less dangerous work and the mill's ability to operate steadily in a more stable market undoubtedly contributed to the lack of unionization.

The wood products industry was king, but agriculture also was gaining in importance. According to census figures, the number of county farms increased from 1,024 in 1900 to 1,813 in 1910, the decade being one of overall prosperity state-wide following the tumult of the 1890s. A full 118,328 acres were in farms, and 34,126 of those acres were improved. The introduction of dynamite around 1905 was instrumental in clearing land and expanding improved acreage. For the first time the huge stumps that dotted the average farm could be eliminated fairly easily.

Dairying was developing into a substantial economic activity as the huge condenseries in Monroe, Stanwood, and later Arlington were both a product of and a stimulus to the dairy industry. The Monroe Commercial Club, primary promoter of that town's condensery, had to confirm there were at least 2,000 cows in the area as a condition for locating the plant there. Once the facility opened, it could handle the milk from many additional animals. Whereas a creamery might measure its daily output in thousands of pounds, a condensery could handle hundreds of thousands of pounds. The mild climate, good soil, favorable growing season and increased amount of cleared land all bode well for the production of a variety of crops. Successful farmers bragged of harvesting up to 100 bushels of oats, 50 bushels of wheat, and 80 bushels of barley per acre. Root crops such as carrots, rutabagas, parsnips, and beets did particularly well. A good potato patch might yield up to 400 bushels per acre. Many fruit growing farms developed. There were both orchards and berry farms. Large strawberry farms near Edmonds were said to be producing up to 400 cases per acre, a number far exceeding the famous berry farms near Hood River, Oregon.

The growth of the agricultural economy also spawned the development of the granges throughout the county. Begun in the Midwest as means of improving the lives of

Shopping in the Early Twentieth Century

John F. and Daniel L. Ashe operated the Ashe Brothers hardware and blacksmith business in Granite Falls. Many items were sold from kegs and barrels rather than the shrink wrapped plastic of a century later. (Courtesy Granite Falls Historical Society)

Interiors of these three Everett businesses were photographed in the summer of 1907. The Japan Bazaar was located at 1410 Hewitt Avenue and operated by Chinese merchant Charles Kan, advertising its Japanese fancy goods, novelties and souvenirs. These were acceptable, whereas Chinese people and objects were not, a hang over from the violence of the 1880s. (Courtesy Everett Public Library)

Confectionery shops were popular throughout the county. They ranged from specialties at the Union Billiard Parlor in Edmonds to stores which featured candies, hot lunches and fancy ice creams such as Wildeys at 2811 Colby Avenue in Everett to the exotically named Palace of Sweets in Granite Falls. (Courtesy Everett Public Library)

Meat markets featured locally raised products, sawdust floors, carcasses hanging in cold storage, and portions freshly cut and weighed at the house wife's request. With no home refrigeration or freezers, a stop at the meat market was a frequent task. (Courtesy Everett Public Library)

farmers, the grange movement had made its way to Washington State by the 1880s. The first subordinate grange organized in Snohomish County was Kellogg Marsh No. 136 in 1903. Located north and east of Marysville, it was the only one in the county for four years. Then came Fidelity No. 206, also near Marysville, followed by several others. By 1922 there were 20 Snohomish County granges. These became important social and political centers for the rural population.

Rural and urban lifestyles sometimes collided in controversies that seem amusing by twenty-first century standards. Around 1905 Marysville, Snohomish, Stanwood and Monroe all were involved in heated discussions about whether farm animals should be prohibited from roaming the streets and yards of their communities. In Snohomish an election was held in March 1906 with the vote in favor of keeping "Bossy" off the streets. The following month the city council enacted an explicit Running-At-Large of Animals ordinance. Similar action was taken in the other communities.

While the timber and agricultural industries flourished, the mining industry was not so fortunate. There were starts and stops, moments of excitement, and some productive operations. Essentially, however, mining was caught in a downward pattern that would lead to its demise as a viable part of the county's economy. The Everett & Monte Cristo Railway was rebuilt in 1900. Both Silverton and Monte Cristo bristled with excitement, and the Mystery and Pride mines were among those that resumed operation. For the next three years there was a rebirth of mining. By 1902 the mines were producing around 1,000 tons per week, and the community of Monte Cristo was viable again. In Everett the smelter was operating continuously. This productivity did not dissuade John D. Rockefeller from wanting to rid himself of the whole enterprise. In 1903 he completed a transaction which left the mines and the smelter in the hands of the American Smelting and Refining Company. ASARCO, as it was known, was a processing monopoly in North America, similar in nature to the steel trust that closed the nail works. A Guggenheim property, ASARCO became another example of outside capital controlling county devel-

opments. The company was interested only in the smelter. In December 1903 it closed the mines. From that point on there would be flurries of activity, but the overall decline would not be reversed. Sam Silverman, a Pacific Northwest regional mining operative, planned to build a large arsenic plant in Monte Cristo. The national financial Panic of 1907, prompted by the fight over Butte, Montana's copper mines, dried up funds and scuttled Silverman's plans. Even the railway was broken up and sold off in parts to the Northern Pacific, which through it gained access to Everett. The

The Sunset was the region's largest copper mine, located up Trout Creek on the North Fork Skykomish River above Index. With many breaks in operation, it produced 1,500 ounces of gold, 156,000 ounces of silver, and 12,912,000 pounds of copper from its five levels and 12,000 feet of workings. (Lee Pickett photograph, courtesy Index Historical Society)

154

section from Hartford east became a branch line, only sporadically maintained and poorly serviced. When the last hotel in Monte Cristo closed in 1912, the once booming hamlet had become a ghost town. That same year the Everett smelter shut down, and operations were transferred by ASARCO to Tacoma.

The number of county banks and the total deposits grew substantially in this period. By 1910 Granite Falls, Edmonds, Marysville, and Sultan each had one bank; Arlington, Monroe, Snohomish, and Stanwood had two each. There were three banks in Everett. The banks' biggest challenge of the era was the swift, devastating, but, fortunately, short-lived panic of 1907. To meet the demands for cash, county banks through their Clearing House Association issued certificates of promise, which could be negotiated only in the county. All local banks survived the year, but the Everett Scandia Bank did fail in 1908. The number of financial institutions grew steadily after 1910, reaching a total of 20 by 1920. The additions were the Bank of Lake Stevens, State Bank of Silvana, First National of Stanwood and four new ones in Everett. The First National Bank of Everett, bolstered by a merger with the American National Bank and its affiliate Everett Trust and Savings in 1909, was easily the largest in the county, and its president, William Butler, one of the most powerful individuals. Initially Butler had come to Everett as a young man to manage the smelter interests for the Rockefeller syndicate. He was from a well-connected east coast family that included brother Nicholas Murray Butler, long time president of New York's Columbia University. Young Butler soon gained control of the First National Bank and led the firm to its preeminent position. A reserved, reclusive individual, Butler bankrolled many of the timber operatives and quietly manipulated the destinies of companies and people. He effectively kept out other industries, which might threaten his domination of mill town Everett. His influence spilled into politics, where he wielded considerable behind the scene control and supported rock ribbed Republicans such as Roland Hartley, whose pursuit of elective office eventually led him to the state governorship.

While banks represented the legitimate financiers, a county growing as rapidly as Snohomish was bound to have its share of illicit financial operators also. One of the bigger swindles involved the Snohomish Valley Railway Company, which was organized in 1906 to bring a feeder line into the area. According to the Snohomish *Tribune*, one Charles M. Meeker, passing himself off as an agent for a legitimate New York bank, took off for Europe to sell the railroad stock. The news of a decision not to build the line came too late for London, Antwerp, Paris, and Berlin investors to whom Meeker had peddled thousands of dollars of what became useless paper. Reportedly, the organizers of the Valley Railway group spent much time and effort trying to track down Mr. Meeker. Another scam involved the scenic waterfront south of Stanwood. Seattle real estate promoter Clarence Hillman bought 12,000 acres of logged off land about 1906 and then attempted to sell tracts for Birmingham, a future seaport city where he bragged "the sun shines 276 days a year." Drumming up rumors such as one about a steel mill coming to the area, he excited prospective buyers and actually hauled them to the site via three special "Hillman" excursion boats from Everett and Seattle. Hillman's grandiose promises and limited intentions finally caught up with him. He was convicted of fraud and found a different kind of waterfront paradise at McNeil Island's federal prison. Residents later rejected the Birmingham name, and the vicinity became known as Warm Beach. However, Clarence Avenue still runs through the area.

County politics of the day were dominated by the Republicans. In the elections between 1900 and 1910 they swept virtually every office. The Democrats were the other major party, but the Socialists and later the Prohibitionists also ran candidates. For a time, the Socialists maintained a loyal following, and frequently their candidates in county races finished third behind the Republicans and Democrats. With the exception of superintendent of schools, everyone elected to a county office or sent as a representative to the state or national government was a male. Some women occupied the school position, including Lizzie Jones and Eva Bailey. The county also provided two different state officials during this time, both from Everett. Sam Nichols was elected secretary of state in 1900 and Walter Bell attorney general in 1908. W.W. Black was one of the few Democrats to buck the Republican trend. Elected to the superior court judgeship in 1904 and 1908, he was the successful candidate for Congress in 1910.

On the afternoon of August 2, 1909 a probable arson fire destroyed the Iles & Newman carriage and wheel factory on the northwest corner of Pacific and Wetmore avenues. Burning debris spread to the roof of the courthouse across the street to the east and also caught it on fire. Fortunately, key records were saved. The building's main arches were incorporated into the new mission style building which still stands on the original site. (Courtesy Everett Public Library)

County government suffered a blow in 1909 when the courthouse burned down. It was one of several Everett fires that occurred on the same day. August Heide, architect of the original, was called back to design the new one. In a tribute to his versatility, he created an entirely different building out of the remains. Spanish Mission in appearance, the 1910 building featured a clock tower and a white stucco-like exterior. Three original arches on the west entrance were the only reminders of its Romanesque predecessor.

At about the same time of the courthouse fire, the county was getting an opportunity to show its wares at the Alaska-Yukon-Pacific Exposition (AYP) in Seattle. Promoted to showcase Washington's evolution from frontier primitiveness to a civilized society with cultural, educational and business opportunities, the big show opened June 1, 1909, on the site later occupied by the University of Washington. Snohomish County participated in many ways. The mammoth four-foot thick, 30-foot high wooden pillars in the Forestry Building reportedly came from the town of Hazel. Arlington offered samples of bog iron ore for display. Clay deposits from Sultan were also exhibited. Commercial exhibits were prepared by Everett Pulp and Paper, Ferry Baker Lumber, and the Robinson Manufactur-

Typical of the county's many rural school districts was Lake Roesiger No. 44, formed in 1890 to serve families north of Monroe. In 1938 it consolidated with Forest Grove, and then in 1946 became a part of the Snohomish School District. (Courtesy Bob Heirman)

ing Company. A miniature mountain and mine with models was the work of Emily Shultz of Index. Copper and gold specimens from Index, Darrington, Monte Cristo and Gold Basin were on display. Snohomish residents D. A. Davis and Joseph Nokes took first and second place, respectively, in the Old-Time Fiddle contest. There was a "Snohomish County Day" on August 3, with special trains and passenger boat runs for Snohomish County residents who wished to go to the fair. The county delegation gathered in downtown Seattle and marched into the fair with banners flying. Index was "The Switzerland of the Northwest," and Stanwood was "The Garden Spot of the State." Monroe hailed its condensery and the Carnation brand milk it produced. Mukilteo proclaimed, "Seattle is a Suburb of Mukilteo." In an afternoon speech, the Snohomish County State Senator, J.A. Falconer, asserted, "the most stalwart men and women on God's green earth live in Snohomish County."

While most Snohomish County residents seemed to enjoy the AYP, there was an undercurrent of ambivalence. Boosterism was fine, but some wondered how well the county could shine in an event hosted in King County. There was the fear of coming off as the younger and less desirable sister. The situation wasn't helped when Snohomish County was relegated to share exhibit space with Island County, each having a 15-foot by 30-foot display area. The cheap labor brought in to rush the fair to completion brought the wrath of labor unions. Significantly, the Everett based *Labor Journal* newspaper didn't even mention the exposition. Everett, still carrying a grudge from losing the Great Northern terminus to Seattle, suffered ignobly when the twice-postponed "Everett Day" never did occur. To further exacerbate Everett's misfortune, "Snohomish County Day" was the day following the courthouse fire. A part of Everett's exhibit never even made it to Seattle on the big day. Several of the Everett banners hinted at a thinly veiled discontent: "Not the Largest, but Absolutely the Best", "Did You Ever See Everett's Townsite? It's the Best in the West." "You'll Like Tacoma, You'll Love

Edmonds High School, built in 1909 on land donated by community founder George Brackett, was typical of the creation of secondary education buildings throughout the county. Improved transportation and the demand for additional schooling led to the consolidation of smaller districts into ones with larger tax bases and more eligible students. (Courtesy Edmonds-South Snohomish County Historical Society)

Seattle, but You'll Settle Down in Everett." AYP was, for the most part, remembered fondly in the Puget Sound area. For Snohomish County, though, it carried mixed feelings.

Snohomish County growth brought a tremendous surge in school enrollment. By the 1907–1908 school year, there were more than 10,000 students county-wide. Everett alone had more than 3,600 students in the public schools and another 400 in parochial schools. Secondary education was becoming more common, and several communities erected substantial new facilities. Arlington, Edmonds, Everett, Marysville, Monroe and Stanwood all constructed new brick high schools in the period from 1907 to 1914. In a sense, each of these substantial structures served notice that the community had come of age. A source of pride often they were the centers for community

It was a big day for Snohomish County when President William Howard Taft visited on October 9, 1911. Here Taft is shown on the temporary platform which was erected in front of Everett High School. The lady next to Taft, holding the megaphone, is Everett High faculty member May Long. The first president to use the automobile as an official means of transportation, Taft was transported around Everett in on open touring car owned by local lumberman David Clough. (#353, courtesy Snohomish County Museum and Historical Association and Everett Public Library)

events. When President William Howard Taft visited Everett in October of 1911, he delivered a major address in front of the high school, a magnificent Beaux Arts building which is still in use. Parent-Teacher Associations also formed at this time. Everett's first was in 1909. Stanwood had one by 1913. One thing that was not increasing was the number of school districts. The consolidation process, as illustrated by the Haller City/Arlington town merger, was underway. Cost efficiency, ability to expand program offerings with larger student populations, improved transportation, and the easing of local "turf" issues all contributed to the merging of districts. Over the next half-century the number of county school districts would be reduced to 15.

Religious organizations were growing significantly too. The 1910 *Polk City Directory* identified 103 churches in 20 different communities. The greatest number was in Everett. Of its 43 congregations, the denomination with the most churches was Lutheran, a reflection of the large numbers of Scandinavians in the community. The lodges and orders of "Secret Societies" still were gaining in numbers as well. The 1910 *Directory* lists 61 individual groups from 44 different orders. Odd Fellows (IOOF), with seven, had the most lodges. Women's organizations continued to grow and develop. The same *Polk Directory* identifies 20 different women's groups. Many of these

Lodges and fraternal organizations were key components in the social life of communities through the middle of the twentieth century. The Redmen and their Pocahontas women's lodge traced their origins back to the Revolutionary War Sons of Liberty and Boston Tea Party, thus the garb shown by these Granite Falls members. (Courtesy Granite Falls Historical Society)

This is the façade of the Everett Theater when it opened in 1901. A project of the Everett Improvement Company, the theater was designed by noted Seattle architect Charles Herbert Bebb and set a new standard for Snohomish County performing arts facilities. In 1923 the theater was gutted by fire and then rebuilt. When it reopened the next year, there was a new façade, the one in existence presently. After transitioning from live performances to motion pictures, the facility eventually fell on hard times and closed in 1989. Through the efforts of the Everett Theater Society, the building was restored and reopened for both live performances and films. (Courtesy Everett Public Library)

were affiliated with the State Federation of Women's Clubs, an association with significant influence. From 1917 through 1919, Snohomish's Margaret McCready served as president of the state group. A county Federation chapter was formed in 1913. A directory in 1914–1915 noted 17 county affiliates, the largest being the Arlington Civic Club with 86 members.

This period also saw an expansion of leisure, sports and entertainment activities. The 1,200 seat Everett Theater was a stop for the major touring live-performance groups. Noted performers Lillian Russell, Al Jolson, Roscoe "Fatty" Arbuckle, Helen Hayes, and George M. Cohan were among those who appeared on the Everett stage. By 1916 the motion picture was being viewed regularly in the Everett Theater and other popular county locations such as Stanwood's Folly and Edmonds' Pavilion. Carl McKee, of Everett's Orpheum Theater, was explaining to his fellow Rotarians the necessity of charging a 20-cent admission fee to his establishment. Music continued as a county favorite. If an event were to include a band, there was a good chance the Stanwood or Silvana ones would be there. Both were county prizewinners.

Baseball was still a popular sport. Fred Schock gained local fame and then was even mentioned in a 1902 *New York Clipper* article as a pitching sensation from Walter Thornton's independent team of Everett, Washington. Thornton himself was a local legend who had played professionally in Chicago. A few years later Edmonds' Lester Wilson cracked into professional baseball. Following a stint with the Boston Red Sox, the outfielder played on the 1912 Seattle team that won the coast pennant. Football began to be recognized as a

With its double balcony and elegant motif, the 1200 seat Everett Theater was a fitting venue for leading performers of the stock and vaudeville era. Audiences packed the house to see the likes of Al Jolson, Lillian Gish, George M. Cohan and Lillian Russell. Although the double balcony became a single one with the 1924 rebuild, the Everett continued as the county's premier showplace. Although Everett of the early 1900s had the reputation of being a tough blue collar town, it is evident here that a large portion of the citizenry was capable of sprucing up for an evening at the theater. (Courtesy Everett Public Library)

premier sport in Everett. Under the leadership of coach Enoch Bagshaw, Everett High School started producing juggernaut teams that simply overwhelmed most opponents. Posting victories like the 174-0 shellacking of Bellingham in 1913, Everett garnered several Northwest championships during the decade. Hunting also had developed as a favored sport, with the 1912 Stanwood area results described as fabulous. The hotels and lodging houses were filled with eager sportsmen who flocked in. In 1908 Everett hosted the North Pacific International Tennis Association's tournament. One of the county's more spectacular sporting events occurred at Lake Stevens in summer 1912. Boats reputed to be the fastest in the United States gathered for a great race. Local driver Bailey Hilton, known for his daredevil auto and motorboat stunts, was an early leader. Power from dual engines was said to have stood his craft on its stern. A recollection in the 1989 Lake Stevens Historical Society Memory Album booklet concludes, "As with many part-nerships, there was dissention between the two motors, and before he could reunite the two powers, even the slower boats on the lake had passed Hilton on the way home."

Another period characteristic was the development and refinement of communication, utility, water, and power systems. The Sunset and the Pacific were among the early telephone companies. In 1916 the Puget Sound Telephone Company emerged to dominate the county. W.N. Winter was largely responsible for the consolidation that brought Puget Sound into being, and he became president of the company. About the same time, Everett was abandoning Wood Creek, near Lowell, as its water source and turning to the Sultan River for its supply. This was the beginning of a high quality, high volume system that eventually would be envied throughout the nation. One of the more enterprising water

Baseball was the great sporting pastime, with Everett taking on the role of the pioneering Snohomish Pacifics in the early 1900s. Led by major league pitcher Walter Thornton, first as a player and then as manager, the Smokestakers lost this 1905 game to Bellingham 9-5 before 4,500 fans (out of a total Everett population of only 15,000) but won the Northwest professional championship. Thornton convinced the city to build this new field at its fairgrounds near Silver Lake. (Courtesy Snohomish Historical Society)

and power systems was developed by Arlington in the early 1900s. The Arlington Power and Water system built a wooden dam on Jim Creek, a tributary to the South Fork Stillaguamish River. Washed out a year later, it subsequently was replaced by two different concrete structures. The final concrete dam, reputed at the time of its construction to be the highest hyroelectric dam in the world, remained in operation until 1935 when it was removed with dynamite.

In 1908 an agency which ultimately would have a substantial impact in the wooded wilderness of eastern Snohomish County first made its appearance. The United States Forest Service was authorized by Congress at the urging of Republican President Theodore Roosevelt in 1905 and then was organized three years later into regions, forests and ranger districts to manage better the huge federal forest reserves, which had been set aside by President Grover Cleveland in the 1897. Created by Gifford Pinchot and guided by the utilitarian philosophy developed by Jeremy Bentham and John Stuart Mill of "the greatest good for the greatest number," the new entity brought the application of scientific management to the federal forestlands. There was, for example, a small tree nursery developed near Silverton, the first in the Pacific Northwest. Seedlings raised here were used to replant burned areas on Long Mountain and Mount Dickerman which were not regenerating themselves, experiment with Eastern varieties of trees which might prove valuable in the region, and provide stock for burns near Snoqualmie Pass and Lester in the Green River Valley of Pierce County. Though the Forest Service would not significantly affect logging until more operations moved farther inland and upward to the federal lands, the Forest Service did negotiate its first timber sale near Darrington in 1908. The Hazel Mill Company was contracted to cut 7.86 million board feet of fir, hemlock and cedar near French Creek, while the Gold Basin Lumber & Shingle Company erected a mill to cut National Forest timber at that settlement in 1910.

The 1910 census figures documented a decade of dramatic growth throughout much of the western United States, including the state of Washington. This surge had begun with the effects of the Klondike gold rush and would not be surpassed until the years following World War II. In Snohomish County population had jumped from 23,950 in 1900 to 59,209 in 1910, an increase of nearly 150 percent. Growth in Everett was even more dramatic. Population had tripled from 7,838 to 24,814, making Everett the state's fourth largest city behind Seattle, Tacoma and Spokane. Nearly 42 percent of the county residents now lived in Everett. The city of Snohomish was still the second largest urban center with 3,244 residents. Monroe, Arlington, Marysville and Edmonds were the next largest towns, in that order. The Stanwood area probably was next, but its census was divided between its rival communities.

The number of racial minorities still was small, and there were actions that demonstrated they were not entirely welcome. While Japanese who toiled on railroad crews and at Crown Lumber in Mukilteo generally were accepted, the situation was much different in Darrington. In 1907, 100 Darrington residents signed a manifesto which read in part, ". . . we earnestly request every citizen, employee and merchant of Darrington and vicinity to cooperate by absolutely refusing said Japanese or Chinese laborers employment of any kind." Despite this document, the U.S. Mill owners hired 20 Japanese workers in 1910. The furor which followed finally culminated on Monday, June 13. About 100 men, summoned by a pre-arranged noon hour bell, gathered on a street corner and marched *en masse* to the mill. As Elizabeth Poehlman describes in *Darrington: Mill Town / Timber Town*, the men rounded up the Japanese workers and paid their way out of town on the train that day. Even three Japanese who were allowed to stay and round up belongings were run out of town on foot two days later because they were "lingering longer than was deemed necessary."

Relations between the owners and the townspeople already had been very strained that year over the issues of prohibition and then town incorporation, the residents seeking self-government as a device to remain "wet." They feared that the county-wide vote affecting all unincorporated areas would go in favor of the "drys." In this they were correct. The U.S. Mill owners actively opposed their efforts and successfully brought suit against them, blocking incorporation and its probable legalization of liquor.

Despite the racial prejudice, a progressive reform movement was evidencing itself by 1910. For Snohomish County it was as if a place that had grown too much too fast was now finding time to build a "better society" on the dream which had attracted so many to the area. This grass roots endeavor to improve the human condition was in concert with a state and national movement of the same nature. Marked both by efforts to curtail perceived abuse (alcohol prohibition, for example) and enhance opportunity (women's suffrage, for instance), progressive reform included a special emphasis on the disenfranchised and more vulnerable members of society. Attention was given to youth, as when ordinances were passed in Snohomish, aimed at keeping underage boys away from saloons. Meaningful changes in education, such as those promoted by C.R. Frazier during his 1910 to 1918 term as Everett's school superintendent, were in the progressive reform spirit. He pioneered a hot lunch program, challenged and changed the system of failing students until they were three or four years older than their classmates, instituted programs for special education students, and started night and summer schools. He also stressed and gained community support for high school manual training and commercial courses for those students not necessarily academically inclined. During his superintendency both the Vocational and Commercial buildings were built on the Everett High campus.

In another venue, Monroe was a direct recipient of state progressive reform when the 1907 legislature acted to create a "reformatory" just west of town. The institution, which would be planned for the rehabilitation of state offenders between the ages of 18 and 30, was the brainchild of Christian enthusiast Corwin Shank. After 10 years of lobbying Shank saw his dream come to fruition through the support of Governor Mead and the cooperation of liberal Democratic and Republican legislators. The eleventh reformatory in the United States, it started with a meager state allocation of $30,000. Property was acquired near Monroe, and by the summer of 1908 about 40 inmates, under the supervision of 11 guards, were living in temporary frame buildings and preparing the

Traditionally, American policy had allowed virtually unlimited immigration, and Snohomish County has had a significant foreign-born population throughout its history. The European wave crested during the first two decades of the 1900s, as anti-foreign feelings and "100% American" pressures followed World War I, leading to sharp restrictions in the successive Johnson Acts of 1921 and 1924. (#0592, courtesy Everett Public Library)

From 1896 to 1903 members of the Monroe Methodist Episcopal Church were the first and only religious congregation in the community. They took an active role in the prohibition movement, signing pledges of abstinence and circulating them in the Skykomish and Snoqualmie valleys. (#301, courtesy Monroe Historical Society)

site for permanent structures. Funds were limited, progress was slow, and cost over-runs staggering, even though the construction itself was being done by the inmates under the supervision of Monroe craftsmen. Using bricks that had been made on site, the crew finally finished an administration building in July 1911. A month later a superintendent's mansion with eight bedrooms and four bathrooms, soon criticized for its extravagance, was completed. Then the main building with 320 cells was begun. Work at the site would drag on until 1920. The cellblock building originally budgeted for $46,000 cost nearly $180,000. Billed popularly as the "University of Another Chance," the institution seemed from the outset to be in conflict with itself. While the concept was the reform of youthful offenders, the facility had the physical design of the classic prison. There was little or no recognition that a reformatory program might require a different kind of facility. The institution, nevertheless, would become a major Monroe employer and landmark and eventually become a complex larger than the state penitentiary in Walla Walla.

Arguably, the two keystone issues of progressive reform were women's suffrage and prohibition. Generally, the latter would be more easily achieved after the former was accomplished, although the issue really wasn't all that simple. The state organizations that championed the two were strangely disassociated; there was no brilliantly orchestrated master plan to franchise the woman voter as a prerequisite to enacting prohibition. Some locales, in fact, instituted prohibition before women had voting rights. Women's suffrage came into being in 1910 in Washington behind the grass roots effort of organizations such as the Edmonds Equal Suffrage Club, which had formed in 1907. At the same time county reformers, including Edmonds' colorful newspaper executive Mrs. Hanna, were working for alcohol abolition. Liquor, in the minds of many reformers, was at the root of vice. Prostitution, gambling, corruption, and crime, they claimed, could all be traced to alcohol. Throughout the county the opportunities to acquire liquor had been plentiful. In 1910 there were more than 110 saloons in 24 different locales. Everett's Hewitt Avenue, with its 36 drinking establishments, was the undisputed saloon row champion.

Reformers were determined to snuff out the evil drink, and they knew the way to do it was at the polls. Fiery Ellen Thayer of the Everett Woman's Book Club said it well, "I am not advocating a Carrie Nation campaign, as much as I would enjoy it, but we must agitate until some action is taken." For Everett, action would occur in November of 1910. Voters narrowly approved a local option, which shut down the saloons. The vote was accomplished without the women; as state suffrage was approved at the same time. The issue proved to be economic as well as moral, however. In short order, without income gener-

John E. Campbell and the Women's Eight-Hour Workday Bill in Washington State

By Margaret Riddle

John Campbell was confident that he had the votes he needed. The young state representative from Everett met with the Joint Committee on Labor and Labor Statistics in Olympia on the evening of January 26, 1911 to discuss passage of House Bill 12. If passed, it would give Washington women an eight-hour workday.

Seattle activist Alice Lord had led the way, organizing Seattle waitresses in the early 1900s and beginning the struggle for shorter working hours. Ten hours was the state standard, with women primarily employed in the fisheries, canneries, laundries, breweries, hotels, restaurants, and confectioneries. Many worked 14-hour days, seven days a week. Lord found an effective supporter in Campbell, who authored and introduced the bill during his first term as state representative in 1909. In that year, however, the measure failed.

While the struggle for an eight-hour day was a cause championed as early as the 1870s by the American Federation of Labor, few workers actually had it. But in the dawning years of the twentieth century, Washington lawmakers supported many progressive causes, and John Campbell was one of the state's influential Progressives.

In 1908 Campbell had been elected to the Washington State legislature on the Republican ticket. It was a time of political turmoil, the party splitting over issues and candidates. Increasingly irritated with the power east coast investors (particularly the railroad tycoons) held over their economic fates, west coast states fought for regional control. Populism and reform gained significant strength in the West. Many followed Theodore Roosevelt as a reform champion who advocated conservation programs as well as government control over big-money trusts. Many Republicans began calling themselves Progressives. John Campbell won his second house term and a state senate seat (1913-15) on the Progressive ticket.

SENATOR J. E. CAMPBELL

Campbell was business manager for the Everett-based *Labor Journal*. The position afforded him the media access he needed for editorializing and running campaign advertisements. This allowed him to make a successful jump into politics. Campbell's strong support of women's rights included the right to vote, an issue that held considerable popular support in the region in the century's first decade.

Washington women gained suffrage in 1910. Passage of the state suffrage act gave Campbell and Lord a new constituency—voting women. In partnership, they began to work for passage of the eight-hour bill. Women's clubs, churches, religious organizations, and organized labor now supported the measure. Women's rights leaders May Arkwright Hutton of Spokane, Emma Smith De Voe of Tacoma, and a Stanwood woman we know only as Mrs. D'Arcy joined Alice Lord in successfully lobbying for the cause and gathered signatures in support of the measure.

But on that January 1911 evening a number of influential employers, and some of their female employees, arrived by chartered rail car to fight the bill's passage. Seattle businessmen spoke of the grave hardships an eight-hour workday would bring. Production speed, they insisted, would need to increase in order to balance the loss of hours. The Spokane Chamber of Commerce representative pleaded that dire economic times would result and that manufacturers would choose to locate their businesses elsewhere, should the bill be passed. Some women workers testified against the measure, fearing a cut in pay or the loss of their jobs. Upon being questioned, however, most agreed that they would be happy working only eight hours if they would receive the same pay.

Campbell presented the committee with the petition of signatures supporting the bill, which he unrolled from his speaker's podium to the length of the room and back again. It was such dramatic flair that had earned John Campbell the respect of his colleagues and the nickname Dynamite Jack.

Fisheries and canneries were important to Washington's economy. They exerted strong influence in the legislature. Representatives agreed to pass the measure only with an amendment that would exclude these trades. With this wording, the bill was forwarded to the senate. The amendment, in all probability, would have led to enough legal entanglements to nullify the measure.

As it turned out, the senate supported the bill as originally drafted. Accusing the legislature of being dominated by special interests, Senator Ralph Metcalf of Pierce County declared that the eight-hour bill should apply to all female workers alike, and in March 1911 the bill passed the senate, without compromise, just as Campbell had written it. Presented by Senator Jesse Huxtable of Spokane, House Bill 12 / Senate Bill 74, entitled "An act to regulate and limit the hours of employment of females in any mechanical or mercantile establishment, laundry, hotel or restaurant; to provide for its enforcement and a penalty for its violation," was read for the first and second times and immediately passed. Only five senators voted against the measure, and Washington State women were granted an eight-hour workday.

Campbell continued his efforts for labor and women's issues, next authoring a bill that provided for the state's first female Deputy Labor Commissioner. He also supported women's compensation bills and improved working conditions for railroad employees.

Campbell had been a laborer himself. Born 1880 in Burnside, Michigan, he traveled to Everett with his family at age 22 and began working in various lumber camps and mills. He also worked as a shingle weaver for a time. In 1905 he purchased an interest in the *Labor Journal*, published in Everett, and became its business manager, a position he held until 1912.

Politics led Campbell back to journalism following his senate term, and he very briefly served as business manager for the *Port Angeles Herald*. This venture seems to have been more political than journalistic, an arrangement to weaken a rival paper. That quickly effected, Campbell moved on. From 1917 to 1921 he worked for the State Department of Fisheries, and from 1921 to 1924 served as deputy in Everett for the State Department of Labor and Industries.

John E. Campbell's life and career were brief. He contracted spinal meningitis and died on June 14, 1924, at age 43, in Everett's Providence Hospital, and was buried in Evergreen Cemetery. He left a wife, Phoebe, two brothers, and a sister, and a significant legacy of accomplishments. Campbell not only served in one of Washington State's most productive legislative sessions, he was an effective reformer for the Progressive cause.

ated by the liquor business, city coffers were empty, and drink was voted back in two years later, even with suffrage in effect. By now the campaign had reached the state level. Everett children, 1,500 strong with banners calling for "Less Booze, More Shoes" were among the campaigners for Initiative Measure Number 3, which if passed would close the saloons. In a narrow victory the measure was approved in November 1914. It would take another vote four years later fully to outlaw Washington's liquor industry.

It was November 1912, however, when the progressive movement had its biggest impact at the Snohomish County polls. That year, county citizens abandoned their usual

Transportation Before World War I

Left: A number of interurban rail lines were proposed in the first decade of the century, but only two were completed. In 1903 service began between Snohomish and Everett along the Northern Pacific tracks north of the river via Lowell. In 1910 a new line was established to link downtown Everett with downtown Seattle, running past Silver Lake and what became Alderwood Manor. This was its first departure. (Courtesy Everett Public Library)

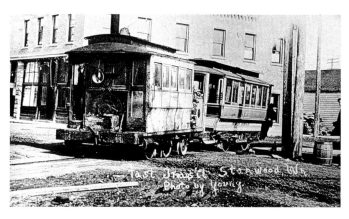

After the Great Northern Railway bypassed Stanwood to the east, John Hall built the mile-long H&H Railway in 1904 to carry passengers and freight from the depot to the town. Operating for three decades, it was nicknamed the world's shortest steam railroad. (Courtesy Stanwood Area Historical Society)

Passenger and freight steamers such as the *Verona* were the mainstay of county transportation until the 1920s, when the growing network of paved highways and inexpensive automobiles drove them out of business. (Courtesy Everett Public Library)

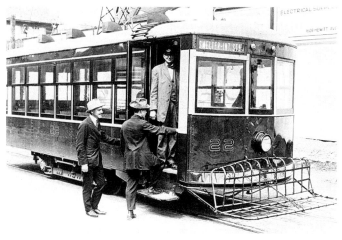

The Everett streetcar system began in the 1890s. By the time this photograph was taken in 1911 a network of tracks connected different parts of the city. In 1923, Everett prided itself in being one of the first cities in the nation to abandon streetcars in favor of a trackless bus system. (Courtesy Everett Public Library)

Where passenger traffic was too light to justify regular train service, gasoline powered rail cars such as this McKean model were used to provide branch line accomodations. This one ran between Arlington and Darrington for the Northern Pacific. (Courtesy Bob Miller)

Republican course and elected several Progressive candidates. One of these was labor leader John Campbell who defeated his Republican and Democratic opponents for a position in the state senate in a career which vastly improved the working conditions for women. After Teddy Roosevelt split the Republican Party and lost his 1912 bid as a Progressive candidate for president to Democrat Woodrow Wilson, the movement lost its steam. In the county, the Republicans were back in control for the 1914, 1916 and 1918 elections. Democrat W.W. Black from Everett was the state Democratic nominee for governor in 1916, but the Supreme Court ruled he could not accept the office because he was serving as a judge on the bench. His replacement Ernest Lister won the election.

The year 1910 saw a major improvement in county transportation with the completion of an interurban rail line that connected Everett with Seattle. Origin of the line could be traced back to 1900 when Fred Sander incorporated the Everett and Interurban Railway Company. By 1907 Sander had reorganized his firm into the Seattle-Everett Interurban Railway Company and constructed a line north from Ballard to Halls Lake in south Snohomish County. Within a year, Stone and Webster, a Boston-based holding company with a national monopoly on streetcar systems, had acquired all of the Sander's company stock. Stone and Webster envisioned the Seattle-Everett connection as part of a network running from Vancouver, B.C. to Olympia. The Seattle-Everett Traction Company, Stone and Webster's wholly owned subsidiary, was incorporated in February of 1909. In spring 1910 the line was completed from Halls Lake to Everett. After an April 30 inaugural trip, regular service started on May 2. The electric trolleys could make a regular run from Everett to Seattle in a 1 hour and 35 minutes. With new cars, that time later was cut by about a half-hour. Stops along the way averaged about one per mile. Transformed in name to the Pacific Northwest Traction Company in 1912, the interurban served as a key transportation link and a stimulus for development of the then sparsely settled south county. The system remained in operation until 1939. The rail connection north to Mt. Vernon never was built because of the expense of crossing the Snohomish River delta area and the Stillaguamish River. There was a bus line to Mt. Vernon as part of the system and a rail line interurban from Mt. Vernon to Bellingham.

Snohomish County obtained its last transcontinental railroad connection when a branch line of the Chicago, Milwaukee, St. Paul and Pacific was built from Cedar Falls in eastern King County to Everett in 1911. The line traveled from Cedar Falls to North Bend,

In 1911 the last of the three northwestern transcontinental railroads reached the county when the Chicago, Milwaukee, St. Paul and Pacific, the "Milwaukee Road," built a branch line from Cedar Falls north down the Snoqualmie Valley to Monroe and then on to Snohomish and Everett along the Snohomish River. Its depots in Everett and in Monroe still were standing in 2004. (Courtesy Everett Public Library)

along the Snoqualmie River to Monroe, down the Snohomish River to Snohomish, and then into Everett. There were several covered bridges along the route. The 450-foot span over the Skykomish River at Monroe was reported to be the longest covered railroad bridge in the world. Regularly scheduled freight runs began in August 1911. Numerous sidetracks and spurs were built to get freight to the mainline, serving such businesses as the Snohomish Iron Works. The start of passenger service on April 21, 1912 was cause for celebration. About 450 Everett, Snohomish, Monroe, and Duvall residents traveled to and from North Bend for a day of festivities. Later, a gas-electric motor coach would provide regular service between Everett and Monroe. Commonly known as the "Milwaukee Road," the line was plagued by financial difficulties and was never a strong competitor for trans-continental passenger traffic.

Transportation of another type was beginning to appear. Lew Paramore, a Snohomish druggist, was reported to have had an automobile as early as 1901. A horseless carriage driven by W.O. Nelson made a noteworthy appearance in Everett that same year when a frightened pedestrian plunged through the Pioneer Drug Store display window. In 1902 Everett got its first resident automobile, a Grout Brothers steam car, made in Massachusetts and owned by print shop operator Wilde Knisely. It would be another three years before other Everett drivers joined Knisely as automobile owners, but soon cars were showing up throughout the county. A touring automobile driven by Charles and Claude Roy created great excitement when it rolled into Monroe in 1904. By 1909, eight automobiles were owned by appreciative Monroe residents. Stanwood could boast of three vehicles by 1907—all of them described as "beauties." Car ownership increased dramatically after Henry Ford began mass-producing his basic, inexpensive Model T in 1909 as automobiles no longer remained an expensive luxury item. *The Everett Tribune* reported that 70 autos were owned in Everett in June of 1910, while Snohomish instituted a 12-mile an hour speed limit that same year. Edmonds' first automobile owner was A.M. Yost in 1911, with an Everett-30. A few years later he opened a Ford dealership, one of the first car sales agencies in Edmonds, and followed that with an "auto stage" bus line to Seattle. Car agencies such as Yost's repair shops and automotive supply stores were appearing in several county communities as a car care infrastructure gradually began to develop. John Gardner of the Everett Auto Company, for example, prepared a 1911 map as a road guide for motorists who wished to travel throughout western Snohomish County. A car even arrived at Index in 1911, although it mired in the mud and had to be towed out by a steam donkey engine.

The advent of the automobile prompted an interest in the expansion and improvement of the primitive county transportation routes. The Snohomish County Good Roads Association organized in 1906 with Dr. W. C. Cox, an early Everett auto enthusiast, as president. The association was successful in organizing a more systematic approach to county road building, but unsuccessful in attaining passage of bonds for major projects. After defeats in 1908 and 1912 the association mounted a vigorous campaign for $1,813,000 bond issue that would be submitted to voters on December 28, 1915. In order to attract the widest support possible, the bonds would fund a carefully crafted plan including something for every part of the county. The costs and locations for paving 140 miles were thoroughly explained to county residents. Sam Hill, son-in-law of James Hill and promoter of the Washington Good Roads Association, even was brought in to stir up the positive vote. The December 29, 1915 *Everett Daily Herald* banner headline announced, "Bonds Win by Good Margin." Congratulatory telegram messages from Governor Ernest Lister and Sam Hill were on the front page. County commission chairman T.C. Fleming effused, "This is the best thing that ever happened to Snohomish County." Dr. Cox, still president of the association, saw a decade-long dream come true, as work on the projects started quickly. One of the early contractors was Everett resident Henry J. Kaiser, whose later ventures into fields of shipbuilding, aluminum production, and construction would make him one of the United States' leading industrialists. Still, roads were primitive, and most travelers continued to use the established rail and steamboat service, the interurbans to Seattle and Snohomish, and the electric streetcars in Everett.

Growth continued after 1910, but not at the rate of the previous two decades. The county seemed to be maturing into its role as the state's fourth most populous. On the social side, interest was sustained in the usual lodges and orders, but new kinds of service organizations also were appearing. The Everett Rotary Club, destined to be the largest of the county service clubs, was launched by 50 business and professional men in December of 1916. The first Lions Club soon would soon follow. New youth organizations also were formed. The first Boy Scout troop was organized in 1914, and the Campfire Girls came into existence three years later.

Although it would be short-lived, a relative calm settled over the lumber and shingle industry in 1912. The shingle weavers and mills had negotiated a contract that guaranteed a fixed schedule of wages and hours through 1914 in exchange for a no-strike pledge. The 1912 Labor Day parade in Everett was said to be the biggest and best ever. A new optimistic Everett Commercial Club had emerged from a marriage of the Business Association and the Chamber of Commerce. New timber operations still were arriving, as the Walton Mill in Lowell, and many of the older, smaller operations were being merged with larger companies. The Wisconsin Lumber Company in Stanwood, for example, became a Clough operation, while John McMasters of Marysville consolidated several small concerns into a 50-employee mill that cut 200,000 shingles and 10,000 board feet of cedar siding daily. Timber was rolling out of the eastern hills in enormous quantities, with *The Arlington Times* reporting that on October 19, 1916 the Darrington train brought down 80 carloads of logs.

From its earliest days in Everett, Weyerhaeuser Timber had talked of a giant mill in the city. It finally came into being in April of 1915. Located on the Snohomish River site of the old barge works and known as Mill B, it dwarfed any previous county mill. Its initial capacity was 400,000 board feet per eight-hour shift; that soon was increased to one million. Run entirely by electricity, the new plant was hailed by American lumbermen as "one of the largest and most up-to-date sawmills in the United States." The 203-foot main smokestack became a community landmark. The plant had a work force of several hundred, and Weyerhaeuser was now the biggest employer in the city of Everett, an honor it would hold for several decades.

As the forest industry rolled along, mining sputtered toward its end. Darrington mining activity had pretty much petered out by 1920. The Boston-American Mining Company invested in Monte Cristo around 1913, but their operations were brought to a halt by the outbreak of World War I. Agricultural pursuits, on the other hand, expanded. The increase in fruit growing led to the organization of the Snohomish County Fruit

169

A County Road System Is Begun

Following the 1916 county road bond issue, paved concrete was laid, some so strong that it still is in use. This crew is working on the Vernon Road between Cavalero's Corner and Marysville, designated the Pacific Highway until the mouth of the Snohomish River was bridged a decade later. (Courtesy Snohomish County Department of Public Works)

Succesful contractors such as Henry J. Kaiser of Everett (later a noted industialist) set up complex truck and rail systems to haul crushed rock to the road work in 1916. (Courtesy Snohomish County Department of Public Works)

Right: Early county roads were so bad that northern county residents threatened to secede if they were not improved. Nevertheless, early motorists vied to see who could reach distant places first. This car made it to Index in 1911 on the new county road but required a steam donkey engine to pull it out of the mud. (Lee Pickett photograph, courtesy Index Historical Society)

Driving across the Snohomish River flats from Cavalero's Corner to Everett always has had its adventuresome side. The original road was on the valley floor. At the west end a bridge across the river from Everett Avenue required a 90 degree turn and resulted in many wrecks. (Courtesy Snohomish County Department of Planning and Development Services)

When the flooding season began in November the high waters often inundated the ground level road from Cavalero's Corner. Motoring and business interests demanded a solution: build a trestle! (Courtesy Snohomish County Department of Planning and Development Services)

Roads often paralleled railroad lines, which in turn had followed ancient tribal routes. Here a 1912 Cadillac is loaded with both passengers and freight outside the store at Lochsloy, mid-way between Lake Stevens and Granite Falls on the west bank of the Pilchuck River. (Courtesy Granite Falls Historical Society)

Growers Association in 1916. A 200-acre pear orchard near Startup was touted as being the largest in the state. The Snohomish County Dairymen's Association was formed in 1917 and soon established an Arlington condensery with the capability of processing 100,000 pounds of raw milk per day. Poultry, too, emerged as a major industry, particularly after the Puget Sound Mill Company began selling off its logged-off south county land in five-acre ranchettes that were billed as perfect for poultry operations. One of the outgrowths of increased farm production was the development of the canning and packing industry. By 1918, the Lien Brothers Packing Company of Stanwood, for example, was using 125 seasonal employees to pack 40,000 cases of vegetables annually. The American Packing Company in Everett was another large operation. Fishing and its related businesses were also developing into a sizeable industry. The Everett Packing Company on the waterfront had the capacity to produce 3,500 cases of canned salmon per day.

As the county moved toward the 1920s, there were signs of more appreciation for the physical setting. In the whirlwind days of the late nineteenth and early twentieth century the natural environment was seen as little more than something to exploit. Mountains were for mining; rivers were for floating logs; trees were for cutting; land was for farming. While the exploitation would continue, there was a growing awareness of nature's beauty and fragility. Index was heralded for its picturesque scenery. The Mountaineers, organized in 1906 to "explore, study, enjoy and preserve," regularly were traversing the Cascades of eastern Snohomish County. Noted Western author Zane Grey was awed by the forest surroundings when he fished Deer Creek, a tributary to the North Fork Stillaguamish River in 1918. His writings helped spread the word about the county's beautiful forestlands. More artists, photographers, and naturalists in the spirit of a John Muir ventured in and spread the gospel of appreciation and preservation.

February of 1916 will always be remembered as the time of the Big Snow. The biggest lowland snowfall in recorded

Automobiles became common in county towns before World War I. These are a 1905 one-cyclinder Cadillac on the right and a 1905 or 1906 Olds on the left, parked on Granite Avenue in downtown Granite Falls. (Courtesy Granite Falls Historical Society)

The Photographic Studio of Rigby & Rigby

By Margaret Riddle

Iowa born Alice and Clara Rigby arrived in Everett, Washington at the dawning of the 20th century and did what few other women of their time dared to try: they owned and operated a professional photo studio. From 1905 to 1915, the Rigby and Rigby Photo Shop successfully competed with prominent local photographers J. D. Myers and Bert Brush, as well as half a dozen smaller firms, and found a niche for themselves in a profession dominated by men.

The Rigby sisters were part of a growing number of women in the early 1900s who sought social and economic independence, and the West was fertile territory for this progressive kind of thinking. Issues of the day included the rights of working women and, more significantly, a woman's right to vote. By 1910, Washington State would grant women suffrage.

But the need for independence had more immediate and personal roots for Alice and Clara. As the result of an unhappy marriage, their mother, Delia, encouraged her daughters to seek professions, not husbands. And, in like manner, Delia's sister, Emma Sarepta Yule, was a highly successful and independent lady. Arriving at the Everett townsite in 1891, Emma Yule became Everett's first schoolteacher. When other teachers were hired, Emma became Principal. From 1897 to 1900, she served as Everett's Superintendent of Schools. In 1900, Emma Yule left Everett to teach in Alaska. Showing such independence, intelligence and ability, Emma was likely a significant role model for her young nieces.

The Rigby sisters chose professions that were considered acceptable for women of their time: Alice became a teacher, and Clara pursued photography. In Washington State, female teachers could not be married, a requirement that continued until after World War II. However, photography was, as the Kodak Company advertised at the turn of the century, an appropriate occupation for women. It was considered a proper artistic endeavor, and work could be done in or near the home. Photography studios routinely employed women in this era, though most worked as silent partners in the darkroom or as retouchers, their identities invisible behind a male studio name.

Rigby family stories recall that Delia came to Everett with daughters Clara and Alice at the turn of the century, but city directories indicate otherwise. Alice seems to have come to Everett first, arriving alone in 1900. She is listed that year as teaching at Lincoln School, in the elementary grades, and living with Aunt Emma Yule at Everett's elegant Monte Cristo Hotel. That year, however, Ms. Yule became involved in a dispute with the school district over her pay and departed to teach in Alaska.

Clara began her career working as a retoucher in 1892 for the J. C. Wilson Studios in Cherokee, Iowa, moving next to Colorado where she did similar work for various studios. In 1904, she and her mother came to Everett. Photographer Loren Seely hired Clara as his retoucher. One year later, she bought the Seely studio, acquiring both his studio location and negative collection. Alice quit teaching to work with Clara, and for nearly 10 years the Rigby sisters operated the business with considerable success.

Rigby family members say that the sisters called their studio *Rigby and Rigby* in an attempt to conceal the fact that they were women, but Clara and Alice soon found ways to capitalize on the pluses of their gender. The Rigbys advertised themselves as "Portraitists" who specialized in baby pictures, and it can be imagined that Alice drew on her teaching experience to aid in photographing the young.

By 1900, times were changing economically for the region. With the severe depression years of the 1890s now in its past, the Pacific Northwest was once again feeling prosperous and optimistic, and Everett gained its share of new arrivals, many of them immigrants, seeking to better their lives in a new place. In the century's first decade, Everett's population tripled.

Everett now had families, and families had "Kodaks". By 1900, photographic advances and cheaper prices made it possible for amateurs to take their own pictures. Working with either a small glass-plate camera or a new popular roll film model known as the postcard Kodak 3A, they photographed their families, their homes and businesses, as well as activities on their city streets. They also recorded heavy snowfalls and floods and documented their vacations and trips abroad.

Often poorly exposed and usually of poor composition, these photographs were, nevertheless, priceless ways of sharing experiences with family and friends miles away. Studios processed and duplicated these amateur views, often printing them as postcards, which could be mailed. Over the years these amateur postcard images have become historical treasures because they often show events of everyday life in a way that studio views do not.

Film processing offered steady work, and the Rigbys gained their share of this business. However, more money was being made in portraiture and commercial photography. Professional portraits were highly prized. Photographed with balanced lighting, set against a studio background and retouched to make its subjects look their best, the professional portrait was considered a work of art, and professional photographers were held in high regard. Competition was keen, and to prosper in the work, a practitioner needed to be good at business as well as art. The Rigby Sisters skillfully balanced both and survived in competition with other excellent photographers. The Rigbys even opened additional studios in Monroe, Snohomish, and Arlington, and commuted by train between towns.

In 1913, they temporarily closed their studios to visit Japan. Photo albums assembled by the sisters document their trip. Upon returning to Everett the Rigbys relocated their studio at 2802 Colby. But the joyful years were behind them. Alice soon was diagnosed with cancer and died at 44 years of age. Clara continued the business for only a few months after Alice's death, then closed the studio for good.

The Rigby negatives were stored for many years and then dispersed, some finding their way into the files of Lee Juleen, now housed at the Everett Public Library. It is a shame that few of their photos remain. Only a small number of negatives and postcards in the Everett Public Library collection are easily attributed to them. What the Rigby family has retained are priceless photos that Clara and Alice took of each other, showing the fine quality of their portraiture.

In the 1920s Clara married James Casperson, an employee of the Everett Pulp and Paper Company. The couple moved to California, where they grew and marketed nuts. Clara eventually returned to live in Everett. She died August 27, 1953.

Rigby descendants speak of Alice as the quieter and gentler sister, but while Clara was a stern and imposing figure to her relatives, it is Clara they remember, since she lived long enough to be a presence in their lives. What made the sisters different from other Snohomish County women working in photography at that time? Were the Rigbys wealthy enough to be able to buy a photo studio while the average retoucher was not? "No," the family says, "they didn't have money." Perhaps just the skill, the drive and the dream. And that, the sisters certainly had.

Snohomish County history began on January 31 and continued for three days. Officially more than 30 inches fell in Everett in one 36-hour period. Many outlying areas reported considerably more. In Stanwood the snow was said to be four to five feet deep, and the Stillaguamish River was frozen all the way across. Snow depth was reported to be 42 inches in Snohomish and 48 inches in Marysville. South county seemed to have it a little better. The Edmonds' snowfall was said to be about two feet. Generally, traffic was paralyzed, including the interurban; business and industry could not operate; schools were closed; roofs sagged, and shovelers gave up until the onslaught was over. A few roofs collapsed, including a church in Granite Falls, but most buildings survived unscathed. Digging out was an arduous task, and there were some problems with subsequent flooding. Through the stories that have passed from generation to generation, and the wonderful photographs that still bring reactions of disbelief, the Big Snow is entrenched in county lore.

By summer 1916 the Everett shingle industry peace had erupted into a vicious strike in which neither side would budge. The shingle workers had struck on May 1 after the mill owners reneged on a promise to restore the wage scale the workers had lost during the 1914 downturn following the outbreak of World War I. Expressing opposition to the wage restoration and support for the open shop principle, the owners' intent was to trigger the strike and use it to crush the union. Strikebreakers were brought in to operate some of the mills. Physical confrontations between strikers and strikebreakers had occurred, with Everett police condoning mill owner violence. To the chagrin of moderate union leaders such as Ernest Marsh, who had orchestrated a new shingle weavers union constitution, the maverick Industrial Workers of the World (IWW) entered the fray. Sensing that if Clough, Hartley, Irving,

When Snohomish County winter weather is discussed, 1916 is the year against which all others are measured. In early February, record amounts of snow were dumped on the county. More than 30 inches fell on Everett in a 36 hour period, and in outlying areas the amounts were even greater. This view looking south on Stanwood's Market Street shows the town after the thaw began. Snowfall in this part of the county was said to be between four and five feet in a two day period. (Courtesy Stanwood Area Historical Society)

and Jamison won, then wages would be cut throughout the Northwest, the "Wobblies" initiated a "free speech" movement on Everett street corners. Essentially, "free speech" was a frequently used Wobbly strategy to flood the community with speakers in expectation that they would be jailed for violating ordinances restricting their right to speak and organize on the streets—a device frequently used against them but not applied to rival groups trying to appeal to workers, such as the Salvation Army. When one speaker was arrested another would replace him, and so on. Soon the local jail would be overflowing. The strain on a community's budget and the undesirable publicity of violation of constitutional rights could result in some compromise with the Wobblies. Such had been the case in Spokane in 1909 when the city council, under this kind of pressure, succumbed by repealing an ordinance against street meetings. It had failed badly later in San Diego, when sheriff's deputies cordoned off the city, at night systematically beat up every arrested speaker jailed during the day, then dumped the men outside of town with warnings never to return.

Preaching a brand of radicalism that advocated revolution and power to the workers through one big undivided industrial union, the Wobblies roused the ire of the mill owners and much of the business establishment. With their backing, Sheriff Donald McRae began arresting the IWW and local Everett speakers on downtown streets. However, more filtered in from Seattle and other places to challenge the sheriff and carry on their free speech campaign. Eager to avoid a Spokane situation and willing to use violence, McCrea and the Everett Commercial Club organized a semi-private army of over 500 armed men to cordon off the city and stop public speaking. Everett's mill owners and businessmen had chosen the San Diego response. On October 30, with the strike weakening, McRae and his deputies intercepted 41 IWW members arriving among steamer passengers from Seattle and that night drove them from the county jail south to Beverly Park next to the interurban tracks. There they beat them mercilessly.

Although the incident was not reported in Everett newspapers, nearby residents had witnessed the incident, blood and pieces of clothing were found, and many of the injured men were hospitalized after making their way back to Seattle. In response, Everett labor leaders and other citizens invited Wobblies to return the following Sunday morning for a peaceful parade, picnic, and round of speeches at Clark Park to explain what had happened. They thought the sheriff would not use violence in daylight. Around 400 union members responded in Seattle the morning of November 5, 1916 for the boat trip to Everett. About half boarded the passenger steamer *Verona,* and the rest waited for the *Calista*.

Everett officials had been alerted to the arrival. McRae and a large group of deputies were at City Dock to greet the *Verona*. They were well armed, and there were handguns in possession of some of the Wobblies. Deputies were posted on Pier One to the south, on the shore to the east, and in the warehouse and waiting room on the dock to the north, where the sheriff stood between the buildings, awaiting the ship with several men at his side. As the *Verona* slid into dockside and began to tie up, Sheriff McCrea is reported to have shouted, "Who is your leader?" "We're all leaders," was the reply. The Sheriff barked, "You can't land here." "The hell we can't," the Wobblies yelled, crowding around the gangway. A shot was fired, from where no one can be sure. Then more. Then many. Amidst a hail of bullets, the *Verona* was thrust into reverse, snapping the mooring line and backing away from the lead, which was riddling its woodwork. Rifle fire continued even as the boat made its way back toward Seattle, warning off the *Calista*. Seven died officially—five Wobblies and two on the dock. Six to a dozen others were missing from the boat, and about 50 total were wounded, including Sheriff McRae. Undersheriff Jefferson Beard was among the dead, his wife always contending that he was struck by deputy crossfire.

This episode traumatized the city. The shingle weavers' strike, which had precipitated the Wobblies involvement, ended days later with no concessions from the mill owners. The class division, which had always characterized mill town Everett, was more pronounced. The Wobblies were burned out and threatened with death when they attempted later in November to reopen an Everett office. Seventy-four surviving Wobblies on the *Verona* were charged with first-degree murder, but all charges were dropped when the first of the group was acquitted in a widely publicized trial. No deputy ever was charged. Thus the incident, which would become known as the "Everett Massacre," had ended. The most infamous event in Everett, and perhaps Snohomish County history, it left scars that would last for decades.

Attention shifted from the still tense local scene to the European front when the United States declared war on Germany on April 6, 1917. The first Snohomish County men, members of the Sixth Division of Federal Naval Volunteers, were called into action immediately and left Everett the morning of April 7. Two Coast Artillery Companies, the 12th Company, Washington C.A. and the 5th Company, Washington C.A., left on August 1. The 12th consisted of mostly Everett residents. The 5th was made up of personnel from Snohomish, Monroe, Arlington, Bothell, Duvall, Lake Stevens, Machias, and other vicinities. In addition there were hundreds of enlistments. The day President Woodrow Wilson

The Everett Massacre

Right: Shingle "weavers" stood in rows at their machines, reaching automatically to the left to pull a shingle from the blade while focusing on the clipper saw in front to trim out imperfections. The pace was set by the circular saw machinery, and the sawyer had to match it for 10 hours per day. (Courtesy Everett Public Library)

Formed in 1905, the radical Industrial Workers of the World attempted to unite all working people into "One Big Union" to oppose spectacular corporate concentration and power in America's major industries. In August 1916 they opened this office on lower Hewitt Avenue to support striking shingle weavers belonging to the American Federation of Labor. (Courtesy Everett Public Library)

This photograph taken by court order in 1917 shows the steamer "Verona" as she was during the shooting on November, 5, 1916. The tide was six feet higher on the day of the clash, and access to the dock was blocked both by rope and armed men where the solitary figure stands next to the telephone pole. (Courtesy Everett Public Library)

These were some of the IWW members locked up in the Snohomish County jail for the killing of deputy Jefferson Beard and Lt. Charles O. Curtis. The jail was located on the east side of the 3000 block of Rockefeller Avenue and bordered by an "L" shaped alley. It was observed that the jail only held 74 prisoners, thus 74 were charged. (Courtesy Everett Public Library)

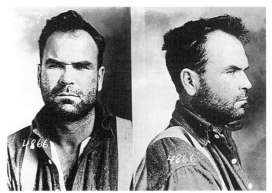

"Mug shot" of IWW member Thomas Tracy, who was aboard the "Verona." He was tried for first degree murder in King County following the killings on the Everett waterfront. When he was acquitted, similar charges against the 73 other jailed "Wobblies" were dropped. (Courtesy Everett Public Library)

Although the IWW and the striking millworkers lost their battle, they succeeded in their portrayal of local millowners and politicians as enemies of free speech and civil rights. This IWW cartoon illustrates their view of the "besmirched beauty" of Everett. (Courtesy Everett Public Library)

Shingle mill workers were highly skilled and productive, but the unguarded saws and thick dust took fingers, limbs, and lives. This Seaside Shingle Co. "knee bolter" saw removed a young man's arm in 1907, years before there was a state workmen's compensation law or mandated safety standards. (Courtesy Everett Public Library)

World War I

Left: This May Day 1916 school parade in Stanwood demonstrated growing support for United States' entry into the war, which began for the country on April 6, 1917. (John T. Wagness photograph, courtesy Stanwood Area Historical Society)

Above: Tremendous support for the Red Cross began with the declaration of war. William Howarth, president of the Everett Pulp & Paper Company in Lowell, led the organization. Over 19,700 residents had joined its eleven county branches by the end of 1918, providing assistance to service men, their families, and European refugees. (Courtesy Everett Public Library)

Above and right: Showing their patriotism, citizens with small flags marched in impromptu ranks along Hewitt. These parades were part of the effort to sell war bonds and rally the home front. (Courtesy Everett Public Library)

signed the declaration of war five Everett High School boys, Fred Spence, Roscoe Spence, Thornton Sullivan, Karl Hultman and Clarence Eddy became the first to enlist from that community. More than 5,000 county residents registered for the initial draft. The first three to be called were Ole Berge (Everett District), Vern Gist (District No. 1), and Takashi Kobasha (District No. 2). Before the war was over the county had provided more than 3,000 young men for military service. In addition a number of young women elected to serve overseas as Red Cross nurses. The R.L. Johnstone family of Arlington and the W.D. Morse family of Snohomish each furnished five sons for duty. Even though they were not United States citizens, several Native Americans from the Tulalip reservation entered the military.

As the European battles raged, the news came home about the heroics—and the deaths. Everett's Earl Faulkner lost his life in a machine gun battle at Chateau-Thierry. He was awarded a posthumous Croix de Guerre and a citation from the French General Petain. The first Distinguished Service Cross to a Snohomish County man was awarded posthumously to Jacob Teiseth of East Stanwood by General John J. Pershing. Private Charles Hall from Everett was wounded in action as a member of the famous "Lost Battalion" which survived six days cut off from its division. Bernard Stiefvater of Lowell died when a German submarine torpedoed his vessel. Malcolm, one of the five Johnstone boys from Arlington, was killed by a high explosive shell while serving at Chateau-Thierry. The list grew on an almost daily basis.

On the home front, the citizenry had mobilized quickly into a war support organization. The Snohomish County Red Cross was formed on April 7, 1917 in Snohomish. A drive the next month produced 14,470 members for the local branches. By fall 1918 there were 17 branches in the county and 45 auxiliaries among the churches and schools of Everett. William Howarth was the leader of two highly successful Red Cross drives. Everett banker Robert Moody chaired three of five Liberty Loan drives, which were equally successful. Communities prided themselves in how much they could raise. In the second Red Cross campaign Sultan, Arlington, Granite Falls, Three Lakes, and Stanwood all exceeded their quotas by more than 500 percent. Giant parades were part of the home front effort. Nearly 8,000 people marched in a 1917 parade organized by the Everett Elks. There were six bands and various organizations from around the county with all kinds of banners. One from Arlington proclaimed, "We Want Peace and Will Fight For It." Arlington hosted a crowd estimated at 6,000 at a parade of its own a year later while these Everett parades of 1918 and July 4, 1917 also were said to be huge.

Despite the general patriotic unity, the home front war effort was not without complications. In Arlington, for example, a segment of the rather large German American population was reluctant to endorse an attack on the Fatherland. They had cautiously watched as others, like the Johnstones, agitated for America's early entry in the conflict. When Malcom Johnstone died in battle, they may have wondered if the senior Johnstones secretly regretted their enthusiasm for America's involvement. The German American issue had another side, too. Some county families found themselves ostracized, ridiculed and even threatened because of their German surnames. In another development, the Wobblies, who had not been dealt a knockout punch in the Everett Massacre, re-emerged on the scene. They were instrumental in the organization of a strike that closed most western Washington logging and milling operations in summer 1917. Prompted by war

179

production needs, the federal government intervened. Leaders of the IWW were arrested and union records seized. Long prison terms or deportation resulted. To produce spruce lumber vital for the fledgling aircraft industry, loggers were taken into the Army's "Spruce Division." Spruce cutting camps were organized at Arlington and Darrington and railroads built by the government to access new stands of timber. The woods shut down was resolved when the mill owners agreed to the strikers' major demand of an eight hour day with the traditional ten hour pay. Eager to wipe out the Wobblies, the lumbermen embraced and encouraged a new employer-friendly labor organization that was created by the federal government. The Loyal Legion of Loggers and Lumbermen, better known as the "4L," was a combine of workers and employers. Barring Wobblies, promoting patriotism, and focusing on the production of the lumber for war, the 4L flourished for the remainder of the hostilities.

For most, the home front response permeated virtually every aspect of community life. Stanwood High School hung a service flag above its stage and then sadly added its first Gold Star when word came that Frank Hancock from that community had been killed in action. Everett High School prepared its own flag, sent discarded books to Camp Lewis south of Tacoma, and featured a ready-for-action sailor on the cover of the 1917 yearbook. Snohomish unveiled a woolen 12-foot by 20-foot flag, provided by Cascade Mill employers and employees. The federal government encouraged food economy, and Snohomish residents responded with recipes of austerity. Members of the Everett Woman's Book Club prepared a service flag and volunteered as "Minute Women" to assist in the sale of War Savings bonds and Thrift Stamps. The Red Cross auxiliaries from the Marysville area were knitting sweaters, wristlets, and woolen socks to be sent to Belgium. The Boys Comfort League in the same community packaged goodies that were sent to the boys overseas. In Edmonds a service flag was completed, and "Smileage" books, which could be used by servicemen for admission to camp entertainments, were prepared. A quartet from the newly formed Everett Rotary Club gained national fame for its renditions of patriotic songs. One of the more unique activities had students in the Snohomish area harvesting sphagnole, a common bog moss that was discovered to be an excellent filling in surgical dressings. After the violence at home and abroad during the decade, it was fitting that materials for healing as well as of war might come from the county.

The military effort on the front lines, with support from home, finally achieved the desired result. On November 11, 1918 the armistice took effect, and the great war was over. More than 3,000 Snohomish County men served in the military, with 124 men and two Red Cross nurses killed or dying in the service, according to W. H. Mason in his history of the war years.

The 1920s

As the 1920s dawned, *The Everett Daily Herald* knew what its Snohomish County readers wanted. The *Herald's* front page on New Year's Day, 1920, was devoted to the national mythical high school football championship, the game played at the city's Athletic Park on "a sloppy field that was covered by a mist of slippery mud." Small fires helped thaw frozen bits of turf, but cold, rain, and fog could not deter over 3,000 spectators. Wearing an Everett rooter's hat, Governor Louis Hart placed the ball for the kickoff, and a "battery of cameras, including moving picture machines" recorded the game. If the final 7-7 tie with Scott High School of Toledo, Ohio, disappointed local fans, there were few apologies. City and county took great pride in the young athletes and their already legendary coach, Enoch Bagshaw. "The Everett team showed championship class in every department, dominating the first half before being forced into an entirely defensive stand against the aggressive visitors."

Elsewhere, editors cheered, "Nineteen-twenty looks good to Everett." The closing year—indeed, the nearly 14 months since World War I ended—had brought substantial growth and placed Everett on a "solider foundation" than ever. Recent labor problems had faded before industrial peace and good will: "we are out of the worst of the doldrums into which unsettled policies and industrial unrest have lured us . . . It doesn't require the gift of prophecy to see that it's sure to be a good year." A good decade as well, the writer might have added. Yet, editorials could not have been as compelling as the quarter-by-quarter account of the day's major local event. Throughout the nation, the 1920s were marked by enthusiasm for high school and collegiate sports and the local and national heroes they fostered. The excitement that New Year's Day at the mill town on Port Gardner Bay proved the rule.

Decades do not begin and end with "January firsts" and "December thirty-firsts," so much as with those signal events that define their character. The 1920s were framed by the armistice ending World War I and the October 1929 stock market crash that signaled the onset of the Great Depression.

Word of the armistice reached Pacific coastal states shortly after midnight on November 11, 1918. Suddenly, it seemed more like midday, however. The *Herald* that day reported that in Everett "Telephone calls[,] noisesome automobiles and other announcements awakened the people of the city, causing hundreds to arise from their beds and hasten down town." Folks from outlying communities came in, and the streets thronged with celebrants of all ages. Carrying an American flag and a cartoon of the Kaiser, Commissioner of Public Safety T.J. Kelly led a parade along Hewitt Avenue from downtown to the river. Elks, Boy Scouts, Rotarians, a fife and bugle corps, mill workers, and store employees followed along the thoroughfare while more crowds watched curbside. Strings of tin cans clanged behind cars. Rotarians trucked a bell that had once rung over City Hall and "awaken[ed] many a citizen with its clarion note." With official permission, Scouts placed "generous deposits of explosive material" on streetcar tracks which "gave forth a sound sufficiently loud to please . . . the most exacting celebrator" when cars rolled over. Come daytime, most mills, stores, and civic buildings remained closed.

Other county towns also celebrated. At 1:00 A.M. the condensery whistle and "the shrill shrieks" of the fire siren awakened Monroe residents who streamed into the streets for an impromptu parade and a bonfire. During the day and into the night, "hilarious people paraded the streets, with fifes and tub drums, and tin-pan tambourines, making merry," according to the local newspaper. At Edmonds, mill whistles joined church bells and cowbells to celebrate the event.

There was, however, additional cause to celebrate. An enemy even more pervasive and frightening than the Hun had visited the Pacific Northwest that September, "Spanish" influenza. The epidemic had raged for over a month, with at least 1,700 attacks and 34 deaths in Everett alone. Now it seemed to be subsiding. Citizens were no longer required to wear gauze masks, and schools, theaters, and churches could reopen. That relief was premature. The scourge increased again, peaking in early December and lasting until Christmas, to the dismay of citizens tired of deprivations and anxious to move on with normal lives.

There were other sobering notes. One hundred twenty-four service men and two Red Cross nurses would never come home to Snohomish County after the War. Alongside the

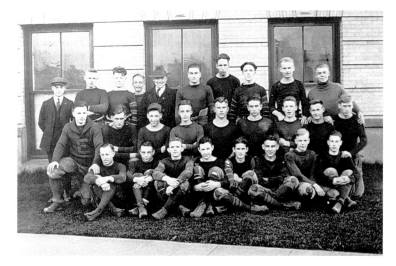

Everett High's 1920 football team was one of several champions coached by the legendary Enoch Bagshaw, who went on to become head coach at the University of Washington. He is standing in the back row, fifth from the left. (Courtesy Everett Public Library)

Home from the War

Right: Victory Parade, Bond Ave. Marchers and county citizens filled the streets along the route, starting at the Great Northern Railway depot on Bond Street above Port Gardner Bay. (Courtesy Everett Public Library)

Left: On March 12, 1919 the 63rd Coast Artillery Company returned from France to an Everett parade. County men had served in two companies before the war, one from Everett and the other from Snohomish, Monroe, Arlington, Machias, and Lake Stevens. The 65th Artillery, C.A.C., fought at St. Mihiel and the Argonne Forest and came home in February. (Courtesty Everett Public Library)

Right: The November 11, 1918 Armistice Day brought an end to World War I and celebratory parades along Everett's Hewitt Avenue. (Courtesy Everett Public Library)

Herald's account of armistice festivities peered the face of a uniformed 21-year-old marine dead in a Virginia naval hospital. Edmonds citizens would make a 67-star flag to commemorate local residents who had served; five stars were gold for those killed, and four silver for men wounded.

Now the time had come to move on. With 67,690 residents, Snohomish County was the state's fourth most populous in 1920, although the extremely rapid growth during the first two decades since statehood slowed markedly between 1910 and 1940. Everett, the largest of the county's 11 incorporated towns, had 27,644 residents; it would add fewer than 3,000 newcomers during the decade. Yet, Everett had far outgrown the city of Snohomish, its older, onetime rival. With fewer than 3,000 residents and a slowly declining population, Snohomish was the county's second city. Monroe (with 1,675 residents), Arlington (with 1,418 residents), and Marysville (with 1,244 residents) rounded out the towns hauling over a thousand population. Most communities experienced only slight gains during the decade, and upriver towns in mountains and foothills such as Gold Bar, Granite Falls, and Index lost population numbers.

The war took 124 men and two Red Cross nurses out of over 3,000 county residents who served in the American and allied forces. Memories of those lost were still fresh for those who visited gravesites in France. (Courtesy Snohomish Historical Society)

The years just after World War I brought on economic confusion and doubts, and the roller coaster of changing demands and costs alarmed players in the Pacific Northwest timber industry. Postwar adjustments created an immediate, short-lived slump that ended with an increased demand for wood products and higher prices during 1919 and 1920. Then, as suddenly as they had come, the favorable times collapsed, only to revive again in 1922. New buildings and homes were being constructed; Panama Canal traffic helped develop markets along the Atlantic coast of the United States; and Japan wanted Pacific Northwest lumber as it rebuilt following the devastating Tokyo earthquake of 1923. In sum, the 1920s were something of a mixed era for wood industries in Snohomish County.

As the decade began, the county was preeminently engaged in manufacturing lumber, claiming to have more standing timber than any similar area in the United States, and at least 130 lumber and shingle mills. Thirty more establishments dealt in pulp and paper, box making, sash and door manufacturing, and specialized milling. Most towns and many

Military concerns were far from most people's minds during the 1920s, but the coastal defense forts guarding the entrance to Admiralty Inlet and Puget Sound still were the scene of reserve training activities, as Snohomish men from Battery K fire the Tolles Battery guns at Fort Worden in 1925. (Courtesy Snohomish Historical Society)

isolated spots had mills; but large rivers flowing from wooded valleys and forested hill-sides brought countless logs to the Port Gardner tideflats and made Everett the principal lumber producing city. Long dubbed "The City of Smokestacks," Everett claimed responsibility for an eighth of the entire national lumber production in 1920. *Polk's Directory* pumped it as "the leading lumber, logging and shingle center of the Northwest, in fact, it might be said, of the entire world." The Clough-Hartley shingle mill alone, "the largest of its kind in the world," produced 1.5 million shingles each day, a third of the city's total shingle output. Everett also claimed to mill 3.5 million board feet of lumber daily. At mid-decade the *Herald* boasted that annual lumber production had reached 8 million feet with shingle production over a billion. "In addition, Everett plans to turn out 2,275 million boxes, 190,000 doors and 23 million square feet of plywood, or veneer as it is commonly called, a year." Everett, the newspaper claimed, produced almost a fifth of the state's lumber output, comparing favorably with many states and out-producing the traditional lumber state of Michigan.

Mills dominated Everett. The Weyerhaeuser Timber Company was the principal player, although it did not realize its full potential until the 1920s. In 1907 Weyerhaeuser's regional manager George S. Long had lured William H. Boner away from the Simpson Company to run its Everett operations. Boner, as broadly based and far-sighted as Long had hoped, ran the Everett operation with considerable autonomy. At Mill A, located on the bayside, he installed a planing mill and one of the first bandsaws on the Pacific Coast. He carefully directed the combined efforts of that and the huge Mill B on the Snohomish River, and he turned a profit even when the economy was weak. The acquisition of additional companies and timber lands increased supplies, and log selection procedures were improved; modern advertising techniques and better sales promotion were inaugurated. Boner and Long argued that the Panama Canal created a legitimate market for Everett mills on the eastern seaboard, and they acquired a lumber-

As the lowland forests disappeared, major operations such as the Wallace Falls Lumber Company began to cut the Skykomish Valley floor and sidehills around Startup and Gold Bar. (Darius Kinsey photo #3708, courtesy Gold Bar Historical Society)

Logging Dominated the Decade

Right: Logged off, burned over uplands had virtually no value once the trees were cut. Logging slash was a constant summer fire hazard, and replanting was not economically viable. (Photograph #65001, courtesy U.S. Soil and Water Conservation Service)

Climax geared locomotives #3 and #4 carried logs 11 miles down the North Fork Skykomish River to the saw and shingle mill of the Index-Galena Lumber Company until it closed at the end of the decade. (Courtesy Bob Miller)

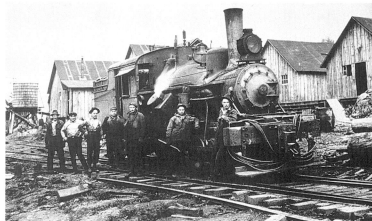

The Sultan Railway and Timber Company's "3-Spot" Heisler geared locomotive provided power to move its logs down to the mill. (Courtesy Bob Miller)

Left: High timbered trestles spanned rivers, swamps, and ravines for the steam engines, as the county was interlaced with temporary railway grades, abandoned once the timber was cut. Some routes still may be traced in second growth forests by the names left behind (as Merrill & Ring or Monroe Camp), and through moss covered rotting pilings. (Courtesy Bob Miller)

yard in Baltimore and then other locations on the Atlantic Coast. In order to ship their own products, they purchased two surplus government steamships, each capable of carrying six billion feet of lumber. After this venture proved successful, additional ships were acquired. Defending the near million dollars spent developing the Baltimore yard, Long admitted that though costs seemed alarming, they were more than offset by the potential rewards.

In 1922 Everett produced 226 million feet of lumber and sold an additional four million. Significantly, prices climbed in one year from $20.07 per thousand board feet to $22.03, but that amount was almost doubled when sold in Baltimore.

The Weyerhaeuser Timber Company was proving it could not only produce lumber but also sell its product and initiate new markets. During the 1920s Weyerhaeuser led the industry by establishing consistent standards and quality with uniform sizes, by selling milled ends, and by packaging molding and other products. Moreover, the company developed ways to use materials previously wasted, creating such new products as wallboard, Pres-to-logs for fuel, and other composition materials. Although these were not necessarily developed locally, they resounded to the success of the Everett operations. In mid-decade Boner built a third Everett mill. Modern and innovative, it cut hemlock, a species commonly wasted in the past but useful for certain needs, as fir stands diminished. The directions Boner had established continued after he died early in 1925, as his successor, William H. Peabody, had come to Everett straight from college and worked up to becoming superintendent of Mill B.

Everett was important, but the economy of much of the rest of the county also remained timber-based. Logging camps were scattered throughout the woodlands and hills from Darrington to Index, Bryant to Three Lakes. Sawmills and shingle mills operated in most towns, in small hamlets, and in forest clearings. Wood products were manufactured in many communities.

Mukilteo was home to the Crown Lumber Company from early in the century until it closed in 1930. Spread along hillside and waterfront where its pier extended into Puget Sound, Crown ran a traditional company town. It owned the houses where its workers and their families lived. A general store supplied most needs and kept records, deducting purchase prices from the workers' paychecks. Farther south, 11 shingle mills had once lined the Edmonds shoreline; the five that remained in 1923 were still a major source of local income. Several burned down during the decade, although one, the Quality mill, was quickly rebuilt as an all-electric plant and outlasted all others. When local timber supplies dwindled, three Edmonds mills cooperated to raft cedar south from British Columbia.

Fire was a constant threat everywhere, and the 20-year-old Rucker Brothers' mill at Lake Stevens burned in the mid-1920s. Surrounded by logging camps, the Index-Galena Lumber Company mill at Index, which once employed 150 people, suffered from strikes, floods, and declining timber resources during and after World War I. The mill shut down in 1929, although small ones endured in the outskirts.

Many business leaders and ordinary residents held lingering fears of radical labor, born from the 1916 Everett violence, the Seattle General Strike of early 1919, and the Centralia "massacre" the following November. Such concerns were only slightly alleviated by government raids and prosecution against the radical Industrial Workers of the

187

Manufacturing and Mining

Sumner Iron Works produced heavy machinery for the mining and logging industries of the county from its first factory on Ebey Island until a 1913 fire, then moved across the Snohomish River to the Lowell side, where it continued operations until selling to Black, Clawson. (Juleen photograph, courtesy Everett Public Library)

Freighters and lumber schooners could tie up at Mukilteo's Crown Lumber Company mill on the waterfront east of downtown, a site chosen both for its deepwater acess and Great Northern Railway service. (Courtesy Pete Hurd)

Left: Mining demanded hard physical work to remove the rock in heavy iron cars from the working face to the outside dump. Often companies employed two shifts, one to drill and blast, followed by the second to load and move cars. (Courtesy Granite Falls Historical Society)

Above: Copper prices held up during the 1920s, allowing deep penetration of ore deposits. These miners are looking at a "stope" inside the Sunset Copper Mine on Trout Creek above Index. (Lee Pickett photograph #4481, courtesy Index Historical Society)

Above: Northeast of Granite Falls above the South Fork Stillaguamish River the Wayside Mine produced over half a million dollars in copper and other minerals during its operating years. It featured a deep shaft with seven levels, six of them under water, which needed continual pumping. (Courtesy Granite Falls Historical Society)

Below: At the northeastern corner of Lake Stevens the Rucker brothers of Everett constructed a major sawmill and cut timber from Tulalip to Skagit County. They platted the townsite of Lake Stevens, sold lots, built a bank, took over the rail line to Monte Cristo, and operated until fire destroyed their mill. (Courtesy Jack O'Donnell

World, which effectively destroyed "the One Big Union." Its effective replacement after the war continued to be the Loyal Legion of Loggers and Lumbermen, the "4-L" a company union created by the federal government with the enthusiastic support of industry. Both loggers and mill workers were required to join in order to have a job, and known activists from the I.W.W. and A.F. of L. were excluded from membership. Within two months after the 4-L was organized, Weyerhaeuser's manager at Everett reported most of his employees had enrolled.

The closing years of the decade were poor ones for Northwest timber. Overproduction, declining construction starts, and rising competition from other regions helped create a precarious position. Although some leaders expressed perennial optimism, the industry as a whole faced a slump even before the national depression hit.

Local boosters argued, however, that Everett was more than just a lumber town. In 1918 business and civic leaders and a willing electorate created the Port of Everett, which soon acquired a World War I shipyard site. In time its properties expanded and its influence increased. Seven years later, Everett had three commercial piers and crowded lumberyards; The *Herald* proclaimed it "the largest shipping center of its population on the Pacific coast," exporting a million tons of products yearly. The Everett Pulp and Paper Company in Lowell manufactured book and tablet paper in one of the area's oldest plants. Iron, steel, and machinery production continued to develop with the Sumner Iron Works and the Washington Stove Company in the forefront.

Agriculture was a traditional county mainstay that affected both rural and urban areas. The poultry and egg industry was growing, as was dairying, and the production of berries and other fruits increased. The new settlement of Alderwood Manor centered around a demonstration egg and poultry farm on logged-over Pope and Talbot lands. A fruit, vegetable, and jam cannery in Everett employed over 400 persons, and there were at least two major seafood-packing companies.

The increase of local produce surely inspired the construction of the Grand Central Public Market at Colby and California avenues in late summer 1922. With modern lighting, plumbing, refrigeration, and decor, the spacious building was described by the *Herald* as "a department store in the fullest sense of the term." Fruits and vegetables, butter, fish, poultry, cheese, plants and flowers, bakery goods, coffee, and short order meals were available in the market's 17 stalls.

The public market and other buildings helped make Everett a true city. Over several years the original river and bayside settlements had crept toward each other, marked by the construction of significant buildings. During the 1920s the downtown business district solidified north of the courthouse. That decade was marked nationally by increased urbanization and the consolidation of downtown areas that

Gurnsey champion "Primrose of Valley Gem" brought Christmas greetings from Valley Gem Farms owners John and Fena Wrage to their many friends for several years late in the decade. (Courtesy Loren Kraetz and the Stillaguamish Valley Pioneer Association)

Dairy Products Increase Their Role

During the decade the Carnation Milk Company condensery in East Stanwood provided processing facilities for dairy farmers in the region. The plant was constructed originally by the Pacific Coast Condensed Milk Company in 1914 and later became a Stokely-Van Camp food processing center. (Courtesy Stanwood Area Historical Society)

The Arlington condensery was operated by the Snohomish County Dairymen's Association between 1921 and 1957 to produce condensed and powdered milk. In was sold to Twin City Foods, which erected a new freezer building for the peas, corn, and beans it processed at Stanwood. (Courtesy Stillaguamish Valley Pioneer Association)

Left: Dairy products also were sold by the scores of small stores throughout the county, including Olaus Braaten's Braaten Cash Grocery on 1532 Broadway in Everett. In 1923 it featured staple and fancy groceries, household drugs, notions, and a confectionery. (Courtesy Everett Public Library)

Right: Householders had door-to-door delivery from their milkman. This is a Pioneer-Alpine Dairy truck in front of their Pacific Avenue plant in Everett on December 23, 1925. (Juleen photograph #1023, courtesy Everett Public Library)

191

had graded streets, department stores, multi-storied office buildings, public transportation lines, street lighting, service buildings, and other amenities. Everett was right in line, transformed from a pioneer town to a mid-sized metropolis. Beyond downtown, a ring of smaller towns with suburban characteristics began to manifest themselves. The 1920s were, in short, a period of prosperity, growth, and consolidation for Snohomish County's largest city and seat of government.

This lumber based wealth led to a record $1.7 million worth of new construction in Everett in 1924; the next May over half a million dollars worth of construction permits set a new monthly record. Several of the new downtown buildings were designed by the Seattle architectural firm of Earle Morrison and V.S. Stimson: the seven-story, Renaissance style Medical-Dental Building, the six-story Central Building, the Central Lutheran Church, two junior high schools a short distance out, and a fire station headquarters. Adding to the building boom were Everett General and Providence hospitals, two parochial schools, and two five-story buildings: Rumbaugh's Department Store and the Hodges Building.

Fittingly, the decade ended with construction of a new city hall, a four-story Art-Deco masonry structure that was nestled among other government buildings in the city's commercial section. Designed by A.H. Albertson, the Seattle architect known for that city's Northern Life Tower, the building's central pavilion gave a monumental aspect appropriate for a significant building, though one critic ridiculed the structure as "a great toad sitting in a hole."

The jewel of this new construction was the new Monte Cristo Hotel, which opened on May 29, 1925 with Governor Roland Hartley cutting the ribbon at the most glittering event in the social history of the city. Its name, honoring the nearby mining district which had once promised great wealth, had been used by an 1892 hotel that was the center of Everett's social life for a decade and later become the site of Providence Hospital.

In the 1920s a group of Mount Vernon businessmen, mindful of the automobile age and tourist possibilities, envisioned the new hotel. The local chamber of commerce undertook a fund raising drive, and some 300 citizens purchased $120,000 of stock. Designed by Henry Bittman, a Seattle architect and leader in structural steel design, its contractors used local firms, products, and workers, bringing additional income to Everett. The hotel set a local standard for elegance. "It was the original decor, including sumptuous draperies and hangings, diffused lighting effects, and overstuffed furniture, which gave the hotel interior its aura of luxury," a reviewer later wrote. The 140 guest rooms were small, but each had outside natural light and ventilation, and there were four bridal suites. A mezzanine circled the main lobby, which had a terrazzo floor and baseboards of Belgian marble. Three wrought iron chandeliers with glass prism pendants and parchment shades hung from the ceiling. A huge concrete fireplace with a sculptured cast stone mantel dominated the north side of the lobby, and overstuffed furniture enhanced the room. A 33-foot by 64-foot banquet hall was decorated with columns and painted wall panels and had a glassed skylight. There was a coffee shop and dining room off the lobby. For several generations the Monte Cristo gave a touch of elegance to Everett and its environs. It was a place for the well-to-do to visit and for ordinary folk to celebrate special occasions, and it lured conventions to the city. An object of continuing civic pride, the

Alderwood Manor

Left: This overview of the Alderwood Poultry Farm looks to the east and shows the community hall and interurban tracks in the foreground. Prominent structures in the background are (left to right) the hotel, the superintendent's cottage, and the water tower, with other farm buildings interspersed among them. (#/1/, courtesy Alderwood Manor Heritage Association)

Right: The old wooden school was used in the 1919–20 school year, then was remodeled with a brick outer wall into a commercial structure, with the Puget Mill Company selling its five-acre "ranchettes" from the south end. On January 17, 1921 the new W. A. Irwin School to the southwest opened with much fanfare. Other commercial buildings shown face south on Trunk Road, now 196th. (Parsons & Co. photograph, courtesy Everett Public Library)

The Everett-Seattle interurban car is stopped next to Wickers' store in Alderwood Manor in 1921. It provided easy access to the two cities between 1910 and 1939, when it was put out of business by growing automobile traffic. (Courtesy Everett Public Library)

Edward and Jenny Gyldenfeldt were Danes who had lived in Oregon and Seattle before moving to Alderwood Manor and their own chicken farm in 1914. Poultry raising was a complex process involving a great amount of time, hard work, and diligence. (#9457, courtesy University of Washington Libraries)

Everett's Urban Renaissance

Downtown Everett went through a major building boom during the period, erecting much of its core retail and office space. All photos courtesy of Everett Public Library.

On the corner of Colby and California the city's tallest structure at seven stories was under construction in 1925, the Medical & Dental Building.

Looking north on Colby from Hewitt Avenue.

A new YMCA building was opened in 1921 to replace the one destroyed by fire on March 30, 1920. Under the leadership of William Howarth, the community raised over $183,000 in a massive one-week fund drive for its construction. Japanese businessman T.Y. Nabatame alone donated $5,250.

Right: The fire department's new station #1 at the corner of Oakes and California avenues became its headquarters facility. With its many mills and lumber yards, the city had a history of major fires.

Right: A new Monte Cristo Hotel was erected in 1925, on the corner of Hoyt and Wall to provide luxurious facilities for guests and civic social events. This replaced the earlier wooden structure of the 1890s which had become the site of Providence Hospital. (Juleen photograph #1219)

Above: The large, open Grand Central Market provided an important outlet for urban customers. It was located first on the northwest corner of Colby and California avenues, then moved down a block to the southeast corner of California and Wetmore. (Juleen photograph #2076)

The Hughes Memorial Methodist Church in downtown Edmonds, built in 1926 and shown here two years later, was, with its Spanish influence, one of the most imposing buildings in the community. (#122.16, courtesy Edmonds-South Snohomish County Historical Society)

Monte Cristo helped Everett and Snohomish County come of age.

Downtown construction was emulated in residential areas and suburbs. Similar changes, if a bit less spectacular, were occurring in smaller towns such as Arlington, Snohomish, and Sultan. Among the more impressive were the new $50,000 county farm and hospital at Monroe and the mission-style Hughes Memorial Methodist Church in Edmonds.

As Everett dominated the county, many rural towns and isolated villages also acquired more characteristics of community during the 1920s. Few were more remote than Darrington. The valley below Whitehorse Mountain had experienced mining and logging ventures for several decades, and a tiny settlement developed around stores and a lumber mill. During the 1920s growth accelerated, needs were met, and amenities created that assured permanence and gave Darrington the character of a solid town.

An automobile road built into Darrington foreshadowed change. In 1922 Standard Oil opened an auxiliary supply station for gasoline and stove oil, another opened shortly thereafter, and an auto stage line presaged the end of passenger trains. In 1926 two local citizens brought electrical power upriver. Initial service was undependable; some homes had only a single, infrequently used light bulb, and sufficient power for electric ranges and other appliances remained in the future. The Sauk Valley Baptist Church, which shared its pastor with Sedro-Woolley, was organized to become Darrington's second congregation, alongside the older Methodist one. The Rex movie theater opened in 1923, showing "River's End" and "Toonerville Trolley" as its first features.

Growth brought problems, however. One longtime resident, Sam Strom, complained to *The Arlington Times* that a "night-howling, night prowling conglomeration of chronic drunks, bootleggers and petty larceny thieves operating around Darrington like a bunch of Chinese highbinders need[ed] taking care of." Strom viewed such publicity "as the

Westwold was the mansion of David Whitcomb, who founded Woodway Park, an affluent residential community of winding wooded lanes set on the bluff above Puget Sound. Early in the 20th century Whitcomb acquired 320 acres which he sold off as large estates. His home was one of the most elegant. (Photograph from a painting montage by Diane Van Dlac in the town hall, courtesy Town of Woodway)

best booster for the promotion of the common good of the community." By 1923 he led other law-abiding citizens to secure a jail—the perennial symbol of a tamed and civilized community—to replace the railroad boxcar that had sufficed.

The formation of the Darrington Improvement Club in 1924 clearly marked the town's emergence. Its several dozen members quickly undertook activities and promotional efforts to better their town. They planted shade trees and put in street lights; they cut a new road through to the elementary school. In 1925 the club helped form a 29-member volunteer fire department and then raised funds for hoses and pump cans to mount on a light truck. They joined with the Arlington Commercial Club to purchase 20 acres of virgin timber for a park, where they helped clear underbrush, build shelters, and make other improvements. By the decade's end this site held the only stand of virgin timber left in the area. Also in 1925, the club distributed an illustrated brochure entitled "Darrington, Where the Trails Begin" to stimulate tourism.

That year the club sponsored perhaps the liveliest Fourth of July celebration in the town's history. Some1,200 celebrants entered such events as foot, bicycle, and tricycle races, a greased pole climb, a log-bucking contest, a greased pig contest, and a baseball game between bachelors and married men: the latter won in seven innings. Fireworks completed the day. The following year the club forsook the festivities in favor of supporting the fledgling fire department; however, that 1925 celebration was remembered for 20 years as the town's biggest event, the coming together of citizens in true fellowship. During the 1920s Darrington changed from a frontier village to a solidly based community with a distinct identity. To a considerable extent its story is that of other settlements about the county where the decade marked an extension of hometown development, boosterism, and pride.

Snohomish County was home to large numbers of persons of western European and especially Scandinavian descent, reflected in any list of its most prominent citizens. County officials in 1923 had such surnames as Williams, Hulbert, Turner, Fickel, Alverson, Miller, Hassell, Roscoe, McCulloch, Jacobson, Ramstad, Fleming, Henning, and Morgan. Peter and Marie Jackson, Norwegian immigrants whose young son was destined for the United States Senate, typified working class Scandinavian families. About to enter a career spanning congress, the Senate, and the governorship was Everett jeweler Mon Wallgren. The communities of Stanwood and Silvana were especially known for their half-century of Scandinavian heritage.

Other ethnic and national groups were sparse. Five hundred Native Americans from seven tribal affiliations had been moved onto the Tulalip reservation where they farmed, logged, and fished under white paternalism. A few Native Americans struggled to hold on to traditional practices. Over 200 children from throughout the Northwest lived and were educated by white instructors at the Indian Boarding School there, while other native families continued to live on traditional sites. In the 1920s Japanese workers continued to live in the gulch near Mukilteo where their families had been brought as employees of the Crown Lumber Company. White children later retained warm memories of their Japanese classmates.

Several Caucasian groups offered diversity. The "Tarheel" population centered at Darrington had unique characteristics, and their numbers increased during the decade.

As the hardwoods of the Appalachian region in the southeastern United States were giving out, families began moving toward softwood logging in the Cascade foothills. These North Carolinians influenced their community with a distinct southern mountain culture reflected in their soft dialects, their cuisine, religious persuasion, and craft work, including quilting. A Greek community that may have reached 3,000 early in the century lingered in Everett's Riverside district, along with many Italian families. Originally consisting largely of single bachelors working in the mills, they included families and businessmen by the 1920s, united by religion, social customs, and a common language, which they intermixed with English. Some ran coffee houses or other food service businesses. Balkan families clustered on Bayside, close to their fishing and packing interests, while a sprinkling of small shops owned by European Jews and Lebanese added to the flavor.

There also were signs of nativism and unrest in the 1920s, reflecting nation-wide disillusionment with the Treaty of Versailles following World War I and support for restricting southern European immigration, which had dominated America's population growth since 1890. Early in July of 1924 white paint lettering "K.K.K. Stanwood, July 12" appeared on several paved roads. It was an ominous invitation. That Saturday an estimated 8,000 Ku Klux Klansmen and 2,000 curious spectators from along the West Coast attended a huge outdoor initiation ceremony on a field just east of town. As a band played patriotic tunes, a solitary horseman carried an electrified crimson cross to lead a train of white robed, hooded Klansmen who formed a semi-circle; one spectator called it "a long ghostly blur against the darkened western sky." Speakers described the organization as a militant group pledged to uphold the law; they also proclaimed white supremacy. Several thousand initiates took their oaths. That evening three large crosses burned against the evening sky, followed by 15 minutes of fireworks before the crowd headed home on country roads. This was no isolated incident in Washington; such initiations were held in other years elsewhere in the state. Three years later 200 knights from across Washington held their state convention in Everett and paraded through town in white robes and hoods. Several times Klansmen interrupted church services to present flags and envelopes containing money to the pastors and urged their congregations to clean up immoral situations.

Most county residents, however, enjoyed more conventional activity. In the county, as across the nation, radio was transforming lives, instantly bringing people together in a way never known before. The county's first station, KFBL, became one of the state's earliest when it when it was licensed in 1922; eight years later its call letters became KRKO. It was started by Robert and Otto Leese, two automobile repairmen whose fascination with the new medium had prompted an amateur effort in 1920. Although its first broadcast was on August 25, 1922, operating on 1340 kilocycles with 10 watts, KFBL apparently did not go into full operation until 1925. It served the few receiving sets in the community a mix of recordings and local news and entertainment. During its early years the station broadcast from a two-story hotel building on Rucker Avenue. Poor soundproofing and the activities of transient guests in surrounding rooms provided some harried moments. An early account of the station by Everett historian Edward Friberg recalled, "the noises of wild drinking parties, furniture smashing and vigorous amorous

197

activities . . . sometimes intermingled with the program being broadcast. Youthful yukulele [*sic*] twangers and aspiring female vocalists would come out from the studio only to find themselves in the midst of a crowd of longshoremen aglow with moonshine and girls clad in gaudy kimonos being assembled for a ride to the hoosegow."

The first movie theaters had appeared before World War I, but they now blossomed with distinctive architecture, brilliant marquees, and elaborate interiors. Such popular spots as the Star, Orpheum, Rose, and the remodeled Everett in downtown Everett, the Gem in Everett's Riverside, the Princess in Edmonds, the Ideal in Stanwood, and the Bijou in Marysville helped promote community pride and togetherness. Their openings were often major community events, as on the October evening in 1924 when a thousand people attended the opening of Brown's Theater in Snohomish. Owner Lon Brown appeared on screen to welcome guests and introduce several films interspersed with live singing acts. "The evening developed into a rather gala occasion for the entire city," according to a later account in the community history *River Reflections*, "with restaurants and confectionery shops filled to overflowing after the show."

Now and then, starstruck locals participated in the movies. Walter Reece, a mill operator, ventured into film making centered partially around his town of Edmonds. He hoped to open a movie studio at the family-owned Brookside Inn, and he incorporated the Edmonds Development Corporation. An early production made in California appeared at the Princess Theater. Then Reece produced a short film called "Edmonds-on-the-Sound" with local actors. A larger venture, "Above the Clouds," was filmed at Mount Rainier and featured Eddie Bacon of Edmonds. Filming was cut short when a camera crashed on mountain rocks, but there was at least one local showing, and the movie was acclaimed for its scenery. In March 1928 Hollywood was attracted to the phenomenon of a small town with baseball teams made up entirely of sons of two families. Crews from Metro-Goldwyn-Mayer and Fox came to Stanwood to film a game between the J.W. Wagness sons and the John Sande sons. The Sande boys won, and the film, though apparently not widely distributed, was shown with much hoopla at the local theater.

Few towns could muster teams made up entirely of brothers, but in the 1920s athletics was as popular in Snohomish County as it was elsewhere. Enoch Bagshaw concluded his career as the Everett High football coach with a 1920 season of lopsided victories, such as 90-7, 67-0, 28-0. Then the team avenged the tie of the previous New Year's Day by defeating a Cleveland, Ohio, team 16-7 to win the national high school championship. Bagshaw moved on to the University of

Movie houses operated in many Snohomish County towns during the decade. The Princess Theatre, still operating as the Edmonds Theater, opened with much fanfare on Edmonds' Main Street in November 1923. (#160.20, courtesy Edmonds-South Snohomish Historical Society)

Washington, taking along several Everett players. One of them, All-American back George Wilson, was later named the greatest player in the first half-century of University of Washington football. Bagshaw's illustrious career lasted the decade, but he died at age 46 in Olympia. In death he remained a legendary Everett athletic hero whose teams united mill owners and mill workers in a sense of local pride, cohesion, and identity, and he influenced a tradition of football preeminence in the city and county. The site of the games was renamed Bagshaw Field and was holding athletic contests into the twenty-first century.

Another illustrious athletic career was just getting underway as the decade ended, that of Snohomish baseball outfielder Earl Averill. The hometown hero returned from his rookie season with the Cleveland Indians in October 1929 to a celebration with bands, fireworks, a parade, and dinner. The city's most famous son went on to over a decade in the major leagues and remains the only Washingtonian in baseball's Hall of Fame.

Most communities had teams, especially in baseball, which became rallying points for entertainment and civic pride. When a group of Mukilteo enthusiasts decided in 1922 to field a team in the county league, they held an organizational meeting, elected officers, and made schedules. More daunting was the challenge to create a playing field near the beach between tidelands and swamp. Volunteer laborers diked the area and erected poles only to have them sink; they moved down the beach, built more dikes, worked by kerosene lamp, and fought mosquitoes in order to complete a field and grandstand. Local merchants helped provide supplies and uniforms, and then the townspeople accompanied their team to spirited contests around Puget Sound. "Members of the Mukilteo Baseball Team," the manager's daughter recalled years later in *Mukilteo: Pictures and Memories*, "developed skills, sportsmanship, and a certain camaraderie in their involvement with the game, and . . . provided the town with a great deal of entertainment over the years."

Howard Earl Averill is in the Baseball Hall of Fame in Cooperstown, New York for his the major league career. Between 1929 and 1941 the Snohomish native played for Cleveland and Detroit in the American League and Boston in the National League, where he compiled a .318 lifetime batting average. Snohomish also has contributed Earl Torgerson, who played 15 years in the majors and led the 1948 World Series with a .389 average for the Boston Braves, and Averill's son Earl. Other big leaguers from the town are Walter Thornton (1890s), Roy Grover (early 1900s), Jim Ollom (1960s), and Adam Eaton, who debuted with the San Diego Padres in 2001. (Averill at the 1982 Mariners' Old Timers' game, courtesy *The Herald*)

In the mid-1920s county historian William Whitfield told of baseball teams, horse races, shooting and cycling clubs in the town of Snohomish that went back several decades. He concluded that "the innumerable home gatherings, socials, dances, picnics, boat rides and lodge meetings . . . show that the city was filled with energetic, fun-loving people abound with life and vigor, generous, often rash, but always lovable." The experiences of Mukilteo and Snohomish were common to other towns as well.

By the early 1920s, the role of women in society was changing in the nation, in the state, and in Snohomish County. As more and more emerged from home ties to enter the

Movies in Snohomish County

By David Dilgard

Motion pictures arrived in Snohomish County communities at the dawn of the twentieth century, turning up as a novelty displayed in jury-rigged storefronts, often as a "chaser" on vaudeville bills. The earliest documented movie showing took place at the Central Opera House in Everett in April of 1901, when the Searchlight Moving Picture Company presented a program of short films, including the funeral of Queen Victoria, travel footage of Windsor Castle, and an odd sequence involving a cigar-smoking baby.

By 1903 George Melies' *A Trip to the Moon* had found its way to Snohomish County, but it was to take nearly a decade and a half for movies to truly establish themselves as an independent entertainment medium. Early Everett storefront nickelodeons like the Scenic (1906), the Grand and the Midway (both 1907) were cramped and makeshift but soon had counterparts in other communities. Within a year or two the Gem in Arlington, the Star in Edmonds, the Electric in Granite Falls, the Star in Monroe, and the Acme and Lyric in Snohomish were offering motion picture fare. As in Everett, these little theaters were usually short-lived ventures installed in vacant stores and shops, but in November of 1909 the Star Theatre in Everett opened for business, the first moviehouse in the county built expressly for that purpose.

Safety issues plagued early film exhibitors. Flammable nitrate film and unreliable equipment made insurance coverage difficult. More than once the failure of a hand-cranked projector spoiled a show. The Iroquois Theatre fire in Chicago in 1903, though not film-related, spurred many American communities to pass and enforce theater safety codes, but for Snohomish County another event produced a similar reaction. A projection room blaze at the Lyric Theatre in Snohomish in the spring of 1909, though miraculously inflicting neither serious injury nor death, seems to have convinced many other towns in the county of the need for stringent enforcement of theater safety regulations.

The Orpheum Theatre, 1615 Hewitt Avenue in Everett, operated between 1911 and 1929. (Courtesy Everett Public Library)

Film epics like *Birth of A Nation* and *Intolerance* began to attract their own audiences during the Great War, and the drawing power of film performers like Chaplin, Pickford and Valentino quickly transformed motion pictures into an entertainment force to be reckoned with. By the early Twenties storefront nickelodeons had been replaced by custom-built movie theaters, like the Princess in Edmonds (1923) and Brown's in Snohomish (1924). An indication of the dramatic change was the Everett Theatre, a 1200-seat "opera house" built in 1901 to present live entertainment. Occasional film attractions had appeared there as early as 1905. After a 1923 fire it was rebuilt as a motion picture venue which could accommodate an occasional live performance.

Movies in Snohomish County quickly evolved from local, independently operated businesses into holdings of large regional and nationwide exhibition companies, a process that began soon after the Great War and has continued to the present day. Weathering competition from vaudeville, radio, the Great Depression, and perhaps most daunting of all, television, the county's movie business moved into the early post-WWII period without much new theater construction. As with talking pictures in the late '20s, innovations such as Cinemascope and 3-D were retrofitted into existing facilities.

The notable exception was the drive-in, a post-war phenomenon that enjoyed considerable popularity from the late Forties through the Sixties. The first of these was the Sno-King, opened in June of 1948 on Highway 99 south of Alderwood Manor, followed by Everett's Sky-Vu Drive-In in May 1950 and the Everett Motor Movie in April of 1951. Although they represented a successful convergence of two of the most powerful cultural forces of the century, the automobile and the motion picture, drive-in theaters were

200

destined to collide initially with television and finally with the daunting competition of the mall multiplexes of the 1970s. As the century drew to a close, only the Puget Park Drive-In survived, perhaps more profitably used as a swap meet site than as a theater.

The postwar exodus to the suburbs eventually had a profound impact on the movie business. Efficient, streamlined multi-screened theaters began to appear, often in shopping malls where parking was conveniently close at hand.

The idea of multiple screens was introduced to Snohomish County in November of 1966 with the addition of a second screen to the 3-year-old Lynn Theater on Highway 99 in Lynnwood. This created the 1600-seat Lynn Twin. But the county's first custom-built mall multiplex was General Cinema's Everett Mall Cinema I-II-III which opened in February of 1974. From that point forward multiple screen theaters have dominated the county's movie business, with large corporations such as Cineplex, General Cinemas, Act III and, recently, Regal competing for patronage.

world of work and politics, many embraced the term "municipal housekeeping," which suggested women's traditional chores could be applied to a wider sphere. In a host of new organizations, observed historian Karen Blair, "women initiated a staggering range of civic projects—public libraries, parks, vocational education, and street lights, to name a few."

Several dozen such clubs existed in the county in the 1920s, including local affiliates of national women's organizations, auxiliaries of men's groups, and cultural clubs, some with a very specific focus. Many began early in the decade: the Altrusa Club, the Dickens Club, the Women's Republican Club, the Auxiliary of the Sons of Union Veterans of the Civil War, the Deaconess Children's Home, the Business and Professional Women's Club, and, in 1926, the Executive Council, which consisted of their presidents.

Oldest and perhaps chief among them, the Everett Woman's Book Club was founded in 1894 to establish a library; it succeeded, and by the 1920s was promoting varied activities. The Book Club set the pace, raising funds for worthy community projects and promoting a moral civic climate. They provided bus fare for poor kindergartners, campaigned for wholesome movie content, encouraged bakers to wrap bread, honored new citizens at receptions, raised funds for local orphanages and other charities, and promoted musical and other cultural programs. They urged citizens to boycott the films of comedian Fatty Arbuckle, who was tainted by a lurid sex scandal, and they urged strict Prohibition enforcement. The club undertook civic beautification by planting trees in Forest Park and led state efforts by the Washington Federation of Women's Clubs to create a park in a grove of virgin timber along the highway to Mount Rainier, the Federated Forest State Park. Clearly the club saw its community role as one of civic betterment and moral suasion.

Women undertook similar programs in other towns. The Women's Civic Club of Arlington supplied undernourished children with fresh milk and developed a city park. At Stanwood the Monday Club and the Four Leaf Clover Club dined at nicely served luncheons and enjoyed a taste of culture, after which they tackled such civic needs as establishing cement sidewalks, planting trees, and creating a public health center.

In 1921 a group of Marysville women grew discontented preparing lunch while their husbands were clearing land and building a log cabin kitchen at a community park. They

Improvements in Medical Care

In February 1924, the Everett General Hospital opened in the 1300 block of north Colby Avenue, a non-profit community owned facility which later added a wing for teaching student nurses. (Photograph #0603, courtesy Everett Public Library)

From 1905 to 1924, Everett's original Monte Cristo Hotel building served as Providence Hospital, under the auspices of the Roman Catholic Sisters of Providence. It was then razed and replaced with a modern brick structure on the same site. (Courtesy Bernie Webber)

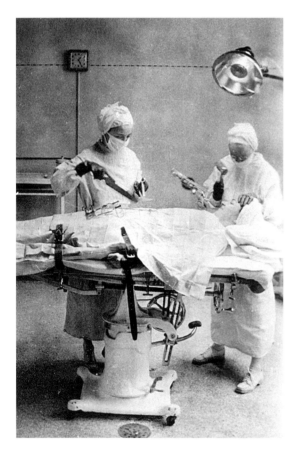

Dental services were widespread in the county, with almost four dozen practices available for patients by 1925. The large majority were located in Everett, followed by Snohomish and Arlington, with single doctors from Darrington to Seattle Heights. (Courtesy Everett Public Library)

Left: This operating room at Providence Hospital illustrates then-current technology. The Sisters of Providence arrived at Fort Vancouver in 1858, opening the first non-military hospital in Washington Territory that year. By 1905, local doctors had organized the Snohomish County Medical Society. (Courtesy Everett Public Library)

1920s Daredevil, Al Faussett of Monroe

By Louise Lindgren

The 1920s were a time of high hopes and wild aspirations. All across the country daredevils were taking on challenges such as going over waterfalls in strange craft, doing stunts on the wings of biplanes or vying for titles of "the best, the biggest, the only." There was even an Australian who came through on his world tour and floated feet-first down Canyon Falls on the Skykomish River in a deep-sea diver's suit with a kayak paddle for stability.

No one could symbolize the "high times" better than Monroe daredevil and ex-logger Al Faussett. On May 30, 1926 his choice for a challenge was Sunset Falls on the Skykomish River. Although at least 20 people had drowned in the whirlpool at the base of the falls, Al felt he could design a canoe that would make it over safely.

His knowledge of trees helped as he chose a huge spruce log to create a 32-foot craft halfway between a rowboat and kayak. It had a steel front cover for protection from battering on rocks and was fitted with strong vine maple branches, which stuck out at angles to deflect the craft from boulders.

Inside, Al would wear a belt with a quick release buckle to anchor him to the canoe, similar to ones that aviators were using at the time. He also invented a breathing device with a rubber tube connected to an air tank.

Newspapers publicized the event for days in advance. Bridges were built and land cleared to afford a better view. A special Great Northern train was arranged to carry spectators from Everett; special stage services and many motorcycle parties were expected.

A newspaper described the falls: "... a drop of 104 feet in a distance of 275 feet with water speed more than 60 mph. Huge saw-logs, 70 feet in length, shoot over the falls, disappear from sight and come to the surface, completely stripped of bark, their ends shooting skyward, to be hurled from the whirlpool at the base of the canyon."

Al was pushed into the water about a thousand feet east of the drop-off. His own words, quoted in the *Everett News* the following day tell the story best. "People will never know, and little did I dream of the power of those treacherous waters in the falls. When I went under the water hit me with a crushing force and hurt my lungs. It twisted my body and head …. The line to my air tank had broken with the first meeting of the fast water and I was forced to hold my breath as best I could against the crushing water …. It was all over in a few seconds, and when I saw the light of day as I rode out of the turbulent waters, I thanked God that I had ridden safely through."

The thrill whetted Al's appetite for more. On Labor Day 1926, he was back on the Skykomish river at the top of Eagle Falls—a narrower channel, equally or more dangerous.

He had designed a new craft that looked like a big cigar or submarine without a turret. It had a hatch which closed completely, forcing the occupant to lie down inside, not seeing a thing as the wooden cocoon tumbled down the rapids.

The day after the jump the *Everett News* put the headline in 1½-inch letters: "AL FAUSSETT RIDES FALLS, PERILOUS TRIP MADE IN SAFETY". "On to Snoqualmie and Niagra, says Al Faussett. The water was low and showed many jagged rocks on the perilous descent but Faussett's specially constructed canoe made the hazardous trip over the angry looking 'white water' without a mishap."

Al's dreams grew of bigger and better jumps with increasing honor and glory. Over the next three years he tackled Spokane Falls; Willamette and Silver Creek Falls in Oregon; and Shoshone Falls in Idaho. For Shoshone, he had designed a canvas cigar-shaped craft, where he lay surrounded by pneumatic tire tubes.

After all his adventures, Faussett died, not in a raging river, but in his own bed in 1948. His son is quoted in a last tribute. "Dad was just nutty about jumping over precipices. He never thought about anything else. Hoped to make the Niagra leap some day, but never got back there."

determined to organize themselves for civic betterment, naming their new group after the structure the men were building. The Log Cabin Club raised funds for a pool, fountain, restroom, bandstand, and kitchen in the park; the club then turned to building a new city hall and a public library, for which they provided books and bookcases.

Civic endeavors of women's clubs could become vehicles toward political power, as the town of Edmonds learned in December 1925, when Alice U. Kerr was elected mayor. She was among the first women mayors of any city and most likely the first in the state, taking office three months before Seattle's Bertha Knight Landes. The manner of her election was also unique: she was a last-minute "sticker" candidate elected by write-in votes. Just days before, election fliers with their boldface heading: "ATTENTION VOTERS" circulated about town announcing that her candidacy had been solicited by "an earnest group of representative citizens of Edmonds wishing a change in city administration."

Kerr had lived in Edmonds barely six years. Born and raised in Chicago, she married James H. Kerr in 1879 and moved to a prairie town in Nebraska and a way of life she later described in a brief memoir. There she began the pattern of community involvement, which continued after moving to Edmonds in 1919. As with other women in politics during that period, including Landes, Kerr entered government through women's activities and civic clubs. She was prominent in the Baptist church and its missionary work both locally and statewide, and in the Edmonds Coterie and the Music and Art Study Club. Narrowly defeating the incumbent mayor, she pledged "no radical" changes but offered a clean government and efficient administration. During Kerr's term the mayor and council quarreled over whether children should be allowed in pool and card rooms—even to purchase candy. Kerr also encouraged civic beautification, with flower and shrubbery planting. Other civic advances involved purchase of a new Reo fire truck and the expansion of cross-sound ferry service. It was apparently her own decision not to seek a second two-year term. In 1931 her husband died. Kerr remained in Edmonds until her death in 1949 at the age of 91.

Women still were a rarity in politics, and the county's leading politician was Roland H. Hartley. In November 1926 over 86 percent of Snohomish County voters—an unprecedented number—turned out to help send Everett's most prominent citizen to the Governor's office. Canadian-born and raised in Minnesota, Hartley had arrived in Everett in 1902 at the age of 39. Having worked at several jobs, mostly in lumber, Hartley was like many others who moved west as the timber stands of the North Central states diminished. He had the additional advantage of being the son-in-law and one-time private secretary of David H. Clough, former Minnesota governor who had become powerful in the Everett lumber industry since arriving in 1900. Clough had helped found and manage the Clark-Nickerson Lumber Company. Hartley invested in the company and, his biographer Albert Francis Gunns wrote, "followed his money to Everett." Economic and political power intertwined in the careers of both men.

Alice Kerr of Edmonds and Bertha Landes of Seattle were two of the state's and nation's earliest women mayors. This meeting occurred shortly before Landes' inauguration. (Courtesy Edmonds-South Snohomish County Historical Association)

Hartley immediately engaged in numerous activities in the lumber industry and in other companies operated by the Cloughs and Hartleys, for other members of both families had also come west. He took part in civic, social, and fraternal organizations and, despite unsuccessful political ventures in Minnesota, he veered toward politics once again. In 1909 he was elected mayor of the city of 24,000 citizens. By that time he had parlayed an honorary commission from Governor Clough into the title "Colonel" and was, in Everett historian Norman H. Clark's words, "an articulate and even flamboyant spokesman for . . . cast-iron Republican conservatism."

Mayor Hartley and the city council bickered over many issues, and critics labeled him a tool of corporations. He countered that his business acumen helped restore Everett to a sound financial basis, although the cutting of staff and services left the population in dismay. Prohibitionists claimed he failed to enforce "dry" laws. Hartley did not run for re-election when 1911 rolled around. Three years later, however, he was elected to the state legislature by a considerable majority even as Progressives captured other offices. Hartley voted consistently with his Republican colleagues against the liberal proposals advanced by Democratic governor Ernest Lister. He was never a conspicuous leader in the house. Yet he apparently left Olympia convinced he could become governor, and he began to prepare for the 1916 campaign. He took a strong business stance and opposed the union shop, but he was little known statewide and lost the Republican primary. Hartley then tried a short and unsuccessful campaign for the United States Senate. In 1920 Hartley was back in the governor's race again. Against the background of post-war fears of radicalism, he ran a pro-business, anti-labor, "Americanism" campaign, but lost the primary to Louis Hart, the incumbent since the death of Lister.

Even as his interests moved statewide, Hartley remained a conspicuous leader in Everett; during the 1916 shingle weavers' strike and resultant killings, for instance, he was a significant player in the business community and Commercial Club. However, his chief goal had become the quest for higher office. The nation was taking a more conservative stance during the twenties, although Republican party splits tended to pit urban counties against rural ones. The now well-known Hartley finally won the Republican nomination for governor and then swamped a lackluster Democratic candidate. Then, in January 1925, Everett's most prominent citizen became governor.

Hartley's two terms were arguably the most turbulent in the state's history. He railed against those "interests" he accused of ruling the state, including labor, education forces, and the logging industry, which was personified by his personal political rival, Speaker of the House Mark Reed. "In a remarkably short time," wrote Norman Clark, he "quarreled publicly and bitterly with virtually every state elected official, most persistently with the secretary of state, the state treasurer, and the superintendent of public instruction, making it clear that he resented their constitutional powers and that he intended if he could to seize their power bases and make them his own." He opposed major expenditures for roads and schools, and engaged in an acrimonious dispute with University of Washington President Henry Suzallo. Yet, he had allies within government and among the public, and he was reelected in 1928.

However, the nation was moving into the depression years. In 1932, Hartley, who seemed little aware that the faltering economy was changing public attitudes, sought to become the first governor elected to a third term; but he lost in the primary to the lieutenant governor. He then retired to his Rucker Avenue mansion, his governorship became virtually forgotten.

During the 1920s a whole new culture was developing around the gasoline-powered automobile. By the mid-1920s, Henry Ford and other automakers were turning out cars rapidly and fairly inexpensively. Ordinary persons found new mobility, related infrastructure appeared, and social life was transformed. The number of motor vehicles in the state increased almost three-fold between 1920 and 1930, from 187,000 to 463,000, and it may be assumed that the ratio in Snohomish County was comparable. New services and businesses developed around automobiles, as the 1919–1920 county directory published illustrated advertisements for cars and four pages of related products and services. Twenty dealers were listed, along with categories for accessories, garages, manufacturers, parts, repairs, storage, supplies, tires, tops, trimmings, and trucks. Most were located in Everett, but they existed in other towns and even small communities. A decade later, there were 36 dealers, almost half in Everett. New categories included awnings, cushions, commercial cars and trucks, used cars, freight transportation, garages, glass, auto laundries, painters, parking, restoration, and wreckers.

Automobile owners converted woodsheds and barns into garages. The well-to-do might have touring cars, while mill workers used secondhand autos, and many had motorcycles. Riverside resident Helmer Malstrom recalled his neighbors' vehicles: "Velie, Chandler, Ford, Chevrolet, Studebaker, Haynes, Willys-Knight, and Premier."

Automobiles required hard surface roads to replace old routes that turned into virtual quagmires during the rainy months. Congress sought to encourage suitable road building as early as 1907, but the principal responsibility fell to state and local governments. Bond issues for road construction were regularly placed before Snohomish County voters, often losing because they tended to pit towns, which favored the bonds, against rural opponents. Thus, passage of the $1.8 million bond issue in 1915 for country road paving was a considerable victory. A decade later the county could boast of 1,620 miles of highways, most paved in some fashion; the overwhelmingly common surface was macadam, although 149 miles were cement.

Everett lumberman, former mayor, and state legislator Roland H. Hartley campaigns (unsuccessfully) in his first bid for governor in 1916. A decade later he would serve two terms. (Jacobs Photo Shop, courtesy Everett Public Library)

Community leaders organized and petitioned to secure hard surface roads in local areas, and the opening of new stretches of highways occasioned celebrations. *The Stanwood News* regularly recounted town-by-town which portions of the Pacific Highway (later U.S. 99) were completed and which were not. When the stretch to Mount Vernon opened late in 1920, local residents were relieved: "At last after more than two years of intolerable detours, two years of shimmying from one side of the road to the other in a frantic effort to avoid bumps or easing out of one shell hole into another; after two years of 'busted' springs, loosened bolts, twisted fenders and shivered steering gears . . . [the] boulevard is to be opened to the public."

The Pacific Highway provided a north-south land route along Puget Sound parallel to the traditional water route. The crossing of the Snohomish River delta between

Roland H. Hartley

By Thomas M. Gaskin, PhD

The riot which became known as the "Everett Massacre" occurred November 5, 1916, when approximately 250 Industrial Workers of the World (Wobblies) and sympathizers aboard the *Verona* from Seattle attempted to land at Everett city dock. Thousands of Everett residents watched on the hillside above the waterfront as Sheriff Donald McRae and several hundred deputized members of a citizen army tried to prevent the Wobblies from coming ashore. A murderous gun battle ensued with seven known dead and fifty (including McRae) wounded.

The Wobblies had come to Everett on "Bloody Sunday" to aid striking Everett millworkers, to respond to a vicious beating 41 Wobblies received a week earlier by a group of Everett vigilantes, and to establish the right of free speech which had been curtailed by the influence of a few wealthy "lumber barons" who controlled the community boastfully described by the mayor's stationery as a "City of Smokestacks." Roland H. Hartley, co-owner of the Clough-Hartley Mill on the bayside of the city, the greatest producer of red cedar shingles in the world, was one of the most influential of the sawdust elite.

Before the *Verona* arrived, the 5-foot-6-inch, 140-pound Hartley organized resistance to the Wobblies. He told 300 deputized citizens the city should be made too "hot" for "agitators and trouble breeders." After the bloody conflict, he asserted that the IWW "came here to burn Everett and to burn the mills. The citizens had to arm to repel the invasion." Few facts support Hartley's claim. However, throughout the remainder of his life, he did not vary his convictions or allegiances. Years later, as a reward for McRae's resistance to the Wobblies, Hartley, who was governor, named the down-and-out sheriff superintendent of the state capitol grounds.

Hartley's dislike for unions was spurred by his faith in individualism and his image of himself as a self-made man in an era of "root, hog, or die." Born June 26, 1864 in the Canadian community of Shogomoc, New Brunswick, Hartley moved to Minnesota when he was 12. After working in logging camps and as a farmer, Hartley's big break came when he became the personal secretary of lumberman David Clough and subsequently married his employer's daughter. Not surprisingly, when his father-in-law moved to Everett in 1900 to take advantage of greater economic opportunities, Hartley followed two years later.

Because of smart investments in the logging industry and the 1906 San Francisco earthquake and fire, which sent lumber prices soaring in the Pacific Northwest, Hartley became one of the wealthiest sawdust barons of the city. He became a spokesman for industrial conservatism and achieved a popularity which he fashioned into a 321-vote victory in the 1909 mayoral contest.

Hating taxes as much as he detested unions, Hartley immediately faced a crisis in 1910 when the city inhabitants voted to close its 41 saloons in a fit of prohibitionist fervor. Since a large part of the city's revenue came from saloon license fees, Hartley ordered a third of the police force laid off, the street lights extinguished, and all of the city street cleaners dismissed. Protest was muted, until the navigational and aromatic difficulties resulting from a horse drawn transportation system convinced city residents to voluntarily contribute $40,000 to replace the lost license fees. During much of Hartley's two years as mayor (1910-11) he wrangled with the city council over taxing the big lumber companies. On one occasion, Hartley had the chief of police throw the president of the city council out of the meeting room, upon which the departing dignitary yelled, with some accuracy, that the mayor was nothing but a "corporation tool."

Cautioned by his physician in 1911 not to run again for mayor (critics said it was the advice of his polltakers), Hartley returned to private life, until elected state legislator from the 48th District in 1914. Serving in Olympia (1915-16), he distinguished himself as an arch conservative, voting against an eight-hour work law for women and authoring bills to prevent labor from picketing and to prevent the teaching of the social sciences in school.

Convinced he possessed the ability, Hartley unsuccessfully attempted to become the Republican gubernatorial candidate in 1916 and 1920, losing both times in the primary elections. Accentuating a pledge to bring business methods to state government, Hartley won a narrow victory in the 1924 primary, assuring election against his Democratic opponent. Once in office he proceeded to alienate the legislature and most department heads under his control by trying to centralize authority and cutting taxes. He called his critics "lame ducks, political tramps and ne'er-do wells...disgruntled politicians, grafters, greedy promoters, uplift agitators, and all other hounds of Hell." He attacked the child labor law enthusiasts as "bolshevists" and "pusillanimous blatherskites." In 1926 he fired two members of the University of Washington Board of Regents, replaced them, and then had the new board fire university president Henry Suzzallo. A recall effort, the first in the history of the Washington State governorship, lost steam and did not reach the ballot. Despite Hartley's contentious first term, in 1928 he campaigned for re-election across the state with a barbershop quartet, a 75-pound brass cuspidor from the new capitol building to demonstrate extravagant state spending, and a black bag he said contained evidence to put all of his enemies in jail. The tax-hating voters were satisfied and continued Hartley in office for four more years.

The ensuing economic depression of the 1930s undermined Hartley's popularity. He doggedly held to his beliefs that the state government should not spend money to help the downtrodden, but instead should cut taxes. His lack of compassion for the common person, which he demonstrated as a mill owner, had not changed. He had become an anachronism. In 1932 he was unable to win the Republican nomination for governor. Four years later, Hartley was the Republican candidate, but suffered a decisive defeat by incumbent governor Clarence Martin. Until his death in 1951 his remaining years were passed in semi-retirement in Everett, undisturbed politically except when a group of Republicans gave the former governor a warm round of applause, mistakenly thinking he was one of the co-authors of the anti-union Taft-Hartley bill.

Everett and Marysville in August 1927 prompted so noteworthy a celebration that Marysville historians have suggested that the excitement surrounding Charles Lindbergh's Atlantic flight that May "paled in comparison." Local bands led parades down the main streets of the two towns and met at the north end of the draw span for the traditional ribbon cutting. Remarks by Governor Hartley, a picnic dinner, and evening fireworks highlighted the event. The cutoff soon "made life a lot easier" for residents north of the river. Marysville merchants discovered new customers, and small businesses like Hazel's Place and Lola's Place sprang up to provide gas, water, oil, air, and light meals to travelers. Auto camps were started, and bus transport began. The city of Marysville discovered a new revenue source—traffic fines—and acquired an early reputation as a speed trap.

Farther south on the Pacific Highway, about midway between Seattle and Everett, Carl Keeler provided varied services at a station that was a sign of entrepreneurship to come. When Keeler's Korner was placed on the National Register of Historic Places, its nominator wrote that it had been "an oasis for motorists and soon became a noted local landmark. . . . Keeler's Korner provided the automobile driver with fuel, oil, tires, batteries, automotive accessories and mechanical service. However, the establishment also catered to residents of the local area with a stock of hardware and groceries. Also, from its inception the station served as a bus stop."

North from Edmonds, "Snake Road" wound above the winding shoreline; locals believed it was the first concrete road in the county, replacing slippery red brick. Another highway that significantly affected Snohomish County was shared with both Chelan and King Counties: the Cascade Scenic Highway over Stevens Pass. A car had crossed the route late in 1924 when four men set out from Everett apparently hoping to dramatize its potential. After driving to the end of the existing road, they were carried up a logging incline by cable; then, in the words of historian JoAnne Roe, they "bumped along behind a freight train on the railroad ties, over frighteningly high trestles, through claustrophobic tunnels and snow sheds." Several passengers fainted from fumes. After pushing the car through snow and mud, they were pulled over the summit by a contractor's team before descending toward Wenatchee on existing switchbacks.

The three counties had undertaken construction of local portions of a highway costing about two million dollars, but boosters soon realized that the hodgepodge of roads would have to be replaced by a primary state link. Snohomish County supporters included County Commissioner Thomas C. Fleming. Efforts began to encourage the state to complete a scenic highway, mostly over old railroad switchbacks. On May 15, 1925 it opened, the second route across the state following that over Blewett and Snoqualmie passes. Described as a "high gear" road, it had minimal grades and few hazards and could remain open most of the year. The route had clear commercial benefits, connecting western and eastern sections of the state and opening timber and other resources. Yet the *Herald* thought it primarily a scenic road that progressed through virgin timber in "a country of snow capped peaks, mountain streams and waterfalls" on the west and "fertile valleys dotted with orchards and grain fields" on the east. Amenities for travelers, including auto camps and hotels, soon appeared.

The automobile affected other means of transportation such as boat traffic on the Sound. Automobile ferry service on the gas powered *Whidby* had started between Mukilteo and Whidbey Island in the late teens. In the next decade the Whidby [*sic*] Island Transportation Company was running two boats between Everett and the island. In October 1922 the Edmonds City Council leased a portion of the city wharf to the Joyce Brothers of Mukilteo as a terminal for a proposed run. The next May, service to Kingston opened on *The City of Edmonds*. The city's Park Band played while Edmonds citizens enjoyed picnic lunches on the inaugural cross-sound trip. Two months later, ferry service across Hood Canal gave the east side of the Sound a direct auto route to the main part of the Olympic Peninsula. Edmonds and Port Ludlow were connected by another route a year later. In 1928 investors from Seattle and San Francisco inaugurated service between Edmonds and Victoria, B.C. aboard the steel steamer *City of Victoria*, acclaimed as the largest and fastest auto ferry under American registry. The ship made two round trips daily and had 100 staterooms, including several suites. There were hot and cold running water and a glass enclosed observation deck. Edmonds remained a major terminal of the cross-sound route for autos, trucks, busses, passengers, and freight with a profound effect on that community.

New opportunities offered by the gasoline

The Edmonds Park Band played on the deck of the auto ferry "City of Edmonds" when service was inaugurated across Puget Sound to Kingston in May 1923. The 56-foot boat could carry 12 cars. (#221.4, courtesy Edmonds-South Snohomish County Historical Society)

Street Scenes of the 1920s

Regular ferry service to Whidbey Island began from Mukilteo, ending the era of "Mosquito Fleet" passenger and freight steamers which had called at the small island communities. (Juleen photograph #973, courtesy Everett Public Library)

Downtown Snohomish retained its business core along First Street and provided an active commercial center for its agricultural hinterland. (Courtesy Everett Public Library)

Left: Lake Stevens depended upon the Rucker Brothers' mill and was surrounded by small farms, along with drawing recreationists and summer residents to the lake shore. (Juleen photograph #378, courtesy Everett Public Library)

Left: Darrington made major civic improvements during the decade, while the completion of an automobile road spelled the end for railroad passenger service. (Courtesy Darrington Historical Society)

Above: Silvana retained its rural Scandinavian character, serving nearby farmers and dairymen, but also catering to increasing numbers of automobile owners and travelers in the lower Stillaguamish Valley. (Juleen photograph #738, courtesy Everett Public Library)

engine affected other forms of transportation. Logging trucks were in use by the mid-twenties, and in 1923 Everett became one of the first cities in the nation to replace electric streetcars with small, gas powered jitney busses. Outlying areas were affected. The beloved "Dinkie," the railroad car that carried passengers to such foothill towns as Index, became a casualty. For years the daily arrival of the train at Index "was the major excitement of the day. Residents met to talk, to see who came and went, to get mail and goods they had ordered from the outside world." Tourists came to hunt or fish. Over time, though, automobiles began to travel over even inadequate roads, and in 1924 the "Dinkie" was discontinued and replaced by a more efficient but less colorful bus. Gasoline powered rail cars also came into use on less traveled lines, as the Hartford Eastern and Northern Pacific.

The newest, most exciting mode of transportation, however, was in the skies. In the aftermath of enthusiasm for Charles Lindbergh's cross-Atlantic flight in spring 1927, Everett sought to build an airport. Using an old shipyard site for occasional flights, the Commercial Air Transport, Inc. was organized in July 1927 and capitalized at $100,000. A permanent site was needed, so a new field with hangars was built near Steamboat Slough between Everett and Marysville. Its formal opening in late April 1928 drew "Ten Planes and as Many Thousand" spectators along with state and federal dignitaries. As Governor Hartley spoke, stunt flier Tex Rankin circled above in the sister-ship of Lindbergh's monoplane before landing; later he treated some 300 passengers—the governor among them—to rides above the city. No mishaps clouded the celebration, but "Daredevil" Thompson's anticipated parachute jump was canceled due to concerns that his cotton 'chute was inadequate. The event was yet another occasion for civic pride, as leaders boasted that their new airport surpassed the few others in the state. Air traffic had entered Snohomish County.

More new businesses began to cater to drivers and tourism. The Monte Cristo Hotel set the standard for counterparts in smaller towns. Mountain hostelries catered to recreation-minded visitors. Since early in the century hotels had drawn visitors to Silverton, and in the 1920s, some entrepreneurs had grander ideas. "Rude hotels in picturesque mining towns were fine for a short stay," Monte Cristo historian Philip R. Woodhouse conceded, but sophisticated tourists were likely to prefer "comfortable housing, as well as golf course, tennis courts, a choice of easy or difficult hiking trails, and other diversions." The pioneering Rucker brothers of Everett decided to develop a choice site on United States Forest Service land in the flat at the base of Big Four Mountain. Safe from avalanche threats and on their Hartford Eastern Railway right-of-way, the spot had a "splendid" view. They abandoned plans for a mill in favor of a hotel and requested permission from the Forest Service even as the carpenters began work!

Airport christening of Everett Skylark. May 31, 1928 (Jeleen photograph #1586, courtesy Everett Public Library)

In 1921 the Ruckers opened the $150,000 Big Four Inn. Its main lodge had 35 sleeping rooms. Common places included the lobby with a massive double fireplace that remained a landmark for decades after the hotel burned to the ground in September 1949. Electricity was generated from Perry Creek, and there was hot and cold running water. The main lodge was ringed by small cabins, tent cabins, a small golf course, tennis courts, and an artificial lake; mountain trails led to a suspension bridge across the Stillaguamish River toward the Big Four Ice Caves. Built for railroad passengers, the Inn became a destination for of auto tourists after the railroad was scrapped in 1936 and the Mountain Loop Highway extended from Silverton in 1938.

Eight miles farther into the mountains, the former mining town of Monte Cristo was changing. The old industry had already declined, and a tourist trade was underway by 1920 when a destructive avalanche on the railroad tracks hastened the end of mining. The new opportunities excited John Andrews, an Illinois investor in the mining venture.

Outdoor fun and education were provided to Campfire girls who stayed at Camp Sah-hah-lee east of Silverton. It was located beyond Big Four Inn, with access via the Hartford Eastern Railway gas cars through scenic Robe Canyon. (Juleen photograph, courtesy Everett Public Library)

He renamed the old Royal Hotel the Monte Cristo Inn and developed it into a recurring tourist destination, its recreational and scenic attraction enhanced by the vestiges of an authentic mining town. Other facilities in the vicinity included small lodges and campgrounds, Boy Scout Camp Mathews at Lake Kelcema above Silverton, and Campfire Girl Camp Sa-ha-lee a mile beyond Big Four Inn. Woodhouse noted, "summer followed summer, and tourists flocked into the mountains in their little gas cars."

Recreation lured tourists to other spots difficult to frequent a decade earlier. Warm Beach and Camano Island attracted daytime and overnight outings. Auto camps allowed travelers to make overnight stops as they journeyed through towns. At Stanwood citizen volunteers built and manned an increasingly popular auto camp for persons on their way to Camano. Country life changed as roads connected farms and villages and people became more mobile.

Local authorities were compelled to establish driving regulations. Stanwood, with only 700 residents, enacted a "motor code" that set a 25-mile-per-hour speed within city limits and 15 miles on curves. A full stop was required when school buses were loading. Cars were required to have rear view mirrors, windshield "swipes," signal devices, and two headlights or spotlights, but there could be no stickers on the windshield. Driving while embracing another person was illegal; "No 'spooning' was permitted; drivers must be free and unhampered while operating cars." Clearly, the automobile had become more than just a means of transportation.

Stories of police chases and tragic accidents along with minor scrapes and turnovers became commonplace, and there were some spectacular crashes. *The Stanwood News*

Big Four Inn

The Rucker Brothers leased the former Everett & Monte Cristo Railway tracks from Hartford to Monte Cristo first for logging and then to bring tourists to their hotel above Silverton. Self-propelled cars and light rail busses were utilized for passengers, often with open trailer cars providing spectacular scenery through Robe Canyon. Major flooding in 1932 led to the end of rail service and gradual construction of the Mountain Loop Highway between Granite Falls and Darrington. (Juleen photograph, courtesy David Cameron)

Big Four Inn was opened by the Rucker Brothers in 1920 and provided a spectacular mountain setting for their quality resort complex. They sold it in 1929. Depression hit hard, followed by flood damage and abandonment of the railway link. During World War II the Coast Guard used the inn for its service men. Attempts to create a state park on the scene after the war ended when the building burned in September 1949. (Juleen photograph, courtesy Everett Public Library)

Centered around the huge stone fireplace, large lobby areas were created for guests, who entered up a short flight of steps directly off the rail cars. Bedrooms were upstairs, while the inn also provided small cabins and wooden floored tents around the central field facing Big Four Mountain. Remains of the fireplace and chimney still may be seen at the site. (Juleen photograph, courtesy Enid Nordlund)

Left: Entertainment was provided for guests in a large dance hall attached to the north end of the inn. Babs and her all-girl band were featured in 1924. Hiking trails, a ski run, a nine-hole golf course, an artificial lake, and the nearby ice caves gave outdoor enthusiasts ample opportunities to enjoy the mountain setting. (Courtesy David Cameron)

reported that a local garage owner towed seven cars involved in wrecks to his garage in a single week: "a Stutz Sports touring car, an Overland touring car, a Ford sedan, Studebaker touring and several others . . . " A tragic downtown accident killed longtime Everett fire chief W.A. Taro. Speeding toward a reported fire, his car crashed into a pumper truck headed for the same spot. The chief's car flew 75 feet through the air, while the truck jumped the curb and demolished a cigar store. Two firemen were killed. Chief Taro died two weeks later from his injuries; an estimated five thousand mourners lined the streets as his cortege traveled to Everett's first "state funeral." The call turned out to be a well-intentioned false alarm.

In November 1918, the same momentous month when World War I ended, Washington voters favored Prohibition two-to-one in a statewide referendum. Two months later Washington ratified the 18th amendment prohibiting the manufacture and distribution of intoxicating liquors nationwide. Then Everett historian Norman H. Clark discerned a mood "of self-sacrifice, dedication, moral unity, frustration, intolerance, and fear, and these feelings interacted to bring the Prohibition movement to its greatest triumph." Prohibition dominated America's social atmosphere during the ensuing decade.

Initially there seemed little objection to the laws enforcing Prohibition, and immediate reactions portended success. The mayor of Everett remarked in 1921 that he had seen only one drunken man during the past year, a notable change from the past. County berry growers optimistically predicted that their industry would grow as fruit juices replaced booze. Yet, the general enthusiasm for reform, including Prohibition, was declining along with general progressive and moralistic fervor. Illegal liquor began to enter the nation, and the Puget Sound area became a favorite site for clandestine activity because of its many coves, harbors, and islands and the proximity to Canadian liquor supplies. Clark summarized that, "Wet goods came down across the border in automobiles, trucks, boats, airplanes, and railroad cars, in coat pockets, hubcaps, suitcases, and gunny sacks." Inadequate funding, public indifference, and open opposition added up to lax, irregular enforcement. Neither governors Louis Hart nor Roland Hartley, the former Everett mayor, were enthusiastic about enforcement.

That task largely fell to county sheriffs and municipal police, and those who attempted enforcement were often frustrated by less honest colleagues or officials at higher levels. A team of Everett officers who were aroused by a suspicious plane circling overhead searched it upon landing. To no surprise, they found liquor, only to have the offender's conviction later dismissed by the State Supreme Court. One local and futile encounter involved the man who was to become the region's most celebrated rumrunner. Early on a March morning in 1920 prohibition agents who had spent several days staking out a beach near Meadowdale finally spotted men unloading a cargo of liquor from a tugboat. Threats, gunfire, and a roadblock did not prevent the wild auto escape of Roy Olmstead, the Seattle police lieutenant who was switching from one side of the law to the other. Later apprehended and fired from his police job, Olmstead paid a modest fine and then embarked on a lucrative career as "King of the Rumrunners" in the Pacific Northwest. He prospered for several years until his ultimate conviction and imprisonment.

According to local legends, most communities were alive with bootleggers, moonshiners, and rum runners. Meadowdale's chronicler relates that the "woodsy spot" between Canada and "big retail outlets in Seattle, Tacoma, and points south, proved to be an ideal spot for the rum runners to unload their boats." Moreover, "the thick brush found on some of the cutover lands made it a favorable place for moonshiners to set up their kettles," and enforcement vessels made frequent visits. Tulalip Bay had similar advantages, and illicit stills catering to loggers abounded in the wooded area overlooking Marysville that continues to be called Whiskey Ridge.

Camano Island attracted rumrunners whose cars regularly sped through Stanwood. In an unusual incident a female suspect who fled during a gun battle later spotted her own car and flagged it down only to be arrested by deputies who were using it to drive injured men to a doctor. On another occasion, *The Stanwood News* reported that an "exciting rum-runner chase was staged thru Stanwood . . . after a mad drive of 55 miles over slippery highways, from the gravel pit about seven miles north of Mount Vernon to a gasoline station in Everett." Shots hit the speeding car, and a female passenger later fled, but "20 cases of high grade liquor" were confiscated when the driver was captured in Everett.

Remoteness and "a cooperative county sheriff" enabled upriver taverns to operate as if Prohibition did not exist. On weekends, nearby loggers swarmed into Darrington to celebrate. Different groups had their favorite taverns, with Swedes patronizing one and Tarheels another. Late night confrontations between rival groups were not unusual. In time, residents from downriver discovered that Darrington was a source of illicit booze, and it gained a reputation as "an especially wild and wooly place" according to town historian Elizabeth Poehlman.

At least one teenager discovered it was easy to become a bootlegger. "It was against the law to make the damn stuff," Ed Kaye recalled in *Voices from Everett's First Century*, "but you could buy all the equipment you wanted: corks, teasers and kegs anywhere from a gallon to fifty. You could buy the ingredients in the hardware and feed stores and there were stores that sold nothing but that. If you were buying sugar the guy in the store wasn't going to say some guy bought a ton of sugar that was income to him. You didn't make your purchases all at one place anyway, you spread it around so it wouldn't be too big a shipment." Stills were built from easily found materials and were generally hidden in spots unlikely to be located. In the early 1920s a quart bottle of "moon" sold for $20, but kegs were popular and easy to handle. The young man soon learned how to dodge agents who put pressure in different locations at different times; also, agents and deputies were easily bribed. Eventually this bootlegger was caught and served five months in jail.

Encounters also took place in urban locations. Occasionally road houses, business places, and private homes around Edmonds were raided, for instance. In Everett drinking, gambling and prostitution flourished in a "notorious" district between downtown and the bay. An adolescent Henry M. Jackson delivered newspapers there during the 1920s and was troubled by what he saw. A decade later, when he was elected as prosecuting attorney, though Prohibition had ended, his early moral outrage influenced other strong cleanup efforts against slot machines and vice.

In the national consciousness the 1920s was an era of spectacular crimes and illustrious criminals. Occasional crime sprees did occur in the quiet environs of the county. The generally peaceful, law-abiding town of Edmonds was a case in point. In the middle of an October night in 1923 a quartet of masked bandits bound and gagged two night attendants at the Yost Auto Company garage and began to crack the safe. A luck-

Recreation and Resorts

Left: Silver Lake was a popular day time destination, on the paved Bothell-Everett Highway and close to the interurban line. (Courtesy Everett Public Library)

The waters of Garland Mineral Springs were developed as both healthful and enjoyable and drew visitors deep into the mountains above Index. Fire destroyed the isolated lodge in 1961, while floods wrecked much of the pool and spring area in 1980 and 1990. (Lee Pickett photograph, courtesy Index Historical Society)

Canyon Creek Lodge east of Granite Falls was created by Mrs. Joe Muller into a destination site for fishing and vacationing, while trails were built into the mountains for hiking and horse expeditions. Eleanor Roosevelt visited the lodge in the following decade. (Courtesy Jack O'Donnell)

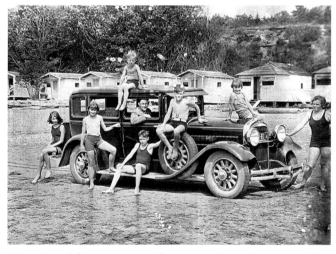

Warm Beach became a popular summer home location on Port Susan. The Hawkins Allen Motor Company of Everett featured it in this July 9, 1929 automobile promotion. (Juleen photograph #1711, courtesy Everett Public Library)

More Motor Vehicles Equals More Wrecks

This wrecked Dodge probably was photographed for evidence in a case involving the J.O. Fisher Motor Company, the Dodge dealer in Everett. (Courtesy Everett Public Library)

Not much remains of this Studebaker, as the wooden body construction, lack of safety protection, and unreliable parts made even low speed impacts often fatal. (Courtesy Snohomish Historical Society)

The Eastside Garage has a customer, as this early tow truck brings in a disabled automobile. Vehicles were far less dependable than later, had to contend with short lived tires, and rural roads especially were muddy and rutted. Yet automobiles gave access to isolated county residents and allowed shopping trips to larger towns, especially after the relatively inexpensive Model T Ford became widely available. (Courtesy Snohomish Historical Society)

A truck and motorcycle tangle. Motorcycles were popular early in the century due to their relatively low cost and the condition of the roads, and races were popular attractions. Solid rubber tired trucks, however, were clear winners, even if the farmer's fence line was not. (Photograph #0675, courtesy Everett Public Library)

217

less customer who interrupted was also bound and gagged, and the culprits proceeded. When the safe exploded, its door flew through a plate glass window and into the street. Escaping with $500 cash, the men stole a Buick touring car, which was later found at the University of Washington stadium. On another wild night thieves first blew open the safe at the Edmonds post office and then at the poultry cooperative office in Alderwood Manor before returning to Edmonds to enter a feed store. With only $45 to show for their rampage, they then stole a car to escape north out of town. Other robberies and offenses were less spectacular, but they did occur.

Then there was 27-year-old Edward Sickles, a local desperado fit for a dime novel who hid out in east county woods during three frantic months in spring and summer 1927 while authorities searched for him. His escapade began on the morning of March 2, when an observant hardware merchant in Sultan alerted officials to a coupe suspiciously parked near his own store and the Citizens State Bank. Investigation showed that the car contained two .30 caliber rifles and 110 rounds of ammunition which town marshal Percy Z. Brewster quickly confiscated. Sickles approached to ask what was going on and was arrested. While the marshal and the merchant were placing him in the small town jail, Sickles suddenly turned on the two and fired a hitherto concealed automatic weapon at Marshal Brewster, who died shortly. Sickles fled. Townspeople and officers began a search that proved successful that afternoon when Sickles, a convict with a record in several states, was arrested under an alias and booked into the county jail. Within three weeks Sickles was tried for murder, found guilty, and sentenced to hang.

Yet that did not end the saga. On the night of April 30 the condemned slayer picked a lock on his cell door and, with apparent outside help, pried through a window casing, sawed through bars, and escaped. The search for him continued for three months, during which Sickles apparently disguised certain of his features, moved about with some freedom, stole cars, and committed other crimes. Deputies eventually traced him to a secluded cabin hideaway near an abandoned mill site up an unused railroad grade five miles east of Granite Falls. A task force was sent to capture him. The four men traveled up "a trail ungraded and rutty. Low hanging boughs screen[ed] the road for most of the distance and scrape[d] the men as they move[d] through the foliage and brush for almost three miles. At the end of the narrow roadway is a turn around, also hidden by a heavy growth of alders and timber where Sickles parked his stolen cars and unloaded his provisions which he was compelled to pack for the remainder of the short distance to his cabin," reported the *Herald*.

Sickles and a woman companion drove to this spot and were walking toward the cabin when deputies ordered him to stop. According to the deputies, he refused to put up his hands, but instead fired at them, whereupon they retaliated and killed him instantly. The woman and other alleged accomplices were arrested. Sickles' cabin proved to contain expensive radio equipment along with bedding and suitcases, and a still was

Disguised as a private mansion overlooking Possession Sound south of Mukilteo, owners of the Waldheim manufactured whiskey in the basement and secretly sent out the finished product through underground tunnels to boats waiting below. "Smugglers' Gulch" was aptly named. (Courtesy Jack O'Donnell)

Prohibition and Vice

Left: This large still was displayed by deputies in front of the county jail on Rockefeller Avenue across from the court house on June 8, 1925. Illegal alcohol manufacturing and importing from Canada were widespread during the decade. (Juleen photograph # 1252, courtesy Everett Public Library)

Right: A railroad spike hammer made short work of slot machines, but illegal gambling flourished outside town boundaries, and enforcement policies had their variations. (Courtesy Everett Public Library)

Left: Rural moonshining operations ranged from the simple to the highly complex. Typical was this whiskey plant in the woods near Lake Ketchum east of Stanwood. Loggers' double bitted axes were handy tools for destroying the wooden barrels, as well as the interiors of clubs and confectioneries suspected of operating as saloons. (Courtesy Stillaguamish Valley Pioneers Association)

found nearby. The shooting of Sickles in a wooded outpost brought an end to one of the county's most spectacular manhunts.

The year 1929 began well in Snohomish County, as in the rest of the nation. Everett merchants celebrated New Year's Day with memories of what the *Herald* called one of the greatest buying and selling Christmas seasons ever. As the paper promoted four new comic strips in the Sunday edition, it also noted that Edmonds pioneer L.R. Rap took his new seat as a county commissioner, the Clark-Nickerson mill on the waterfront reopened after a week's shutdown for repairs, and $525 would buy one a brand new Chevrolet—$10 more for a two-door Whippet sedan. Within months people would remember these as "the good old days" and yearn for "the second coming of prosperity." The boom still had time to expand, but its days now were numbered.

The Great Depression: 1929–1939

No one really knew what caused the Great Depression. Its effects were so severe that government officials ever since have studied and worked to ensure a similar event never would reoccur. Their unease is compounded with the knowledge that it only ended with the massive infusion of foreign and domestic expenditures for military arms to fight the worst war of the twentieth century.

Nevertheless, economists and historians propose a number of probable causes and effects, often interrelated, for the collapse. These include the Treaty of Versailles that ended World War I, but saddled Germany with impossible reparations and prevented it from contributing to the world economy. Additionally, overproduction on farms (following wartime demand) reduced farm prices to dangerous lows, and a growing disparity between rich and poor, lax regulation of financial markets (with the resultant speculation on Wall Street), and the British government's default on gold payments to foreigners, resulted in similar actions by more than two dozen other countries and lead to a reaction that slowed world commerce. An especially important factor that served to increase the downturn was the Smoot-Hawley Act of 1930, which Congress passed establishing prohibitive tariffs on foreign goods entering the United States. With the highest rates in the nation's history, it was intended to protect American manufacturing, but it had the opposite effect when foreign nations imposed similar duties on American products, greatly diminishing our overseas sales. Congress passed and President Hoover signed it, despite a petition signed by 1,000 economists urging a veto.

The most visible sign of economic disaster to the people of Snohomish County was the New York Stock Exchange crash in the fall 1929. For at least an entire generation people throughout America and the world looked back on that meltdown as the beginning of the decade of privation.

That world still seemed good when it all began. Despite Prohibition, there were speakeasies where gin flowed freely, roadsters with rumble seats, and young women with flat chests and short skirts. Young men wore coonskin coats and carried hip flasks of hard liquor. Moving pictures were becoming a major source of entertainment, as sound was added to the flickering images on the screen with Warner Brothers' *Don Juan* in August 1926, followed a year later with the same studio's Al Jolson in the first talking film, *The Jazz Singer*. Gradually the county's theaters were replacing the traditional, and more expensive, live entertainment with the movies. In Everett the Fox Company owned the Everett, Granada, and Balboa theaters, all within two

Walt Disney recognized early on the possibilities of marketing Mickey Mouse movies with merchandise and toys. With the coming of sound in his cartoons, youngsters identified with Mickey, and Disney organized Mickey Mouse Clubs throughout the country. Children signed up with local busnesses, such as Meadowmoor Dairy ("Every Meadowmoor Dealer is an Official Mickey Mouse Ice Cream Dealer," ran the club newsletter ad), then went to the theatre for contests, prizes, and free admissions for members, and even marched in the Fourth of July parade. (Courtesy Everett Public Library)

blocks of the downtown area. The independent Roxy would open in May 1935 across Colby Avenue from the Everett. Theaters elsewhere in the county during the period included the American in Arlington, Lake in Lake Stevens, Marysville in Marysville, Avalon in Monroe, Ideal in Stanwood, and Brown's on First Street in Snohomish.

Everett's radio station KFBL was a local addition to the Seattle signals from KOMO, KOL, KJR, and KIRO that were broadcast into Snohomish County. By 1930 the Leese brothers were broadcasting for 10 hours a day. The depression years were the heyday of radio and the period when it became a major source of news and entertainment. Local reporters covered nearby stories, while the networks increasingly provided national and international news as well as big-name entertainment shows, often by former vaudeville performers such as Bob Hope, Jack Benny, and Fred Allen. Just before dinner time the air was filled with children's programs such as "Little Orphan Annie" and "Jack Armstrong, the All American Boy." Radio was maturing during the 1930s. Despite that, the Depression hit KFBL hard. The Leese brothers gave up, and Lee Mudget took over the station in 1933, changing the call letters to KRKO. The station had a staff of 12, including announcer Cliff Hansen, who eventually would become the president of KWYZ, which rose as KRKO's local competition in the mid-1950s. In 1938 KRKO signed on with the Mutual Broadcasting System, but even by 1939 it only could stay on the air from 7:00 A.M. until noon, then return from 4:00 to 7:00 P.M.

Cars had replaced horses for transportation by the end of the 1920s, and it was easier to go to town for a meal and a show or to drive to the country for a picnic or sightseeing. "Sunday driver" became a popular term for people who went out for a ride with no particular destination in mind. By 1939 buggies were an anachronism, as was the interurban to Seattle, killed off by the automobile and the refusal of the car makers who held the patents to upgrade technology. Everything it seemed was "streamlined" by then, from new car models to locomotives, toasters to vacuum cleaners.

Perhaps best of all as the 1920s rolled to a close, for those who had money, there were stock margins that could make one rich. It was easy: borrow 97 percent of the price of a stock from the broker and buy the shares, then watch their price rise. Almost every company qualified. The value of America's stocks doubled between March 1928 and September 1929. The market was going up, ever up. RCA jumped 12¾ points in one day. Its low in 1928 had been 85½. In 1929 it soared to 549.

The future seemed bright almost beyond belief. While Herbert Hoover was campaigning in 1928 for election as president, his Republican party promised, "With the Help of God, the abolition of poverty." When he was inaugurated in March 1929, the promise seemed to be valid. During the first six months of his administration the index continued its upward thrust so strongly that it was called the "Hoover Bull Market." People flocked to the brokers to buy stocks with money they raised any way they could: bank loans, home mortgages, by selling their low yielding but much safer government securities Billions of dollars went into the market, and for those who could afford to play, the country was riding high.

There were warnings. Farm prices had been low for years, so low that many farmers were forced into bankruptcy. Northwest lumber prices had fallen, leading to production cutbacks and the scrapping of older, less efficient mills, most notably in Everett and Granite Falls. Iron and steel production fell in the United States. Interest rates in Britain rose to 6.5 percent, attracting European capital that had been in the United States money market. Yet, the good times seemed endless, and the buying frenzy on the New York Stock Exchange continued unabated until September 29, 1929. On that day the market fell, then rose, then fell again more rapidly. The newspapers and financiers remained optimistic through October 22. Then on Thursday October 24 stock prices plunged again, on huge volume. A group of financiers ostentatiously bought stocks that afternoon, and the market steadied the next day. However, on Monday sellers again drove down prices, and on Tuesday October 29 prices collapsed: the day went down in history as "Black Tuesday." Thousands of people who held stock on margin saw their money disappear as they were unable to meet broker calls to pay what they owed or lose their investment. A record 16.4 million shares changed hands, and the Dow Jones Industrial Average plummeted 30.57 points.

Economists, newspapers, and the government assured the country there was no threat of a business

Construction of the Pacific Highway northward from King County to Mt. Vernon opened a major north-south route for motorists and stimulated both faster travel times and the growth of services for travelers. The highway later was designated as U.S. 99, the main throroughfare from Canada to Mexico. This is a Model 30 Caterpillar with a Thirty Leaning Wheel Grader working on July 25, 1931. (Caterpillar Tractor Co. #4318, courtesy Everett Public Library)

depression, but by the end of the year stock values had fallen by $15 billion. President Hoover and Secretary of the Treasury Andrew Mellon assured the nation that the economy was fundamentally sound and that "Prosperity is just around the corner." Yet banks failed, factories closed, commodity prices fell, and unemployment rose in a deflationary downward spiral. The "Roaring Twenties" went bust, and with or without the acknowledgment of the administration, the country was in the early stages of a depression of major proportions, the worst since the Panic of 1893.

On September 17, 1930 a tremendous shock wave rolled over Port Gardner Bay. Shattering windows, knocking over stacks of boxes at the canneries, and causing residents to fear a major disaster, the Puget Sound & Alaska Powder Company plant between Mukilteo and Everett blew up tons of dynamite and nitroglycerin. The plant (shown here intact years earlier) was destroyed, but casualties were limited to only eight injuries. (Courtesy Everett Public Library)

County residents didn't immediately become aware of the economic avalanche that was surging across the country from the east. Local people were acquainted with bad economic times, of course. Old timers remembered that Everett nearly died when the Everett Land Company went bankrupt 40 years before. Younger people had lived through the Depression of 1920–1921, when Weyerhaeuser sales fell 50 percent and small mills closed throughout the county, even though mill hands asked the owners to reduce wages so they would have work. Some fathers then had faced the winter without enough to feed their families. Although there was, in Everett at least, an unspoken understanding that it was not to be discussed, adults had vivid memories of the Everett Massacre of 1916, when mill owners refused to honor salary agreements. Striking workers and the radical IWW had found themselves facing police violence and gunfire, breaking the shingleweavers' attempts to organize and negotiate on an even basis. However, few of the county's businessmen and fewer still of its farmers and mill hands understood how much the stock market was an invisible force in their lives, since few Americans actually owned stock or had retirement plans then, and news of the crash in 1929 only slowly sank in.

On October 22, a week before Black Tuesday, the major local story in the *Herald* was a contest for the national amateur billiard championship, which was being played out in the Everett Elks Lodge. Participants were the title holder, Percy Williams of Chicago, playing against Everett's native son Mon Wallgren, who later would become a United States congressman, a senator, and governor of Washington. That story ran under a four-column headline at the top of page one. Near it was a two paragraph Associated Press report that, "The stock market staged one of its characteristically violent comebacks today after more than a week of severe decline, which culminated in yesterday's avalanche of selling." The article noted that the volume was well below the previous day's.

The next day, the *Herald* offered near the bottom of page one a single paragraph noting that, "Bear pressure again sent share prices into a headlong decline." That note ran beside a long story which reported that Enoch Bagshaw, who had led an unbeaten Everett High School football team to an unofficial national football championship, then took the University of Washington team to its first Rose Bowl game, was being fired as the university's coach after a series of losing seasons. There was no way to know it then, but clearly, Wallgren's future was brighter by far than that of either Bagshaw or the economy

On Black Tuesday itself there was promising news at home, if one ignored the swirling financial markets. Everett Masons announced plans for a $50,000 renovation of their lodge. The Fisher Co. moved its department store into new quarters in downtown Everett after spending $80,000 on renovations to the building. An estimated 6,000 people attended the grand opening. Everett's C.B. shingle mill finished construction of a 12,000 square foot storage building. The *Herald* began printing comics and a weekly magazine on its new color press. There were unfounded rumors that the giant Zellerbach Company had bought property on the Everett waterfront and planned to build a large paper plant. Perhaps best of all, the Puget Sound Pulp and Timber Company announced it would build a huge new pulp mill on the waterfront. Things looked good (if you could believe the news), and the *Herald* on November 24 printed an editorial in which it quoted *The Nation* magazine as saying the market crash did not mean the country was headed for a calamity.

However, Snohomish County residents who looked closely might have noticed a report in the November 19 paper that shingle production in the Northwest was down 50 percent. Then, 11 days later, the paper ran a story under a headline that said, "Lumber Buying Shows Decrease." The story beneath it reported that lumber dealers were buying only for "immediate use or replacement." In a county where forest products were the foundation of its industrial base, that kind of news could only mean trouble.

It all began in the east, where most of the victims of the stock market crash were licking their wounds. The crash had swallowed so much money that it completely destroyed many investors, some of whom had been capitalists who helped make the country's economic wheels turn. Investors who survived the crash were gun shy, and even people who had taken no part in the wild speculation suddenly realized that the high flying economy of the 1920s was fragile: prudence dictated that they hoard their resources. The ripple effect went to the retail stores where stock they had expected to sell stayed on the shelves. The stores reduced the orders to their suppliers who, in turn,

225

bought less from the manufacturers who took up the slack in their revenues by laying off workers and cutting the pay of those they kept. The workers were forced to reduce their buying, and the cycle started all over again. Stores went out of business. Factories closed. Debts went unpaid. Banks failed, taking people's savings with them.

The catastrophe moved inexorably toward Snohomish County. However, for a time, few in the county were aware of what was happening. The Everett *Herald* was able to report on December 29, 1929, for instance, that local merchants had done a record business during the Christmas season, and that construction in Everett during 1929 exceeded $1.65 million more than that of 1927 or 1928. On New Year's Day the paper said the coming year promised continued growth throughout the county.

It was wrong. As the months of 1930 passed, the signs of economic slowdown began to appear. In early December the good news that holiday shoppers were jamming the stores and that large new construction programs were being planned began to be neutralized with reports that President Hoover had signed an emergency bill making $116 million available for unemployment relief, and by Christmas wire stories were talking openly about the existence of a depression and growing unemployment in the nation. On December 20 the *Herald* published an editorial declaring that new business construction "while not startling in its size is nevertheless welcome at this time of the year when relief agencies are taxed to look after the wants of those in distress because of unemployment." The building plans were a sign, the paper said, "definitely indicating an upward trend." Three days later the paper's editorial said that Christmas business was "a good finish to an otherwise ordinary year which we have looked on as one of general depression." The paper was beginning to understand something had gone badly wrong, but it still did not comprehend how terrible the situation was becoming.

However, the facts of the Depression were becoming more and more obvious to the community at large. The crush hit a wide range of people in Snohomish County, just as it had in the remainder of the country. The most severe consequences were to the common workers, the people who worked the factories and the mills scattered along the county's waterways and among its communities. Even during the easy times of the mid-1920s, they had lived from payday to payday with little surplus to put aside for bad times.

In July 1930 expansion was taking place at the Monroe Reformatory, which had laid its cornerstone in 1910 and served to handle young men sentenced to terms inside its walls. (Juleen #1906, courtesy Everett Public Library)

Sultan River Water Supply 1929-1930

The city of Everett provides water service for much of Snohomish County, thanks to a system based on diverting the flow of the Sultan River twenty-five miles to the east. The first diversion dam and pipeline were begun in 1915. Between 1929 and 1930 a major upgrade was accomplished with the construction of of a new dam and tunnel, which sent the water into Lake Chaplain and allowed for using 50 million gallons a day and storage of 1.4 billion gallons. The following construction photographs were taken by Baar and Cunningham, Consulting Engineers. (All photos courtesy Everett Public Library)

New pipelines to Everett were set in trenches and backfilled When they reached the Snohomish River valley it was necessary to build long trestles and lay the pipes on top, while submerging them beneath Ebey Slough and the river.

Much of the work still was hand labor, with men moving those sections along temporary rails.

Crossing Ebey Slough required scows and a diver. Notice his helmet in the water between the timbers.

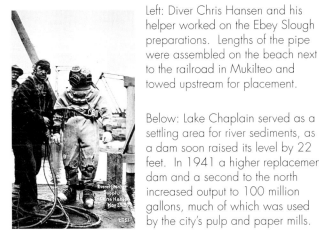

Left: Diver Chris Hansen and his helper worked on the Ebey Slough preparations. Lengths of the pipe were assembled on the beach next to the railroad in Mukilteo and towed upstream for placement.

Below: Lake Chaplain served as a settling area for river sediments, as a dam soon raised its level by 22 feet. In 1941 a higher replacement dam and a second to the north increased output to 100 million gallons, much of which was used by the city's pulp and paper mills.

Away from the water, sections of pipe were hauled by railroad flatcars and heavy trucks.

As the orders for lumber, shingles, paper and paper pulp dried up, the mills that were the county's economic foundation did what they could to survive. That meant cut production, lay off workers and reduce the wages of those who remained. Often the plants were forced to shut down entirely, sometimes permanently.

The economic situation began to seem chaotic. Frank Platt, who was a teenager in Everett at the time, remembered that, "The mills mostly would close, then open when they got a little business then close down again. The Fourteenth Street Dock on [Everett's] Bayside had four or five small mills, and they all were pretty much shut down. But that was true all over, and a lot of mills never did open again, places like Blackman Point, Hingston Box Factory, Parker Poyner, National Pole, K 'n' K. The Canyon Mill shut down and was sold to a junk dealer, but they bought it back before it was torn down. Even the large mills like Hulbert, C.B., and Jamison would close down from time to time." Platt became personally familiar with the desperation of mill hands unable to find work because his mother owned the small Bayview Grocery store at Twelfth and Grand in a blue collar

The Sultan River Bench construction site, July 29, 1930.

The diversion dam was hit with serious flooding in September and October 1930, with water flowing five feet over its top on October 17.

neighborhood of Everett. "She carried her customers on credit, sometimes for years, because she knew they needed the food for their families." That was an example of how people responded to each other's need during what they called "the bad times." It also was an indication of the community's character that all but two of those customers eventually paid their debt to the little grocery store that had helped them. Some paid just a dollar or two at a time.

Conditions became exceedingly difficult, especially in 1932 and early 1933. Young people were especially hard hit, as marriages had to be delayed and the birth rate fell. Elderly parents might be dependent upon the earnings of a single son, while others who had known lives of comparative luxury found themselves coping with the psychological collapse of becoming unemployed or competing for scarce blue-collar jobs. Compared to 1929, the number of production workers employed nationally was down to 68.9 percent, but an even lower 59.1 percent in Washington. The gross national product was halved, 75 percent of the value of the stock market had evaporated, while the home and residential construction industry had dropped by more than 80 percent. Downtown commercial buildings, which had replaced many earlier wooden structures in the 1920s now stood

228

Automobile Row in the 1930s

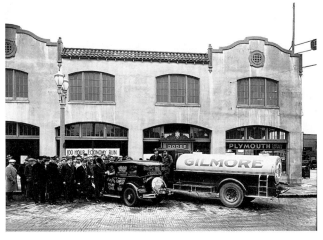

As money and jobs grew scarcer, automobile dealers stressed mileage and economic performance. This is the J.O. Fisher Company promoting Gilmore oil for its Plymouth cars and Dodge trucks on February 17, 1931. (Juleen #1974, courtesy Everett Public Library)

In 1934 Fisher succumbed to the Depression, leaving a major vacancy on Everett's auto row at the southwest corner of Hewitt and Rucker avenues. The building survives to the present and served as a revived Dodge-Plymouth dealer location until late in the century under the ownership of Dwane Layne. (Juleen #2306, courtesy Everett Public Library)

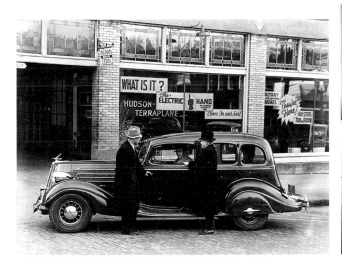

South of the Fisher building, Miller O. and Marie G. Swenson operated their Swenson Motors at 3020 Rucker, selling and servicing Essex and Hudson cars and Reo trucks. This is the Hudson Terraplane, illustrating the new trend toward streamlining everything from trains to toasters. (Juleen #2224, courtesy Everett Public Library)

Service stations were handy and widespread throughout the county. Walt Maahs sold Shell gasoline from his at the corner of Wall and Rucker, with the price of gasoline prominently posted on November 10, 1937. (Juleen #2059, courtesy Everett Public Library)

partially empty or vacant, no one renting or buying. Combined with a drop in lumber exports to less than half of 1929 levels, those communities in the county most dependent upon logging and timber milling were hurting badly.

Many of those who held their jobs found pay scales reduced by hard pressed employers, hours cut, and positions turned into intermittent or part time statuses. Some who lost their homes or felt burdensome to their families became itinerants who wandered the country by road, rail, and foot following rumors of jobs. Forced to work temporarily, beg, or even steal what they needed to stay alive, they camped in hobo "jungles" often near railroad tracks and met mixed receptions from local communities and residents. Splitting and throwing in loads of firewood in return for a meal from houses they had marked as being friendly, pooling gleaned bits of food into a "hobo stew" to be shared with others, and sharing news of which police or railroad detectives to avoid were daily routines. Others found some unoccupied land where they built shacks of whatever material they could scrape up or floated by along the rivers. There were no organized "Hoovervilles" in Snohomish County as there was on the tideflats of Seattle, but abandoned logging camps were taken over, placer gold mining increased along the streams, and many people took what the land provided in game, berries, and wood. Everett High School teacher Ruth Stephenson recalled bringing her lunch from home but regularly giving most of it to her students who had none. Others fell asleep in class, exhausted from nighttime fishing and crabbing to bring in food for their families.

Statewide, individual incomes fell 55 percent between 1929 and 1933, business failures were above national averages, and there was a net out-migration from the Pacific Northwest. Some communities, such as Granite Falls, lost half their population when key industries closed (in this case Waite's saw mill southeast of town) and logging camps did not reopen after normal winter shutdowns. More isolated attractions, including Big Four Inn above Silverton, found their businesses drying up and were forced to shut their doors, leaving only caretakers to keep an eye on the buildings and hope for better times. Severe flooding in 1932 only added to the problems, forcing closure of the Hartford Eastern Railway from Hartford to Monte Cristo. Four years later it was scrapped. When a fire destroyed the main shed and its traveling crane at the Index granite quarry in May 1932, an era came to an end: reinforced concrete would be used in the future, as the remains of the once bustling operation were scavenged for chicken grit.

One direct result of the Depression was to make some urban residents rethink the possibilities of making a new home in the country, even though agricultural commodity prices had dropped to the point, for example, where neighboring Chelan county growers were ripping out apple orchards for firewood and dumping fruit into canyons and the Columbia River. Hopes to provide jobs for unemployed men to pick the unsellable crops and haul them across Stevens Pass and give them to the needy in Snohomish, King, and Pierce counties also failed, as fruit rotted on trees and pickers crossing the mountains in search of seasonal work found no help wanted.

Making a living in the rural areas always has been difficult, and in economic down times the conditions are even harder. Shacks, houseboats along the lower rivers, and shelter in old logging camps sometimes were necessary. Populations fell as mills closed, beginning in 1927. Granite Falls, for example, lost half its population by 1933 and stabilized at 500. These girls lived in the Three Lakes area northeast of Snohomish. (#FA008, courtesy Snohomish Historical Society)

Employees of the Washington Cooperative Egg and Poultry Association pose by their building on Everett's Riverside on November 3, 1931. County poultry production had boomed in the 1920s, stimulated by projects such as Alderwood Manor and improved breeding of layer hens. Prices, however, plummeted in the years following. (Miller photograph, courtesy Everett Public Library)

While many townsfolk dug up back yards to plant large gardens, others strove for more self-sufficiency by creating fruit/berry, small dairy, and poultry operations, utilizing cheap marginal or cutover lands and selling or bartering their surpluses. In 1930 the United States Census of Agriculture listed 4,262 farms in the county, a number which rose to 6,026 in 1935 and then 6,231 in 1940. Although the raw numbers increased, their total value shrank with deflation, the 1930 figure of $31,735,500 dropping to only $24,995,612 in 1935 and then rising partway back to $28,520,393 in 1940. Farm acreage rose with the increase in activity, as the 1930 figure was 160,310. By 1935 it reached 185,171, then in 1940 188,304. Larger farms increased seasonal job opportunities, especially in labor-intensive tasks such as berry picking, tying up pea vines, and harvesting lettuce. Packing, canning, and transportation also benefited, as the county maintained a complex agricultural infrastructure through the decade.

Another phenomena of the Depression years sometimes was called "doubling up," as people moved in with relatives or friends to reduce living costs and pool their resources. One example of this was the experience of Carl Ramstad. His family had moved from Canada to Snohomish County in 1910 when he was six years old, and he had lived here until he entered the University of Washington. After studying forestry at the university he held several jobs in various parts of the Northwest. Shortly after Black Tuesday he took a job with the contractors who were building the huge new Puget Sound Pulp and Timber Company pulp mill on the Everett waterfront. He was paid 50-cents an hour. Nearly 70 years later, he recalled, "When the plant was finished two other young men and I started working as technicians in the laboratory." He stayed with the plant through several owners until he retired. "I really never knew much about the Depression. About 1932 the mill shut down for three weeks. Then it shut down again in 1933 or 1934. Each time we were called back we took a 20 percent pay cut. I recall that the last time the mill shut down it was because it couldn't pay the interest on the bonds. But the bond holders took over, and they reopened the plant. My pay got down to 29 cents an hour, but I was young and single and without responsibilities, so none of that really affected me very much. When I was out of work I just moved in with my brother Arthur until the plant opened

How Snohomish County Coped with the Great Depression

By Nellie E. Robertson

The late Ruth Wade of Everett summed it up very well. "It took the worst of times to bring out the best of people," she said when talking about the Depression years.

While the men tilled the soil and scratched for a few pennies here and there, the women managed the meager funds and stretched the assets as far as they could.

Ole Eide, now in his 90s, was raised on a Stanwood farm. His family felt the lack of money, but they had enough to eat. They picked up any odd jobs they could find to augment what they grew. He finally got a permanent job in 1934 with the state game department, where he worked for 35½ years.

"A strange thing," he said. "Everybody cooperated. We were all in the same boat. We had a good time socially." They got together in homes and played cards.

Ruth Yost of Arlington had similar experiences. Her parents lived on a small farm with their six children during the Depression.

"We had a cow, chickens, and good neighbors," she said. Her mother, an Arlington native, made the family's clothes out of hundred-pound sacks that had contained sugar and flour. Her father had contracted to build roads. "But the government closed down. He finally went to work for WPA in 1936 for $48 a month." Yost had one school dress and one play dress. Some folks traded work for groceries and necessities. "The church was a big part of our lives," she concluded.

Walt Taubeneck witnessed the Depression at the ripe old age of six in Marysville. His father worked at the L.E. Witt grocery store nine hours a day, six days a week, for $50 a month. "Our family of four got along okay. My mother was a good manager. She knew where every penny went. She was a good cook and a good seamstress." Although they raised no food, they never went hungry. "We always had wood in the woodshed and a fire in the stove." The family's Model-T Ford took them to a weekly movie in Everett and on Sunday drives. Gas

sold for less than 20 cents a gallon. When his father received the second half of his WW I bonus, he bought another car and paid off the property tax just before the county forgave real estate taxes. "My mother would make me an extra sandwich for school. I'd put it on my desk for the teacher to pick up to dole out to others."

Marion Van Trojen remembers property taxes and mortgages well. Her mother continually intoned, "We have to clear the mortgage." They paid only the interest for years on the small Sultan farm. Her mother canned what they raised and the wild blackberries they picked. "She was so pleased with her jars."

Like many of her classmates, Van Trojen picked berries to buy her school clothes. As a Sultan High School student, she regretted that the Depression robbed them of class rings and annuals. "We did have class pictures and the junior-/senior banquet, though."

The four children in the family wore hand-me-downs from neighbors. "That was before Sanforizing," she said. "It was just the way it was. We never felt inferior." Her father worked in the big mill over the hill as a shingle weaver, and his two sons worked there as well. To make ends meet, her mother took in boarders.

Everett's Shirley Small shared memories of her parents and her research into Depression living. "Our parents protected us from the harsh realities of the Depression. We had no money. Daddy took apart old buildings, board by board, and straightened the nails." He used the lumber for his own building projects. As the number-one winner in Weyerhaeuser's garden project, he grew fruits and vegetables that her mother canned. "She had to boil the jars for hours to can them." Every vacant lot had a garden. Parents didn't discuss finances with their children. A Weyerhaeuser employee, her father cut cedar shakes when the mill shut down.

"My mother was the focal point of the home," Mrs. Small remembered. "She had empathy for everybody and helped everyone. She taught by delegation." She gave her children jobs to do in the garden and in the home. Many people knocked on the back doors of Everett homes asking to trade work for food. For fun, "we played hide and seek in Forest Park, played store with leaves for money, and had bonfires. We had a chance to use our imaginations," Small said.

Walter Gobiet of Snohomish, in his early 20s during the depression, worked at a wholesale house for 30 cents an hour. "You worked until you got through," he said. "If you didn't want to work, you could go down the road." A Snohomish resident for 50 years, he said they had good neighbors. It was all woods and sawmills then. "When the mills were running, there was some money. When they closed down, there was no work."

Marguerite Graden Ellwanger, born in 1900 on a Monroe farm, had six children to provide for during the Depression. They lived on a small farm. "We fared a lot better than some," she said. "We raised our own meat, had a cow, raised a garden, and canned everything. We never saw any money. You made do with what you had. Once in a while Paul picked up a job." One time her husband, Paul Graden, found a job making pea stakes for a Tualco farmer. He made the stakes, 20 to 25 feet long, from old growth cedar on their farm. He carried bundles of 25 stakes on his shoulder half a mile to the road for pick up.

"We never felt deprived," Mrs. Ellwanger said. "Nobody had any extra, we were all in the same boat. We managed to hang on to our place. We never had a mortgage." Their small farm was near where the Wagner Community Hall now stands. "They called it Hungry Hill in those days, even when things got better."

Grace Kirwan tells of those days in Monroe. Teachers were paid with county warrants that paid four percent interest, with the call dates published in the newspapers. Mary Rosenzweig, a Monroe teacher, sold her warrants for immediate cash at a 10 percent discount, a practice followed by many. The buyer received face value plus interest when they were due.

The entire Monroe Union High School salary budget for 1932-33 amounted to $25,000. The average teacher salary was $100 a month.

Milk, seven cents a quart, was home-delivered daily twice a day in summer, since there was no refrigeration. Sugar cost $5 for a 100-pound sack. One farm wife sold whipping cream for 25 cents a quart, but customers had to go get it. The cream had the consistency of mayonnaise.

Mrs. Kirwan's father owned Camp-Riley Drug Co. and sold ice cream sodas and milkshakes for 10 cents during the Depression.

A hobo jungle grew on the southeast corner of U.S. 2 and North Kelsey St. in Monroe where the Rite Aid store stands in 2004. The nearby railroad tracks offered easy transportation. Hoboes would go door to door offering to work for food. The encampment frightened local children, who were warned to stay away from there.

After Franklin D. Roosevelt was elected president, he declared a moratorium on banks for a week. Mrs. Kirwan, in school at the College of Puget Sound in Tacoma, received a crisp $20 bill from her father to tide her over the bank closure, but depositors in the Monroe bank didn't lose a penny.

The Frye lettuce farm, just west of Monroe and now a rapidly growing area of housing and industrial development, made it possible for many to survive during the Depression. Whole families worked in the fields and in the packing sheds. When Frye raised the pay from eight cents to 10 cents an hour, the word spread like wildfire through the town. Workers received 10 cents an hour for a 10-hour day. When lettuce hit a bad year in the late 1930s, the farm closed down, but it had been in business long enough to sustain many in the community through the Depression years.

Pulp, Plywood, and Pres-to-logs
Diversified the 1930s Timber Industry

Above: Canyon Lumber Company on 24th Street and Snohomish River in Everett had been organized at the head of Robe Canyon on the South Fork Stillaguamish River at Robe, then moved down to a better location by its owners, C.A. Dean, Jack Theurer, and Richard Hambridge. (Courtesy Everett Public Library)

Left: Millions of "Pres-to-logs" were manufactured by the Weyerhaeuser company at Mill B to utilize waste sawdust. Most homes heated with slab wood and planer ends from the mills, and buildings utilized "hog fuel" waste from huge hogger machines which chewed up the debris for the steam boilers. These new artificial logs (shown here in June, 1938) were popular with older people and those using "trash burner" stoves while cooking with newer gas and later electric kitchen stoves. (Juleen #2616, courtesy Everett Public Library)

Left: Huge sections of old-growth Douglas fir had their bark removed by hand, than were spun past long, razor sharp blades to peel off sheets of veneer. These were then glued in sheets with alternating grain patterns to provide strong pieces of wood of varying thicknesses. This is at the Robinson Manufacturing Company on the Everett waterfront, 19th and Norton. The plant later was purchased by its employees and renamed Everett Plywood & Door Company. (Courtesy Everett Public Library)

Photographer Everett Murray was known for his fascination with the power and drama of modern technology. Here a log comes dripping out of the water bound for the head rig saw, while behind are the rounded waste burner and belching smokestack. (Everett Murray photograph, courtesy Everett Public Library)

Weyerhaeuser's sulfite digesters. (Courtesy *Everett Herald* Archives)

The huge new Soundview pulp mill dominated the central waterfront of Everett and today remains as the sole survivor of the four mills which came to be located in the city. Able to supply the huge demand for fresh water, a nearby source of wood, and major transportation routes, the city dominated the industry and became known for its pungent reek which was noteworthy for years. (Courtesy Everett Public Library)

again." Arthur Ramstad was a long-time history teacher and coach at Everett High School, where the staff were paid in interest-bearing warrants because the district did not have enough tax money coming in to pay salaries. The warrants could be cashed in at a bank for a portion of their value, the bank holding them for collection of interest and future redemption when the times improved.

For many of Carl Ramstad's fellow workers, men with families and responsibilities, the situation was much more serious, as people throughout the county were being left jobless and destitute. Employees at the mill asked the company to reduce its payroll by cutting the work day to four or six hours rather than lay off some workers entirely. That was a last, desperate effort by helpless people to keep at least some income. The company complied by setting a six-hour day for those working on an hourly basis.

Snohomish County residents who escaped the worst effects of the Depression used the meager resources they had left to help the destitute, especially the children. The *Herald* sponsored a milk fund, raising money through activities such as dances, exhibition football games, and a circus organized by local firefighters. Milk purchased with the proceeds was distributed through the schools to undernourished children. A dental clinic for needy children was sponsored by the Elks Club women's group and the Parent-Teacher Association in Everett. The Red Cross distributed thousands of sacks of government flour, while volunteers from that institution used cotton supplied by the government to hand-make clothing for children of Snohomish and Island Counties. Churches organized relief programs such as the "Harvest Day" at the Lake Stevens Union Sunday School, which collected food for the poverty stricken. In Snohomish, the Central Elementary School organized a soup kitchen to serve hot lunches to hungry pupils. Parents, teachers and pupils all contributed. In Everett the Earl Faulkner Post of the American Legion acquired 185 acres near the northern tip of the city and employed idle men to begin clearing 60 acres for a park—but the money soon ran out.

As the Depression deepened, more people were left destitute at the same time as it became more difficult for the charitable institutions to find new resources to meet the demand. Local governments were in the same predicament as the country's other institutions. The governments' revenues plummeted as many of their tax sources disappeared and others simply were unable to pay. Snohomish County Auditor John Haugen reported in November 1932, for instance, that the county's funds in 1931 had decreased $136,093.62 from 1930, while the county collected only 84.23 percent of the taxes due during 1931. Nevertheless, by 1932 local governments, alarmed by the huge numbers of families stricken by overwhelming poverty, were doing what they could to provide relief. Everett provided garden plots in empty sections of parks and other lands. Park Board Directors Jacob Anthes and W.R. Confers organized the program, which allotted the plots and provided seeds and tools for persons unable to provide their own. By April 1932 park tracts had been assigned to 450 persons who represented 1,800 dependents. The city also assisted another 200 persons who obtained plots on other lands. Two hundred more were on a waiting list. In November park officials reported that 60 percent of the gardens had been "successful." Twenty percent had been "fair", and the remaining 20 percent had "failed."

The program the following year was limited to gardeners who had plots in a Riverside neighborhood park the previous summer, and they were warned that, "The Park

Conservation, Land Improvement, and the CCC

Red alders are planted by this CCC crew, working as a team to space the trees correctly across logged and burned over lands near Granite Falls. (J.G. James photograph, #WN50002, 2/22/39, courtesy USDA Soil Conservation Service)

Much of the county had become cut-over stump land, abandoned after the passage of logging and essentially worthless. Large parcels reverted to the county to satisfy unpaid taxes, and thousands of acres burned. (J.G. James photograph, #WN50004, 2/22/39, courtesy USDA Soil Conservation Service)

Left: Construction of campgrounds, trails, and the Mountain Loop Highway up the Sauk River occupied much of the time of young men working out of the Darrington CCC camp next to the ranger station. (Courtesy Everett Public Library)

Dressed in his Civilian Conservation Corps war surplus uniform, an enrollee with a bag of seedlings plants trees near Granite Falls in February 1939. (J.G. James photograph, #WN50003, 2/22/39, courtesy USDA Soil Conservation Service)

- and All the King's Horses and All the King's Men -

BREAK YOUR MATCH -

BE SURE ITS OUT!

Can't Put the Forest Together Again

Fire prevention was a major public and private concern and received strong support from the forest products industry, federal and state governments. This Forest Service poster made an emotional appeal in the days before Smokey the Bear became its symbol. (Courtesy David Cameron)

238

Snohomish County benefitted greatly from public works and conservation projects created as part of the New Deal. This is Darrington Camp F-15 and its complement of CCC Company 934 under the leadership of First Lieutenant C.H. Adams on October 11, 1934. (Courtesy Everett Public Library)

Snohomish County benefitted greatly from the New Deal emphasis on public works to increase employment. This is the Veterans Camp in Sultan, which began a site which still benefits the community. Later it would serve as a state fire crew base, a city hall, and presently for public works and a river access park. (Courtesy Everett Public Library)

Board was assuming no obligation nor proffering any assistance." As with private charities, the city's resources were too thin to do more than a bare minimum for the ever-growing numbers of unemployed.

If there were a developing national mood in the United States it was one of bewildered helplessness. The carefree prosperity of the Roaring Twenties gradually became the confusion of the desperate thirties. The downturn continued to worsen, and there wasn't a good explanation of why. Yet if the American people didn't understand the causes of the Depression, they were convinced that something had to change. President Hoover didn't agree. Early in 1930 he had reacted primarily by exhorting the people to have faith in the system and by providing small increases in the national public works expenditures. However he considered direct governmental intervention to be Socialism, and he fought what he called "pork barrel" spending proposed by the Democrats to create jobs. Republicans controlled the Congress, so the minority Democrats were stymied. Passage of the Smoot-Hawley tariff in June 1930 backfired, drying up trade and pressuring the banking industry, plagued with bad debts and declining asset values.

Across America 1,300 banks failed in 1930 and another 2,300 in 1931. The Hoover administration created the Reconstruction Finance Corporation to lend funds to troubled banks and ease restrictions on their assets, but by early in 1933 America's banking system was close to collapse, as R.F.C. funds were seen to go to millionaires such as Bank of America's A.P. Giannini to pay off their loans, while smaller institutions were allowed to go under.

Snohomish County also felt these pressures, as the number of local banks decreased from 19 at the end of 1929 to 16 a year later, 13 in 1933, and only six by 1939. Sales and mergers took their toll here as well as in other areas of business.

In the fall of 1931, two-term governor of New York Franklin D. Roosevelt declared himself a Democratic candidate to run against the Republican President

Rosehill School, shown here on August 24, 1932, was the educational center for the Mukilteo area. After the original wooden building burned on St. Patrick's Day 1928, the new structure was erected with such speed that it opened for classes that fall and served until 1973. In 1976-77 it was converted to a community center. Mukilteo students were sent to Everett for their high school years until the district decided to build Mariner High School in 1968. (Juleen #980, courtesy Everett Public Library)

Hoover in 1932. He defeated Hoover by more than seven million popular votes, nearly the same number by which Hoover had defeated Democrat Al Smith four years earlier.

Americans did not stop with changing the person, the policies, and the philosophy that controlled the White House. They extended their mood for changes to Congress as well. Republicans in the House shrank from 237 to 117, less than half their 1930 number, while the Democrats sharply expanded theirs from 195 to 313, with five independents. In the Senate, the Democrats' slight advantage of 48-47 with one Independent in 1930 became a solid 59-36 majority with one Independent in 1933.

There was a similar Democratic avalanche in Washington and Snohomish County. In 1932 conservative Republican governor Roland Hartley was sent home to Everett when he lost his attempt at a third term to Democrat Clarence Martin. Democrat Homer T. Bone unseated incumbent Senator Wesley L. Jones in the Senate election. Following the 1930 census Washington had gained a Congressional seat, and now the state went from four Republicans and one Democrat to all six in Roosevelt's column, where they remained a solid bloc until 1942. In the Fifth District the Republican candidate, J.A. Drain, failed even to get enough votes in the primary to have his name appear on the ballot for the final election. In 1934 Senator C.C. Dill did not run for another term. Lewis B. Schwellenbach won the seat handily, keeping it Democratic. Everett's Democratic pool champion, Mon Wallgren, was elected in the Second Congressional District with a 49,002-30,780 majority over Republican Lindley Hadley.

The Democrats' overwhelming victories extended all the way down to the county level. The Snohomish County Auditor's records show that in 1928 the Democrats failed even to find candidates to run for two open seats on the Snohomish County Commission or for county assessor. In the only contested county election Republican Charles R. Denny overwhelmed Democrat A.W. Swanson 14,337-8,546 in the county prosecutor election. All that changed in 1932. Democrats not only fielded two County Commission candidates (Charles A. Smith and William Mero), but both defeated their Republican opponents by wide margins. The 1932 Democratic avalanche was the beginning of that party's dominance of Snohomish County politics that lasted for the rest of the century. One result of that was the election of Henry M. "Scoop" Jackson as prosecuting attorney in 1938 in a landslide election that unseated the incumbent. Jackson, an Everett native and the son of poor Norwegian immigrants, went on two years later to win a seat in congress.

After 1932 it was clear that voters throughout Snohomish County and the nation wanted drastic changes in policy, and clearly they were giving a mandate to the Democrats to make that change. Change is what they got.

The incoming President's campaign promise had been to bring a new deal to the country and its people, and "New Deal" came to be the slogan for his programs to restore prosperity. The administration in its first month produced a flurry of bills, proclamations, messages and executive orders so intense that it amazed the newspapers and nearly exhausted his aides. In his Inaugural Speech on March 4, 1933 Roosevelt said, "Let me assert my firm belief that the only thing we have to fear is fear itself." That line became the centerpiece of his early administration as he sought to reassert confidence, beginning with the nation's failing banking system. On May 5 he declared a "Banking Holiday" which closed the banks until federal officials determined their solvency.

The three banks in Everett (Security National Bank, First National Bank, and Everett Trust and Savings Bank) were all reopened for restricted business on March 9, 1933. The president announced three days later that solvent banks were authorized for full service. Later that year, the Glass-Steagall Act created the Federal Deposit Insurance Corporation, which at first guaranteed the safety of deposits up to $10,000. Although the bank holiday and FDIC combined to restore confidence in the financial system, many people still became accustomed to having some spare money tucked aside "just in case," remembering when they had to face the future with only the change in their purse or pocket.

Numerous other programs seemed to pour out of the White House and Congress, all designed to invigorate the economy and to create jobs for roughly one third of the labor force, as 16 million people were unemployed. Two of the programs that had major direct effects in Snohomish County were the Civilian Conservation Corps (CCC) and the Works Projects Administration (WPA). The WPA was renamed the Works *Progress* Administration in 1939.

Forest Service Expansion

Left: In 1936 the U.S. Forest Service created the new Monte Cristo Ranger District, with its headquarters at Verlot on the Mountain Loop Highway, which also was under construction. The compound was designed in a distinctive style, with its architecture and decorative touches typical of the 1930s mountain lodges and interiors. (Courtesy Darrington Ranger District, U.S. Forest Service)

The Verlot office and garage, along with residences for the district ranger and protective assistant and a large warehouse on the flat above, were constructed by CCC crews, who also planted a variety of trees to create a living arboretum. (Courtesy Darrington Ranger District, U.S. Forest Service)

Atop Blackjack Ridge south of Silverton lookout Gene Slocum staffed his new station in 1936. The vital Osborne fire finder was located in the cupola. During World War II the building served as part of the Aircraft Warning Service. It was intentionally burned around 1960. (Courtesy Bill Rawlins)

Guard stations, such as those at Index, Barlow Pass, Bedal, and on the Suiattle River (shown here) provided seasonal bases for patrolmen and fire fighting crews. They were linked with lookouts and the headquarters ranger stations with No. 9 wire telephone lines, whose repair and restringing after winter storms and snows always heralded a new fire season. (Courtesy U.S. Forest Service)

The CCC was one of the first of the programs Roosevelt (dubbed FDR by headline writers who couldn't fit his full name into their headlines) asked Congress to adopt. The law was approved by Congress on March 30, 1933 and signed by the President the following day, less than a month after he took office. Even as he signed it, the Department of Labor was preparing to enlist the 250,000 young men the new law directed them to hire. Most of the enrollees were to be unemployed and unmarried males who were United States citizens 17 to 28 (later 24) years old. They would live in work camps supervised and disciplined by Army officers, but they would work in outdoor settings for state or federal land agencies such as the United States Forest Service. (At that time, only the Army had the capacity to take on such a huge program on such short notice.) The goal was to improve and expand the country's forests and parks while taking young men off the streets and providing them with food, shelter, and other necessities as well as training and education for future civilian jobs. Their pay was set at $30 a month, but the enrollees received only $5. The rest was sent home to their often destitute families.

The program had immediate and long lasting effects in Snohomish County. By early April 1933, just weeks after the President signed the law, the government announced it would establish 42 camps in Washington, four of them in the Mount Baker National Forest, which included a large portion of Snohomish County. Forest Supervisor L.B. Pagter had already announced tentative plans to establish a camp at Darrington, and county welfare boards throughout the state began registering young men for the 3,250 jobs available for Washington citizens. Fort Lewis, south of Tacoma, was designated the headquarters for the Fort Lewis District of the CCCs and was preparing to provide for thousands of young men from all parts of the country. Within 30 days the first companies of some 200 men began arriving, as the number of camps in the district would peak at 54 in 1935.

In Snohomish County the number varied as new ones were created and old ones disbanded according to need. Among the camps were major ones at Darrington, Index, and Sultan. Others operated at Roosevelt (east of Snohomish), Perry Creek near Big Four Inn, Verlot on the South Fork of the Stillaguamish River eleven miles east of Granite Falls, the Forest Service station at Texas Pond north of Darrington, and Bedal, at the forks of the Sauk River 16 miles southeast of Darrington.

One of the earliest camps was the one established in April 1933 at the United States Forest Service ranger station at Darrington. Barracks were built across the railroad tracks from the compound. The enrollees lived there for 16 hours a day under the Army officers assigned to the camp and worked the other eight hours for the Forest Service.

An historical sketch of one of the companies assigned to the Darrington camp (CCC Company 6439) records that the company was organized at Fort Oglethorpe, Georgia on July 16, 1940, as part of Roosevelt's strategy was to break down barriers by having young men get to know others by working in regions away from their homes. The company commander was Caldwell Dumas of Paris, Tennessee. The second in command (with the title of subaltern) was Mack White of Hayesville, North Carolina. Of the 202 enrollees, 198 were from Tennessee; three from Georgia, and one from Alabama. They spent a week at physical conditioning at Fort Oglethorpe then boarded a train for Washington State, arriving at Darrington on July 26. Company Commander Dumas was replaced on August 10 by Jefferson H. Fulton, and some of the men refused to go to work. Fourteen of them were discharged three days later. The rest were assigned to work projects under older

243

men (called local experienced men, or LEMs) who could teach them what they needed to know about forest crafts.

Over the years, hundreds of young men from near and far were assigned to Camp Darrington. In addition to work and work training they were given opportunities to attend class. Some learned to read and write, as each camp had a library. Some earned high school diplomas. Classes were taught by professional teachers such as Maurice Thompson, who later became a popular and revered history teacher at Everett High School.

While many of the enrollees at Darrington were from other parts of the country, a number of others were from Snohomish County. One of those was Lloyd Larson of Everett. The son of a logger who was working in a lumber camp, Larson arrived in the Darrington CCC Camp in 1935, when he was 16 years old. Sixty-two years later he remembered:

There were five barracks in the camp with 20 to 25 men in each and one man chosen to be in charge. The Army ran the camp, and the officers were in charge of the discipline, so we had roll call in the morning; we stood at attention during the flag salute, and we had inspection every morning to make sure everyone and everything was clean. I was assigned to work in the forest. I planted thousands of trees, worked on bridge construction, road construction, did (bulldozer) work, fought forest fires. I worked for a while on a gas-operated donkey machine that pulled logs to a central location where they could be loaded onto trucks. At first I worked out of what they called the Sauk side camp about 10 miles from Darrington. In the winter there was too much snow to work in the woods, so we came out of the side camps to Darrington and rebuilt "cats" (Caterpillar tractors). Dad used the $25 they sent him to help out my two younger sisters and also gave me some to spend when I came home on leave. Forest Service trucks would take us to Arlington or Everett for weekend leave. On workday nights we could play poker or go to Darrington for a gallon of wine. The essence of the CCCs was to take the boys out of the work force and reduce competition for jobs. But it was good experience, too. I learned how to work and something about what not to do when I wasn't working. There were several ways you could get out of the CCCs after you signed up. One was to go to the end of your six-month term. Another was to join the Army, and another was to get a civilian job. The only other way I know was to screw up and get sent home. I remember one bunch of rowdies came in from New York. They didn't last long until they were on their way back to New York.

Stanley Lloyd joined the Darrington camp in fall or winter 1940, shortly after he graduated from high school in Arlington. He describes his experience this way:

I worked on trails for a little while, but it was cold, and it kept raining, and I wasn't sure that was where I wanted to be. Then I learned that because their work hours were irregular the assistants in the mess hall worked five days one week and only two days the next. The mess hall was warm and dry. The work was easy, and I could go home on my days off, so I volunteered and got the job. I liked it so well that when my six-month enlistment ended I signed up for another term. Then they closed the Darrington Camp, and I was transferred to Camp Naches near Mount Rainier, where I worked on maintaining telephone lines to Forest Service fire lookouts on the mountain tops. About five months into my second term I got a job in a service station at home, so I left the CCCs.

244

Over the years thousands of young men worked at the Darrington camp, leaving a legacy of healthy forests and improvements that lasted beyond the next century. Among them are the former ranger station headquarters building at Verlot on the Mountain Loop Highway, Gold Basin campground, plus numerous trails, roads, and bridges. Many of the young men went on to become leaders in business and professions in Snohomish County and elsewhere. One of the noteworthy individuals was Bill Moore, who served three terms as the mayor of Everett late in the century.

The CCCs were only the beginning for the President's New Deal. Even as the bill that created the agency was working its way through Congress he was preparing more programs to rebuild the nation's economy and relieve the suffering the Depression was causing. Some of those bills were geared to assist farms and agricultural areas. One of them paid growers to take land out of production in an attempt to reduce surpluses and allow farmers to get higher prices for their produce. Another was the Rural Electrification Administration, created in 1935 to extend electrical service to rural areas and to create jobs.

A key early program was the National Industrial Recovery Act, which created the National Recovery Administration to regulate business, in order to reduce over-production and create fair prices. With its widely publicized Blue Eagle symbol and massive publicity campaign, the main effect of the NRA locally was to stabilize the timber industry. Company leaders met in Washington, D.C. to work out codes for forest product manufacturers which had the force of law behind them and which would be administered by the NRA bureaucracy. Loggers, small mills, and the major corporations such as Weyerhaeuser, Simpson, and Bloedel-Donovan would cooperate to limit production and divide the market fairly, one which had fallen to only 42 percent of 1929 levels for both 1933 and 1934.

Forest conservation gained a boost from the act, as did labor, neither favored by the industry. Yet in 1933 both pulp and saw mill workers organized their own AF of L locals in Everett, with the pulp mills granting a contract the following year. These complex operations were extremely expensive to shut down and restart, and the companies needed a steady cash flow. In the area of conservation, it was agreed that with federal financial help companies would work toward creating a sustained yield from their lands rather than cutting over and abandoning them, fire fighting would become a higher priority, and old-growth timberlands would receive special tax benefits. The argument over adopting selective cutting of timber rather than the widespread practice of large clear-cuts also was raised, but no binding agreement to switch was possible. A strong proponent of the selective approach was University of Washington forestry professor Burt P. Kirkland, who as supervisor of the Snoqualmie National Forest had created the first public tree nursery at the Silverton Ranger Station between 1909 and 1916. The desire to reduce fire losses also led to an emphasis on the building of access trails and fire lookouts on both state and federal lands, providing much faster detection and suppression.

During 1934 it became obvious that the codes were unworkable, as smaller mills started up and demanded quotas, some companies blatantly cheated, pricing all the variations in wood products was a nightmare, and the government failed to stop violators. Joe Irving of Everett stated openly that the loggers' association would ignore fourth quarter allocations, while the big companies led by Weyerhaeuser caused the West Coast Lumbermen's Association to take action against the code. In June 1935 the NRA was

declared unconstitutional by the United States
Supreme Court, and the forest products industry
returned to its competitive ways. Merrill & Ring
Lumber Company's Timothy Jerome bitterly
remarked that anyone who had voted for the
Democrats in 1932 should "be taken out and
shot at sunrise."

The New Deal's Public Works Administration was a major expansion of Hoover's approach
of preferring to spend federal money building
roads, bridges, dams and similar projects to
alleviate unemployment rather than granting
direct relief funds to individuals. In 1935 the
Works Projects Administration allowed local
communities to match federal funds and hire
workers to perform needed tasks. Congress
appropriated what in those days was considered

Public park construction and improvements provided many jobs during
the decade and improved facilities for families to enjoy. This is the new
concessions building at Everett's Forest Park. (Courtesy Everett Public
Library)

an enormous $4.88 billion for projects in 1935 alone. Local governments were to pay
workers slightly less than prevailing wages but more than would be received if on direct
relief. A novel idea was administrator Harry Hopkins' agreement that women should be
paid at the same rate as men.

In Snohomish County, officials desperate to find relief for the destitute had been
taking advantage of the federal relief programs from the beginning. In Everett, for instance, Park Board President Dean S. Ashton
applied in the fall of 1933 to the local welfare
body for approval of three projects to provide
improvements in Riverdale and Forest parks as
soon as the first funds would be distributed.
Thinking the earliest proposals would be the
most likely to be approved, he made the application without taking the time to notify the other
board members. The welfare body had approved
the application, provided 300 workers and, after
further negotiation, agreed to pay for their tools
before Ashton got around to letting the others
know. Ashton apparently chose those projects
from among a wish list they had adopted November 9, contemplating providing 3,550 man-
months of work to the unemployed and improving numerous parks. One desired item was the
development of an 18-hole golf course at Legion
Park. It is not clear how many on the list were
completed, but the Legion Park Golf Course

Major landscaping, road improvements, and a public kitchen shelter
were new attractions at Forest Park, along with a small zoo. (#1033,
courtesy Everett Public Library)

eventually became a major part of the city's park system and continued in that role into
the 21st century. Ashton and the other park board members followed up those early ideas

with numerous other WPA improvements to the city's recreational facilities. From there, work relief projects spread throughout the county, most of them administered under WPA programs through a state bureau established to distribute money to local governments and oversee their progress.

Giving the federal government the responsibility (and power) to intercede in local economics and in the financial misfortunes of individuals was a revolutionary inversion of the American tradition of independence and self reliance and of the concept that charity should be a matter of neighbor helping neighbor, and at least some people were concerned about the changes that took place in the 1930s. However, community leaders throughout Snohomish County were faced with such overwhelming numbers of destitute unemployed and with budgets so diminished that they no longer were able to provide minimal necessary services. They must have seen the advent of the WPA as a combination near miracle and horn of plenty. It was a way of providing subsistence with at least a little less of the humiliation involved in outright charity. At the same time, it was a way of providing communities with services and improvements that they could not afford without help.

Crews soon were working throughout the county. Even an incomplete list is long. One of the larger projects was a $200,000 program to clear the Marysville water shed.

An outdoor wading pool near the playground and shelter gave children a safe place to play in the water at Forest Park. For a more challenging experience, youths and adults swam in the salt water at City Beach next to the mouth of Pigeon Creek below the park. (Courtesy Bernie Webber)

About the same time a fish hatchery was built at Cicero between Arlington and Darrington. It was designed to provide from two million to five million trout a year for state streams and lakes. Elsewhere, WPA workers in numerous communities were building recreation facilities, including field houses, parks, tennis courts, play fields, football fields, and many others. New county parks were built at Clearview and Meadowdale, and new athletic fields went up at Edmonds, Alderwood Manor, Stanwood, Arlington, Granite Falls, Snohomish, Lake Stevens, Lake Goodwin, Silver Lake and Monroe. School gymnasiums were built at Maltby, Lakewood, Mukilteo and Sultan. WPA crews created city halls in Stanwood and Granite Falls, and the Monroe City Hall was remodeled.

The early program was expanded to include work for professional and business people, along with other highly skilled victims of the Depression. Many of the slots were designed for people such as writers and artists, and more than 30 Snohomish County communities had activities involving teachers, recreation specialists and sewing rooms where unemployed women made clothing and other articles. Eventually there was a WPA school in Snohomish, where people were taught skills needed in the defense industry, which was growing swiftly by 1940. In that year the agency was sponsoring 12 types of what it called professional and service projects in the county, including an adult-education center in the Everett High School. There also were household workers training schools in Everett, Alderwood Manor, East Everett, East Sunnyside, Edgewater, Intercity, Lake Stevens, Lowell, Maple Heights, Marysville, Mukilteo, Pinehurst, Shoultes, Silver Lake, Swan's Trail, and Tulalip.

In 1940, five years into the program, State WPA Administrator Carl W. Smith reported that thus far in Washington State the administration had constructed more than

10,533 miles of roads and streets, as well as 866 bridges and 365 miles of sidewalk. Nearly 2,000 buildings had been built or renovated. Civic features such as parks, swimming pools, water and sewer systems, as well as telephone and electrical distribution lines were also completed.

For many of the elderly in 1935 the New Deal brought a safety net in the form of Social Security, an attempt to provide pensions for the aged and also to help remove them from the labor market. Retirement was set at 65 for those covered, which at the time excluded a number of categories of people, notably agricultural workers.

Not all creative attempts to ease the effects of the Depression came from the New Deal, however. The Darrington Pioneers' Cooperative was formed by a number of individuals who donated their time for credit in order to come together and create jobs, sell firewood for cash, purchase food supplies, build a small sawmill, and even erect housing. It was a difficult, ongoing effort, but the times demanded it. Others thought in units of energy to create a new economy, the Technocracy movement. It promised a scientific operation of America and had a county office well into the 1960s. Some promoted the Share-Our-Wealth Society and "Every man a king" panaceas of Louisiana governor and senator Huey Long, even after he was assassinated in 1935 and his dictatorial political machine exposed. For the Townsend Club members, the "second coming of prosperity" would be when people over 60 would be given free money certificates which would have to be spent in a short amount of time. This had a natural appeal for older Americans, but others wondered where the tax money would come from in order to pay for the plan. After the abortive attempt by fringe and emotion-driven groups to mount a challenge to Roosevelt's re-election in 1936 most of them quietly faded away.

Unexpected windfalls for Snohomish County cities were rare indeed during the Depression, but they sometimes occurred. One such was the $75,000 bequest of Leonard Howarth to the city of Everett. Howarth was vice president of the Everett Pulp and paper Company plant in Lowell and the brother of William Howarth, the president of the company. Leonard Howarth died suddenly at the age of 63 on May 12, 1930 while staying in his winter home in Santa Rosa, California. The executors of his estate consulted with a committee of citizens and city officials, then decided to replace the Carnegie Building on Oakes Avenue at Wall that had served as the city library since early in the century. The city acquired a $10,000 grant from the Washington Emergency Recovery Program and a $23,000 grant from the federal Public Works Program. Those grants, and the interest accrued while preparations were being made, brought the new library fund to a total of some $110,000. Architect Carl Gould built the solid, ornate structure at 2702 Hoyt Avenue for $102,930. The building was dedicated on October 3, 1934. With additions and renovations, it continued to serve the community into the next century.

In addition to the large reading room and other facilities, the library featured a series of four metal alloy sculptures titled the "History of Books" in the lobby. The 1930s style sculptures by Dudley Pratt survived the renovations of the building and are one of Everett's major cultural attractions. The cost to the city was $590, $60 less than budgeted.

The Public Works Administration, which added a $23,000 grant to the Howarth bequest for the library, also funded numerous projects throughout the state and nation, including many large ones such as the first Lake Washington floating bridge, the Tacoma

A New Library Emerges for Everett

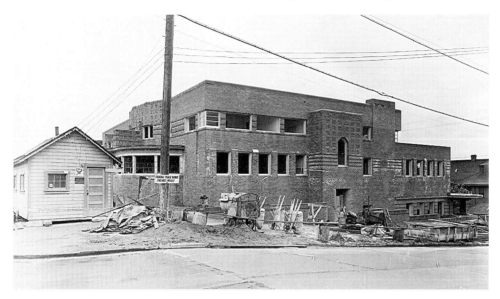

Left: In 1934, a new Everett Public Library was constructed on the southwest corner of Hoyt and Everett avenues to replace the Carnegie building. Designed by architect Carl Gould, it was financed by a $75,000 bequest from the estate of Leonard Howarth, vice president of the Everett Pulp & Paper Company, plus $33,000 more in federal and state grants. (Juleen #2163-A, courtesy Everett Public Library)

Left: Artist Dudley Pratt created four large decorative panels on the history of books for the library entry. These were made of hammered sheets of Britannia metal, an alloy similar to pewter, and designed to harmonize with the building, materials, and figures. This is primitive man carving pictographs on stone, then more formal symbols. (Courtesy Everett Public Library)

Another panel illustrates early printing, this an edition of Shakespeare. Pratt, an asistant professor of art at the University of Washington and trained in Paris, completed the four panels for only $590. (Courtesy Everett Public Library)

The distinctive finished library is shown in this Juleen portrait. Later major additions and remodeling retained the original lines. (Courtesy Bernie Webber)

Paine Field
By Margaret Riddle

The Beginnings

One of Snohomish County's largest relief projects of the Great Depression was the building of Paine Field, originally called the Snohomish County Airport. Planned by local Works Progress Administration officials and the U. S. Commerce Department for the development of a "super airport," the project was designed to bring both jobs and economic growth to the Pacific Northwest.

Lt. Topiff Paine

First recommended by pioneer Northwest aviator Elliott Merrill, the chosen site consisted of 640 acres, then owned by Merrill and Ring Logging and the Pope and Talbot Company. Situated 8 miles southwest of Everett and 17 miles north of the Seattle city limits, the location was unpopulated, offered reportedly fog-free conditions at an elevation of 576 feet, and was on a direct route from Portland to Vancouver, B.C. and Alaska.

Snohomish County matched federal dollars, and the project commenced September 10, 1936. More than 300 workers were hired to clear, grub, and excavate land in the initial work phase. A well was drilled to provide water for boilers of construction locomotives, Puget Sound Power and Light installed a power line, and temporary buildings were constructed on skids and moved as the work progressed. When completed, the airfield was to have four runways.

World War II

World War II changed both the usage of the airfield and its name. By the spring of 1941 the first Army Air Corps contingent arrived at the airport to develop a military base that would support the nearby Bremerton shipyards, the Boeing plant, and the Seattle airfield, which housed B-17 and B-29 bombers. The airport was renamed Paine Field, in honor of Army Lt. Topliff Olin Paine, an Everett native who was killed in 1922 while flying in the Air Mail Service.

The Air Corps' stay lasted from 1941 to 1946, with some personnel on site until 1948. During that time the military improved runways, installed and improved lighting, constructed more buildings, and added concrete aprons to the runways. Among the fighter aircraft stationed here were P-38s, P-39s, and P-40s.

In the early 1940s Alaska Airlines established its overhaul and repairing service at Paine. They were joined by the Willard Flying Service, which offered training sessions and commuter services. Both enterprises continued at Paine for over a decade.

Snohomish County Supervision and the Korean War

The military presence decreased following World War II. By 1946 administrators began turning over operations to county supervision, in hopes once again of creating a county airport. Plans were only beginning when a new war interceded, this time the Korean conflict. Following his tour of Pacific Northwest defense installations, Washington State Senator Henry M. Jackson recommended more military presence in the area, and Paine Field was reactivated as an airbase. This time there was not an exclusive military presence at the site. In a shared use agreement, the county relinquished most of its commercial facilities to house Air Force personnel and installations. The military operated the control tower.

Paine Field was considered a vital Western Defense Command post, an alert-status military base with tactical radar installations and jet interceptors. F-89C fighters were the first generation of jets at Paine, and by the 1960s the field was able to accommodate the F-102 and F-106. The field was now part of the 25th NORAD (North American Defense) region and supported the 25th Air Defense Command stationed at McChord Air Force Base in Tacoma. It was part of a horizon radar system of stations along the coastline that linked to a central computer system able to transmit to all ADC bases.

The Civil Aeronautics Administration once again opened the way for economic expansion of Paine in 1953, allowing business and industry unrelated to aviation to become established at the site. This combination of military and commerce brought economic strength to the region. Now with sleek, supersonic jet interceptors, the military portion of Paine Field was expected to defend the Northwest against air attacks. An Aerospace Defense Command unit was stationed at the field in 1951, and land surrounding the Paine site was appropriated for military facilities and extended runways. The federal governments acquired 205 acres east of the airbase in August 1957 for construction of a Bomarc Missile site that became obsolete before it was completed.

George Forbes was hired as the first manager of Paine Field's commercial endeavors. Erecting a substantial terminal and civilian hangar, and planning expansion of air terminal facilities as well as businesses, Forbes hoped that profits from business and industry at Paine would pay for improvements on the site. It was Forbes' plan to begin running regularly scheduled commercial flights. Money would also be earned from the rental of hangars, buildings and tie-down costs from emergency landings.

In 1960 George Petrie, an ex-Naval Commander and businessman flier, was employed as Paine Field's new manager. The county commissioned a comprehensive planning study by the firm of Anderson, Bjornstad and Kane, which recommended "incubator complexes." The incubator idea was to grant short-term leases to small, startup firms, allowing them the low overhead needed for fast business expansion. Paine Field followed this course, and within six years, 16 tenants were listed in the city directory for the industrial park. In addition, there were aviation-related businesses selling aircraft, offering charter flights, and providing flight instruction.

Boeing Arrives

In 1968 the Air Force quit operations at Paine Field when enemy missiles replaced manned bombers as the major threat and made ADC units obsolete. Military withdrawal from Paine Field once again left the site ready for either greater economic expansion or creation of a regional airport. The Boeing Company determined the course taken when the company purchased property north of Paine Field in 1966 for the site of its 747 plant. By 1969, Boeing was firmly established at this location. And there was still talk that the region needed a better airport.

Airport Planning and Growth: 1970–2004

By the mid-1970s, a sizeable population inhabited the area near Paine Field and Boeing. When Paine Field was considered as a possible commercial air-carrier airport, local residents protested. Citing rising noise levels, devaluation of property, and lessened personal safety issues, the populace demanded alternatives. In 1978, a coalition of the Snohomish County Planning Commission and public interest groups began working on plans to determine Paine Field's future.

Four options were considered, ranging from leaving Paine as it was to developing it as a major air-carrier airport. On April 11, 1978 the County Commissioners board approved a combination plan that allowed light aviation, commuter services, and aviation-related activity at the field. Improvements and additions were allowed to provide new hangar space, as well as maintenance and service terminals. A noise abatement plan was undertaken.

By the 1990s Paine's mixed use as an airport and aviation commerce site was well established. In addition to being vital to Boeing, Paine Field was also one of the county's largest source of jobs, employing more than 5,000 people. Claiming 1,320 acres in 2004, the site suggests great potential for development in the new century.

Narrows Bridge, and Grand Coulee Dam. In Snohomish County the Everett School District was a major beneficiary, receiving $200,000 toward the construction of the Everett Civic Auditorium and other additions to Everett High School, construction of the Lincoln Elementary School, and a new gymnasium for South Junior High School. The local $244,000 share of the cost was provided through a $164,000 tax levy and $80,000 the district had in cash.

Another New Deal project with a long-term significance to Snohomish County was Paine Field. A number of pilots early recognized that the high plateau southeast of Everett was ideal for an air field because the topography left it clear of fog even when much of the rest of the Puget Sound area was hidden. One record indicates that the site was marked by an airmail pilot in the days when the mail was flown in planes of "wood, wire and fabric," and pilots who sat in one open cockpit strapped the bags of mail into another open cockpit. The flyer noted time after time that the site was the only fog free spot for miles around, and he dropped a bag of flour, which made a white splotch so the place could be recognized from the ground.

Until 1935 little was done to follow up on the flour bomb. Commercial aviation was beginning to come of age, Boeing and other companies were vying for contracts to build immense new four-engined bombers, and the China Clipper was being prepared for its first scheduled flight from San Francisco to Canton, China, carrying mail and 14 passengers with stops in Hawaii, Midway Island, Wake Island, Guam, and the Philippines. With all that in mind the federal Department of Commerce set out to build 10 super airports in various sections of the country over a five-year period. The agency earmarked $180 million for the project, with communities all over the country, including Snohomish County, vying for designation as one of the locations.

Early that year Elliott Merrill, a pioneer Northwest aviator, flew with an official of Pope and Talbot's Puget Mill Company over the plateau. The passenger commented that his company owned the land. Merrill mentioned its aviation potential and suggested the mill man work to develop it as an airport.

The sequence of events after that is shrouded, but Theodore Bowden, an Everett banker, lifelong Democrat, and a WPA executive, persuaded the Snohomish County Commission to take an option on 1,000 acres and reported that "every assurance has been given that the Snohomish County site would be selected" by the government as an airport. The project would begin with an expenditure of $200,000 and be expanded over 10 years to $5 million. Two weeks later the federal Commerce Department did announce approval of $17 million in WPA airport projects in 31 states, and local officials said they believed the proposed Snohomish County project was included. The news got better on November 15, when the WPA's Bowden announced that the Snohomish County Airport and another being sponsored by Arlington near that city were on a list of projects that had been "approved or tentatively approved." Then 10 days later a *Herald* editorial noted, "Seattle is doing everything it can to obtain this airport." Hopes sank on December 4 when the paper reported that the county airport was removed from the list, although the Arlington site was approved on December 20. Six months later federal officials announced that Boeing Field had been granted a "resurfacing and improvement" project employing 130 men and also mentioned in passing that Snohomish County's super airport was "again under consideration." Whatever behind the scenes activities caused the uncertainty, the problem was resolved in favor of the Snohomish County, as the project went ahead with few hitches after the announcement.

Construction began in 1936, as the second-growth forest began to give way at a swift pace to long, clear runways. Bill Moore, who later became a three-term mayor of Everett, was a 12-year-old boy living a half-mile away when construction started. He could not see the field from his home, but 50 years later he remembered the noise of machinery that "seemed to go on forever." On September 9, 1937 the *Herald* reported that a crew of 260 WPA workers equipped with two steam shovels and three miles of railroad with a 20-ton locomotive and 16 cars was completing the first phase, moving 2,500 yards of dirt a day. Urged on by the military, which was planning a string of air fields in Washington state, the WPA was applying for an additional $250,000 to complete the first phase. A week later a private plane piloted by Mark E. Thorely of Seattle developed an overheated engine and became the first plane to land on the field, much to the surprise of the crews that were working to make it usable.

The story of Arlington's airport was much the same as the county's. It was conceived in February 1934, a month after it was learned that the federal government had appropriated $1.5 million for construction of small landing fields across the country. Mayor Henry Backstrom and the Arlington Commercial Club noted that the large, level area south of the city would be an ideal place for a 4,000-foot landing field. He estimated it could be built for $9,867 and the construction provide work for 50 to 60 men. The city signed a five-year lease on the land, and crews started on March 1. Work was suspended briefly in April when the Civil Works Administration went out of business but was resumed under the Washington Emergency Relief Administration. The first plane landed there on June 13, ten days before completion. The field saw increasing use for the next several years as barnstorming aviators and flying circuses put on shows. By 1935 the city had enlisted the aid of county officials in promoting the field as a military base, and the WPA announced plans for building a cross runway as its share of the Commerce Department approval.

Other transportation changes were happening in the county at the same time. A major improvement for Everett was construction of the Hewitt Avenue Trestle, completed in 1939. The trestle and its accompanying bridge across the Snohomish River raised the roadway between Everett and Cavelero's Corner above the flood plain and, consequently, above the high waters that periodically closed the ground-level route, notably in 1932. The trestle and bridge also now aligned with Hewitt Avenue, eliminating the former Everett Avenue access with its two dangerous, sharp-angled turns which took traffic over the river and resulted in numerous serious accidents as drivers failed to negotiate them. The faster route also encouraged traffic between downtown and the east side of the valley, resulting over the years in new growth in that area, especially around East Everett, Lake Stevens, and north of Snohomish.

The trestle also provided improved access to the county's magnificent backcountry and stimulated visitor traffic. The Snohomish County Good Roads Association, under the leadership of Perry Black, saw a need to create more scenic routes and began to work toward providing a through road for cars that would go between Granite Falls and Darrington deep in the Cascade Mountains. The Verlot to Barlow Pass portion of the Mountain Loop Highway was built starting in 1936 with contracts from the Bureau of Public Roads, later extending to Monte Cristo and then almost to Glacier Falls in the early years of World War II to provide access to the mines. The Forest Service and CCC took responsibility for the portion of the route from Darrington to Barlow Pass. This section was completed in December of 1941, within days of the Japanese attack on Pearl Harbor, which brought the United States into World War II. Gasoline rationing and closures meant there would be very little use of the route until the war ended.

The portion which began in Granite Falls largely followed the right-of-way of the abandoned Everett and Monte Cristo Railway from Verlot over Barlow Pass, while part of the Darrington portion followed the former grade of the Sauk River Lumber Company tracks, which had reached as far as the old Bedal homestead at the forks of the Sauk River before turning east. The two railroad rights-of-way were converted to use by cars, and a stretch of scenic new road for seven miles along the old 1892 wagon road up the banks of the South Fork Sauk River connected them.

Prohibition still was in effect throughout the nation when the Depression began, and so was bootlegging, which had become a significant part of both the social and economic climate of the nation despite sporadic, and not always genuine, efforts to control it. In

Automobile routes improved with the Pacific Highway to the point where by 1939 interuban rail lines joined steam boat passenger service as out-of-date and unprofitable. The bridges across the Snohomish River delta especially cut travel time from Everett north to Marysville, eliminating the older route easterly across the flatlands to Cavalero's Corner, then curving northerly along Sunnyside Boulevard and the edge of the valley. (Ellis post card #1419, courtesy Jack O'Donnell)

Snohomish County one result was a series of night spots, many along U.S. 99 and especially in the South County area close to the lucrative Seattle and King County trade. They dealt in illegal liquor and also gambling and whatever other enticements that would attract money.

Prohibition came to a rather sudden end after President Roosevelt and the new Democratic Congress took office in 1933. Congress and the states approved the Twenty-first Amendment to the Constitution, nullifying the Eighteenth Amendment, which had provided for the prohibition laws that had gone into effect 13 years earlier. Repeal did not automatically make the bootlegging night spots disappear. Many of them continued to

Snohomish Remained the County's Number Two City

Left: Although the automobiles and businesses would change, the physical setting of First Street (viewed to the west) would remain largely intact into the twenty-first century and thus become a major attraction for visitors. (Juleen #488, courtesy Everett Public Library)

Left: The Snohomish County Fruitgrowers Association actively promoted locally grown products, as the community had a strong agricultural infrastructure. (#BU908, courtesy Snohomish Historical Society)

Also in 1938 the town received a new post office building on the west side of Union between First and Second streets, with the dedication on May 11 of that year. (Courtesy Snohomish Historical Society)

One major landmark which was razed was the county's first courthouse building, which went down in June 1938. Used as a school following the transfer of the county seat, it was replaced by a new Snohomish High School. (Kleppinger photograph, courtesy Snohomish Historical Society)

operate for years as legitimate restaurants and entertainment establishments, while sale of alcohol now was a closely regulated state monopoly.

Lakeside resorts, which had been recreational sites in Snohomish County since early in the twentieth century, continued to operate despite the economic bite of the Depression. Most offered boating, fishing, and swimming. Some had attractions such as athletic fields, stores, restaurants, dance halls, and cabins. They provided a relatively inexpensive place where families could get away for a few hours or a few days, and people took advantage of the opportunity. Many of the resorts were located on the shore of Lake Stevens, including Lundeen's, the Purple Pennant, and Davies' Resort, as well as other smaller ones. They attracted as many as 3,000 people on a busy day. Lake Goodwin had four major resorts and several smaller ones. The busiest places on Lake Goodwin included Leonard's, Schuh's, the Lake Goodwin Resort, and Cedar Grove Resort. Saltwater docks and boathouses also were popular, renting boats and often cabins for longer visits.

Davies' Resort on Lake Stevens provided a mix of outdoor activities after the weather began to warm up in June. It and Lundeen's on the north side of the lake were popular destinations for several decades of swimmers, picnickers, and boaters. (Juleen #462, courtesy Everett Public Library)

The Depression was the cause of untold misery and deprivation for innumerable citizens of Snohomish County. However in other ways, it was the beginning of social and economic developments which unexpectedly benefited the county's future generations. Infrastructure grants provided by New Deal programs, for instance, while designed primarily to provide jobs for workers and meager help for their needy families, resulted in numerous improvements such as new roads, buildings, airports, and other projects that might never have been accomplished if it had not been for the hard times.

Another key development, which took place during from the middle of the 1930s, was the resurgence of organized labor in Snohomish county. The shock of the Everett Massacre in November 1916 resulted in a new realization that the labor movement was a permanent part of the community and its economy. Slowly, usually grudgingly, management accepted the organization of its workers, although the preceding decade had been one of union retreat under pro-business governments and early economic downturn. In 1929, the 1,500 member Snohomish County Labor Council built a new Labor Temple at 2610 Lombard, next door to the frame store front building that had served the movement as headquarters, meeting place, and social hall since 1901. The new 120-foot by 50-foot brick building was designed by Architect C. Ferris White and completed just months before the stock market crash. It cost some $40,000. A significant portion of the cost was donated by some 136 businesses and businessmen.

As economic conditions worsened, the number of industries in Everett fell from 101

Logging Slowly Revived Late in the Decade

The Lervick Logging Company of East Stanwood posed its crew by one of the diminishing number of huge old-growth giants. It measured 11' 10" across at the undercut, which still was being made by fallers using crosscut saws and standing on spring boards. (Courtesy David Cameron)

Railroad logging, however, was on its way out, as was the age of steam. Lervick crews utilized caterpillar tractors, logging trucks, and diesel powered yarders to bring in the logs. (Courtesy David Cameron)

Above: Old skills and stories were kept alive for younger generations of loggers by events such as Darrington's Timber Bowls, which flourished after the war years. Caulk boots and double bitted axes were required to compete in this speed chopping contest. (Courtesy Darrington Historical Society)

Right: Small shingle mills continued to operate sporadically during the lean years, while some men and women returned to the 19th century practice of hand splitting shingles at home to help make ends meet. This mill operated near Monroe in 1938. (Courtesy USDA Soil Conservation Service)

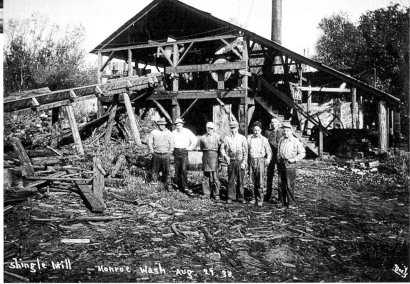

with payrolls totaling some $7 million in 1929 to 89 with payrolls of $6 million in 1933. The city's population fell from 38,000 to 30,000 during the same period, while the Pacific Northwest actually witnessed a rare out-migration of population. The value of industrial production in the city plummeted from nearly $29 million to $18 million. Wages in the logging camps dropped from an average $5.80 per week to only $3.11 in an industry which was operating at barely 35% capacity in 1931 and 19% by early 1932. Willam C. Butler, the dominant force in county banking and finance, observed, "In the lumber district liquidation is complete."

With the election of Roosevelt the tide began to turn, stimulating both the economy and the labor movement, and including legislation such as the 1935 Wagner National Labor Relations Act, which gave workers the right to organize and required employers to bargain with unions.

During the decade there was bitter infighting along with the growing power of organized labor, especially in the timber industry, which continued to dominate the economy of the county. Although it did not erupt into major violence here as in 1916 or to the extent of the riots in Tacoma at the end of June 1935, feelings ran high enough for Governor Clarence Martin to send National Guardsmen to Everett and other mill towns to calm tensions caused by a long, hard strike by the AF of L, seeking union recognition and bargaining rights from Long-Bell and Weyerhaeuser. Thirty thousand Northwest workers walked out. Industry had utilized its Loyal Legion of Loggers and Lumbermen, the "4L", against first the IWW and then the American Federation of Labor, but after 1937 it faded away as workers became free to choose their own representation. They had lost the 1935 battle but eventually won the war.

Inexpensive outdoor recreation flourished, while many people also fished and hunted to supplement their families' food supply. Resorts furnished boats for both salt and fresh water use, and mountain lakes were stocked with trout by groups such as the Trailblazers. This is Lake Roesiger, with Mt. Pilchuck in the background. (Courtesy Bernie Webber)

This led to divisiveness between the traditional craft union orientation of the AF of L and the industrial union philosophy favored by supporters of the new Congress of Industrial Organizations, which split away from the parent organization and quickly gained millions of supporters, including the newly formed International Woodworkers of America in 1937. Whereas the older, more conservative organization was formed along the lines of skilled jobs such as printers and boilermakers, the CIO favored organizing all workers in an industry such as coal mining or automobile manufacturing into a single, unified structure, the better to oppose the huge new corporations of the twentieth century, and would include both skilled and unskilled workers.

Dominated by the carpenters' union, the AF of L locals fought the IWA for control over virtually every mill in the Pacific Northwest, and employers were faced by ongoing jurisdictional strikes. Nevertheless, the workers managed to increase their salaries, foil wage cuts, and ensure a 40-hour workweek. This was especially impressive given the

Fishing and Packing Were Major Waterfront Activities

Above: A double line of women trim, wash, and check the cleaned fish as they move along processing belt at Fisherman's Packing Company. Fruits and vegetables were treated similarly. (Juleen #1725, courtesy Everett Public Library)

Above. The American Packing Company plant on Everett's Bayside employed many workers and shipped its products regionally via its Great Northern Railway spur. (Courtesy Everett Public Library)

Left: On November 3, 1930 this catch was unloaded dockside at the Fisherman's Packing Company plant in Everett, beginning the start of a series of standardized steps which were repeated by every cannery, regardless of location. (Juleen #1947, courtesy Everett Public Library)

Above: Cans are filled by hand before being sealed and then loaded into steam retorts for cooking. (Juleen #1725, courtesy Everett Public Library)

Left: Wooden boxes assembled on site are filled with cooked, cooled, and labeled cans. From here they are stored until being loaded into rail cars and shipped. (Juleen #1725, courtesy Everett Public Library)

return of serious depression conditions in 1938, when Weyerhaeuser in Everett actually was running at a loss. The company had opened a new sulphite pulp mill in 1936 on the site of its original Mill A on the south end of the Everett waterfront, and profit margins continued close. Everett Pulp and Paper had a more solid niche and steady employment at Lowell, as it met a fairly stable overseas demand for its higher-grade products.

Conditions did improve as the economy partially recovered, but they would not return to pre-crash levels until orders from Great Britain and war preparations stimulated demand in 1940 and 1941. In 1932 perhaps 50 percent of the woods workers had been unemployed, and the 1935 average hourly wage in the sawmills was just 57-cents per hour. In 1938 the wages had risen to 73-cents. For loggers the average wage rose from 66-cents to 84-cents per hour. By comparison, Helene Cameron recalled that women working in canneries on the Everett waterfront in 1938 still made only 27.5-cents per hour when work was available, and they might have to wait around the plant unpaid until a shipment of fish or fruit came in and they were called back to the processing line. Men were paid 35-cents per hour. Both she and her sister Ruth were working at the Bugge Packing Plant and met their future husbands there: Alex Cameron, who was supporting both his widowed mother and his brother, and Monte Holm, who found welcome work after being asked to leave by a new stepmother at age 13 and surviving his depression years as a young hobo and sheepherder. Helene and Alex pooled their resources to get married, but before they could do that the cannery closed permanently. All of them were out of work again. More time would have to go by before they too found stability, which gradually was taking hold as the economy began to improve in 1939 after 10 years of contraction.

As the decade drew to a close, many people sensed an end to economic uncertainty and their delayed dreams. Americans had looked inward during the 1930s, trying to cope with their own crises at home and rejecting foreign involvement. As they did so, they ignored the dangers of rising military threats, which were starting to engulf the nations of the world. For the Depression generation an even greater challenge was only months away, and the issues of the New Deal soon would lie in the past.

World War II: 1940–1945

Battered by a decade of economic woes, most Snohomish County residents welcomed 1940 as a harbinger of better times. Locally there were hopeful signs. In Everett building permits reached the highest levels since 1930, postal receipts set an all time record, and most businessmen reported increased retail sales. Also, despite the Depression, the 1940 U.S. Census indicated the county population had grown to 88,754, an increase of nearly 10,000 since 1930. Interestingly, the growth had taken place outside of Everett, which declined slightly from 30,567 residents in 1930 to 30,224 in 1940. The rest of the county actually grew by more than 20 percent in that 10-year period. Snohomish, with a population of 2,794, was still the second largest urban area, followed in order by Marysville, Monroe, Arlington, and Edmonds. The census continued to show a population with very few racial minorities. In the language of the day there were 151 "Negroes" and 648 "other races." Nearly all of the African Americans lived in Everett, and a large percentage of the "other races" were Native Americans on the Tulalip Indian Reservation.

As Snohomish County and the rest of the nation eased out of the Depression, attention increasingly turned to the war in Europe and Japan's growing menace in the Far East. A formal state of war had developed in Europe following the September 1939 German invasion of Poland, but save for the division of that hapless country with the Union of Soviet Socialist Republics and the subsequent Russian attack on neighboring small Finland, no great outbreak had occurred on the scale of 1914–1918. America had not wanted to enter another foreign war, but to growing numbers of citizens involvement seemed more probable. This was especially true following the collapse of first Scandinavia, then the Low Countries and France in late spring 1940. Holding a letter from relatives in occupied Norway and seeing it stamped with a black swastika on the back from the German censor came as a disturbing shock to the Gulbrandson family of Everett, who had emigrated early in the century and now learned to look for hidden messages. On the back of a stamp was written, "We are starving."

By late summer the county was experiencing at first hand the effects of President Roosevelt's resolve to make the United States an "arsenal of democracy." When the National Guard was federalized in 1940, units in Snohomish and Everett were placed on active duty. On Monday morning, September 23, 1940, the 104 members of Snohomish's Battery C, First Battalion of the 248th Coast Artillery left for Fort Worden in Port Townsend. Under the leadership of Captain Joe Aprill, the unit was scheduled for a year of training. That same day Everett's Headquarters Company L and Company M, Third Battalion of the 161st Infantry marched through town and then boarded trucks bound for their year in Camp Murray and Fort Lewis in Pierce County. Reporting the departure, *The Everett Daily Herald* noted that family members "said their farewells with tears streaming unashamedly down their cheeks." Perhaps there was a premonition that this would be more than a year in training. When war broke out these units were shipped into battle and experienced much of the bloodiest combat. Many of the boys who left Snohomish and Everett that day were killed or wounded.

At the same time the guardsmen were leaving, county men between the ages of 21 and 35 were preparing to register for military duty as required by a new federal law. The nation's first ever peacetime draft was about to begin. In January 1941 notices of induction began to arrive. Local newspapers reported Victor Corti, Alderwood Manor; William O. Porter, Edmonds; and James De Vries, Alderwood Manor as among the first county men to receive induction notices. By late spring Defense Savings bonds and stamps were being

Onlookers enjoy a float in the 1940 Marysville Strawberry Festival parade, a celebration which began in 1932 when the Commercial Club responded to new Marysville *Globe* editor Leon Stock's call to liven up the town. Over 3,000 plates of strawberry shortcake were served the first year, and the event became an annual affair, save for cancellations during the war years of 1942–1945. (Courtesy Marysville Historical Society)

A portion of the 100 National Guardsmen of Snohomish's Battery C, 248ᵗʰ Coast Artillery are shown in this 1938 photograph. Federally activated in September 1940 along with the Everett unit, they were to have received a year's intensive training as part of the regular army and then return home. Events cancelled those plans. County guardsmen were among the first Americans shipped overseas, and their casualty rates were high. (Courtesy *1939 Historical and Pictorial Review of the National Guard, State of Washington*)

sold throughout the county to help finance the national defense program. Meanwhile, the federal government started free local programs to train potential employees for defense production jobs at the Boeing Aircraft Company or the shipyards. Classes at Snohomish's old Emerson School (which had closed for many years as a fire hazard) had by the fall of 1941 produced 194 graduates who were working at Boeing for a beginning wage of 87-cents an hour. The pay seemed like a fortune for those who had suffered through the Depression.

There was action, too, that would create a significant local military presence. A portion of the Snohomish County Airport was taken over by the Army Air Corps in 1940. In spring 1941 the Air Corps personnel began to arrive. Under the direction of Lieutenant Colonel A.C. Strickland, at first the 34ᵗʰ Pursuit Group was housed in tents at the airfield and at Everettt's National Guard Armory. With the continued use of WPA labor and a $1.2 million federal government contract, major airport improvements were completed. Barracks, hangars and other buildings were erected, and some 4 million cubic yards of dirt were moved to improve the runways, one of which now was over a mile long. By the summer 1941 the Army had formally acquired the entire airport and named it Paine Field in memory of Lt. Topliff O. Paine, an Everett native and pioneer World War I Army pilot who had lost his life in 1922 while serving in the Air Mail Service. His parents attended the dedication. In early December 1941 word arrived that another $1.5 million in U.S. defense funds was being allotted for further improvements. Meanwhile, the Paine Field buildup was accompanied by the erection of federal housing units in south Everett. Eighty-five homes for non-commissioned officers and civil service employees at the base were under construction.

Residents of the Arlington area were excited by the fall 1940 announcement that the U.S. Navy was taking over their airport 2½ miles south of the town. It would be auxiliary to the Naval Air Station at Sand Point on Lake Washington in Seattle. *The Arlington Times* billed the site of the 1934 vintage field as "by far the most desirable in Northwest Washington, lying, as it does on a large plateau with a porous sand soil providing perfect natural drainage." In the summer of 1941 the Austin Construction Company completed major improvements, including a graded and surfaced runway on the 278-acre site. By fall the facility was being used as an adjunct flight training location for the overflow from Sand Point.

Amidst the preparation for war, the Everett School District Board of Directors took the bold step of starting the county's first full-fledged junior college. Although the same board would govern it, the college would be an entity separate from the Everett School District. Housed in the recently constructed Lincoln building at 25th Street and Oakes Avenue, a facility which the board decided was not needed for grade school purposes, Everett Junior College opened its doors in the fall of 1941. Immersed in controversy over the revised use of Lincoln and soon to be hit by the loss of students to the military and defense jobs, the college had a challenging first year. The board's willingness to make the building available at no charge and the establishment of contracts with local hospitals for the training of nurses were instrumental in keeping the junior college afloat. It was a rocky start for the educational institution that eventually would be the largest in the county.

Although people had sensed and seen the defense buildup and were aware of the deteriorating international situation, no one was prepared for the suddenness with which America was launched into war with Japan, followed shortly by declarations of hostilities from Germany and Italy. The shock of the December 7, 1941 Japanese attack on Pearl Harbor, followed by the destruction of American air forces in the Philippine Islands a few hours later, triggered immediate and momentous responses. On December 8 local men flocked to the Armed Services Recruiting Offices. Everett resident George Winnie typified the willingness to serve. By 10:00 A.M. on December 8 his papers were complete, and he was on his way to Seattle for induction into the Navy. The first county "blackout" under wartime conditions occurred that night.

Everett Junior College opened in September 1941 in this building at 25th and Oakes. After a precarious existence during the war years, the college proved an essential county asset when the campus was filled after the war with temporary buildings from Paine Field and enrollment surged. In 1958, it relocated north near the Americal Legion Memorial Golf Course at 8th Street and Wetmore Avenue. (Courtesy Larry O'Donnell)

Lights from all sources—residences, businesses, industries, farms, even vehicles—had to be turned off or shielded from external view. There was to be no evidence that could provide a target for enemy aircraft. The blackout was deadly serious business: no automobile traffic was allowed; only busses using parking lights and trains could operate; police and wardens entered buildings to turn off the switches of violators. In Everett on the first night the only major exception was the federal building on Colby, since no one could figure out how to darken the bulbs on the second floor. Regardless, radio stations went off the air to eliminate aircraft honing in their signals, outside smoking and flashlights were

Block Warden Glenn O'Donnell and his five-year-old son Larry are shown in a 1942 family photograph. Civil defense was serious business, and the warden's role was to be responsible for neighborhood activities, including enforcement of the nightly blackout rules. O'Donnell's area was on Tulalip Avenue north of Laurel Drive in Everett's Bayside section. (Courtesy Larry and Jack O'Donnell)

forbidden, and even service station battery chargers had to be unplugged lest their small glow be visible.

Since the aircraft carriers of the Japanese navy had disappeared following their stunning victory, there was genuine concern that the same kind of surprise attack that hit Pearl Harbor might well fall on the vulnerable facilities in Puget Sound. The State of Washington was virtually defenseless, with few fortifications, anti-aircraft guns, heavy artillery pieces, or placements for defense– and none in the Snohomish County! Civilian defense units quickly were activated, and a description of air raid signals was printed regularly in the local newspapers. Volunteers poured in to learn first aid, augment the fire departments in case of incendiary or high explosive bombs, and to staff the county's air raid observation stations around the clock. In Everett the station was atop the Medical & Dental Building; Snohomish first used the old Emerson School and then built a new tower nearby; Arlington's post was on the roof of the high school. Local Red Cross units started a $35,000 war fund drive with a "Remember Pearl Harbor" slogan. *The Everett Daily Herald* reminded the citizenry that "the bombs that rained on Pearl Harbor were the final answer of aggression to those who ever believed that tyranny and democracy can share the same seas, can breathe the same air." Continuing, the *Herald* called for "130 million Americans speaking with one voice and this voice directed toward one objective and only one objective." That objective was to win the war.

Within a few weeks after Pearl Harbor it was announced that the newly formed Everett Pacific Company would locate on the Everett waterfront to build a $3 million dry dock. It was expected that a workforce of 400 would start within 30 to 60 days and take a year to complete the project. This was the beginning of an industrial plant which would be the largest to that point in the county's history. The Piggott family, associated with the Pacific Car and Foundry of Seattle, had contracted with the Navy to operate the shipyard. Known initially as Everett Pacific and later renamed the Everett Pacific Shipbuilding and Dry Dock Company, the firm located on a Bayside site known as Tract O. The land, approximately at 21st Street, at first was leased. Later the Navy purchased the property from the Port of Everett for $250,000. Ground was broken on February 16, 1942. The keel for the dry dock *Rebuilder* was laid on May 15. It was launched in October and delivered to the Navy in March 1943. The *Rebuilder* was sent to the South Pacific, where it was used for on-the-spot repair of damaged warships.

At the same time three other county firms also were joining the marine vessel business. Everett Marine Ways, at the foot of Hewitt Avenue on Everett's bayfront, contracted with the Army for two huge wooden ocean-going barges. In Stanwood the Carl E. Edlund Shipyard, later known as the Stanwood Shipyard, also was gearing up to build similar craft. Located along the Stillaguamish River, the plant was on the site of the former Stanwood Lumber Company. (The shipbuilder changed its name when Edlund sold his interest to Horace Kelsey just before the first barge was launched in 1943.) The third plant was operated by the Pointer-Willamette Company, which took over the location of the A.M. Yost and Sons lumber yard in Edmonds. This firm would build Army barges as well, but these would be of steel. It was estimated that 35 to 50 men would be employed for at least four months to complete that work.

The Pearl Harbor attack accelerated the expansion at Paine Field. Word spread that upwards of 3,500 officers and enlisted men would be stationed at the base. By 1942 the federal government had spent $2.597 million for acquisitions and improvements. In addition Snohomish County had contributed over $375,000 to the project. At Arlington the Navy presence briefly was usurped by the Army, which envisioned the base as an adjunct to Paine Field. Later the Navy again would occupy the facility and use it as a training site for specialized aircraft assigned to small Navy aircraft carriers. Another government defense project developed in Mukilteo, where a 1,200-foot bayfront pier and a 1,100-foot railroad approach were constructed. These were used for loading from rail cars to ships ammunition stored in bunkers built at Tulalip. Bill Humphrey, whose father worked for the railroad, lived in Mukilteo at the time. Years later he recalled that he and his boyhood pals would watch the dozen or so rail cars be disconnected and rolled out to the pier for unloading. "There were armed guards when they did that. My buddies and I would watch with binoculars like we were spies or something. We thought it was pretty neat."

With the National Guard activated and many of the young men off to the service, local guard units were formed to protect the citizenry in event of enemy attack. Stan

The Everett Pacific Shipbuilding and Dry Dock Company was Snohomish County's largest industrial plant during the war years and employed over 6,000 workers. Housing and transportation were sharply limited due to wartime constraints, but the yard still launched over 50 vessels and dry dock units. (Courtesy Everett Public Library)

Dubuque, later the Snohomish County auditor, was a member of the Snohomish Home Guard. "We would drill at night," Dubuque recalled. "We had old model rifles and old khaki overalls for uniforms." In Edmonds a Washington State Guard Reserve was organized in the spring of 1942 and immediately began to drill. Some four decades later former Edmonds Mayor Gordon Maxwell remembered the early days of the Reserve as being even more primitive than what Dubuque had described. "Members wore coveralls, and they didn't have any guns. I guess they were supposed to hit the enemy over the head with clubs." While the Edmonds Reserve drilled, they were reminded of battle by the "ack-ack" of real guns. Antiaircraft weapons installed on the waterfront north of the Union Oil Company facility were utilizing an Army test area to fire at sleeve targets towed by planes in the skies above Puget Sound.

Meanwhile, Seattle's Boeing Aircraft Company dramatically expanded its workforce to produce airplanes for the war effort. In early 1939 the company had about 3,000 employees. By 1943 that number had soared to 78,000 with still a need for at least 9,000 more. The company began to explore sites for satellite plants which could assemble parts for its B-17 "Flying Fortress" heavy bombers. Both Everett and Stanwood were among the Snohomish County locations considered, with Everett eventually selected.

A unique business took shape at the Monroe condensery, a building vacated when the plant closed under competitive pressures in the late 1920s. In large part that competition had come from Darigold, which local farmers had helped organize in response to condensery milk tests which they considered unfair. After President Roosevelt declared flax a strategic war material, the Pacific Fiber Flax Association bought the condensery building and began to remodel it for use as a processing plant. In conjunction, local farmers were induced into growing the crop with promises of $1,000 a ton for their product. By early 1944 remodeling had been completed, and 40 employees were busy converting the raw material into linen. However the business was short lived when early on March 23, after just three weeks of operation, the plant exploded in flames when 600 tons of stored flax ignited by spontaneous combustion. Intensely hot fire reduced the business to ashes, and those fighting the blaze were hard pressed to save nearby buildings. As the plant was not rebuilt, only its landmark concrete smokestack remains as a stark tribute.

While many new companies existed solely for the purpose of war production, the county's typical peacetime industries also filled military demands. Businesses such as Everett's Weyerhaeuser Timber Company and Washington Stove Works, Lowell's Sumner Iron Works, Snohomish's Nepa Construction Company, and Monroe's Bozeman Canning Company were being counted on to produce their quotas for war.

One thing was certain: the Depression was over. Labor shortages now replaced job shortages. Federal employment programs such as the Civilian Conservation Corps closed down in 1942 as companies struggled to find enough workers, while the reforming zeal of the Roosevelt domestic New Deal programs faded before a successfully strong Republican backlash. Roosevelt was willing to let them go in order to gain support for the war effort.

Many adults held more than one job, and high school students routinely raced from school to work, some of them serving during the summers as Forest Service fire and trail crew members. Farmers faced the special challenge of finding enough employees at harvest time. Local high school students were sometimes dismissed from school to assist

267

them. Years later Sylvia (Strotz) Dycus, a lifelong Arlington resident, remembered being excused from high school early to help at the Valley Gem Farm. "We had to report to school first, and we had to keep our grades up. Then we could go out and help with the beans, potatoes and such." The farmer's life also might be complicated by his holding a second job. Long time Monroe resident Sam Mann typified many of those in agriculture. In 1991, at the age of 90, he reflected on his World War II years. He had a herd of 27 cows at his Wagner Hill farm, and he milked 16 or 17 a day. He also worked swing shift at Boeing, leaving home at 2:00 P.M. and arriving back at 2:00 A.M. in time to whistle the cows in for the milking. "I hardly knew my kids at that time," he said. "They'd come home after I left for work and be in bed when I came home. I was sleeping when they got up." Finally, his daughter Kathryn took over the milking, saying, "It's too much work for you, Dad."

Along with job security, the war brought many other homefront realities. A new set of expectations, restrictions and sacrifices permeated virtually every facet of everyday life. The Federal government had priority on all goods and services. Rubber for military purposes was an immediate need, and civilian tire rationing began in January of 1942. Sugar, gasoline, and coffee rationing were in effect before the end of the year, and many other items would be similarly affected in 1943 and beyond. Ration book stamps and the "points" required to buy food became as important as cash in the trip to the store – and far more confusing to compute. Within months the supply of passenger cars disappeared as automobile makers converted to the production of tanks and other military vehicles. Snohomish County was permitted to sell only 98 new cars already in stock between March 2 and May 31, 1942. The vehicles went only to those allowed by the government to buy them. In future war years none were available. The first war bond campaign began. Scrap and salvage drives started for all kinds of material that could be processed for use in the war effort including: rags, scrap metal, bottles, rubber tires, plus household fats and greases. A July 1942 effort by Snohomish's Zion Lutheran Church resulted in the collection of 1,750 gunnysacks, needed for food marketing and storage. This was typical of the scrap drives throughout the county.

Civil defense also continued as a serious community effort. Piles of sand were placed in strategic locations for use in case of an incendiary bomb attack.

War in the Pacific and the German submarine offensive in the Atlantic and Caribbean, along with the massive military buildup, soon brought rationing to the civilian population. With rubber supplies cut off, gasoline was restricted to reduce automobile use. Red meat, butter, sugar and other commodities soon followed. Everyone was issued a ration book, which contained "points" which had to be surrendered when purchases were made. Grocery advertisements typically included both the price of a product and the number of points required. (Courtesy David Cameron)

Thousands attended first aid classes, while laundry and other delivery truckers trained and organized as volunteer ambulance drivers.

Additional defense against aerial attack was undertaken by creation of the Aircraft Warning System in 1942. A network of observers was established. Men and women were trained to recognize the various planes and telephone to filtering centers reports of all aircraft passing within four miles of their observation posts. As a part of this program a number of fire lookouts and guard stations were staffed year-round from early 1942 until late autumn 1943, usually by married couples willing to undergo the rigors and isolation of a Cascade mountain winter in structures designed for summer use only. These included French Point, Rinker Point, Whitechuck Bench, Barlow Pass, and Blackjack Ridge, as well as Green Mountain lookout on the Suiattle River near Glacier Peak. The extremely successful program ended its role with praise for its accuracy, closing when the Japanese threat no longer was realistic.

Region-wide blackouts also were monitored closely by local authorities and volunteers. More than a half century after the war, lifelong Snohomish resident Donna Harvey vividly recalled the blackouts of her girlhood years. "Many houses had blackout drapes that could be closed to totally shut off light. They were very heavy, kind of like blankets." Loren Kraetz, who in 1999 still lived on the Arlington area farm founded by his family more than a century before, remembered the blackouts from his childhood days. "It was a challenge for the farmers. No light was supposed to leak out, so many of the farmers used special shutters which fit into the barn windows. I imagine there are still a lot of those devices sitting in barn lofts around the county." Kraetz recalled the blackouts as being frightening. "I didn't like them. It was eerie. Everything was dark except the beacon from the Arlington airport." He also wondered about the value of the farmers' efforts with airport light illuminating the area.

The influx of military personnel to Paine Field, Arlington, and the new Whidbey Island Naval Air Station, along with workers for the defense industries such as Boeing and the Everett shipyard, also created a severe housing shortage. As during the Depression, virtually no new private homes were being built. Local boards were created to find available shelter and to solicit government funding for new housing projects.

In a move that later would be viewed as one of America's most shameful World War II episodes, the federal government acted in 1942 to ship Japanese Americans living west of the mountains to interior regional internment camps. The Mafunes of Edmonds were among the families so affected. Densaku and Kura Mafune had been in Edmonds since the early 1930s operating greenhouses. Their three children had been outstanding students, with the youngest, Teiko, being the first girl elected Edmonds High School student body president. Teiko later recalled, "Edmonds was an excellent school for us to go to, because there wasn't any prejudice or anything like that." She acknowledged that Pearl Harbor changed the attitude of some residents, and then the announcement came that the family must dispose of all its property and prepare to move. In June 1942 the Mafunes left for the Tule Lake relocation center in Northern California. Suffering from the effects of a stroke, Densaku was taken against the advice of his physician. He died the first day at Tule Lake. Not until after the war did any of the family come back to Edmonds. Kura and daughter Ryoko returned to start a flower shop from scratch. Two years later Teiko joined them in running the business. Kura was killed in a 1984 hit-and-run accident. She had died a few years short of formal United States government acknowledgement that it had acted improperly in forcing the Japanese Americans from their homes.

While the domestic front scrambled to adjust to early wartime realities, the news from overseas depicted the truly grim realities on the battlefronts. After Pearl Harbor news came that Sgt. Charles Cole of Granite Falls and Navy Seaman First Class Daniel Guisinger, Jr. of Everett had died on the battleships *USS Arizona* and *USS Oklahoma,* respectively. The early battles went to the enemy, and Snohomish County men were among those losing their lives in previously unheard of places such as Bataan, Corregidor, and the Java Sea. Word arrived that Edmonds' James Howard Kerr had been killed in the early Japanese attack on the Philippines. It was the beginning of a long list which would unfold with somber regularity over the next few years.

By 1943 the military tide had begun to change. The Allies were on the march in the African, European, and Pacific theaters. The homefront was on the march too. Snohomish County had congealed into a well-oiled machine that would function productively for the remainder of the war. In March of 1944 it was announced that $114,450,000 in federal government war supplies and facilities contracts had been issued in Snohomish County from June 1940 through December 1943. A good percentage of those dollars were directed to the Everett Pacific Shipbuilding and Dry Dock Company. The firm continued to garner contracts for the huge dry docks and expanded its scope of work to produce other types of marine vessels. Then a repair yard was added. Almost 6,000 employees were launching some kind of craft at a rate of one every month, a total of 36 by February of 1945. They included the floating dry docks, sectional dry dock units, netlayers, harbor tugs, and barges. By war's end another five vessels had been launched and were being prepared for delivery, while the keels for 23 more harbor tugs had been laid.

Jim Cunningham, one of the last surviving members of the shipyard management team, reminisced about the yard shortly before his death in 1997. "In the first year, the shipyard was a mess. Then in early 1943 the Piggotts brought in Barkley Knerr as manager. He straightened things out and brought in new sub-bosses. The shipyard was always fighting with the unions. The government seemed to back the effort to keep wages down. With Everett being a strongly unionized town, it was a never-ending battle. I don't remember that we had any 'black' or 'brown' employees, but we did have around 100 to 150 women laborers. Some were painters, and there was a group known as 'tarbabies'. They coated the insides of vessels with a black gooey substance. It was hard work, and the women would crawl out each day covered from head to toe with the black goo. They were treated poorly by other workers, too, especially the men."

On a smaller scale, the county's other shipbuilders also were producing craft. In a brief ceremony in July of 1943 the first of the two ocean-going barges constructed by Everett Marine Ways was launched. Approximately one million board feet of lumber were used in the vessel's construction. The next year the company was busy building Navy tugs and a fireboat. A photo of the large crane barge built at Edmonds' Pointer-Willamette plant was featured on *The Everett Daily Herald* front page on August 20, 1943. The Stanwood Shipyard launched its first ocean-going barge on July 22, 1943. Six more had been completed by August of 1944, when it was announced that a contract had been secured for ten steel barges.

Production at the Everett Shipyard

SHOWN during self-docking operations is one of three YFD's constructed in the yard. Designed for service at remote bases, these three-sectional mobile dry docks have an all-over length of 622 feet and a lifting capacity of 18,000 tons.

Three floating dry docks were built at the plant, YF 21 (the *Rebuilder*), YF 62, and YF 63. The keel for the first was laid on May 15, 1942 and delivered to the navy on March 11, 1943. The last was laid on March 6, 1944 and delivered on January 23, 1945. (Courtesy Everett Public Library)

Ten navy netlayers (top), four army ordnance barges, and two navy freight barges (below) were ordered by the federal government. The netlayers were launched between March 1943 and July 1944, carried the designation AN, and were numbered from AN 38, the *Ailanthus*, to AN 47, the *Canotia*. (Courtesy Everett Public Library)

Work began in February 1942 and escalated as orders came in, first for net layers and then for battleship sized sectional dry dock units. The demand for labor increased the city's population by 16 percent during the war years, most of them drawn to the higher paying shipyard jobs. (Courtesy Everett Public Library)

A repair facility was added later in the war to aid in reconditioning naval vessels. Puget Sound became a center for such work on the West Coast, given the intensive needs of the Pacific war. (Courtesy Everett Public Library)

In August of 1943 Boeing announced plans for its sub-assembly plant in Everett. The Universal Machine Shop building at the southwest corner of Grand and California avenues would be used to assemble parts for the B-17. A call went out for workers—men 16 years and older, women 17 years and older. In a few short weeks a workforce of several hundred was participating in the Boeing effort that produced 387 of the Flying Fortresses every month. Many of the employees were women. With the ever-present labor shortage, busses were bringing workers in each day from as far away as Arlington. Before the war ended Boeing opened another Everett facility, this one at the northeast corner of Pacific and Rucker avenues.

The county's military establishments also were in full swing. The 54th Pursuit Group; the 20th, 33rd, 55th and 329th Fighter Groups; the 465th Army Air Corps Base Unit, the 1021st Air Service Squadron, and detachments of the 102nd Army Airways Communication Squadron and the 24th Weather Squadron were among the units stationed at Paine during the war. Pilots and crews operating P-38, P-39 and P-40 type aircraft had the principal mission of providing air defense for the Pacific Northwest and training pilots and other service men for overseas duty. In June of 1943 the base welcomed its first women

These Boeing Airplane Company employees personify the "Rosie the Riveter" term used to personify female workers in war industries. Faced with massive labor shortages, companies hired thousands of women to fill traditionally male jobs, such as these assembling an aircraft part in one of the Boeing plant buildings in downtown Everett. (Courtesy Everett Public Library)

During the war the American military still was segregated, with most African American units given support rather than combat roles. Mail call was a most welcome time, regardless of race. (Courtesy Snohomish County Museum and Historical Association)

"Loose lips sink ships" and similar slogans had serious meanings during the war years, as espionage by the Axis powers was of great concern to the Allies. Soviet intelligence gathering also was active on the West Coast. Failure of the 1944-45 Japanese balloon project was in large part due to tight security imposed on all reports of sightings, and most Americans cooperated out of a strong sense of patriotism. (Courtesy Everett Public Library)

Paine Field, shown here around 1943, had a multi-million dollar expansion by the U.S. Army Air Corps. At war's end many of these structures were removed, several to Everett Junior College and one still in use as the Memorial Community Church at 710 Pecks Drive in Everett. (Courtesy Everett Public Library)

military personnel. Initially designated as part of the Women's Auxiliary Army Corps, the women were redesignated as part of the regular army two months later. The word "Auxiliary" was dropped, and the women labeled the WACs (Women's Army Corps). The base also saw the arrival of an African American unit. The military was segregated until 1947, and the "colored," as they were identified in the base newsletter, had their separate organization. Augmenting the several thousand military personnel was a cadre of civilian employees. Paine Field evolved into a community of its own. There was a myriad of activities for the base personnel, ranging from a post library to infant care programs and organized sports leagues. A newsletter titled *Ace Pursuiter* was published regularly.

Base personnel loved sports, and they watched with interest when the Fourth Air Force Flyers, a football team laden with ex-college stars, squared off against the University of Washington varsity at Husky Stadium in 1944. Drained of its best players by the war effort, the Huskies lost 28 to 0. Although the regular units were segregated, the Flyers were not. Jimmy Nelson, former All American from the all-white University of Alabama, was a backfield star. African American Woody Strode, ex-UCLA standout who later gained Hollywood fame in such movies as *Spartacus*, excelled as a Flyer end. Strode, in fact, scored two of the victors' touchdowns.

At the Arlington airport the Navy was back in control by early 1943. Work by the Austin Company continued, and in May *The Arlington Times* reported its understanding that 750 Navy personnel would be assigned to the base that summer. On June 26, 1943 some 2,000 to 3,000 people swarmed to the dedication when the airfield was officially designated as "U.S. Naval Auxiliary Air Station, Arlington, Washington." Soon the facility, which had now expanded to 1,162 acres, was in full operation. An official June 26, 1943

Arlington Airport in World War II

Above: Lined up on the warm up apron are Grumman fighters designed for aircraft carrier service with the Pacific fleet. In 1940 the F4F Wildcat was the first successful monoplane fighter, with wings that folded up for more compact storage and landing gear which lifted flush with the fusalage. Its F6F Hellcat successor came on board in 1943 with more power, speed, and high altitude performance to outclass the Japanese Zero models. (Ellis #1838, courtesy Stillaguamish Valley Pioneer Association)

Above: On June 26, 1943 the U.S. Naval Auxilliary Air Station, Arlington, Washington was dedicated, under the command of Lt. Leland L. Wilder, U.S.N.R.. At the airport over 3,000 pilots were given advanced training for the war in the Pacific. (Ellis #1840, courtesy Stillaguamish Valley Pioneer Association)

Left: The naval station had its own fire department, a vital part of the support system given the amount of high octane fuel, number of planes, and training role of the base. Army fire crews first were stationed at the field, then were transferred to Paine Field in the summer of 1943 and succeeded by naval personnel. Arlington firemen also were available in case of a serious incident. (Ellis #1942, courtesy Stillaguamish Valley Pioneer Association)

Left: Both army and navy improvements were made at the field, but in early 1943 naval construction to complete a full training base was undertaken by the Austin Company, which by the middle of the summer had erected these barracks, the fire hall, hangar, heating plant, service building, and other facilities. Married men's housing became a serious problem later in the war, as the county simply had too few homes and apartments for the influx of service men and defense workers. (Ellis #1826, courtesy Stillaguamish Valley Pioneer Association)

274

U.S. Navy description (not declassified until May 10, 1995) described the station as having two completed 5,000-foot runways, another under construction, 33 buildings, barracks for 850 enlisted men, and quarters for 116 officers. The base function was identified as follows: "…this station maintains and operates facilities and furnishes services for the support and training of naval aircraft units and aviation personnel." Proud of its military neighbor, Arlington residents took special care to make the newly arrived service men feel welcome. Among other activities, the citizenry refinished and equipped Robertson's Hall in downtown to be the Arlington Service Men's Recreational Center. Young women between the ages of 17 and 35 signed up to be Junior Hostesses there.

Army and Navy planes now were commonplace in the local skies. Loren Kraetz remembered how the farm animals were terrified by low flying aircraft. "I think some of those pilots kind of liked buzzing the cows," he recalled later with a wry smile. Others discovered that many Forest Service fire lookouts now were women. Trudy Woll on Mt. Pilchuck dutifully reported all passing aircraft as well as spotting fires, returning the smiles and waves of young men circling too close to her perch. They did not know that her heart was with her husband Carl, far away with the Seabees in the South Pacific.

There also were mishaps and crashes, some of them fatal. The first wartime death at Arlington involved Dudley Pope, a civilian employee from Sand Point. He was killed when his parachute, a new type he had invented, failed to open after he had bailed out at 10,000 feet. At Paine the flag flew at half-mast after First Lt. Charles E.R. Blair, base operations officer, was killed in a crash of a P-39 fighter. Pope and Blair were two of several who lost their lives in various training exercises.

The air bases also sparked romances between local girls and servicemen, many of which led to permanent commitments. Retired Arlington couple Julius and Sylvia Dycus were volunteering their time at the Stillaguamish Valley Pioneer Museum half a century later, but they vividly remembered the World War II circumstances that brought them together. "I was living in Farwell, a little town in the Texas Panhandle, when I enlisted in the Navy," said Julius, who preferred to be called JY or Dyc. "After Ordnance school my squadron was sent to Arlington Naval Air Station. That was December 1943." Sylvia, her sister and her mother were working at the time in Everett's Boeing plant, catching the bus each morning from Arlington. Sylvia recalled, "Arlington had a roller skating rink downtown. It was a great place to have fun and meet people." "Yeah, I met her at the roller rink," JY chimed in. After a short courtship, they married in April 1944. Two months later JY was sent to California and then in October shipped out for duty in the South Pacific on the carrier *U.S.S. Salamaua.* "We lost men when we got hit by a suicide plane. We were lucky. It just missed the fuel tank. Then we got hit by a huge typhoon that peeled back part of the flight deck. After the war that ship was scrapped," JY recalled. When the war ended JY returned to Arlington, where he and Sylvia raised a family. "We have three girls," the couple continued, "one in Alabama, one in Seattle, and one next door." Numerous Snohomish County couples could tell stories similar to that of JY and Sylvia.

While the military bases prepared personnel for overseas duty and the defense plants fulfilled their contracts, other local industries were meeting or exceeding war production quotas. Snohomish's Nepa Construction Company expanded its cargo pallet plant to meet the demand for this critically needed product. By mid-1943, 120 pallets an hour, or 11 railroad carloads a day, could be produced. In March of 1943 the Sumner Iron

Works between Everett and Lowell became the first Snohomish County firm to be awarded the coveted "M" honors from the United States Maritime Commission. The honors came for Sumner's outstanding record producing steam steering engines and anchor windlasses for the famed "Liberty Ships," the mass-produced cargo haulers of the war. In May of 1944 Everett's Washington Stove Works was the only Pacific Coast stove company to earn the Maritime Commission's "M" award. Ranges from the Everett plant were going into every western built "Liberty Ship." Monroe's Bozeman Canning Company was presented the distinguished Achievement "A" award in September 1944. The award was given in recognition of the 1943 season, when the plant produced its largest pack ever of frozen fruit and vegetables, much of it for delivery to Army and Navy bases. The county agricultural community also was receiving honors. In the summer of 1944 the farmers, ranchers, livestock producers and agricultural workers were presented a State Agricultural War Board certificate which enrolled them on the Food for Freedom Honor List. Noting the shortages of equipment, supplies and labor, W.A. Wolfe, chairman of the State Department of Agriculture War Board, remarked that, "farmers of Snohomish County, in particular, did an outstanding job in spite of all these difficulties and made possible record production." The truth of Wolf's comment was shown by the Snohomish

In 1944, reknowned Northwest artist Kenneth Callahan painted a series of murals for the Weyerhaeuser Mill B cafeteria portraying the men and technology of the timber industry. Recently the works have been re-installed at the Everett Transit Center. The Callahans hosted an active artists' gathering place at their Robe Ranch east of Granite Falls and practiced scientific forestry on their land. (*Weyerhaeuser Murals* by Kenneth Callahan: Paul Bunyan Detail, Courtesy City of Everett Public Art Collection)

County Dairymen's Association's record-setting production of 76,018,512 pounds of milk in 1944. The lumber industry also was doing its share. Companies such as Weyerhaeuser, struggling with manpower and log shortages, still were meeting production schedules. When the national need for lumber was approaching a crisis stage in early 1945, Jim Stevens of the West Coast Lumbermen's Association stated, "The brightest spot in the picture is Everett."

For the hardworking citizens, the never-ending war bond campaigns and other drives became a way of life. There were seven bond drives during the course of the war, and each met its multi-million dollar goal. Workers were encouraged and coaxed into bond purchases. Children trudged off to school with pennies to buy stamps for their stamp book. When $17.50 worth of stamps had been purchased at 10 or 25 cents a stamp, the book would be turned in for a $25.00 bond. Bond promotions ranged from light-hearted gatherings on the courthouse lawn where a movie star such as Veronica Lake, of the peek-a-boo hairdo fame, might give the pitch, to gut wrenching ads which sought to motivate by guilt. One such ad featured the ghostly figure of a helmeted G.I., one eye concealed in shadow and the other balefully staring out at the reader. "I Died Today…What Did You Do?" the caption read. As the months and then years of war continued, the scrap and salvage drives involved virtually everyone. Housewives were asked to collect and contribute household fats and grease; they were used in the making of glycerine and explosives. An Edmonds scrap drive resulted in a massive pile of discarded items on a vacant lot at Fourth and Main Streets. In one Snohomish drive, school children turned in 7,000 metal keys. Each student who turned in 10 keys got a 10-cent war stamp. Students at Everett's Garfield School were pictured in *The Everett Daily Herald* with the thousands of glass bottles they had collected. Even a historic cannon at Snohomish's G.A.R. Cemetery was sacrificed. It yielded 2,250 pounds of metal for salvage.

People generally adjusted willingly and often creatively to the shortages and rationing of everyday goods. With no new cars available and tires and gasoline rationed, carpooling was commonplace. At the Everett shipyard shift change, for example, automobiles would be lined up along Norton Avenue with four to six people in each vehicle. Many depended on the bus for getting around the county. The Index Stage Line, with its home depot in Monroe, became the popular travel means to Seattle and Everett from all the towns in the Skykomish Valley. Norman Hartzell, who drove for line at that time, remem-

This tangled mass of debris in a downtown Edmonds vacant lot is the result of a community scrap metal drive during the war. It illustrates the seriousness with which county residents rounded up and donated materials needed for the war effort. In Edmonds people who added to this heap often were rewarded with movie tickets for the nearby Princess Theatre. (Courtesy Edmonds-South Snohomish County Historical Association)

Logging in the Early 1940s

Left: Assisted by a "cat," a Lervick truck moves a donkey engine through logging slash to a new setting. Diesel tractors, logging trucks, and diesel powered donkeys were more efficient than steam power and enabled crews to reach higher up mountain slopes and into more remote valleys in search of fresh timber to cut. (Courtesy David Cameron)

Lervick Logging Company of East Stanwood paraded a huge old-growth Douglas fir through Snohomish, cut into lengths for its trucks to haul. (Courtesy David Cameron)

Jack Earlandsen has tools of the high climber's trade as he prepares to climb a spar tree with his spurs and rope. Climbers were a small elite in the woods, their skills originating with sailors in the 19th century and adapted to topping trees, hanging pulleys, and rigging complex systems of wire rope. (Courtesy Gold Bar Historical Society)

Left: Where once steam locomotives were posed for the photographer, now trucks were the company pride. (Courtesy David Cameron)

Right: Following the parade, the logs were dumped into the river for rafting down to the mills in Everett. (Courtesy David Cameron)

Left: Hard working tugboats towed the log rafts down the rivers and around Puget Sound to the large booms maintained by the salt water mills. Water storage of logs kept them from deteriorating but also added large amounts of sediments to the estuaries. (Courtesy David Cameron)

bered that extra buses to Seattle were added on Sunday night to carry valley folks back to resume their weekday defense jobs or to check into military establishments. Housewives studied the newspaper ads of grocery stores such as June's, which operated in several county locations, checking both the prices and the accompanying numbers listing the points needed for rationed items. Then they negotiated with neighbors and friends, swapping stamps in a bartering arrangement that seem to benefit all. The same kind of exercise occurred for shoes and other rationed goods. For some menu items, however, even ration stamps couldn't help. Except for rare instances, food items from the tropics had long since disappeared: pineapples, coconuts and bananas could not be found. Most shoppers discovered the value of sticking with one grocer. When some rare commodity was available, the grocer might hide it under the counter and then slip it quietly to his most loyal customers. Fred Howard, who operated Everett's Farm Products Grocery, remembered being approached by one lady who coyly asked if he had any bananas under the counter. "You know, Mr. Howard, I do all my shopping here," she stated. Howard replied, "Well, lady, you sure must not eat very much."

For many the victory garden was at least a partial answer to the food issue. Encouraged by the federal government, Snohomish County residents were among the millions of Americans who planted vegetable gardens in their backyards. Whereas the rural family always had been relatively self-reliant, the prospect of providing their own food could be a new adventure for the city family. Predictably, the results varied. Digging through the cinder blackened dirt at the base of Rucker Hill in Everett, several families found they lost the battle to worms and insects. "Only my rhubarb and horseradish made it," complained one shipyard worker. For others, the experiment was successful. Betty Morse, a teenager on Snohomish's Avenue G during the war, later remembered a thriving, productive garden. "We grew beets, potatoes, carrots, rutabagas, all kinds of onions, beans, corn, peas – and I'm sure a lot more I don't remember. We canned lots of things. We also had several fruit trees: egg plum, mulberry, apple, and pear. We even had chickens — all this on a small city lot." Betty also recalled the gardens as part of general neighborliness. "Everybody shared their produce with everyone else. Everyone was so generous. It was a time when we all needed each other in a lot of ways. The victory gardens were one of the things that pulled us together."

The irony of the economy was that people had money to spend but little to buy. The average hourly wage of $1.27 at the Stanwood shipyard, for instance, exceeded the daily amount for which many had worked during the Depression. Spending increased, but not at the level it would have if major goods had been available. Items with metal—refrigerators, stoves, washing machines, tools, toys, etc.—just weren't being produced for civilian consumption. Some synthetic rubber products became available, but the quality was often questionable. At birthdays or Christmas time children learned it was futile to ask for the electric train or the new tricycle. Instead they might crawl up on Santa's lap and proudly announce they wanted a War Bond for Christmas. While they secretly longed for real toys, kids had to settle for cheap cardboard and paper playthings that never matched the extravagant pictures on the boxes.

The movie was one available luxury, and people flocked in record numbers to the theaters. Along with newsreel with its carefully edited action pictures which people scanned for familiar faces and cartoons with stereotypical Nazis and buck-toothed Japa-

Henry M. Jackson began his lengthy career in Congress when he was elected to the House of Representatives in 1940. Only 28 years old, he was the youngest person ever elected to that office from this state. Re-elected by a hefty margin in 1942, he enlisted in the army in 1943 but was transferred to reserve status early the following year when President Roosevelt released all members of Congress from active military duty. (Courtesy Everett Public Library)

nese being foiled by the likes of Bugs Bunny, there was a plethora of patriotic films with heroes such as John Wayne leading the Yanks to victory. Nobody noticed that the Japanese usually were portrayed by unwilling Filipinos. Betty Grable, the G.I.'s favorite pinup girl, seemed to show up in a new movie nearly every weekend. Light comedies, westerns, and musicals, though, helped to let the mind drift off for several hours from the reality of war.

While the radio served as an indispensable source of war news, it also provided escapism from the conflict's harsh realities. People gathered in the living room to listen to the latest antics of comics such as Jack Benny or Fibber McGee and Molly. Housewives glued their ears to the radio as Helen Trent lived out the question, "Can a woman over thirty-five find romance?" The radio broadcast of a Joe Louis boxing match could prompt neighborhood conversation for days before and after, while the legendary voice of Seattle Rainiers baseball announcer Leo Lassen recreating the action of an away game from the cryptic code of the Western Union wire often was the last sound of the night for a drowsy youngster slipping off to sleep.

One of the war year changes was the shifting of power to a new generation of county leaders. The massive infusion of federal dollars altered county economics and politics. The role of the local Congressman increased in stature and influence. Henry M. Jackson, the young Everett Democrat who had first been elected to the U.S. House of Representatives in 1940, emerged as a potent force. Announcements about the awarding of major federal contracts for county firms almost always came from the his office. In keeping with the patriotism of the day, Jackson, only 29 years old when America entered the war, enlisted in the military. However, he was called back to Washington, D.C. by President Roosevelt, who cited a federal law prohibiting members of Congress from serving in the military at the same time. By 1944 Jackson had compiled an enviable record of accomplishments and had further strengthened his reputation as an earnest, hard worker. In his campaign for re-election that fall he pointed to specifics, such as helping bring the shipyards to Everett and Stanwood and the air base to Arlington. His Republican opponent, Payson Peterson, spoke in generalities and lost by an almost three to one margin. There would be several Jackson/Peterson repeat races, all with the same final results. Jackson had exhibited the qualities and political savvy that eventually would land him in the United States Senate and very nearly in the White House.

At the same time Jackson was rising to power, William Butler, the Republican Everett banker who was arguably the most powerful county resident in the first half of the 20th century, was ending his reign. He retired in 1942 and two years later died. Ironically, some 20 plus years later, Jackson and his family moved into the beautiful home Butler had built on Everett's Grand Avenue. Jackson used to laugh that Mr. Butler would turn over in his grave if he knew that a Democrat were living in his house.

Mon Wallgren of Everett was another influential county figure during the era. A former U.S. Congressman, he was in the U.S. Senate during the early war years. His name and Jackson's frequently were mentioned together in federal announcements affecting local residents. In 1944 he campaigned successfully as the Democratic candidate for state

Mon C. Wallgren

By Thomas M. Gaskin, PhD

National Amateur Balkline Billiards Champion (1929) Mon Wallgren is the only politician to be elected to the U.S. House of Representatives, the U.S. Senate and as governor of the state of Washington.

Born in Iowa in 1891, Wallgren carne to Everett with his Scandinavian parents in 1901 from flood devastated Galveston, Texas. Attending Everett High School, he helped his father run the family jewelry and watch repair business. Wallgren enrolled at the Washington State School of Optometry in Spokane, graduating in 1914. Later his diploma allowed political supporters to say that Wallgren could speak with professional certainty about the shortsightedness of his opponents. During World War I, Wallgren served in the Washington National Guard as a heavy artillery instructor of at various forts on the Puget Sound.

As a civilian once again, Wallgren continued in the jewelry and optometry businesses, participated in a variety of fraternal organizations, and increased his reputation as a stellar billiards player. In a three-day match played before a large crowd at the Elks Club in Everett, Wallgren defeated Percy Collin of the Illinois Athletic Club of Chicago for the National Amateur 18.2 Balkline Championship. In somewhat of an understatement, Collins admitted in defeat, "considering the location, lack of competition, and size of the town, Wally is tough."

Mon C. Wallgren

In 1932 Wallgren entered politics as the Democratic candidate for the Second Congressional seat in the House of Representatives. He promised to help farmers by supporting lower freight rates. He sought the votes of those in the timber industry by urging a protective tariff on forest goods, and he stated that military preparedness and economic fairness required that a portion of the Pacific feet should be brought to the Northwest from California, with a permanent navy base established on Puget Sound. A Democrat had never won election to the 2nd District, but as part of the Democratic landslide of 1932 Wallgren emerged victorious by 18,000 votes.

Re-elected to office in 1934, 1936 and 1938, Wallgren demonstrated that he was a consistent supporter of Roosevelt's New Deal policies. His most important legislative achievement during these years was the introduction of legislation in 1938 which created Olympic National Park. To protect private business from being excluded from much of the valuable resources of the peninsula, the timber industry, the National Park Service, and Governor Clarence Martin all worked for a small park of 440,000 acres. Wallgren's bill created a 634,000-acre park with the important proviso that presidents in the future could increase the park to near 900,000 acres. A Seattle Chamber of Commerce spokesman denounced the Olympic National Park by saying, "How are you going to get 500,000 tourists into the park in one year as Wallgren claims. Why, how are you going to get even 50,000 tourists a year into that park?" Today, the park covers 923,000 acres and over two million tourists visit each year.

In 1940 Wallgren defeated Stephen Chadwick to become a U.S. senator. Appointed to the Senate Committee to Investigate the National Defense Program (the Truman Committee), he helped stop production of defective military airplane engines and poor quality "Liberty" ships. In the process the committee saved the nation $15 billion and Wallgren became the close friend of the chairman, Senator Harry S. Truman.

Prevailed upon by the Democratic Party to save the state from the Republicans in 1944, Wallgren defeated incumbent Arthur B. Langlie by a scant 28,000 votes to become Washington State's 13th governor.

Liberal in his use of Eau de Cologne and shaving lotion, Wallgren gained a reputation as the best smelling governor in the history of the state. Governor Wallgren also was liberal in his policies, being credited with creating the nation's most generous unemployment compensation law ($25 a week for 26 weeks) and supporting public power funding.

In 1948 Langlie attacked Wallgren for driving two state owned Cadillacs, for encouraging the state Department of Fisheries to buy a $15,000 yacht for his personal use, having two bars in the governor's mansion, and appointing union leader and high school dropout Dave Beck as a regent of the University of Washington. Concerning the charge of extravagance, Wallgren remarked, "If the voters don't want to go first class, they better get another governor." They did: Arthur Langlie.

Wallgren moved his family to the Wardman Park Hotel in Washington, D.C. and waited for his friend President Truman to appoint him to a government job. Truman named him chairman of the National Security Resources Board in charge of coordinating the nation's resources in times of war. Before the Senate could confirm the nomination, Harry P. Cain, Republican senator from Washington, charged in a six and three quarter hour speech that Wallgren was unfit for the job. In case anyone missed the speech, Senator Cain had a 261-page book with 78,300 words published explaining Wallgren's deficiencies. After a three-month fight, Truman withdrew the appointment. Embarrassingly, the Congressional Directory had come out prematurely listing Wallgren as NSRB chairman. In October 1949 Truman nominated Wallgren to the Federal Power Commission. The senate quickly approved, and in the next year Wallgren was made chair of the commission, a position he held until he retired at age 60 in 1951.

As a politician Wallgren was known as a gregarious individual, a raconteur of Swedish-dialects, an avid hunter, a fisherman, a low handicap golfer, and of course as an expert billiard player. In retirement he lived in Palm Desert with summer residences in Olympia and Everett. He took great pride in his southern California blue ribbon grapefruit, and he also helped found Shadow Mountain Golf club in the Palm Springs area.

On July 8, 1961 a flat tire stalled his car on the Nisqually Bridge outside of Olympia. A 22-year-old National Guardsman, Gerhard Schock, stopped to help. A drunk driving a pickup truck slammed into Wallgren and Schock. Schock died immediately, and Wallgren died two months later at age 70. Mon Wallgren was buried in Everett's Evergreen Cemetery, having achieved in a 20-year political career a record of public office holding which has not been duplicated.

governor. When he bowed out of the Senate he was replaced by his handpicked successor, Hugh Mitchell, a former Everett newspaperman. Mitchell, who had been serving as Wallgren's secretary since 1932, was succeeded in that position by Jack Gorrie, another former Everett newspaperman. In addition, Governor Wallgren appointed Everett's Clarence Hickey as state highway director. Citing these appointments and the prominence of Henry M. Jackson, *The Everett Daily Herald* stated flatly, "Olympia is the site of the state capitol, but Everett is the political center of the state."

Of all the changes on the homefront perhaps none was more momentous than the role of women. Due to the war-caused manpower shortage, women entered the workforce in greater numbers than ever before, assuming new responsibilities and experiencing new opportunities. Females were not only working in greater numbers; they were doing such traditionally male ones as welding, riveting and shipfitting. They even went to work in trousers, a move that prompted Everett High School girls to ask why they couldn't come to school in slacks. That change wouldn't occur, however, for almost another three decades. School districts did ease up on the policy of hiring women teachers only if they were unmarried. The Everett School District, for example, began to employ married women with the caveat that this was an emergency measure to be terminated at the war's end. Even with the changes the labor shortage continued, as most women preferred if

Federal Housing

(All photos courtesy Everett Public Library)

Low cost, basic housing units provided shelter for families, as wooden and then cement block units were laid out in rows. Each building was divided into several smaller living spaces.

Floor space was concentrated, but the buildings were new and clean if not very soundproof, and bus service connected the Baker Heights project on 12th Street to the shipyard and downtown shopping. Distance from amenities was a problem, especially with gasoline rationing and long hours when men were away at work.

The Everett Public Library brought its venerable 1924 Ford bookmobile, the "Pegasus," staffed by Willa Jameson with reading materials and programs for project children. Over half a century later the Baker Heights area in north Everett still is in use, while the Pegasus has been found and is being restored.

Most families had radios and all had to provide their own furniture. A two-building elementary school of similar simple wooden construction, each room heated with its own coal stove, provided a spartan educational setting and began classes in 1943 at the corner of 12th and Poplar. In 1952 it was replaced with the brick Hawthorne school.

Right: Having the federal government as the landlord made for uniform and predictable rents. Private sector housing starts had virtually dried up during the depression years, shortages restricted civilian materials during the war, and only the government had the resources necessary to reduce the housing crunch.

given a choice to maintain their roles as wives, mothers, and caregivers – especially important with the number of husbands and sons in the service. The Norman school was forced to close in 1943 when it couldn't find a teacher. Many industries survived by having workers often put in double shifts. The mills suffered with the loss of employees to better paying defense industry positions until the federal government "froze" workers on their jobs to eliminate the practice. Even so, at one point, Weyerhaeuser's giant Mill B sawmill shut down one of its head rig saws for lack of workers to run it. It was the first time this had happened since the mill's opening in 1915. In the summer of 1944 Mexican laborers were recruited to work on the Snohomish Valley farms in the *bracero* program.

The housing shortage also persisted. Drawn by military bases and defense industries, county population grew significantly. By the spring of 1944 the state census board reported that Everett had grown to a population of 35,000, an increase of 4,776 or 16 percent since 1940. Snohomish had grown by nearly 10 percent to 3,050. Private residential construction still was practically non-existent. In Everett, for instance, only 15 residential building permits were issued in 1944. The situation was alleviated partially by the construction of federally funded housing units. By 1944 a total of 1,275 public housing units had been provided, the bulk in a big northeast Everett project. This large complex created the need for its own grade school. Housed in temporary wooden structures similar to the project around it, Baker Heights at 12th and Poplar streets became more than a school. Staff who worked there remembered it as being the focal point for the residents. Christine (Rindal) Dorsey, who served as principal, later recalled substandard facilities but "a wonderful core of teachers and such appreciative parents. The school was the center of their lives. They poured their hearts out to us."

For a significant number of women the war stimulated a breaking out of the local mold and a venture into the larger world via the military. The services needed young women, and those of Snohomish County were among those who answered the call. Marysville's Aloha Hammerly was one of the first. After completing training at Everett's General Hospital, she received her orders to report for service in the Army Nurses Corps where she was commissioned a 2nd Lieutenant. Betty June Lloyd was one of three from Everett in the Marine Corps Women's Reserve. Erva Buckley, who grew up in Lowell, served in the Navy WAVES. Alice Strand of Edmonds was not in the military, but she did serve overseas as a Red Cross secretary. Even for the majority of women who stayed in their traditional homemaker roles there was change and additional responsibility. Many served in volunteer capacities, while others performed such home-based tasks as the preparation of surgical dressings for wounded servicemen.

In short, the war years were a time of patriotic zeal. In early 1942 *Snohomish County Tribune* Editor Tom Dobbs observed, "Snohomish now has approximately 240 men in the fighting forces; the local training school for aircraft workers had graduated 470 men of which 100 were from the Snohomish area and 350 citizens were involved in civilian defense. That's about 700 doing their bit to help the nation—pretty good for a town of 2,800." As involvement increased, Dobbs continued to point with pride to the local contributions. Sentiments similar to his were being expressed by every region of the county. For everyone—from small children to the elderly—the mission was clear: Win the War. While virtually everyone participated in, or at least knew of, defense work, bond campaigns, salvage drives, civil defense, and rationing, also there were other unheralded and unique contributions. Anson Moody, whose yacht was considered the finest in the Everett harbor, made the vessel available without compensation for full time use by the U.S. Coast Guard. Mrs. Carl Hagedorn used her telegraph and telephone experience and fine short-wave receiving radio to gather information about prisoners in Japanese war camps and send that information throughout the nation to families of the prisoners. When the war department put out a call for human blonde hair of soft texture, of the highest quality, untouched by hot irons or chemicals and not less than 14 inches long, nine-year-old Caroline Howland of Snohomish cut her tresses and sent them off. The War Department had discovered that blonde hair of the qualities described was the perfect material for use in certain critical meteorological studies of air currents at the 60,000-foot level. Young Howland received an impressive certificate and money, which she reportedly donated to the Red Cross.

"Jimmy" Kyes (second from right) shown with his father James, mother Elizabeth, and younger brother Montana at Monte Cristo in 1920, captained the destroyer U.S.S. "Leary" when it was torpedoed by U-275 in the North Atlantic on Christmas Eve, 1943. Giving his life jacket to an African American crewman, Jimmy was lost with his ship. Kyes Peak and a U.S. Naval Academy memorial at Monte Cristo bear his name. (Courtesy Enid Nordlund)

Citizens related to the altruistic notion that America was locked in a struggle for national survival, but for most the great motivator was the knowledge that local youth were among those on the battlefields. Almost every county resident knew someone in combat. For many it was a family member—husband, father, son, uncle or cousin. Anxious families and friends waited for the news that filtered in from overseas. Reports came in about harrowing battles and heroes. Major Edward Nollmeyer, later a Snohomish County Superior Court judge, earned the Silver Star as a daring pilot in the famed Flying Tigers of the China Volunteer Flying Corps. Sultan's Private First Class Frank Chimenti, Jr. was awarded the Distinguished Service Cross for his action on the Pacific island of New Georgia. As an infantry runner he took over an automatic rifle from a fallen comrade, attacked with abandon, and saved a machine gun squad from Japanese fire. Later the same day he rescued a wounded officer pinned down by hostile fire. Technical Sergeant Robert B. Good of Marysville distinguished himself as a member of the vaunted "Black Death" Marauder group in Western Europe. Everett native James Kyes, a 1930 graduate of the U.S. Naval Academy, was commander of the destroyer *Leary* when it was sunk by German torpedoes in the Atlantic. Kyes was last seen handing his life preserver to a member of his crew. Some twenty years later, a memorial to Kyes' memory would be unveiled in the old mining mountain town of Monte Cristo where the navy hero had spent much of his early life. The bronze plaque, donated by the U.S. Naval Academy Alumni Association, was placed on a concrete pedestal near a mature subalpine fir which, as a seedling, had been planted in the hotel garden by young Jimmy Kyes.

By 1943 the casualty lists were awesome. The reports rolled in steadily, and no part of Snohomish County was exempt from the news that hometown boys were being lost.

Duane Lewis, Granite Falls; Manuel Surdyk, Snohomish; Robert Barnes, Lake Stevens; Richard Solver, Cedar Valley; Arthur Espe, Arlington; and Danny Hess, Stanwood; were among the fatalities. In addition to those lost in combat, there were the prisoner of war deaths, including Howard Jubb of Hartford and Harold McCann of Everett.

Men from the Everett and Snohomish National Guard units activated in 1940 distinguished themselves in battle and were hard hit by casualties. Scattered throughout the armed service, the Snohomish area Battery C men saw more than a third of its original unit rise to commissioned officer ranks. Harvey Winoski and Leland Wallace of Snohomish and John Hedlund of Monroe were among the guardsmen who never returned. For the soldiers of the 161st Regiment fighting in the Pacific, losses were high, and awards for gallantry in action often posthumous. Everett High School buddies Dave Ritchie, Bob O'Brien, Dave Oswald and Duane Pepple were among those who lost their lives in battle and were honored for bravery. A June 1, 1944 front page *Herald* photograph showed a "Camp Ritchie" sign. After Ritchie's death it had been erected at a South Pacific bivouac by men who had served with him. After O'Brien's death, a battle hill on an island was named for him. This quartet was joined by many others who made the supreme sacrifice.

On the northwest corner of the Snohomish County courthouse grounds the war memorial was dedicated on August 28, 1943 with over 60 names. Within months the number had grown to more than 160. A report from the Washington State Department of Veterans' Affairs identifies the final number of county war dead as 273. (Courtesy Everett Public Library)

For families, nothing was more devastating than the arrival of a telegram reporting their loved one had been killed. There also was the dreaded "missing in action" notice, which too often only postponed the dreaded news. Occasionally, however, there were exceptions. On May 12, 1942 Mr. and Mrs. Rolf Galde of rural Arlington received a Western Union telegram stating that their son Burton Galde was missing after his ship the *Canopus* had been scuttled in Manila Bay. The telegram related "no report of injury or death" and that Burton "may be a prisoner of war." Confirmation of his status did not come until August of 1943 when another telegram from the Navy informed the Galdes that Burton indeed was a war prisoner. Later the parents received postcards from their son, and at war's end he was liberated from Japanese custody. He returned home in late September of 1945 after sending a letter dated September 17 from Guam in which he said he expected to fly to the U.S. four days later. Sadly, Mr. Galde had died before his son's return. A couple of months later Burton received a letter from President Harry S. Truman welcoming him home and thanking him for his service in combat and his steadfastness while a prisoner of war. Galde stayed in the Navy until his retirement at the rank of Chief Boatswain's Mate in 1959. He died on October 30, 1995. In the 1990s his crisp, white dress uniform, along with an explanation of all his World War II experiences became a featured display in Arlington's Stillaguamish Valley Pioneer Museum.

The county honored its fallen servicemen with the erection of a war memorial on the courthouse lawn. In the August 28, 1943 ceremony, the Paine Field band performed, and Representative Henry M. Jackson was the featured speaker. The plaque on the memorial already included the names of more than sixty men. When servicemen began returning from overseas, they were welcomed by proud and appreciative communities. A huge throng gathered at the corner of Hewitt and Colby in downtown Everett on June 8, 1944 to greet Frank Batterson. Sergeant Batterson had flown in early combat missions over Germany and then spent time in a prisoner of war camp after his Flying Fortress was shot down. He was the county's first repatriated war hero, and his arrival was cause for celebration by a local citizenry which all too often had occasion to mourn.

In a time when almost all news centered around the war effort, the county was rocked by a non-war episode that received national press. At noon on Thursday, January 27, 1944 nearly all the students in East Stanwood's Lincoln High School walked out in protest of what they and some parents called rigid discipline and a too stringent grading system. Hardly anyone appeared for classes the next day, and school was suspended until Monday. Student strikes were virtually unheard of, especially during this time when obedience was viewed as a hallmark of patriotism. Now bucolic, traditional East Stanwood had one. Marathon weekend meetings between school authorities and parents finally eased the situation, and students began to trickle into school on Monday. By Wednesday, enrollment was back to normal. The strike had gotten the attention of the lower Stillaguamish Valley communities and probably was a factor in the ultimate unification of the Stanwood, East Stanwood and Warm Beach school districts. East Stanwood Superintendent Alfred Tunem resigned, and in Stanwood a new superintendent, George Moore, was brought in with an understanding between the two boards that he would serve as head of a unified school district in a coming consolidation election.

D-Day came to Normandy in June 1944, and then the push across France to Germany began as the slow offensive in Italy continued into another year. In the Pacific, Allied forces were island hopping the way to Japan. These bloody assaults also brought a major increase in casualties, as the nation's armies now were fully involved against Germany, while the Soviet Union's forces pushed enemy forces into Central Europe. In the Pacific the battles were even more vicious, with Japanese troops trained to die rather than surrender.

As the final months of the war approached, a remarkable story emerged about an Everett sailor named Joe "Eddie" McCann. In December 1941, 13-year-old McCann was a student at Everett's North Junior High School. After Pearl Harbor he was among the first to volunteer for duty as an air observer, but his real goal was to get into the Navy. He ran away to Canada thinking it would be possible to enlist in the Canadian Navy. When that failed he headed to Seattle. After more than fifty years, retired and living in Everett, McCann related the story: "I was living in Seattle when I found a pair of welders' gloves. I sold them for five dollars. Then I found a derelict and told him I would give him five dollars if he would sign this paper that he was my dad and I was 17 years old. He signed, and I got in the Navy." So, McCann became, at age 13, the youngest county resident to enter the military. By age 14 he was in charge of an LCVP (landing craft) and was trans-

The U.S.O.
Helping Service Men and Women

The United Service Organizations operated a busy center for armed forces personnel at 2816 Wetmore Avenue in Everett. Its many activities were designed to provide a wholesome "home away from home" environment. Many in the military were single and far from their families for the first time. Holiday dances and parties, local and traveling entertainers, and local residents such as the Camp Fire Girls all helped maintain morale. In Arlington The Robertson Building at the corner of Fourth and Olympic became the service men's club, not qualifying for the U.S.O. due to fewer than 2,000 personnel stationed at the Arlington air field.   (Courtesy Everett Public Library)

289

porting men from a larger vessel to the beach in battles at Tunis, North Africa, Sicily, and Salerno, Italy. He saved lives in a tragic Normandy landing practice known as Exercise Tiger. German torpedo boats slipped in, sinking allied vessels and killing more than 700 servicemen. The episode, which was shrouded in secrecy for nearly four decades after the war, may have claimed more lives had it not been for heroes such as McCann braving the flames on the oil slickened water to fish out survivors. McCann piloted a leading landing craft to Omaha Beach on D-Day. By the time Navy officials caught up with him, the war was almost over, and 16-year-old McCann still wasn't old enough to be in the Navy. They let him stay, and he was training for the invasion of Japan when the war ended. Modest about his contributions, McCann later maintained, "I never felt like a hero." The record speaks otherwise.

As the war reached its waning months, the homefront strain was showing in various ways. Everett Rotary historian E.B. Wight expressed outrage toward the civilian population. "We Americans, here at home, have been spared the horrors of war," he wrote. "Vacation, recreation, gratification fill our days. Borrowing from the future, we are growing corpulent upon war's spoils." Mrs. J.A. Falconer, a member of the Everett Woman's Book Club lamented the tragedy of war, "Why do not the women of the world stop it? Of course now that we have it I believe it is necessary to carry it through and sacrifice for it, but of all things—war seems so senseless as well as wicked. Will the human family ever learn to cooperate instead of fight each other?" A few months after Mrs. Falconer's comment the county's only World War II female military fatality occurred. Margaret Billings of Lowell was an Army nurse on the hospital ship *Comfort* when Japanese *kamikaze* suicide planes attacked it. She died at her post in surgery when the ship was hit.

The trauma of war may have been showing on the homefront, but the basic patriotic pride was undiminished. A crowd estimated at nearly 27,000 swarmed into Paine Field on Sunday, April 8, 1945 to view Boeing's B-29 bomber and to watch Everett's Bud Johnson receive a Silver Star for gallantry in action. The event marked the first time since the Army take over that the field had been opened to unrestricted visiting. There was speculation this was the largest group of people ever assembled in the county. The huge B-29 symbolized the sense of victory that was in the air. Known as the Superfortress, the aircraft was bigger and better in every way than its B-17 predecessor. Within a few months the B-29 would deliver the final, telling blows for the Allies.

As those bombers flew from their bases toward the Japanese home islands they encountered a previously unknown natural phenomenon, the jet stream. This strong river of westerly flowing air which brings our weather fronts in from the Pacific Ocean forced the big planes to buck its headwinds as they flew at high altitudes. On the receiving end of their bomb loads meanwhile, the Japanese Imperial Army had perfected inexpensive 33' tall by 100' in circumference helium balloons which could be launched from the home islands to catch the jet stream and carry incendiary bombs to North America. Perhaps 9,000 in all were sent aloft from November 3, 1944 through April 1945. Sped along by powerful winter winds out of Siberia, the bombs were devised to retaliate for American attacks which had begun with the Doolittle raid by American medium bombers in 1942, as well as to raise civilian morale and tie up American and Canadian resources in fighting their effects. The bombs turned out to be major disappointments for the Japanese. Northwestern forests would not burn during the wet winter months when most of the balloons were airborne, but Japanese intelligence hoped to gain sufficient information from the effort to generate a much more deadly campaign for the coming summer and early autumn.

Bombers were diverted to attack the balloon infrastructure and launching sites as Allied authorities immediately clamped a total news blackout on their existence to deny the Japanese any way of evaluating their effectiveness. People were warned to be on the lookout for odd, unknown devices they might find, while civil defense and military units were trained on how to defuse the payload, which had a small explosive as well as the incendiaries. On March 13, 1945 one of the balloons landed near Paine Field. Recovered were the damaged envelope, ballast gear which controlled its flying height, and a five kilogram incendiary bomb. This was the only recorded enemy attack on the county. Twenty eight balloons came down in the state, over 300 in North America, with most lost over water and probably a number never found. Three days before the Paine Field incident the Japanese inadvertently shut down the top secret Hanford Engineering Works when near Toppenish a balloon tangled in the main transmission power lines from Bonneville Dam, causing the project to shut down automatically. It took three days to restart the piles creating plutonium for one version of the atomic bomb.

President Roosevelt died on April 12, 1945. This sad news soon was tempered by the May 7 announcement of Germany's unconditional surrender. Local celebrations were subdued. A grim citizenry, familiar with the "fight to the death" Japanese ethic, was warned the conquest of Japan could take three more years at the cost of a million or more Allied lives. All that changed when a single B-29 dropped an atomic bomb on the Japanese city of Hiroshima on August 6, followed two days later by a declaration of war on Japan by the Union of Soviet Socialist Republics, which immediately invaded Japanese-held Manchuria. On August 9 an atomic bomb built at Hanford, Washington fell on Nagasaki, Japan causing undreamed destruction and loss of life. On Tuesday August 14 the Japanese announced their intention to surrender. Word was relayed to lookout Trudy Woll on Mt. Pilchuck, and she entered into her logbook in huge letters: "4:12 p.m. War is Over!"

Snohomish County, with the rest of America, was exuberant. In Edmonds the Methodist Church bell began ringing. Soon the city fire siren, mill and ferry whistles, and automobile horns joined in. Firecrackers popped, and guns were fired. The telephone service was overwhelmed with calls. In Everett the shipyard and mill whistles shrieked incessantly. A delirious crowd spilled into Hewitt and Colby under a shower of paper. *The Everett Daily Herald* billed it "the greatest demonstration ever to be staged in this city." A group of the Everett shipyard "tarbabies" crawled out of a vessel's interior to announce that they had given their all—now they were through. A throng gathered at the USO Club in the evening. Snohomish and other county towns had similar celebrations, although the liquor stores and taverns were closed early to curtail revelers' excesses. Most county retail stores shut down and remained closed for the next two days. Gas rationing ended the morning of August 15. Many motorists, although they weren't going anywhere, rolled into stations just so they could say, "Fill 'er up."

The war was over, but the price of victory was horrendous. More than 250 Snohomish County armed service members had lost their lives. No one knows the exact number wounded, disabled, or those suffering from the mental trauma of what they had experienced, nor of the civilian casualties inflicted by the conflict. Among the American citizenry there were those who expected a return to a simpler life they called normalcy.

That wouldn't happen. The war had changed the nation and Snohomish County dramatically and irrevocably.

One of the best kept secrets of the war was the Japanese use of balloon bombs to experiment with kindling forest fires, divert manpower and resources into combatting the threat, and sow panic among the civilian population of North America. Artist Bernie Webber has caught the feel of Lockheed P-38 vs. the envelope carrying its load of incendiary and high explosive bombs. (Original painting for this book by Bernie Webber)

1945 –1965

During World War II Snohomish County as with all of America and most of the world, devoted its energy and economy to winning the war. That continued until early August 1945, when the Japanese government surrendered without the necessity of an invasion of its home islands. The thrust of over a half-decade of war and war preparation suddenly was reversed. As the troops came home, the country dismantled its military machinery and began converting to a world at peace. Yet, it also was not a return to the years of depression, as some feared. Pent-up demand for civilian goods (caused by money earned, but little to buy), an economy unaffected by war on its shores, and the emergence of the country as a victorious world leader all helped ensure a period of growth and prosperity not seen since the years following the 1898 Klondike Gold Rush.

In Snohomish County as elsewhere military bases, camps, and stations disappeared. The Naval Air Station at Arlington was transferred to the town and became the Arlington Municipal Airport. Paine Field reverted to the county. The naval facilities on the Everett waterfront were closed. The army radio stations in Everett reverted to the City Parks and Recreation Department. The station located between Edmonds and Alderwood Manor, in what was to become the heart of Lynnwood, continued to operate for a time, but was soon abandoned to deer and coyotes. Decades later, the station was devoted to public facilities, including the then newly-created Edmonds Community College campus. Throughout the county "temporary" structures constructed by the military during the war were converted to businesses, homes, and schools, including portable classrooms at Everett Junior College on Oakes Avenue near Clark Park. Just as the military bases, camps, and stations

Alaska Airlines Comes to Paine Field

Alaska Airlines operated from the field following the war and its return to civilian status, ending the Army Air Force's presence. These are the company's control tower and hangar in May 1948. (Willard Flying Service photograph, courtesy Everett Public Library)

Inside the hanger ground crewmen tend to maintenance and repair. In the foreground are biplanes which were used with the EJC training program that autumn. (Willard Flying Service photograph, courtesy Everett Public Library)

Radio communications utilized the bulky vacuum tube technology of the time, keeping contact between aircraft and ground control. (Willard Flying Service photograph, courtesy Everett Public Library)

Above: With simple passenger boarding ramps and open access around the field, air service was far simpler than soon would be the case when the company moved to larger facilities at Seattle-Tacoma International Airport and bore no resemblance to conditions after the September 11, 2001 anti-terrorist restrictions were imposed. (Willard Flying Service photograph, courtesy Everett Public Library)

The simple operations building was war surplus, but it was adequate at the time for the developing airline. (Willard Flying Service photograph, courtesy Everett Public Library)

Business operations also occupied the spartan former military facilities, creating a small, closely knit company unit. (Willard Flying Service photograph, courtesy Everett Public Library)

294

began to disappear, many of the people who had moved to the county as part of the war effort also left to go home. Others who had left to work or to fight, returned.

Snohomish County soon settled down to its prewar experience of harvesting trees and processing logs— but only for a little while. There were some 12 million young men and women in the United States armed forces when the war ended; about seven million of them overseas. The vast majority left the service, as many as 1.5 million a month, and headed to a homeland where there had been little beyond subsistence production

With the strong growth in civil aviation following the war, Everett Junior College taught a program at Paine Field to train students for careers in that field. (Willard Flying Service photograph, courtesy Everett Public Library)

for civilians for four years. Some of the veterans went to school on their G.I. Bill benefits. Others just looked for jobs or took a little time to settle down after their service. Soon, however, nearly all began to look for homes of their own in a country where there was very little housing available and where material for a time was still so scarce that it was difficult for the economy to provide the new homes that were needed. The veterans made do with whatever shelter they could obtain in basements, attics, garages, or wherever else there was a roof. Those who did not have families soon created them, making the demand for suitable housing that much more pressing.

As the market grew and materials became available, a major construction spree began throughout the United States. In western Washington, its early phase occurred in Seattle and in King County, but a scarcity of vacant land plus strict (for that time) permit requirements made building there more difficult and more expensive than the young veterans could afford. Contractors looked for more hospitable places. They found one just north of the border in Snohomish County. That started a growth period which continued with few interruptions into the next century.

Beginning in the extreme southwest, nearest the Seattle job market, local population growth eventually radiated out to all parts of the county. During the first years of the twentieth century the number of county residents had risen from 23,950 in 1900 to 88,754 in 1940, a nearly 400 percent in-

Over the years enlargements and remodeling have increased the capacity of the Mukilteo ferry terminal, but traffic on the Whidbey Island route has increased faster, making a major impact on the community. (Courtesy Everett Public Library)

SNOHOMISH COUNTY and VICINITY SOUTH

JUNE 1946

SCALE: 1" = 2 MILES.

Classroom throughout the county were filled to overflowing with the "baby boom" following the war and increased in-migration of people looking for jobs in the expanding economy. These are Granite Falls Elementary School students in 1949. (Courtesy Everett Public Library)

crease. That was greatest during the first decade, then virtually flat during the Depression era. Then wartime job opportunities and peacetime family growth led a surge to 111,580 by 1950. The pace continued to increase during the next two decades, reaching 172,199 in 1960 and 265,236 in 1970. Jokes circulated that there was no one left in the Dakotas: they had all left the farm and come west.

This growth strained the ability of existing governments to serve their communities, especially in the southwestern part of the county where the influx started. One of the early manifestations occurred in 1945 when the volunteer fire department at Seattle Heights incorporated as the first county fire district, officially Snohomish County Fire Protection District No. 1. The volunteers had operated out of Carl Eisen's garage and service station at the intersection of U.S. 99 and 212 Street S.W. since they bought a 1925 Reo Speedwagon fire truck from Edmonds in 1937. State law provided for establishing special-use districts in places which had grown so much that rural services no longer were sufficient, but not yet enough to support those of a city. The volunteer fire department had only the resources it could scrape up with community events and donations. Now as an official fire district the fire fighters would be entitled to a small portion of the property tax, as well as the right to obtain war surplus materials and equipment from the government.

The chief of the volunteers was Clarence Crary, who operated a well drilling service in Seattle Heights. Eisen was the assistant chief. He had arrived as a teenager when his family operated a resort on Halls Lake. The two of them worked with the volunteers, members of the Seattle Heights Community Club, and others to organize the district, which continue to serve the community into the twenty-first century.

Everett, which began the twentieth century with 7,838 residents in 1900, tripled in size to 24,814 by 1910. It mirrored the county pattern when the timber industry reached a plateau in the 1920s and depression followed. Adding only 6,000 from 1920 to 1940, it grew by another 3,000 during the 1940s and 6,000 the following decade. In the northern section of the county, Arlington had 1,476 people in 1910 (the first census after the city incorporated), but still only 2,261 by 1970.

However, in the far southwestern corner, Edmonds (then the county's only incorporated city south of Everett) grew from 474 in 1900 to 1,288 in 1940, then mushroomed to 23,989 in 1970, even as the four new neighboring cities of Mountlake Terrace, Lynnwood, Woodway, and Brier were incorporated and the adjacent non-incorporated county areas also heavily expanded their populations. The Puget Sound region was becoming a metropolitan "Pugetopolis"—bedroom suburban communities focused on the Seattle urban core for employment, information, and entertainment and made possible by both the sharply rising standard of living and the development of the American automobile culture.

The early growth in what became known informally as "South County" was primarily in Edmonds School District 15. In 1940 there were four schools in the district with a combined enrollment in 1941 of 1,213. By 1953 it had more than quadrupled to 5,032. The total population of the district rose to 10,000 in the census of 1950.

The school district's economic and social core was Edmonds. That community traced its origins to the logging and milling of the original old growth forest covering the lowlands. Throughout the early years the city was supported by lumber and shingle mills that lined the waterfront. At the high point there were a dozen or more, mostly steam operated with boilers, which spewed thick smoke out of their tall stacks. Fires, storms, and economics gradually forced their closure, and on June 1, 1951 the last of the originals, the Quality Shingle Company, shut down. In August of that year the Skyline Lumber Company built an all-electric mill, but it failed soon after starting, and Edmonds became basically a bedroom community for people who worked elsewhere.

Inland at Alderwood Manor, the few residents who had survived the collapse of the small farm and poultry plan of the Puget Mill Company and then the abandonment of the interurban railway in 1939 saw the gradual movement of the commercial center of the area westward toward U.S. 99, especially to its intersection with 196th Street S.W.

One day in 1944 Ed McCollum, a sales manager for the Armour Company, went home to the house in Richmond Highlands, south of Edmonds, where he lived with his wife Dorothy and preschool aged son David. He looked a little strange, and Dorothy asked him if he had one of his periodic headaches. "Never felt better in my life," Ed replied. "I quit my job. We're going into business."

Business, Dorothy learned, was groceries in an unimposing building on the northwest corner of 196th Street S.W. and the highway. They sold their home in Richmond Highlands to buy stock for the store. As it turned out, the apartment (in a converted Alderwood Manor chicken coop) where they had expected to live had already been rented to someone else. The wartime housing shortage was underway and no place else was available, so at first the little family moved into the back room of the store. There was water, but toilets and sewers were under wartime rationing, and they could not get the necessary permits to install them. They used the toilet in a nearby gas station and bathed wherever they could. Many of their meals were in Mrs. McKinney's little restaurant across the street. It was not an auspicious beginning, but it was a major step in what eventually became the city of Lynnwood. However, Mountlake Terrace formed first.

Albert LaPierre was an imaginative developer and organizer; Jack Peterson was an innovative builder. Neither seemed to know or care much about the other's specialty, but together they made a formidable team as Peterson-LaPierre, Inc. They had built some small developments together in north King County and prospered, but as King County land and building permits became more expensive they began looking northward. In 1949 they purchased an abandoned airport just across the Snohomish County line between 60th and 61st Street S.W. When they inspected the property, they noticed that the flat runway seemed like a terrace and that they could see both Lake Washington and Mount Rainier from some parts of the property. They named it Mountlake Terrace and started building homes designed for the World War II veterans who were becoming more and more desperate for a place to live and raise their new families. The houses were simple and, even by the standards of those days, tiny. Consisting of only two bedrooms, a living room, a kitchen, and a bath, they measured 20 by 30 feet and had concrete floors and concrete-block exteriors. An oil stove in the living room heated the entire house. Yet, they were warm and dry and much better than the garages and basements where so many of the veterans had lived while they hunted for something better. The houses sold for $4,999 and, as a bonus, for a small extra amount on the 30-year mortgage the kitchen could be supplied with an automatic washing machine, a dryer, and a refrigerator.

Peterson established what amounted almost to a ground level assembly line. Individual crews of specialists prepared the land, built the foundation, and put in the plumbing, which was imbedded in the concrete floor. Bricklayers put up the exterior walls, carpenters built the interior walls and roof, and so on. Painting and landscaping were left for the purchasers to do themselves. The system produced an inexpensive but solid structure that was completed in a few weeks. They sold even faster than they were built, as Peterson-LaPierre expanded to the north, the east and later the west, building houses as fast as they could obtain the land and selling them before they were built to new young buyers. With a roaring economy and growing families the demand in a few years grew for larger, more attractive housing, and Peterson-LaPierre met that with somewhat larger structures and more adornment. Yet their product was still less expensive than others, and their sales kept pace. So many people moved in so quickly that the company built an L-shaped shopping complex south of the King County line. It was quickly filled with a supermarket, drug store, hardware store operated by Gilbert and Glee Geiser, and barber shop operated by George Wickman and Coy Wilson. Later the company built another, larger shopping center in the vicinity of 56th Avenue W. and 232nd Street S.W.

By 1954 the little houses had filled much of the land between 244th Street S.W and 216th Street S.W. The east and west boundaries extended as far as 48th Avenue W. and 68th Avenue W. County officials established the population at 5,104. The average age of adults was 26, according to Peterson-LaPierre sales records. Nearly all the families included children, and most of the children in the early days were of preschool age.

By then the community had vastly overtaxed the infrastructure that had been designed to support a few scattered homes amidst thick forests of second-growth trees. People who moved in were surprised to learn they would have to wait a year to have a telephone installed. When they did get one, it was a 10-party line shared with nine other families. There were no paved streets and only one block of paved sidewalk. Storm drains were open ditches. When the ditches clogged there was no one to clear them. Water mains were completely inadequate even for cooking and washing, let alone for watering lawns or fighting fires. Each house had only a septic tank in the back yard for sewage. After a time, some of the tanks failed, and raw sewage flowed to the surface. Police protection was provided by the sheriff's office 15 miles away in Everett. Often the sheriff had only one or two cars on the road to patrol the entire county. Sheriff Tom Warnock organized and trained a volunteer Mountlake Terrace Sheriff's Patrol of local residents, with Bob Fox elected captain. The group raised money to buy an ancient panel truck, which they rebuilt for police service. Peterson-LaPierre Co. donated $600 to buy a police radio to communicate with the sheriff's dispatcher in Everett. They patrolled diligently,

Mountlake Terrace is Formed

The Peterson-LaPierre company's budget homes division stressed its low prices, attracting young World War II veterans eager to provide a place of their own for their new families. (Courtesy Pat McMahan)

This 1949 aerial photograph shows the first cleared area and rows of homes which were constructed in Mountlake Terrace. (Courtesy Seattle Post-Intelligencer)

Jack Peterson, the building half of Peterson-LaPierre, developed a system based on a factory production line to erect their homes quickly and inexpensively. In the early days the homes sold faster than they could be finished, as the veterans snapped them up. (Courtesy Patrick McMahan)

A teen canteen soon was organized to provide recreation for the community's young people. (H. Scott Wilson photograph, courtesy Patrick McMahon)

Right: Among the first actions after incorporation was the formation of a fire department, with Patrick McMahon as chief, and a police department, with Robert Shriber as its chief. Both agencies worked extensively with youngsters in the community. (Courtesy Patrick McMahon)

One of the tangible pieces of evidence that Mountlake Terrace had become its own city was the creation of its first post office. Prior to that, mail had come through Edmonds. (Courtesy Patrick McMahon)

but the volunteers all had daytime jobs, making them available only in the evening.

To assist with fire protection, Peterson-LaPierre built a fire station for Fire District One in Mountlake Terrace. As with the sheriff's patrol, its volunteers often were not available during the daytime. The captain was Patrick McMahan, a professional fire fighter in Seattle who was highly critical of the equipment supplied to the station, the lack of a reliable water supply, and of organizational problems such as each of the four stations in the district having individual telephone numbers. This required residents to know in advance which station would respond to their homes and what to do if that station were out of service, making it necessary to call a secondary one.

By 1953 it was obvious to many Mountlake Terrace residents that it was time to think about incorporating as a city, but nothing was done until one summer night shortly before the Mountlake Terrace Sheriff's Patrol was formed when someone attempted to break into the home of McMahan while he was on duty in a Seattle fire station. Whoever it was threw a rock through a window but apparently was frightened off when he realized McMahan's wife Beverly was home. The sheriff's office was called but did not respond until 4 P.M. the next day. The deputy explained that there was only one car available for patrol the previous night, and they were responding to calls in the order they were received. Forty-three years later, McMahan remembered that he quickly decided the community needed a better system.

In July 1953 he attended a meeting of the Edmonds city council to ask if they were interested in annexing Mountlake Terrace. He quoted Mayor Paul McKibbon as saying, "Son, you are five miles away, and we will never go beyond Ninth Avenue." As McMahan left the meeting, one of the council members followed him and introduced himself as Warren Bishop, a member of the University of Washington Governmental Affairs Department. He suggested McMahan contact the department for help in conducting a study of ways to solve Mountlake Terrace's problems.

McMahan contacted the department, and with their help and the guidance of Bishop he organized what came to be called the Mountlake Terrace Study Committee. He and another resident, Fred Smethurst, were named cochairmen. Levy Johnston, a local attorney, volunteered to provide the legal work, later joined by Bill Hennessey, another local attorney. For several months the group gathered information from the university, governmental agencies and other sources. With the facts in hand they obtained the required signatures on a petition asking the county commissioners to set a date for an election on incorporation as a third class city with the council-manager form of government. The commissioners approved the petition and scheduled the election for November 23, 1954.

A turbulent campaign followed. Study group members and their supporters favored forming a city. Opponents hired Oliver Neibel, a local attorney, to speak against the proposal. The ballot would have two issues, the first to decide the question of annexation, the second to name the five residents who would serve on the first city council if the incorporation were approved. Nineteen people filed for election. After the filing period ended Beverly McMahan, the wife of the fire chief, announced she would be a write-in candidate. Officials of the county, Fire District One, and the Alderwood Water District noted that incorporation could fragment services. They tended to oppose the incorporation. None lived in the proposed area, so they were unable to take a personal part in the campaign, but the fire district commissioners fired Pat McMahan from his volunteer job as captain of the Mountlake Terrace fire station on the grounds that his promotion of a city was not in the best interests of the district. Public reaction caused the commissioners to reinstate him, but many residents shared the officials' concerns. A local weekly newspaper, the *County Line Reporter*, published by Scott Wilson, a member of the study group, covered the issues extensively, as did the Everett *Herald*, which had a news bureau in the community.

The campaign reached a climax the evening of November 16, when about 100 residents attended a meeting in the Mountlake Terrace Elementary School all-purpose room to hear opponents, proponents, and 15 of the 20 candidates speak. The wide ranging discussion covered subjects such as potential street improvements, police and fire protection, reduced fire-insurance rates, sewers, garbage disposal, and the potential for revenues, in addition to the $9.00 per resident to be supplied by the state. On Election Day, exactly 1,000 voters cast ballots. The tally was 517 in favor of incorporation, 483 against. Elected to serve on the first council were Gilbert Geiser, Lester Steele, Harley McFarland, Scott Wilson, and Patricia Neibel. The average age of the council members was 32. Neibel, the wife of opposition leader Oliver Neibel, had filed for election saying that people should vote against incorporation, but if they voted for it they should at least see that someone who questioned the need for a city was on the governing council. She received the fourth highest number of votes. The next day the new council elected Geiser as the first mayor under the new city's council-manager form of government. Within a few weeks they appointed Evan Peterson the first city manager. For a week or so, Peterson told people that City Hall was the pile of papers in the back seat of his car, but he soon rented an empty two-bedroom house, installed a little furniture, and transferred the papers to this new city hall. He appointed Lucille Foard as city clerk and Bob Schriber as police chief. Bill Hennessey became the city attorney and Levy Johnston judge of the municipal court.

One of the reasons Mountlake Terrace developed first and fastest was that Peterson-LaPierre were among the leaders in seeing the need for quick, inexpensive housing for the influx of World War II veterans. Additionally, their development was concentrated and fast selling, which made it possible to advertise and promote on a large scale, bringing an ever larger number of residents. It was just that success that brought on the need to incorporate as a city to alleviate the problems associated with a high concentration of people.

At the same time, new housing was going up throughout much of the area roughly delineated by the boundaries of School District No. 15. That development was by individual builders who erected one or a few houses at a time on a more scattered and leisurely pace than the highly concentrated construction at Mountlake Terrace. Nevertheless, throughout the school district the population gradually became significantly concentrated in isolated places.

The first to feel the pressure was Lynnwood, partly because U.S. 99 had moved the transportation center (and thus business and population) from Alderwood Manor, and partly because Ed McCollum recognized that potential and took advantage of it.

The little grocery store in the small, weathered building on the northwest corner of 196th Street S.W. and U.S. 99 did well almost from the day Ed and Dorothy opened it in 1944. They were able to buy a house on 196th Street S.W. and were about to move in, but Ed needed a butcher to help in the store. After a lengthy search, they found one in Everett, but in those days of wartime rationing the butcher was not eligible for enough gasoline to commute between Lynnwood and Everett, so they rented the house to him. The McCollums moved into a cabin on Norma Beach. The cabin had no sewer or water. They carried drinking water two blocks in a bucket and used rainwater to wash.

At the intersection of U.S. Highway 99 (top) and 196th Street (right), the Lynnwood Square was the crossroads of the community. Featured businesses were Everybody's at upper right, Grocery Boys' Thriftway, and at lower right, Conklin Appliance. (Courtesy Larry O'Donnell)

The store continued to prosper, and shortly the McCollums were able to pay $9,000 for the vacant property diagonally across on the southeast corner of 196th and the highway. A Seattle real estate man told them they were crazy and would "lose their shirt." Undaunted, in 1949 they joined with McCollum's brother-in-law, Russell Starr, to build a new store called Ed's Market on the property. By the standards of the following century the operation was small, but for that time and place it was full-sized, large enough for a well-rounded stock and to allow the McCollums to buy in bulk lots and sell at low prices. Much to the chagrin of other merchants, customers came from many parts of the surrounding area. As with its predecessor, the new store prospered, and McCollum and Starr built the Lynnwood Shopping Center behind it, which quickly filled with thriving new shops.

South county infrastructure was overwhelmed by growth and demand, as this silt buried fire hydrant graphically illustrated. With photographs such as these in hand, concerned residents demanded better roads and utilities. (Courtesy Patrick McMahon collection)

By 1955 the center had expanded into two blocks on eight acres. That attracted more people and more business to the area. McCollum worked with United States Senator Henry M. Jackson to obtain a small post office for a corner of his market. He was the acting postmaster until Howard Sievers, a long time Lynnwood resident, was appointed the first permanent postmaster of Lynnwood. That made "Lynnwood" the official name of the community, a name that had started as a development plat created by Seattle realtor Karl O'Beirn. It was a blend of his wife's name Lynn and "wood" from both Alderwood Manor to the east and Maplewood to the west. Clarence Fulton picked it up when he started a lumber yard on the plat east of U.S. 99 and called it Lynnwood Lumber, while the Lynnwood Cabinet Shop was opened the following year on the west side. Several more businesses adopted the name. Then in 1946 a group of businessmen formed the Lynnwood Commercial Club, erecting signs bearing the name at the four major entrances to the community and helping publicize it. Within a few years Lynnwood had established itself as the business center for much of southwest Snohomish County, developing into a viable neighborhood with the additional efforts of the Lynnwood Commercial Club. The precise geography of that would change when I-5 was built, but the community itself would retain the position of business center well into the new century.

In the late 1950s McCollum and Starr sold the shopping center to Al Forsgren, who had lived as a child on an Alderwood Manor chicken ranch. In the 1930s he and his older brother N. Richard Forsgren operated a gold mine in Alaska. When that was closed by the wartime economy, he became a lumber dealer in Everett, while his brother became a professional golfer and course designer. Richard Forsgren opened a jewelry store in the shopping center after his brother bought it. He later became a member of the first Lynnwood City Council and a then a county commissioner.

McCollum and Starr also sold their market. The new owners, Arb Thorne and Ted Wilson, changed the name to The Grocery Boys and moved it to new, larger quarters on the south end of the shopping center. McCollum and Starr concentrated on the real estate business, but McCollum joined with Barry O'Conner and Orville Danforth and Danforth's wife Helen to found the Lynnwood *Enterprise* weekly newspaper. The previously existing Lynnwood *Reporter* had been founded in 1949 by S. Al Wilcox and Grant M. Donohue. They sold it in the mid-1950s to Sim Wilson, Jr. who also owned the *Marysville Globe* and *Arlington Times*. Wilson's son, Sim Wilson III, was editor of the Lynnwood *Reporter*. O'Connor and the Danforths were employed by the *Reporter* until they helped found the *Enterprise*. The Grocery Boys placed its advertising in the *Enterprise*. Other businesses followed, and the *Reporter* soon ceased publication.

As more new commerce was attracted to Lynnwood many new structures were built to house it. A major one was the James Village shopping center on the northwest corner of the main intersection at 196th Street S.W. and U.S. 99. It was built in 1959 by Frank James, the son of the man who had rented Ed and Dorothy McCollum the store where they began their business. By then, the 3.5 square miles surrounding the Lynnwood Shopping Center had a population of 6,000 and 250 businesses. It also had many of the same problems that had caused Mountlake Terrace to incorporate five years earlier. Septic tanks were failing, and raw sewage was floating to the surface. The fire district did not have the resources to provide adequate fire service. The Alderwood Water District was extended beyond its capacity. A volunteer South End Sheriff's Patrol had a long and distinguished record of service, but it helped the sheriff's office patrol the entire county and did little to help cope with the law enforcement needs of the highly concentrated population of Lynnwood. As in Mountlake Terrace earlier, it seemed obvious to many residents that the community would have to incorporate if it were to solve its problems.

By 1955 Mountlake Terrace had been an incorporated city for a year, and its success seemed assured. It had effective police and fire protection. There was a rudimentary public works department to maintain streets and clear clogged ditches. A small library was operating. The city was replacing inadequate water mains, some of them wooden, and was working with the Alderwood Water District to improve water supplies. Officials were discussing preliminary plans for installing a sewer system to replace the septic tanks that were becoming less and less satisfactory. Perhaps the most important improvement was the fact that there was a city hall where people could make requests or lodge complaints without going 15 miles to Everett.

That success was a strong argument for supporters of incorporation in Lynnwood. Nevertheless there was a great deal of skepticism. From the beginning Mountlake Terrace had a sense of cohesiveness. It had been created over a few years by a single developer. It had a single name and a feeling of community. Lynnwood, on the other hand, was a conglomeration of communities created over a period of generations. Each had its own history and sense of belonging. People in places such as Cedar Valley, Alderwood Manor, and Seattle Heights thought of Lynnwood as a place to go for shopping. They did not feel it was home.

Nevertheless, in 1955 the Lynnwood Commercial Club created a committee to study incorporation, gathering facts on the community's needs, population, and potential revenues and estimated costs of services and the procedures for incorporating. The committee worked for a year, and then came forward with an ambitious plan calling for creation of a 6.7 square mile city with a population of 10,744 and an annual budget of

$219,000. The city would have a mayor-council form of government. It would contract with the fire district for fire protection, but it would have its own police department and street department. A Lynnwood Incorporation Committee was formed with Richard Fox as chairman. It circulated a petition asking for an election to incorporate a city somewhat smaller than that envisioned by the commercial club. It would have 6.59 square miles and 8,500 population. The committee obtained 600 signatures on

Typical of many split-level houses built during the suburban boom of the late 20th century is this Everett home as it appeared in 2003. (Courtesy David Cameron)

the document and submitted it to the county commissioners, who studied it for a few weeks, then announced that the legal description included some land that already was in Mountlake Terrace. Thus they rejected the petition.

Supporters reorganized, circulated a revised plan, and submitted it in August 1958. The county commissioners called a public hearing. About 20 people attended, some supporting incorporation, some opposing it, and some just asking that their neighborhoods be eliminated. State law said that if the commissioners reduced the size by more than 20 percent the petition would be invalidated. Following the hearing they eliminated Seattle Heights and areas on the north and west ends of the proposed city and called for an election.

Then Loren Wiltfong, a resident of the area, brought a lawsuit asking the courts to reject the proposal. He fought it all the way to the state Supreme Court, which finally declined to act. At the same time the Edmonds city council received a petition for annexation from residents of the area around the new Edmonds High School at 76th Avenue and 212th Street S.W. The council scheduled a hearing. Lynnwood supporters, noting that part of the annexation area was in their proposed Lynnwood city limits, went to court. After a trial, Superior Court Judge Thomas Stiger issued an injunction prohibiting Edmonds from holding its hearing. When an election finally was held on the Lynnwood proposal, voters rejected the incorporation by a vote of 890 to 848.

Loren Wiltfong's reason for opposing the incorporation was simple and straight forward. He said he simply could see no benefit in it. Proponents' reasons were more complex. A major concern was the constant and obvious growth of the area, the problems that brought, and the promise that it would continue far into the future. That promise was expressed succinctly in a study by the four-county Puget Sound Regional Planning Council. The study, issued as Lynnwood was discussing incorporation, indicated the population of Snohomish County would grow from the 1950 figure of 112,000 to 371,000 at the end of the century. Further, the study indicated that the county would see only minor industrial growth, limited to "large-area, small employment" oil refineries and some small increase in the wood and pulp industries. Therefore, the planners said, population expansion would be almost entirely west of the Snohomish River because most residents would commute to Seattle and Tacoma, and traffic congestion would make it unlikely they would locate farther east. The planners could not know that the Boeing Company in a few short years would build a massive new plant in Everett. Nor could they know that huge numbers of high technology plants would follow soon after. Their estimate of the population in 2000 was nearly 100,000 less than the actual number for 1990, and they were wrong about where the newcomers would settle, but even with discounting those errors the population, cultural, and economic changes which loomed over the southwestern region could overwhelm the county's ability to cope, and the incorporation proponents made that case.

It was obvious that change already was flooding the once relatively stable county of forests and mills, farms and small towns. It also was obvious that some residents were responding to that growth. Even as Lynnwood was discussing incorporation, Mountlake Terrace had increased its population by 50 percent since it incorporated five years earlier. The council of that city was opening bids on construction of a city-wide sewer system and discussing with Edmonds a joint "little metro" sewer project. The planning commissions of both cities were preparing to approve large new residential developments, and both cities were acting on petitions for annexation. The county planning commission changed the zoning of a 2.5 square mile area northwest of Lynnwood from rural to single family residential use, and John Porter, the acting superintendent of School District 15, was warning that even though the district had already built several new schools and was planning more, it would be 79 classrooms short in 1961 when the student population was expected to grow to 15,300 from the current 11,500.

Meanwhile up north, Everett also was feeling change. The Hulbert mill, one of the larger of the city's early lumber producers, announced it was about to close down, continuing a process of closures and consolidations of the industry that had been the city's bread and butter since its inception. Yet, at the same time, *The Everett Daily Herald* opened its large new plant at California and Grand avenues to replace the one at the northeast corner of Colby Avenue and Wall Street which had been damaged in a fire in 1956, and Everett officials were working on plans for a dam in the Sultan basin that would bring huge new additions to its water supply and its ability to attract new businesses and

Paine Field was reactivated for the Korean War, with new jet fighter squadrons stationed at the base. When operations were transferred to McChord Air Force Base south of Tacoma, Paine's F-102 aircraft went there as well. (Courtesy Bernie Webber)

307

new residents to Everett and to much of the rest of the county.

However, Lynnwood, despite its dense population, could use only the meager resources of the county and the special-use governments such as the water and sewer districts to meet its problems. The defeat of its first incorporation election surely disheartened the supporters. Nevertheless, they reorganized and set out to hold, and win, a second election. They started by consulting University of Washington experts who helped draw new boundaries, excluding areas where "no" votes had been heavy.

Then came the legwork of circulating the petition for another election and of campaigning for enough "yes" votes to win. Nearly 40 years later, Dr. J. Richard Roos, a dentist who had moved to the county in the late 1950s, remembered spending many hours knocking on people's doors to spread the incorporation word. "The incorporation committee produced a little pamphlet pointing out the community's problems and the difficulty of solving them without a city," Roos recalled. "And we set out to leave one at every door." The supporters divided the proposed city into segments that were assigned to specific people. The newly arrived dentist worked with Dean Echelbarger, a part owner of a family heating oil business that had grown up on an Alderwood Manor chicken ranch. They would go out after work trudging through the rainy night leaving pamphlets at people's houses. "We were pretty determined," Roos said.

The campaign received an unintended boost from developers who bought up structures in the right-of-way of the proposed new I-5. They moved many of them to new locations in Lynnwood, even though some of them were ramshackle and neglected. The county had no regulations governing this, and neighbors were outraged.

Incorporation supporters approached J. Gaylord Riach, a recently arrived attorney, for free legal advice. He agreed to help, but advised that it would make more sense to annex to the existing city of Edmonds rather than to try to organize a new city and at the same time solve its growth problems. Edmonds, however, showed no interest in going east of 76th Street S.W., because that was the brow of a ridge, and any sewer system beyond that would depend on an expensive pumping system rather than gravity to take sewage to Puget Sound. Eventually the petitions were signed and delivered to the county commissioners, who set April 14, 1959 as the election date. That was the beginning of the second phase of the campaign, persuading the voters to approve the incorporation. The supporters were not always certain of what kind of reception they would receive. Dr. Roos remembered one public meeting sponsored by the Lynnwood Chamber of Commerce. "They appointed me to be the master of ceremonies; I think because I had been in the area the shortest time and was the least able to say no. The meeting was in a bowling alley, and I didn't know what to expect. But it went very smoothly. People asked questions, said what they thought, and everybody went home. There weren't any fireworks."

The election carried, 490 to 208, establishing a city of three square miles and a population of 6,000. Jack Bennett, owner of a real estate office and a former Alderwood Manor chicken rancher and tavern owner, was elected the first mayor by a vote of 442 to the 156 received by his opponent, Ralson Steproe. Members of the new city council were N. Richard Forsgren, Dean Guth, William Chadwick, Erwin Buxton, Harry Moore, Edward Martin, and Harry Morrison. Russ Haggard was elected city clerk, Edith Smith was to be the part-time treasurer, and J. Gaylord Riach was the city attorney.

Beginnings of the new city government were only slightly less humble than Mountlake Terrace's pile of papers in the back seat of Evan Petersen's car. In Lynnwood the pile sat on a corner of a desk in the new mayor's real estate office—where it quickly became obvious that the desk was no more satisfactory than the car seat. Mayor Bennett moved as quickly as city manager Peterson had in finding a new home for the city. He called the first meeting of the city council for April 20, 1959, six days after the election. The first item on the minutes of that meeting is a report by the mayor that the use of his office was inconvenient. The council approved a motion for $100 per month to rent space Bennett had arranged in a small professional office building at 197th Street S.W. and Scriber Lake Road. Three days later the county commissioners approved the city charter. On the following day, Mayor Bennett and city council member Forsgren drove to Governor Albert Rosellini's office in Olympia, where the governor presented them with a certificate of corporation. Bennett announced that Ken Killien, an incorporation supporter and manager of the Lynnwood branch of the Everett First National Bank, had agreed to accept $10,000 worth of the city's interest-bearing warrants. That gave the city its first bank account.

On May 9 some 300 people attended an "Inaugural Ball" in the Lynnwood Junior High School, and, by the end of September, the new city had adopted its first zoning code and annexed two small areas that had been excluded from the original incorporation. It also had adopted its first ordinances, contracted for fire protection from Fire District One, created police and street departments, appointed Joe Swontkoski municipal judge, Marvin Listoe city supervisor and Al Glandt police chief. In October the city bought a house on 196th Street S.W. as the new city hall, and by the end of the year four more areas had annexed to the city, including portions of Alderwood Manor and Seattle Heights, two communities that predated Lynnwood by many years.

The incorporation of Lynnwood was the direct result of the post-war growth that simply overwhelmed residents of the informal communities, which had existed more or less unchanged for decades. Many of the families in those communities had been in their homes for several generations, living on multi-acre lots, usually covered with tall, second growth trees. Some commuted to work in Edmonds, Everett, or Seattle. Others were self-sufficient, often operating small businesses. Sometimes they raised gardens or kept livestock to add to their incomes. When the immense rush of growth came, all that changed. Suddenly the rudimentary two-lane roads became insufficient for the traffic. The

Scriber Lake in Lynnwood is a natural area preserved in the heart of businesses and residences, a reminder of what existed prior to the years of development. (Courtesy Lynnwood *Enterprise*)

water district could not keep up with demand. Telephone service became slow and unreliable. Bit by bit the forest was replaced by houses, and storm water runoff became a problem. Sometimes raw sewage ran down the ditches, while it was no longer safe for children to walk to and from school on narrow roads without shoulders. Without wishing it, their community had changed within a few years, and there was nothing they could do to stop it. Some adjusted their lifestyles. Others simply sold out to eager developers and moved to some place not affected by masses of people.

In the 1930s the Black Ball Line had replaced the old steam powered ferries with diesel-electric vessels from San Francisco Bay when the Golden Gate Bridge was completed. When financial and service problems increased, the Washington State Ferry System bought out Black Ball in 1949 and continues to operate the Mukilteo-Clinton and Edmonds-Kingston runs (shown here). (#135.9, courtesy Edmonds-South Snohomish County Historical Society)

For Edmonds residents the shock of post war growth was softened and delayed a bit. Their community was small but nevertheless, a city. People were used to having neighbors next door, shops and stores nearby, plus the benefits of a small, professional police department and their own volunteer fire department. For the urban amenities of a sewer system, regular garbage service, and close-by government officials they were willing to pay the necessary taxes.

They knew, of course, that growth was taking place. From 1949 to April 1959 (when Lynnwood incorporated), Edmonds accepted 30 annexations totaling almost 1,065 acres, nearly doubling the size of the city and quadrupling the population from roughly 2,000 to 8,000. During that period, the last of the mills, which had supported the community from the beginning, closed. At the same time, roads and highways were improved enough to make it practical for affluent people from Seattle or Everett to move to Edmonds and commute to work, much as was happening in the neighboring areas. All that modified both the local economy and attitudes. Still, in 1953 when Pat McMahan approached Edmonds to ask that Mountlake Terrace be annexed, Mayor McKibbon was quite serious when he said the city would never annex beyond its traditional edge on Ninth Avenue.

A preeminent cultural event in Snohomish County is the annual Edmonds Arts Festival, which began in 1957 to exhibit and sell regional art. Its scope includes arts and crafts booths, artists in action, entertainment, and foods. This scene at an early festival illustrates the informal, outdoor flavor. (Courtesy Edmonds-South Snohomish County Historical Society)

The futility of that course became apparent when the rush of new students overwhelmed Edmonds High School, which had been located since early in the century in the heart of the city. The school board converted that building to Edmonds Junior High and built a new Edmonds High School at the southwest corner of 176th Avenue W. and 220th Street S.W.

It was apparent that if the city did not annex the area the new Edmonds High School might very well be in Lynnwood. Edmonds already had annexed to Five Corners, where 84th Avenue W. intersected with Bowdoin Way and an extension of Main Street, a mile beyond that hoped-for Ninth Avenue boundary. Now Edmonds Mayor Gordon Maxwell (who had once been a hero on the high school football team) let it be known that the community was less than thrilled at the prospect of the new building being in another city. When residents of the area submitted a petition to annex to Edmonds, the council moved as quickly as it could to accept, adopting the ordinance on December 15, 1959 and putting the school safely inside Edmonds. It also added some 200 homes and 600 people to the city, extended the border another seven-eighths of a mile east, and made it obvious that the city's dream of remaining a tiny, isolated community beside Puget Sound had succumbed to growth. The town threw the dream aside and annexed as far as it could go, a process that continued through the end of the century.

By the time of the Edmonds High School annexation, the facts of growth and change and what to do about them were major questions throughout the southwestern areas of the county. A bewildering number of proposals to incorporate new cities or annex to one

From Point Wells at the southern county boundary with King County, this 1953 view is northward toward Woodway and Edmonds. (#152.2, courtesy Edmonds-South Snohomish County Historical Society)

that already existed had begun after Mountlake Terrace broke the ice. Many of the proposals were based on the fear of being taken over by an existing city and losing local identity. Sometimes that resulted in the attempt to form a new municipality, and other times neighborhoods simply annexed to one city in order to stay out of another.

For instance, in 1964 a developer, Thomas A. McGrath, sought to annex property he owned east of the city to Mountlake Terrace. He said he wanted his property inside the boundary so he could take advantage of its sewer system for any houses he might build there. Residents of the nearby unincorporated area banded together to prevent the annexation, protesting that they did not want sewers and that they feared that annexation would mean that Mountlake Terrace would zone the area for small lots, making for denser population. They submitted a petition for incorporation of a city to be called Brier, after a real estate development in part of the area. The petition was accepted by the county commissioners and the required public hearing held. The resulting election on February 2, 1965 carried by an overwhelming vote of 461 to 194, with Richard Balser, a leader of the incorporation campaign, elected the first mayor. McGrath sued to overturn the election, contending that the county commissioners had not properly established the population of the proposed city. He went to the state Supreme Court but lost, and the city was official with a population of 2,168.

Eight years earlier, the Esperance Community Club had proposed that the large Esperance neighborhood south of Edmonds be annexed to that city. They included the tiny, upscale community of Woodway Park in their proposal. Woodway residents protested, and the community club dropped that area from its plans, but Woodway leaders said the only way to be sure they would not eventually become part of Edmonds was to incorporate as a fourth class town. Their petition for an election was approved, and the February 18, 1958 election carried by a vote of 99 to 80. Chesley M. Cook was the first mayor of the town, which encompassed 800 acres with about 400 residents and had first year revenues estimated at $7,712. The Standard Oil Company, which had a nearby storage area, donated a small, surplus building for a city hall, and one of the city council's first tasks was to find a place to put it. Meanwhile, the Esperance Community Club's proposal to annex to Edmonds failed.

Other incorporation attempts by residents of Meadowdale and Alderwood Manor also failed, and the communities eventually annexed, Meadowdale to Edmonds and Alderwood Manor to Lynnwood. The Alderwood Manor post office, which had existed long before there was a Lynnwood, eventually became part of the Lynnwood one which had started in a corner of Ed McCollum's market.

One effect of the post war multiplication of cities in south Snohomish County was that the resources to prepare the infrastructure needed for the new people were fragmented as the mayors and councils of the cities and the governing boards of the county and the special-purpose districts each established their own goals and policies. While they often cooperated on matters such as fire department mutual aid, police departments backing up each other, and joint sewer and water facilities, they often competed on matters such as annexation, street location, and zoning.

The major entity directly serving all the southwest portion of the county was School District 15. It, too, was sorely pressed to cope with the flood of new population. When the war ended in 1945 the district buildings totaled four: Edmonds High School, built in 1910;

Esperance Elementary School, built in 1911; Alderwood Elementary School, built in 1921; and Edmonds Elementary School, built in 1928. In 1965, 20 years after the war, the district had 33 school buildings, including four junior highs and three high schools. The struggle to construct, staff, and operate those facilities put a major burden on the entire community. The board of directors called elections year after year to approve special levies, and bond issues to raise funds for the local share of the cost of new schools. The special taxes were not popular among the older people of Edmonds and similar places, many of whom no longer had young children and who were less than enthralled over the sudden influx of newcomers. They tended to vote against the special taxes. On the other hand, Mountlake Terrace residents, nearly all of whom had children in school, or about to begin, voted heavily in favor. It sometimes was so close that the district had to double shift, provide portable classrooms, or rent buildings, but it always was able to provide classrooms for all the children.

Major symbols of the area's growth and increasing maturity were the creation of Stevens Memorial Hospital and of Edmonds Junior College, which later became the Edmonds Community College. Plans for the hospital were publicly announced for the first time in August 1958, during a meeting of the Edmonds City Council by Kenneth Caplinger of the United States Small Business Administration. He was president of the organization that was proposing the hospital. Dr. Olav Sola, a Lynnwood physician who had grown up in Everett, was vice president. Their organization put together a program based on citizen activity that included such projects as a door-to-door effort to sell bonds to help raise funds for the local match for federal grants. Ground breaking ceremonies occurred in 1962, and the hospital opened in 1964. Some local doctors were reluctant to support the new institution and continued to send their patients to Seattle hospitals. That caused a financial crisis, but eventually it was resolved, and the hospital became an important fixture in the community.

The college was born as a division of School District 15, as the school board created a special advisory committee to organize and prepare plans for the institution. One hundred acres were obtained on unused property in the Lynnwood commercial area, which had been the site of an Army radio station during World War II. After the war the station was abandoned, so the federal government transferred it for college and other public purposes. Byron Norman was named acting president, succeeded by Carlton Opgaard, who had been principal of Edmonds High School. Classes began in 1967 in the new Woodway High School building, which had been built but not yet occupied by students. After a year, the college moved to portable classrooms on the permanent campus, as the first permanent structure was not completed until 1970. Also in 1967, the state legislature changed the status of two-year colleges from divisions of their school districts to part of 22 separate statewide community college districts. Under that law both Edmonds and Everett colleges became part of Community College District 22, with Dr. Paul McCurley appointed president and offices at Paine Field. In 1981 the district was divided when the legislature created a new District 23 for Edmonds. Both institutions saw major growth as the dawning technology era increased the need for new skills, more Snohomish County students sought to continue their studies after high school, and older students (especially women) returned to the classroom to pursue their education.

Much of the change which took place in the county during the post World War II

313

period was in the southwest corner, and much of that change was spill over from Seattle. While Edmonds and, to a lesser extent, Mountlake Terrace maintained strong ties to King County, the rest of the area tended to keep a more independent attitude. Thus, while many South County people worked and shopped in King, their community governments worked more closely with Snohomish County and Everett. One example of that tendency occurred when Seattle proposed a metropolitan government, which would include territory up to Everett. Alarmed at the possibility of losing its self-determination, that city quickly proposed a Snohomish County Metropolitan government, which would preclude King County Metro from going north of the county line. Voters in both Everett and South County approved it handily, although Snohomish County Metro quickly became dormant as the communities resolved their region-wide problems through negotiations and contracts. One major example of such cooperation was the collaboration between Everett and the "South County" communities to provide water supplies to the area. Another was the number of cooperative sewer projects the cities worked out.

Everett also reached south. When the Everett *Herald* opened its South County Bureau in May 1954 the newspaper had no door-to-door circulation in School District 15, while the Seattle dailies had large numbers of customers there. Twelve years later the bureau was producing a separate *Western Sun* edition of the *Herald*, and its circulation in the area was larger than the Seattle *Post-Intelligencer* and not much less than the Seattle *Times*.

While the county's major post war growth occurred in its southwest corner there were also developments, real and potential, elsewhere. The central, northern, and eastern portions of the county were more mature and had more foundations of their infrastructure in place. Also, since

At the base of 6852' Mount Whitehorse, the Whitehorse Cash Store on Highway 530 west of Darrington had a picturesque setting. When pioneer Fred Olds' white horse ran off, a neighbor helping search pointed out a horse-like snowfield on the nearby mountain and quipped, "There it is above us!" and gave the peak its name. (Courtesy Darrington Historical Society)

population growth tended to spread northward from Seattle along the highway system, the influx of new residents in those areas was slower but, nevertheless, was taking place. While in 1940 Edmonds had a population of 1,288 and was the only city in South County area, 30 years later the combined population of what had become the five cities in the southern areas of the county area was 46,489, not counting the large number of residents in the unincorporated areas. During the same period, the other cities in the much larger remainder of the county added only 32,171 to their population. Three of the communities that had long been part of the county's unincorporated history also became incorporated cities: Darrington as the war ended in 1945, Lake Stevens in 1947, and Mukilteo in 1960. That increase in number partly was offset in the early 1960s when Stanwood and its adjacent neighbor East Stanwood found they needed sewers and neither was able to finance them independently. A committee organized by attorney Ed Jones and others petitioned for consolidation, failing in the first election, but winning in a second attempt,

Over half a century of rivalry ended when East Stanwood (foreground, along the railroad track) and Stanwood finally decided to merge. The "neutral ground" between the two is visible in the middle, with the meandering Stillaguamish River to the left. (Ellis photograph #326, courtesy Stanwood Area Historical Society)

bringing the total number of cities outside of the southwestern corner of the county to 13.

Although expansion in the rest of the county was slower than in the Edmonds School District 15 vicinity, it was enough to cause growing pains. In Everett, for instance, job creation actually began during World War II, the result of Paine Field and other military installations as well as defense industries such as the shipyard. The Everett School District No. 2 increased from 5,990 students in 1941 to 6,876 as the war ended in 1945. The district then increased to 11,628 in 1951. That was a considerably smaller percentage than the post-war growth of School District 15 but still put a strain on the Everett District's resources. As with the rest of the country, the district had been restricted by the government from new construction to meet the needs of the additional students during the war, but it began playing catch-up in 1947 when it completed both the new Madison Elementary School and the Everett Memorial Stadium at 38th Street and Oakes Avenue. With additions and renovations, the stadium continued to be the home field for Everett athletes, both public school and professional.

That was just the beginning. In 1949 the district opened the new Jackson and Whittier elementary schools, utilizing the old wooden Jackson structure to house seventh graders for nearby South Junior High. During the 1950s the district built five more elementary schools, including a modern replacement for the castle-like white wooden Lowell Elementary. The 1950s also saw construction of permanent quarters for the

315

Everett Junior College on property adjacent to Legion Park at the northern tip of town, and the new Evergreen Junior High School became the district's third, as population growth shot up in the newer south end. In 1961 Cascade became the district's second high school and quickly one of the biggest in the state. A major glitch in the district's struggles to keep up with its burgeoning student count came in 1964, when voters turned down propositions to provide $6 million for site acquisition and capital improvements. That threw a hitch into the construction program, but district officials pared it back and put a $3.75 million bond issue on the ballot the following year. It passed, and the district continued providing for a growing student body.

If the northern and eastern portions of the county appeared relatively stable, it was only on the surface. Agriculture and timber products, the traditional economic foundation of the county, both began almost imperceptibly to diminish in importance. Lumbering in the county began to decline after 1925 when 45 mills produced 1,033,699,000 board feet of Douglas fir timber. After wartime demand ceased, the 1949 cut totaled only 470 million board feet in 57 mills, as much of the private land had been logged off. After that the cut within the county diminished to some 220 million board feet, not enough to feed the county's plants, which had to bring in large, old growth timber from other parts of the Puget Sound Basin and the Olympic Peninsula. Time was running out for the ancient forest cover and the gigantic complexes such as Weyerhaeuser's Mill B at the mouth of the Snohomish River, which sawed them.

Change also was occurring in the technology of logging. First, oxen hauled out the heavy trees to the rivers for transportation to distant mills. This was followed by the advent of steam donkeys and then steam railroads. In the late 1940s the last major use of steam came to an end with the closure of the Sauk River Lumber Company's operations south of Darrington. Rails were pulled up, racking diesel truck sounds replaced the whistles of Shay, Heisler, and Climax locomotives in the woods, and the roar of chain saws ended the quiet rustle of crosscuts for falling and bucking the logs into lengths. The war also provided readily available surplus machinery, which could be modified for use in the woods, enabling a generation of "gyppos," small, independent operators, to take on timber sales at more difficult locations and compete with the remaining giant corporations.

Timber continued to be the foundation of the county's economy for some time, largely supplied after 1953, National Forest sales, when Republican Dwight Eisenhower became president and Secretary of Agriculture Ezra Taft Benson ordered a change in policy to harvest these public lands. The Forest Service rapidly changed from largely a conservator over much of eastern Snohomish

As postwar children grew up, so did organized athletic programs for them. Little League baseball was the most popular, drawing widespread community support and recognition. These are the 1961 champions from Arlington Heights. (Courtesy Stillaguamish Valley Pioneer Association)

Postwar Woods Activities

Right: Portable sawmills cutting smaller trees were developed to assist small operators and landowners, with technological innovation encouraged by the federal government. Many of the formerly wasteful logging practices ended, along with the age of steam and railroads, replaced with diesel power and trucks on roads. (A.F. Harms photograph, courtesy USDA Soil Conservation Service)

War surplus equipment and smaller volume timber sales, especially from National Forest lands after 1952, made it possible for many more enterprising loggers to strike out on their own as independents, or "gyppos." This unit was built in Gold Bar in 1946. (J.G. James photograph, courtesy USDA Soil Conservation Service)

Technology also advanced in the milling and pulp industries, as older and inefficient plants closed, while more modern ones hired skilled union workers at far better salaries and working conditions. (Courtesy Darrington Historical Society)

Left: Farmers and rural land owners found a favorable market niche by beginning to grow trees as a crop and joined the tree farm movement. Real estate tax benefits, new wood products, and mills cutting smaller diameter trees all factored in to stimulate reforestation. (J.G. James photograph, courtesy USDA Soil Conservation Service)

County to an organization whose employees were judged on how well they "got out the cut." As a result of this activity substantial money flowed to local school and road funds, while a network of logger-built roads opened much of the backcountry to recreational and fire fighting access.

However, the future of the industry throughout Western Washington began to grow precarious when Congress adopted the National Wilderness Act of 1964. The House version was written by Second District Democratic Congressman Lloyd Meeds, who represented most of Snohomish County and the area north to the Canadian border. The Senate version was written by Everett Senator Henry M. "Scoop" Jackson. He had spent much time during his youth hiking, climbing, and camping in the Cascades and was seen by many as the father of the nation's wilderness system. Both he and Meeds were responding to a widespread belief that even though new trees were planted to replace those that were harvested, the harvesters were taking more than were being planted and that the original forests people used for recreation, watersheds, and wildlife habitat eventually would disappear. That concern later was expanded to one of maintaining entire ecosystems for their own sake, as well as for preservation of endangered and threatened species.

With the strong support of such outdoor groups as The Mountaineers, Sierra Club, and The North Cascades Conservation Council, the 1964 act set aside millions of acres of National Forest land where logging and mining were banned. The Glacier Peak Wilderness area of 458,505 acres already had been created in 1960 by the Forest Service, and now it was given

Lloyd Meeds followed the path of Senator Jackson, serving first as a successful Democratic county prosecutor and then second district congressman. Both men advanced the cause of environmental protection, while Meeds also is deeply interested in educational issues. After serving seven terms in Congress, he left to become an effective Washington, D.C. lobbyist. (Courtesy Larry O'Donnell)

congressional protection. Much of this is located in Snohomish County. The law also set the stage for more land to be set aside later. Indeed, four years after the 1964 Wilderness Act was adopted, Congress established the 675,000-acre North Cascades National Park adjacent to the Canadian border.

Fishing and mining had permanently ended as major economic factors by the end of the 1940s. Derbies still brought in catches of salmon for proud anglers, but the backbone of the industry had shifted to offshore and Alaskan waters. Puget Sound became the off-season home and repair site for the fleet, but no longer a serious producer. Mining had declined to an activity for hobbyists and rock collec-

Camp Mathews at Lake Kelcema above Silverton served the Evergreen Area Council of the Boy Scouts of America from the late 1920s until its abandonment 30 years later. Bernie Webber decorated the interior timbers. After repeated vandalism, the Forest Service burned the lodge and shelters. Here it is at Christmas 1959. (Courtesy David Cameron)

318

Completion of the Granite Falls fish ladder in 1954 allowed returning salmon and steelhead better access past the falls and into narrow Robe Canyon. Unfortunately, deep clay deposits and erosion farther upstream by Gold Basin and Eldred Creek add to the amount of silt in the river and make it less productive than the North Fork Stillaguamish River. (Courtesy Granite Falls Historical Society)

tors, save for the immense deposits of sand and gravel which provided rich sources of building material for the booming development of the county. Thanks to the glacial deposits in the Puget Sound lowlands, companies such as Associated Sand and Gravel could locate large operations adjacent to urban areas and bid successfully for highway and building construction jobs.

Farming still was a viable way of life in the postwar period, but had settled in to a long, continuing decline. The number of Snohomish County farms (6,259) and acres devoted to farming (194,687) had peaked in 1945. Rural farm population was 17,174 in 1950, about 15 percent of the total for the county. Some 3,636 people were listed as employed on those farms, about 10 percent of the number of people with jobs in the county. Occupations with more workers than farming were manufacturing with 10,301, retail and wholesale services, 7,463, and miscellaneous services with 7,141 workers.

By 1954 there were 441 fewer farms than 1949, but the average size increased from 37.7 acres to 38.2. The size was still far below the state average of 270.7 acres. In 1955 4,345 farms were operating on 166,133 acres, mostly in the fertile soils of the Stillaguamish and Snohomish Valleys. They ranked third in the state in dairy production and fifth in poultry. Many of those in agriculture worked only part time on their land, obtaining much of their income from other sources in order to sustain themselves. On the other hand, in June many urban residents flocked to the large fields of strawberries and then raspberries, helping bring in the harvest for wages and for home eating and processing. Much of the activity was centered on the sandy soils north of Marysville, which continued its popular annual Strawberry Festival. The days after school ended saw hundreds of youngsters join older workers, Native Americans, and others in harvesting the quickly ripening berry crops, staples for local markets and processed export from the county. Wheezing old yellow surplus school busses, pickup trucks loaded with children, and carloads of women with their work clothes on and sack lunches packed were common early morning sights on the roads to the long rows of berries awaiting them at producers such as Leifer and Due in north Marysville, Cooper and Pilchuck near Lochsloy, and Hansey west of Monroe.

319

County Street Scenes

State Avenue in Marysville appeared quiet and efficient in this photograph, but as traffic grew during the 1950s it no longer could function during weekend gridlock in its dual role as U.S. Highway 99. By the middle of the decade police were required to direct southbound travelers on summer Sundays, and demands grew for a new route parallel to the city. (Ellis photograph #5701, courtesy Jack O'Donnell)

Downtown First Street in Snohomish retained its flavor of buildings dating back to the community's days as county seat and territorial center of business and culture. (Courtesy Jack O'Donnell)

Main Street in Monroe was the commercial center of the Skykomish valley, hosting a number of long-term businesses such as Camp-Riley Drugs. Later it would decline when U.S. Highway 2 would bypass it to the north, followed by State Route 522 to the west. (Ellis photograph #6600, courtesy Jack O'Donnell)

The intersection of Colby and Hewitt bustled with business and traffic, a vibrant core for the county's largest city. Within a few years the major companies and many of the buildings which housed them would all be gone. (Courtesy Bernie Webber)

Agriculture also figured in the industrialization of the county's economy during the post-war period. One major example was the Twin City Foods plant in Stanwood. Founded in 1945 by lumberman Ole Lervick and his sons Art, Magnar and Arnie, the plant prospered, and by the mid-1960s was providing seasonal employment for hundreds of people from many parts of the county. It only gradually became apparent that industry would continue to be the county's future despite the decline of timber and its related products. One indication of change occurred when the John Fluke Company moved its large electronics facilities from Seattle to Mountlake Terrace in 1959, then in 1981 to even larger quarters in south Everett.

Another major indication of change in the postwar county was the formation of the Snohomish County Public Utility District No. 1. As government agencies set plans for immense power dams on the Columbia and Snake Rivers, it became apparent that there would be large amounts of inexpensive electrical power available throughout the region. An initiative election in 1930 allowed local communities to form utility districts to provide water, sewer, or electrical service, but left it up to local communities actually to establish the utilities. Some communities felt that local control would mean they would be able to control their own destinies. Others feared such action would constitute social-ism, and there was a great deal of controversy. Snohomish County created the P.U.D. as a water utility to serve areas where water service was inadequate or non-existent in 1936 but took little action actually to begin functioning. Thirteen years later, on September 1, 1949, the P.U.D. completed negotiations, paid Puget Sound Power and Light Company $16,945,000, and took over the electrical service for Snohomish County and Camano Island. At that point it had no generating capacity of its own, and as a result contracted for supply with the hydroelectric resources of the Bonneville Power Administration.

Entertainment also changed during the years after the war. Everett's second radio station was founded as KQTY in June 1957 by Wally Nelskog, an Everett native with an affinity for owning them. He founded several in the Pacific Northwest and had equities in as many as seven. KQTY broadcast the "top 20" sound of popular music, and, with KRKO, competed for listeners with the numerous sta-tions in Seattle, including those with network affilia-tions that broadcast big name programs. Even before that, in the late

Ongoing work continued to protect valley farm lands from flood damage. In April 1949 county trucks were busy spreading gravel to raise low spots along the road near Swans Trail on the Snohomish River. (A.F. Harms photograph, courtesy USDA Soil Conservation Service)

Resorts in Snohomish County

By Bob Laz

My brother and I came from Chicago. We remembered well the fun we had as kids, going to family picnics at Opatrny's Grove, a resort on the Fox River in Illinois, beginning in 1921. We went swimming, had baseball games, pitched horseshoes. A few of the family drank some, and everyone had fun.

In 1946 we made up our minds to come to Snohomish, Washington, to build a resort. We figured it must be fun to run one. We built Wonderland Park on Flowing Lake. It was first-class: dance floor, boats, canoes, swimming, baseball diamonds, horseshoes, ping pong tables—we had it all. What we didn't think about or pay attention to was that there were three other nearby resorts, two on Storm Lake that were dying and one on our lake that was already closed. We didn't question how come, because we were going to have the best resort around. And we did.

Adams' Resort on Storm Lake was built in approximately 1920 with a dance hall and the whole ball of wax. Loggers in particular found it a good place to let their hair down. Adams sold to Lyon, who after a couple of years sold to Alexander, who closed the dance hall and eventually, in the early 1950s, closed the resort. Potter's just had boats, and that dried up with the opening of a public fishing area next door to him. Leckie's on Flowing Lake had the most beautiful grounds and beach anywhere and was eventually sold to the county for a park in the 1960s.

Lake Goodwin had four major resorts and a number of smaller ones. Leonard's was closed and shortly will be a county park, while Schuh's is now subdivided and into homes. Cedar Grove and the Lake Goodwin Resort survived by converting to recreational vehicle parks. RV traffic was building, and they saw the trend. The Lake Goodwin Resort has 66 hookups, four boats, a store, and a gas station, with Karen Ryan as the manager.

Lake Roesiger was discovered by Richard Roesiger in 1885. He established residence in 1887 and started his resort business in the early 1900s "with a few dugouts that reached nowhere. I had boats built in Snohomish and hauled out here." That was in 1918. Lyons' Den opened in the late 1920s. Both resorts closed after the state put in a public boat launch and fishing area access.

The most popular lake, Lake Stevens, was the largest and most easily accessible in the county. It was also the closest to major population centers. Most of the resorts were developed about 1905 through 1910. Lundeen's and the Purple Pennant had baseball fields that attracted some of the better minor league baseball teams. They had everything, including food service, dance halls, beaches, boats, canoes, and daredevil equipment out over the lake. They attracted crowds up of to 3,000 people. Davies' Resort wasn't far behind. Except for the baseball field they had every major attraction. There were also smaller resorts with some boats and cabins around the lake, and of course there were resorts on the many other county lakes.

When World War II came and took so many young men, the resorts began to hurt and then deteriorate. After the war more and more people built homes around the lake, and with sewage leaching into the water, that became an environmental concern. The sewage lines that followed were then assessed by the foot, and since the resorts had large chunks of lake frontage, the assessments also put a large drain on their financial resources.

"HEY, GEORGE! BRING the other CAN!"

When the state began buying up frontage and putting in public access areas in the 1950s, and the counties began buying lake properties for parks in the 1960s, well, that was like selling ice cream cones next to a guy who was giving them away. A decline in the number of resorts became an epidemic. Most of us, in order to get our lakes stocked with more fish, built our own scaffold to hang ourselves. We signed on to and supported the Washington Department of Game program.

That, however, wasn't the only problem. Television came along strong in the late 1940s and early 1950s and began televising sporting events on weekends. That kept a big chunk of the resort clientele off the market. Another factor was that automobiles took people on better roads throughout the state. Resorts in eastern Washington, where the weather is warmer and more reliable, grew in number.

After the war, with more people moving to the Puget Sound area for its natural wonders, and the more affluent bidding up the value of the properties these resorts sat on, there was no way for anyone to afford to buy out the deteriorating resorts and refurbish them. The final nail in the coffin came from the insurance companies. As people became more litigious, and the lawyers in the yellow pages looked for clients, the vulnerability of resorts to all sorts of accidents put them off limits as far as getting insurance coverage.

Without insurance and with nowhere to get it, you simply closed the doors. We know we did at the end of the season in 1961, when Wonderland Park, almost the last one to go, finally gave in to the pressures and closed its doors. Nearly all the resorts suffered this same fate.

Bob Heirman deserves most of the credit for this report. He must be forever remembered as part of the history of the outdoor life, picnicking, and fishing in Snohomish County. He has seen its greatness and has fought its decline, as more people have moved into our area and developers spread into the countryside. Thank you, Bob! I also have to thank Bob Tuerk, Bill Pardee, Jim Mitchell, and Newell Dana, four major players in shedding light on the history of Lundeen's, Davies', the Purple Pennant, and a number of smaller resorts on Lake Stevens.

Editor's Note: Bob still lives on the site of Wonderland Park, where he and his twin brother George raised their families and worked to create their dream. After retiring, Bob took the advice of a county tax assessor and began growing Christmas trees on the land, starting with the former baseball diamond. This venture coincided with a rush of others doing the same thing. Planting more than 3,000 trees a year, he and his son Gary never sold more than 1,500 during a holiday season.

One day Gary remarked as they labored, "This is an exercise in futility! Why don't we build a golf course?"

"When do you want to start?" replied Bob, without straightening up. In 1991 Flowing Lake Golf Course became a reality.

1940s, television began what eventually became a major source of news, information, and entertainment. Snohomish County did not have a station of its own through the twentieth century, but the signals of Seattle reached far into the hinterlands. In the early days the three network radio stations in Seattle, KING, KOMO, and KIRO, expanded into television and were the primary stations here, followed by Tacoma and then Bellingham signals. At first these transmissions were weak, especially in the northern areas and those below the line of sight, and houses sprouted huge, awkward antennas on their roof. Eventually cable service was established, bringing more and better signals into people's homes for a price,

Sculptor Dudley Carter carved the "Maiden of the Woods" for the 1947 MGM film "Giant Tree Sculptures of the Pacific Northwest." Work stopped as soon as the shooting ended, but the giant cedar became a popular attraction at Verlot. A lightning strike burned the tree despite the best efforts of Forest Service fire crews. (Fred Shaw photograph, courtesy Jack O'Donnell)

Everett School District No. 2 created a major new sports complex with the opening of Memorial Stadium on 39th and Broadway in 1947. Built on land next to Longfellow Elementary School which was donated by the Everett Elks lodge, Governor Mon Wallgren gave the dedicatory speech. The site has served high school, community college, and professional baseball teams, as well as civic and religious events. (Courtesy Everett Public Library)

Left: KING-TV star Stan Boreson and his dog No-Mo-Shun entertain a crowd of young fans at the Everett Theatre. (Courtesy Everett *Herald* Archives)

Arlington maintained its traditional economic base of agriculture and forest products during the period, growing steadily and having a vibrant downtown. This view is from May 1963. (Ellis photograph #1805, courtesy Stillaguamish Valley Pioneer Association)

Trains on the 28 mile long Northern Pacific Railway branch line from Darrington west to Arlington brought as many as 250 car loads of logs down from the mountains each day earlier in the century and still were busy as steam power ended in the 1950s. Mikado #1612 is shown pulling the Darrington Logger on May 25, 1955. (Courtesy Stillaguamish Valley Pioneer Association)

Swenson's auction barn at Snohomish, shown here in June 1953, was a busy scene for livestock sales. As Mr. Swenson rattled off his well practiced auctioneer's line, handlers brought cattle through from pens, and observers in the hard wooden seats sought with critical eyes to find quality animals at the lowest possible price. (Juleen photograph, BJ009, courtesy Snohomish Historical Society)

and the antennas largely disappeared, along with vacuum tubes, then black and white sets.

One of the stars of the early regional programs on TV was Stan Boreson, a young man from Everett who was a talented accordion player as well as an attractive personality. After graduating from Everett High School in 1944, he went overseas to help big name entertainers such as the Andrews Sisters, who were touring the USO circuit to entertain troops. Then he became a business major at the University of Washington. He and piano player Art Barduhn took part in a zany campus show, were seen by a representative of KING-TV, and were hired to perform on the station's first live show. They combined comedy and music in their program, which went on the air in 1949. After Barduhn left to take a group of his own on the road, Boreson continued with KING-TV and developed a highly popular children's show with a sleepy basset hound named No-Mo (a take-off from the favorite Seattle hydroplanes *Slo-mo-shun IV* and *V* of record breaking racer Stan Sayres), No-Mo made a big hit by not doing anything. Boreson hosted the show for 15 years.

As television became more prevalent and people stayed home for entertainment, theaters found it more difficult to make money. In Everett three downtown movie theaters survived the war, but the Balboa (at 2812 Wetmore Avenue) was closed in May 1953, and the Granada (at 2926 Wetmore) ceased operation in November 1954. The larger Everett Theater, which was opened in 1901 to feature vaudeville and road shows, was remodeled in 1952 and survived commercially until 1989. Eventually, the Everett Theater Society took on the task of restoring it as an historical showcase. Theaters in the county's other communities struggled to survive, and their numbers diminished despite renewed interest in movie going with the passing phenomena of drive-in theaters located for the rising automobile traffic along U.S. 99 between Marysville and north Seattle.

The Puget Sound region received a sudden and unwelcome thrust into the national news at 11:55 A.M. on April 13, 1949 when an earthquake with a magnitude of 7.1 struck near Olympia. By the next day eight people had died and many millions of dollars in damage had been done, much of it to older brick structures that collapsed under the shock. Snohomish County was at the northern edge of the impact area, and damage was relatively light. There were no serious injuries in the county, but there were some reports listing power outages, brick chimneys twisted or shattered, cracked plasterwork, and objects knocked to the floor from shelving. Such reports came from throughout the county including Arlington, Granite Falls, Startup, and Sultan. In Index three six-inch water mains were broken. In Everett a railroad car loaded with coal broke loose from its blocking, rolled down a grade, and derailed. This was the county's greatest earthquake experience of the century.

At that date, the violent possibilities of Pacific Northwest geology were not yet well understood. Cascade volcanoes "appeared" dead, short-term weather patterns random, and earthquakes totally unpredictable. Yet, just a few years later, those "appearances" would change when the ash of Mt. St. Helens began to drift down over the county. Despite this, the growing stream of incoming residents and economic change, which, by the end of the century would spread the pattern of the southwest corner throughout the Puget Sound lowlands region of Snohomish County, did not abate. Timber would give way to aircraft, strawberry fields to housing developments, new freeways to gridlock, downtowns to malls. As a result, a virtually unbroken urban area from Fort Lewis north to Smokey Point was created.

1965 – 2004

Any discussion of the last three and a half decades of the twentieth century and the beginnings of the twenty-first in Snohomish County would have to focus on the issue of growth. As the trend had begun in the southwestern corner of the county immediately after World War II, so it continued to expand with only one significant dip throughout the ensuing years. Everett had 40,304 residents in the 1960 census. During the following decade, for example, population filled in southward with annexations from 52nd Street to the Casino Road area of Beverly Park and reached 53,688 in the 1970 count. By 2004 the number was 95,473, more than doubling the amount of only 40 years earlier as the boundaries passed Silver Lake. Everett's numbers, however, paled compared to other parts of the county. In the mid-1960s the total Snohomish County population was about 265,000 and expected to reach 400,000 by the turn of the century. Instead it passed that mark in 1990 and raced past 600,000 a decade later, with planners predicting 712,244 by 2012. In South County Edmonds, Woodway, Brier, and Mountlake Terrace grew, as did Lynnwood, swallowing up Meadowdale and the last of Alderwood Manor, while Bothell expanded north from King County.

Even the more rural towns did not escape the growth. Snohomish expanded north-ward toward Lake Stevens, which met Marysville at S.R. 9. Marysville and Arlington met and absorbed Smokey Point, which had grown enough to necessitate a high school in Lakewood to the west. Monroe expanded north, boasted new subdivisions in the Fryelands just west of town, and surpassed Snohomish in size. Sultan had developments of new earth-tone homes and felt the paralysis of weekend and rush hour traffic tying up access to U.S. 2. Up the Skykomish valley Gold Bar cul-de-sacs and even gated communities created morning commuter traffic lines beginning at the base of the Cascades. Cathcart and Maltby were not so remote after construction of S.R. 522 linked Monroe with the burgeoning job market of King County. Stanwood, not really that far from an Interstate 5 commute to Boeing, was undergoing tremendous growth on the hills east of town. Perhaps the best indicator of all that most of the county was part of Pugetopolis was the opening of a McDonald's drive-in restaurant in the former timber town of Granite Falls the summer of 1997. Only the most isolated eastern mountain communities of Darrington and Index remained relatively unaffected, the former hit by the collapse of its logging industry and Index protected by its tiny mountain-ringed land base and a strong citizen desire to maintain its small town quality of life.

Most impressively, by 1998 for the first time Snohomish County was adding more

The tiny Wayside Chapel, located one mile west of Sultan on U.S. 2, is a place of respite for those wishing to pause, rest, and worship. Sponsored by the Christian Reformed Church in Monroe, it is open to all faiths. (Clifford B. Ellis post card #SP448, courtesy Jack O'Donnell)

people annually than even King County and absorbing 35 percent of the total population increase in the Puget Sound region. Only a few "sun belt" counties were growing faster, such as those surrounding Phoenix, Arizona, Los Angeles and San Diego, California, and Palm Beach, Florida. Unfortunately for commuter traffic, however, the explosion in Puget Sound area jobs has been taking place in King County to the south where affordable housing is in short supply. Most of our new residents are living here but working in Seattle and east of Lake Washington.

The year 1965 opened with a continuation of the boom the county had experienced during that decade. In Everett, Providence Hospital was erecting an addition, which was a part of a project that eventually would replace the old cross-shaped structure of the 1920s. General Hospital also was planning a new tower. On the waterfront Scott Paper

Company's new four-story addition was nearing completion, while the Port of Everett was planning a new boat storage basin at 14th Street, which would be the largest north of Seattle. County government was looking forward to some growing space in the form of a new five-story office expansion, which would replace the old annex to the courthouse Mission building, which had survived the 1909 fire. Not only was this building going up, but also a more visible structure was under construction at Hewitt and Colby Avenues for Seattle First National Bank, replacing the original red brick one. At seven stories it would be Everett's tallest, displacing the 1925 Medical & Dental Building and its north wing addition of 30 years later. This major project warranted a viewing

Spada Lake, impounded by Culmback Dam, serves the City of Everett and the Snohomish County P.U.D. for power and water. The Morning Glory Spillway with a diameter of 80 feet allows excess water to pass through the dam by way of a 615 foot long, 34 foot wide tunnel. (Fred Shaw photograph, courtesy Jack O'Donnell)

This 1971 view looks northeast over the interchange at 164th Street S.W. and Interstate 5. Although there was some economic development along 164th Street (Martha Lake Road), this would change dramatically after it was widened to five lanes and became the major route to Mill Creek. (Pete Kinch photograph #1565-3-71, courtesy Everett Public Library)

grandstand on Hewitt Avenue so shoppers could watch the progress. Downtown Everett was experiencing its biggest building boom since the 1920s. In Lynnwood the Lynn Theater was talking of adding a twin auditorium to become the county's first multiplex theater. Proposed apartments in Edmonds included the Ebb-Tide, Edgewood, Townhouse, Jangard, and Reef. John Fluke was ready to double its electronics plant in Mountlake Terrace. Marysville was anticipating the new Snohomish-Island County Regional Library headquarters building. In a joint project between Everett and the Snohomish County Public Utility District No. 1, construction of Culmback Dam was creating Spada Lake in the Sultan Basin, its huge morning glory spillway carrying overflow through a tunnel to the old river bed. The resulting water and hydroelectric power would be welcome with the influx of new people to the county and provide the P.U.D. with its only local generating capacity.

On February 3, 1965 Rose Clare Menalo of Meadowdale High School, Miss Sno-King, cut the ribbon which opened the long awaited 19.7 miles of the Everett to Seattle section of the new I-5 freeway. Leaving Eastmont, the limited access highway roughly paralleled the old interurban line on its route south. At Alderwood Manor it sliced through the northwestern part of Puget Mill Company's old Demonstration Farm. From there it continued southwesterly, cutting east of Halls Lake and through the valley in Mountlake Terrace before entering King County. With its open lanes and fast speeds it was instantly popular. Names such as 128th, 164th, 196th, and 44th soon replaced Post Road, Martha Lake Road, Filbert Road and Cedar Way as part of the freeway commuter vocabulary. In Lynnwood and Mountlake Terrace split diamond interchanges were built at 44th, 196th, 220th, and 236th respectively. Providing access in one direction only, they were adequate at the time of construction, but growth and traffic that followed soon overloaded them, challenging the highway department for the next three decades. Yet opening the freeway was not the end-all to congestion at the time. In Everett traffic funneled into the old highway route along Broadway, and it was not uncommon on a late Sunday afternoon for travelers to be stalled as far south as Eastmont or as far north as Marysville because of this bottleneck. Broadway became infamous statewide, and many would have welcomed the chance to go as fast as the 28 M.P.H. posted to make the traffic signals. It would be three long years before Megan Mardesich, daughter of Democratic State Senator and Mrs. August Mardesich, joined Republican Governor Daniel J. Evans to cut the ribbon for the Everett section between 41st Street and the Snohomish River, which had sliced through its original Riverside neighborhood and taken out many older historic commercial buildings and homes on lower Everett and Hewitt avenues. It was still another year later when on May 14, 1969 Debbie Herivel, Miss Everett, and Katherine Smith, Miss Marysville, snipped the ribbon of the four-mile stretch across the Snohomish River flats to open a route free of traffic signals and draw bridges, finally linking Canada and California. Harold Walsh, state highways commissioner from Everett, was master of ceremonies at the dedication taking place on the new Steamboat Slough bridge. North of Marysville, where there was already a divided highway, it was mostly a matter of gradually widening lanes and building overpasses along Highway 99 at such places at Island Crossing, Lakewood, and Stimson Crossing. President Eisenhower's dream of an interstate freeway system for national defense in his Highway Act of 1956 was reaching fruition in Snohomish County.

Meanwhile in 1965, another key highway project was under way, a two-lane trestle paralleling the original to provide a divided highway across the Snohomish River and Ebey Island between Everett and Cavalero's Corner on U.S. 2. In April 1969 the new bridge and trestle were opened, reducing a major bottleneck and eliminating head-on collisions. This time it was Monica Mardesich cutting the ribbon with Donna Granity of Bellingham, whose father had been killed in a fall from the old trestle. Much of the credit for this project went to the perseverance of the Riverside Commercial Club, one of Everett's oldest service organizations.

On February 11, 1965 the new Monroe-Woodinville Cutoff was opened prematurely. Monroe's Main Street had to serve as the temporary route because the final link up to U.S. 2 and the new Monroe bypass would not be finished until much later. There were only a few grade level crossings on the new two-lane highway, and two major hills were prepared for eventual passing lanes. The 11-mile stretch was expected to cut off a half hour for those traveling from Seattle to Stevens Pass. Instead it provided critical new commuter access to the area, causing Monroe to surge in size, and turning the bypass into a clogged commercial strip. As the direct result Monroe became the dominant town of the Skykomish Valley as King County's available land for development disappeared, bringing that expansion north and commuters south. This ensuing growth helped make S.R. 522 one of the most dangerous in the state and led to ongoing demands for widening, overpasses, and better control over traffic flow.

On the morning of April 29, 1965 Western Washington was rocked by an earthquake that measured 6.5 on the Richter Scale. Centered south of Seattle, it caused seven deaths and over $12.5 million (1965 dollars) in losses throughout the Puget Sound region. Snohomish County sustained relatively minor damage. Chimneys were knocked down in Stanwood at the Masonic Lodge and an apartment. Huge boulders rolled down Mt. Persis near U.S. 2 between Gold Bar and Index. In South County pupils were evacuated from the fourth floor of Edmonds Junior High School after plaster fell off walls, while Stevens Hospital officials reported their third floor was rolling and rocking. A fissure developed near downtown Edmonds at 8th Avenue and C Street, while bricks fell from the Edmonds Safeway store and the old gas plant along the Snohomish River at the foot of California Street in Everett. The high hose tower in front of the Mountlake Terrace Civic Center swayed up to 18 inches, and there were several small cracks in the center's walls. Cans and bottles cascaded off shelves in stores county-wide. Utility lines came through the quake fairly well, although the Alderwood Water District suffered breaks in its supply line from Everett as well as in a four-inch line at Meadowdale. One of the Sultan River supply pipelines into Everett ruptured along a welded seam, spouting geysers which defoliated trees north of the Hewitt Avenue trestle 25 yards away and shut down the Weyerhaeuser and Scott Paper Company pulp mills in Everett. Closed for engineering examinations were the old Lincoln Building portion of Marysville High School and Monroe High School. The most serious damage was at the 1894 Monroe School in Everett's Riverside, where the west wall separated from the structure. Teacher Edythe Pavish and principal Bob Timm reported that the students never returned to the building, which was razed and the name bestowed on a new school near Silver Lake. This was the area's worst earthquake following that of April 13, 1949 and the last major one to affect the county for the rest of the century.

On December 22, 1965 William Allen, president of Seattle's Boeing Company, and Juan Trippe, president of Pan American World Airways, signed a statement of intention that Boeing would build a huge new airplane designated the 747 and that Pan American would buy and operate 25 of them. This decision would send the county on a course of growth the likes of which it never had seen. In the spring of 1966 the news gradually became public. On May 2 *The Everett Daily Herald* carried the headline, "Boeing Considering Paine Field Area for Site of 747 Jumbo Jet." To add fuel to the fire a June 17 story read that if Boeing built its new 747, it would be assembled in Everett. Actually Boeing already had an option on 780 acres of Modern Home Builders' land adjacent to the Snohomish County Airport (Paine Field). In April the firm had announced that it would indeed build 25 of the huge jumbo-jets for Pan American, the critical mass of orders deemed necessary to go into production. Formal announcement for the go ahead came on July 25, but by this time the Boeing boom already was under way.

Mukilteo was impacted immediately. To move materials to the building site by rail it was necessary to obtain an easement for construction of a spur from the Great Northern

333

Boeing Comes to Paine Field

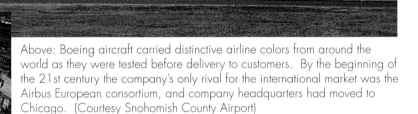

Below: On February 9, 1969 bands played, speeches were made, and a huge crowd watched the roll out of the first 747. (Courtesy Snohomish County Airport)

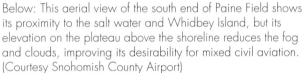

Above: Boeing aircraft carried distinctive airline colors from around the world as they were tested before delivery to customers. By the beginning of the 21st century the company's only rival for the international market was the Airbus European consortium, and company headquarters had moved to Chicago. (Courtesy Snohomish County Airport)

Below: This aerial view of the south end of Paine Field shows its proximity to the salt water and Whidbey Island, but its elevation on the plateau above the shoreline reduces the fog and clouds, improving its desirability for mixed civil aviation. (Courtesy Snohomish County Airport)

Above: Air fairs drew substantial crowds to the field, as shown in 1993. From 1946 to 1967 they were sponsored by the Everett Elks Club and Everett Jaycees, co-ordinating with the U.S. Air Force and Snohomish County Airport. After the military presence ended, the Lynnwood Rotary Club took over from 1968 to 1992, bringing in attractions such as the Air Force Thunderbirds and Navy Blue Angels. The event ended in 1994. (Courtesy Snohomish County Airport)

Railway main line at Edgewater up to the building site. This new route up Japanese Gulch became one of the world's shortest and steepest. Mukilteo widened Front Street, and lanes were added for workers along Casino Road in the far reaches of south Everett. Plans and construction soon were under way for both the new State Highway 526 freeway link to Interstate 5 and the connection of Interstate 405 from Bothell to Interstate 5 at Swamp Creek.

Soon thousands of Austin Construction Company workers were employed at the site. It was a study in superlatives for an assembly plant that would require a work force of at least 10,000 to build the aircraft. At 228 feet in length the jetliner was longer than the first Wright Brothers' flight. The main assembly building, large enough to contain the Pentagon and Rome's Colosseum, would be the world's largest by volume, larger even than the structure being built at Cape Kennedy, Florida to house the Saturn moon rocket. All-

Casino Road (heading west on the far left in this 1969 view) immediately was inadequate for carrying traffic to the Boeing 747 plant. Soon Highway 526, the "Boeing Freeway," was under construction to fill this need. Casino Road eventually was widened and many apartments constructed along the corridor to accomodate workers. In the lower right is the K-Mart, opened in 1966 along the Evergreen Way strip. (Pete Kinch photograph #266-11-69, courtesy Everett Public Library)

335

in-all, the building and auxiliary facilities would cover over 2.3 million square feet.

By the end of the year almost 100 of the planes had been ordered at an estimated cost in excess of $1 billion. To add to the excitement Boeing won the design race for the proposed supersonic jet transport, and the Everett plant possibly would figure into its construction and testing. A spectacular era was forecast for Snohomish County. By the first of the year Boeing's 15,000-employee payroll was generating new business and new population. After its completion new permanent residents to the county (many transferred from the Wichita, Kansas plant) needed places to live, which sent real estate prices skyrocketing and construction of new homes and apartments to record levels. By the end of 1967 Snohomish County was one of the fastest growing counties in the nation. The boom was going strong in 1968 when on the last day of September the first 747 was unveiled to government and business leaders. However, the inaugural flight was delayed until February due to testing delays and an unusually severe winter. As the decade ended,

In 1969 the Everett Mall was under construction next to I-5, with the Bothell-Everett Highway in the foreground, Eastmont interchange, and Cascade High School to the north as the Boeing Freeway curved to the west. Before construction of the Pacific Highway 40 years before, the Bothell route was the main north-south highway between Seattle and Everett. (Pete Kinch photograph #266-33-69, courtesy Everett Public Library)

This 1998 view looks north over Interstate 5 and the Alderwood Mall. In the lower foreground is the new crossing of Alderwood Mall Parkway (formerly 28th Avenue West and originally Manor Way), with the recently built food court on the southeast. (Courtesy Alderwood Mall)

Left: Compare the mall photograph with this one taken of the 1896 cabin of the Elizabeth and William Morrice homestead, on which the mall later was built. Elizabeth was known for her rose garden and honored for her community generosity, while William became justice of the peace and a founder of the Masonic lodge. (Courtesy Edmonds-South Snohomish County Historical Society, photo #306.5)

business activity and growth stemming from the Boeing plant caused optimism to carry into the 1970s.

The boom was changing the face of Snohomish County. In September 1965 Klein Motors, a Ford distributor, was the first to abandon Everett's old Rucker Avenue auto row downtown for a larger site south on 52nd and Evergreen Way. By May 1966 a new shopping center anchored by a Wigwam variety store was under construction opposite it. Less than a decade earlier both would have been just outside of Everett's city limits at 52nd Street. At the end of December 1965 the S.S. Kresge Company unveiled plans for a new K-Mart department store on 79th and Evergreen Way. This, the first new such big-box complex on old Highway 99, gave a whole new definition to the old "dime stores." It covered 11 acres and had parking for 1,000 cars. Another K-Mart followed on Old Highway 99 in Edmonds, while Valu-Mart opened a similar store on the same road. It became obvious that the earlier highways would not become backwaters, but instead the busy new thoroughfares of commerce, requiring new lights and significant widening as traffic intensified.

With much of Everett at saturation point in terms of new housing and further expansion to the west, north, and east limited by its peninsular location, many developers turned south to Lynnwood. The opening of I-5 had the effect of moving the center of activity from the 196th Street S.W. crossroads with Highway 99 easterly back toward old Alderwood Manor, as freeway Interchanges at 196th and 44th Avenue W. caused those two arterials to become Lynnwood's new main thoroughfares. A relatively unknown Portland based company had plans for the intersection of the two newly widened streets that would redefine the city. On December 4, 1968 Fred Meyer had a grand opening of its first outlet in the Puget Sound area. At 185,000 square feet it was reportedly the largest single floor store in the Pacific Northwest. The opening was a significant enough event that the mayors of Edmonds, Mountlake Terrace, Brier, and Woodway joined Lynnwood Mayor Merle Hrdlicka for ceremonies that included pop singer Tiny Tim, Minnesota Twins baseball slugger Harmon Killebrew, and local children's television heroes J.P. Patches and Gertrude. Now shoppers in South County had a new place to shop for food, apparel, pharmaceutical products, and a variety of other items all under one roof. Additionally, there were new housing developments east of Lynnwood, such as Mays Pond in the Everett School District off 180th Street just east of the Bothell-Everett Highway, which opened October 17, 1969.

One down side of the growth in Lynnwood came with the decision when widening 196th to eliminate the route around Scriber Lake and go right next to it. Since the area was a bog, fill materials such as logs and brush tended to float. Engineers finally overcame the problem, but the resulting road accelerated the lake's aging process, breaking it into two smaller bodies of water. Today the area is a city park, providing respite in a busy community.

Strategically located between the Everett and Edmonds school districts, the residents of the Mukilteo School District found themselves with a difficult choice. The new Boeing plant with its substantial property tax base and influx of working families was located within its previously mostly rural boundaries. After intensive debate, they decided to open their first high school, Mariner, at the southern edge of the district miles away from the original pioneering town. Up to this time most students in the district had attended high school in Everett.

338

As early as summer 1966 a sign was erected advertising the proposed Broadway Center along the Broadway Cutoff south of Everett. The 40-acre mall, anchored with a new Sears, Roebuck Company outlet replacing the downtown Everett department store on Colby and Everett avenues, was to open in 1968. The actual ribbon cutting for the Sears store was on February 12, 1969. A month later Allied Stores announced construction plans for the Alderwood Mall, an even larger regional shopping center, to be located north of 196th Street and west of I-5 on the homestead of area pioneers William and Elizabeth Morrice. Prior to all this the county's closest was Aurora Mall, which had opened in 1959 just across the King County line on Highway 99.

Malls destroyed downtown shopping, appealing to customers with acres of free parking, volume of stores from which to choose, restaurants and entertainment, and anchored by a major retail outlet—often all under one roof. Built to formula, they depended upon open inexpensive land outside core areas with easy highway access. How to save abandoned downtowns from resulting decay and urban blight troubled city governments and merchants associations from then on.

Not all of the boom was good news. Some people were frustrated with the change that took place as neighboring stands of trees gave way to new housing developments and country roads became suburban arterials. Other rued the transformation of strawberry fields between Marysville and Arlington into residential subdivisions. County agriculture was threatened by higher taxes, loss of available land, and disappearing infrastructure of processors and dealers, while more dairy farms were going out of business. Although home building went on at a frantic pace, it could not keep up with demand, and therefore real estate prices reached new highs. Eventually price replaced volume as the biggest housing problem, an issue which continued throughout the era. In Lynnwood, 165 permits for multiple family dwellings were issued in 1968. Such apartments, often in large complexes, commanded rents beyond what middle and low-income families could pay.

All public services were strained. The item that held back the proposed new town of Olympus, for example, was sewer construction. Planned for the vicinity of 164th and the Bothell-Everett Highway, the city was projected by its developers to eclipse Everett in just 10 years, with a population of 200,000. Water shortages to meet projected growth faced the Snohomish and Skykomish valleys. Health care was more expensive as room rates jumped at Providence and General Hospitals in Everett and Stevens Hospital in Edmonds. Law enforcement agencies were burdened with jumps in crime rates, including wider use of alcohol, marijuana and narcotics, as Edmonds Police Lieutenant Les Newert estimated that half the high school students in that city had experimented with drugs. Vandalism was up, as were armed robberies in Everett, Lynnwood and Mountlake Terrace. In Snohomish traffic violations tripled and burglaries doubled. In Monroe there was an increase in car thefts. Sultan had an invasion of "hippies" and a bank robbery. However, in spite of all the changes, most people were enjoying the good times.

Then, as quickly as it had begun, the boom was over as a nation-wide recession set in. Once the first 747s were in production, employment began dropping at the Boeing plant. These cutbacks were expected, but the situation was more severe as the airlines industry floundered and orders slowed on the jumbo-jets. The situation was exacerbated when the United States Senate cut funding for the proposed Super Sonic Transport (SST) in 1971. From a manpower high of about 25,000 at the Everett plant, employment collapsed to a low of 4,700 in 1972. Naturally the bottom fell out of the real estate market.

From Marysville to Mountlake Terrace the lay-offs forced newcomers simply to walk away from their new homes and mortgages. It was a rare block in Everett or Lynnwood that did not have an F.B.I. warning sign in the front window of a vacant repossessed home owned by the federal Department of Housing and Urban Development. In the Puget Sound region there was a net out migration of 53,000, equal to the population of Everett. A billboard erected by two Seattle area real estate salesmen seemed to say it all: "Will the last person leaving SEATTLE—Turn out the lights."

In the fall of 1969 the Edmonds School District had continued its construction program with the opening of College Place, Evergreen and Hilltop elementary schools. Yet, less than two years later, the school board had the grueling task of deciding which three elementary schools to shut down. After 20 years those young families of World War II veterans whose acute need for housing had led to the population boom in Mountlake Terrace and then throughout South County had passed beyond their child-rearing years. Sharply declining enrollments led to doors closing at Cypress, Maplewood, and Woodway elementary schools. Edmonds elementary school followed in 1970, then eventually Martha Lake, Forest Crest, Alderwood, Esperance, Maple Park, and Melody Hill elementary school, plus the Edmonds junior high school.

Everett School District No. 2 also endured a major reduction and shifts in enrollment patterns, losing the Mukilteo high school students to Mariner and then families to the economic decline, a total of 3,000 students between 1969 and 1972. Meanwhile the trend of young families buying new homes to the south continued, leading to closures in the older neighborhoods. The original Jefferson School built in 1894 on Pacific and Hoyt avenues last was used for classes in 1959, then after an interim career as central office space was torn down in 1964, the land used for the new Everett post office. Other elementary schools followed: the 1911 Longfellow next to the Memorial Stadium in to office space in 1971, 1929 Roosevelt in Beverly Park into the New Life religious center after 1973, and 1908 Washington on north Oakes recycled into the Washington Oakes retirement apartments.

As businesses failed and the local economy lurched with the bust (the cleared acreage for the Alderwood Mall became a haven for dirt bikers and model airplane enthusiasts, for example) it also was a turbulent time for the nation. A new generation was questioning American values in a way that shook the very foundation of the country. It was a time of protest—a time of demanding equal rights for women and minorities and a time to protest the industrial destruction of the environment. Nothing brought young dissenters together more than the United States' military involvement in Vietnam. When the decision was made to invade Cambodia in the spring of 1970, college campus demonstrations erupted nationwide. At Kent State University in Ohio four students were killed by national guardsmen in a riot, causing even more tension among youth. Everett Community College philosophy instructor David Houghtaling suspended his classes in protest against the invasion of Cambodia and the National Guard action against the "Kent State Four." His grievances were about the Black liberation movement, Asians suffering from American imperialism in Southeast Asia, and American GIs in Vietnam. While they did not block the freeway as in Seattle and Bellingham, a crowd some 75 strong marched from the college parking lot over to Colby Avenue and downtown to the Selective Service office and courthouse. At Cascade High School approximately 100 students cut first period classes for a gathering in the cafeteria to discuss the Ohio student casualties. Students at the new Edmonds Community College came together to consider a strike. Adding to the confusion, there was dissension among the young people. Other Everett Community College students drafted a resolution condemning the strike, while anti-protesters at Cascade High announced that they were at the school for an education and not to demonstrate.

Students also were showing their feelings by questioning school dress codes, which were modified as a result. This, in part, helped women challenge them as well. In January 1971 women teachers in Everett were allowed to teach in pantsuits, only a beginning of the liberation women would find in the coming decades. Women who were urged into the work force during World War II and then laid off when the men came home were moving permanently from roles limited to housewives, nurses, secretaries, and teachers to major positions of leadership. Eleanor Fortson was elected to the State House of Representatives, while Diane Woody and Susan Gould served in the Senate. Everett even had a policewoman by March 1971. Changes also affected youth organizations, as Campfire no longer was solely for girls or Explorer Scouts for boys, while physical education classes in the public schools also became co-educational, and girls' athletic programs moved toward equality with boys' due to federal legislation banning discrimination based on gender.

Citizen activism in government also increased when Martha Lake resident and furniture salesman Bruce Helm set out to reverse a pay hike state legislators had granted themselves in the recent session. He gathered about 700,000 signatures to ensure Initiative 282 would go to the voters. The measure, which passed four-to-one, rolled salaries back to the 5.5 percent increase accepted under federal guidelines.

As county population grew and demands on government continued to increase, county commissioners erected a $5.6 million administration building just east of the old courthouse Mission Building. Voters earlier had rejected selling bonds for the project earlier, but the county insisted it needed the office space and construction jobs would be created. Funding instead came from sales tax revenues. Additional facilities developed when a Thurston County judge ruled in 1981 that the overcrowded Snohomish County jail in the top floor of the courts building was inadequate. The site chosen for a new jail at Wall Street and Lombard Avenue was two blocks east of the courthouse. The $12 million facility was completed in 1986. With 11 stories, it was equipped to handle 257 men and 20 women, with the majority of the inmates being held for no more than 72 hours before being assigned to housing or released. As population grew, however, even this was not enough. Law and justice became even greater costs to county government, demanding an increasing percentage of the budget.

On a September evening in 1973 county motorists joined long lines at area gas stations to fill up, fearing a boycott by service station owners might cause a petroleum scarcity for the next few days. Dealers were protesting President Richard M. Nixon's price freeze on retail gasoline. Not all honored the boycott, and some who stayed open did run out. These lines were an omen of what was to come. The fragile peace in the Middle East once again was broken on Yom Kippur, when Egypt and Syria suddenly attacked Israel. American assistance to the Israelis resulted in the employment of a new tactic by the Arabs, an oil embargo. Major population centers were hardest hit, and the Puget Sound region was no exception. Residents were beginning to wonder if they ever would be able

The venerable Everett Pulp and Paper mill in Lowell, shown here in its 1950s heyday when it was sold to the Simpson Timber Company (later Simpson-Lee), became antiquated and expensive to operate. Closed in 1972, it was dismantled soon after, and the community lost a major economic asset. (Courtesy Everett Public Library)

to drive up to a pump again without a long wait. Typical were lines at the Mobil station in Stanwood, where the dealer had a 10-gallon limit and closed at 6:30 P.M. Drivers gladly pumped their own gas. A complicated system of flags was implemented which signaled when gas was available, but then maybe only to regular customers. Eventually, motorists were allowed only to buy gasoline on odd or even dates according to the last digit of their license plate numbers. With the shortage the oil companies closed some of their outlets, and the old gas station on every corner adage began to change. As far as the scarcity went, there never did seem to be much difference in the number of county teenagers heading for Everett on Friday and Saturday nights for a session of "cruisin' Colby." Real or not, the shortage did bring about some things that would not change. There were fewer service stations, brands such as Gulf, Amoco, and Phillips 66 retreated back across the Cascades, most stations became self-service, and gas prices went up substantially. American taste turned for a while toward smaller and more fuel-efficient cars, many of them foreign, as Detroit was slow to catch on. This trend lasted until the prosperity of the late 1980s and 1990s, when four-wheeled drive sports utility vehicles and light trucks again were known for their gas guzzling.

Snohomish County awoke to a shock on January 15, 1974 with news of the brutal murder of Sheriff Donald Jennings. While vacationing near the Mexican resort city of

Mazatlan, Jennings, his wife, and his mother-in-law were shot to death in their motor home. Robbery was immediately suspected as the motive. Later other theories surfaced. Some suspected a conspiracy, others thought that anti-Americans did it, or perhaps the blame lay with Mexican police and a cover-up. Most leads led to dead ends, and while suspects were held by Mexican authorities, no arrests were made. Years later, the case was still as puzzling. Some believed that the travelers were mistaken for drug traffickers by undercover Mexican "federales" and shot when they tried to escape. Others believed the murders were committed by a small band of Mexican nationals getting revenge on wealthy Americans. Those from Snohomish County agreed that, at best, Mexican police work was poor, as police were caught in lies and evidence was tampered with or destroyed. In addition, two of the Mexican officers investigating the case were later convicted of murdering six Mexican nationals the night the Jennings party was killed. Even after 25 years had elapsed, Sheriff Rick Bart said he still wanted to see the case closed before he left office.

Less than a month after the Jennings murder, on the foggy Saturday morning of February 9, 1974, a crowd gathered near the old car wash in the Simpson-Lee parking lot in Lowell. It was on this site that the substantial home of A.H.B. Jordan, one of the owners of the Everett Pulp and Paper Company mill, once had stood. The onlookers came to witness the end of an era with the implosion of the plant's 50-year-old smokestack, long a fixture of the Lowell skyline. Closed over a year earlier rather than meet the costs required to comply with air and water pollution standards, most of the pioneer mill already had been dismantled and its work force laid off. The heavy fog did not lift, so after the thud of the blast the spectators strained to see the stack slowly sink to the ground. With its collapse a key link to the founding of Everett was severed, and Lowell had lost its once stable economic base. Cut off by the freeway on the hill above and bounded by the Snohomish River below, Lowell had become only an isolated neighborhood of older houses and a few small businesses.

The gloom of the day extended beyond Lowell, as the county's timber, pulp, and paper industry was fading into history with more closures and layoffs. While the Boeing Company was rehiring, it had not held its promise of being the next secure industrial base for the area, and service sector jobs would not pay anything comparable to the wages and benefits skilled unionized workers had fought to obtain in the mills. Although almost every group had shared in the increasing national wealth of the past 30 post-war years, now an ever-increasing gap began to grow between rich and poor, with the middle class shrinking and two wage earners in the family becoming the norm.

For valley residents, floods in Snohomish County are not uncommon, but those of December 1975 were notable for their severity. During the worst floods in a half-century the Snohomish, Skykomish, Snoqualmie, Pilchuck, Sultan, Stillaguamish, and Sauk Rivers swelled and overflowed their banks. The Snohomish at Snohomish was well above flood level, while a failed dike put Ebey Island under 15 feet of water. As usual, the old Snohomish-Monroe Highway and the road to Duvall were affected. Agriculture and dairying suffered a critical blow, with the destruction of the French Creek Flood Control project upstream from Snohomish allowing torrents of water swiftly to inundate the lowlands. The Burlington Northern Railway tracks were closed due to washouts, while the eastern approach to High Bridge over the Snoqualmie River washed away. At Monroe the

343

Lewis Street bridge fishing access was under several feet of the Skykomish River. The nearby Sergeants Road area was evacuated, as were the Sky View River Tract and the Twin Rivers mobile home park at the confluence of the Snoqualmie and Skykomish rivers southeast of Monroe. Farther east, downtown Sultan businesses were threatened as water came up Main Street. Tunnel Creek washed out part of the west bound lanes of U.S. 2 below Stevens Pass, and nearly half the roads in the Mt. Baker-Snoqualmie National Forest were damaged. To the north there was a 30-foot break in the dike on Hatt Slough near the mouth of the Stillaguamish River. In all more than 300 people were evacuated, 50,000 acres of lowlands were inundated, and damage ran into millions of dollars, as Governor Daniel Evans declared the county a disaster area. In the aftermath one particularly gruesome task was the disposal of 1,300 animal carcasses from the French Creek break, as hundreds of dead cattle were buried at the Bryant landfill. As muddy waters receded, revealing the massive extent of the damage, busy young volunteers from FFA classes and Snohomish High School helped farmers with the cleanup work.

By the mid-1970s the economy had rebounded. The federally owned vacant houses were being sold by lottery, and gone were the days when $30,000 would purchase a three bedroom home with 160 feet of waterfront on Lake Stevens. The situation had improved enough for United Development Corporation, a subsidiary of Tokyo Corporation and Ohbayashi Corporation, to create a new up-scale planned community centered about an 18-hole golf course and located where Olympus had been proposed earlier near 164th Street and the Bothell-Everett Highway. Originally called "Klahanie" (Chinook for open, free, or outdoors), the developers felt it sounded too Japanese and opted instead for "Mill Creek." The first occupants moved into their homes in spring 1976, the same year the course was completed. Affordable then by less than six percent of the county's population, many of the high-end homes overlooked the fairways. In the early years most of the governmental duties were overseen by a homeowners association, which also enforced the many restrictive property covenants. However, it was soon obvious that incorporation was a more attractive option for preserving community standards than were relying on county services or being annexed into less restrictive Everett or Lynnwood. In September 1983, voters approved incorporation with a majority, and Sid Hanson was elected the first mayor of the city of approximately 3,000. As population grew, the Everett School District responded with the construction of Mill Creek Elementary, Heatherwood Middle and Jackson High Schools in 1988, 1990, and 1994 respectively. By the end of the century Mill Creek's population reached 10,000, as it created a vibrant civic and business center west of the Bothell-Everett Highway and expanded northward toward a meeting with Everett.

The economy also was strong enough for the DeBartolo Company of Ohio, which had purchased the Alderwood Mall site from Allied Stores in 1976, to go ahead with their plans. In late 1977 the 100-acre parcel,

Willis Tucker (right) and Bob Drewel, both Democrats, became the first two County Executives in Snohomish County government when the commission form was revised to a council and executive. Tucker, from Snohomish, had a long career as an Everett *Herald* newspaper writer, while his successor Drewel, from Arlington, had served as president of Everett Community College before his election. (Courtesy Bob Drewel)

344

which had sat vacant for a decade, began to be transformed into the county's largest shopping center. In 1979, 10 years after it was first announced, the Alderwood Mall finally became a reality and set off a building boom in the northeast part of Lynnwood.

In December of 1977 Lloyd Meeds, Second Congressional District Representative, announced his decision not to run for reelection in 1978. A graduate of Monroe High School, Everett Junior College, and Gonzaga University Law School, he also had served in the United State Navy. He began as a deputy prosecuting attorney in Spokane and Snohomish counties, and later served as Snohomish County Prosecutor. Meeds had represented the district (which included all but the southwestern part of the county) since 1964. As he bowed out, Bellingham radio announcer and fellow Democrat Al Swift was elected to the position. For the first time since the Depression the 2nd Congressional District was represented by someone outside of Snohomish County, a situation which did not change until 2001 when Democrat Rick Larsen succeeded retiring two-term member Republican Jack Metcalf of Langley.

Changes also came to county government. The 21st amendment to the state constitution in 1948 had allowed counties to adopt home rule. Snohomish first had taken advantage of this in 1968, when a 15-member Board of Freeholders was elected to write a new charter, but this proposal was defeated at the polls. In November 1979 voters adopted a home rule charter developed by 21 newly elected Freeholders. The reorganized executive/council form of government went into effect May 1, 1980. The charter provides for the elected offices of County Executive, five council members chosen by districts, plus the positions of Assessor, Auditor, Clerk, Sheriff and Treasurer, which eventually were made non-partisan. In the years since the elimination of the three-commissioner system, three Democrats served as Executive, Willis Tucker of Snohomish, Bob Drewel of Arlington and Aaron Reardon of Everett. Reardon gave up his state senate seat and won the executive's position in November 2003 when term limits required Drewel to step aside. Control over council direction has been more contentious, with Republicans controlling District 3 in the southwest, Democrats District 2 in Everett, and the remaining three dependent upon current issues, personalities, and voter mood swings.

Heavy rains and melting snow on Christmas Day 1980 caused severe flooding once again. This time it was the upper elevations that sustained the ravages of the swollen rivers. Rampaging floodwaters of the North Fork Skykomish River at Index carried off two blocks of Avenue A and seven houses, as people's lots on the west side of town became river bottom. Worsening the situation, the Reiter Road into town from Gold Bar was under water and the town's sole water line destroyed. Farther east, Snohomish County never reopened the road up to Mineral City and its historic mining district after a massive landslide collapsed a portion of the road into the canyon of Silver Creek. Over the ridges to the north the South Fork Stillaguamish River claimed parts of the Mountain Loop Highway between Red Bridge and the Silverton school camp and another section at Boardman Creek, as well as inundat-

In 2004 at age 33 Democrat Aaron Reardon became the third County Executive, following five years of service in the state legislature. (Courtesy Snohomish County Executive's Office)

ing a dozen homes northeast of Granite Falls. Along the Sauk River there were several disasters. The warm rains caused a clay slide on the road to Monte Cristo to slough down into the river, while bridge approaches were washed away and deep piles of debris swept down the mountainside, isolating the families of Jerry and Eileen Rosman and Jim and Del Thompson. The county never repaired the damage or bridges. As a result the Monte Cristo Preservation Association was formed in 1983, in part to continue public access to the historic mining and alpine area. Downstream the Mountain Loop Highway was eroded away in several places, the worst spots below Monte Cristo Lake, scoured-out Bedal Creek, and loss of the bridge serving isolated residents at Reece's Hideaway. Churning waters reached 16 feet in a few hours at Darrington, forcing evacuation as at least three homes were swept

In 1980, the floods began the day after Christmas, devastating communities and cutting roads in the Cascade Mountains and foothills. The North Fork Skykomish River did not "yield," sweeping away the homes, trees, road, and utilities in Index and cutting the town's water system. Damage took years to repair, while some roads and bridges in the county were abandoned permanently. (Courtesy Kem Hunter)

away and nearly 40 others damaged, including those splintered by floating logs. In the lowlands damage was less, but there were heroic tales such as that of John Gonsalves, who clung to an alder tree south of Monroe for two and a half hours while waters of the Snoqualmie raged below him. Downtown Sultan once again was awash and evacuation necessary. U.S. 2 was closed at Monroe, as was S.R. 530 between Silvana and Stanwood. Altogether damages topped $4.5 million.

Population growth during the 1970s led to the State of Washington gaining a ninth member to the House of Representatives and set off the inevitable redistricting fight between Republicans and Democrats to see which party would gain. Everett found itself little more than a tail on the 1st Congressional District dog dominated by south Snohomish County and north Seattle. Protests came almost immediately, enshrining Everett resident Peggy Doph in *Doph v. Munro*, the case against the new boundaries. A very vocal committee from Everett wanted the city restored to the 2nd District, where it had been the largest and most powerful municipality. The fruits of the committee's work finally paid off when Republican Governor John Spellman signed into law House Bill 1038, restoring Everett to its traditional 2nd District position.

The early 1980s were years of contradictions. On the surface industry appeared to be healthier than ever. Chinese Vice Premier Deng Xiaoping had visited the Boeing 747 plant in 1979 in a gesture which seemed to presage new commercial orders, while the company rolled out its new 210-seat 767 model in August 1981. Also, although a new Seaway Boulevard north of the Boeing plant dead-ended into a chain link fence, the promise of a new technology corridor between Everett and Bellevue seemed certain. Editors of *Time* magazine broke tradition when, instead of naming a Man of the Year in 1982, they chose the computer as the Machine of the Year. Snohomish County was right in step, with electronics company Hewlett-Packard building a plant on Soper Hill west of Highway 9 between Marysville and Lake Stevens, Eldec in the Martha Lake area continu-

In 1979 another victim of the declining lumber era was Weyerhaeuser's Mill B, once the largest all-electric saw mill in the world. The company's sulphite pulp mill A on the Everett waterfront closed two years later and the kraft pulp mill in another decade. By 1990 the county's once largest employer had ended Everett's reputation as "Milltown." (Courtesy Bernie Webber)

347

Index: Coping with Isolation and Change

Following the disastrous December 1980 flood, residents of the town pulled together to restore their damaged water system, roads, and homes and create a new sense of community pride. A Fourth of July parade grew out of having a celebration for the children, as well as for the country. This was the 1984 version. (Courtesy Louise Lindgren)

The issues and their implications related to salmon and bull trout as endangered species still are developing, but the Skykomish and North Fork Stillaguamish rivers continue to provide excellent opportunities for fishing. James "JJ" Jotblad has a winter steelhead. (Courtesy Louise Lindgren)

A rapidly growing sport on the eastern whitewater rivers of the county is rafting and kayaking, which has led to the creation of skilled guide services, expedition outfitters, and seasonal employment. The Skykomish River from Index to High Bridge is especially known for its challenging rapids and famous Boulder Drop. (Courtesy Louise Lindgren)

Regulations on land and water use, growth management, and urban growth boundaries have been very divisive in the county, often sparking political changes and heated debates. Citizens here gather outside the Index General Store to argue the issue of being assessed a surface water management fee. (Courtesy Louise Lindgren)

ing its growth, and Honeywell Marine Systems building in the Harbour Pointe area west of Paine Field. John Fluke, another electronics firm, moved from its Mountlake Terrace plant to the old Valu-Mart building on Evergreen Way while it planned a new headquarters north of Boeing.

Both the ports of Edmonds and Everett were growing. The Port of Everett was filling in a new area north of the old shipyards at 18th Street, which would become a diversified terminal, creating new jobs. As in cities all over the country, the waterfronts were being improved for recreational uses. Both had large new marinas, and as with Mukilteo, were becoming people places offering nearby fine restaurants and shops. The glass fronted Wall Street Building at Wetmore Avenue and Wall Street at 10 stories became Everett's tallest, while the new 254-room Everett Pacific Hotel and convention center on Pacific Avenue at I-5 would employ 200. *The Everett News Tribune*, a branch of the *Snohomish Tribune*, began publishing its weekly on May 20, 1981.

In reality, though, it was a time of recession. Dependent upon sales tax revenues for much of its income, the state was having financial troubles. Airlines were not ordering the wide-bodied jets, so once again Boeing made deep cuts at the Everett plant, its work force of 18,000 in 1980 dwindling to 12,500 just two years later, and company stock values plummeted. The economy suffered with record high inflation, interest rates, and unemployment, sharply slowing the wood products and home building industries. Scott Paper Company announced lay-offs to an area already suffering cutbacks by Bayliner Marine Company, a recreational boat manufacturer in Arlington. On the north Everett waterfront, new third-generation family management policies at he E.A. Nord Door Company led to a long, brutal strike, which evoked reminders of the 1916 IWW atmosphere.

Downtown Everett was moribund. In the mid-1970s the city had attempted to retain shoppers and retailers with new sidewalks and landscaping on Colby Avenue, trees down Hewitt Avenue, and a sculpture where the two met, defining the heart of the retail section. The area was much more attractive, but that was not enough to buck the national trend of large chain stores locating in the malls, flagship department stores moving out, grocery stores abandoning their older and smaller outlets in favor of huge facilities with massive parking lots, and family owned businesses fleeing with them or forced to close. The area actually approached a rare no-growth population period.

On a positive note, Everett voters passed a paramedic levy, as calling 911 for emergency health needs gradually became effective throughout the county. Fire districts and urban departments created staffs of both professional and volunteer members highly trained in medical responses, centrally dispatched, backed up with mutual aid agreements, and coordinated with the region's hospitals. Aid calls now became more common than those for fires. Snohomish County Search and Rescue units, assisted by Everett Mountain Rescue and under the command of daring sheriff's deputies such as renknowned Sergeant John Taylor provided back country assistance which also saved many lives.

As industry and population grew rapidly in the county, so also did the need for electrical energy to serve them. The Washington Public Power Supply System (WPPSS) dated back to 1957, when 17 public and privately owned electrical utilities including the Snohomish County P.U.D. No. 1 formed a joint operating agency authorized by the Washington State Legislature. Its first project was a small hydroelectric plant at

Packwood, in Pierce County. Based on the nuclear industry's optimistic cost estimates and Bonneville Power Administration market projections that energy use would continue to soar, WPPSS now expected to build five separate nuclear power plants for less than $2 billion, operate them for 40 years, and sell the output for less than a penny per kilowatt. However, WPPSS was a late entrant in the nuclear construction field, and it quickly fell victim to poor management, engineering problems, safety issues, contract disputes, and cost overruns, which already plagued the industry. As construction cost skyrocketed, utilities raised rates to pay for the increasingly expensive projects.

Members of the AquaSox, Everett's Class A Northwest baseball team, sign autographs for eager young fans. In 1984, Bob and Margaret Bavasi brought the franchise here and affiliated with the San Francisco Giants. In 1995 the team switched to the Seattle Mariners and became the AquaSox. Mark and Joan Sperandio purchased the club after the 1998 season, continuing the tradition of "real baseball on real grass." (Courtesy the Everett AquaSox)

Snohomish County P.U.D., the state's largest, also had the largest participant shares, 13 percent of the public ownership in all five nuclear projects. To meet its obligations under the billing agreements the P.U.D. raised the cost of electricity in Snohomish County and Camano Island almost 400 percent in a space of three years. As the cost of electricity went up, public confidence went down. Heating and lighting bills, traditionally among the cheapest in the nation, now were bigger than mortgage payments for a number of older homeowners. The grass roots organization Fair Use of Snohomish Energy (FUSE) urged the utility to end its involvement in the nuclear program. In 1982 a FUSE leader, Matt Dillon, filed for a seat on the P.U.D. Board of Commissioners, promising to "end the P.U.D.'s love affair" with nuclear power. Dillon offered voters a choice between the status quo and the possibility of reform. Outspent five to one and opposed by interests including his employer, the Boeing Company, the young union electrician won a bitterly contested election with 53 percent of the vote. By the time Dillon took office WPPSS was in a tailspin out of control, and investors had lost confidence in the supply system's ability to manage costs. The joint operating agency now thought it would take 12 times its original estimates, or $25 billion, to build the reactors. As utilities increased the price of electricity to pay for the cost overruns, the demand for power naturally dropped, a point missed in the BPA projections. The shortages and brownouts of the 1970s vanished, and utilities struggled with a combination of falling revenues and a huge oversupply of electricity, which would last until population growth and energy deregulation (begun in 1995) absorbed it. Then the cycle of increased demand and looming shortages began again, touched off by California deregulation, energy trading company corruption, a shortage of new generating capacity, and heavy requirements for more power from the "high tech" industries, along with unceasing population growth. Badly burned by the nuclear experience, new generation favored natural gas, which also had supply limits.

In the summer of 1983 the Washington State Supreme Court finally ruled that the state's publicly owned utilities did not have the authority to enter into participant agreements in two of the WPPSS nuclear projects. This ruling forced the Snohomish County P.U.D. commissioners to repeal a 16.5 percent rate increase they had approved a few months earlier. Unable to attract investors or find buyers for the unfinished projects, WPPSS defaulted on its obligation to repay $2.3 billion worth of bonds it sold to finance the fourth and fifth reactors. This action, the largest municipal bond default in the nation's history, set off a tangle of lawsuits between the 88 participating utilities, BPA, bond holders, brokers, banks, underwriters, engineering firms, contractors and suppliers. After a decade of litigation in state and federal courts, bond holders recovered only a fraction of their investment, saving county residents from having to pay off bonds over the next 30 years for electricity they never would receive. Only one of the five nuclear projects was completed by WPPSS, and its performance did not live up to expectations, as most of the plant's output cost more to generate than it was worth. Snohomish County P.U.D. no longer had the cheapest electrical rates in the country, and by early in the new century had some of the highest.

On the evening of September 1, 1983 county residents were stunned with news of the sudden death of Senator Henry M. Jackson. Everett's favorite son had died at his Grand Avenue home of a massive heart attack. Born in 1912 of Norwegian immigrants, "Scoop" had begun his political career as Snohomish County prosecuting attorney. He was successful in his bid to the House of Representatives in 1940 and joined the U.S. Senate in 1952. In 1972 and again in 1976 he campaigned for the Democratic presidential nomination, taking the Massachusetts and New York primaries before Governor Jimmy Carter of Georgia seemed to come out of nowhere. For years he and fellow Washington Senator Warren G. Magnuson had been two of the most powerful members of Congress. His funeral, held at Everett's First Presbyterian Church, brought such luminaries as Vice President George H.W. Bush, Massachusetts Senator Edward M. Kennedy, former Secretary of State Henry Kissinger, and Supreme Court Justice Warren Burger. Although he spent over three decades in the Senate, he never forgot his roots in Snohomish County.

Many institutions such as Henry M. Jackson High School in Mill Creek ended up carrying his name. It also lived on appropriately in the Henry M. Jackson Wilderness area. Located in the easternmost part of the county, adjacent to the Glacier Peak Wilderness, it included Goat Lake and much of the old Monte Cristo mining district, a place Scoop had hiked as a youth. He had backed the creation of wilderness areas, a concept which had bipartisan support despite environmental complaints that proposed lands were not large enough and forest products industry concerns that too much prime timber land would be included. In Snohomish County that would include enlarging the Glacier Peak and creation of both the Boulder River and Jackson wilderness areas. Congress approved the Washington Wilderness bill in June 1984, with President Ronald Reagan quietly signing it a month later. Among those present at the August dedication near Goat Lake were Jackson's widow Helen Jackson, Republican Senators Dan Evans and Slade Gorton, and Democratic 2nd Congressional Representative Al Swift, who was the prime force behind preservation of the Boulder River through his staff member and environmentalist Rick McGuire.

One of Senator Jackson's dreams was realized on along the Everett waterfront. In May 1983 Everett and Seattle became finalists for a new navy homeport. Jackson, always a strong supporter of national defense, favored the Everett selection. Ironically the

Henry M. Jackson

By Tom Gaskin

Henry Martin ("Scoop") Jackson's remarkable congressional career, spanning 43 years (12 years in the House of Representatives and 31 years in the Senate), came to a sudden end when Jackson died of a heart attack at age 71 in 1983. During his impressive political career, Jackson served in congress while nine different presidential administrations were in office and became one of the nation's most important political figures. He twice campaigned for Democratic Party's presidential nomination.

Born on May 31, 1912 in the mill town of Everett, Jackson was the youngest of four children. His oldest sister, Gertrude, nicknamed Henry "Scoop" after a comic-strip character in the Everett *Herald* who constantly escaped doing work. Jackson's parents, Peter and Marine, had migrated from Norway to the Northwest before they met and married. Peter excelled at building solid concrete basements as a contractor. Marine create equally strong family values in the Jackson home.

As a paperboy for the *Herald* in the 1920s, Jackson earned an award for fewest customer complaints three years in a row. Scoop's route took him down the south side of Hewitt, from Colby to the bay. That was a rough part of town in a tough community of loggers and longshoremen. Many of the hotels were infested by ladies of the night (although they also worked during the day). The illegal drinking, gambling, and prostitution (all openly tolerated by city officials) bothered the young paperboy. Reflecting on these experiences years later, Jackson remarked, "I saw this going on, and I said, 'I want a chance someday to do something about that . . . .'"

After graduating from Everett High School in 1930 and the University of Washington Law School in 1935 during the heart of the Great Depression, Jackson worked briefly for the Federal Emergency Relief Agency. Later, he joined the Everett law firm of Lloyd Black and Jasper Rucker. Although his father was a staunch Republican, in 1938 Jackson filed as a Democratic candidate for Snohomish County prosecutor, heeding Lloyd Black's advice, "Well Henry, if you want to be in business, be a Republican, but if you want to be in politics, be a Democrat."

With corruption so visible and the county solidly Democratic as a result of the Depression, Jackson (only 26 years old) became the youngest prosecutor in Snohomish County's history. Immediately, he set out to earn his $250 a month salary. He led raids against providers of illegal liquor and owners of pinball machines that made cash payoffs. In 1939 he tried Edward Bouchard in the county's first robbery-murder case since 1926. The *Herald* described the arrest and conviction as "one of the quickest and most dramatic sequences in the annals of major crime in this county." When Mon Wallgren decided to leave his Second Congressional seat to run for the Senate, Jackson rode his widening popularity as prosecutor to a 1940 congressional election victory.

He would be elected to six terms as a member of the House of Representatives. During World War II Jackson supported the relocation of the Japanese Americans to detention camps and suggested, according to the Seattle *Post Intelligencer*, "that pro-Japanese influences still exists in the United States, having gone underground only temporarily." In 1943 Jackson waived his congressional immunity to the draft and entered the Army as a private. He served 15 of the 17 weeks of basic training (half of that time was spent in an Army hospital with an infected foot) before President Roosevelt called congressmen in the military back to Washington, D. C. As a member of the House, Jackson voted against the creation of a permanent House Un-American Activities Committee, for upholding President Truman's veto of the anti-union Taft-Hartley Act, and promoted hydroelectric resources of the Northwest, as well as nuclear power.

In 1952 Jackson challenged the arch conservative Senator Harry Cain, a man even *Time* magazine called one of the Senate's most expendable members, for his upper house seat. Cain's highly publicized extra-marital affair with his secretary helped Jackson become only one of two Democrats to defeat Republican senators in the Eisenhower landslide of 1952.

As a senator, Jackson warned that the United States suffered a "missile gap" with the Soviet Union. When the Russians launched Sputnik in 1957 and the U. S.'s initial space efforts failed (dubbed "flopnik" by the Soviet leader Khrushchev), Jackson's political stock soared. Incorrect about the missile gap, Jackson's popularity and close friendship with Senator John Kennedy made the Washington senator a contender, although unsuccessful for the Democratic Vice-Presidential nomination in Los Angeles in 1960.

In 1961 Jackson and Helen Hardin married. Previously New Mexico Senator Clinton Anderson's receptionist, the newly-wed Mrs. Jackson remarked demurely to newspapermen after the honeymoon, "Some of Scoop's political friends have told me that it must be true love, because I come from a state which has so few electoral votes." In 1963 Anna Marie was born, and, three years later Peter Hardin completed the Jackson family. In 1970 Jackson was named "Father of the Year."

His concern for the environment garnered him other awards. An environmentalist long before it was popular, Jackson the former Boy Scout who had traipsed through the Cascades as a youth, helped steer the Wilderness Act of 1964, the Redwoods National Park Act of 1968, North Cascades National Park Act of 1968, and the Natural Environmental Policy Act of 1969. The Sierra Club, the Baruch Foundation and the National Wildlife Federation all presented Jackson awards for his conservation efforts.

Jackson tried to win the 1972 Democratic presidential from rivals George McGovern and George Wallace. Unable to do so (despite what McGovern workers felt was Jackson's attempt to describe the senator from South Dakota as the candidate of "amnesty, abortion, and acid"), Jackson's chances for the White House appeared better in 1976. The Watergate scandal and Ford's pardon of Nixon encouraged voters to elect a candidate outside of the Washington beltway: Jimmy Carter.

Domestically, Jackson with the aid of Senator Warren C. Magnuson (the so-called "Gold Dust Twins") brought vast amounts of government expenditures to Washington State. As two biographers of Jackson note, "In some years during their powerful reign, the amount of federal money that flowed into Washington State was three times as much as their constituents sent back to the capital in federal taxes."

Although Jackson made contributions shaping the legislative agenda in almost every major area in American life, he is probably best known for his opposition to the Soviet Union. As he liked to say, "It was clear to me that the Cold War was going to be the great challenge of my time." That fear of communism, however, did not shake his faith in the ability of the American public successfully to respond to the threat.

During the early 1950s, when Jackson entered the senate, hysteria over communist infiltration into the federal government gripped the nation. Senator Joe McCarthy of Wisconsin did much to encourage the "Red Scare." On one occasion he sarcastically remarked, "I don't think we need fear too much about the communists dropping atomic bombs on Washington. They would kill too many of their friends that way." Jackson did not share McCarthy's paranoia.

During the televised Army-McCarthy hearings in 1954, 20 million Americans saw the boyish looking Jackson methodically undermine McCarthy's credibility. When Jackson ridiculed a McCarthy staff proposal suggesting overseas communism be fought by distributing pinups and bumper stickers with democratic slogans, McCarthy threatened to "get" Jackson. He never did.

If Jackson rejected the danger of domestic communist subversion, throughout his senate career he remained an implacable foe of what he saw as a worldwide conspiracy of domination directed by the Soviet Union. As early as 1955 Jackson told reporters, "If we don't stop Russia in Southeast Asia, we might as well sign a quitclaim deed to the balance of Asia and grant Soviet entry into the United States." As the U. S. effort in Vietnam escalated in the 1960s, Jackson advocated an expanded war. Students at the University of Washington opposing the war started buying Henry-Jackson-suffers-from-a-military-complex posters for their dormitory room walls. When opposition to war became increasingly vocal, Jackson responded, "I'm neither a hawk nor a dove. I'm just interested in seeing that we don't become a pigeon out there." Evidently, the voters agreed with Jackson. In 1970 he was re-elected by an astounding 82.4-percent of the votes. Years later, Jackson reflected proudly that he had opposed both McCarthys: Joe and Eugene, the anti-war senator from Minnesota.

Tied to his fear of the Soviet Union were his interests in arms control and human rights. Jackson reluctantly supported the Nuclear Test Ban Treaty in 1963 and strongly criticized concessions made to the Soviet Union in the 1972 Strategic Arms Limitation Talks Treaty. He forced the Carter administration to withdraw the SALT II agreement from senate consideration, calling it "appeasement in purest form." Trying to increase the opportunity of Soviet Jewry to immigrate to Israel, Jackson (sometimes called the "Senator from Israel" for his unwavering support of the Jewish state) coupled improved trade relations with the Soviet Union to a change in their immigration policies. Jackson's anti-Soviet ideology became so legendary even he could kid about it. In a gathering in 1981, Jackson confirmed the President Nixon had in 1969 offered to appoint him Secretary of Defense, "but it was not true that I turned it down because he refused to give me one free shot [atomic attack] at Moscow."

Jackson did not live long enough to see the collapse of the Soviet Union, although he remained a "cold warrior" to the end. In his last major public statement of the day on the day he died he denounced the barbarity of the Soviet Union and the blasting of Korean Airlines flight 007 out of the sky.

proposed base would be on the very land of the shipyard, which he was instrumental in bringing to Everett during World War II. Almost as soon as the announcement was made, however, those against the base mobilized. Questions about the environment, depletion of health and social services resources, higher volumes on roads, demands on the public schools, concerns that the navy would attract a negative element to the area, as well as worries of having nuclear powered vessels in Everett and the threat of nuclear attack, were aired.

In April of the following year the final selection of Everett for the homeport was made. Polls indicated that the general populace favored the idea, but opponents through the Port Gardner Information League pushed for an advisory election. At first the Everett City Council was against such a vote, but members relented, and an election was held in November. The Navy League mounted a strong yes-vote campaign, and the outcome of the November referendum indicated Everett voters favored the base two-to-one. Perhaps after living the past decade and a half at the whims of the airline industry and its boom-bust cycles the majority of the voting public simply wanted a major industry in the area that was safe from recession. The facility, which would have an aircraft carrier and several

Support for preservation of federal lands in the eastern county led to creation of the Henry M. Jackson and Boulder River Wilderness Areas in 1984, and added to the already existing Glacier Peak acreage. In 2002 and again in 2003, Democrats Congressman Rick Larsen and Senator Patty Murray sponsored an expansion of 106,000 acres as the Wild Sky Wilderness Area. Merchant and Gunn's Peaks (as viewed from Index) were prominent summits in the proposal. (Courtesy Bernie Webber)

support ships, would create a projected annual payroll of $400 million. By August 1985 it was official that the Navy would build in Everett. On November 9, 1987 the groundbreaking ceremony was held on land purchased from Western Gear Corporation and the Port of Everett. The project continued, overcoming environmental concerns, local challenges, and funding problems. Four years later on September 5, 1991 a ribbon cutting ceremony initiated a $27 million project for six buildings and the main gate. The last major threat to the project came in 1993 after construction was well under way. The Everett homeport was put on a cut list, which might have led to its closure as a money saving measure. However, the Navy opted to shut down the older homeport in Alameda, California, assuring that $190 million would be spent over the next two years to complete the local facility. Also nearing completion was the Navy Support Complex in north Marysville. Containing the commissary, exchange, family services and many other support facilities, it attracted newcomers to the burgeoning Smokey Point area between Marysville and Arlington. The resulting homeport became a pride of the community, with the commons building the site of many civic events and celebrations. By October 1995 there were 104 officers, 745 enlisted personnel, and 426 civilians involved in base operations. The largest of the ship crews was that of the aircraft carrier *USS Abraham Lincoln* with 203 officers and 2,981 enlisted personnel.

In the late 1980s the local economy did rebound. However, it was not the United States Navy making the biggest difference: it was Boeing again. This comeback began about the same time as the Navy announcements. In 1985 the company sold 390 civilian aircraft, with sales of nearly $15 billion, triple those of the previous year. By 1988 orders had climbed to $29 billion. In the 1990s, to accommodate production of the new 777, a jet to fill the niche between the 747 and 767 (also built in Everett), the world's largest building was enlarged from 59 acres to over 96, with over 30,000 employees involved at the plant. In late 1992 Boeing announced a reduction of its Puget Sound work force by 19,000; however in Everett the layoff would be counterbalanced by 777 production. Also, airline workers received a morale boost when President Bill Clinton visited the 747 plant on February 22, 1993, pledging support for the airline industry.

Despite all the economic upheaval, some county residents still treasured physical evidence of their past. As early as 1974 the Snohomish city council had approved the establishment of two historic districts, as nationwide people were questioning the "newer is better" philosophy that was causing the loss of historic buildings at an alarming rate. The community of Snohomish was the logical place to start in the county, since much of its turn-of-the-century character was intact in both districts, downtown and in the residential neighborhood on the hill immediately to the north. Only a few years earlier Snohomish had considered an urban renewal project which would have seen the destruction of many structures on First Street, but that had been rejected in favor of preserving its historical landmarks, including the county's first brick buildings, erected almost a century before when Snohomish was the region's dominant town. This decision helped stimulate tourism, create a regional mecca for antique businesses, and provide the setting for a number of major films.

Everett followed suit with an historic ordinance and a National Register of Historic Places district in the Rucker Hill neighborhood. The city also adopted an innovative historic overlay district along north Grand and north Rucker avenues that required or

355

encouraged design review for new construction or remodeling, with the objective of keeping the changes in harmony with the historic neighborhood. All over the county individual properties have been nominated and accepted for the National Register of Historic Places and the Washington Heritage Register, although the county lagged behind in creating one of its own until 2003 when the Bryant store became its first listing. These designations, along with tax incentives and an American nostalgic desire to return to the past, breathed life into old buildings and helped preserve threatened sites throughout the county. Even tiny Index saved its wooden framed Redmen's Hall, while diners flocked to the Maltby Cafe with its "petroliana" motif. In Lynnwood, a community more aware of its future than its past, residents also took notice when the state highway department announced plans in the 1990s to revise the inadequate split diamond freeway interchange at 196ᵗʰ Street. The remaining buildings of the Puget Sound Demonstration Farm and the old Wickers Foods and co-op buildings, all dating back to the beginnings of Alderwood Manor, would be lost. Largely through efforts of the Alderwood Manor Heritage Association, concerned neighbors and school children, and a sympathetic city government, the Wickers Food building and Demonstration Farm superintendent's cottage and water tower were moved to temporary locations until permanent new homes could be found for them. To coordinate their efforts and create a network of historical, genealogical, and old-time

Naval Station Everett, dedicated in 1994, is homeport to six Navy ships, one Coast Guard ship, and one Military Sealift Command ship, including the aircraft carrier USS ABRAHAM LINCOLN (CVN 72) and the USS SHOUP (DDG 86), a newly constructed Aegis destroyer. NAVSTA Everett has a total population of 6,550 Sailors and civilians and supports more than 9,100 additional reserve military, spouses and children within a 20-mile radius (excluding Whidbey Island). (Courtesy United States Navy)

Winner of the 1985 Washington Trust for Historic Preservation Award, these small cottages once were used by laundresses who labored for the workers at Blackman's Mill, thus their nickname "Soapsuds Row." Without the efforts of the Housing Authority of Snohomish County and local preservationists, they probably would have been demolished. Mirrors to the past, they now provide affordable housing for senior citizens and are a credit to the community in the heart of Snohomish's National Historic District. (Courtesy Darlene Huntington)

special interest groups the League of Snohomish County Heritage Organizations was created in 1983. At the same time, a very effective county committee began to organize a host of activities celebrating the state centennial in 1989. These included the blowing of a large glass bell by William Morris to represent the county in the state bell garden in Seattle and a depiction of Snohomish County in an intricately sewn quilt designed by Betty Parks and created by dozens of volunteer quilters. It hung on permanent display in the courthouse hearing room.

From territorial days communities in Snohomish County had been club towns. The fraternal and lodge organizations for the most part still were going strong during the 1960s. However, by the 1970s, they began to fall onto hard times. Many men of the postwar generation, perhaps with longer commutes, were not willing to spend their free evenings in lodge meetings, while more and more women entered the work force and found it difficult to combine both job and household duties. With television entertainment and family responsibilities, many people were more content staying at home. Some had been drawn by gambling to organizations which had rows of slot machines, but that no longer was legal. Others came because they could have liquor by the drink, which was not allowed to the public until 1948. Drinks could be purchased with scrip on Sundays. The repeal of the Blue Laws and the state liquor control board's decision in 1967 to allow Sunday liquor sales in restaurants caused a new kind of competition for the clubs. Driving after drinking also grew much riskier as the state cracked down on driving under the influence and lowered legal blood alcohol limits, much to the credit of Mothers Against Drunk Driving (MADD). Private insurance and death benefits no longer were needed, due to employer and federal programs. Fraternal organizations also faced the stigma of being sexist, even though many had "women's nights" and auxiliaries. Racism was another issue. Finally, many lodges were saddled with large and aging buildings. Declining memberships and rising property valuations meant that those remaining had to pay more to keep what they had. Both men's and women's organization were affected. Over the years some stayed on in their facilities, some merged, others moved to smaller quarters, and still others disbanded completely.

With a population nearing half a million, there were bound to be some tragic stories. One was that of Charles Rodman Campbell of Edmonds. In 1974 he was convicted of

Pilchuck Glass School

By Catherine Lange

Since its founding in 1971, Pilchuck Glass School, located northeast of Stanwood in Victoria Heights, has been a source of education and inspiration to artists working in glass. After three decades, Pilchuck continues to serve as a melting pot for the international glass art community, bringing together faculty and students from traditions as diverse as those of Venice and Japan, Switzerland and New Zealand to share, to work, to learn and to create.

The story of the founding of Pilchuck has been told and retold so many times that it has taken on the lapidary gloss of legend. In 1971, Dale Chihuly, then Chair of the Glass Department at Rhode Island School of Design, and Ruth Tamura, Chair of the California College of Arts and Crafts, won a $2,000 grant to run a summer glass program. Inspired by the example of the Haystack Mountain School of Crafts in Maine, Chihuly sought to create an opportunity for artists to work with and learn about glass amid the spectacular beauty of his native Northwest forests. Only two weeks before the program was scheduled to begin, with sixteen students and two instructors already on their way, Chihuly found the ideal location for the school: a corner of the Pilchuck Tree Farm, offered by owners and long time arts patrons John Hauberg and Anne Gould Hauberg.

The site had its own magic—a hilltop meadow surrounded by deep sheltering forests—and it offered a spectacular view of the Skagit River Delta with the Straits of Juan de Fuca glimmering in the distance. But it had no buildings, no electricity, no plumbing. "Nothing," Chihuly has said, "but cows."

During the first days of that rainy summer, Pilchuck's students and faculty worked side by side to build the school. In just two weeks, the furnaces were fired up and the first glass was blown— an awkward, amorphous cobalt blue goblet. Once the furnaces were finished, the students and faculty turned their attention to the next priority—building shelter for themselves. Pilchuck's residents scavenged the local junk yards and army-surplus stores and constructed shelters of found lumber and tents. Some of these early buildings—such as Chihuly's cabin and Buster Simpson's tree house—remain today as inspiring reminders of the school's bootstrap beginnings.

Although Pilchuck was conceived as a one-time, experimental workshop, interest in the school spread quickly, and students returned with enthusiasm for a second summer and then a third. Pilchuck's faculty and students in its early years included many "big names" in today's glass art movement: Jamie Carpenter, Toots Zynsky, Fritz Dreisbach, Cappy Thompson, Richard Marquis, Therman Statom, Sonja Blomdahl, Dan Dailey and Marvin Lipofsky were among those attending the school in one capacity or another.

Much of Pilchuck's appeal came from Chihuly's philosophy of teaching: if you invite good artists to make art, then students will learn from them. Pilchuck also benefited from its spectacular setting, which insulated the resident artists from the day-to-day business of life, allowing them to focus on the creative challenges at hand.

It soon became apparent that Pilchuck had a life of its own, and Chihuly, with the Haubergs, began to establish a lasting infrastructure for the school. In 1973 Thomas Bosworth, chair of the Architecture Program at the University of Washington, was hired to create permanent campus buildings. His first design was for Pilchuck's signature Hot Shop, sited in a meadow just up the hill from the original outdoor furnaces. During the next few years, Bosworth went on to design and supervise construction of the

Cold Shop (for cutting, engraving and polishing glass), the Flat Shop (initially intended for stained-glass work and now used primarily for flame-working and neon) and the architectural award-winning Lodge, where the campus population still gathers for meals, slide shows and social events.

Today Pilchuck still retains its experimental spirit, attracting novice and professional artists from more than 37 states and 25 countries. From May to September each year, the school offers a series of intensive residential sessions. Five classes run concurrently through each 2½ week session. All classes are limited to 10 students, and most offer a focused inquiry into the potential applications of a particular technique or set of techniques including glass blowing, casting, fusing, slumping, neon, stained glass, flame-working, mixed-media sculpture, cutting, polishing and engraving.

Pike Powers, the school's Artistic Program Director, works closely with each faculty member to develop courses which emphasize experimentation, teamwork and the development of an individual creative voice. Instructors include leading international and American glass artists and university faculty. With a ratio of one staff person to every student, twenty-four hour access to many studios, and sophisticated facilities, Pilchuck gives both new and experienced glass artists the opportunity to make tremendous conceptual and technical progress in a very short period of time.

As the level of public interest in glass art has skyrocketed in recent years, Pilchuck has expanded its educational efforts to include special symposia targeted at collectors, curators, academics and others. Two summer intensives have focused on the interface between art and architecture, drawing internationally recognized architects such as Stephen Holl. More recently, spring programs for museum curators have drawn attendees from the Smithsonian, The Metropolitan Museum of Art, and London's Victoria and Albert Museum. Together, Pilchuck's academic programs, symposia and public events attract over 20,000 participants each year.

The Pilchuck Experience

After 30 years Chihuly's vision of Pilchuck as a place for artists to come together and create in glass has become a reality. Pilchuck has become much more than a school. It is an experience. Powers says of this experience that it "is less about amassing a body of work, or technical training, than it is about active participation in a community of people who thrive on creative challenge. Often it is impossible to express all that you absorb at Pilchuck. A notebook of sketches and a handful of experimental artifacts may be the only immediate, physical fruits of your efforts. However, these often become the fertile seeds that perpetuate new work and new experiences in years to come." Therman Statom, who first attended Pilchuck as a student in 1972 and returned as an instructor, has much the same to say: "Pilchuck is definitely a place where a person (can) go and come out different."

Notes:

1. Lloyd E. Herman, *Clearly Art: Pilchuck's Glass Legacy* (Bellevue, WA, The Whatcom Museum of History and Art, 1992), page 21.
2. Ibid, page 24.

sodomy and assault against Renae Wicklund. While on a work release program out of the state reformatory in Monroe, he returned to the scene of the crime in Clearview and murdered Wicklund, her 8-year-old daughter Shannah, and neighbor Barbara Hendrickson. Campbell was apprehended, convicted of murder, and after much legal haggling finally executed at the state penitentiary in Walla Walla. Just as tragic was the fate of Matthew Eli Creekmore of Everett, who at age three was fatally kicked in the stomach by his father Darren. The case caused a serious examination of the state's child protective services. If the dark cloud had a silver lining, it brought nation-wide attention to the problem of child abuse and resulted in state legislation mandating 20 years to life sentences to anyone convicted of inflicting such punishment on a child. Such was the sentence of Darren Creekmore. The saga of Paul Kenneth Keller, fodder for a made-for-television movie in 1995, was one of arson. From August of 1992 to January of 1994, fires were set in a swath from Everett into King County. The worst, at a retirement home in north Seattle, claimed three lives. Finally George Keller, father of the arsonist, made the difficult decision to turn in his son when he recognized similarities between Paul, police profile information, and artist sketches. Arrested in February, Keller, a well-dressed advertising salesman, pleaded guilty to starting 32 fires and admitted starting 44 others. As a young boy Keller had been caught setting fire to a neighbor's house. Well-known to county fire departments, the fire buff showed a real passion for fires and firefighting. He had gone through a difficult period after a 1991 divorce, and there was recent evidence of drug and alcohol abuse. Keller was sent to Clallam Bay Corrections Center to serve sentences of 75 years for arson and 99 years for murder.

There also were the unusual stories. On October 20, 1982 the *Al-Ind-Esk-A Sea*, a World War II cargo vessel converted into a food processing ship, was in Port Gardner Bay for repairs. At 2:15 P.M. a fire broke out, believed caused by a welder's torch. Six crewmembers were safely evacuated, and the ship was allowed to burn. Forty-four hours later, in what one observer called a "marine freak show" she heeled over and sank stern first to a murky grave half a mile off shore in about 200 feet of water. Most of the oil and other toxic chemicals had burned off, while wind and waves helped disperse the smoke and a negligible spill, sparing the area an environmental disaster. Stranger was the September 24, 1984 blaze south of the old Everett city dump near the Snohomish River. On fire were five acres of discarded tires. This second, and much more serious, such tire fire in less than two years raged out of control. Because of heat, firefighters were helpless to do anything. Flooding was ruled out because of the pollutants that would be sent into the nearby river. "Mt. Firestone," as locals called the four to five million tires, sent a plume of black, sooty smoke over the city, closing North Middle School and causing pedestrians to leave black, oily footprints at Hewitt and Broadway avenues. By the year's end the tire fire had died down to just a few hot spots.

Once again, Chinook winds blowing heavy, warm rains into the county from the Hawaiian Islands onto the early snow pack brought record high waters from Stanwood to Index, this time twice in November 1990. In Gold Bar two houses were lost to the Skykomish River. Darrington and Stevens Pass were cut off at times, while Ebey Island and the Tualco area were especially hard hit hard. Although minor compared to the loss at the same time of the old Mercer Island floating bridge across Lake Washington, perhaps the most memorable county story was of the old 125-foot ship *Seatac*. The unmanned

Major damaging floods struck the river valleys in 1975, 1980, twice in November 1990, and in 2003 as heavy subtropical rains melted early mountain snowfalls and filled the drainages with water. The Stillaguamish lowlands have been especially hard hit. (Courtesy Snohomish County Public Works Department)

freighter, which was being used as a dwelling, was plucked from its moorings along Riverview Road midway between Snohomish and Everett and sent on a strange journey down the swollen Snohomish River. Upon reaching the U.S. 2 draw bridge it became lodged with a log jam against one of the piers of the span. A futile attempt was made by a tugboat to pull it upstream against the roiling current. An hour later, shortly after noon, it slowly began to list and finally capsized. A large window in the stern broke open as it sank, scattering contents of the dying vessel downstream in the muddy brown waters.

On President Bill Clinton's Inauguration Day in 1993 morning windstorms swept the lowlands, knocking over utility poles along 196th Street in Lynnwood and darkening parts of southwest Snohomish County for days until repairs were made. Students at Cascade High School enjoyed an unexpected break from semester final examinations when suddenly the power went out and classes had to be cancelled. In 1995 the November flood season brought a major washout of the Lowell-Snohomish River Road as the dike gave way and surging waters carved a huge basin nicknamed "Norwegian Bay" for the Army Corps of Engineers experts who had to deal with repairs. The route remained closed for seven years, awaiting settling and relocation of the bypass road. The most unusual weather of the decade came late in 1996. A heavy snowfall in November was a prelude of what would happen at the end of the year, when the area would be buried in over a foot and half of snow. The wet, dense downfall caused a furniture store along Everett's Evergreen Way, as well as many other less substantial sheds and outbuildings around the county, to collapse. Particularly hard hit was the Edmonds marina, where roofs over the boats gave way and tumbled onto the pleasure craft. As the storm reached its peak, snow turned to rain—and, it continued to rain until the snow was gone. The area, then com-

361

pletely saturated, had many basements flooded for the first time in decades. Cars were completely submerged on Meadowdale Drive in Lynnwood. Worse were the slides. All along Puget Sound the bluffs slipped, causing much damage and closing roads and rail lines. Tulare Beach on the Tulalip Reservation was cut off from the rest of the county, and Howarth Park in Everett was closed due to mudslides. Particularly hard hit was the bluff near Woodway, where entire tree-lined hillsides dropped off toward the sea. Elsewhere the Lowell-Larimer Road and the Fire Trail Road near Lake Goodwin were closed.

During the last 20 years, land use battles became more common as adversaries such as property rights backers and preservationists, or open growth proponents and controlled growth advocates, fought one another. More people involved themselves in such decisions, as changes became subject to governmental review, sometimes involving environmental impact statements. With denser population and a greatly diminished open land base, new developments which would have gone unchallenged in the 1960s were stopped in their tracks or modified to meet concerns. In the early 1960s the Atlantic Richfield Company (ARCO) set out to build a large oil refinery at Kayak Point northwest of Marysville. Concerned about the objectivity of county officials and worried about the effect a refinery and oil tankers might have on her community, Marilyn Sherry began organizing beach communities around Port Susan Bay. Snohomish County changed its comprehensive plan as ARCO asked and granted the oil company a rezone. Disappointed by the county's posture, area property owners turned to the justice system. The trial court voided the county's actions, and the Washington State Supreme Court rejected appeals by the county and oil company. Fears that the combined resources of the two would overwhelm them discouraged the local group, yet Joe Chrobuck, president of the citizens' organization, his wife Betty, and neighbor Peter Newland worked tirelessly to raise money and keep spirits high. The residents spent more than $50,000 defending themselves against the county and the oil company. In the end, Snohomish County bought 640 acres, including the entire salt-water frontage, from ARCO for use as a public park. Shadow Run, a project to be built on an old gravel pit in Everett, was another project which was modified. When demand for wood chips and small diameter timber caused total clear-cutting of second and third growth stands near Lake Roesiger reminiscent of the nineteenth century practices, neighbors there raised an unsuccessful furor. There also was a long review process before Costco was allowed to build its discount warehouse near Silver Lake. On the other hand, west of Monroe the Fryelands development was built on the floodplain site of the old Frye lettuce farm, which the rapidly expanding city then annexed, while the new Hewlett-Packard plant on Soper Hill successfully violated Lake Stevens' comprehensive plan shortly after it was adopted. Later the fate of commercial development on Cavalero's Hill southwest of Lake Stevens became an issue as that section grew swiftly in density. Fights between developers and environmentalists boiled over into county council races, especially the swing districts one and five in northern and eastern Snohomish County. Realtors and developers found favor with Republicans Shirley Bartholomew, Don Britton, John Koster, Jeff Sax, plus Democrat "Swede" Johnson, while proponents of limited growth supported Democrats Peter Hurley, Ross Kane, Barbara Cothern, Dave Somers and Dave Gossett.

One of the most high-profile battles was that over CSR Associated's proposed quarry northeast of Granite Falls along the Mountain Loop Highway. The process to rezone the land from forestry to mineral conservation began in 1992. CSR Associated cited the need for more sand and gravel for ready-mix concrete and drainage tiles, as its operations in southwest Everett were nearly exhausted. The environmental impact statement of 1995 was rejected by county hearing examiner John Galt, so the process was drawn out longer. The Stillaguamish Citizens Alliance, headed by Bruce Barnbaum, opposed the quarry. They argued that it was too close to residential areas and would add unnecessary traffic to Granite Falls' already overcrowded single road through town. Environmental concerns also were raised about blasting vibrations disturbing salmon spawning, pollution of the aquifer with arsenic, and the risk of contamination from fuel leaks. The county hearing examiner again ruled against CSR Associated in 1998 on the basis that the project was incompatible with the low-density neighborhood. As the decision was appealed to the county council, CSR Associated countered that it was compatible and said that they were good neighbors at their quarry surrounded by far more residences in Everett. They also reported that they were helping the local economy with jobs and keeping down the price of sand and gravel. As the project was modified to half the size they had originally proposed, there would be a streamside buffer along the Stillaguamish, and they offered $4 million for traffic mitigation. Finally, they were committed to restoring the environment after the sand and gravel was taken. After limiting the amount of information the hearing examiner could consider, the county council then approved his final recommendation that requirements were met and voted to allow the company to mine the 425 acres. Granite Falls in turn began a multi-year process to plan and build a truck bypass, which would move heavy quarry traffic away from its schools and out of downtown.

As the rapidly expanding urban areas absorbed nearby neighborhoods, most citizens opted for annexation. Few were as successful as Woodway or Brier in maintaining their independence, as Smokey Point discovered in April 1999 when Superior Court Judge Charles French denied their hopes, fended off Marysville, and awarded the 614 acre prize to Arlington.

Hang gliders, ultra-lites, experimental and historical aircraft, aerobatic shows, and a friendly atmosphere of owners camping out near their planes have been typical of the Arlington Airport summer air show. These models were part of the July 1997 event. (Courtesy Louise Lindgren)

Another area which had hoped to incorporate was bounded by Puget Sound, Mukilteo, Everett, Highway 99, Lynnwood, and Edmonds. Highland Bay, this proposed city of 24,000, was a grass roots effort early in 1989 which was questioned almost immediately, as opponents saw the move as a thinly disguised ploy to control growth in and around Paine Field. Those against the incorporation included Everett, Lynnwood, Fire Districts 1 and 11, Boeing, the Honeywell Corporation, and several landowners and

residents within the proposed boundaries. The
Snohomish County Boundary Review Board also had
concerns about fiscal and political ramifications. While
the proponents said that taxes would go down, opponents
countered that the opposite would happen. The review
board delayed its decision but eventually said the county
would not fund a $40,000 impact study, citing the fact
that $100,000 had already been spent studying the area.
In the end the county rejected the incorporation, citing
boundary and financial questions. Although not successful, this effort did raise questions about the area's future.
Two years later, with state law encouraging annexation
over incorporation, Mukilteo annexed Harbour Pointe and
Chenault Beach, nearly doubling the city's population,
even as Everett and Lynnwood made further plans to
whittle away at the remainder. Highland Bay was a dead
issue, while in Mukilteo the annexation caused a financial
crisis and actually shifted much of the city's political base
to Harbour Pointe.

Cleaning up arsenic contamination from the Puget Sound
Reduction Company smelter in northeast Everett became a
highly controversial issue a century after its dumping, as
legal issues swirled in court. Some homeowners were
bought out by ASARCO, their houses razed, and the area
cordoned off with cyclone fencing. (Courtesy David
Cameron)

As in the nineteenth century, again some wanted out of Snohomish County. Part of a
trend in the Puget Sound area in the early 1990s was the collection of petitions for
breakaway counties. Citizens in the proposed jurisdictions, suspicious of big government,
urban areas, and growing restrictions on land use, accused county leaders of mismanagement. Freedom County with 50,000 residents would have taken the northern half of the
existing county, while Skykomish County (with a population of 40,000) would have taken

the land east of Snohomish as
well as the Skykomish area in
King County. After much legal
haggling, the northeastern seces-
sionists, led by Thom Satterlee of
Darrington, found themselves
with few adherents. Skykomish
County missed a deadline to
apply, while Freedom County
fought on after having appealed
unsuccessfully to the United
Nations for help. Finally the state
Supreme Court dismissed their
case, ruling that the petitions
gathered had to be a majority of
registered voters, not just a
majority of those voting in the
last election. The high court also
ruled that the secretary of state
did not have the authority to
certify a new county, and that

Mt. Pilchuck State Park was the dream of H.A. "Happy" Annen of Everett, who led the
drive for its creation. Skiing on the north side lasted for only a few years, however, as
the closeness of the site to Puget Sound did not make up for the often wet, heavy snow
and failure to make a profit. (Courtesy Jack O'Donnell)

Modern-day urban boundaries (dark gray)

Darrington

Index

Gold Bar

Everett (water supply only)

Sultan

Granite Falls

Lake
Stevens

Marysville

Monroe

Snohomish

Stanwood

Arlington

Mill Creek

Everett

Mukilteo

Bothell

Lynnwood

Brier

Edmonds

Mountlake
Terrace

Woodway

such a decision would have to be made in the state legislature. Given the opposition of Senator Mary Margaret Haugen of the 10th Legislative District (which included northeast Snohomish County), that would not happen. Property rights arguments, the Posse Comitatus movement of the early 1970s, opposition to school levy elections, and the militia movement of the mid-1990s all had their local adherents, but the new county issue drew the most popular support.

The case of the old ASARCO smelter in northeast Everett drove home the point that all can be held accountable for the use of land, as ASARCO and taxpayers worked to rectify a mistake made more than a hundred years ago. Dating from the Rockefeller boom era and designed to process gold, silver, and lead from Monte Cristo and southern British Columbia, the smelter was purchased by ASARCO, closed in 1912, and dismantled two years later. In the 1930s and 1940s houses were built on the site. In 1990 the Weyerhaeuser Company notified the Washington State Department of Ecology that soil and ground water samples from their land adjacent to the spot contained higher than normal levels of arsenic, cadmium and lead. Further testing confirmed that there were indeed potentially dangerous amounts of the toxic materials. ASARCO and the Department of Ecology entered into an agreement with the Snohomish Health District, City of Everett, Everett Housing Authority and two north end neighborhood associations to work collaboratively in cleaning up the smelter site and surrounding neighborhoods. ASARCO spent $10 million to purchase houses in the neighborhood and erect barrier fencing to secure the site, while 22 houses in the most contaminated section were demolished. This cooperation extended until July 1998 when Ecology dropped out of talks with ASARCO about the amount of soil that had to be cleaned and ASARCO countered by filing a lawsuit. Even though the issue went to the courts, the state decided to go ahead with the clean up as funds allowed due to the seriousness of the health risk. ASARCO agreed in 2004.

Gold and silver had come down from Monte Cristo and Silverton by the trainload, but returning coaches also were filled with sightseers, fishermen, vacationers, and organized excursioners from the lowlands heading up to enjoy the county's mountains, lakes, and streams. Snohomish County always has put a high priority on its recreation. Three state parks, Wenberg on Lake Goodwin, Wallace Falls near Gold Bar, and Mt. Pilchuck are located in the county. A ski area, for years promoted by H.A. "Happy" Annen, briefly operated on the north slopes of Mt. Pilchuck but unfortunately proved to be a financial failure due to a series of years with a poor snow pack and closed in the 1970s. Its lodge, support buildings, and tows eventually were dismantled, but the Everett Mountaineers restored the 1921 fire lookout atop the summit as a state centennial project in 1989. Similarly, Mukilteo Lighthouse Park resulted when deep budget cuts forced the state to turn over its former site to the city of Mukilteo in 2003.

Both the county and individual cities have been active in acquiring new land for recreation and maintaining their existing parks. Rails to trails became a popular theme, helping preserve the old interurban grade between Lynnwood and south Everett. Another popular route for walking, running, skating and biking is the Centennial Trail, along former Northern Pacific Railroad tracks between Snohomish and Hartford and planned eventually all the way to Lake McMurray north of Arlington. The old Everett and Monte Cristo Railway route through Robe Canyon is being developed by Snohomish County

Parks and The Friends of Robe Canyon, led by Steve and Nancy Dean, but just as the original, continues to be plagued by flood damage. Spencer Island in the Snohomish Delta between Marysville and Everett is a protected wetland habitat for fish, birds, and other wildlife. One of the newest regional parks is on Lord's Hill, overlooking the Snohomish River between Snohomish and Monroe. Altogether the county's 30 parks offer 7000 acres of land from Puget Sound to the Cascades. There also is some interest in creating a greenway and historic route along the Stevens Pass Highway from Everett to Wenatchee, while the rails to trails conversion of the Northern Pacific spur line from Arlington to Darrington awaits further funding.

Women continued to make major contributions in government and other executive positions during this period. Democrat Maria Cantwell represented part of South Snohomish County in the United States House of Representatives, became a technology company millionaire, then returned to politics in 2000 to defeat long-time incumbent Republican Slade Gorton for the United States Senate in an election decided finally by a recount. Val Stevens, Pat Scott, Jeanette Wood, Jeralita Costa, Jeanine Long, Renee Radcliffe, and Jean Berkey have represented county constituents in Olympia. Liz McLaughlin, Karen Miller, and Barbara Cothern followed Shirley Bartholomew, serving on the county council. Kay Anderson and Pam Daniels served as County Clerk, while Gail Rauch and Cindy Portman have served as County Assessor. Cities have woman mayors, including Joyce Ebert in Everett, Tina Roberts in Lynnwood, Margaret Larson in Arlington, Rita Matheny in Marysville, Leila Dempsey and Joyce Jones in Darrington, Carla Nichols in Woodway, Pat Cordova in Mountlake Terrace, Donnetta Walser in Monroe, and Rella Morris in Granite Falls. Five major school districts had superintendents who were women: Susan Torrens in Edmonds; Jane Hammond, and Carol Whitehead in Everett; Ginny Tresvant in Snohomish; Linda Whitehead in Marysville; and Linda Byrnes in Arlington. Mill Creek's city manager was Joni Earl, who went on to the county executive's office and then a leadership role with Sound Transit. Evelyn Odom was an executive with GTE. Margaret Bavasi, who with her husband Bob brought pro baseball to Everett, went go on to chair the board of directors of Everett Mutual Bank. Viola Oursler became well known as a vocal activist in her northeast Everett neighborhood. Cheryl Wilson was the Monroe police chief, while Cynthia First and Kathleen Vaughn are P.U.D. commissioners.

Greater numbers of African Americans also found roles of leadership. Betty Cobbs and Shirley Walthall became principals in the Everett School District. For a period of time in the 1980s three top level Edmonds School District administrative positions were held by African Americans, Harold Reasby as superintendent, Evelyn Freeman assistant superintendent, and LeRoy Drake director of personnel. Ron Gipson followed in the footsteps of his father, Carl, and was elected to the Everett City Council, joined there by David Simpson. Runner Herm Atkins operated a sports store in south Everett.

By 1990 racial and ethnic minorities were making their mark on the county, as their numbers rose from 4.3 percent in 1980 to 6.7 percent a decade later. Hispanics, number-ing over 15,000, have found niches in Monroe and Lynnwood, where four grocery stores in a two-mile area served people with roots from all parts of Latin America with what they could not find elsewhere. Nearby was a used-car dealership owned by a woman from Mexico, while a Latino Fair was held at the Las Americas Business Center. Asian and Pacific Islander Americans became the largest minority group. The Chin family pioneered

Carl Gipson

By Tony Stigall

Carl Gipson, a young black man from the farm country outside of Little Rock, Arkansas, decided to follow his dream to "go west, young man." The pursuit led him to Everett, Washington where he set a series of firsts and wrote his name on the pages of Snohomish County political history. He arrived as a sailor, stationed in Oak Harbor in 1943, and stepped into the political arena in 1972.

Following the war, Gipson and his family moved to Everett. At their first home on north Hoyt Avenue they found gun-toting residents and threats of violence awaiting them. He had moved into a neighborhood that was thought to be off limits to blacks during the 1940s and 1950s. There were very few blacks in Everett at the time. It was not easy for minorities to make it in Snohomish County in the 1950s. Racism, bigotry and intolerance abounded. During World War II some neighborhoods had enacted restrictive covenants barring nonwhites, a practice which lasted until it was outlawed in the 1960s. Needing to support his family, Gipson found his first job at the Sevenich Chevrolet dealership washing cars. He worked his way up and became the first black shop foreman at a West-Coast Chevrolet dealership. The white employees initially refused to work under him, but they cried when he left 11 years later in 1960. Fairness and tolerance were his mainstay in dealing with and relating to his fellow employees. He carried this principle into his own businesses ventures the following year, starting with a service station on Hewitt and Rucker avenues, and into his life in politics, which was to follow. Tuberculosis almost got the best of him in 1967, but that also gave him an opportunity to explore ways of making a better community. He made his initial bid for the Everett City Council in 1971, the same time as he began his role as the Human Rights Specialist for Snohomish County. He ended his business career and devoted his time to his county and city responsibilities.

Gipson had a great concern for public safety. He led the city council effort to bring aid cars under city jurisdiction. This concept met with some resistance. However, the ordinance passed, with one of the white city council members receiving the credit. Gipson went on to spearhead the successful effort to build the first public swimming pool in Everett, the popular facility in Forest Park. He was mentored by and worked with Seattle City Councilman Sam Smith, considered to be the dean of black politicians in the Puget Sound area. Henry "Scoop" Jackson also supported Gipson and admired his honesty. In spite of his accomplishments and his integrity, he was the only black applicant and the only one of 67 men who applied, who was denied membership in the Elks Club in 1977, during his second term on the Everett City Council.

Gipson believed that his role was that of bringing people together. His focus was inclusion, bringing citizens closer to their government and service to all people. Gipson was convinced that each person has a right to contribute to the political process and has a right to be heard. He felt that elected officials often lose their ability to relate to people. As a councilman he would typically conduct public meetings throughout the city so that the citizens would have their time to be heard. He was a member of the Association of Washington Cities and National Association of Cities throughout his tenure on the city council and was actively involved in municipal matters on the state and national levels.

There was still a lot of unfinished business when Gipson left the city council in 1996. The one thing he had hoped to do was to inspire and increase minority participation in the political process. He has seen both the good and bad of Everett. He also believes that the racial climate has changed considerably since the day when he and his wife Jodi first moved to Everett. He believes that more minorities should pursue government as a career option.

A great void exists, and there is still more work to do in making Everett a better community. Gipson's hope is that government will become truly reflective of the multicultural, multiethnic community and that color and race might be cast aside to reach that end.

serving Chinese food, with restaurants in Everett and Lynnwood, and numerous other ethnic establishments flourished as American cuisine continued to adapt to new tastes. With waves of people from Japan, Korea, and more recently Southeast Asia following the Vietnam War, there was a far greater Asian ethnic diversity. One could say Snohomish County changed from lutefisk to kimshi, as more Asian dishes were introduced. Perhaps just as notable as the McDonald's in Granite Falls was the Thai restaurant in Jack Webb's old gas station. The Mekong store in downtown Everett served the local Vietnamese population, while Middle Eastern and then Russian groceries opened on North Broadway, and downtown office workers could choose from menus with Russian, Indian, Japanese, and Philippine flavors.

For immigrant children trying to make the transition to America and fit in with their classmates, school districts created English as Second Language (ESL) programs. Barbara Vadset began that teaching assignment in 1980 at Edmonds High School, and then it was moved to Lynnwood High School in the 1990s. The largest number of students she saw during those 20 years were Vietnamese, the first wave coming in the 1980s as children from educated families who had supported the South Vietnamese government during the war. A later group from Vietnam came for five years during the late 1990s, children of parents imprisoned and later released after the Communist takeover. All of these students were high achievers. Large numbers of Cambodians also came in the early years of the ESL program. In the mid-1980s there was a wave of Amerasians. Following the demise of the Soviet Union in 1989 Russian and Ukrainian students began entering, many of them religious refugees. Throughout the years there were consistent numbers of Koreans and

In the spring of 1962 a group of local musicians who were members of the Bremerton Symphony were returning home by ferry and questioning why they should travel so frequently instead of starting their own community symphony. Thus the Cascade Symphony was born, centered in Edmonds and gaining a national reputation under the leadership of Robert Anderson. In 2000 the group dissolved when most members resigned at the changing directions of the orchestra and formed a new "Classic Cascade Symphony," which turned to its roots and soon its original name. This portrait was taken November 10, 1970. (Photograph #221.5, courtesy Edmonds-South Snohomish County Historical Society)

Hispanics. Mrs. Vadset also worked with children from such places as Bosnia, Iraq, Iran, Pakistan, India, Sudan, Puerto Rico, and Peru. She considered it a rewarding job, as the students were happy with their new lives in Snohomish County.

To the north, the long-anticipated renaissance in central Everett had begun in the mid-1990s. New construction included the Colby Square project with the 14-story Everett Mutual Tower and adjoining Everett Community Theater, Colby

At the intersection of state highways 9 and 204 the Frontier Village shopping center has grown from its original wild west theme to become the economic hub of the Lake Stevens area. (Courtesy Jack O'Donnell)

Center with new quarters for Frontier Bank, Colby Place, a large addition to the public library sympathetic with the original building, a P.U.D. expansion with an auditorium, and the Group Health Clinic on Riverside. National Register of Historic Places properties were restored, including the Monte Cristo Hotel and the Commerce Block. The old Rumbaugh-MacLain/Bon Marche department building was made over for office space, the top two floors going to the Navy and the lower ones to Henry Cogswell College, which also took over the former post office/federal building on Colby Avenue. Everett High School's 1910 Beaux Arts building was restored. In addition, as part of a water main replacement, three blocks along Colby Avenue received new sidewalks, replacing much of the work done in the 1970s. Streetlights from an earlier era were also installed. In 2003 the city's new Events Center opened at Hewitt and Broadway avenues, while the county courthouse complex underwent major expansion with an underground parking garage, new jail, and nine-story administration building all due for completion in 2005. The total effect showed that a strong downtown was going to be part of the city's future. It was not likely to return as a major retail marketing area, but was firmly established as a business, financial and governmental center.

Other cities in the county also redefined themselves. Snohomish, bypassed and insulated from gridlocked traffic, flourished with antiques. In Monroe U.S. 2 became a congested commuter, recreational and commercial route. Most of all, the strip became Monroe's business center. Meanwhile its downtown, centered on Main and Lewis Streets, maintained its small town charm. Sultan repaved its main street, adding an attractive tree-lined median in the residential section and erecting an award-winning new community center. Most of Mukilteo's downtown disappeared decades ago, but what remained was teeming with activity with the beach front park, picturesque lighthouse campus, busy ferry, and several fine eateries. The city also had a waterfront opportunity after the removal of the 1950s storage tanks. Edmonds found a special niche for its downtown with upscale shops to serve the immediate environs and those waiting for the Kingston Ferry.

370

In 1989 the city replaced utility poles with underground wiring and installed historic lamps along Main Street. Edmonds shoppers also were served by Old Milltown, Harbour Square, the Waterfront, Edmonds Shopping Center, Westgate, Five Corners, Firdale Village, the Highway 99 strip, and Perrinville.

Mountlake Terrace was encouraging no setbacks at the sidewalk in new construction along 56th Avenue to give its downtown more pedestrian appeal. The southern part of the city east of I-5 also was developed. Lynnwood had meetings about creating a downtown. Lake Stevens, struggling to hold onto its village quality, was considering re-creating a main street feel that was lost when most of the commercial buildings were razed in the 1950s and 1960s, or moved to Frontier Village west of the lake. Granite Falls retained a business district remarkably intact and perhaps likely to stay so despite the pressures of gravel hauling. New housing to the northwest and west filled with commuters moving in and wanting its small town feel. Marysville compromised its downtown by tearing down most of the buildings on the west side of State Avenue to build a shopping mall. However, in doing so it worked to keep the area commercially vital, even though it was in the southwest corner of a city which had expanded to former strawberry fields to the north and east and created a commercial strip all the way to Smokey Point. There was much activity on the west side of the freeway just inside the Tulalip Indian Reservation with its hotel and other business enterprises and major tribal commercial development at Quil Ceda Village with its new casino and retail site several miles to the north.

Arlington kept its quintessential downtown along Olympic Avenue, at least on the surface. However, the city was challenged as more and more businesses move closer to I-5

The Weyerhaeuser office building was barged from Mill B down the Snohomish River under the old Highway 99 draw bridges in 1994 and placed at the corner of 18th and Marine View Drive on the Everett waterfront. It was the second such move, as originally it had served as the offices for Mill A a mile to the south of its new home. In its new location the ornate building which was made of every kind of lumber produced in the Pacific Northwest served the Everett Chamber of Commerce. At present its future is uncertain. (Courtesy James Arribito)

and south to Kent Prairie, while then mayor Bob Kraski closed his furniture store, long a cornerstone business on Olympic Avenue and car dealer Dwayne Lane fought an agricultural land use struggle to move his operations westward to Island Crossing. Arlington resident Sue Pace wrote fondly of her new found home town in a *Newsweek* magazine article, pointing out that in order to keep it a "Blue-Plate Special Town" citizens would have to support downtown stores. Joining the traditional Blue Bird Cafe was a restaurant run by the Love Israel family, a communal religious group transplanted from Seattle to a woodland farm southeast of Arlington and known for its annual Garlic Festival. However, the family was in financial trouble, forced to declare bankruptcy and move to Eastern Washington. In Darrington much of the business along Darrington Street moved four blocks north to S.R. 530 along Seeman Street. Both of Stanwood's centers were alive and well, despite major commercial development on the hills east of town through Cedarhome. The older billed itself as Stanwood's "Historic West Side." Old East Stanwood had a comfortable Western feel and retained much of its Norwegian character.

A commuting and growing society greatly affected pressure on the county roads. Even in the 1980s, writers were conjuring up such terms as Broadway Brake Test, Trestle Tango, Lynnwood Lineup, Marysville Muddle, Lake Stevens Snarl, High-Tech Tie-Up and Freeway Freeze. Added to this were the Stanwood Standstill, Casino Crapshoot, and Swamp Thing. Many agreed that the biggest misnomer was the Mukilteo Speedway which required widening. The Bothell-Everett Highway added lanes to accommodate growth in the area south of Mill Creek,and then planned for more around Silver Lake. Every afternoon freeway traffic slowed to a crawl from Eastmont to the Hewitt Avenue trestle. Morning jams formed well north of Marysville and thickened from Lynnwood south. State Route 522 sometimes was jammed for hours by head-on wrecks. To combat this developing gridlock the adoption of the Regional Transit Authority (RTA) was put to the voters in March of 1995. Although it passed by a narrow 51 percent margin in King County, it was soundly rejected in Pierce and Snohomish counties. The highest opposition was in Everett, where a lawsuit was filed challenging the RTA's plan to stop its rail line short of town at 164th Street. Only in Edmonds did county voters support the plan. Planners for RTA returned successfully to the electorate with a scaled down version which included more high occupancy vehicles on the freeway, improved bus service, and the use of existing rail lines instead of building new. Ground was broken for Everett's new transportation center in July 2000, with Sound Transit train service begun in 2003 along the Burlington Northern Santa Fe Railway tracks, stopping at Edmonds.

By the later years of the twentieth century the county's once-dominant timber industry was but a shadow of its former self. Shingle packers at Darrington's Summit Timber Company (now an affiliate of Portland-based Hampton Affiliates) continue to practice a disappearing trade. (Courtesy Darrington Historical Society)

As community groups, government, and social service agencies found budgets strained by increasing costs and demands for services, more and more tasks have been taken on by volunteers. Retired sheriff's department Sergeant John Taylor, his former county search and rescue friends, and Monte Cristo Preservation Association members continued to rebuild public access into the old mining town and Henry M. Jackson Wilderness Area. (Courtesy Louise Lindgron)

Non-transportation related construction also flourished at the end of the decade, including the Stillaguamish River-Haller Bridge on Highway 9 at Arlington, bachelor enlisted quarters at the Naval Station, an Instructional Technology Center at Everett Community College, a new Evergreen Middle School in Everett, a Park and Ride lot at 164th Street, the Alderwood Mall Boulevard connector, Sonoma Villero and other apartments in Bothell, and the University of Washington-Bothell Branch Campus.

A group of issues (labeled Ascent 21) was put to the voters in November 1998, a five-part property and gas tax plan advocating five steps to control sprawl. These included directing growth away from rural areas, improving local roads to ease traffic jams, building more parks and playgrounds, setting aside critical habitat areas and providing for clean water and flood control. All five propositions were turned down by voters, who interpreted the proposals essentially as an attempt by development interests to create more local infrastructure necessary for much greater growth. In a move to restrain that growth the county council proposed an emergency ordinance placing a three-month moratorium on new applications for denser subdivisions, but voted it down three to two. Snohomish County Executive Bob Drewel actively welcomed more expansion and jobs but stated he planned to spend more time working on ways to increase the standards for development.

Health and welfare services also faced new challenges. In 1983 there was one known case of Acquired Immuno-Deficiency Syndrome (AIDS) and no reported deaths. By 1997 the numbers were 425 and 242. Group Health Cooperative opened a large new facility near the freeway in Everett, while the Everett Clinic continued to expand into a regional medical system. Providence and General hospitals merged under the auspices of the Sisters of Providence, combining operations and reducing costs. Elderly care also was enhanced with the move of Bethany Home residents from their outmoded facility on Broadway Avenue to several floors of Providence's Pacific Campus, while the Hospice program gave dignity to and assisted those patients who were in terminal condition. In Arlington rising costs forced Cascade Hospital into seeking new ways of providing services while still staying financially viable, and Valley General Hospital in Monroe erected a totally new facility to replace buildings dating back to the County Poor Farm as debate

373

continued nationally on how to improve affordable health coverage for all citizens.

As populations grew, work weeks again expanded beyond 40 hours, and the necessity for two-income families reduced parental time with children and the elderly, more social support systems also began to appear. Pre-schools were widespread, assisting working mothers. Private education also expanded, notably with a growth in religiously supported institutions, which catered to parents concerned with a perceived lack of Christian values taught in the public system. Equi-Friends gave horse experiences to disabled children, while for troubled youth the Cocoon House provided a shelter better than the streets, and Housing Hope offered homes for desperate families. The Everett Gospel Mission opened a new facility, as did the Snohomish County Center for Battered Women, St. Vincent de Paul, and the Volunteers of America. All received widespread religious and public support. Food banks such as those coordinated by the Volunteers of America now had become a mainstay for an increasing number of needy people, no longer just an emergency assistance program, and could be found in almost every community. Senior centers had an equally wide distribution, with a growing number of elderly and low-income housing units also available, along with community assistance and financial programs publicized through *The Third Age* newspaper.

The issue of abortion brought forth deep divisions in viewpoints during the last decades of the century. Protests sometimes became violent, including the firebombing of a women's clinic in Everett across from the county court house and the sentencing of the perpetrator to time in prison. Confrontations happened on the streets, in front of clinics, and before schools as demonstrators urged their points of view. It also helped bring more people into political activity, notably evangelical protestant Christians to the conservative wing of the Republican Party and its subsequent success in electing candidates.

Mukilteo resident and businessman Tim Eyman reflected that smaller government philosophy and became a household name when he sponsored Initiative 695 in 1999. Filed in January, by June it had twice the required number of signatures and passed with ease. Its intent was to limit excise taxes to $30 on state motor vehicle excise taxes, plus prohibit state and local governments from raising taxes without a vote of the people. While Eyman promoted the results as a victory for the little guy, opponents characterized it as a tax break for the wealthy and took the case to court. Here it was nullified as containing an unconstitutional two subjects rather than the allowed one. However, the state legislature bowed to popular will and passed the reduction, though not agreeing to give up its taxing powers. Undaunted, Eyman continued to develop new initiatives to allocate state monies toward new highway construction rather than aiding mass transit and to limit property taxes. His image as a highly principled citizen crusader, however, took a major hit when he broken heartedly admitted to taking money for personal use from his campaign and was assessed a $50,000 fine. Bouncing back in the summer of 2002, he announced plans to become a salaried professional initiative sponsor, although under terms of his settlement with the state he had to promise never again to control the financial end of future drives. Elatedly, he proclaimed to the public, "This is full-bore, vintage Tim Eyman, not the bawling boob they saw in February. This is Tim Eyman, swinging the bat, the guy who shakes up the status quo."

On August 28, 1996 a blaze destroyed the old Twin City Foods plant in Stanwood. Founded in 1945 by the Lervick family, it packaged frozen peas and cut corn, potatoes and mixed vegetables. Three hundred fifty workers were out of jobs until it was rebuilt. The temporary loss of the processing plant reminded residents of the closure of many other packing plants countywide. With the loss of agricultural infrastructure the trend toward more loss of farm income and lands seemed inevitable. Nevertheless, at the start of the 21st century, the county still ranked third statewide in the number of dairy cows and pounds of milk produced, second in broiler production, fifth in eggs, and third in strawberries. Over 74,000 acres remained in agriculture, with 1255 farms and 6,500 employed in the field. A welcome recognition of the role farming has played in county history was the honor paid to those families who had maintained their operations for a hundred years. This was done for the state centennial and revived annually in 2000 by county historic preservation planner Louise Lindgren, when seventeen received their centennial farm awards at the Evergreen State Fair from County Executive Bob Drewel.

Another mainstay of the early local economy that changed was the fishing industry. Although the Boldt Decision limited how many fish could be taken commercially, the real problem was that the salmon run counts hit new lows. Despite conservation and hatchery programs by state, federal, and tribal agencies, in 1999 the Puget Sound chinook runs were declared threatened under the Endangered Species Act, shortly thereafter joined by the bull trout. The development and implementation of rules to protect and enhance the salmon habitat are ongoing, complex processes that will take considerable time before their effectiveness may be evaluated.

In November 1998 a lone spotted owl, far off course, landed and spent the night in a downtown Everett tree. Onlookers were curious, watching as the bird was captured for release in the wild near Index. Reactions had to be mixed. Some probably saw the spotted owl as a savior. Because of its endangered species status, its habitat, the national forests, were closed to most logging, thus saving the remaining old growth forests. Others must have looked at the owl seeing lost jobs in the timber industry because of the shutdowns. Whatever the case, environmentalists and mill workers had to look down on the water-front with dismay as raw logs were loaded on freighters for Asia. Gone were virtually all of the lumber and all but one of the pulp mills. Weyerhaeuser, once the county's largest employer, no longer even was a presence, closing their Kraft mill in 1993. Only Kimberly Clark (formerly Soundview and Scott Paper) with its tall stack remained in "The City of Smokestacks." Miller Shingle Company in Granite Falls and Summit Timber Company in Darrington (since sold to the Hampton Affiliates of Portland, Oregon) were among the few survivors of the old resource-based economy. However they had to go far afield for logs and compete with the highly efficient Longview Fiber Company small-diameter mill across Stevens Pass in Winton. Those heading for the ski slopes might wonder at truck-loads of second growth timber going east over the mountains rather than to struggling local processors.

The United States Forest Service also had downsized, combining the Mt. Baker and Snoqualmie National Forests in 1972 with headquarters eventually at Mountlake Terrace, closing its Monte Cristo Ranger District at Verlot 10 years later, and sharply reducing both staff and services. Illustrative of the collapse of the county's timber industry is that in 1964 the total cut on the two forests had been 418 million board feet. In 1995 it was three million. With the emphasis on timber harvest over, the agency focused more on watershed restoration, fisheries enhancement, and marketing recreation, including "user fees" for many activities such as walking on forest trails and contracting with private companies for campground operations. It also began a major program of closing its forest roads, built during the preceding three decades for timber harvest but now too expensive to maintain properly. Utilization of Washington State forestlands swung first toward environmental interests under Jennifer Belcher, then back toward more industry friendly policies after 2000 with the election of Doug Sutherland as state Lands Commissioner.

Snohomish County awoke on September 11, 2001 to news that shocked the world and again would emphasize the ongoing cyclical nature of the local economy. On that morning two Everett-built Boeing 767s were hijacked by terrorists and used as weapons, crashing into the World Trade Center twin towers in New York City, causing them to topple. In addition, two 757s also were taken, one hitting the Pentagon in Arlington, Virginia and the other going down in the western Pennsylvania countryside. Security immediately was stepped up here as well as nationwide. At the Everett naval station additional personnel were placed at Harborview Park to watch the facility, neighbors on Grand Avenue above the base were asked to watch for suspicious activities, and armed guards closely quizzed visitors who passed through a maze of concrete barricades at the station gates. Naval and Coast Guard reserve units were called to active duty, and over the next year county-based naval ships headed for Persian Gulf and Indian Ocean waters.

An acute airline crisis was set off by the September events, triggering an immediate shut down of all air travel and then resulting in greatly increased costs due to improved screening, higher security, and a drop in both business and tourist travel. Corresponding with a sharp drop in financial markets, which had begun the year before, aircraft orders dropped. Boeing announced within a week that it was laying off 30,000 employees. Added to these concerns was the company's decision to move its headquarters from Seattle to Chicago, while its workers feared more job losses to overseas nations as a part of Boeing's marketing strategy and did not go on strike in the summer of 2002.

By that time the Pacific Northwest was in recession, with the state's unemployment the highest in the nation and slow to recover. In the preceding decade the county's population had grown to over 600,000 and surpassed that of the entire state of Wyoming. As an average of 51 people per day moved in over the last half century, now the county's number of school children alone surpassed the entire total of residents half a century earlier. Demographers concluded that the two leading factors for this continued growth were affordable housing and a booming regional economy. If they remained intact, growth would continue well into the following decade. These now seemed in danger.

When war developed in Iraq, the naval station ships departed to their stations in the Persian Gulf and took part in the fighting, as did many service personnel and reservists once more called to duty. Erratic oil prices, continuing high unemployment, and ongoing overseas news were constant reminders that the county no longer was isolated in a far corner of the country, but instead was thoroughly integrated into the rest of the complex world.

In the space of two lifetimes the landscape had been altered from a place of vast old growth forests and a small native population concentrated along the salt water and inland river valleys to a largely urban scene typical of metropolitan America. Changes had come so rapidly and completely that it is well to remember the story of how it occurred. Perhaps this knowledge will help us when we make decisions for the future.

References

Chapter 1

Alt, David and Donald W. Hyndman. *Northwest Exposures: A Geologic Story of the Northwest*. Mountain Press Publishing Co., Missoula, MT., 1995.

Collins, June McCormick. *Valley of the Spirits: The Upper Skagit Indians of Western Washington*. University of Washington Press, Seattle, 1974.

Gower, Howard D., James C. Yount, and Robert S. Crosson. *Seismotectonic Map of the Puget Sound Region, Washington*. U.S. Geological Survey, Washington, D.C., 1985.

Gerstel, Wendy J., Matthew J. Brunengo, William S. Lingley, Jr., Robert L. Logan, Hugh Shipman, and Timothy J. Walsh. "Puget Sound Bluffs: The Where, Why, and When of Landslides Following the Holiday 1996/97 Storms." *Washington Geology*, Vol. 25, No. 1. Washington State Department of Natural Resources, Olympia, 1997.

Haeberlin, Hermann and Erna Gunther. *The Indians of Puget Sound*. Vol. IV, Number 1 of the University of Washington Publications in Anthropology, Seattle, 1930.

Hollenbeck, Jan. *A Cultural Resource Overview: Prehistory, Ethnography, and History. Mt. Baker-Snoqualmie National Forest*. USDA Forest Service, Pacific Northwest Region, 1987.

Harris, Stephen L. *Fire & Ice: The Cascade Volcanoes*. rev. ed., The Mountaineers, Seattle, 1980.

Murphy, Leonard M. and William K. Cloud. *United States Earthquakes, 1955*. U.S. Department of Commerce, Coast and Geodetic Survey, U.S. Government Printing Office, 1957.

Murphy, Leonard M. and Franklin P. Ulrich. *United States Earthquakes, 1949*. U.S. Department of Commerce, Coast and Geodetic survey, U.S. Government Printing Office, 1951.

Nelson, Charles M. "Prehistory of the Puget Sound Region." *Handbook of North American Indians*. Vol. 7. Smithsonian Institution, Washington, 1990.

Neumann, Frank. *United States Earthquakes, 1932*. U.S. Department of Commerce, Coast and Geodetic Survey, Serial Number 563, U.S. Government Printing Office, 1934.

Pojar, Jim and Andy MacKinnon. *Plants of Coastal British Columbia*. Lone Pine Publishing, Vancouver, B.C., 1994.

Von Hake, Carl and William K. Cloud. *United States Earthquakes, 1965*. U.S. Department of Commerce, Environmental Science Services Administration, Coast and Geodetic Survey, U.S. Government Printing Office, 1976.

___ ___, ___ _____. *United States Earthquakes, 1969*. U.S. Department of Commerce, Environmental Science Services Administration, Coast and Geodetic survey, U.S. Government Printing Office, 1971.

Waitt, Richard B., Larry G. Mastin, and James E. Beger. "Volcanic Hazard Zonation for Glacier Peak Volcano, Washington." United States Geological Survey Open-File Report 95-499, 1995.

White, Richard. *Land Use, Environment, and Social Change: The Shaping of Island County, Washington*. University of Washington Press, Seattle, 1980.

Yates, Richard and Charity. *Washington State Atlas: A Political and Economic View of the Evergreen State*. rev. ed., The Information Press, Eugene, OR, 1987.

Chapter 2

Amoss, Pamela T. "The Indian Shaker Church." *Handbook of North American Indians,* vol. 7, *Northwest Coast.* Smithsonian Institution, Washington, DC. 1970.

Carlson, Roy L. "Cultural Antecedents." *Handbook.. of North American Indians,* vol. 7, *Northwest Coast.* Washington, DC: Smithsonian Institution, 1970.

Collins, Gary C. "Indian Policy, Government Treaties, and the Chehalis River Indian Council," *The Pacific Northwest Forum.* 5:2. Cheney, WA: Eastern Washington University, Cheney, WA, Summer-Fall 1992.

Collins, June McCormick. *Valley of the Spirits: The Upper Skagit Indians of Western Washington.* University of Washington Press, Seattle, 1974.

Crooks, Drew. "An Expedition Against the Snohomish Indians As Recorded in the Journal of George Gibbs, March 1854." *The Pacific Northwest Forum.* 4:2, Eastern Washington University, Cheney, WA, Summer-Fall 1991.

Fish, Jean Bedal. *Glimpses of the Past.* unpublished manuscript.

Gibbs, George. *Indian Tribes of Washington Territory.* Ye Galleon Press, Fairfield, WA, 1978.

Haeberlin, Hermann and Erna Gunther. *The Indians of Puget Sound.* Volume IV, No. 1 of the University of Washington Publications in Anthropology, Seattle, 1930.

Hanson, Timothy R. "The Autobiography of Charles Huntington." *The Pacific Northwest Forum.* 4:1, Eastern Washington University, Cheney, WA, Winter-Spring 1991.

The Herald, Everett, WA, various issues.

Hollenbeck, Jan. *A Cultural Resource Overview: Prehistory, Ethnography, and History.* Mt. Baker-Snoqualmie National Forest. Mountlake Terrace, WA, 1987.

Janes, Diane. Conversations with David A. Cameron, January 9 and March 31, 1999.

Joseph, Norma. Conversation with David A. Cameron, November 8, 1999.

Joseph, Lawrence and Norma Joseph. Conversation with David A. Cameron, November 4, 1998.

Josephy, Alvin M., Jr. "The American Indian and Freedom of Religion: An Historic Appraisal." *The Changing Pacific Northwest: Interpreting Its Past.* David H. Stratton and George A. Frykman, editors. Washington State University Press, Pullman, WA, 1988.

Kew, J.E. Michael. "Central and Southern Coast Salish Ceremonies Since 1900." *Handbook . . .*

Marino, Cesare. "History of Western Washington Since 1846." *Handbook . . .*

Mierendorf, Robert. Conversation with David A. Cameron, March 30, 1999.

Nelson, Charles M. "Prehistory of the Puget Sound Region." *Handbook . . .*

Page, Michael. "The Office of the Commissioner of Indian Affairs." *The Pacific Northwest Forum.* 4:1, Eastern Washington University, Cheney, WA, Winter-Spring 1991.

Rader, Maryann. "Indians and Education in the Pacific Northwest." *The Pacific Northwest Forum.* 4:1. Eastern Washington University, Cheney, WA, Winter-Spring 1991.

Report of the Commissioner of Indian Affairs for the Territories of Washington & Idaho, and the State of Oregon for the Year of 1870. Ye Galleon Press, Fairfield, WA, 1981.

Ruby, Robert H. and John A. Brown. *Esther Ross: Stillaguamish Champion.* University of Oklahoma Press, Norman, OK, 2001.

Sampson, Chief Martin J. *Indians of Skagit County.* Skagit County Historical Society, Mt. Vernon, WA, 1972.

Treaty Fishing Rights and the Northwest Indian Fisheries Commission. Northwest Indian Fisheries Commission, Olympia, WA, 1980.

Tulalip Tribal 1991 Bibliography Project. 6 vols. Tulalip Tribes, Marysville, WA, 1991.

Tweddell, Colin Ellidge. *A Historical and Ethnological Study of the Snohomish Indian People: A Report Specifically Covering their Aboriginal and Continued Existence and their Effective Occupation of a Definite Territory.* Docket No. 125, Ct Ex No 10, Seattle, August 1953.

Utley, Robert M. *The Indian Frontier of the American West 1846-1890.* University of New Mexico Press, Albuquerque, NM, 1984

Whitfield, William, supervising editor. *History of Snohomish County, Washington*. vol. 1. Pioneer Historical Publishing Company, Chicago-Seattle, 1926.

Zucker, Jeff, Kay Hummel, and Bob Hogfoss. *Oregon Indians: Culture, History & Current Affairs, An Atlas & Introduction*. Western Imprints, The Press of the Oregon Historical Society, 1983.

Chapter 3

Anderson, Bern. *Surveyor of the Sea: The Life and Times of Captain George Vancouver*. Seattle: University of Washington Press, Seattle, WA, 1960.

Buerge, David M., "The Wilkes Expedition in the Pacific Northwest," *Columbia: the Magazine of Northwest History* 1:18-32, Spring 1987.

Cook, Warren L. *Flood Tide of Empire: Spain and the Pacific Northwest, 1543-1819*. Yale University Press, New Haven and London, 1973.

Goetzman, William H. *New Lands, New Men: America and the Second Great Age of Discovery*. Viking, New York, 1986.

Henderson, Daniel. *The Hidden Coasts: A Biography of Admiral Charles Wilkes*. William Sloane Associates, New York, 1953.

Hitchman, Robert. *Place Names of Washington*. Washington State Historical Society, Tacoma, WA,1985.

An Illustrated History of Skagit and Snohomish Counties: Their People, Their Commerce and Their Resources, with an Outline of the Early History of the State of Washington. Interstate Publishing Company, Chicago, IL, 1906.

Marshall, James Stirrat, and Carrie Marshall. *Vancouver's Voyage*. Mitchell Press Limited, Vancouver, BC, Canada, 1955.

Meany, Edmond S., ed., *Diary of Wilkes in the Northwest*. University of Washington Press, Seattle, WA, 1926.

Meany, Edmond S. *Vancouver's Discovery of Puget Sound: Portraits and Biographies of the Men Honored in the Naming of Geographic Features of Northwestern America*. Binford & Mort, Portland, OR, 1957.

Phillips, James W. *Washington State Place Names*. University of Washington Press, Seattle and London, 1971.

Wilkes, Charles, U. S. N., *Narrative of the United States Exploring Expedition During the Years 1838, 1839, 1840, 1841, 1842, in Five Volumes and an Atlas*. Lea & Blanchett, Philadelphia, PA, 1844; esp. Vol. IV.

Chapter 4

Ackerman, Dolores Dunn, compiler. *Census of Snohomish County, Washington Territory 1889*. Stack Enterprises, Bellingham, WA, 1986.

An Illustrated History of Skagit and Snohomish Counties, Their People, Their Commerce and Their Resources, with an Outline of the early History of the State of Washington. Interstate Publishing Company, Chicago, IL, 1906.

Bruseth, Nels. "A History of the Stillaguamish Valley in Washington State." Ms., n.d., ca. 1910.

Bruseth, Nels. "Short History of Silvana, Formerly Stillaguamish." Ms., n.d.

Conroy, Dennis. Written comments to author on Utsalady, Stanwood, and the lower Stillaguamish valley. January 2000.

Cox, Thomas R. *Mills and Markets: A History of the Pacific Coast Lumber Industry to 1900*. University of Washington Press, Seattle, 1974.

Dilgard, David. *Dark Deeds: Snohomish County Crimes*. Lowell Printing & Publishing, Lowell, WA, 1991.

Dilgard, David. "The Adventures of Old Ferg." *Journal of Everett & Snohomish County History*. Nos. 2 and 3, Everett Public Library, Everett, WA, 1981, 1982.

Dilgard, David. " The Tulalip Settlement of 1853." *Journal of Everett & Snohomish County History*. No. 1, Everett Public Library, Everett, WA, 1981.

Dubuque, Ron. "Origin and History of all School Districts in Snohomish County, Washington." Ms., January 1970.

The Eye. Snohomish City, W. T., 1883-1887.

Ficken, Robert E. *The Forested Land: A History of Lumbering in Western Washington*. University of Washington Press, London and Seattle, 1987.

Index to Snohomish County Marriages. vol. 1, 1867-1899. Sno-Isle Genealogical Society, Edmonds, WA, 1992.

Johansen, Dorothy O. *Empire of the Columbia.* 2nd ed. Harper & Row, New York, 1967.

Joergenson, Gustav B. *"History of the Twin Cities"* series. *Twin City News*, Stanwood, April 1, 1948 - October 27, 1949. Also exists in manuscript form as *Stanwood - East Stanwood: And With Its Great Surrounding Settlement and How It Started.*

Monroe, Robert D. "Sailor on the Snohomish." *Journal of Everett & Snohomish County History.* Nos. 4-8, Everett Public Library, Everett, WA, 1982-1989.

Morgan, Murray. *Skid Road.* University of Washington Press, Seattle, WA, 1982.

Neil, Dorothy and Lee Brainard. *By Canoe and Sailing Ship They Came: A History of Whidbey's Island.* Spindrift, Oak Harbor, WA, 1989.

Newell, Gordon R. *Ships of the Inland Sea.* Binfords & Mort, Portland, OR, 1951.

____,_____. *SOS North Pacific.* Binfords & Mort, Portland, OR, 1955.

The Northern Star. Snohomish City, W. T. 1876-1878.

Our Pioneer Ancestors: Of the Stillaguamish Valley and of Snohomish County, Washington. vol. 1, Stillaguamish Valley Genealogical Society, Arlington, WA, 1997.

Peohlman, Elizabeth, S. *Darrington: Mining Town/Timber Town.* Gold Hill Press, Kent, WA, 1979.

1870 Federal Census. Washington Territory: Snohomish County. Stillaguamish Valley Genealogy Society, Arlington, WA, 1988.

1880 Federal Census. Washington Territory: Snohomish County. Stillaguamish Valley Genealogical Society, Arlington, WA, 1989.

Schwantes, Carlos A. *The Pacific Northwest: An Interpretive History.* University of Nebraska Press, Lincoln, NE, 1989.

Smith, Dr. Henry A. " A Trip to the Snohomish." *Journal of Everett & Snohomish County History.* No. 1, Everett Public Library, Everett, WA, 1981.

Trimble, William J. *The Mining Advance into the Inland Empire.* Ye Galleon Press, Fairfield, WA, 1986.

White, Richard. *Land Use, Environment, and Social Change: The Shaping of Island County, Washington.* University of Washington Press, Seattle, 1980.

Whitfield, William, supervising editor. *History of Snohomish County, Washington.* 2 vols., Pioneer Historical Publishing Company, Chicago and Seattle, 1926.

Chapter 5

Adams, Kramer. *Logging Railroads of the West.* Superior Publishing Company, Seattle, WA, 1961.

Anderson, Eva. *Rails Across The Cascades.* 5th ed., World Publishing Company, Wenatchee, WA, 1989.

Barrett, Maude and Pat Olsen. *Reflections of Marysville: A Pictorial History, A Centennial Look at the Past.* City of Marysville, WA, 1991.

Berry, Don. *The Lowell Story: A Community History.* Lowell Civic Association, Everett, WA, 1985.

Bohn, Dave and Rodolfo Petschek. *Kinsey, Photographer.* vols. 1 and 2,Chronicle Books, San Francisco, CA, 1986.

Broom, Judith. *Lynnwood: The Land, The People, The City.* Peanut Butter Publishing, Seattle, WA, 1990.

Brownell, Francis H. *When Everett Became the County Seat.* Everett Public Library, Everett, WA, reprint January 1998.

Bruseth, Nels. "History of Silvana, Formerly Stillaguamish." Ms. n.d.

Cardle, Doug. *Snohomish County Toponymy.* Coastal Press, Seattle, WA, 1988.

Caryl, Delmar H. *With Angels to the Rear: An Informal Portrait of Early Meadowdale.* The Dilemma Press, Edmonds, WA, 1960.

Chronicle of America. Chronicle Publications, Mount Kisco, New York, 1989.

Clark, Norman. *Mill Town: A Social History of Everett, Washington from its Earliest Beginnings on the Shores of Puget Sound to the Tragic and Infamous Event Known as the Everett Massacre.* University of Washington Press, Seattle, WA, 1970.

Cloud, Ray V. *Edmonds: The Gem of Puget Sound, A History of the City of Edmonds*. Edmonds-South Snohomish County Historical Society, Edmonds, WA, 1983.

Cornwell, Grace. "Stanwood and the Gold Rush." Ms., n.d.

Dilgard, David. *Everett Chronology*. Lowell Printing and Publishing Company, Everett, WA, 1992.

Dilgard, David and Margaret Riddle. *Journal of Everett and Snohomish County History*. Vols. 1-8, Everett Public Library, Everett, WA, 1980-1985.

Downstream Doggerel: The Courthouse Fight in Rhyme and Song. David Dilgard compiler, Everett Public Library, Everett, WA, January 1998.

Dubuque, Ron. "Origin and History of All School Districts in Snohomish County, Washington." Ms., 1970.

Duncan, Don. *Washington, The First One Hundred Years, 1889-1989, An Anecdotal History*. *The Seattle Times*, Seattle, WA, 1989.

The Enterprise Showcase Centennial Edition, February 15, 1989. The Enterprise, Lynnwood, WA, 1989.

Essex, Alice. *The Stanwood Story*. 3 vols., *Stanwood/Camano NEWS*, Stanwood, WA, 1971, 1982, 1998.

Everett, Washington City Directories. R.L. Polk and Company, Detroit, MI, 1893-1900.

Ficken, Robert E. and Charles P. LeWarne. *Washington: A Centennial History*. University of Washington Press, London and Seattle, 1988.

Getting Acquainted With Our Valleys, Historical Edition. Tabloid Supplement to *The Monroe Monitor* and *The Sultan Valley News*, June 2, 1982.

A Guide to Marysville. Pamphlet, Marysville Historical Society, Marysville, WA, 1991.

"Guide to the Gold of Monte Cristo." Pamphlet, Monte Cristo Preservation Association, Granite Falls, WA, n.d.

The HERALD. Everett, WA, 1891-1900.

Hidy, Ralph W. *Timber and Men: The Weyerhaeuser Story*. MacMillan, New York, 1963.

Historical Background Information: Major Burlington Northern Predecessor Companies. Booklet, Burlington Northern Railroad, St. Paul, MN, ca. 1980.

Hofstadter, Richard, William Miller, and Daniel Aron. *The United States: The History of a Republic*. Prentice-Hall, Englewood Cliffs, NJ, 1957.

Humphrey, Robert M. *Everett and Snohomish County: Pictorial History*. Donning, Norfolk, VA, 1984.

Inventory of the County Archives of Washington, No. 31 and Snohomish County, Historical Sketch and Governmental Organization and Records System. Preprint Edition Prepared by the Washington Historical Records Survey, Division of Community Service Programs, Work Projects Administration, Seattle, WA, March 1942.

Iron Goat Trail. Booklet, Volunteers for Outdoor Washington and Mt. Baker-Snoqualmie National Forest, Seattle, WA, ca. 1993.

"James J. Hill." Pamphlet, Minnesota Historical Society, St. Paul, MN, 1999.

Joergenson, Gustav B. "Stanwood – East Stanwood and Its Great Surrounding Settlement and How It Started". Meadowmoor Dairy of East Stanwood and Everett, WA, n.d.

Kraetz, Loren. Interviews with author, October 5, 1998, 1999.

The Labor Journal. 85: 45, July 2, 1976.

Lake Stevens Historical Society Memory Album. Booklet, Lake Stevens Historical Society, Lake Stevens, WA, 1989.

Lindgren, Louise. "Perspective on the Past: Silvana's Lively Past May Surprise You." *The Third Age*, December 1997.

Lydecker, Ryck. *Pigboat…The Story of the Whaleback*. Sweetwater Press, Duluth, MN, 1973.

McConnell, Opal. *Mukilteo Pictures and Memories*. Mukilteo Historical Society, Mukilteo, WA, 1977.

Meany, Edmond S. *History of the State of Washington*. MacMillan, New York, 1910.

Memories of the Courthouse Fight: 1949 Interviews with Joseph Irving of Everett and William Dolsen of Snohomish. Pamphlet, Everett Public Library, Everett, WA, January, 1998.

Monte Cristo Historical Tour, Booklet, David A. Cameron, Mt. Baker–Snoqualmie National Forest, 1976.

O'Donnell, Lawrence E. *Everett: Past and Present, a Centennial History of Everett, Washington*. Cascade Savings Bank, Everett, WA, 1993.

O'Donnell, Lawrence E. *Everett School District: The First 100 Years.* Peanut Butter Publishing, Seattle, WA, 1992.

O'Donnell, Lawrence E. *Woman's Book Club of Everett, Washington, Centennial History, 1894-1994.* Woman's Book Club, Everett, WA, 1994.

Poehlman, Elizabeth S. *Darrington: Mining Town/Timber Town.* Gold Hill Press, Shoreline, WA, 1995.

River Reflections: Volume I, 1859-1910, Volume II, 1910-1980. Snohomish Historical Society, Snohomish, WA, 1975, 1981.

Robertson, Donald B. *Encyclopedia of Western Railroad History, Volume III, Oregon and Washington..* Caxton, Caldwell, ID, 1995.

Robertson, Nellie. Skykomish Valley mining history. *The Monroe Monitor/Sultan Valley News*, Monroe, WA, February 20, 1985.

Robertson, Nellie E. *Monroe: The First Fifty Years, 1860-1910.* Bill and Nellie Robertson, Monroe, WA, 1996.

Roe, JoAnn. *Stevens Pass.* The Mountaineers, Seattle, WA, 1995.

Sandborg, Sandy. *Picnic Point Pathways.* Peanut Butter Publishing, Seattle, WA, 1997.

Satterfield, Archie. *Edmonds: The First Century.* City of Edmonds, Edmonds, WA, 1990.

Schuler, Lynda Hansen. *And We will Not Forget, History of the Snohomish School District, 1866-1994.* Snohomish School District, Snohomish, WA, 1994.

Snohomish Walking Tour. Pamphlet, Snohomish Chamber of Commerce, Snohomish, WA.

Stanwood's Historic West End Walking Tour. Pamphlet, Snohomish County and the Stanwood Area Historical Society, 1998.

Stevens, John F. "An Engineer's Recollections." Ms., Pacific Northwest Collection, University of Washington Libraries, Seattle, WA, ca. 1933.

United States Census. Various official documents, 1890-1900.

"Welcome to Historical Monroe." Brochure, Monroe Historical Society, Monroe, WA, n.d.

Wilterding, John H., Jr. *McDougall's Dream: The American Whaleback.* Lakeside Publications , Green Bay, WI, 1969.

Whitfield, William, supervising editor. *History of Snohomish County, Washington.* 2 vols., Pioneer Historical Publishing Company, Chicago and Seattle, 1926.

Woodhouse, Philip R., with Robert Wood. *Monte Cristo.* The Mountaineers, Seattle, WA, 1979.

Chapter 6

Adams, Kramer. *Logging Railroads of the West.* Superior Publishing Company, Seattle, WA, 1961.

Anderson, Eva. *Rails Across The Cascades.* 5th ed., World Publishing Company, Wenatchee, WA, 1989.

Barrett, Maude and Pat Olsen. *Reflections of Marysville: A Pictorial History, A Centennial Look at the Past.* City of Marysville, WA, 1991.

Berry, Don. *The Lowell Story: A Community History.* Lowell Civic Association, Everett, WA, 1985.

Bohn, Dave and Rodolfo Petschek. *Kinsey, Photographer.* 2 vols., Chronicle Books, San Francisco, CA, 1986.

Broom, Judith. *Lynnwood: The Land, The People, The City.* Peanut Butter Publishing, Seattle, WA, 1990.

Brownell, Francis H. *When Everett Became the County Seat*, Everett Public Library, reprint January 1998.

Bruseth, Nels. "History of Silvana, Formerly Stillaguamish." Ms., n.d.

Cardle, Doug. *Snohomish County Toponymy.* Coastal Press, Seattle, WA, 1988.

Caryl, Delmar H. *With Angels to the Rear: An Informal Portrait of Early Meadowdale.* The Dilemma Press, Edmonds, WA, 1960.

Chronicle of America. Chronicle Publications, Mount Kisco, New York, 1989.

The City of Everett, State of Washington, U.S.A.. Booklet, *The Daily Independent*, Everett, WA, 1900.

Clark, Norman. *Mill Town: A Social History of Everett, Washington from its Earliest Beginnings on the Shores of Puget Sound to the Tragic and Infamous Event Known as the Everett Massacre.* University of Washington Press, Seattle, WA, 1970.

Clark, Norman. *The Dry Years: Prohibition and Social Change in Washington.* University of Washington Press, Seattle, WA, 1965.

Cloud, Ray V. *Edmonds: The Gem of Puget Sound, A History of the City of Edmonds.* Edmonds South Snohomish County Historical Society, Edmonds, WA, 1983.

The Coast: Alaska and Greater Northwest. 14:4, The Coast Publishing Company, Seattle, WA, October 1907.

The Coast: Alaska and Greater Northwest. 15:5, The Coast Publishing Company, Seattle, WA, 1908. Reprint 1973.

Cornwell, Grace. "Stanwood and the Gold Rush." Ms. n.d.

Dilgard, David and Margaret Riddle, editors. *Journal of Everett and Snohomish County History*, vols. 1-8, Everett Public Library, Everett, WA, 1980-1985.

Dubuque, Ron. "Origin and History of All School Districts in Snohomish County, Washington." Ms., 1970.

Duncan, Don. *Washington, The First One Hundred Years, 1889-1989, An Anecdotal History.* The Seattle Times, Seattle, WA, 1989.

Early History of Lake Stevens. Booklet, Lake Stevens Community Development Study, Lake Stevens, WA, May 1957.

The Enterprise Showcase Centennial Edition, February 15, 1989. The Enterprise, Lynnwood, WA.

Essex, Alice. *The Stanwood Story.* 3 vols, *Stanwood/Camano NEWS* , Stanwood, WA, 1971, 1982, 1998.

Everett, Washington City Directories. R.L. Polk and Company, Detroit, MI, 1900-1918.

Ficken, Robert E. *The Forested Land: A History of Lumbering in Western Washington.* Ficken, Robert E. and Charles LeWarne. *Washington: A Centennial History.* University of Washington Press, London and Seattle, 1988.

Forest History Society, Inc., Durham, North Carolina and University of Washington Press, London and Seattle, 1987.

Getting Acquainted With Our Valleys, Historical Edition. Tabloid Supplement to *The Monroe Monitor* and *The Sultan Valley News*, June 2, 1982.

A Guide to Marysville. Pamphlet, Marysville Historical Society, Marysville, WA, 1991.

"Guide to the Gold of Monte Cristo." Pamphlet, Monte Cristo Preservation Association, Granite Falls, WA, n.d.

The HERALD. Everett, WA, 1891–1919.

Hidy, Ralph W. *Timber and Men: The Weyerhaeuser Story.* MacMillan, New York, 1963.

Historical Background Information: Major Burlington Northern Predecessor Companies. Booklet, Burlington Northern Railroad, St. Paul, MN, ca. 1980.

A History of the State of Washington. Vol. 2, Lloyd Spencer, Editor-in-Chief; The American Historical Society, New York, 1937.

Hofstadter, Richard, William Miller, and Daniel Aaron. *The United States: The History of a Republic.* Prentice–Hall, Englewood Cliffs, NJ, 1957.

Holbrook, Stewart. *Wildmen, Wobblies & Whistle Punks.* Oregon State University Press, Corvallis, OR, 1992.

Holl, Jack M. and Roger A. Pederson. "The Washington State Reformatory of Monroe." *Pacific Northwest Quarterly*, 67:1, pp. 21-28. January 1976.

Humphrey, Robert M. *Everett and Snohomish County: Pictorial History.* Donning, Norfolk, VA, 1984.

Inventory of the County Archives of Washington, No. 31 and Snohomish County, Historical Sketch and Governmental Organization and Records System. Preprint Edition Prepared by the Washington Historical Records Survey, Division of Community Service Programs, Work Projects Administration, Seattle, WA, March 1942.

Iron Goat Trail. Booklet, Volunteers for Outdoor Washington and Mt. Baker-Snoqualmie National Forest, Seattle, WA, ca. 1993.

"James J. Hill." Pamphlet, Minnesota Historical Society, St. Paul, MN, 1999.

Joergenson, Gustav B. "Stanwood – East Stanwood and Its Great Surrounding Settlement and How It Started." Meadowmoor Dairy of East Stanwood and Everett, WA, n.d.

Kaiser, James G. *Crown Lumber Company and The Early Growth of Mukilteo.* Packrat Press, Oak Harbor, WA, 1990.

Kraetz, Loren. Interviews with author, October 5, 1998, 1999.

The Labor Journal. Everett, WA, 85:45 and 1909.

Lake Stevens Historical Society Memory Album. Booklet, Lake Stevens Historical Society, Lake Stevens, WA, 1989.

Lindgren, Louise. "Perspective on the Past: Silvana's Lively Past May Surprise You." *The Third Age*, Everett, WA, December 1997.

Major Industrial Potential of Snohomish County Washington. Booklet, Snohomish County Public Utility District No. 1, Everett, WA, 1950.

McConnell, Opal. *Mukilteo Pictures and Memories*. Mukilteo Historical Society, Mukilteo, WA, 1987.

Monte Cristo Historical Tour. Booklet, David A. Cameron, Mt. Baker–Snoqualmie National Forest, 1976.

Nesika-Kodak. Everett High School, Everett, WA, June, 1917.

O'Donnell, Lawrence E. *A History of The Everett Rotary Club*. Booklet, Everett Rotary Club, Everett, WA, 1996.

O'Donnell, Lawrence E. *Everett: Past and Present, a Centennial History of Everett, Washington*. Cascade Savings Bank, Everett, WA, 1993.

O'Donnell, Lawrence E. *Everett School District: The First 100 Years*. Peanut Butter Publishing, Seattle, WA, 1992.

O'Donnell, Lawrence E. *Woman's Book Club of Everett, Washington: Centennial History, 1894-1994*. Woman's Book Club, Everett, WA, 1994.

Poehlman, Elizabeth S. *Darrington: Mining Town/Timber Town*. Gold Hill Press, Shoreline, WA, 1995.

Riddle, Margaret. Sheet about John E. Campbell, Everett, WA, 1998.

River Reflections: Volume I, 1859-1910, Volume II, 1910-1980. Snohomish Historical Society, Snohomish, WA, 1975, 1981.

Robertson, Donald B. *Encyclopedia of Western Railroad History, Volume III, Oregon and Washington*. Caxton, Caldwell, ID, 1995.

Robertson, Nellie. Skykomish Valley mining history. *The Monroe Monitor/Sultan Valley News*, Monroe, WA, February 20, 1985.

Robertson, Nellie E. *Monroe: The First Fifty Years, 1860-1910*. Bill and Nellie Robertson, Monroe, WA, 1996.

Roe, JoAnn. *Stevens Pass*. The Mountaineers, Seattle, WA, 1995.

Sandborg, Sandy. *Picnic Point Pathways*. Peanut Butter Publishing, Seattle, WA, 1997.

Satterfield, Archie. *Edmonds: The First Century*. City of Edmonds, Edmonds, WA, 1990.

Schuler, Lynda Hansen. *And We will Not Forget: History of the Snohomish School District, 1866-1994*, Snohomish School District, Snohomish, WA, 1994.

Snohomish Walking Tour. Brochure, Snohomish Chamber of Commerce, Snohomish, WA.

Stanwood's Historic West End Walking Tour. Pamphlet, Snohomish County and the Stanwood Area Historical Society, 1998.

United States Census. Various official documents, 1900-1920.

"Welcome to Historical Monroe," Brochure, Monroe Historical Society, Monroe, WA.

Wilterding, John H., Jr. *McDougall's Dream: The American Whaleback*. Lakeside Publications, Green Bay, WI, 1969.

Whitfield, William, supervising editor. *History of Snohomish County, Washington*. 2 vols., Pioneer Historical Publishing Company, Chicago and Seattle, 1926.

Wing, Warren W. *To Seattle by Trolley*. Pacific Fast Mail, Edmonds, WA, 1988.

Woodhouse, Philip R., with Robert Wood. *Monte Cristo*. The Mountaineers, Seattle, WA, 1979.

Chapter 7

Berry, Don. *The Lowell Story: A Community History*. Lowell Civic Association, Lowell, WA, 1985.

Broom, Judith M. *Lynnwood: The Land, the People, the City*, Peanut Butter Publishing, Seattle, WA, 1990.

Caryl, Delmar H. *With Angels to the Rear: An Informal Portrait of Early Meadowdale*. The Dilemma Press, Edmonds, WA, 1960.

Clark, Norman H. *The Dry Years: Prohibition & Social Change in Washington*. rev. ed. University of Washington Press, Seattle and London, 1988.

Clark, Norman H. *Mill Town: A Social History of Everett, Washington, from Its Earliest Beginnings on the Shores of*

Puget Sound to the Tragic and Infamous Event Known as the Everett Massacre. University of Washington Press, Seattle and London, 1970.

Cloud, Ray V. *Edmonds, The Gem of Puget Sound: A History of the City of Edmonds.* Edmonds South Snohomish County Historical Society, Edmonds, WA, 1953.

Dilgard, David. "The Automobile in Everett - Its Initial Decade," *Journal of Everett & Snohomish County*, No. 7, Everett Public Library, Everett, WA, Autumn 1985.

Dilgard, David and Margaret Riddle, editors. "Enoch Bagshaw, Man and Legend," *Journal of Everett & Snohomish County*. No. 7, Everett Public Library, Everett, WA, Autumn 1985.

Essex, Alice. *The Stanwood Story.* 3 vols., Stanwood/Camano NEWS, Stanwood, WA, 1971, 1982, 1998.

Gunns, Albert Francis. *Roland Hill and the Politics of Washington State.* M. A. Thesis, University of Washington, 1963. Malstrom, Helmer. *Memory Lanes of Old Everett and its East Riverside, Revisited by Helmer Malstrom.* The Estate of Helmer Malstrom, Mill Creek, WA, 1986.

Poehlman, Elizabeth S. *Darrington: Mining Town/Timber Town.* Gold Hill Press, Shoreline, WA, 1979, 1995.

Schmid, Calvin F., and Stanton E. Schmid. *Growth of Cities and Towns in Washington.* Washington State Planning and Commnity Affairs Agency, Olympia, WA, 1969.

Whitfield, William, supervising editor. *History of Snohomish County, Washington.* 2 vols., Pioneer Historical Publishing Company, Chicago and Seattle, 1926.

Woodhouse, Philip R., with Robert L. Wood. *Monte Cristo.* The Mountaineers, Seattle, WA, 1979.

Chapter 8

Cameron, Helene. Interview with author, November 14, 2000.

CCC Company 6439 historical file, Darrington Ranger District, Darrington, WA.

Clark, Norman. *Mill Town: A Social History of Everett, Washington from its Earliest Beginnings on the Shores of Puget Sound to the Tragic and Infamous Event Known as the Everett Massacre.* University of Washington Press, Seattle, WA, 1970.

Daniels, Jonathan. *The Time Between the Wars.* Doubleday, Garden City, New York, 1966.

Ellis, Edward Robb. *A Nation in Torment.* Kodansha International, New York, 1995.

Everett Park Board, minutes, various dates.

Ficken, Robert E. *The Forested Land: A History of Lumbering in Western Washington.* Forest History Society, Inc., Durham, North Carolina and University of Washington Press, London and Seattle, 1987.

"50th Anniversary of Paine Field," one page flyer, November 4, 1986.

Garrotte, John A. *The Great Depression.* Harcourt, Brace, Jovanovitch, New York, 1986.

The HERALD. Everett, WA, 1929-1939.

Holm, Monte. *Once A Hobo: The Autobiography of Monte Holm.* Proctor Publications, Ann Arbor, MI, 1999.

Johansen, Dorothy O. *Empire of the Columbia.* 2nd ed., Harper & Row, New York, 1967.

Kennedy, David M. *Freedom From Fear: The American People in Depression and War, 1929-1945.* Oxford University Press, New York, 1999.

Larson, Lloyd. Interview with author, October 10, 1996.

Lloyd, Stanley. Interview with author, January 15-17, 1997.

May, Allan and Dale Preboski. *The History of Everett Parks.* Donning, Norfolk, VA, 1989.

O'Donnell, Lawrence E. *Everett: Past and Present, a Centennial History of Everett, Washington.* Cascade Savings Bank, Everett, WA, 1993.

Platt, Frank. Interview with author, October 14, 1996.

Poehlman, Elizabeth S. *Darrington: Mining Town/Timber Town.* Gold Hill Press, Shoreline, WA, 1979, 1995.

Prochnau, William and Richard Larson. *A Certain Democrat.* Prentice-Hall, New York, 1972.

Ramstead, Carl. Interview with author, October 14, 1996.

The Seattle Times, March 17, 1957.

Snohomish County Auditor, archives.

Steen, Harold K. *The U.S. Forest Service: A History*. University of Washington Press, Seattle, 1976.

World Almanac and Book of Facts, 1933.

Chapter 9

Ace Pursuiter. Paine Field weekly newsletter from the Army Air Force Special Services Office and Post Exchange of Paine Field, Washington, several issues, 1944-1945.

Adams, Kramer. *Logging Railroads of the West*. Superior Publishing Company, Seattle, WA, 1961.

Arlington Municipal Airport, 1934-1946, The Formative Years: An Historic Scrapbook. Neill D. Mullen compiler, ed., from articles in *The Arlington Times*, Arlington, WA, 1997.

Barrett, Maude and Pat Olsen. *Reflections of Marysville: A Pictorial History, A Centennial Look at the Past*. City of Marysville, WA, 1991.

Broom, Judith. *Lynnwood: The Land, The People, The City*. Peanut Butter Publishing, Seattle, WA, 1990.

Cardle, Doug. *Snohomish County Toponymy*. Coastal Press, Seattle, WA, 1988.

Chronicle of America. Chronicle Publications., Mount Kisco, New York, 1989.

Cloud, Ray V. *Edmonds: The Gem of Puget Sound, A History of the City of Edmonds*. Edmonds-South Snohomish County Historical Society, Edmonds, WA, 1983.

Cunningham, James. Interview with author, April 30, 1993.

Dubuque, Ron. "Origin and History of All School Districts in Snohomish County, Washington." Ms. 1970.

Duncan, Don. *Washington, The First One Hundred Years, 1889-1989, An Anecdotal History*. The Seattle Times, Seattle, WA, 1989.

Dycus, Julius and Sylvia. Interview with author, March 7, 1999 and September 14, 1999.

Essex, Alice. *The Stanwood Story*. 3 vols., *Stanwood/Camano NEWS* , Stanwood, WA, 1971, 1982, 1998.

Everett High Kodak. Everett High School, Everett, WA, several issues, 1940-1944.

Everett Junior College documents: Everett School District No. 2 Board of Directors' Meeting Minutes; *Integrand*, 1941-1943, First Everett Junior College Annual; Reports to the Board of Directors from the College, including budget and enrollment.

Everett Port Commission Meeting Minutes, several meetings, January 5, 1942 through October 4, 1943.

Everett, Washington City Directories. R.L. Polk and Company, Detroit, MI., 1940, 1944.

Ficken, Robert E. and Charles P. LeWarne. *Washington: A Centennial History*. University of Washington Press, Seattle and London, 1988.

"50th Anniversary of Paine Field," one page flyer, November 4, 1986.

Flight Path, A History of the Boeing Company. The Boeing Company, Seattle, WA, 1990.

Galde, Burton G. information from various documents on display at Stillaguamish Valley Pioneer Museum, Arlington, WA, 1999.

"Guide to the Gold of Monte Cristo." Pamphlet, Monte Cristo Preservation Association, Granite Falls, WA, ibid.

Guisinger, Mrs. Al. Interview with author, September 16, 1999.

The HERALD. Everett, WA, 1939-1947.

Hofstadter, Richard, William Miller, and Daniel Aaron. *The United States: The History of a Republic*. Prentice-Hall, Englewood Cliffs, NJ, 1957.

Humphrey, Robert M. *Everett and Snohomish County: Pictorial History*. Donning, Norfolk, VA, 1984.

Humphrey, William. Interview with author, winter 1998-spring 1999.

Inventory of the County Archives of Washington, No. 31 and Snohomish County, Historical Sketch and Governmental Organization and Records System.

Preprint Edition Prepared by the Washington Historical Records Survey,Division of Community Service Programs, Work Projects Administration, Seattle, WA, March 1942.

Kraetz, Loren. Interviews with author, October 5, 1998, 1999.

Major Industrial Potential of Snohomish County Washington. Booklet, Snohomish County Public Utility District No. 1, Everett, WA, 1950.

McCann, Joe "Eddie" and Helen. Interview with author, March 2, 1999, with numerous newspaper articles supplied by the McCanns.

_____. "Outline of My Story." Ms., ca. 1990.

1939 National Guard of the United States, State of Washington, Historical and Pictorial Review: A tribute by the Military Department of the State in observance of the 50th Anniversary of Washington's Statehood. Army and Navy Publishing Company, Baton Rouge, LA, 1939.

O'Donnell, Lawrence E. *A History of The Everett Rotary Club*. Booklet, Everett Rotary Club, Everett, WA, 1996.

O'Donnell, Lawrence E. *Everett: Past and Present, a Centennial History of Everett, Washington*. Cascade Savings Bank, Everett, WA, 1993.

O'Donnell, Lawrence E. *Everett School District: The First 100 Years*. Peanut Butter Publishing, Seattle, WA, 1992.

O'Donnell, Lawrence E. *Woman's Book Club of Everett, Washington, Centennial History, 1894-1994*. Woman's Book Club, Everett, WA, 1994.

Pacific Northwest Goes to War. Art Ritchie and William J. Davis, 1944.

Paine Field materials, Snohomish County, ca. 1990.

River Reflections, Volume I, 1859-1910, and *Volume II, 1910-1980*. Snohomish Historical Society, Snohomish, WA, 1975, 1981.

Robertson, Nellie. Sam Mann article. *The Monroe Monitor-Valley News*, April 24, 1991.

Robertson, Nellie. "Index Stages, Inc., a part of Monroe's History". *Heritage Herald*, Monroe Historical Society, Monroe, WA, First Quarter, 1998

Satterfield, Archie. *Edmonds: The First Century*. City of Edmonds, Edmonds, WA, 1990.

Schuler, Lynda Hansen. *'And We will Not Forget, History of the Snohomish School District, 1866-1994*. Snohomish School District, Snohomish, WA, 1994.

Startup, Richard. Interview with author, September 1, 1993.

Three Years of Service: Everett Pacific Shipbuilding and Dry Dock Company, Everett, Washington. Booklet, Everett Pacific Shipbuilding and Dry Dock Company, February 1945.

United States Census. Various official documents, 1940.

"Welcome to Historical Monroe." Pamphlet, Monroe Historical Society, Monroe, WA. n.d.

Woodhouse, Philip R., with Robert L. Wood. *Monte Cristo*.The Mountaineers, Seattle, WA, 1979.

"*World War II*." Associated Press Tabloid Supplement to *The Everett Daily Herald*, October 20, 1945.

Chapter 10

"Agriculture in Snohomish County," Snohomish County Department of Planning and Development Services, n.d.

Agriculture Series of 1956. "Snohomish County Agriculture." Washington State Department of Agriculture, Olympia, WA.

Broom, Judith. *Lynnwood: The Land, The People, The City*. Peanut Butter Publishing, Seattle, WA, 1990.

Clark, Hazel. *An Informal History of the Everett Public Library*. Lowell Printing and Publishing, Everett, WA, 1996.

Cloud, Ray V. *Edmonds: The Gem of Puget Sound, A History of the City of Edmonds*. Edmonds-South Snohomish County Historical Society, Edmonds, WA, 1983.

Edmonds School District archives.

The *Enterprise*. Lynnwood, WA, various issues.

"The Entrance Sculptures." Pamphlet, Everett Public Library, Everett, WA, n.d.

"Everett Community Profile." Pamphlet, Greater Everett Chamber of Commerce, Everett, WA, n.d.

"50th Anniversary of Paine Field," one page flyer, November 4, 1986.

Guide to the Gold of Monte Cristo." Pamphlet, Monte Cristo Preservation Association, Granite Falls, WA.

The HERALD. Everett, WA, various issues.

Humphrey, Robert M. *Everett and Snohomish County: Pictorial History*. Donning, Norfolk, VA, 1984.

O'Donnell, Lawrence E. *Everett School District: The First 100 Years*. Peanut Butter Publishing, Seattle, WA, 1992.

Our Glorious Century. Readers Digest Association, Pleasantville, New York, 1994.

Public Utility District No. 1 of Snohomish County, archives.

The *Reporter*. Lynnwood, WA, various issues.

Satterfield, Archie. *Edmonds: The First Century*. City of Edmonds, Edmonds, WA, 1990.

The Seattle Times, various issues.

Snohomish County Directories. R.L. Polk and Company, Detroit, Michigan, various dates.

The Third Age, Everett, WA, August 2000.

The *Tribune*. Edmonds, WA, various issues.

U.S. Department of Commerce, Technology Administration, National Technical Information Service.

Chapter 11

Bakken, Don. *Lomcevak!: The Story of the Lynnwood Rotary International Air Fair*. Gorham Printing, Rochester, WA. 2000.

Bennett, Geoff. "Mill Creek, Washington, A Brief History, 1983-1987," Everett School District, Everett, WA, n.d.

Berry, Don. *The Lowell Story: A Community History*. Lowell Civic Association, Everett, WA, 1985.

Beyers, William B. "From Seattle to the World, and Vice Versa: The Evolution of Boeing's Subcontracting Strategies in Aircraft Manufacture," University of Washington, Seattle, WA, March 6, 1993.

Broom, Judith M., *Lynnwood: The Land, The People, The City*, Peanut Butter Publishing, Seattle, WA, 1990.

Cameron, David A. "Snohomish County History," Everett School District, Everett, WA, June 1987.

Citizen Link. Snohomish County, April, 1997.

Duncan, Don. *Washington, The First One Hundred Years, 1889-1989, An Anecdotal History*. The Seattle Times, Seattle, WA, 1989.

"Edmonds: 100 Years for the Gem of Puget Sound, A Special Commemorative Issue Presented by The Edmonds Paper and The Edmonds/South Snohomish County Historical Society," Edmonds, WA, December 1990.

Essex, Alice. *The Stanwood Story*. vol. 3, *Stanwood/Camano NEWS* , Stanwood, WA, 1998.

Everett Herald Business Journal. Everett, WA, various dates.

Ficken, Robert E. and Charles P. LeWarne. *Washington: A Centennial History*. University of Washington Press, London and Seattle, 1988.

"Healthy Communities for Snohomish County". Brochure, The Healthy Communities Vision for Snohomish County, 1997.

The HERALD. Everett, WA, various dates.

"Homeporting History." Information sheet 1983-1990, Everett/Snohomish County Impact Coordinating Council, n.d.

"Know Your County." Pamphlet, League of Women Voters of Snohomish County, Everett, WA, March 1966.

Monroe *Monitor*. Monroe, WA, various dates.

Newland, D. Peter. Interview with author, January 15, 1999.

O'Donnell, Lawrence E. *Everett: Past and Present, a Centennial History of Everett, Washington*. Cascade Savings Bank, Everett, WA, 1993.

Pace, Sue. "A Blue-Plate Special Town," *Newsweek*, September 30, 1999.

Pavish, Edythe. Interview with author, July 17, 1998.

"Political Pioneers: A Study of Women in the Washington State Legislature," Washington Commission for the Humanities, October 1993.

Public Utility District No. 1 of Snohomish County. *Annual Report*. 1966.

Satterfield, Archie, *Edmonds: The First Century*, City of Edmonds, Edmonds, WA, 1990.

The *Seattle Post-Intelligencer*. Various dates.

The Seattle Times. Various dates.

Snohomish County Department of Planning and Development Services, Planning Division, Selected Demographic Tables, Graphs, and Maps.

"Snohomish County's Supply of Sand and Gravel is Running Out." Brochure, CSR-Associated Sand and Gravel Company, October 1998.

Vadset, Barbara. Interview with author, June 21, 2000.

Voss, Frederick S. *Faces of Time: 75 Years of Time Magazine Cover Portraits*. Little, Brown, Boston, 1998.

Washington Biographical Dictionary, Somerset Publishers, New York, 1996.

Woodway Park. The Woodway Centennial Committee, Woodway, WA, July, 1989.

Snohomish County: An Illustrated History

Appendix

TREATY WITH THE DWAMISH, SUQUAMISH, ETC., 1855

Articles of agreement and convention made and concluded at Múckl-te-óh, or Point Elliott, in the Territory of Washington, this twenty-second day of January, eighteen hundred and fifty-five, by Isaac I. Stevens, governor and superintendent of Indian affairs for the said Territory, on the part of the United States, and the undersigned chiefs, headmen and delegates of the Dwámish, Suquámish, Sk-táhl-mish, Sam-áhmish, ,Sinalh-kamiah, Skope-áhmish, St-káh-mish, Snoquálmoo, Skai-wha-mish, N'Quentl-má-mish, Sk-táh-le-jum, Stoluck-whá-mish, Sno-ho-mish, Skágit, Kik-i-állus, Swin-á-mish, Squin-áh-mish, Sah-ku-méhu, Noo-whá-ha, Nook-wa-cháh-mish, Mee-sée-qua-ġuilch, Cho-bah-áh-bish, and other allied and subordinate tribes and bands of Indians occupying certain lands situated in said Territory of Washington, on behalf of said tribes, and duly authorized by them.

ARTICLE 1. The said tribes and bands of Indians hereby cede, relinquish, and convey to the United States all their right, title, and interest in and to the lands and country occupied by them, bounded and described as follows: Commencing at a point on the eastern side of Admiralty Inlet, known as Point Pully, about midway between Commencement and Elliott Bays; thence eastwardly, running along the north line of lands heretofore ceded to the United States by the Nisqually, Puyallup, and other Indians, to the summit of the Cascade range of mountains; thence northwardly, following the summit of said range to the 49th parallel of north latitude; thence west, along said parallel to the middle of the Gulf of Georgia; thence through the middle of said gulf and the main channel through the Canal de Arro to the Straits of Fuca, and crossing the same through the middle of Admiralty Inlet to Suquamish Head; thence southwesterly, through the peninsula, and following the divide between Hood's Canal and Admiralty Inlet to the portage known as Wilkes' Portage; thence northeastwardly, and following the line of lands heretofore ceded as aforesaid to Point Southworth, on the western aide of Admiralty Inlet, and thence around the foot of Vashon's Island eastwardly and southeastwardly to the place of beginning, including all the islands comprised within said boundaries, and all the right, title, and interest of the said tribes and bands to any lands within the territory of the United States.

ARTICLE 2. There is, however, reserved for the present use and occupation of the said tribes and bands the following tracts of land, viz: the amount of two sections, or twelve hundred and eighty acres, surrounding the small bight at the head of Port Madison, called by the Indians Noo-sohk-um; the amount of two sections, or twelve hundred and eighty acres, on the north side Hwhomish Bay and the creek emptying into the same called

Kwilt-seh-da, the peninsula at the southeastern end of Perry's Island, called Sháis-quihl, and the island called Chah-choo-sen, situated in the Lummi River at the point of separation of the mouths emptying respectively into Bellingham Bay and the Gulf of Georgia. All which tracts shall be set apart, and so far as necessary surveyed and marked out for their exclusive use; nor shall any white man be permitted to reside upon the same without permission of the said tribes or bands, and of the superintendent or agent, but, if necessary for the public convenience, roads map be run rough the said reserves, the Indians being compensated for any damage thereby done them.

ARTICLE 3. There is also reserved from out the lands hereby ceded the amount of thirty-six sections, or one township of land, on the northeastern shore of Port Gardner, and north of the mouth of Snohomish River, including Tulalip Bay and the before-mentioned Kwilt-seh-da Creek, for the purpose of establishing thereon an agricultural and industrial school, as hereinafter mentioned and agreed, and with a view of ultimately drawing thereto and settling thereon all the Indians living west of the Cascade Mountains in said Territory. *Provided, however*, That the President may establish the central agency and general reservation at such other point as he may deem for the benefit of the Indians.

ARTICLE 4. The said tribes and bands agree to remove to and settle upon the said first above-mentioned reservations within one year after the ratification of this treaty, or sooner, if the means are furnished them. In the mean time it shall be lawful for them to reside upon any land not in the actual claim and occupation of citizens of the United States, and upon any land claimed or occupied, if with the permission of the owner.

ARTICLE 5. The right of taking fish at usual and accustomed grounds and stations is further secured to said Indians in common with all citizens of the Territory, and of erecting temporary houses for the purpose of curing, together with the privilege of hunting and gathering roots and berries on open and unclaimed lands. *Provided, however*, That they shall not take shell-fish from any beds staked or cultivated by citizens.

ARTICLE 6. In consideration of the above cession, the United States agree to pay to the said tribes and bands the sum of one hundred and fifty thousand dollars, in the following manner—that is to say: For the first year after the ratification hereof, fifteen thousand dollars; for the next two year, twelve thousand dollars each year; for the next three years, ten thousand dollars each year; for the next four years, seven thousand five hundred dollars each years; for the next five years, six thousand dollars each year; and for the last five years, four thousand two hundred and fifty dollars each year. All which said sums of money shall be applied to the use and benefit of the said Indians, under the direction of the President of the United States, who may, from time to time, determine at his discretion upon what beneficial objects to expend the same; and the superintendent of Indian affairs, or other proper officer, shall each year inform the President of the wishes of said Indians in respect thereto.

ARTICLE 7. The President may hereafter, when in his opinion the interests of the Territory shall require and the welfare of the said Indians be promoted, remove them from either or all of the special reservations hereinbefore made to the said general reservation, or such other suitably place within said Territory as be may deem fit, on remunerating them for their improvements and the expenses of such removal, or may consolidate them with other friendly tribes or bands; and he may further at his discretion cause the whole or any portion of the lands hereby reserved, or of such other land as may be selected in lieu thereof, to be surveyed into lots, and assign the same to such individuals or families as are willing to avail themselves of the privilege, and will locate on the same as a permanent home on the same terms and subject to the same regulations as are provided in the sixth article of the treaty with the Omahas, so far as the same may be applicable. Any substantial improvements heretofore made by any Indian, and which he shall be compelled to abandon in consequence of this treaty, shall be valued under the direction of the President and payment made accordingly therefor.

ARTICLE 8. The annuities of the aforesaid tribes and bands shall not be taken to pay the debts of individuals.

ARTICLE 9. The said tribes and bands acknowledge their dependence on the Government of the United States, and promise to be friendly with all citizens thereof, and they pledge themselves to commit no depredations on the property of such citizens. Should any one or more of them violate this pledge, and the fact be satisfactorily proven before the agent, the property taken shall be returned, or in default thereof, of if injured or destroyed, compensation may be made by the Government out of their annuities. Nor will they make war on any other tribe except in self-defence, but will submit all matters of difference between them and the other Indians to the Government of the United States or its agent for decision, and abide thereby. And if any of the said Indians commit depredations on other Indians within the Territory the same rule shall prevail as that prescribed in this article in cases of depredations against citizens. And the said tribes agree not to shelter or conceal offenders against the laws of the United States, but to deliver them up to the authorities for trial.

ARTICLE 10. The above tribes and bands are desirous to exclude from their reservations the use of ardent spirits, and to prevent their people from drinking the same, and therefore it is provided that any Indian belonging to said tribe who is guilty of bringing liquor into said reservations, or who drinks liquor, may have his or her proportion of the annuities withheld from him or her for such time as the President may determine.

ARTICLE 11. The said tribes and bands agree to free all slaves now held by them and not to purchase or acquire others hereafter.

ARTICLE 12. The said tribes and bands further agree not to trade at Vancouver's Island or elsewhere out of the dominions of the United States, nor shall foreign Indians be permitted to reside in their reservations without consent of the superintendent or agent.

ARTICLE 13. To enable the said Indians to remove to and settle upon. their aforesaid reservations, and to clear, fence, and break up a sufficient quantity of land for cultivation, the United States further agree to pay the sum of fifteen thousand dollars to be laid out and expended under the direction of the President and in such manner as he shall approve.

ARTICLE 14. The United States further agree to establish at the agency for the district of Puget's Sound, within one year from the ratification hereof, an agricultural and industrial school, to be free to children of the said tribes and bands in common with those of the other tribes of said district, and to provide the said school with a suitable instructor or instructors, and also to provide a smithy and carpenter's shop, and furnish them with the necessary tools, and employ a blacksmith, carpenter, and farmer for the like term of twenty years to instruct the Indians in their respective occupations. And the United States finally agree to employ a physician to reside at the said central agency, who shall furnish medicine and advice to their sick, and shall vaccinate them; the expenses of said school, shops, persons employed, and medical attendance to be defrayed by the United States, and not deducted from the annuities.

ARTICLE 15. This treaty shall be obligatory on the contracting parties as soon as the same shall be ratified by the President and Senate of the United States.

In testimony whereof, the said Isaac I. Stevens, governor and superintendent of Indian affairs, and. the undersigned chiefs, headmen, and delegates of the aforesaid tribes and bands of Indians, have hereunto set their hands and seals, at the place and on and year herein before written.

Isaac I. Stevens, Governor and Superintendent. [L. s.]
Seattle, Chief of the Dwamish and Suquamish tribes, his x mark. [L. s.]
Wats-ka-lah-tchie, or John Hobtsthoot, Sub-chief of Snohomish, his x mark. [L. s.]
Pat-ka-nam, Chief of the Snoqualmoo, Snohomish and other tribes, his x mark. [L. s.]
Smeh-mai-hu, Sub-chief of Skai-wha-mish, his x mark. [L. s.]
Chow-its-hoot, Chief of the Lummi and other tribes, his x mark. [L. s.]
Slat-eah-ka-nam, Sub-chief of Snoqualmoo, his x mark. [L. s.]
Goliah, Chief of the Skagits and other allied tribes, his x mark. [L. s.]
St'hau-ai, Sub-chief of Snoqualmoo, his x mark. [L. s.]
Kwallattum, or General Pierce, Sub-chief of the Skagit tribe, his x mark. [L. s.]
Lugs-ken, Sub-chief of Skai-wha-mish, his x mark. [L. s.]
S'hootst-hoot, Sub-chief of Snohomish, his x mark. [L. s.]
S'heht-soolt, or Peter, Sub-chief of Snohomish, his x mark. [L. s.]
Snah-talc, or Bonaparte, Sub-chief of Snohomish, his x mark. [L. s.]
Do-queh-oo-satl, Snoqualmoo tribe, his x mark. [L. s.]
Squush-um, or The Smoke, Sub-chief of the Snoqualmoo, his x mark. [L. s.]
John Kanam, Snoqualmoo sub-chief, his x mark. [L. s.]
See-alla-pa-han, or The Priest, Sub-chief of Sk-tah-le-jum, his x mark. [L. s.]
Klemsh-ka-nam, Snoqualmoo, his x mark. [L. s.]
He-uch-ka-nam, or George Bonaparte, Sub-chief of Snohomish, his x mark. [L. s.]
Ts'huahntl, Dwa-mish sub-chief, his x mark. [L. s.]
Tse-nah-talc, or Joseph Bonaparte, Sub-chief of Snohomish, his x mark. [L. s.]
Kwuss-ka-nam, or George Snatelum, Sen., Skagit tribe, his x mark. [L. s.]
Ns'ski-oos, or Jackson, Sub-chief of Snohomish, his x mark. [L. s.]
Hel-mits, or George Snatelum, Skagit sub-chief, his x mark. [L. s.]
S'h'-cheh-oos, or General Washington, Sub-chief of Lummi tribe, his x mark. [L. s.]
S'kwai-kwi, Skagit tribe, sub-chief, his x mark. [L. s.]
Whai-lan-hu, or Davy Crockett, Sub-chief of Lummi tribe, his x mark. [L. s.]
Seh-lek-qu, Sub-chief Lummi tribe, his x mark. [L. s.]
She-ah-delt-hu, Sub-chief of Lummi tribe, his x mark. [L. s.]

Tse-sum-ten, Lummi tribe, his x mark. [L. S.]

Kwult-seh, Sub-chief of Lummi tribe, his x mark. [L. S.]

Klt-hahl-ten, Lummi tribe, his x mark. [L. S.]

Kwull-et-hu, Lummi tribe, his x mark. [L. S.]

Kut-ta-kanam, or John, Lummi tribe, his x mark. [L. S.]

Kleh-kent-soot, Skagit tribe, his x mark. [L. S.]

Ch-lah-ben, Noo-qua-cha-mish band, his x mark. [L. S.]

Sohn-heh-ovs, Skagit tribe, his x mark. [L. S.]

Noo-heh-oos, Snoqualmoo tribe, his x mark. [L. S.]

S'deh-ap-kan, or General Warren, Skagit tribe, his x mark. [L. S.]

Hweh-uk, Snoqualmoo tribe, his x mark. [L. S.]

Chul-whil-tan, Sub-chief of Suquamish tribe, his x mark. [L. S.]

Peh-nus, Skai-whamish tribe, his x mark. [L. S.]

Ske-eh-tum, Skagit tribe, his x mark. [L. S.]

Yim-ka-dam, Snoqualmoo tribe, his x mark. [L. S.]

Patchkanam, or Dome, Skagit tribe, his x mark. [L. S.]

Twooi-as-kut, Skaiwhamish tribe, his x mark. [L. S.]

Sats-Kanam, Squin-ah-nush tribe, his x mark. [L. S.]

Luch-al-kanam, Snoqualmoo tribe, his x mark. [L. S.]

Sd-zo-mahtl, Kik-ial-lus band, his x mark. [L. S.]

S'hoot-kanam, Snoqualmoo tribe, his x mark. [L. S.]

Dahtl-de-min, Sub-chief of Sah-ku-meh-hu, his x mark. [L. S.]

Sme-a-kanam, Snoqualmoo tribe, his x mark. [L. S.]

Sd'zek-du-num, Me-sek-wi-guilse sub-chief, his x mark. [L. S.]

Sad-zis-keh, Snoqualmoo, his x mark. [L. S.]

Now-a-chais, Sub-chief of Dwamish, his x mark. [L. S.]

Heh-mahl, Skaiwhamish band, his x mark. [L. S.]

Mis-lo-tche, or Wah-hehl-tchoo, Sub-chief of Suquamish, his x mark. [L. S.]

Charley, Skagit tribe, his x mark. [L. S.]

Sloo-noksh-tan, or Jim, Suquamish tribe, his x mark. [L. S.]

Sampson, Skagit tribe, his x mark. [L. S.]

Moo-whah-lad-hu, or Jack, Suquamish tribe, his x mark. [L. S.]

John Taylor, Snohomish tribe, his x mark. [L. S.]

Too-leh-plan, Suquamish tribe, his x mark. [L. S.]

Hatch-kwentum, Skagit tribe, his x mark. [L. S.]

Ha-seh-doo-an, or Keo-kuck, Dwamish tribe, his x mark. [L. S.]

Yo-i-kum, Skagit tribe, his x mark. [L. S.]

Hoovilt-meh-tum, Sub-chief of Suquamish, his x mark. [L. S.]

T'kwa-ma-han, Skagit tribe, his x mark. [L. S.]

We-ai-pah, Skaiwhamish tribe, his x mark. [L. S.]

Sto-dum-kan, Swinamish band, his x mark. [L. S.]

S'ah-an-hu, or Hallam, Snohomish tribe, his x mark. [L. S.]

Be-lole, Swinamish band, his x mark. [L. S.]

She-hope, or General Pierce, Skagit tribe, his x mark. [L. S.]

D'zo-lole-gwam-hu, Skagit tribe, his x mark. [L. S.]

Hwn-lah-lakq, or Thomas Jefferson, Lummi tribe, his x mark. [L. S.]

Steh-shail, William, Skaiwhamish band, his x mark. [L. S.]

Cht-simpt, Lummi tribe, his x mark. [L. S.]

Kel-kahl-tsoot, Swinamish tribe, his x mark. [L. S.]

Pat-sen, Skagit tribe, his x mark. [L. S.]

Pat-teh-us, Noo-wha-ah sub-chief, his x mark. [L. S.]

S'hoolk-ka-nam, Lummi sub-chief, his x mark. [L. S.]

Ch-lok-suts, Lummi sub-chief, his x mark. [L. S.]

Executed in the presence of us—

M. T. Simmons, Indian agent.

C. H. Mason, Secretary of Washington Territory.

Benj. F. Shaw, Interpreter.

Chas. M. Hitchcock.

H. A. Goldsborough.

George Gibbs.

John. Scranton.

Henry D. Cock.

S. S. Ford, jr.

Orrington Cushman.

Ellis Barnes.

R. S. Bailey.

S. M. Collies.

Lafayetee Balch.

E. S. Fowler.

J. H. Hall.

Rob't Davis.

Authors and Artist

David A. Cameron, Ph.D., (author and editor), is a retired teacher of history and philosophy at Cascade High School. He has also been an instructor of history for Antioch University and Western Washington University. Throughout his career he has served as a leader of heritage projects; written articles and news columns on county and forest history; chaired the county's committee for the state centennial; and worked for the U.S. Forest Service on historic interpretation projects.

Charles P. LeWarne, Ph.D., retired from teaching at Meadowdale High School, co-author of Washington state's official centennial history. Other publications include a widely used state history textbook and works on the communal movement including *Utopias on Puget Sound, 1885-1915*. He is a leader in local and regional historical organizations and former chair of the State Advisory Council for Historic Preservation.

M. Allan May, M.A., retired from a full career in the newspaper business, serving as reporter, editor, and general manager for *The Western Sun/Everett Herald*. He is the author of travel guide and outdoor books on the Washington Cascades and Olympic Peninsula, as well as Everett Parks.

Jack C. O'Donnell, B.A., continues in a long career of teaching in public and private schools. He has written a history of Everett based on historic postcards and has long served as "historic perspective" columnist for *The Herald* newspaper. As a noted local historian he has been active in Everett historic preservation efforts, including membership on that city's historical commission.

Lawrence E. O'Donnell, M.A., retired as a school administrator, having had a life-long interest in local history and photography. He has written numerous books on historic topics, including the Everett centennial, Everett High School athletics, the Boy Scouts, and the Y.M.C.A.. Community service has always been his focus as his membership in numerous service organizations attests.

Bernie Webber was named Snohomish County's Artist of the Year for 2003. His portrayals of local and regional scenes have enjoyed widespread popular and commercial appeal. His works of art range from those commissioned by the U.S. Navy and governments requesting historical murals to capturing the essence of seascapes and Cascade Mountain towns. Community activities include service on the Snohomish County Airport Commission.

Contributors

Catherine Currie, B.A., works in the Office of the Mayor at the City of Bainbridge Island, where she coordinates City communications and public relations. She previously served as Director of Executive Relations for the Pilchuck Glass School.

David Dilgard serves as history specialist at the Northwest Room of the Everett Public Library. He is the author of many articles and several books, including *Milltown Footlights: The Theaters of Everett, Washington.*

Thomas M. Gaskin, Ph.D., twice was named teacher of the year by students at Everett Community College, where he has taught history since 1976. He is especially interested in researching the early career of Senator Henry M. Jackson.

Roger Kelley, M.Ed., is a Watershed Educator for Snohomish County Public Works Surface Management's Watershed Education Program, co-ordinating and teaching a variety of youth and adult courses. A regional environmental education resource and a project manager for volunteer salmon surveys, he is an avid mountain hiker and waterborne explorer of the Snohomish River estuary.

Bob Laz left Chicago in 1946 with his brothers and their families to follow their dream of creating a popular resort from an "overgrown jungle of trees, brush, rotting logs and stumps" on the shores of Flowing Lake, northeast of Snohomish. His book *The Epic of*

Wonderland Park describes their (mis)adventures in humorous, honest, and heart warming form. Bob died in 2005.

Louise Lindgren is in the graduate program for Cultural Resource Management at the University of Victoria. The Senior Planner for Cultural Resources for the Snohomish County Department of Planning and Development Services, she also is an exhibit designer, writer, museum technical consultant, and coordinator of county heritage activities. She conceived the idea of writing this book and provided vital support throughout the process.

Karen Prasse, M.A., is a researcher, writer, and a volunteer for the Stanwood Area Historical Society and League of Snohomish County Heritage Organizations, Karen worked for the University of Washington libraries and now is with the Sno-Isle Regional Library System.

Margaret Riddle, M.A., is a history specialist in the Northwest Room of the Everett Public Library. Margaret writes articles on local history and edits library's historical publications. Her work with the library's photography collection was a major contribution to this publication.

Nellie Robertson spent many years writing for two weekly community newspapers, retiring as Lifestyle Editor for the *Monroe Monitor/Valley News* in Monroe. She earned five writing awards from the Washington Newspaper Publishers Association and has published two Monroe history books, along with three novels, two of which were based on Snohomish County locations and historical facts.

Tony Stigall, M.S. and M.U.P., is an Environmental Planner for the Snohomish County Department of Public Works, after serving as a planning director and city manager in Alaska, as well as being a self-employed planning consultant for many years. He has been on the faculty of Kuskokwim Community College and Columbia College in Missouri and enjoys both singing and the study of history.

The Tulalip Tribes Cultural Resources Department Lushootseed Program has its goal of keeping the language alive by speaking it, teaching it, and retrieving it from archives in which it sleeps.

Index